The University of New Mexico
At Gallup

Zollinger Library

The Lumberman's Frontier

The Lumberman's Frontier

THREE CENTURIES
of
LAND USE,
SOCIETY,
and
CHANGE
in
AMERICA'S FORESTS

Thomas R. Cox

Oregon State University Press

Corvallis

The paper in this book meets the guidelines for permanence and durability of the Committee on Production Guidelines for Book Longevity of the Council on Library Resources and the minimum requirements of the American National Standard for Permanence of Paper for Printed Library Materials Z39.48-1984.

Library of Congress Cataloging-in-Publication Data
Cox, Thomas R., 1933-
  The lumberman's frontier : three centuries of land use, society, and change in America's forests / Thomas R. Cox.
      p. cm.
  Includes bibliographical references and index.
  ISBN 978-0-87071-579-2 (alk. paper)
  1. Lumbermen—United States—History. 2. Lumbering—United States—History. 3. Lumbering—Social aspects—United States—History. 4. Frontier and pioneer life—United States. 5. Logging—United States—History. 6. Forests and forestry—United States—History. 7. Land use—United States—History. 8. Social conflict—United States—History. 9. Social change—United States—History. I. Title.
  HD8039.L92U537 2010
  338.1'74980973--dc22

                                                           2009047314

Oregon State University Press
121 The Valley Library
Corvallis OR 97331-4501
541-737-3166 • fax 541-737-3170
http://oregonstate.edu/dept/press

To

Rachel, Rita, Ruth, Matthew, Joshua—and Max:
May they find their own frontiers

Table of Contents

Maps

Illustrations

Preface

This is not the book I set out to write. Several years ago Ray Billington approached me about preparing a short volume on the lumberman's frontier for the American Frontiers series of which he was then the general editor. Knowing a good bit had already been done, having completed considerable research in the field myself, and thinking I could quickly synthesize the literature and fill the gaps therein with additional research, I agreed. But the gaps were far larger than I dreamed, and new works kept appearing to reshape our understanding of environmental and American socio-economic history, forcing me to rethink much of what I had to say. This study is thus the product of over forty years of probing and questioning—and, I trust, more valuable than the modest volume I originally envisioned.

A word or two about my approach is in order. Both in portions that rest on the work of others and those that primarily depend upon my own archival research, I try to keep the principals at center stage and let them speak for themselves, for I believe personal values and perceptions drive events. To be sure, individuals are partially shaped—and certainly limited— by the *zeitgeist* of time, place, and class, but participants on the lumberman's frontier differed so much in outlook and actions that we generalize at our peril. This is, in short, not a study of the political economy, but of individuals, their varied accomplishments, and the results thereof.

Nor is this a study of the use of forests throughout American history. I define the lumberman's frontier more narrowly, arguing it existed only at times and places where trees drew settlement into an area. Felling trees to clear land for farming—even when one might sell the products of such labor—is, I contend, a part of the agricultural, not the lumbering, frontier. And when the process of drawing settlers to new areas is over, I conceive of the lumberman's frontier itself as having ended even though timber harvests and other forms of forest utilization might still be going on. Except for a brief epilogue, both modern industrial lumbering with its emphasis on permanent operations and post-industrial forms of forest use are beyond the scope of this study.

Needless to say, during the years I worked on this project I received help and encouragement from too many individuals for me to mention most, let alone all, of them here. Nonetheless, some played roles so central I must acknowledge them. Ronald J. Fahl and Harold K. Steen, then with the Forest History Society, lent support, encouragement, and ideas as I set to work; Judith Austin, of the Idaho State Historical Society, introduced me to material on the Mountain states about which I then knew little; Richard Judd of the University of Maine provided hospitality and help as I wrestled with the colonial and early national periods; Raymond Starr of San Diego State University reviewed chapters on the colonial period and the South and helped me from going astray therein; and Gene Stuffle and Sarah Hinman of Idaho State University provided computer and cartographic expertise which my generation of graduate students never had to acquire. The staffs of various libraries and archives were helpful, but those of the Forest History Society in Durham, North Carolina, the Hill Memorial Library at Louisiana State University, and the Warren County Historical Society and Clearfield County Historical Society both in Pennsylvania went the extra mile. To all these—and to many others—I will be forever grateful. Special thanks are also due to the Laird-Norton Foundation, the San Diego State University Foundation, the Forest History Society, and the Henry E. Huntington Library for research grants that helped to make this study possible. Above all, I owe special thanks to my wife Mary, who suffered through a project that she must surely have thought would never end but who hung with me nonetheless.

In the end, I alone am responsible for what follows. The interpretations are mine, as are any errors in this study. I ask that readers consider the former and try to forgive the latter.

McCammon, Idaho
April 2009

CHAPTER ONE

Colonists and Trees:
Lumbering before the Lumberman's Frontier

Many things lured European settlers to North America, but the continent's forest wealth was not prominent among them. Accounts of explorers and early visitors made clear the new land was cloaked with trees. Many an observer discussed the potential value of these for medicinal purposes, staves, and shipbuilding. Policymakers considered the potential of forests as a source of naval stores and masts. Still, most settlers were not drawn by such considerations, but by the availability of agricultural land and opportunities for trade and freedom of worship.

Indeed, forests long seemed an obstacle more than a source of opportunity. As the abode of Indians and dangerous animals, as places outside the sphere of Christian civilization, and as landscapes so different from long-settled western Europe that they seemed dark and dreary rather than uplifting, the forests of the new land were used, but little treasured and never loved. In 1747 Jared Eliot lamented how the first settlers, "tho't themselves obliged to stubb all Staddle [i.e., saplings] and cut down or lop all great Trees; in which they expended much Cost and Time, to the prejudice of the Crop and impoverishing the Land." As they "began the world a New," as he put it, they sought to recreate on the western side of the Atlantic what they had known on the eastern, a land of permanent settlements, fixed fields bounded by fences, and open meadows with but a few scattered trees.[1] Forests hindered the process of building an agricultural society. In 1681 Thomas Markham wrote of Pennsylvania: "It is a very fine Country, if it were not so overgrown with Woods." A visitor to Britain's mid-Atlantic colonies explained, "[A]t the beginning in the nearer, and latterly in the farther reaches of America, wood has been everywhere in the way of the new planter [and] . . . people have grown accustomed to regard forests . . . as the most troublesome of growths."[2]

Although settlers neither loved nor valued the forests of British North America and were not drawn to the continent to exploit them, they made extensive use of them nonetheless. From the first, the ubiquitous forests provided building materials, fuel, and material for a host of everyday uses. Wood was much more widely used in the New World than in the old, leading one British visitor to warn his countrymen that in America they would have to accept "a Wooden Town in a Wooden Country & a wooden bred set of Tavern-keepers."[3]

Colonists everywhere drew upon the woods. The first English arrivals exported oak staves from Virginia in 1607, and their counterparts to the north did the same from Plymouth in 1621, William Bradford reporting the *Fortune* "was speedily dispacht away, being laden with good clapbord as full as she could stowe." Following the usage of the time, Bradford surely meant oak barrel staves, not wainscoting—the clapboards of a later generation.[4]

Colonists generated these first exports by riving logs with wedges and mauls, but sawmills soon sprang up from the Carolinas to Maine. The Virginia Company was "very solicitous for the erection of saw-mills," sending Poles and Dutchmen to build them. The first mills had indifferent success, but after mid-century "saw-mills became as numerous as grist-mills" in Virginia. Three mills operated in New Netherland in 1623, and the number was increasing rapidly. By the time the English took over in 1664, there were some forty sawmills in the colony, more even than in New Hampshire. Sawmills also appeared at an early date in New Jersey, Pennsylvania, and North Carolina, especially in the Cape Fear region from whence sawn pine became a staple export.[5] To the north, employees of John Mason erected a mill on Salmon Falls River in 1634, thus laying the groundwork for a huge export trade from the Piscataqua and its tributaries that soon became the economic backbone of New Hampshire and southern Maine. In Maine, sparsely settled though it was, there were twenty-four sawmills by 1682.[6]

Regional differences in forest utilization quickly developed, reflecting local conditions. In the South, where the fall line was far from the coast, the number of sawmills grew slowly, but production of staves (for tobacco barrels), naval stores (from the highly resinous pines of the area), and charcoal (to fuel Virginia's iron smelters) burgeoned. Local specialties added to the output. In Georgia, William Knox's plantations were kept going until his agricultural enterprises began to pay off by producing and selling hand-split bald cypress shingles.[7] In Pennsylvania and New York, potash (made from the ashes left from burning hardwoods) was a by-product of turning forests into farmland, vast quantities of staves poured forth to meet the demands of commerce, and huge amounts of fuelwood went to nascent urban centers. Northern New England, with a plethora of millsites near the coast but limited agricultural potential, came to be the great area of lumber production, although it had a large output of staves and fuelwood too; masts from the area's magnificent white pines were a regional specialty. Coastal New Hampshire and extreme southern Maine were the transition zone between predominantly deciduous forests to the south and evergreen forests to the north. They were the area of softwood lumber production most accessible by sea to the growing cities of Boston, New York, and Philadelphia, and their residents responded accordingly.[8]

No records exist adequate to determine the precise quantities of forest products turned out by colonial Americans. Records of foreign trade give clues to their importance—and to the relative importance of various types of forest products in different places—but they omit both commerce internal to the colonies and products that did not enter commercial channels, such as those consumed on farms. Moreover, statistics in extant documents are often little more than estimates, one might even say informed guesses. Still, the repeated statements of contemporaries and the results—thousands of acres of cleared and cutover land, hundreds of wooden ships, and an almost endless list of wooden products in everyday use—attest that colonial America was a wood-intensive society heavily dependent upon the forest.

Not everyone saw opportunities in this. In 1687 New York's Collector of Customs wrote, "[I]f the Indian Trade bee disturbed or distroyed it will be Impossible for Inhabitants of this Province to provide themselves with Clothinge and other nessisaries from England their beinge Little else then furrs Sutable to make returns." Lord Bellomont, the colony's governor, was more sanguine; the potential advantages to the Crown from forests "are infinite and inestimable," he reported. "[T]is most amazing . . . that the value of these Plantations to England has not been seen."[9]

Profits on early timber exports encouraged later ones. One sea captain's success, Lord Bellomont reported in 1700, "has set all the country agog."[10] As a result of this and similar shipments, colonists from an early date drew upon the forests so heavily and in so many ways that shortages and other problems associated with deforestation began to appear.[11] As early as 1693 John Nelson wrote of the area along the Piscataqua: "[M]any parts of it [are] almost exhausted by the Continual Exportation" of lumber. Not long after, Lord Bellomont echoed the complaint. The residents of New Hampshire, he told the Board of Trade, had taken "what tracts of land and woods they pleas'd . . . [so that now] they are forc'd to go 20 miles up into the country to get a good mast for the use of the navy."[12] The following year, he noted with alarm the number and size of sawmills in New York. Especially ominous was one built by "a Dutchman lately come over who is an extraordinary artist at those mills. A few such mills will quickly destroy all the woods in the province at a reasonable distance from them."[13] In 1729 another official reported, "[T]here is Scarse a Tree Standing anywhere within 6 or 7 miles of waterside between this [the Saco River] and [the] Kennebeck that is worth halling to the Bank." Local residents, he explained, "think it less labour to Logg than to do anything else."[14]

The effects of forest depletion were widely felt. Settlers on Cape Cod were especially hard hit. When it was first settled by whites, the cape's abundant trees stabilized the sandy soil while providing shade and browse for domestic animals and building materials and fuelwood for the area's human inhabitants. But by the mid-1700s, overgrazing combined with burning and overcutting had set off a chain reaction of environmental degradation. Streams and springs dried up, meadows and fields succumbed to encroaching sands, and the carrying capacity of the land plummeted. In Truro "[f]ormerly fifty bushels of Indian corn were raised to an acre; but the average produce [is now] not more than fifteen or twenty. . . . Large tracts of land have now become unfit for cultivation." Eastham was even worse off: "[W]hat was once a fertile spot, has become a prey to the winds, and lies buried under a heap of barren sand."[15] Devastation was so pervasive that not only farmers, but also fishermen and others less directly dependent upon the land suffered.

A mass exodus soon followed. Many areas that Cape Cod's residents moved to—New Hampshire, southern Maine, and the Penobscot Valley— were well forested, but the overwhelming majority of these emigrants were farmers seeking a more inviting location for agrarian pursuits, not pioneers of the lumberman's frontier. They described themselves as farmers and viewed tapping forests near their new homes as an essential part of agricultural life.[16]

Less dramatic degradation took place in other early-settled parts of Massachusetts. As a commercial economy developed in Boston, Salem, and nearby areas it buffered the effects of forest depletion and, by offering alternative sources of employment, slowed out-migration, but in places that remained dependent upon agriculture, the effects were disastrous. From causes such as these the Yankee diaspora would later spring.[17]

Well before independence, criticisms of Americans as wastrels of the forest were common, and colony after colony enacted legislation to slow forest depletion or at least rationalize use and insure the maximum public benefit from it. In spite of such regulations, deforestation continued. In New York by the mid-1700s, "many Streams of Water which in the beginning came from Wood Lands, and carried Gristmills and Saw Mills, when these lands were cleared vanished . . . and became dry, the Mills ceased, and in some Parts the Cattle could not be conveniently watered." A contemporary in Pennsylvania voiced a similar complaint: "Our runs dry up apace; several of which formerly wou'd turn a fulling Mill are now scarce sufficient for the Use of a Farm, the Reason of which is, when the Country was cover'd with Woods and the Swamps with Brush, the Rain that fell was detain'd by These Interruptions," but with the land no longer cloaked with trees and brush, desiccation had resulted. Moreover, fuelwood shortages had become a major problem in Philadelphia and elsewhere.[18]

Critics of forest utilization in early America often overlooked the realities faced by settlers. Living in societies painfully short on both labor and capital, they had to utilize extensively that which they had in abundance—the land and the products thereof. As Benjamin Vaughan explained, "Wood is too abundant & labor too scarce in a new country, to admit of other than coarse operations for clearing lands."[19] Colonists developed land-clearing techniques such as girdling and burning, which destroyed vast quantities of wood later generations might have valued, but in the process they provided themselves with a source of livelihood—useable agricultural land—without expending excessive amounts of that most scarce colonial resource, labor.[20]

In colonial America forest utilization was so intimately tied to agriculture the two can hardly be separated. One authority noted, "Early settlers were of necessity lumbermen." Income from the sale of lumber, potash, staves, and other by-products of clearing went far toward paying the costs of transforming forests into farms. In place after place, the author of *American Husbandry* noted in 1775 (and Tenche Coxe two decades later), such products generated sufficient income to pay for indentured servants to do the clearing, leaving landowners in the end with valuable farmland obtained with a minimal outlay of capital. Even when a farmer did the work himself, the products of clearing were vital, providing income until agricultural output was sufficient to support his family.[21]

Forest production remained vital to farm life even after adequate crop- and pastureland had been cleared. Forests provided fuelwood, building materials, and a host of other products essential to the farm family during "America's Wooden Age."[22] Some of the more affluent farmers had small water-powered sawmills they operated seasonally to supply their own needs and generate goods for sale. Those who did not drew upon the forests too. They cut logs for others' mills, rived planks and split shingles by hand, and cut fuelwood for sale.[23]

The by-employment such activities generated fit the seasonal rhythms of agricultural life, for felling and hauling logs could be done in winter when farmers had time on their hands. So too could turpentining, tar burning, stave making, and most other employment in the woods. Only in spring did the demands of forest and farm conflict, for not only was it the season for plowing and planting but also the time when streams ran full, making water-powered mills their most efficient and providing the means to float logs to mills and rafts of forest products downstream to market.[24]

Even settlers' agricultural pursuits were often tied to tapping the forests. Farmers produced and sold hay to feed the oxen that pulled logs from the woods and large quantities of corn, potatoes, grain, and dairy products to feed those working in the woods. By creating a nearby market, timber harvesting thus helped make agricultural enterprise feasible on many a remote and otherwise unpromising tract.

The economies of forest and farm complemented one another so well many families would have been reduced to bare subsistence if forced to depend on either alone. The early years of Winthrop, Maine, provide a case in point. Winthrop was five miles from the Kennebec and, being newly settled, roads were poor. As a result, one observer wrote, "Inhabitants cannot have the advantage of Lumbering as People that live on Kennebeck River; their whole dependence being upon what they Raise from the land, the said Inhabitants are poor in General and of Consequence money [is] very Scarce among them."[25]

The more marginal the farmland, the greater and more long-lasting the role of forests in supporting those who resided on it—and the less the attention paid to agriculture. In North Carolina the incentive to labor in the woods was limited because, as William Byrd put it in 1726, "there is no place in the World where the Inhabitants live with less labor." Due to "the easiness of raising provisions ... [they] are extremely cheap, and extremely good, so that a people may live plentifully at a trifling expense."[26] In northern New England, by contrast, agriculture was risky and provisions dear; there farmers turned readily to the forests to augment the meager output of their farms—often to the latter's neglect.

The experience of one early resident of Brunswick, Maine, is illustrative. When he bought a farm in the area in 1780, the township had been settled for half a century, but agriculture was still poorly developed; the farm "was in but poor condition, the former owner having stripped it of all the most valuable timber which was convenient to the river and had not improved the land or buildings."[27] The area around Portland was no different. The Reverend Thomas Smith, a city pioneer, recalled: "The attention of the people had been turned so much to lumbering operations that they neglected the cultivation of the land. Lumber was in constant demand and afforded a quick remuneration for labor. . . . Agricultural pursuits continued to be neglected so long as there remained a supply of timber to be manufactured." The pattern was familiar in many another marginal agricultural area as well.[28]

Farmers were not alone in recognizing the value of forests to would-be agricultural settlements. When a group of Massachusetts proprietors won control of a tract on the Androscoggin River in what became Topsham township, they sought to encourage its settlement. These Pejepscot proprietors, like George Mason before them, envisioned agrarian estates ruled over by a prosperous rural gentry—themselves—but realized the forests of Maine were an economic asset that would have to be tapped to make their project feasible. One of their first actions was to order the building of two sawmills on their grant. Moreover, when dividing the land among themselves, the proprietors directed that each "shall be accomodated with a Place for a Mill . . . so that each Partner may finally have one Mill to himself in Propriety."[29]

Recognizing reality, the proprietors agreed in the 1730s to take payment for tracts sold to settlers "in wood or timber, or in such farm products as can be spared."[30] A chronicler described the result. In winter, when Indians retired to the interior, settlers "employed themselves in getting lumber and firewood to be sent to Boston as soon as the spring opened." The area was marginal for agriculture, so there was rarely any surplus. Payment in wood stuff became the norm.[31]

The proprietors had been midwife to a monster they could not control. As timber on the settlers' lands grew scarce and inaccessible, they turned to cutting elsewhere—which usually meant on lands still belonging to the proprietors. In spite of the efforts of the proprietors' agent, Belcher Noyes, settlers spent a good part of the year felling trees on proprietary land and sawing the resulting logs into boards and planks. Noyes protested vehemently:

> I am sorry to hear your People have so generally combined in the old Trade of destroying the Lumber on the Proprietors Interest. This is very abusive treatement & convinces us you have no Regard to the Laws of God and Man, for such a small frontier settlement to live in such an abandoned State in open violation of all Law, will expose you to the vengeance due such Behaviour. It will one day fall heavy on your heads—For shame then, be persuaded to leave such actions.[32]

Cutting continued unabated. When attorney Enoch Freeman went to investigate, one settler told him that if he were sued for illegal cutting he would refuse to pay the proprietors for his land. Freeman suggested the proprietors settle with most, if not all, of the trespassers "should they be willing to pay value of the Trees or near it."[33] He pointed out that mills at the river's falls have "no Timber but what must come from off of Proprietors Land. I am persuaded they will have it either by fair means or foul and there will be great Difficulties in procuring Evidence" should the proprietors resort to legal action.[34] It was sound advice, for, one resident noted, people in the area were too jealous of large property owners to find for them in a court of law; "all the Causes brought into the Court are first tryed in the Tavern and judgement passed there before its Tryed in a Court of Justice."[35]

The social and economic standing of the more successful timber thieves gradually improved, and they became leaders in Brunswick township, carved from Topsham in 1739. Once in authority, they levied heavy taxes on remaining stands of timber. In so doing, they not only transferred the burden of taxation to non-resident proprietors, but also sought funds from one of the few sources available; in spite of having been settled for years, the area's farmlands were inadequate to support the local government. Not surprisingly, the proprietors were outraged. For decades, their agent complained, proprietors' lands had been "plundered by the Inhabitants; Some of whom have made themselves rich [thereby]. . . . Now the town wants to tax the land & sell for a penny an acre [if the proprietors default on their taxes]. What abominable Injustice this is!"[36]

The importance of forests to early agriculturists can be seen in other ways too. Farm settlements tended to grow up around sawmills, which supplied necessary building materials for farmers and merchants and others on whom farmers depended. It was a reciprocal relationship. Recognizing the importance of forest products to their own economic success, farmers settled where sawmills were present to supply them; potential operators of small sawmills, realizing nearby farmers would be ideal consumers for their cut, erected plants where agriculture was feasible.

The farm-mill connection was evident early in northern New England. The pattern in which mill development encouraged agricultural development, sometimes even preceding it, a pattern introduced along the Piscataqua in the 1630s, was followed time and again in subsequent years. Edmund Littlefield, perhaps the first permanent white resident in the area of Wells and Kennebunk, Maine, built a sawmill there in 1641 or 1643. Others followed, obtaining lumber for their buildings from Littlefield. Settlers huddled on tracts near the coast "where there were the fewest trees to be felled, and where there were meadows and marshes for the ready supply of food for whatever animals they might be able to obtain. . . . The sea and the [tidal] flats were important adjuncts to every homestead."[37]

Settlers also seem to have regarded mill privileges as of great importance, for "there was no other source of immediate profit." The main centers of population continued to cluster near the sea until the end of Indian hostilities in 1678. With peace came a rush to acquire good, if more distant, millsites on the Mousam and Kennebunk. Settlement quickly spread, for a "saw-mill in those days was always a nucleus for a village."[38] The same was true on Casco Bay. A report of 1680 describes the area's first sawmill, built by Garth Gidney, as "the Maine & chiefe Incoradgement to the first settlement . . . without which we Cannot se at present a likelyhood of any convenient progresse."[39]

Farmers and their needs were not alone in stimulating the tapping of forests in early America. As commerce grew during the colonial period, forest products came to play a larger and larger role. Boards, planks, staves, spars, naval stores, potash, and other forest products were major items of trade; moreover, the very vessels that carried the commerce were crafted from trees that had once graced the American landscape.

Forest products were important items of trade almost everywhere, but nowhere more than in New England. Leaders of Exeter, New Hampshire, made the point clearly when royal authorities sought to ban lumbering in the region so as to guarantee a supply of masts for the Royal Navy. They argued that if the ban were not lifted trees unfit for masts would go to waste, hundreds of people whose estates were in mills would be impoverished, New England's shipping (most of which was engaged in the timber trade) would be idled, and the West Indies would go unsupplied with lumber. They petitioned that, as soon as trees reserved for masts had been marked, they be allowed

> to Improve [i.e., log] the remainder, without any lett, or paying any acknowledge't. . . . And whereas the Winter season is so farr advanced and our teems lye unemployed . . . that we may forthwith bee permitted to Improve them, in our usual way of logging; which otherwise will render the succeeding summer altogether useless.[40]

The growing commercial importance of timber and other forest products encouraged farmers, especially those in areas marginal for agriculture, to spend more time in the woods and less in their fields. Nowhere was this truer than in northern New England. Fishing, not farming, had led to the first settlements in Maine. This, coupled with the threat from Indian and French resistance, long kept English settlement huddled along the rocky, storm-swept coast and on offshore islands. When settlers finally began to move inland, they found the soil better and the area more protected from winter storms, but conditions were still far from ideal for agriculture. The growing season was short, killing frosts could occur in almost any season, and winters were severe. Yet there were forests that could be tapped to

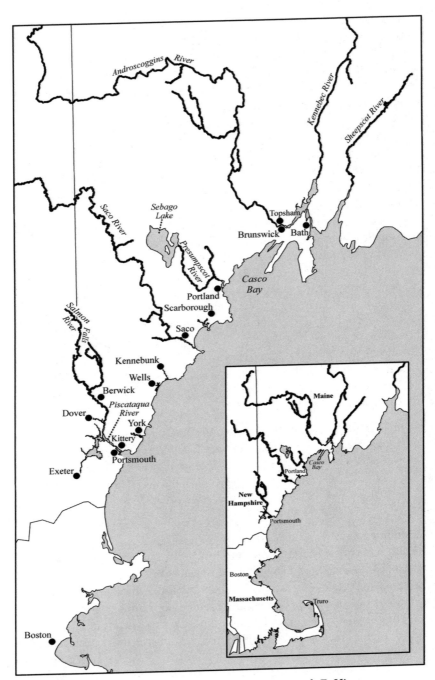

Early Maine-New Hampshire forest frontier. Map by Sarah E. Hinman.

supplement the bounty of the fields, and the region had ready access to colonial markets that needed forest products—as well as the catch of its fisheries, which continued to prosper. As a result, northern New England early developed an economy based on farm, sea, and forest. The place of forests in the economic mix grew as the difficulties of farming in northern New England became manifest even as the inland population grew.[41]

Geographical factors worked to make lumber the primary product of northern New England's woods. The region was near the main urban centers of colonial America; it was graced with white pine, a species that yielded high-quality softwood lumber much in demand both there and in the maritime markets that merchants from those cities served; it had good harbors that remained ice free in winter; and, with a fall line close to the coast, it had numerous millsites that could be developed while the interior was still the domain of Indians, sites from which lumber could easily be rafted to anchorages accessible to ocean-going vessels. Combined with the agricultural limitations of the area, these factors made forest utilization more-than-normally important from an early date. In contrast, coastal North Carolina, although a source of softwood lumber too, was plagued by fewer, poorer, and more distant millsites; shallow, shoal-ridden approaches; greater distances to the main colonial centers of demand; and weaker social, cultural, and commercial ties with them.[42]

The Piscataqua, formed by the joining of the Salmon Falls and Cocheco rivers and enlarged by the Exeter and other tributaries, was especially favorably endowed. It was close to Boston. It had a broad, deep, and protected estuary where both small coasting vessels and larger ships bound for the Caribbean could call and where rafts of lumber could await them in safety. Excellent millsites were a short distance inland. Moreover, the surrounding lands were more level and less stony than those in much of northern New England, and thus encouraged early settlement.

A sizable commerce in timber developed on the Piscataqua early in the seventeenth century and not long thereafter on Casco Bay, a short distance north and another premier location. Within its broad reach, it harbored numerous anchorages that remained ice free all year, most importantly at Falmouth (after 1786 known as Portland). As on the Piscataqua, there were excellent millsites and high-quality coniferous stands grew nearby.[43]

Faced with the necessity of tapping the woods and with a ready demand for softwood lumber, settlers in the two areas developed more and more efficient methods that were to be the basis of operations for Maine's lumber industry when it emerged in the late eighteenth century as a full-fledged operation, independent of agriculture. Quietly and without fanfare, forest-dependant New England farmers were laying the foundations of the first lumberman's frontier.

Colonial sources seldom discuss the technology of such mundane undertakings as getting out logs and manufacturing lumber. Only scraps of information survive. The first sawmills of northern New England were simple, water-powered plants built beside natural falls of rivers and streams. With the fall line close to the coast, these mills were convenient not only to anchorages that could be reached by seagoing vessels but also to the initial settlements clustered in the coastal strip. Under the circumstances, mills proliferated. In 1665 there were over twenty sawmills on the Piscataqua and its tributaries; those on the Salmon Falls River alone had cut 266,281 feet of boards by August 1676. By 1682 there were at least twenty-four sawmills between Kittery, Maine, and Casco Bay, with a collective capacity of two to four million board feet per year. By 1709 one colonial authority charged with protecting mast trees for the Royal Navy reported over seventy mills in the area; two decades later, a successor set the number at a hundred.[44]

As millsites were taken up, competition for those remaining grew intense. Squatters sometimes claimed the best locations, just as they did the best farmland. In the 1740s Samuel and Hugh Wilson built a mill dam at falls on the Androscoggin in defiance of the Pejepscot proprietors. A contemporary later reported, "The Wilsons observed that they would build there, if they pleased, as they had as good a right as any body, and would build in defiance of any body." Their motives seem to have been entirely pecuniary. As Talleyrand observed, the lumberer's "only idea is the number of blows of the axe that he has to use to cut down a tree. . . . If in departing he does not forget his ax, he leaves no regret for the place where he has lived for ten years."[45]

With unclaimed millsites along the fall line becoming scarce, imaginative individuals began looking elsewhere. Among them was Gilbert Winslow, who in the 1720s built a mill on Atwater Creek in North Yarmouth that was powered by the ebb and flow of the area's immense tides. Locals considered it a hopeless speculation and labeled it Folly Mill, and the creek came to be known as Folly Creek. Winslow's undertaking proved successful, however, and was soon followed by other tide mills. Just how many there were is not clear; most seem to have been small and ephemeral, but they were surely numerous. Coastal Maine is dotted with place names suggesting that, like Folly Creek, they once boasted one or more tide mills.[46]

When obtaining sites for sawmills, operators also sought to ensure a log supply. Grants to millmen on Salmon Falls River in 1651 included the right to take "all the timber that can bee Brought to said streme Improufements." In New Hampshire a year later, Richard Waldron obtained a grant of two-thirds of the timber along the river between Cocheco and Bellamy's Bank. In 1680 Silvanus Davis and James English obtained rights to a millsite near Falmouth together with the right to build a dam, to use nearby marshes and swamps for hay for oxen, and to cut timber for three miles on each side of the falls where their mill was to be located as well as on the commons. In 1693 Jonathan Wheelwright obtained a grant to a millsite on the Mousam and "allso of sum timber for supply." The following year he also got permission "to Cut timber on the Province Comons nere s^d Rever." Others also obtained the legal right to take timber they needed.[47] But many did not. As Nathaniel Jones and Nathan Look told the Pejepscot proprietors in 1737, "[I]t has been & is Common Practice of the Inhabitance of the Town [of Topsham] to Cut & cary Logs off of the Remainder of your Claime . . . and carry the same down to the mills at the Falls." The Sheepscot and Skowhegan proprietors faced the same problem, as did royal authorities. In 1739, David Dunbar found thirteen sawmills in the vicinity of Exeter, New Hampshire, illegally cutting lumber from trees reserved to supply masts to the Royal Navy.[48]

At first logs were hauled overland to sawmills. Operators cut primitive roads radiating out to nearby stands and used oxen—a large yellow variety introduced from Denmark by George Mason—to haul logs (either on carts or by skidding them over the snow) to yarding sites on hills overlooking the mills. In time roads stretched as many as a dozen miles into the woods. Some masting operations employed prodigious numbers of oxen. To get out masts, one observer wrote, "they yoke seventy or eighty pairs of oxen, and drag them [the masts] along the snow." Such activity was beyond farmer-loggers, with their limited assets, and in any case they had no chance of getting contracts to supply masts to the Royal Navy. To move smaller logs, a few oxen sufficed.[49]

As accessible stands retreated before the axe, land transportation proved inadequate. Log drives have been reported as taking place first in New York in 1813, but logs were floated down the rivers of New England long before that.[50] Humphrey Chadbourne was perhaps the first to do so. He started logging in the woods near Mason's mill, but soon depleted the supply. Chadbourne then moved upstream and by 1661 was floating logs down the Great Works River (a tributary to Salmon Falls River) to the mill.[51] Others adopted the practice too. In 1680 George and John Ingersoll acquired a millsite on the Presumpscot and the right "to cut such timber as may be conveniently brought down that stream." In 1694, when the General Court of Massachusetts granted Jonathan Wheelwright permission to build a mill on the Mousam, it also gave him "Liberty of the streame to bring timber" to it. However, the General Court specified Wheelwright's grant was not exclusive; others might receive grants for "felling and floating down of Timber" and "Improving" the river for that purpose. In contrast, in 1719 the Pejepscot proprietors, assuming logs would be floated down streams on their grant, sought to insure "the sole right of Said Stream above the Mill" would belong to the person to whom the mill right was given.[52]

Booms appeared at an early date too—at least one was present in the 1640s. Like much of the rest of the technology of lumbering, these floating wooden barriers seem to have been introduced from Europe, probably by the Dutch: the word itself is of Dutch derivation.[53] However, it is difficult to tell when booms began to be used to collect logs floated down the area's rivers. Most early booms seem to have been intended to catch sawn lumber as it dropped from the mill and incidentally as primitive floating bridges for crossing the streams. One at Waldron's mill in Dover, New Hampshire, was "made of three or four pieces of hewn timber laid side by side, wide enough for horses and cattle to pass over in file."[54] Regardless of use, booms sometimes caused confrontations, for they could interfere with river traffic. Probably because of this, in 1738 Ebenezer Hawks received permission to build a mill at Saccarappa Falls on the Presumpscot and "a landing place to lay logs on," but was expressly forbidden to obstruct the passage of logs or rafts.[55]

Although records are vague, it appears booms were used in the early eighteenth century as they were later, as devices for collecting logs floated downstream—and probably for storing them prior to their being sawn in mills. Booms were numerous, and no other uses seem sufficient to justify the frequency with which they appeared at the main sites of lumber production.[56]

References to specialized logging camps in the woods appear as early as 1659 and give evidence of the scale and sophistication operations had assumed. By 1729, David Dunbar reported, there were over one hundred sawmills in Maine, each with winter camps of fifteen to twenty men. Winter was, a contemporary noted, "the best Season to procure Timber for the Supply of their Saw Mills the ensuing summer."[57] As often as not, camps seem to have been located in timber to which the "loggers"—the term was already in use by 1729—had no legal right. They needed logs for their mills and, as the Pejepscot proprietors were told, "they will have it either by fair means or foul." Such actions lay behind Dunbar's scathing denunciation of loggers as "ungovernable people who would be under no Controul and who never will behave as [proper] English subjects." As if to prove the accusation, in 1734 some thirty men attacked Dunbar and his deputies near Exeter, New Hampshire, in an attempt to frighten these representatives of the Crown into abandoning efforts to halt illegal logging.[58]

Techniques used in these pioneer camps seem to have been much like those used later. While large sticks for the mast trade were often pulled from the woods on wheels,[59] from an early date logs for sawmills were placed on sleighs and pulled over ice roads in winter. Thus, in 1729 Dunbar wrote of "Mr Westbrook [who] cutt slay [i.e., sleigh] roads near Casco in the Woods where he intended to cutt ye trees." If no snow comes, Dunbar explained, "they can do nothing but cutt down," but when snow falls "it is soon crusted so hard as to bear carriages of any weight."[60]

From hilltop yards, logs were rolled into quiet impoundments just upstream of the mill and from there maneuvered to the water-powered saws or, on some sites, rolled directly to them. At first most mills had a single reciprocal saw that slowly made its way up and down, cutting planks from logs; where there was a sufficient head of water, operators often replaced these by gangs of saws set parallel to one another and working in unison. The rest of the technology was equally simple, for the English had little previous experience with sawmills and acquisition of knowledge from Dutch, Danish, Polish, and German sources was slow. Not until well into the eighteenth century did simple machinery replace human muscle power in returning and repositioning logs for cutting after each passage through the saws.[61]

Mill dams were a regular feature. They created slack water above the dam in which logs could be impounded after being rolled from the log hill or floated downstream, and they created a head of water sufficient to turn the wheel that powered the saws. As river traffic increased, including more and more free-floating logs and rafts of lumber, dams became a major source of friction, for many were built so as to make passing them without going ashore difficult or impossible. Dams could be a nuisance in other ways too, causing flooding of lands upstream or preventing a sufficient head of water from reaching downstream facilities. To assuage neighbors, Nicholas Shapleigh, a pioneer sawmill operator in Kittery, gave bond in 1651 "to keepe two Cannows [canoes] on the up side of s[ai]d Damme, for their transportation, & likewise w[he]n the s[ai]d inhabitants shall find thejre marshes to be overflowne at any tyme, w[he]n it may hurt them, upon notis from them, to take up the wast gates" to lower the impounded water.[62]

Once sawn, lumber was collected below the mill and floated from there to landings to be loaded onto wagons of local purchasers or rafted to anchorages near the head of navigation, then taken aboard seagoing vessels for the journey to Boston or beyond. Records of Dover, New Hampshire, for 1699 refer to "the usual rafting-place for delivering boards"; this was described three years later as "at the river below the mill where they hall up boards."[63]

In improved and perfected form, the pattern of operations in place in northern New England by the end of the seventeenth century was still present a hundred years and more later, when the first lumberman's frontier was in full flower there, and it was a pattern little different from what followed elsewhere as lumbermen moved on to new stands. Winter logging, skidding logs with oxen, floating logs downstream on spring freshets, collecting them in booms, and sawing them at water-powered mills long remained the norm. So too did the aggressive felling of timber wherever it might be found. Timber trespass, as illegal cutting euphemistically came to be called, continued to plague timber owners and government officials long after the centers of American lumbering had shifted south and west from New England.

Like its modes of production, lumbering's social relations developed patterns in the sixteenth and seventeenth centuries that would long endure. A division between those who labored in the woods and those who milled and marketed their products appeared early. Pioneer historian Jeremy Belknap noted contractors and agents who supplied masts for the Royal Navy "made large fortunes by this traffic; but the laborers who spent their time in the woods . . . were generally kept in a state of poverty and dependence." As lumbering grew in importance, the pattern remained the same: woods workers, he concluded, "work hard for little profit," while sawmill owners and merchants prospered from their output.[64] Central to this development was the fact that, as technology became more sophisticated and sawmills larger, more investment capital was needed to establish a new plant or rebuild an old one. Merchants in Boston and elsewhere came to see investments in sawmills as a way of ensuring a steady supply of lumber to sell while also earning good returns through the production itself. For their part, poor farmers found investments in sawmills increasingly beyond their means.

To be sure, tiny mills were numerous throughout the colonial period and even after, mills at which labor and management were one and the same. In the mid-eighteenth century William Douglass observed "*New-England* abounds in Saw-mills of cheap and slight Work, generally carry[ing] only one Saw; one Man and a Boy attending of a Saw may in 24 Hours saw four Thousand Feet of White-Pine Boards. These Mills mostly stand upon small Streams."[65] Such mills, with their absence of divisions of labor, were concentrated in agricultural districts, where nearby demand was sufficient to absorb their cut and close enough to keep transportation costs low enough to make up for inefficiencies of operations. On larger streams, and in New Hampshire and Maine where local demand was relatively small, bigger and more efficient plants catering to distant markets eclipsed such tiny mills at an early date.

Specialization of function developed at northern New England's larger mills. Separation of loggers, who worked in the woods, from lumbermen, businessmen who owned the mills, was a first step. Loggers were almost invariably "farmers" for whom logging was seasonal by-employment. However, not everyone who settled on the land was a farmer, even if he considered himself one and was so labeled by early observers. Many were gatherers who lived off the land, extracting what they could from the forest's largesse, rather than cultivating and developing it. They had more in common with fur trappers or placer miners than with sturdy yeoman agriculturists. But whether farmers or gatherers, forest dwellers cut and skidded trees in winter and floated them to the mills in spring, thus earning cash that their largely subsistence lifestyles otherwise seldom yielded. Such people had little invested in their logging operations, their work in the woods being labor rather than capital intensive.

Ideological as well as economic factors lay behind the growing separation of lumbermen from loggers. In England, forests held out to the poor the chance of freedom from control by the gentry or the wage system. In the seventeenth and eighteenth centuries, many found a vast new refuge in the forests of North America, where they could acquire a freehold such as they could never obtain in England. They brought with them ideas about the poor man's customary rights to common lands. Transferred to the American forest and combined with the commoners' hostility to the gentry, these ideas (and the long tradition of poaching associated therewith) helped to create a squatter mentality that questioned the claims of either proprietors or the Crown to the right to control the forest. The Wilsons of Brunswick and Topsham were among the most outspoken. One of them stated bluntly that the wilderness "was common land and hee had as good a rite to cut timber thair as anney man."[66]

The attitudes of these forest dwellers were hardly entrepreneurial. Their goal was self-sufficiency, which they considered their best safeguard and surest road to prosperity. They looked forward to an old age as patriarchs on their homesteads, settled among sons and kinsmen with farms of their own. Such people inspired fear and contempt in polite society. They were, William Douglass argued, "more dangerous than any Parcels of despicable straggling *Indians*."[67]

The economic autonomy of simple farmers and gatherers combined with their squatter ideology to lessen the likelihood they would obey commercial contracts. As Jeremy Belknap observed, woods workers "are always in debt, and frequently at law." Since they had little labor invested in their holdings, they could abandon them and move on with minimal loss.[68]

The regulatory activities of royal officials such as Jonathan Bridger were a nuisance, but the claims of proprietors were a greater threat to their dreams of economic self-sufficiency and security. Relations grew especially tense around 1718. As Bridger explained to officials in London, "the People are being persuaded that his Maj[ty] has no right to the Woods in this Countrey by Elisha Cook[e], and on that Opinion they will act next Winter they say."[69] Cooke argued that the Crown had no legitimate claim on the forests of Maine; Massachusetts had purchased the province in 1677 from the heirs of Sir Ferdinando Gorges, the original grantee who had been made Lord Proprietor of Maine in 1639 and given almost sovereign powers. As a private purchase, Cooke contended, Maine did not revert to the Crown when Massachusetts' charter was revoked in 1684. In other words, royal officials seeking to enforce the prohibition against cutting mast trees reserved for the Royal Navy, men such as Bridger, were in fact the trespassers. Not surprisingly, Bridger heatedly denounced Cooke's "unparalleled Insolence [and] republican notions."[70]

Some of the more successful loggers prospered, but most remained poor, isolated from the seats of political and economic power and dependent upon their labor for their income. By 1746, David Cargill noted, these rural folk had become "profitable to the maritime towns . . . by supplying them with wood, timber, boards, staves, &c" as well as butter, cheese, peas, and other agricultural products. In winter they worked in the woods and hunted; in spring and summer they planted, fished, netted pigeons, and worked in sawmills.[71] Plain folk of the interior may have been becoming more important to coastal towns, and to their commercial-mercantile elite in particular, but business dealings continued to be carried out on terms unfavorable to them. A settler near Casco Bay complained he and his fellows had to "labour exceedingly hard from one end of ye year to ye other, at cutting of wood, & notwithstanding all our hard labour we & our poor families are often great sufferers for want of ye necessaries of life; having most of us little or nothing to support our families with but what comes from Boston to us." As a body, they were becoming debtors—a development that deepened the gulf and embittered relations between classes.[72]

Still, some were successful. Notable among them was Humphrey Chadbourne, who arrived on the Piscataqua in 1631 to build the Great House at Strawberry Bank for John Mason and was followed in 1634 by his father and two others who built the area's first sawmill "for Captaine Mason and ourselves" with the assistance of eight Danes. When Mason abandoned his enterprise, Humphrey Chadbourne continued running the mill. In 1643 he obtained a deed to the land from the local Indian leader. Through it all, Chadbourne got out logs for the mill, which continued operating long after Mason left. As already noted, Chadbourne had a logging camp in the woods in 1659; by 1661 he was floating logs to the mill from a camp upstream—a precursor to countless New England log drives to come. Until his death in 1667, Chadbourne was a community leader. He served as a town selectman, a representative to the General Court, and an associate judge. The Wilsons of Topsham and Brunswick, those plagues of the Pejepscot proprietors, also rose to local prominence.[73]

A number of sawmill owners had less humble origins. Many of the first mills in northern New England were the work of relatively well-to-do merchant venturers seeking opportunity where they might find it. In 1651 Edward Rishworth arrived in York, located just a few miles downeast—that is, up the coast to the northeast—from the Piscataqua, to assume the post of Recorder of the Province. As a local historian put it, "[H]e brought with him a spirit of enterprise that easily made him one of the leading citizens of the town for the next half century." Rishworth promptly erected a sawmill and entered the lumber trade. About the same time, William Ellingham and Hugh Gale of Kittery contracted to build another mill in York. They enlisted the aid of two wealthy Boston merchants, Henry Webb and Thomas Clarke, and of Rishworth. Milling in York developed quickly thereafter.[74]

Similar developments took place elsewhere. In 1660 William Phillips, a man of some wealth, moved from Boston to Biddeford, Maine, on the banks of the Saco. Within two years he purchased part interest in one mill and formed a partnership to erect another. In 1680 Benjamin Blackman, acting for a company from Andover, Massachusetts, launched a grand scheme to develop every millsite on the east bank of the lower Saco. Aaron Jewett, a pioneer lumber merchant, built one of the first mills in Scarborough in 1727 and soon had an extensive lumber business. Others followed suit. One local historian observed, "For many years the lumbering business engaged the whole attention of the townsmen. . . . Lumber was even the local medium of exchange." In 1731 Boston merchants Thomas Clarke and Thomas Lake, sensing potential on the lower Kennebec, erected sawmills, built houses, brought settlers to the area, and began building ships there.[75]

So it went in place after place from New Hampshire to Casco Bay and beyond. What was said of North Yarmouth could have been said of countless others: "The inhabitants did not engage much in agriculture, but were employed in procuring wood and lumber for coasting vessels, of which many were owned here."[76]

Of all the centers of the growing lumber trade, none could match the Piscataqua. The efforts of Humphrey Chadbourne and other pioneer sawmill operators on the river lay behind a report of the Council of New Hampshire in 1681:

> *The Trade of this Province exported by yᵉ inhabitants of its own produce, is in masts, planks & boards, staves, & all other lumber. . . . And if they come here, [ships] usually come empty, to fil with lumber: but if hapily they are at any time laden with any fish, it is brought from other parts, there being none made in our Province. . . . Our soil is generally so barren, & yᵉ winters so extreme cold & long, that there is not provision enough raised to supply yᵉ inhabitants.*[77]

Lumbering was central to the economy on the Maine as well as the New Hampshire side of the Piscataqua. In 1701, when New Hampshire imposed a tonnage levy "payable by all Small vessels trading into this river," residents of York County, Maine, protested vigorously. The tax, they feared, would discourage vessels from coming to the port, vessels needed for "Exporting our Lumber, the native product of the place."[78]

Dependence upon timber exports continued for the next half-century and more, even as the trade itself grew larger and more complex. In 1730, the Lords of Trade and Plantations were told:

> *The trade of the province is lumber and fish much the same as it hath been for some years past. . . . The trade of this province to other plantations is to the Caribbee Islands, whither we send lumber and fish, and receive for it rum, sugar, molasses, and cotton; and as to our trade from hence to Europe, it is to Spain and Portugal, from whence our*

*vessels bring home salt [for preserving fish]. . . . Besides what is above
mentioned, the coasting sloops from Boston carry from hence thither fish
and timber.*

The value of the Boston trade was estimated to be five times the combined
value of that to the Caribbean and Europe.[79] The fortunes of Sir William
Pepperell and other leaders in Portsmouth and across the Piscataqua in
Kittery, Maine, depended to a great degree upon the sawmills that filled
their ships, just as did the fortunes of many in Boston, Providence, and
elsewhere to the south.[80]

The pattern was similar in Falmouth, if somewhat slower in developing.
John Phillips apparently built the first sawmill in the vicinity in 1646. For a
long time he and other millmen devoted themselves to supplying the local
community. Not until after the peace of 1726 did lumber exports boom. As
they did, new sawmills appeared, and many inhabitants turned to getting
out logs. By 1735, every millsite of consequence near the community had
its sawmill, and a solid foundation for the future city of Portland was in
place.[81]

From the first, people who erected export mills had little in common
with the simple logger-farmer, and as time went by and their trade grew,
social and economic ties bound millowners ever more closely to the
commercial-mercantile elite of the port cities. Ruralites might depend upon
the lumber trade for desperately needed cash, but their interests in it were
far different from those of sawmill owners and their allies, the merchants
who marketed their cut.[82]

Behind these developments lay the basic fact that Massachusetts, having
depleted sources nearer to hand, was reaching out to New Hampshire and
Maine for timber. As the timber trade grew during the period 1640-1688,
more enterprising individuals moved downeast to make investments in
sawmills. Others invested in ships to carry the cut to market. The bulk of
the vessels in this trade, especially the larger ones, were owned in Boston
or elsewhere to the south. The power such ownership gave outsiders was
exacerbated by the fact they alone had the commercial connections to market
the growing quantities of forest products pouring out of the north. A sort
of "timber imperialism" thus developed in the last half of the seventeenth
century in which outsiders controlled the economies of Maine and New
Hampshire to a great extent. But sawmill owners, as major allies and partners
in this commercial development, suffered from this dependency far less than
the suppliers of the logs that fed the trade. Small wonder that over time the
two were to follow divergent—and hostile—political paths.[83]

A dozen decades of development had resulted by the middle of the eighteenth century in conditions in northern New England ripe for the emergence of a full-blown lumberman's frontier. The value of forests was recognized. The technology of logging, sawing, and transporting wood products was in place; so too were established markets and individuals with vested interests in serving them. All that was needed was a change in perceptions. Enough people had to come to see lumbering as the foundation of their economic welfare to make its potential the primary lure drawing settlers and capital into new areas. That would come with a rush during the last half of the eighteenth century. When it did, a genuine lumberman's frontier quickly emerged downeast in Maine.

CHAPTER TWO

The Lumberman's Frontier Emerges

In the mid-eighteenth century, developments followed one another in quick succession, combining to make residents of northern New England more aware than ever of their dependence upon lumbering. As settlement came to new areas downeast, the place of lumbering in the economy grew ever larger. By the end of the century, a full-blown lumberman's frontier was in place, and by the 1820s community leaders in Bangor, Maine, proudly proclaimed it the largest lumber-producing center in the world. Patterns developed on this first lumberman's frontier spread west and south to shape the industry as it moved into one new area of production after another. Northern New England thus provided not only the first American lumbering frontier, but also the model for much of what followed as the industry moved across the continent.

Imperial policies of the British government were high on the list of factors in the mid-eighteenth century making people in northern New England increasingly aware of their dependence on lumbering. As trade in forest products grew, it drew attention from policymakers in London. Dominated by mercantilist thinking, they sought to regulate the trade for the greater good of Britain and the empire. More and more wood products came under the controls of the Navigation Acts, subsidies were extended to encourage production of naval stores, and the largest white pines were reserved to guarantee a source of masts for the Royal Navy. These actions increased friction between the Crown and Britain's North American subjects, especially in New Hampshire and Maine, whose export-oriented, forest-dependent economy they threatened.[1]

Wars between France and England helped make New Englanders conscious of the importance of the timber trade. These conflicts made Atlantic and Caribbean sea lanes dangerous in the extreme; with merchant vessels bottled up or owners unwilling to risk sailing, demand for the cut of New England's sawmills plummeted. Unable to dispatch cargoes of lumber, fuelwood, and other wood products by sea, rural residents in New Hampshire and Maine fell back on their farms to support their families—and frequently found them inadequate for the task. Farm income fell, for as woods operations ceased, demand for hay for oxen and food for woods workers dried up. Moreover, harassment by France and her Indian allies hampered work in woods and fields. In light of "the great Danger & distressing circumstances" faced by residents downeast, "those unhappy People" lost both direct and indirect sources of income and, save at usurious rates, their ability to buy goods or borrow from the outside. In spite of welfare handouts and frequent reduction or forgiveness of taxes, suffering was widespread.[2]

Huge forest fires helped make clear the dependence upon forests. In 1761 fires began in the interior of New Hampshire and swept toward the coast, encouraged by drought and strong winds. The next year a second series of fires broke out, moving more slowly but even more destructively through the area. Before they were stopped by fall rains, the blazes of 1761 and 1762 consumed some three million acres of forest, two-thirds of it in southern Maine. Farmers who depended on forests as much as on cropland and pastures were devastated. Migration eastward to unburned lands along the Kennebec and Penobscot soon followed.[3]

The settling of Machias speaks clearly of conditions. Machias was "a child of Scarboro"—one of those Maine settlements whose limited, marginal farmland made it especially dependent upon forests. Scarborough was hard hit by interruptions of the timber trade during the French and Indian War. Moreover, by the 1760s its accessible timber was becoming depleted. When the fires of 1761-1762 swept through the area, a number of local residents were ready to emigrate.

People in Scarborough were aware of extensive marshes along rivers east of the Penobscot. They and others had on occasion tapped them for hay for their cattle. In the autumn of 1762 Isaiah Foster, Isaac Larrabee, and others set out in a whale boat to obtain hay desperately needed because of the forest fires and drought. As experienced lumbermen, they also sought a sawmill site. Far downeast, on the Machias and East Machias rivers, they found what they were seeking: extensive tracts of tideland marsh whose salt grass had never been cut, fine millsites near the coast, and beyond both an untouched forest of pine. Moreover, the area sported "an extraordinary Harbour with several ways of entrance into it and a number of Navigable Rivers."[4]

Word of their find spread quickly in Scarborough. That winter Foster and Larrabee joined fourteen others in an association to build and operate a sawmill on the Machias. Thirteen were from Scarborough, Jonathan Carlton from Sheepscot; the remaining two associates were not expected to take up residence in the new settlement. They were Thomas Buck of Plymouth, captain of a coaster brought in to provide the community with a lifeline to the outside, and William Jones, a merchant from Portsmouth who was to furnish the settlers with supplies. What the group sought to build was not another forest-dependent agrarian community, but a lumber town; forests, not farmland drew them. However modestly, a new era had begun.

In April 1763 twenty-four people embarked for the Machias on Buck's small schooner. The venture got off to an inauspicious start. The voyage was long and stormy; when they were almost at their destination, the vessel ran onto a rock and was nearly lost. But the group persevered. They erected temporary log dwellings and, on the falls of the Machias River, a double sash mill.[5] By summer's end, they had cut sufficient boards to cover the log houses. Still, when the women and children arrived from Scarborough in August, the settlement's future remained uncertain. The settlers had been able to cut few boards beyond those needed in the community itself, and provisions were in short supply. Somehow they found the wherewithal to purchase foodstuff brought by the vessel that brought the families and agreed to furnish it with a cargo of lumber the following spring.

Each of the original partners had one-sixteenth interest in the sawmill. It was a modest operation, but they ran it night and day, and in 1764, their first full season of operation, reportedly produced over 1.5 million board feet of lumber. That same year, they laid out eighteen seven-acre lots on a peninsula near the mill, one lot for each partner plus one each for the millwright and blacksmith. The eleven married associates all built small houses on their tracts. At last the settlement was taking on an air of permanence.

By 1765 new settlers were moving in—as before, nearly all from Scarborough. But life was still perilous. As Micah Jones Talbot put it, "[P]eople were poor, [they] used to haul a few logs in the winter and saw them in summer; no one did more than he could do within his own means."[6] During the winter and spring of 1767, supply vessels failed to appear; days dragged into weeks, and provisions ran low. One of the group remembered surviving on "potato sprouts, clams, and a little flour . . . reserved for starch." Too weak from hunger and too inexperienced to succeed in hunting deer and moose, most depended for sustenance on eels and clams they collected. Long after, 1767 was still referred to as the "clam year."[7]

In spite of difficulties, the sawmill continued to run. Soon two settlements—Machias and East Machias—had sprung up, each around its own mill, while a third, Machiasport, was taking shape downstream on the bay. Other mills followed. Like the first sawmill, they were jointly owned. Pioneer memoirs report that almost every settler "went into the woods and logged in winter and sawed his own logs in summer—the time of using the saw[mill] being arranged and agreed upon" among the partners. Each partner appears to have owned his own saw blade, and after completing his turn at sawing took it home with him—for sharpening as well as safekeeping.

Logging was conducted on a shareholding basis, with the output divided at the end of the season on the basis of the shares each partner held. If a partner went into the woods to work, his labor was credited; if he did not, he had to pay a proportionate share of logging costs. Thus practically every man in the area was engaged both in logging and lumber production.[8]

From the first, logs were floated downstream in the spring. To Micah Jones Talbot, a leading lumberman of the next generation, this seemed surprising, for "by drawing them scarcely half a mile . . . [logs] could have been landed at the brow of the hill" above the mill and then rolled down to the saws. But investigators at the time reported, "without the clearing of the Land . . . [logs] cannot be transported . . . without very great expence." In any case, a shortage of labor and oxen made floating logs to the mill a practical necessity.[9]

So isolated was this outpost of European civilization that its founders were unsure to whom they should turn to legitimize their claims. They petitioned first Nova Scotia, then Massachusetts, for township status. Initial requests were denied, but they kept petitioning until in 1770 Massachusetts' General Court finally granted their request. Residents' titles remained in doubt, however, for royal authorities withheld approbation of the General Court's action.[10]

London's failure to approve probably resulted from the actions of Governor Thomas Hutchinson. A strong defender of the royal prerogative, he denounced settlements such as that at Machias, which he deemed illegal and believed gave "incouragement . . . to the waste and destruction of the Kings Timber." Frustrated when the General Court not only failed to take action to remove these trespassers, but actually encouraged them by granting a township, Hutchinson warned of possible "interposition of Parliament . . . for the sake of His Majesty's Timber."[11]

Responding, the General Court appointed a commission of three to examine the settlements. They tailored their report for Hutchinson's eyes, not to reveal the true state of affairs. At Machias, the commissioners said, they found a community with a plentitude of good farmland, an extraordinary harbor, fish in the rivers, "a considerable number of Mills," and a "sober, peaceable, and industrious" population. The pines being cut, they claimed, were not good for masts, being "what is called Saplings," while the charge that the settlers had gone there "for the sake of the Timber and when they have cut that off intend to quit the Land is without the least color of Truth; . . . a great number, perhaps the greatest never was concerned in logging, Masting, or a Saw Mill . . . and in the conclusion those who are least concerned in logging will be the Richest." The commissioners added that illegal cutting of mast trees was rare at Machias, for the area was well settled and such actions thus easily detected.[12]

The report provided a defense against Hutchinson's charges of inaction in the face of despoliation of the king's woods, but tells little about actual conditions. For those, one must turn to other sources, most notably pioneer reminiscences and contemporary records. Those paint a different picture.

From the first, settlements on the Machias depended on the forests. The promise of lumbering called them into being and sustained them once they were established. Before the American Revolution this may have been encouraged by the uncertainty of land titles, which made people loath to spend much time clearing land for agriculture and erecting improvements, but it was primarily because settlers recognized the area's potential for lumbering and went there intent upon seizing the opportunities thus offered.

The settlements at Machias were not alone. The French and Indian War was hardly over before others appeared on the far coast of Maine. By 1764 the Massachusetts General Court had granted thirteen townships east of the Penobscot.[13] The record is not clear for all of them, but several—including Bucksport, Gouldsborough, and a group of settlements on the Union River—were lumbering centers from the first. Captain Jonathan Buck founded the settlement that bore his name by erecting a mill near the mouth of the Penobscot in 1764. Thanks in part to its fine harbor, lumbering increased steadily—by the 1820s Bucksport boasted eleven sawmills. Gouldsborough (now Gouldsboro) was similar, and when Nathan Jones and associates received a grant there, they promptly set about settling it with lumbermen from Falmouth, Saco, and vicinity.[14]

These settlements were all small and poor. In 1764 their total population, including places such as Machias that had not yet been granted a township, was estimated at a mere one hundred and eighty families. Moreover, Governor Francis Barnard noted, all "except 1, 2 or 3 leading men are extremely poor & worth nothing but their lot of land, & the miserable dwelling with the little clearings they have made upon it." Still, they were harbingers of what soon became a surge of population downeast.[15]

Massachusetts' Governor Hutchinson sought to explain this rash of new settlements to the Earl of Dartmouth in 1772:

The inducement of the people to flock from the settled parts of this Province and New Hampshire and to prefer the Sea coast and Islands and Rivers . . . [in Maine] to the inland parts of either Province is the profit which arises from the pine and Oak timber which, being near the Sea, is purchased of Settlers for transportation to Europe or for the supply of the Inhabitants of Boston, Portsmouth &c.[16]

Settlers on the Union River admitted as much. "From the first settlement of these Towns, or Plantations," they reported, "the Inhabitants almost to a Man have applied themselves to the Lumber trade." The same was true at Gouldsborough. As David Cobb, resident manager of William Bingham's immense holdings, acidly commented: "They settled here in the first instance upon the sole principle of plunder."[17]

Since royal approval of their grants had been withheld, Hutchinson believed these settlements were an illegal threat to the king's woods. He told the Earl of Dartmouth, "A very great quantity [of timber] has been carried away to England" from them, "and the King has paid no inconsiderable sum as a bounty for bringing away his own Timber without his license." Worse yet, "As the settlers increase, this mischief increases."[18]

Surging lumber production elsewhere coincided with developments downeast from the Penobscot. In Falmouth, the Reverend Thomas Smith noted construction of a number of mills following the French and Indian War and—after a long period during which the lumber had primarily been consumed locally—a burgeoning export trade. "The ships and other vessels loading here are a wonderful benefit to us," he wrote. "They take off vast quantities of timber, masts, oar-rafters, boards, &c." Up the Presumpscot to Gorham lumbering was forging ahead.[19]

Production was booming in other long-settled areas too. At Wells "demand for lumber rapidly increased, and . . . farmers found the manufacture of boards more profitable than tilling the soil." In nearby Kennebunk, which had done less in the way of agriculture, nearly all its twenty-five families had come "for the purpose of building and operating mills and supplying the lumber market." Sawmill operations also grew rapidly on the Saco. By 1772 operators were obtaining logs from as far inland as Fryeburg—some sixty miles from the coast.[20]

East of Casco Bay, near Bristol and Bremen, similar developments were taking place. A local historian noted that, after 1763, "Agriculture was not entirely neglected, but was not depended upon. People obtained a livelihood chiefly by getting out lumber and wood, or by fishing." Firewood could be obtained for 58 cents a cord and sold for many times that in cities to the south. Profits on sawn lumber seem to have been nearly as great. As a result, "[s]mall sloops and schooners ran frequently to Boston, carrying wood and lumber, bringing in return supplies of West India goods and other articles."[21]

Although still modest at this time, developments on the Kennebec and Penobscot would in the long run prove more important than any of the others. Joseph Berry built a mill at Georgetown, near the mouth of the Kennebec, in 1759. The first mills appeared upstream at Gardiner in 1760 and 1761. With the coming of peace, others followed in rapid succession until, a local historian wrote, "of saw mills there was no end. Where there was a saw mill is not so much of a question as where there wasn't one."[22] After years of struggle, the area entered a period of steady growth. The General Court created Lincoln County in 1760 and made Pownalborough (formerly Frankfort, later Dresden) its seat. By 1764, the county had 4,347 inhabitants, most residing in the Kennebec drainage, and Pownalborough was prospering. Agriculture had been the initial focus, but now most settlers "were occupied in lumbering, legally or otherwise, neglecting their planting for the quick profit" forests offered.[23]

Development on the Penobscot lagged behind that on the Kennebec, both because it was further downeast and because the Indian threat lasted longer there. To be sure, Jonathan Buck erected a mill near the river's mouth in 1764, but the community long depended as much on fishing as lumbering. Not until operations moved upstream, closer to major supplies of sawtimber, did lumbering begin to take firm root. That came in 1771, when Joseph Mansel built a sawmill at Bangor, while John Brewer and Moses Wentworth each erected one at nearby Orrington; by the end of the year there were twenty-two people in the community developing around the two mills, all except Wentworth from Cape Cod or Worcester. In 1772 James Budge also erected a mill in Bangor, and he steadily expanded his operations thereafter. Development began at Orono too. Lumbering on the Penobscot was soon booming.[24]

The sum of these developments can be simply stated: a lumberman's frontier had emerged. Tapping North American forests had been profitable since the earliest European settlements, but it had never been the primary stimulus for development of any large area. In the years immediately following the French and Indian War that is precisely what developed downeast in Maine. Lumbering had become a major stimulus for growth and an important support of the economy.

John Wentworth, Surveyor General of the Woods (as well as royal governor of New Hampshire), was cognizant of the circumstances. Britain's existing forest policy, which sought to protect the king's woods from loggers, was, he later admitted, "merely penal" and worked "against the conveniences and even necessities of the inhabitants." Strictly enforced, it would hold back development of northern New England. Wentworth sought a more reasoned approach. In 1773 he proposed that a new government be created encompassing lands stretching from the Penobscot to Nova Scotia, an area where lumbering not agriculture was the more promising road to progress; that its best forest tracts be set aside as royal reserves; and that settlers be attracted to the area to log these and other stands. Wentworth prophesied: "their labors as lumbermen would bring prosperity to them and the Crown."[25]

Wentworth's proposal was tacit recognition that a lumberman's frontier was emerging east of the Penobscot, but the same thing was happening elsewhere. Indeed, although they were most noticeable in new places such as Machias where there was nothing pre-existing to obscure them, the most significant advances were taking place in older communities such as Falmouth and Saco. There lumbering provided an unwonted stimulus to expand their hinterlands into the interior while at the same time enriching and enlarging the metropolitan center those hinterlands fed.

One must be careful not to overstate the case. Lumbering was not the sole cause of Maine's rapid development after 1763. While lumbermen were moving downeast along the coast, farmers were pouring into the interior, many driven by environmental degradation and population pressures in older parts of New England. Visitors repeatedly remarked on the persistent, grinding poverty of Maine's back country, yet hope for the future continued to draw settlers. The valleys of the Kennebec and Penobscot seemed particularly promising. More fertile than the rocky coastal strip, more sheltered from Atlantic gales, the interior drew a host of settlers. Trapping had eliminated most of the beaver in the interior; their dams, which had once flooded many acres, had fallen into disrepair; and meadows had developed where beaver ponds once stood. Settlers coveted the resulting openings, for they required no arduous clearing. They also turned to hardwood-covered ridges, with their good soil and relative freedom from unseasonable frosts. The bottoms, to which cold air drained, were the domain of conifers, and settlers tended to avoid them although on carefully selected sites, successful farming seemed feasible. Once one pushed so far into the interior as to pass above six hundred feet in elevation, farming became decidedly submarginal; this area too was dominated by conifers and was scrupulously avoided by the well informed.[26]

Records are imprecise, but it seems at this time more people set about carving out farms in the interior than ventured to settlements on the emerging lumbering frontier. Eventually, settlers in the interior would become important to Maine's lumber industry, but for the moment they were largely outside it. Many tapped the forests to supplement the output of their farms; however, in so doing, they represented not something new, but older colonial patterns that had appeared long before a real lumberman's frontier emerged.

Maine developed rapidly during the first decade following the French and Indian War. But as lumbering spread and its importance to the province grew, so too did dissatisfaction with royal regulations of the woods and the timber trade.[27]

In light of the actions of Hutchinson and the royal government he championed, it is hardly surprising that when the Revolution came, settlers on the Machias rallied to the American cause. They successfully repelled British attack, and as the only settlement between the Penobscot and St. Croix remaining in American hands, kept alive claims of the United States to that vast area. But it was not just Machias; Maine as a whole supported the American cause even as many Tories fled there to be closer to British forces in Canada or to escape persecution in areas to the south.[28]

The war years exacerbated social divisions within Maine. Samuel Thompson a "rough-hewn, self-made" sawmill and tavern owner from Brunswick "who had attained prosperity by taking logs for his sawmill from royal and proprietary forests" was one of the district's most prominent revolutionary leaders. In 1774, disturbed by the caution and suspected pro-British views of the leadership of Falmouth and Wiscasset, he led an armed band of farmer-loggers to those and other communities to force people to sign covenants to boycott British goods. The following year he conspired to seize royal mast agent Edward Parry and then H.M.S. *Canceaux*, anchored in Falmouth harbor to guard a shipbuilder constructing a vessel for buyers in England. Hard on the heels of fighting at Lexington and Concord, he briefly captured Lieutenant Henry Mowat, captain of *Canceaux*. Roused by "Thompson's War," militia sharing his views poured into Falmouth from the surrounding area. "The soldiery," a resident wrote, "thought nothing too bad to say of the *Falmouth* gentry. Some were heard to say as they walked the streets . . . 'this Town ought to be laid in Ashes.' "

Thompson had set in motion a chain of events that would do precisely that. In October 1775 Lieutenant Mowat returned with a small fleet to bombard the town and then sent landing parties ashore to fire buildings still standing. Two-thirds of the town was destroyed; the rural militia, rather than fighting the British, looted structures while the fires raged. The Reverend Jacob Bailey, an avowed Tory, described the scene: "[A] multitude of villains were purloining . . . goods and carrying them into the country beyond the reach of justice. . . . The country people were hardly restrained from destroying the houses that escaped the general devastation."[29]

Thompson's growing reputation as a patriot led to his appointment as brigadier general for Cumberland County. The gentry were outraged. To them Thompson was a dangerous radical who failed to treat his betters with deference and who, through his actions, threatened the entire social order. They were absolutely correct. Thompson's views epitomized what Carl Becker had in mind when he wrote his oft-quoted statement: the American Revolution was not only a question of home rule, but also of who should rule at home. Not surprisingly, in 1779 the gentry mounted a campaign to get Thompson removed from command. The towns that rallied to his support and stymied the gentry's effort were nearly all small, poor, interior communities.[30]

Wartime suffering was not confined to Falmouth. Other coastal communities were captured or abandoned. With vital maritime supply lines cut, provisions were scarce and dear almost everywhere. With producers unable to market lumber and fish, unemployment skyrocketed. Maine had an extraordinarily high rate of enlistments in the Continental Army, a reflection of devotion to the American cause, to be sure, but also of the dire straits in which many a family found itself. Uncertain though it was, the promise of food and pay as a Continental soldier seemed the best hope for many a young Maine resident. Sometimes the result was tragic. An estimated one-quarter of the able-bodied men of Bristol died in military service during the war.[31]

Machias provides another case in point. When fighting broke out, the community had only a three-week supply of provisions. Cut off by British seapower, unable to sell their lumber or get supplies from outside, residents turned to the area's waters for sustenance just as they had during the "clam year." They also took up farming as best they could, but there was little good agricultural land and the climate severely limited success. As in 1767, suffering was widespread.[32]

In spite of difficulties, Maine continued to grow during the Revolution. Forests in the interior offered a refuge from the ravages of war and a place beyond the reach of enlistment officers where able-bodied men who wished to avoid service could remain with their families. There was little demand for lumber, so, as at Machias, settlers turned to farming. Utilizing the new "good burn" method of clearing, they were able to raise their first crops without extensive ploughing or even completely removing trees. In time these settlers would provide a reservoir of laborers for the lumber industry, but for the moment their inroads on the forest came primarily through land clearing and fires started in the process. Indeed, so numerous were forest fires in the interior that on May 19, 1780—the infamous "dark day"—smoke

Downeast in Maine. Map by Sarah E. Hinman.

and an atmospheric inversion combined to make it so dark, even in coastal towns, that to see candles needed to be lit at noon.[33]

The end of the war found Machias and many other lumber settlements in dire straits. During the conflict, mills had rotted down while debts accumulated. Now, with both labor and interest rates high, but lumber "in great demand & commanding a great price," owners borrowed heavily to rebuild. But the new mills were barely on line when Britain closed the West Indies to all but a trickle of American commerce—and that only in British vessels. Lumber prices plummeted. Two years of drought followed; at Machias mills had to stop sawing in July for lack of sufficient water to drive the saws. Its people "in the utmost distress," Machias petitioned for a reduction in taxes.[34] Settlements on the Union River did likewise; a spokesmen explained, "the late stagnation and the fall of [prices for] our Lumber . . . sinks us down to that Poverty and distress which we experienced in the War, and obliges us again to cultivate the Pine Wilderness for Bread."[35]

Conditions were little better further south. The area around Falmouth, although considerably wealthier, was plagued by many of the problems facing Machias and the Union River settlements. In addition to the destruction of much of the city, nearly all vessels owned there were lost during the war. In 1785 disastrous floods swept away most of the area's sawmills as well as quantities of logs and lumber. "Great numbers of persons, who depended on their mills for support, are reduced to extreme distress," the *Falmouth Gazette* reported, adding it would probably take years to repair the damage.[36]

Recovery came—and not as slowly as the *Gazette* forecast. As times became better, interest in lumbering grew. Following the Revolution, William D. Williamson wrote in his classic *History of the State of Maine*, "no subjects commanded more lively and universal attention than the settlement, the conditional grants, and the timber of the eastern lands. . . . There was a passion for obtaining settlers' lots, mill sites, and water privileges."[37] Settlements largely dependent upon timber sprang up on both banks of the St. Croix, while on the Penobscot, with Indian as well as British threats eliminated, development rushed ahead. Elsewhere, new settlements appeared one after another, while older ones grew and gained incorporation as towns. Land speculation was rife; as Moses Greenleaf noted, "investments in wild land were considered by many as the surest and most abundant sources of profit." From time to time floods struck, sawmills burned, and local crop failures occurred, but such events were too scattered and infrequent to undermine the general mood of optimism.[38]

Massachusetts encouraged the process. Seeking to aid development, reward veterans of the Revolution, and reduce staggering debts accumulated during the war, it sold and granted eastern lands with abandon. Of the thirty million acres in Maine, an estimated two-thirds had not previously been transferred to private hands. During the twelve years following the war, title to some 3.5 million acres passed from the commonwealth.[39]

Much land went to non-residents. In 1786 the Massachusetts legislature established a lottery commission to bring in money by offering to award fifty townships east of the Penobscot. Only five people from Maine participated, showing the lack of capital there and fueling a belief that wealthy outsiders were engrossing the district's resources. Indeed they were. In July 1791 General Henry Knox of Boston and Colonel William Duerr of New York purchased over three million acres. In January 1793, finding themselves financially over-extended, they sold their key tracts—some 2.1 million acres, one-ninth of Maine—to William Bingham of Philadelphia for 12.5 cents an acre. The *Cumberland Gazette* inveighed against mass transfers on grounds that owning large tracts of land was undemocratic. In spite of such complaints, disposal continued unabated.[40]

Massachusetts was also seeking to bring order to developments. In 1785 the legislature passed an act setting standards for lumber and shingles and requiring each town to name inspectors to ensure compliance. Merchants in Falmouth and elsewhere tended to support the new rules, while producers in the hinterlands often objected. A feeling that the regulations favored the mercantile elite, while penalizing common folk, contributed to demands for separating Maine from Massachusetts; among the leading separatists was Samuel Thompson (who, consistently, was also a staunch anti-federalist and supporter of Daniel Shays).[41] The populist rhetoric of such men aside, the intent of the regulations appears to have been to reduce the glut of lumber on the market and thereby help stabilize prices.

Just how successful the regulations were in ensuring quality is open to question, as conflicting claims and an anecdote in the local press show:

> *A number of sailors, who had been loading a vessel with lumber, for the West-Indies, was a few days ago ask'd by the owner of their opinion of the cargo:*
>
>   —Why, *says one,* bad enough, hardly fit for use.
>   —It is fit for no use, *says another,* except to *burn.*
>   —No, faith, *says a third,* nor is what I have handled fit even for
>   *that!*[42]

The regulations' effectiveness in stabilizing prices was equally doubtful.

Massachusetts also tried to regularize lumbering by forbidding timber cutting on ungranted commonwealth lands and providing for the prosecution of those who did. Further, it attempted to clear up the welter of land claims that clouded titles and added to the risks of lumbering downeast, approved a lottery to raise funds to clear the Saco for log drives, and passed legislation protecting the owners of logs floated downstream and providing punishments for those who removed or defaced owners' brands on them.[43]

Swept along by uncommon prosperity, hunger for timberland grew. The Napoleonic Wars diverted neutral trade to the United States and increased demand for Maine's lumber. Sales for export and construction of wooden ships increased. "There is not a river," Alexander Baring wrote, "on which a mill for sawing boards is not erected and the southern states, as well as the West Indies, are supplied entirely from Maine, [timber in] the old countries being exhausted." By 1801 "public lands were uniformly . . . a subject of great interest," but local leaders—who understood only too well the district's dependence on foreign markets—worried over rumors of impending peace in Europe.[44]

In spite of their fears, prosperity and growth continued. Maine had a population of 42,241 in 1777; by 1800 it had risen to 151,719, most of the increase in newer townships; by 1810 it was 228,767.[45] According to pioneer statistician Moses Greenleaf, five-sixths of the population were "farmers," but as has been shown, the bulk of Maine's farmers depended on lumbering as much as or more than agriculture. In areas like Wells, per capita crop production fell after the Revolution, while that of lumber rose. More than ever, timber was the backbone of the economy. William Morris noted almost all the people "on the coast, and up the Kennebeck, Penobscot, Sheepscut [sic] and other rivers to the eastwards are connected with navigation and lumbering." Alexander Baring agreed, "the only occupations . . . are fishing and lumbering. They are found the most profitable." Indeed, there "is scarcely a settler in the country who has not some direct or indirect concern" in lumbering. One historian summed it up neatly: "Maine's economy at this time, as throughout her history, was very nearly a one-crop economy. Timber was king."[46]

Records from individual communities underscore the point. For the ten years between 1800 and 1812 for which statistics are available, *all* of the 576 vessels sailing from Wiscasset, a fairly typical port located a short distance east of the Kennebec near the mouth of the Sheepscot River, had lumber and other timber products as their primary cargo; only twenty also carried flour, fish, or potash. Wiscasset, Baring noted, had more shipping than all New Hampshire and there "is no small port in Maine that does not own some shipping; the whole coasts swarm with coasters . . . employed in nothing but carrying lumber and firewood to Boston" and beyond. At Blue Hill in 1790, thirty-eight of the town's seventy-eight residents owned timberland but no cropland, while twelve had an interest in one or more sawmills. Hardly the expected figures from a district in which five-sixths of the population was listed as farmers![47]

The erection of new sawmills and the enlargement of older ones accompanied this growth. On the Saco, money poured into mills and ships. Congestion on the waterfront became so great that by 1795 it was necessary to regulate how long lumber could be stacked on wharves before being taken away. In places where production was long established, loggers moved ever deeper into the interior in search of sources of logs. Benjamin Lincoln described the process:

> these people . . . take hay on their sleds, when the rivers are frozen and follow up the streams on the ice, until they find a good spot of timber near the banks. Here they halt, sometimes the distance of forty miles. The timber is cut and thrown into the river, or on the ice, so that on the breaking up of winter, the logs go downstream even into the mill ponds, and often when there is a great head of water, they go over the dams and into the sea.[48]

On the Presumpscot, nearly all accessible timber from the coast to Sebago Lake had gone through the saws by the late eighteenth century. Mills fell into disrepair, and "farmers" in the interior, who depended on logging for their livelihood, were destitute. Those in Gorham Township tried rafting logs across the wide lake and failed repeatedly. However, "the pressure of poverty and a spirit of hardy enterprise induced them . . . to persevere" until they succeeded. Immense quantities of logs were soon moving across Sebago Lake and down the Presumpscot, sawmills were repaired, and Portland's commerce in lumber entered a new era of prosperity.[49]

On the lower Kennebec, accessible timber was also fast disappearing into the mills. By 1792 there were over seventy sawmills on the river, most well built and equipped with two or more saws. Hallowell, which at the end of the Revolution had only three houses, was becoming a major lumbering center. By the end of the eighteenth century, the river's lower reaches had a well-settled agricultural air, but lumber production was still growing as loggers pushed upstream well beyond the line of settlement. The fact the Kennebec could support log drives all the way from its source on Moosehead Lake drew loggers ever further into the interior. Nor did the move inland occur only on the Saco, Presumpscot, and Kennebec. As Alexander Baring noted, coastal Maine had been cleared of "fine timber" almost to the Penobscot "and people [everywhere] go as far as forty or fifty miles back for it."[50]

As loggers moved ever further into the interior, they frequently trespassed on others' holdings. In 1792 the Plymouth Company, disturbed by reports from the vicinity of Skowhegan, appointed Thomas Wallcut to "prevent any strip or waste by cutting of masts or other timber on any of the lands of the Propriety." Further upstream on the Kennebec was a million acres of prime timberland that was part of William Bingham's purchase of 1792. Loggers moved into this too, cutting legally or illegally as circumstances demanded and floating the logs downstream to Winslow, where they were sorted into rafts for distribution to various sawmills. When F. Andre Michaux visited Winslow in 1806, he reported the river was "covered with thousands of logs."[51]

The situation was similar on the Androscoggin, which joins the Kennebec at Merrymeeting Bay. Its main mills were at Topsham and Brunswick (there were twenty-five sawmills at Brunswick Falls by the 1820s), but logs came from the far interior and distances grew ever greater.[52]

Bath served as the shipping point for lumber from the Kennebec and Androscoggin. A modest settlement when Jonathan Hyde arrived in 1792, Bath grew steadily as lumbering expanded and residents took to building ships for the carrying trade. By the early nineteenth century it was one of Maine's premier towns. "Merchants were largely engaged in the West India trade," a resident recalled. "The bulk of outward cargoes was lumber. This was bought here for $8.00 a thousand and sold in the West Indies for $60.00. The return cargoes would consist of rum, sugar, and molasses, on which the profits would equal those of the outward cargo."[53] Ellsworth, Gouldsborough, Machias, and other lumber ports grew rapidly too. Machias shipped millions of feet annually during the 1790s and by mid-decade was building ships of its own to carry its cut.[54]

The greatest growth was on the Penobscot. Bangor, destined to become the largest city on the river, was not even founded until 1769; Joseph Mansel erected the first sawmill in the vicinity in 1771; and by the following year twelve families had moved in. Others followed in rapid succession. At first agriculture attracted much of the attention of settlers, many of whom were from Cape Cod or other environmentally devastated parts of Massachusetts, but by the 1790s, lumber had become the chief staple and more and more ships were calling for it. By the time Talleyrand visited Bangor in the mid-nineties, it was a bustling lumber town. "You know by reputation the settlement of *Bangor*," he wrote. "We have mentioned to you the beauty of the river, where the vessels can enter without a pilot, and it is enough to add that this municipality has fifteen hundred inhabitants, that a fourth of the land is cleared, and that on the *Penobscot River* proper and on an arm named *Custine* [Castine] there are sixty mills." Talleyrand's figures were inflated, but clearly lumber production was high and rising rapidly.[55]

The first settlers in the area, as in many other localities downeast, were squatters. Frequently denigrated by contemporary observers, who had trouble seeing past their poverty and crude ways, many were in fact bright, shrewd men who were worthy and industrious. A good portion had lived in older areas of settlement, where timber was now running short; they moved to the Penobscot country to find fresh sources of pine to allow them to continue their mode of living, which alternated winter logging with simple subsistence agriculture in summer.[56]

The scale of undertakings, as well as their number, was growing. Although one historian noted that at Machias no one yet had enough capital to operate a large business, operations—there and elsewhere—were growing. The earliest mills cost their builders a few hundred dollars, at most; by 1792 it cost some $800 to build a good mill on the Kennebec; in 1801, William Hammond built a mill at Bangor for $1,028. By 1819 there were forty-seven mills at Calais, on the St. Croix; most were valued at $3,000. And while the first mills were almost invariably single or double sash mills, by 1803 there was a fifteen-saw gang mill operating at St. John, just across the border, and similar ones seem to have been present in Maine.[57]

It is difficult to get a precise fix on the increases. Data for the period are fragmentary and notoriously unreliable. The federal census for 1810, for example, does not list a single sawmill in Maine. Illegal cutting was intentionally unreported. Coastwise lumber shipments do not appear in customs house records. Still, tax records make it possible to get a rough estimate of what was transpiring. Between property evaluations carried out for tax purposes in 1786 and those of 1792, the number of sawmills in Maine increased roughly 50 percent, reaching 366 by the latter year. Commercial property increased even more rapidly. Since most commercial property was in ships, wharves, and the like, and since the predominant, if not exclusive, purpose of these was to handle lumber exports, it appears shipments more than doubled during the period. Sawmills obviously were not only more numerous, but also averaged considerably larger in 1792 than they had in 1786.[58]

Like sawmills, woods operations had grown. At first loggers worked alone or with a handful of associates, as had the first settlers at Machias. As late as

1794 many still did. One observer wrote that settlers "supply their timber out of their own woods; convey it to the shore upon their own sledges, drawn by their own oxen, at a time when they are not necessarily employed in any other work; and reckon nothing for their labour, by all of which their small profits are somewhat enhanced." One settler on the Waldo Patent, operating thus, cut one hundred and fifty cords of firewood and one to two hundred large trees in a winter.[59] But by 1800, individual had given way to group effort in many places. Crews of forty or more loggers elicited no surprise. Such crews would have many yoke of oxen, considerable specialization of tasks, and a fairly sophisticated support network. They were primarily made up of young, single men who once would have worked locally hauling logs on their own account but now labored far from home for wages offered by contractors and entrepreneurs.[60]

Farmers made a considerable business out of gathering and stacking hay to meet the winter demands of this new type of operation. Viewing the size of haying operations, some proprietors hastened to sell their land, for they saw in them a sign that loggers would soon be stripping timber from it at an unprecedented rate. Such fears were warranted. Benjamin Lincoln observed that traditionally nothing had been paid for timber cut in the eastern parts of the district: "People have set down on public lands, possessed themselves of the best mill seats, and have cut the timber . . . where it has been most convenient for them, without ever accounting for the same." As David Cobb said of loggers near Gouldsborough: "[T]he inhabitants have practis'd it for such length of time that it has long since ceas'd to be a crime to plunder the forrests of this country—so far from it that the principle is completely revers'd, and he is the criminal that attempts to prevent it."[61]

Not all the increase was a product of thievery. Unlike the number of sawmills, the ownership of woodland property failed to show a significant increase in the period; however, that is hardly proof of increased timber trespass. In fact, during the late 1790s Cobb and others managed to institute a system whereby sawmill owners paid a standard fee to timberland owners for each thousand feet of lumber cut from logs taken from their land. Sometimes this was as low as one-eighth of the cut, but normally higher. This system was easier to enforce than it was to prove timber trespass, for the number of mills was limited and their sites fixed, so determining roughly the amount of lumber sawn was not difficult. The development represented a major step toward systematizing the region's lumber industry.

By 1796 payments for timber based on the quantity of lumber produced were standard on the Kennebec. Thanks to the efforts of local leaders such as Judge Stephen Jones, the system was also adopted on the Union

River, at Gouldsborough, on the Machias, and elsewhere. In December 1800, when a forty-man crew of loggers moved into woods across the low divide separating the Kennebec watershed from the Sheepscot, residents of the latter, "claiming a right of territory, drove them off" until the agent for the trespassers agreed to pay the standard fees. The emerging working relationship between timber owners and sawmill operators brought unwonted stability and order to operations. Timber trespass continued, but it was no longer the norm. Lumbering was moving from its most primitive phase, in which woodsmen gathered logs much as trappers took beaver, and entering the more sophisticated world of business—a world where property rights and legal titles played an increasingly important role, and in which it was no longer essential to steal logs if sawmills were to operate.[62]

Timber owners were not entirely happy with the new order. Despairingly, William Bingham noted that timber was "rising immencely [sic] in value" and ought to be held, but he thought that "when it is so exposed that the most circumspect attention cannot protect it from depredation" one should sell it on "the best terms . . . which the nature of the case will admit." He briefly considered building sawmills, so those felling timber would have to sell their logs to him, but the cost of building enough mills to control his vast domains was too high, the difficulties too complex. In the end, faced with a choice between trying to halt timber trespass or allowing cutting to proceed and accepting one-eighth as payment for stumpage, Bingham joined others in opting for the latter course.[63]

Many loggers were surely unenthusiastic about the change. Like other plain folk, they resented the engrossing of the land by the wealthy, believing they had a right to the products thereof and perhaps even to title. But the legal, political, and economic cards were stacked against them, and the more perceptive realized that a system allowing them to continue logging while indirectly paying fees for the sawlogs they took was the best arrangement they could expect.[64]

Other structural changes were also occurring. The social and economic gap between sawmill operators and woods workers was growing ever larger. So too was the gap between coastal mercantile communities, in which more and more sawmill operators lived, and those who dwelled in the interior. In 1786 five towns—Portland, Pepperelborough, Bath, Scarborough, and York—contained half the commercial property of Maine. The ownership of woodland property was slightly more dispersed, but residents of twelve towns owned half of that reported for the entire district. Since commercial property and woodland ownership were central to Maine's growing lumber industry, combining the value of the two types of property gives a good indication of where control lay. On this combined scale, Portland headed all other communities, followed in order by Hallowell, Berwick, Pepperelborough, and Wells.[65]

Within these and other centers, a handful of relatively wealthy men was coming to the fore. Property ownership was concentrated in fewer hands than in other communities. Among the leaders were merchants, such as Thomas Cutts of Pepperelborough and Thomas Robison of Portland, who became wealthy because outside financial connections allowed them to take advantage of opportunities in the wake of the Revolution; attorneys, whose expert help was essential in the complex world of land titles and whose work gave them information and connections far more important in advancing their fortunes than their fees ever were; and entrepreneurs, such as General Samuel Veazie, who built upon contacts developed during the War of 1812 to become the foremost sawmill operator on the Penobscot. Sometimes it was simply enough to be in the right place at the right time. James Kavanaugh and Matthew Cottrill arrived from Ireland in the early 1780s. Within ten years they were established at Newcastle on the Damariscotta River as successful merchants owning stores, sawmills, shipyards, and vessels.[66]

Merchants and lawyers—men with "connections"—thus formed a working elite beholden to outside capital and the social favors that went with it. Moses Greenleaf spelled out the situation:

> *A considerable proportion of the active capital, employed in Maine . . . has been furnished from other places. . . . A large share of the exports of Maine consists of lumber and fish. To procure these articles, and prepare them for the market, requires an advance of capital, or labor, which amounts to the same thing, from three, to six, twelve, and in some cases eighteen months. The persons annually employed in these pursuits have seldom capital enough of their own to carry on the business to any profitable degree, and wait the slow returns of the eventual sales of their products for their remuneration; but the extensive advances which the [outside] merchants and traders were enabled to make, superseded the necessity of it.*

More succinctly, "Maine, *in its present state*, must owe some part of its prosperity to the use of the capital of persons not residing within the District." Portland, Wiscasset, and Biddeford dominated Maine's West Indies trade, which gave them an advantage over other ports of the district, but much of their trade passed through Boston, a circumstance that helped keep even these favored locations dependent. To make matters worse, per capita wealth in Maine was half that of Massachusetts proper and, following the Revolution, Maine was growing less rapidly.[67]

The participation of coastal towns in the market economy gave them a higher standard of living and more available specie, but the interior was not sufficiently integrated into that economy to get the same advantages. As historian Richard Judd has put it, "Most farmers straddled the worlds of commerce and self-sufficiency," a decidedly precarious position under the circumstances. Moreover, many in the coastal communities, preferring to protect their superior position and hoping to cultivate sources of capital in Boston and elsewhere to the south, took little interest in alleviating economic distress in the hinterlands. They seem to have considered themselves indispensable guides responsible for the development of the eastern country—for speeding and rationalizing settlement while improving the discipline of settlers. Without such leadership, they were convinced, squatter barbarism would bring anarchy and ruin to the commercial state.[68]

David Cobb was blunt. "Lumbermen and Savages add no value to the Soil on which they reside," he wrote, "as they both equally live on the Forest." He advocated building roads to the interior in hopes they would draw settlers away from the rivers, for "the Farmer who setts down on a River in this Country, turns as naturally to a log stealer as the civiliz'd man does to a Savage." Cobb called for the prosecution of "these depridators or this country will be unfit for any civilized character to live in." He even set up model farms to teach "the Yahoos here, these log stealing scoundrels, how to get their living by cultivating the soil."[69]

The rhetoric of squatters was as flamboyant as that of Cobb. Following in the footsteps of Elisha Cooke and Samuel Thompson, Samuel Ely of Ducktrap made himself a spokesman for settlers. He attacked Knox and the "nabobs" mercilessly, denouncing their proprietary claims as invalid and them as grasping speculators who sought to profit from the labors of others while doing nothing to improve the land themselves. Settlers, Ely said, did not ask for much, just clear title to lands they had reclaimed from the wilderness at great personal risk and hardship and to which they had thereby given value.[70]

But to juxtapose such extreme views paints a misleading picture. Not everyone in the seacoast towns shared the views of Cobb and Knox or the goals of speculators like Bingham. William King, a leading merchant-capitalist of Bath, was a spokesman for squatters' rights at the same time that he actively engaged in land speculations of his own. King championed the separation of Maine from Massachusetts and successfully rode the twin sentiments of Jeffersonianism and separation to become the first governor of an "independent" Maine. Others of his class, such as Peleg Tallman of Woolwich and Moses Carlton, Jr., and Abiel Wood, Jr., of Wiscasset, also showed sympathy for the plain folk. No doubt a central cause of such concern was the fact Maine's elite had never achieved the status of a genuine aristocracy. As William Willis noted, "Most . . . were engaged in trade, and the means of none were sufficiently ample to enable them to live without engaging in some employment." To many such men, it was clear Maine's economy was tied to the exportation of lumber and settlers were essential elements in its production. To champion their interests was to champion one's own.[71]

Buoyed by the economic climate, "a spirit of adventure and risque" was abroad by 1805—a spirit that neither frequent financial losses nor insecure land titles could quash. Timberland far removed from sawmills was eagerly sold and resold; its price rose dramatically. William Morris reported land prices increased between 50 and 100 percent between 1785 and 1792. State land, which had sold for an average price of 20 cents per acre between 1785 and 1812, was by the end of the period going for 58.5 cents—and that for more isolated tracts than those sold earlier.[72]

The Embargo of 1807 and the War of 1812 brought the era of prosperity to an abrupt, if temporary, halt. Once again ships were tied up, stacks of lumber went unsold, and settlers were reduced to poverty. By March 1809 some 60 percent of the population of coastal towns was unemployed and soup kitchens were set up in Portland. Seamen and fishermen, like loggers, were driven to find sustenance from the land. Maine's outside sources of capital dried up.[73]

Despairing of the repeated cycles of boom and bust and seeing that much of the timber was already cut in those parts of Maine where subsistence agriculture could best be pursued, settlers began to depart from Maine for more promising lands in the West. "Ohio fever" would in time drain the state of thousands of industrious young men and their families and divert numerous others, who a decade or two earlier might have thought of moving from Massachusetts to Maine, to move west instead.[74]

Even these developments were insufficient to kill the speculative spirit, which in Williamson's words "seemed to float without control." The thirst for Maine's timberlands continued, and with the return of peace in 1815 burst forth in a frenzy of purchasing. Capital flooded into investments in sawmills, and the construction of ships for the lumber trade surged, especially after 1817, when the United States closed its coastwise shipping to foreign-built vessels.[75]

Swept along by these developments, many farmers—rather than departing for the Ohio—sold their holdings in the older parts of Maine and took up new claims downeast. There they found fresh supplies of pine and continued the pattern of simple subsistence farming in summer combined with logging in winter that had long supported many of them but was becoming increasingly difficult in older sections as timber became ever more remote and inaccessible.[76] As they removed to the Penobscot and beyond in search of new stands, these frontier farmer-loggers provided testimony to just how forest dependent life in Maine had become.

On the eve of statehood, Maine's economy rested more than ever on its forests. The lumberman's frontier that had emerged there was its driving force, tying the state to dependence on outside capital and markets, to boom and bust cycles, and to activities that shaped social norms and individual values. Along the coast from the Kennebec to the St. Croix, and far up many another river, the first lumberman's frontier had taken shape since the end of the French and Indian War.

CHAPTER THREE

The Maine Frontier at Floodtide

Maine became a state in 1820; the first lumberman's frontier came into full flower there not long after. The two developments were intimately connected. Lumbering had developed slowly during the colonial and early national periods. Knowledge of the value of the District of Maine's forests, the technology and expertise for exploiting them, and entrepreneurs, workers and others dedicated to doing so had all appeared over the preceding years. By providing employment and exports, Maine's forests contributed to a gradual buildup of the district's economy, infrastructure, and population and brought closer the day when statehood would become well nigh inevitable. After 1820, with statehood providing a freer hand to those desiring to further economic growth by tapping the state's most plentiful resource, the last prerequisite for full development of the forests was in place.

But 1820 marked more than the commencement of statehood. In a more general way, it was the beginning of a new era in the exploitation of Maine's forests. Until then lumbering had been essentially pre-industrial, carried on by individuals who made limited investments in land or equipment, performed a multiplicity of poorly differentiated functions, and engaged in minimal processing. Loggers' activities were those of resource gatherers, while those of lumber manufacturers were more artisanal than industrial—and the separation between the two, loggers and lumbermen, was often from season to season rather than individual to individual.

This had begun to change earlier, but the speed with which modifications came accelerated rapidly after 1820. The older patterns persisted in remote, newly opened areas in the interior, but in more accessible and established locations the size of investments, levels of functional differentiation and processing, and—not least—the mindset of those engaged all changed. Lumbering became at least proto-industrial, and the lumberman's frontier of Maine thus a special sort of manufacturer's frontier. This transition took place not just at the logging and milling levels; transportation and marketing grew more intricate and took on new forms. Of course, there had been a slow but steady growth of sophistication in tapping Maine's forests ever since the days of Humphrey Chadbourne and that first mill near Berwick, but now a qualitative as well as quantitative shift was taking place. Developments at Machias had been a harbinger, but in many ways that community's activity was the result of individual more than collective efforts (remember, each of the pioneer participants owned his own saw blade and used it to cut his own logs at the mill). Now, associations and other forms of business combination far more sophisticated than those at Machias increasingly supplanted individual enterprise. Corporations appeared in ever-larger numbers and, with the advantages they possessed, made bigger-than-ever pools of investment capital available. Larger and more complex partnerships worked in the same direction. Various forms of inter-firm cooperation also emerged, bringing increased complexity to the industry as well as to individual operations.

An insatiable demand for lumber drove the development, leading producers to construct ever-larger plants and to adopt new technologies as they became available: Maine's first steam-powered sawmill went on line in Bath in 1821, and practical circular saws, developed at Brunswick the year before, were used increasingly thereafter, especially in the 1850s. Statehood thus marked the approximate beginning of an era in which not only were the producing units larger and more complex, but also group activities came to the fore, making the term "lumber industry" mean something more than the sum of the efforts of individual operators.[1]

Increased complexity did not come in steady increments. From 1820 to 1836 widespread recognition of the potential for lumbering in Maine spurred a wave of speculation in timberlands. Lands sold and sold again in an accelerating round of price increases. In June 1835 *Niles Register* reported that from daylight to sunset the land office in Bangor was crowded with speculators, many from Boston and New York, and some tracts had increased ten-fold in price since the winter of 1834. Indeed, timberland that a decade before had sold for 6 cents an acre now went for as much as $10.[2]

Some observers saw the speculative fever as assuring a great future for the lumber industry. The *Bangor Daily Whig* noted in 1834: "The vast speculations . . . have served to unfold, in some degree, the real value of our long neglected forests. . . . A calculation may be easily made of the value of the lumber as it stands, to which a reasonable sum must be added as the cost of getting it out, and for half of this sum per acre, lumber lands may be purchased in almost any part of our state." Even after the predictable crash, the newspaper remained sanguine: "In spite of the stupendous frauds perpetrated by a few knavish and worthless land speculators, it is undeniable that there are timberlands in the state worth five times the money which the best have yet been sold for."[3]

Bangor's Isaac Farrar was among those who grew rich during all this. His fortune, a contemporary reported, "is variously estimated at from two hundred to two hundred & fifty thousand [dollars]—mostly made in speculation." Moses Patten, Samuel Veazie, Ira Wadleigh, and other local businessmen shared the speculative fever and led local banks to join in the scramble. The lure of profits from buying and selling, rather than harvesting, timberland diverted much money from productive investments, enriching Farrar and others in the process; but when the bubble burst in 1836, quickly followed by the national Panic of 1837, it left many a victim behind.[4]

Still, the Great Speculation had drawn vast quantities of capital into Maine, and in time a fair portion made its way into productive investments. Between 1820 and 1840 money invested in Maine's manufacturing enterprises increased 200 percent, the number of sawmills ninety-fold, and the capital invested in lumbering 400 percent. Banks tripled in number, and deposits increased by 250 percent. Swept along by it all, Maine's population increased 67 percent during the two decades.[5]

Bangor was a focal point both of the speculative fever and the growth it spurred. Located on the Penobscot River, fifty miles from the sea at the head of navigation for ocean-going vessels, it was ideally placed for lumbering. There were numerous sites for water-powered sawmills nearby, while the Penobscot drainage was not only the state's largest but also the most richly endowed with timber. In 1820 Bangor had a population of only 1,221, but by 1825 it had risen to 2,002 and by the time of incorporation in 1834 had ballooned to nearly eight thousand. New buildings were rising left and right—reportedly as many as five hundred in 1836 alone—but the city still suffered from a housing shortage as new residents poured in. One visitor reported,

> *There is a spirit of enterprize and activity [in Bangor] which I like much. They seem to have the bump of 'go-aheaditiveness' pretty large upon their craniums. . . . The rise of real estate and the accession of population and capital, real capital has given this place a character— and stability which few cities of equal age possess.*

As a result of the building boom, the city's property valuations rose 1,350 percent during the 1830s.[6]

All this fueled community ambitions. City leaders proudly labeled Bangor the "Queen City of the East" and looked forward to contending with Portland and Boston for regional commercial dominance. In 1830 the *Daily Whig* predicted "All our Atlantic cities will have to depend on Maine for their pure pine timber. The supplies on all the rivers to the south of us are getting to be scanty and of inferior quality," so most would have to come from the Penobscot. In 1834 the paper boasted that Bangor "lifts high its head in justly anticipated greatness, speaks of Boston and New York as sisters, and looks upon your lovely city of Portland as no more than a country cousin." High expectations were not unreasonable. Bangor was closer to Europe than either Boston or Portland and had an ample supply of wood, which was much in demand there.[7]

The passage of time seemed to prove the predictions correct. By 1842, the *Daily Whig* was reporting "there is actually shipped from this city more lumber . . . than from any other port in the whole world." It is not clear on what the newspaper based its claim, but quantities were certainly prodigious. In 1845 shippers dispatched from the Penobscot over 171 million board feet of lumber, worth over $1 million, and the city's population had risen to 11,690. By 1850 Bangor was the ninth most active port in the United States—almost entirely as a result of lumber. And trade was still rising. On the single day of 8 June 1854, twenty-seven ships arrived in Bangor and eighteen others departed with cargoes of lumber. By 1860 the annual value of shipments had risen to $3.1 million.[8]

Sailing ships taking on lumber on the Bangor waterfront. Lumber rafts in the foreground brought down the cut of sawmills up the Penobscot. Courtesy Bangor Museum and Center for History, # 87.50.64.

Speculative fever and the more soundly based economic growth that followed made Bangor a vibrant place. Men came from their little farms in the countryside, looking for seasonal employment in the woods and on log drives. Investors or gamblers—the line separating the two was not always clear—flocked to the growing community. Assorted others came too, the whole soon giving Bangor a reputation for being rowdy in the extreme. David Norton, chief clerk for the Penobscot boom for thirty-five years and thus in a position to know, protested that the rowdies were non-resident laborers waiting to go into the woods. Most of these, the *Bangor Daily Whig* claimed, were men "dazzled with the hope of obtaining high wages . . . [who had left] the steady and regular pursuit of farming and the low wages of the interior for employment on our river." After the spring drive they would spend the summer farming and then return to Bangor in the autumn to engage once more in lumbering. Lawrence Costigan was one of the more successful. He had squatted on land up the Penobscot and then began hiring out with his oxen to haul logs. Unusually skillful, he soon developed a reputation as the "king" of the area's teamsters. Feisty and independent, Costigan frequently found himself engaged in fisticuffs and "was always at law with somebody."[9]

There was considerable truth to the claims of Norton and others, but in fact community business leaders were only slightly more sedate than Costigan and his peers. Ira Wadleigh—tavern owner as well as lumberman—forcibly seized three of Samuel Veazie's mills at Pine Island, claiming Veazie, the area's leading lumberman, had encroached on his claim there. Wadleigh's action triggered a rivalry that divided the business community for fifteen years and resulted in court cases, fraud, bribery, and more than one violent confrontation. A separate rivalry led Veazie to wind up in a courtroom brawl with another area lumberman, Waldo T. Pierce, and his supporters. Veazie's son settled the matter out of court soon after; the elder Veazie, "very much grieved," declared, with tears rolling down his cheeks, he "should have licked them." And in a classic case of tax dodging, Veazie maneuvered to get Bangor's north ward, where many of his mills were located, incorporated as a separate town—immodestly named Veazie—so that his own employees could serve as tax assessors.[10]

Rufus Dwinel was no better. A dashing bachelor and daring businessman, he dispatched a group of armed toughs to settle a quarrel with David Pingree, who owned vast stands in northern Maine. After taking over the Penobscot boom from Veazie in 1847, Dwinel ran it in such a heavy-handed manner that he triggered a stream of complaints from other lumbermen. His associate, Jefferson Sinclair, whom Isaac Stephenson considered "the greatest practical lumberman of his time" and called "the Napoleon of lumbering," was not much better, on one occasion threatening to remove by force log rafts tied up to a landing that he planned to use himself.[11]

Bangor's business climate encouraged such actions and such men. The lumber business was volatile in the extreme. If money were made one year, manufacturers increased their production the following year and the market was sure to soon be flooded. Nearly everything was done on credit, and goods and supplies were extremely expensive—seemingly always more so in the years of high production. Under the circumstances, profits were almost impossible to predict and cautious, conservative businessmen were the exception rather than the rule.[12]

Daniel White stood out, for he "never took great risks, and having made one good operation and laid up money, he never risked it all the next year." A local historian noted, "[O]nce having secured a capital, he could hold on to his lumber in dull times when everyone else was obliged to sell, and the next year when his neighbors could not get into the woods [for want of capital], his boards would be pretty sure to bring remunerative prices." But men like White were rare indeed.[13]

The Great Speculation primarily involved the buying and selling of private tracts, but Maine's policies contributed too. In 1820 about half of Maine was still public land. Bit by bit authorities modified laws and policies to encourage the lumber industry. In the process, they contributed to the view that timberland was an attractive investment and thus made speculative acquisitions more common.[14]

To compensate it for giving up its northern district, Massachusetts got title to half the public lands in Maine when the northern district obtained statehood. The older state offered to sell its share to Maine for approximately 23 cents an acre, but the latter rejected the offer. This left Massachusetts owner of a vast acreage in Maine, but since most of the public domain was unsurveyed just what each state owned was unclear. Sorting out their properties took considerable time, diverting attention from questions of policy.[15] Moreover, the presence of two states as landowners made a unified approach difficult, if not impossible, and kept the shift in land laws and policies from being as complete after Maine obtained statehood as one might expect.

George W. Coffin was a further impediment to rapid change. Coffin had served as Massachusetts' land agent in Maine before separation and continued in that capacity for years thereafter. Coffin's continuing presence gave both a personal and, since he seems to have been largely self directing, a philosophical continuity to his state's approach. In contrast, Maine's land agents changed frequently, as did membership on the Commission on State Lands, which directed them. Commission records are scanty, but personnel changes seem to have resulted in occasional re-evaluations leading to policy shifts.[16]

Both states used land sales in Maine as a source of revenue. This was especially important to Maine, for these sales were expected to provide much of the state's income. Sales of stumpage—that is timber separate from land—were made for the same purpose, and in 1824, to maximize returns, Maine's land agent, James Irish, raised stumpage fees by as much as a third. Irish and at least some of his successors were also diligent in the pursuit of trespassers, who continued to be a problem. As Richard Wood noted, for all the complications resulting from the dual ownership of public lands, the arm of the law seems to have grown longer—or stronger—after Maine achieved statehood.[17]

More than increased diligence was involved in the changes in law and policy. Maine's authorities recognized that much land to which the new state held title had little if any agricultural value. In 1820, Governor William King told the legislature it should encourage settlement, but also recognize that "part of the public land is covered with timber . . . [and] is not generally well calculated for settlement." Nevertheless, he went on, its timber "will be highly interesting to the State," for in the future it could supply both revenue and employment.[18]

In spite of King's efforts, Maine did not commence at once to sell timberland to lumbermen. In 1823 Maine adopted a policy of selling lots up to five hundred acres "to actual settlers" and a year later established further rules to encourage agriculturists on its more easterly holdings, the so-called "settling lands." But lumbermen wanted larger tracts, and in 1826 the state dropped the acreage limit; two years later the State Land Commission authorized its land agent to sell eight townships per year, with a maximum of one township per person or company. Lumbermen and land speculators, not farmers, were the likely purchasers of such tracts. In addition, lands were now classified as agricultural, timber, or waste. The commission did not specifically state that the township-sized sales were to be timberland, but that seems to have been its intention.

In 1831 the commission formalized the system toward which it had been moving. It established a minimum price, directed that public lands be surveyed into lots, and required that sales of agricultural land be to actual settlers. Timberland was to be sold separately, and purchasers could buy as much as they wished. Maine's leaders still wanted to encourage agriculture, but in taking steps such as these they were recognizing what federal policy steadily ignored for another half century and more: not all land had agricultural potential, and timberland was not well suited for a system of smallholdings.[19]

Inadvertently, the commissioners' action added to the rampant speculation in timberland. Indeed, in 1835, in response to the speculative fever, the two states temporarily joined in holding timberland off the market. Concerns sparked by the Great Speculation no doubt contributed to a renewed emphasis on encouraging small-scale purchasers and actual settlers. The growing friction with Great Britain over Maine's northern border and a desire to combat "Ohio fever" added to renewed efforts to encourage actual settlers.[20]

Jacksonian democracy grew stronger in Maine during the 1830s, but failed to win a complete reversion to land-to-the-tiller policies. Democrats pushed for legislation restricting the activities of railroads and banks, but did relatively little to restrict lumber companies—which were less often owned or controlled from outside the state and, in any case, supplied markets and employment that many Jacksonian smallholders badly needed.

Moreover, reality was beginning to dawn. Speeded by the opening of the Erie Canal, a great exodus was under way. The out-migration was destined to continue, for it was becoming clear Maine was not the Promised Land for tillers of the soil. Lumbering was another matter, and however much such approaches might have been tarnished by the excesses of speculators, the state continued to implement policies seeking to get timber into the hands of lumbermen, albeit with provisos regularly added favoring small operators and cash purchasers. The emphasis on timber sales both reflected and shaped conditions. Lumbering, the *Machias Union* noted, "was the chief inducement to settlers" in the interior of Washington County, for, although farmlands of the area were productive, settlers attached "little or no value" to them.[21]

In the wake of the Panic of 1837 Maine's land sales fell by 95 percent, and 40 percent of the state's banks failed. By 1840 lumber exports from Bangor, estimated at $3 million in 1835, reportedly had plummeted to only $650,000. Under the circumstances, many Maine residents were unable to pay their taxes, and authorities did not want to eliminate land sales, a potential source of badly needed income. Unlimited purchase of timberlands thus remained an option.[22]

A land policy favoring timbermen was not the only thing done to encourage lumbering. In 1824 Maine passed a law reserving millsites for three years for the first person to build a sawmill thereon; a settler who would erect a mill within three years of the founding of a town would receive two hundred acres as well as his millsite. Laws designed to prevent log theft, allow owners to recover logs stranded on the property of others during downstream drives, and facilitate the building of booms soon followed. Regulations became ever more favorable to lumbermen; for example, in 1836 imprisonment was added to fines as punishment for log theft.

The decade of the 1830s saw the end of unregulated rivers. There was no blanket legislation; each river system was treated separately, as was logical in an age when the legislature issued corporate charters on a case-by-case basis.[23] Yet the effect of these individual actions was quite consistent: on watershed after watershed, lumbermen gained the right to clear obstructions from streams, build booms and other works, and drive logs downstream, often at the expense of other users and uses. In 1839 upriver interests protested that mill dams on the Penobscot interfered with fish runs on which they depended. The *Bangor Democrat* weighed in on the side of these small-time operators: mill dams operated "to the great injury of the public, [and will] almost totally ruin the fishing business in Penobscot waters. . . . Will the time ever arrive," the editor asked, "when the wealthy and influential few will not be permitted to recklessly trample on the rights of the hard working and obscure many?"[24] Such calls to rein in the lumber industry went for naught.

In throwing its weight behind the lumber interests, Maine's legislators were responding not only to pressure from influential groups and individuals, but also to an awareness that lumbering provided the economic foundation on which the prosperity of many of their home districts and the state as a whole rested. However dimly, they understood the role a favorable legal climate could play in encouraging the industry. They might respond to calls from Jacksonian representatives—especially strong in interior districts—for greater regulation of corporations, but they were not about to pass legislation that threatened the lumber industry's survival.

Private citizens were as aware as legislators of the importance of lumbering. An outcry arose in 1827 when operators built a dam that blocked passage of logs down the Piscataquis, a key tributary of the Penobscot. A party of men proceeded to the site and removed the dam "without the consent of the owner." Similarly, when two Bostonians built a mill and put a dam across the Penobscot below Oldtown Falls, lumbermen complained the sluiceway that was supposed to enable rafts of lumber to pass downstream was "of no value." In the face of public pressure, its owners hastened to modify the sluiceway "and the lumber public was accommodated."[25] As Edward Potter noted, "almost everyone in the state was directly or indirectly dependent upon Maine's [leading] natural resources industry." Clearly, in legislating in ways favorable to the industry, the state's government was acting in concert with widespread public opinion.[26]

Only laws regarding timber mensuration seemed to run contrary to the interests of lumbermen. Tied to Massachusetts for its main market as well as investment capital, Maine tended to follow the laws of that state in regard to lumber measurements and standards. Producers complained—indeed "Boston system," a term used to describe the rules, became a pejorative—but there was little they could do, for merchants, not manufacturers, dominated the commerce. Still, even in this acquiescence to standards demanded by outsiders, Maine's legislators showed awareness of the importance of timber exports.[27]

Ironically, even as the state passed laws encouraging the lumber industry, it remained wedded to laissez-faire economic policies. From time to time business interests and National Republican or Whig politicians took tentative steps in other directions—as in 1834 when the state established a Board of Internal Improvements to conduct and finance surveys for a system of canals, roads, and railroads—but little came of these flirtations with activist government.[28] Already earning satisfactory returns on their investments, timberland speculators, lumbermen, and shipbuilders tended to oppose both state interference in their private ventures and intervention on behalf of others. Similarly, business interests in Portland protested development programs that they feared might produce growth for the state as a whole but undermine their dominance. Dismissing Bangor's ambitions as mere pretension, they looked forward to Portland becoming the largest seaboard commercial center north of New York City. Democrats, of course, joined in opposing state as well as federal aid to economic development.[29]

Only in the disputed Aroostook region did proposals for state-funded road building have significant results, and accomplishments there were too limited and the costs too high to inspire the continuation, let alone expansion, of such an approach once the question of the northeastern boundary with Canada had been settled.[30] For Maine's state government to undertake a broader program of economic development would have required either raising taxes or increasing borrowing from outside the state. Neither was politically acceptable. The strong Jacksonian commitments of many, the widespread belief that the people simply could not afford them, and the power of the lumber industry all militated against higher levies. At the same time, hostility to the economic imperialism of Massachusetts fueled a desire to be financially independent. No one expressed this view better than a correspondent to Portland's *Eastern Argus*: "The State was severed from Massachusetts for the purpose of breaking up the influences and avoiding the oppressions, which Boston managers exercised over us; and yet our money institutions . . . are left, bound hand and foot, within the tightening grasp of Boston sharpers." These forces combined to insure both a laissez-faire approach to economic growth and protective legislation against out-of-state businesses and capital.[31]

Maine's lumbermen were suspicious of one another as well as of outsiders, although a grudging cooperation eventually emerged. Those from Bangor fought among themselves with especial vigor. No rivalry was more intense than that between Samuel Veazie and Ira Wadleigh. In 1826 Veazie moved to the area from Topsham, on the Androscoggin, bought interests in land and mills in Old Town, and gradually expanded his holdings. Eventually he controlled some fifty-two mills on the Penobscot, the Bangor and Old Town Railroad, the Penobscot Boom Corporation, and assorted other holdings, making him one of the few millionaires of his day. Veazie's management of the boom put him on a collision course with other lumbermen, who believed he managed it to benefit his own businesses while harming theirs. Among the complainants was Veazie's arch-rival, Ira Wadleigh.

Veazie and Wadleigh also clashed over control of millsites on Pine Island near Old Town, rights Wadleigh and a partner had purchased from Penobscot Indians in 1834. Wadleigh claimed Veazie had encroached on his mill privileges and took him to court. The rivalry took on a new dimension a few years later. At that point each had title to seven mill privileges on the rapids at Pine Island; N. L. Williams owned the other three. When Williams' privileges came up for sale at auction, Veazie and Wadleigh each pulled out all stops to buy them, for the successful purchaser would control one of the key industrial sites on the river. Unable to outbid his rival, Wadleigh tried to rig the auction so Veazie would have to pay an exorbitant price. His ploy failed, and the site went to Veazie for $27,000, a considerable sum but less than Wadleigh had hoped for. However, conflicts over the boom and Pine Island's millsites continued to surface for years thereafter, deeply dividing the local business community.[32]

Similarly, towns and businesses on the Kennebec sought to prevent that river from being controlled by any one of them. Later, as both Portland and Bangor lumbermen began to move into the upper reaches of the Kennebec drainage, its resident interests, seemingly always short on funds, turned to Boston capitalists and railroad connections with that city in an attempt to maintain economic independence from others within their own state. The threat of domination by lumbermen from other parts of Maine was apparently even more frightening than being subservient to Massachusetts.[33]

Although lumbermen feared what control by any one of their number—or a small group thereof—might bring, at the same time they recognized a need to work together. Indeed, the rise of cooperation among lumbermen revealed changes under way in the industry even more clearly than did the evolution of state laws and policies. In spite of internal squabbles, Penobscot lumbermen banded together to protect their collective interests—for example, lobbying to block legislation that might allow lumber from the Aroostook and St. John drainage to make serious inroads into their markets. Cooperation on the Penobscot and elsewhere was even more evident in connection with booming. With large mills clustered along the fall line, where waters navigable by ocean-going vessels and adequate sources of waterpower were close to one another, booms to collect logs for a number of mills became necessary. Boom sites, after all, were far fewer than millsites—and took much more space.

Booms had long been present, but they had tended to serve single mills. Now, huge booms appeared that served several mills at once. Sometimes these were joint projects of leading sawmill operators, as when eighteen men joined to construct the Penobscot Boom above Old Town; at other times they were constructed by one or more entrepreneurs who saw a chance to profit by providing a needed service. The boom at Brunswick, on the Androscoggin, was fairly typical. A visitor described it in 1820:

> *Above the falls, where the river is wide and gently moves, are sunk six piers at great expense, between which timbers are united by irons to stop the logs in the spring freshet. In these places they are secured before they reach the falls. There are five piers below, connected by similar timber to save what pass the piers above.*

Together the twin booms provided some ninety acres of log storage.[34]

The Penobscot Boom was considerably larger. Indeed, it was not a single boom, but a complex of booms managed as a unit by the Penobscot Boom Corporation, an entity started by a consortium of key individuals and

eventually managed by a committee representing all lumbermen of the
area. Begun in the mid-twenties, the complex was expanded repeatedly;
by the 1850s it could corral some six hundred acres of logs, piled several
deep, in holding areas stretching six miles along the river. As many as four
hundred hands worked on its holding and sorting facilities.[35]

The Penobscot Boom introduced radically changed log handling on the
river. Before its construction, each lumberman corralled his own logs as
they arrived downriver and was "obliged to keep crews and boats out night
and day, building large fires upon the shore to make light upon the water,
to enable them to see the logs as they went floating by in the darkness."[36]
By replacing this inefficient system, the boom made possible a burst of
lumbering at Old Town, Orono, and elsewhere nearby and soon made
Bangor, outlet for the production of the entire area, a great lumber port. In
1837 Henry David Thoreau noted there were two hundred and fifty saws
at work above Bangor and local lumbermen seemed to be seeking "like so
many busy demons, to drive the forest all out of the country, from every
solitary beaver-swamp and mountain-side, as soon as possible." A decade
later he returned to find the city

> the principal lumber depot on this continent, with a population of
> twelve thousand, like a star at the edge of night, still hewing at the forest
> of which it is built, [and] already overflowing with the luxuries and
> refinement of Europe and sending its vessels to Spain, to England, and to
> the West Indies for its groceries.[37]

It was a record of accomplishment made possible by the Penobscot
Boom.

Large or small, rivers from the Saco to the St. John sported booms,
and nearly all required some level of inter-mill cooperation to operate
successfully. In addition, since booms were not normally operating adjuncts
of individual mills, but separate entities with their own charters, they stood
as silent witness to growing specialization as Maine's lumber industry moved
beyond its simple, undifferentiated pioneer stage.

Legislative action, as well as cooperation, directed boom use. The state
set the fees boom owners could charge and inserted provisos into both
charters and laws requiring operators to sort promptly the logs collected.
For example, although the boom on the Penobscot was privately owned,
any lumberman had a right to have his logs turned out within twenty-four
hours of requesting it. In spite of such provisos, friction between boom
operators and lumbermen surfaced repeatedly both before and after
Veazie sold his controlling interest to Rufus Dwinel in 1847. Eventually

the situation became so intolerable the legislature chartered the Penobscot Lumbering Association, made up of all local millmen, to rent and manage the boom; Dwinel was left with title and annual rents, but little authority. The legislature's action was extraordinary, but even without such intervention booms could only function effectively if considerable inter-firm cooperation existed; as a result, they represented a sharp shift away from the small, determinedly independent operations characteristic of lumbering during the colonial and early national periods.[38]

Nowhere was cooperation more evident than in log drives. Initially operators drove logs out of the woods with their own crews or contracted with someone to do it. In 1826 Daniel Usher paid a jobber $247.50 to drive 330,000 feet of logs from Moose Pond Bog to the Saco River; similarly, Aaron Babb contracted to drive logs from Black Brook to the main Penobscot boom for $1.25 per thousand feet. But as sawmills became more numerous, rivers became clogged with individual drives; the short driving season that came with the spring freshets meant everyone sought to use the rivers at once, and if one drive jammed all were inconvenienced. Disputes mounted. To bring an end to the chaos, lumbermen on major streams formed associations for collective drives.

There was no single, uniform set of laws on the subject—legislative actions varied from stream to stream—but a general pattern emerged. The owners of logs on a river were empowered to select a committee to oversee operations, hire a master driver to direct the running of the logs in a single drive, and assess costs to members on a pro-rata basis. By the 1840s logging was carried on so far from major milling centers that it was sometimes impossible to drive logs to the mills in a single season. Both costs and the loss of logs mounted as drives became longer, but lumbermen had few alternatives.

On the Kennebec the law was extended in 1837 to give its association a lien on logs to assure payment of an owner's share of expenses and make association members of anyone "who is owner or interested in logs or other timber on said river." The association was charged with disposing of prize logs—that is, unbranded logs or logs stranded during drives so many years earlier that they were now considered the property of whoever recovered them. When sold at auction, prize logs often brought enough to pay the association's overhead. If they did not, members were assessed their proportionate share.

A compromise arrangement long existed on the Penobscot. Owners could form an association, and several did, but individuals were also free to drive their own logs. The association was entitled to charge only those who had contracted with it. Again, disputes were frequent, and in 1846 the legislature chartered a new association, the Penobscot Log Driving Company, empowering it to "drive all logs and other timber that may be in the west branch of the Penobscot river between Chesuncook dam and the east branch to any place at or above the Penobscot boom." The boom company assessed owners for the costs of the drive. When logs bearing unfamiliar brands collected behind the boom, the association published the brands in the local press. If they went unclaimed or the owners failed to pay their share of costs within thirty days, the company sold them at auction. Unlike on the Kennebec, the contract to conduct the drive generally went to the lowest bidder. If all bids seemed excessive, the association appointed its own master driver, although in fifty years of operation this only happened eight times.

The Penobscot Log Driving Company undertook various projects to improve driving conditions on the river. About 1840, Samuel Veazie built the first major undertaking of this sort, a large dam at the outlet of Chesuncook Lake. With this dam Veazie was able to regulate the flow of the West Branch to the benefit of his and other drives, and he profited handsomely as a result. But most subsequent projects on this and other streams were the result of group, not individual effort, and underscore the cooperative turn the industry was taking.[39]

Two key inventions helped make cooperative drives successful. For decades rivermen had manipulated logs with long poles with a hinged hook attached that could move up, down, or sideways—and at crucial moments the hook often slipped to where it was not needed. Generations of loggers roundly cursed these notoriously inefficient "swing dogs." Then Joseph Peavey, a blacksmith from near Bangor, produced an improved tool. He attached the hinged hook solidly to one side, shortened the handle, reinforced it with steel bands, and added a steel spike to the tip of the pole. The result—promptly called a peavey—was a vast improvement and continued to be the main woodsman's tool for generations. By contrast, Maine river boats, known as batteaus,[40] developed gradually as a type that Hosea B. Maynard of Bangor perfected around 1860. High in bow and stern and with sides tapered in sharply to a short, flat, narrow bottom, these vessels were remarkably nimble for their size (thirty-two feet long and six feet wide, they weighed only eight to nine hundred pounds). Their shallow draft enabled them to work almost anywhere on the region's major rivers; they became indispensable to rivermen conducting drives.

Working from a batteau to keep logs moving. The men are using peaveys to pry loose logs starting to jam. Courtesy Bangor Museum and Center for History, #88.2.1.

In spite of subsequent imagery of drivers riding free-floating logs as they hurried on their way downstream, most of the work of rivermen was done from batteaus—and they could do it far better in the perfected Maine river boat than in its predecessors. John Ross claimed that "with a Maynard boat and six men with peaveys he could do more than with twenty men and the old tools." He surely knew whereof he spoke; Ross was one of the toughest and best master drivers on the Penobscot.[41]

Land transportation improved too. As the number of sawmills near Old Town and Orono grew, so did the need for better connections between there and Bangor. Rafts of lumber continued to be floated down the Penobscot after being portaged around or sluiced past Oldtown Falls. Rafts averaged about twenty-five thousand board feet; rafting from Orono cost 75 cents per thousand, from Old Town 92 cents. But the river was crowded, losses during shipping added to costs, and the location of some mills made rafting a less than ideal option; hauling their cut the fifteen or so miles by cart was even less satisfactory. The obvious answer was a railroad to carry at least part of the cut and to transport the increasing upriver traffic in supplies. Entrepreneurs soon emerged to build the Bangor and Old Town Railroad (later known as the Bangor, Old Town, and Milford). The line—Maine's first—opened in 1836, and an engine christened the *Tiger* was soon at work hauling lumber from upriver sawmills to dockside in Bangor. Like so much else in the area's lumber industry, this railroad soon came under the control of Samuel Veazie.[42]

Entrepreneurs built railroads elsewhere too, but on the whole neither their lines nor the turnpikes and roads built by others were as important to the lumber industry as that first short rail link between Old Town and Bangor. Maine's gentle topography meant that, with only minimal improvements, nearly all its magnificent network of rivers was useable for log drives, reducing the need for land transportation. As David Cobb had recognized long before, roads helped reduce the isolation of farmers, giving at least some of them easier access to the logging camps that were a primary market for their output, but otherwise were of little importance to lumbermen.[43]

Developments at sea were another matter. Shipbuilding burgeoned in Maine, spurred by the need for vessels to carry the growing exports of lumber. Bath became a major center, turning out one merchant vessel after another, but shipyards appeared in many other locations as well. Businessmen from Massachusetts and New York invested in Maine's shipbuilding industry, speeding its growth, but much of the industry was locally controlled. Many lumbermen invested in ships and shipyards, partly as a limited forward integration of their operations and partly simply because they seemed good investments. But most shipowners appear not to have been lumbermen. Between 1820 and 1840, the maritime tonnage owned by residents of Maine increased 155 percent. Shipbuilding on the Penobscot, the *Bangor Daily Whig* reported in 1845, was "increasing very considerably . . . and the reputation of eastern built [i.e. Maine] vessels . . . rapidly improving."[44]

Building wooden sailing vessels created demand for construction timber, but not all the wood used came from Maine. Much oak came from sources far to the south, as did many a buyer for the bottoms turned out in the state's shipyards. The trade in construction materials and the sale of finished vessels helped link Maine to the outside world.[45]

The Bangor and Old Town Railroad, a growing maritime fleet, bigger booms, and coordinated drives were all necessary because sawmills were becoming larger and more numerous. A steady stream of improvements in mill technology speeded production, required more and more investment capital to stay competitive, and drove loggers relentlessly as they sought to keep up with the demands of the ever-hungry saws. Innovations in logging technology failed to keep pace with those in sawmills, so operators responded by simply dispatching more men into the forest. Logging camps grew in size and became more numerous. In the 1850s one firm reportedly had twenty-six camps working to generate the logs it needed; another had 1,200-1,500 men and 1,000 oxen in the woods.[46]

As logging operations pushed ever further upstream, they neared the limits of Maine's main river drainages; and loggers increasingly crossed the low, almost imperceptible divides separating the headwaters of one stream from those of the next. Not surprisingly, this led to clashes. In 1834 businessmen from a number of communities along the Kennebec, concerned about dwindling supplies of logs on the lower river, stopped jockeying for advantage with one another and incorporated the Moosehead Dam Company to provide an adequate head of water for driving logs from the vast stands around Moosehead Lake (the river's source) to sawmills downstream. The following year they chartered the Kennebec Log Driving Company to conduct drives the dam would make possible. These actions extended the area tapped by sawmills on the Kennebec, but when the lumbermen attempted to expand even further, they met stern opposition from operators on the Penobscot.

In 1839 Kennebeckers proposed diverting water through a canal from the upper Penobscot into Moosehead Lake. Toward that end, they sought a charter from the state legislature for the Seboomook Sluiceway Company. The added water in Moosehead Lake, they anticipated, would increase the flow of the Kennebec, making possible drives of longer duration and larger size and expanding the area of operations of Kennebec interests well into the upper Penobscot drainage. Bangor's lumbermen steadfastly resisted this raid on what they considered "their" water and timber. Each side sought political and economic allies—and deeply divided the legislature in the process. Repeatedly, Bangor's forces turned back the sluiceway promoters' efforts to obtain a charter, and gradually a vague line of demarcation developed separating operations on the two drainages.[47]

But Bangor's lumbermen were more often on the offense. In 1841 operators from the Queen City, having reached the northern limits of the Penobscot drainage, built two dams at the outlet of Chamberlain Lake, raising the water level eleven feet and reversing the natural northward flow into the Allagash southward through a short canal (or "cut") into little Telos Lake and from there into a tributary of the East Branch of the Penobscot. The next spring lumbermen drove logs to Bangor on water from the Allagash drainage; soon they were treating the entire Chamberlain Lake area as if it were a part of Bangor's natural hinterland.

Like the Seboomook Sluiceway Company, the project became a major source of conflict. In 1846, David Pingree, a Massachusetts investor who owned several townships of timber in the area, collided with Rufus Dwinel, who by then controlled the diversion project and whose ally, Jefferson Sinclair, owned extensive stands in the area. Pingree wanted to sell his logs to Bangor interests, for logs brought twice as much in the Queen City as they would if driven down the Allagash, but he thought Dwinel asked an exorbitant fee for use of his facilities. When Pingree threatened to send logs through without paying, Dwinel dispatched seventy-five armed woodsmen and at gunpoint blocked Pingree's loggers from moving their cut until their employer paid the price demanded.

Dwinel had won a Pyrrhic victory. He had not obtained a charter for his enterprise, arguing that one was not needed since the canal was not a "natural waterway" over which the legislature had jurisdiction. Seeing an opening, Bangor lumbermen applied for a charter for the diversion project for themselves. Belatedly Dwinel countered with an application, but his rivals had more influence in Augusta. Outmanuevered, Dwinel accepted a charter that dictated terms favorable to Bangor's interests rather than lose control of the facilities altogether.

By 1847 lumbermen from the St. John (into which the Allagash drained) had worked their way into the area near Chamberlain Lake, intending to cut timber to float down the Allagash the next spring. When the spring thaw came, the flow on the tributary they expected to use for their drive was so depleted by the diversion into the Penobscot that it proved inadequate for the task. The drive jammed. Distraught, twenty volunteers made their way to one of Dwinel's dams and tore away a ninety-foot section, unleashing a torrent of water that safely floated the logs to their destination and provided "an argument that would be understood" in Bangor. Intermittent struggle continued over the years, but a compromise of sorts, in which the waters of the Allagash were grudgingly divided between operators from Bangor and St. John, generally held.[48]

In similar fashion, in the 1850s Bangor interests sought to construct a rail line into the Moosehead Lake area, thus extending their operations into the forests of the upper Kennebec. The results were negligible, and the division of territory of operators on the two rivers, worked out earlier, remained essentially unchanged.[49]

What emerged from this jockeying was a *modus operandi* that established the rough limits of the hinterlands of Bangor and other lumber centers. These territorial divisions effectively halted the spread of the Queen City's timber imperialism and set a ceiling on its potential for continued growth. At the same time, the various projects that gave rise to these struggles, expensive as they were, illustrated the increasingly capital-intensive turn the industry was taking. Clearly, lumbering was no longer the simple undertaking of colonial and early national times.

⁕

But in many ways the impressive growth in Bangor and elsewhere gave a false impression. After the Great Speculation, while increases taking place in Maine rested on a relatively solid foundation, the state was not keeping up with the rest of the Northeast, the Ohio Valley, or the nation as a whole. While Maine's population grew 67 percent between 1820 and 1840, that of New York increased 82 percent, Ohio 325 percent, and the nation as a whole 80 percent. The ratio of bank capital to population in Maine, a vital measure of the capacity to finance development, fell ever further behind the rest of the country. Railroad construction had a worse record still. In 1840 Maine had the least railroad mileage of any state; Delaware, second from the bottom (and much smaller), had twice as much; and Maine's ratio of railroad mileage to square miles of territory was only 1 to 3,000 (compared to 1 to 10 for Ohio, 1 to 40 for New York, and 1 to 50 for Pennsylvania).[50]

More important than the gap between the rate of development in Maine and the rest of the United States was the Pine Tree State's failure to achieve economic diversification. Lumbering, shipbuilding, farming, and fishing had been and remained its primary supports. Some manufacturing put in an appearance, most notably in textiles, leather, boots and shoes, and iron products. Banks, insurance companies, stagecoach lines, and steam navigation companies became more numerous too, but these tended to be small.

Portland's record was best. With a magnificent harbor, but limited hinterland, its business leaders were forced to lean more on commerce than lumbering. They cooperated to push for construction of the Cumberland and Oxford Canal and various road and railroad schemes they hoped would increase the area their city served—and in the process stirred opposition from towns on the lower Androscoggin and elsewhere whose leaders saw in such projects threats to their own trade. These undertakings were intended to serve general business, rather than open sources of logs for lumbermen. The remaining stands inland from Portland were inadequate to support large export mills, for they had been depleted by decades of cutting, but the canal and railroad projects served to encourage further broadening of the city's economy, already more diverse than that of the state as a whole. Construction of deep-water port facilities on the city's tidal basin came later, but had a similar effect.[51]

In an age when merchants dominated America's business life, Portland was becoming ever more dominant as the state's leading commercial-mercantile center. In 1820 it was the new state's largest town, its valuation 83 percent higher than its nearest competitor and almost double the combined valuation of all the towns on the Kennebec from Augusta to Bath. With control of over half the state's commercial bank capital, it was growing rapidly. New stores were springing up and what William Willis, the city's pioneer historian, called "the accommodations for business" were increasing. The city's population grew by a third during the 1820s and by 25 percent in the 1830s; by 1840 property valuation was double that of 1820 and still climbing. Shipbuilding and commerce were the fastest-growing sectors of its economy. In 1787 not a single ship was completely owned by residents of the city, but by 1820 they controlled over thirty-two thousand tons and by 1849 nearly eighty thousand tons of merchant shipping. Portland led the state in both tonnage and value of exports.[52]

Portland's trade with the West Indies was central to this growth. Before the revolution, England had been the city's main foreign market; after it, William Willis wrote,

> *our trade had to form new channels . . . and in a few years our ships were floating on every ocean, becoming the carriers of southern as well as northern produce, and bringing back the money and commodities of other countries. The trade of the West Indies, supported by our lumber, increased vastly, and direct voyages . . . received in exchange for the growth of our forests and our seas, sugar, molasses, and rum, the triple products of the cane.*

Portland became the hub of Maine's Caribbean commerce, thanks in large part to its well-developed commercial-mercantile infrastructure. In 1826 some 117,000 tons of shipping entered Havana from the United States; 11,600 tons were from Portland, which put the city not only ahead of Maine's other ports but in front of Boston, New York, and Philadelphia as well. The trade, Willis claimed, gave "new activity to all the springs of industry and wealth . . . [and] contributed mainly to the advancement and prosperity of the town."[53]

Sugar processing soon became a major undertaking in Portland, for the refining done in the islands left a considerable admixture of molasses in the end-product. Plants were needed to separate the molasses and layers of various grades of sugar that developed during transit as molasses slowly drained to the bottom of the waterproof wooden boxes in which sugar was shipped. John B. Brown and other Portland entrepreneurs provided these processing plants—and thereby further broadened the local economy. By 1850 sugar, at 20 percent of the total, was foremost among the city's manufactures, considerably ahead of textiles, which held second place.

The two legs of the West Indies trade complemented one another. Sugar shipments from the islands created a huge demand for pine, both for construction spurred by the expanding plantations and box shooks to make the containers used for the exported sugar; in turn, the men in Maine's lumber camps consumed vast quantities of sugar and molasses. As the major distribution center on the northern New England coast, Portland was ideally located to serve this two-way trade.[54]

In some ways, Portland's successes worked against the rest of the state. With a more diversified economy and a developing infrastructure, it came to control more and more of Maine's commercial and business activity. Moreover, although Whigs generally dominated the city's politics, its business interests, finding adequate investment capital for their needs available locally, tended to oppose state action to support economic development elsewhere. At the same time, long-standing hostility to Boston interests served to make Portland's business leaders suspicious of capital investments from Massachussetts and resulted in a variety of barriers to capital from that quarter—capital that was badly needed in other parts of Maine, if not in Portland.[55]

There was an additional problem. Portland and the local markets it served could not consume all the goods her ships brought. Much of the surplus went to Boston for sale, creating links that encouraged affluent Portlanders to shop in Boston and New York, since goods purchased there carried prestige even when the same items were available in state. All this resulted in a variety of ties with its erstwhile rival and served to lessen the impact Portland might have had in helping build a more diversified economy in Maine as a whole.[56]

Bangor provided a sharp contrast. Lumbering accounted for over 50 percent of the manufacturing in Penobscot County, compared to only 2.7 percent in Portland. Bangor's banks had only a third as much commercial capital as those in its rival; what capital there was frequently came from Boston, whose businessmen invested heavily in Bangor's banks, just as they did in its lumbering enterprises. The banks themselves were often owned by local lumber merchants and sawmill operators. Under the circumstances, it comes as no surprise that banks in Bangor frequently showed more interest in investing in timberland than in projects in the city itself. In any case, the need to build or improve sawmills, booms, and ships, as well as to purchase timber, absorbed the bulk of the lumbermen's capital, leaving them little to invest in unrelated businesses in Bangor and vicinity. Moreover, it has been suggested they had little concern for the city's development, since "for them Bangor was [just] a shipping point." The fact that a number of Bangor's businesses were the property of absentee owners probably worked in the same direction.[57]

Bangor's non-lumber manufacturing enterprises tended to be owned by men of limited means who often criticized lumbermen for their narrow, self-interested approach. The *Bangor Daily Whig* agreed, arguing the city badly needed diversification, but concentrating on lumbering impeded progress in that direction. "Too much money has been tied up in the timber and lumber industry," the paper maintained; the "monarchs of the woods" were responsible for the city's narrow and unstable economic base.[58]

According to historian Edward Potter, lumbermen were not alone in creating the situation. Throughout the first half of the nineteenth century, Maine's government adhered to laissez-faire economic policies and directed most of its financial effort to reducing the public debt. By failing to invest in essential internal improvements, as various other states were doing, it helped create a situation where scarce private capital had to be directed to such undertakings, leaving less for diversifying business development. Simply put, Potter argued that far more than the myopia and narrow self-interest of lumbermen lay behind Maine's failure to diversify. His point seems well taken.[59]

If the *Daily Whig* heaped on lumbermen more blame for Bangor's problems than they deserved, the newspaper's fears for the city's future were certainly justified. While Portland continued to show substantial growth during the 1850s, Bangor did not. In the Queen City and nearby areas, lumber production, shipbuilding, and exports all fell. The limits of the white pine on which the local economy rested had been reached, and lumbermen were turning to spruce to keep their sawmills running. By 1861 the output of spruce exceeded that of pine. But spruce was a poor substitute—little valued by consumers, it was harder to market and returned smaller profits. Other lumber-producing areas were capturing more and more domestic and foreign markets from Maine. Bangor continued to lean heavily on the lumber industry—in 1860 it still accounted for 50 percent of Penobscot County's manufacturing—but the city's glory days had passed.

The limits of logging technology long made clearcutting impractical; loggers took only the best trees, leaving others to be cut by later arrivals with greater needs or more advanced equipment and techniques. As Theodore Winthrop observed, "a lumber campaign is like France after a *coup d'etat*: The bourgeoisie are as prosperous as ever, but the great men are all gone." This, coupled with a shift to less-desirable species, helps explain the long continuation of logging in Maine, but in time even spruce sawlogs grew scarce and the Penobscot drainage became primarily a producer of pulpwood. However, paper production centered far upriver at Millinocket and had limited economic benefits for Bangor. Portland, with its considerably broader economic base, no longer had any real competition as Maine's leading city.[60]

⚹

Maine's lumbering frontier left more than a legacy of an extractive, single-industry, boom-and-bust economy. It shaped land-ownership patterns that continue to dominate much of the state. As the Great Northern Paper Company rose to primacy in northern Maine in the late nineteenth century, it was heir to—and extended—the economic system resting on concentrated land ownership that had begun long before. The system, based as it was on inequality, helped to reinforce class divisions and limit opportunities for upward socio-economic mobility for workers.[61]

Nothing illustrates this better than developments in the Aroostook and upper St. John valleys. Farming preceded lumbering in the area, which spanned the border between Canada and the United States. Its first sawmills were tiny operations serving local agrarian needs. By the time larger mills capable of selling their cut in outside markets put in an appearance, most land suited for agriculture had been taken up. The arrival of sawmills tied to the outside commercial economy was paralleled by a similar reorientation in the area's agriculture. The Aroostook Valley, in particular, proved well suited for the cultivation of potatoes, and as railroads penetrated the area marketing them became easier. The advent of potato starch plants in the valley added to demand.

Agriculture and lumbering, long interdependent, were growing apart—and increasingly antagonistic. In 1856, when Maine's Board of Agriculture polled the state's farmers, four-fifths said they considered lumbering a negative influence; in part this reflected the continuing antagonism of smallholders to the engrossing of the land by a privileged few. For their part, timber owners opposed farmers' proposals for market roads across forested areas, for they feared carrying the tax burden to build and maintain them, and shut out settlers from their lands, ostensibly to prevent illegal cutting and wildfires caused by careless land clearing, spite, or efforts to improve grazing.[62]

New sawmills and the logging operations that supplied them provided employment for excess rural population—mostly newcomers and non-inheriting children of older settlers—but, Beatrice Craig notes, they "could not prevent their impoverishment." In both logging and sawmills, wages were low, hours long, and work hard, while agriculture was beginning to prosper as improved transportation tied the area into the larger commercial world. Those in a position to take advantage of the new developments stayed with farming; many even on marginal tracts, hoping for better days, continued to work the land while turning to by-employment in the woods to make ends meet. Since woods work brought marginal farmers supplemental income, rather than their primary economic support, they were willing to work for little and thus helped keep wages in the industry low. The combination of marginal agriculture and poorly paid woods or sawmill work was a dead-end poverty trap. Small wonder so many from rural Maine caught "Ohio fever" and departed for the West.

Non-landowners turned to full-time employment in the lumber industry with no better results. Jobs provided by the advent of commercial lumbering slowed out-migration from the area, but created a poor, non-property-owning class with little social standing, a group viewed with considerable disdain by land-owning agrarians and "polite society" alike. At the same time, workers looked on merchants and capitalists as exploiters and on farmers as a stodgy, unimaginative group blind to the exploitive nature of the wage labor system beginning to dominate American society.[63]

Those holding key positions in the expanding commercial nexus prospered. Downriver merchants accumulated capital, financed lumbermen, and gradually expanded their holdings—and frequently became lumbermen and timber owners in the process. These developments drove them steadily away from the farmers and woods and sawmill workers upon whom they depended. In Bangor and along the Kennebec, as surely as in far northern Maine, merchants and lumbermen dominated the economic and political scene, seeing themselves as responsible for the economic future of their area and underestimating the value of the work of others. Class divisions, long evident in the state, remained deeply etched as lumbering evolved in northern Maine.[64]

For a time the manufacture of hand-made shingles and hand-hewn squared timbers offered an alternative to working for industrial lumbermen. It was an option many preferred, in part because it paid better. Those so employed, by earning a good return on their labor in the woods while working outside the mainstream of the lumber industry, sometimes acquired the capital to gain title to farm and forest tracts of their own, thereby slowing concentration of land and power in the hands of the commercial and business classes. These activities were in fact throwbacks to an earlier age made possible by the peculiar circumstances of time and place. The area's real economic future, for better or worse, was clearly tied to the emergence of commercial lumbering and farming.[65]

Much of Maine was long wedded to the lumber industry and to those interests associated with it, but beyond passing laws that cleared the way for the industry to function, the state could take little credit for what progress lumbering brought. Nor could lumbermen themselves. They were the beneficiaries of circumstances, of being in the right place at the right time, more than they were the agents of the region's economic growth that most seem to have considered themselves. The industry was the result of the magnificent patrimony of forests that blanketed Maine, not of encouragement from its politicians and policy makers nor of the genius of its businessmen.

If those resources produced an extractive, boom-and-bust economy and concentrated patterns of land ownership, rather than a diversified economy with an egalitarian foundation, one should not be too critical. Outside of forests, Maine had only a modicum of assets with which to build a broad-based economy. Unlike the Aroostook Valley and other favored locations, most of the state was poorly suited for agriculture—and even the best farming areas suffered from short growing seasons and harsh winters. Fishing and shipbuilding continued to support a number of communities along the coast, but their benefits did not reach far inland and, like farming, had little potential for expansion. Mineral resources were limited.[66]

Maine's experience as a lumbering frontier brought problems, but it also brought a prolonged—if not very equitably distributed—period of prosperity. Moreover, by turning a good portion of the state's fixed assets into liquid ones that could be used to finance development, both within Maine and in other areas to which the capital was transferred, and by creating a body of experienced workers and improved industrial technology, Maine's lumber industry helped speed the rise and growth of lumberman's frontiers in other areas and to ensure them a future more prosperous than they might otherwise have had. Its legacy could have been far worse.

CHAPTER FOUR

From Farmer-Loggers to Lumbermen in the Mid-Atlantic States

As important lumbering was in Maine during the early nineteenth century, however much it dominated its public image, Maine was not alone as a lumbering state. By 1825 New York reportedly had 4,321 sawmills, nearly six times as many as Maine (although few resembled Maine's large commercial mills sawing for distant markets). By 1840 both New York and Pennsylvania led the Pine Tree State in the number of sawmills, with New York's production more than double that of Maine. The differential continued to grow. Census records for 1850 report New York led all states with 4,625 mills and an output valued over $13 million; Pennsylvania was second with 2,894 mills and a production value of $7.7 million. Maine had only 732 mills, and although they were on average considerably larger, their combined production of $5.8 million was well behind either of the two large Middle Atlantic States. The figures are not entirely reliable—many sawmills went unreported—but the data are adequate to show that by mid-century lumber production was well established in Pennsylvania and New York and present, though less dramatically, in New Jersey.[1]

The Mid-Atlantic's impressive output was not the result of the emergence there of a lumberman's frontier—that would come later—but largely because of the size and health of its agricultural sector. Still, consumption was not entirely agrarian. The steady if unspectacular growth of early New York generated a continual demand for building materials, both on the farm and off. By 1750 New York was the third-largest colonial port and demand from merchants complemented that of farmers. The staple exports were wheat and flour, lumber and other wood products, and furs. Overcutting of readily accessible stands—both by New Yorkers and by stave- and shingle-getters from New Jersey who, having depleted the white cedar stands of their own colony, had turned to cutting in New York—soon led to a lessening of quality of New York's lumber; by 1765 the colony's merchants were seeking regulations "to restore the credit of our lumber" in the marketplace. Depletion also led to rising prices for fuelwood, leading many people by the end of New York's colonial period to shift to coal for heating.

Yet it was a long time before something that could legitimately be called a lumberman's frontier emerged in New York. As in early Maine, it was primarily a quest for farmland that drew settlers to new areas; lumbering was an adjunct, serving to meet farmers' needs and to provide them with supplementary income. But unlike in Maine, agriculture in New York was sufficiently promising that there was less incentive for agrarians to abandon, or even de-emphasize, farming in favor of lumbering. When a lumbering frontier finally would emerge in New York it might have been expected to draw upon men, money, and technology from Maine, thus initiating a pattern of transfer that would be seen in many a subsequent area, but that does not seem to have been the case. New York's lumber industry seems to have been overwhelmingly homegrown.[2]

Initially, events followed a similar pattern in Pennsylvania. Agricultural demand was the main driving force from the beginning, but commercial considerations—the need for exports to make the colony pay—were present too. Johan Printz, governor of Sweden's early colony on the Delaware, received instructions "to examine and consider how and in what manner profit may be derived" from New Sweden's "abundant forests," hardly a surprising directive considering Sweden's own experience with profitable forest operations, including exports to Britain. By the time William Penn arrived in Pennsylvania, there were four Swedish sawmills on the river and shingle and stave making were well established. Production mounted thereafter. By 1760 there were forty sawmills in Philadelphia County alone. They were small, but their cumulative impact was significant. In 1705 one millowner had described his plant: "It occupies a building 32 by 70 feet. . . . We can cut with one saw seven or eight hundred feet of inch boards a day and more sometimes when the water is high." Such a mill might gross £400 per year, and the forty present in 1760 obviously much more.[3] With a reputation as "the best poor man's country" and policies that encouraged immigration, settlers poured into "Penn's Woods." As Swedish visitor Pehr Kalm laconically put it, "it has not been necessary to force people to come and settle here." The resulting clearing of farmland ate steadily into the colony's forest cover, while the farms themselves created a demand for lumber that did the same. Trees yielded shingles, staves, lumber, and potash, all of which helped pay the hired or indentured help used during the clearing process and provided farm families with an income until their cropland could produce a surplus for market. "Their crops in," one authority on Pennsylvania agriculture explained, "the farmer, his boys, and his hired men hied them off to the woods" to log. As a result, for several decades more trees fell to farmers' axes than to those of lumberers.[4]

The importance of agricultural clearing should not obscure the fact that there was considerable commercial manufacturing of lumber and other wood products. Statistics on exports are generally the most reliable measure of colonial forest output, but in the case of Pennsylvania they are misleading. There was a steady production, turned out by a host of small, localized operations with limited capital and using relatively simple technology, which local demand gobbled up almost as fast as it was cut. There were exports—Pehr Kalm observed that in 1748 ships left Philadelphia with timber "almost every day," while Tench Coxe reported that from October 1, 1791, to September 30, 1792, over 1.5 million feet of pine boards and planks left Pennsylvania—but far more was consumed locally, and it left almost no evidence in the statistical records of the period. The combined effect of exports and domestic consumption was predictable. An observer noted in 1775, "[H]owever plentifful it may be in remoter parts of Pennsylvania . . . wood is almost as dear at Philadelphia as it is in some parts of Britain." Shortly after, Isaac Weld described the nearby countryside as having "a bare appearance, being totally stripped of the trees."[5]

Sawpits and sawmills appeared early in New Jersey, as did a host of small-time operators who virtually annihilated the colony's white cedar stands to make shingles. Pehr Kalm, trained as a botanist, described New Jersey's woodlands in 1748. In its northern highlands, he found extensive hardwood forests of oak and chestnut. The Pine Barrens of the southeastern part of the colony included not only the trees that gave them their name, but also oak and white cedar—creating what one historian later described as "a wall between the settlements on the Delaware and the sea."[6] Most of the pines, Kalm reported, were "of considerable height, but they stood every where far enough asunder to permit a chaise to pass through the woods without any inconvenience, there being seldom any shrubs or underwood between the trees to obstruct the way." The colony's pineries, he added, were being busily exploited. Almost daily, shipments of lumber and other wood products left the area's port (New Brunswick) for New York. On the other hand, except in a belt across the center of New Jersey—from the Delaware River to Raritan Bay—much of the land was poorly suited for agriculture; "the ground," Kalm noted, "is almost entirely sand."[7]

By Kalm's visit, most of New Jersey's central belt had been cleared for agriculture—"improved," as the tax records put it. Much of the rest was better suited for yielding forest products than for farming. Under the circumstances and with major markets nearby, sawmills were numerous. Indeed, in West Jersey, where large farms with extensive timber holdings dominated, tapping their forests made many an estate profitable. As a result, Kalm observed that in the portions of New Jersey near Pennsylvania the forests were "more ruined than [those of] any other" province. By 1798 there were nearly five hundred sawmills in the state, and a considerable coastal trade transporting cordwood northward from the Pine Barrens to Philadelphia and New York. Burlington, Cumberland, Gloucester, and Monmouth counties loomed large in the trade. Throughout the pine belt, as elsewhere, sawmills often heralded the advent of settlements, but these rested on a dual foundation of field and forest, and when the thin soil became exhausted, many a community stagnated or died.[8]

Forest as well as soil depletion came early to New Jersey. The boards of proprietors of both East and West Jersey considered their resinous pines of little value. Settlers, sharing the assessment, burned the woods so persistently to make way for agriculture and pastureland that proprietors had to rethink their position and enacted legislation in 1683 prohibiting "firing the woods to the prejudice of the inhabitants." But to no avail. Although by 1700 much of the pineland had been purchased from the proprietors, firing of forests continued. Timber theft was a problem too, leading to an act of March 1713 "prohibiting the common practice of stealing timber, cedar, pine staves, and poles." This too had little effect. Settlers claimed "natural privileges" to fish in the colony's waters and hunt on untenanted land. They seem to have viewed timber in much the same light: it was theirs for the taking in spite of claims of distant proprietors and landowners. As a result, toward the end of the eighteenth century, woodlands in the better agricultural districts had been so overcut that farmers had to purchase distant woodlots to meet their needs.[9]

By 1849 lumber production was rising rapidly in New York and Pennsylvania, while New Jersey lagged far behind, producing a mere 2 percent of the national total. Extensive tracts remained in the Pine Barrens, and smaller stands grew elsewhere, but these had limited commercial value, for few streams large enough to float lumber or log rafts to market flowed through them. For a time, iron and glass manufacturers tapped these forests for charcoal for fuel, but this demand and the coastal fuelwood trade both dwindled with the increasing use of coal. New Jersey's forests, in spite of their closeness to population centers, thus became less and less attractive to those who would turn them to profit, and when farming exhausted the soil and settlers left for more promising locations, scrub pine reclaimed much of the land, soon growing "so thick as to be almost impenetrable to man or beast."[10]

New Jersey was almost 95 percent forested when white settlement began, and forests were cut steadily into the twentieth century, but at no time did New Jersey sport a lumberman's frontier. Forest harvests were at best ancillary to its main economic activities. This was not the case in either

Pennsylvania or New York. Both had early forest-utilization patterns similar to New Jersey's, but they also had areas where in time a true lumberman's frontier would emerge.

It was a long time before timber harvesting in any part of the Middle Atlantic region constituted a lumberman's frontier. As in New England, initial harvesting was but a precursor. Would-be farmers moved into the interior and tapped the forests as a stopgap until cropland could be brought into production—and to provide supplemental income thereafter. What historian David Ellis said of New York in the early national period applied elsewhere as well: "[T]he upstate pioneer was as much a lumberman as a farmer."[11] A better climate and richer soils in many parts of Pennsylvania and New York made many of the farms in those states less marginal than those of most of Maine or New Jersey. But even in the more favored locations, forests played a vital supporting role in agriculture's march into the interior. Indeed, sawmills sometimes appeared even before farms. Their builders knew settlers would need construction materials and sought to position themselves to supply them after they arrived.

Bath, New York, located on the Cohocton, a tributary of the North Branch of the Susquehanna, provides a case in point. It was first settled in 1793, and a sawmill appeared there that same year and two more the following. Mills preceded settlement in Canton, in far northern New York. The first party arrived in 1801 and immediately set to work erecting a sawmill. Having largely completed the task, most of the party returned to Vermont for the winter and then came back to commence sawing the following year, just as rapid settlement began. With ample local demand, the sawmill prospered. Elsewhere too, those who selected mill locations wisely soon had farmers clustered nearby, and prosperity followed. Such mills were not part of a lumberman's frontier; they were adjuncts of an expanding agricultural society—a part of the farmer's frontier.[12]

In the interior transportation was key. Products from forest and farm had to be moved to market if the settlers' economy was to rise above the subsistence level, and in Pennsylvania and New York this usually meant using rivers as highways of commerce. Shipment by sea, which loomed large in Maine, was of limited importance; lumber was normally rafted to its primary markets rather than dispatched in ocean-going vessels.

It is not clear when rafting began on the Delaware; the first shipments from the river's upper reaches may have been made in 1740, but certainly

Middle Atlantic forests. Map by Sarah E. Hinman.

they were present by 1754, for in that year, according to a notice in *The Pennsylvania Gazette*, a raft of pine mast timbers ranging from fifty-five to eighty feet long broke loose some one hundred miles upriver and is "supposed to be drove down over the Falls [at Trenton]." Two years later the paper reported rafts of boards that had been floated to Philadelphia from upriver had broken loose from Stamper's wharf. In both cases, rewards were offered for their return. Similar notices followed in 1762, 1770, and 1771. Various authorities have credited Daniel Skinner with inaugurating rafting on the Delaware in 1764, but the practice was clearly present before then.[13] Still, as late as 1785 rafting seems to have been uncommon, for in that year a notice in the *New Jersey Gazette* stated: "The inland navigation of the Delaware has been so little attended to for several years past, that at present it is imperfectly known to many." The author of the notice—owner of a tract on the Lackawaxen, a tributary of the upper Delaware—estimated he could cut his trees, haul the logs to a nearby mill, saw them into boards, and raft the cut to Philadelphia for 40 shillings per thousand board feet; there, he could sell his lumber for £6 per thousand. In addition, he noted, there was ready demand for boards and scantling in nearby Trenton, also at £6 per thousand.[14]

As settlement moved inland, the importance of transportation loomed larger. In light of the wretched state of early American roads, this normally meant shipment by water. As farmers moved upriver past the Delaware Water Gap, rafting became an essential link to the main population centers.[15] As time passed and upstream settlement increased, such shipments became increasingly important. According to one source, at the height of this work in the early nineteenth century, some ten thousand people were involved in lumbering and rafting along the Delaware "and most of the towns and villages owed their support if not their existence to the industry." Thaddeus Kenderdine, an early resident, later recalled:

> to ambitious people in a lumber business way . . . Delaware valley seemed a paradise for their exploitage. . . . These rivermen, farmers, or woodsmen were as unsentimental as Markham's hoe-man, but if their minds soared but little above the clods of the valley which raised their buckwheat, rye, potatoes and cabbage, they were . . . well attuned to the nature which kept their physical systems going. . . . Farming on a small scale such crops as their begrudging soil and climate yielded . . . was only a side line . . . for getting out logs and running sawmills was their profitable business.[16]

Lumbering may have been more important than agriculture for such settlers, but, as in early Maine, it was the latter that had drawn them, and they continued to think of themselves as farmers.

Huge rafts—sometimes over one hundred feet wide and fifteen hundred feet long—provided the main vehicles connecting farm and market. In 1824 one resident counted over one hundred and fifty rafts passing his home on the Delaware in a single day. So crowded was the river during spring that navigation often became difficult and finding mooring space at night a challenge. For a time, Philadelphia was the main distribution center for this lumber, and until about 1850 the lumber district, located on the river north of Colowhill Street, was called the Barbary Coast "because of the roughness of the characters who brought their lumber . . . down the river." As late as 1878, two hundred million feet of lumber still entered downstream markets via the Delaware River, although Philadelphia was no longer the center for distribution.[17]

The pattern repeated itself as agriculture moved up the North Branch of the Susquehanna and the Hudson. In the upper Susquehanna drainage the population grew and shipments increased in the wake of the American Revolution. When General John Sullivan moved into the area in 1779 to fight the British and their Iroquois allies, many of his Pennsylvania troops were impressed with its fine forests and potential farmland. After the war, a good number returned to take up claims along the North Branch and in the tributary Chemung River valley.

Jacob Lowman was among the postwar settlers. Soon he was shipping rafts of timber cut from his land to Havre de Grace, Maryland. There, where the river emptied into Chesapeake Bay, he sold his rafts, the buyers then transporting them to New York, Philadelphia, and Baltimore for construction and shipbuilding. Lowman may have been preceded in the trade by George McClure, who in 1794 made a seventy-five-foot-long ark, loaded it with staves for Baltimore, and thus created a "sensation" in the upriver country, and by Jacob and Frederick Bartles, who took both arks and rafts of logs and wood products down the Susquehanna soon after McClure.[18]

Lumbering continued to grow. By 1825 there were over four hundred sawmills in the valley of the upper North Branch; in 1826 some fifteen hundred rafts arrived at Port Deposit, upriver from Havre de Grace (which it had replaced as the main terminus of the trade); the next year 1,631 rafts with over four million feet of lumber passed Harrisburg en route downstream; and on April 17, 1829—reportedly an average day for that rafting season—111 board rafts and twenty timber rafts passed Catawissa,

Pennsylvania, headed for downstream markets. During the heyday of the trade from 1833 to 1840, some two thousand to twenty-five hundred rafts of hewn timbers, at least as many rafts of lumber, and a few spar rafts—altogether some thirty million feet of woodstuff—went down the North Branch annually. A half century after Lowman's arrival on the river's upper reaches, his grandson, William, was still engaged in the trade, although by then most rafts were of sawn lumber, rather than timbers.[19]

In addition to the dangers of the downstream voyage—rocks, sandbars, foul weather, and unexpected changes of water level—the trade was bedeviled by uncertainties in the marketplace. In 1848 the younger Lowman, newly married and eager to return upstream to his bride, had to remain in Port Deposit for weeks until he was able to sell his lumber. On March 29 he wrote his wife he "was the first one to come into port with a raft. I hope that I will be the first one to leave the city [too]." Lowman's hopes went unfulfilled. On April 12, he reported, "I am fearful that I will not be able to leave this place before the first of May. There appears to be a backwardness in business matters here." Still in Port Deposit on May 12, he found matters looking up at last:

> From every appearance here I think the Chemung River must be very high. The water is very riley and is rising rapidly in this place and will cause a reaction in business in a few days. Those that buy lumber are waiting for all [the rafts] to come down. This is what has detained me this length of time. They are not willing to pay what it [lumber] is worth until it is ascertained what quantity there is in the market. This freshet will bring rafts down . . . [and] probably make business a little more brisk than it has been.

In the end, Lowman was unable to sell his lumber and return to the Chemung Valley until June.[20]

The situation was similar on the upper Hudson. Albany, Pehr Kalm reported, had a considerable trade with New York in boards, and the trade's potential was great for land along the river "is everywhere covered with woods except for some pioneer farms which are scattered here and there."[21] Above Albany transportation was by raft, and within a few years a virtual flotilla passed down the river each spring. Recalling rafts observed in the 1760s, Anne Grant wrote:

> There is something serenely majestic in the easy progress of those large bodies on the full stream of this copious river. Sometimes one sees a whole family transported on this simple conveyance: the mother calmly

*spinning, the children sporting about her, and the father fishing at one
end and watching its safety at the same time. These rafts were taken
down to Albany, and put on board vessels there for conveyance to
New York; sometimes, however, it happened that, as they proceeded
very slowly, dry weather came on by the time they reached the Flats,
and it became impossible to carry them further; in that case they were
deposited in great triangular piles opposite our door.*

The fact that the river was navigable by ocean-going vessels as far Albany
combined with construction of the Erie Canal in the 1820s turned that
community into the nation's great lumber mart and altered the picture on
the Hudson, but rafting long continued important and its basic patterns
those found along the Delaware and Susquehanna.[22]

Large though this traffic on rivers of the Middle Atlantic States looms in
historical literature (and in folk memory), one recent case study argues that
rafted lumber never represented over 20 percent of the cut in the New York
portion of the Upper Delaware drainage. The author may well be right, and
the percentage was probably not far different in other interior areas that
had access to river transportation, but he misses an essential point. Wood
not rafted was utilized locally as lumber, as cordwood (or a thousand lesser
uses), rendered into potash, or simply burned, but the portion that went
downstream—whatever it was—was vital to the local economy. Moreover,
rafts provided the easiest means of getting whiskey, flour, cash crops,
products of the hunt, and shingles, potash, and other minor forest goods
to market. These items together with the lumber and timber of the rafts
themselves provided a means of lifting settlers in the river valleys above
the semi-subsistence level that dominated in less-favored locations such as
much of western New York's huge Holland Purchase.[23]

In time canals and railroads extended the marketing of the output of
farmer-loggers into new areas and enlarged the hinterland tapped by the
rivers themselves. In nearly all these areas the symbiotic relationship of farm
and forest continued.[24] Nowhere has this been more clearly demonstrated
than in the area around Beekmantown, New York. Located in the hill
country west of Lake Champlain, Beekmantown attracted settlement
in the late eighteenth century. Gradually its population grew and, with
it, timber harvests. Although most residents thought of themselves as
farmers, the area's leading analyst noted "exploitation of forest resources
was fundamental in the economic development of Beekmantown and the
Lake Champlain region." Forest operations provided employment during
agriculture's slack seasons, an outlet for farm products, encouragement

to clear more land for crops, and a means of earning funds with which to buy goods in the more-developed areas on which hinterland communities such as Beekmantown depended. In turn, farms supplied much of the work force used in the woods and on the waterways in getting the forest output to market, and earnings from the woods were sufficient to encourage the extension of agriculture ever further into the surrounding hills. Initially, many shipments went northward on Lake Champlain, then down the Richelieu River to markets in Canada, but with construction of the Champlain Canal in 1822 the flow reversed; Beekmantown's output now joined the growing flood from Burlington, located on the east side of the lake in Vermont, into New York's major markets.[25]

So long as adequate forests remained, Beekmantown rested on a dual economic foundation, and the community prospered. However, decades of exploitation coupled with ever more effective techniques of harvesting and transporting timber pushed back the forest until few trees of commercial value remained. When that day arrived, many farmers around Beekmantown discovered that, by itself, the land they and their ancestors had worked so hard to clear could support them poorly if at all. Much of the farmland was in fact submarginal for agriculture. The community fell on hard times. Its population dropped, and many of those who remained suffered a reduced standard of living.[26]

A similar pattern developed when settlement moved up the West Branch of the Susquehanna onto the Allegheny Plateau. Farmers settled in the upper reaches of the watershed, felled trees, grubbed out fields, and planted corn, potatoes, buckwheat, and grain. During winter they cut timber and skidded the logs to streamside; in spring they rafted them down to markets in Marietta and nearby communities. As one regional historian wrote, each year "every farmer ran one timber raft at least. . . . It was the timber trade that made the pioneer prosperous." Lumbering was the chief occupation of nearly every area resident and landowner.[27] Many a farm had its own little water-powered sawmill, some on streams so tiny there was insufficient flow to operate them except during the spring runoff or following storms—in local parlance they were "thundergust mills." In addition, there were a number of somewhat larger mills located on more adequate heads of water. All in all, by the 1850s there were some four hundred sawmills in Pennsylvania's Clearfield County alone. Other counties on the Allegheny Plateau must have had nearly as many.[28]

Ubiquitous though sawmills were in west-central Pennsylvania, this was still a farmer's frontier, albeit a frontier where occupational labels could be misleading. William Langdon logged and farmed far upstream near Cherry Tree and in the spring ran rafts down the West Branch; in the census he appears as a "lumberman." His father, who lived nearby and followed the same pursuits (although by 1855 he seems no longer to have run rafts), was listed as a "farmer." Similarly, owners of some of the area's larger sawmills—men such as William Irvin of Curwensville, relatively affluent citizens who had a variety of interests—were given various labels, sometimes called lumbermen and sometimes not. Be that as it may, such men had usually begun as farmers and often still were. And regardless of occupation reported to the census taker, they still employed farmers in their logging, milling, and rafting operations, and still supplied lumber to meet the needs of the local agricultural community. For the moment at least, theirs was still a farmer's frontier.[29]

Nothing demonstrates the nature of Clearfield County's economy as well as the pages of the leading local newspaper. Although it was called the *Raftsman's Journal* and its editor, S. B. Row, was a strong supporter of the local lumber and rafting business, its pages extolled the virtues of agriculture and argued that the future of the county lay with farming. Lumbering was viewed as a temporary expedient needed to supplement agriculture during the early years of settlement; farming would not only bring a sounder, more stable economy, but also encourage a better citizenry. However exciting logging and rafting might be, they encouraged a profligate lifestyle.

Row was not alone in condemning the pitfalls of the raftsman's life. One author of the period claimed, "The rafting business . . . kept half the people of Clearfield drunk down the river several of the best months of the year." The charge may have had some validity. A correspondent wrote to Row in similar, if more extended terms, describing Marietta, the trade's main terminus, during the rafting season:

It is quite amusing to loiter around Front Street during the day and observe the modus operandi of fleecing the more ignorant part of the watermen out of their hard earned money. At every alternate door you will observe a small board stuck out with a notice that within the dirty walls cakes and beer are sold. Some of them, and the fewest number too, bear the look of respectable shops; the balance are attended by one or more young females of a rather suspicious character. The hotels on Front Street are crowded to overflowing and free fights are plenty beyond conception. The bad whiskey drank here during the season of rafting would of itself float half the lumber to Peachbottom, or perhaps into the [Chesapeake] Bay. There are several fancy jewelry shops in operation, in which is sold any amount of brass in the shape of breast pins, eardrops,

lockets, and watches to the unsuspecting backwoodsmen and warranted
. . . to be pure gold. . . . Then there are three or four Patent Medicine
venders mounted on chairs and door steps, rendering the streets hideous
with their songs and gulls to come and buy or test the virtues of their
nostrums.

Ballad singers, a lecturer on phrenology, a fat lady said to weigh 550 pounds, and cock fights all joined the competition for the raftsman's money.[30]

Row, and in all likelihood the authors of the above assessments, looked forward to the day when farming would be so firmly established in Clearfield County that rafting would no longer be necessary; but, if one may judge from the pages of Langdon's diary, many found lumbering and rafting far more interesting than agriculture. Langdon himself did not comment on the diversions offered in Marietta (although he did report that while there he went to a circus in nearby Columbia), but his diary's entries, full of vigor and a sense of drama during the rafting season, became terse and dry as soon as it was over.[31]

In spite of recent historical literature to the contrary, the contrast between the values of those pursuing the agrarian and lumbering lifestyles—a contrast to which Row alludes and Langdon's diary reflects—was more than just the product of polite society's biases. Historian Lee Benson, examining two communities in New York's far northern Franklin County—one basically agricultural and the other primarily dependent on lumbering—found a sharp distinction in church membership, voting behavior, and levels of violence and drunkenness. Burke, the lumber town, displayed characteristics apparently also found in other lumbering communities. Its residents tended to vote Democratic and be non-puritan in behavior. Those of Malone, the farming community, tended to vote Whig and have a high incidence of such things as church membership and temperance activity. Benson argues, "[T]he two occupations [lumbering and farming] retained or developed or attracted men who differed in psychological makeup." Farming tended to reward men willing to plan, demonstrate self-discipline, and devote themselves to a long-term daily routine. Such men were the solid yeomanry on whom Thomas Jefferson had hoped the republic would rest; by way of contrast

lumbering required quick spurts of great exertion during which men
destroyed things under conditions of constant physical danger, followed
by long periods in which they were free to act as the spirit moved them
and the spirits flowed. Moreover, it tended to bring quicker returns

*with more fluctuation than did farming, giving it something of the
lure and excitement of gambling. Rafting logs down the Delaware, the
Susquehanna, or the Allegheny in high-water season was a world away
from the dull routine of hoeing weeds in home corn fields.*

The manifest differences between the two communities, Benson concludes,
resulted from "moral attitudes and values" incident to the contrasting ways
of life that dominated them.[32]

Such generalizations must be approached with caution. Benson's image
of rural life and values is clearly based on a settled agricultural society, not
a frontier community practicing what a later generation would call agro-
forestry—a system that required practitioners to stand, as it were, with one
foot on the farm and one in the forest. Editor Row hoped for the day when
Clearfield would become the sort of staid farm town that Benson showed
Malone to be, but that day was still some time off. Indeed, in places like
Clearfield and Beekmantown, both of which were essentially submarginal
for agriculture, for most residents that day would never come.

Proprietors as well as settlers had a vested interest in frontier forests. In
the case of the Holland Purchase, some 3.3 million acres of wild land in
western New York, absentee landlords viewed the first settlers as transient
residents who would pave the way for others by partially clearing the land
and making other improvements. The proprietors anticipated a second wave
of settlers—more stable and better off financially—would take up long-term
obligations, introduce regular cropping on permanent fields, and thus be
able to compensate the proprietors and make up for the delinquencies of
their predecessors.[33]

The hopes of Holland Purchase's proprietors were in vain. The
agricultural and pastoral activities of the initial settlers removed many of
the most valuable trees, introducing unwelcome ecological changes. Scrub
growth came to dominate on many sites. By 1822 Paul Busti, chief American
agent for the company, was complaining to his employers the property was
"overspread by wood-choppers," and the proprietors found their holdings
falling in value. As one company official put it, "[H]alf improved lands
are [of] less worth than the wild on account of the brushes and weeds by
which after a few years they are overspread." Moreover, it was difficult to
resell "badly improved" plots, for newcomers found bringing such tracts
into production "more tedious and laborious" than clearing old-growth
forest. Long before the lumberman's frontier reached western New York,
the forests present when the first whites arrived had undergone extensive
changes: environmental degradation had already set in.[34]

The situation was similar elsewhere. New York grew slowly during the colonial period, but after the American Revolution it developed apace. In 1785 most of the state's population was in the Hudson Valley and near the Atlantic; by 1820 three-fourths of the growth was in the newer counties north and west of Albany. Much of the increase stemmed from a huge influx of New Englanders seeking new and better lands to farm. They brought with them cultural baggage that shaped their activity in their new homes just as it had in their old: they valued hill farms, distrusted proprietors, and considered resources of the forest theirs for the taking. Many came as squatters. Within a generation they almost totally reshaped upstate New York. For example, by 1820 two-fifths of Otsego County, an area lacking permanent residents before the war, had been settled and "improved."[35]

Nathan Ford, resident agent on Gouverneur Morris's vast claim north of the Adirondacks, was repeatedly frustrated by frontier settlers, as had been David Cobb in Maine before him. In 1797 Ford reported an influx of settlers planning "to purchase [tracts] and strip off the timber before payment becomes due, and then give up the land." Two years later, he reported, "There are several persons now cutting timber upon the upper townships. I have no authority [there] . . . but vast injury will take place upon the townships . . . if there are not measures taken immediately" to halt depredations. Most timber, he added, went into staves and hand-hewn square timbers that were rafted down the St. Lawrence to Montreal. The trade "gave employment to many men, and brought a transient population"; several people came who "pretended to settle [but] their motive was only stealing off the timber."[36]

Just when these inroads began is unclear. Franklin Hough reported a "considerable amount of valuable timber" was stolen along "the whole front of the state on the St. Lawrence before there was anyone to assert the title of the proprietors." In Orleans township improvements were begun in 1806 by people who came without acquiring title and squatted on lands of which they believed there was no legal owner; according to Hough, the belief that free land was available "led great numbers, chiefly of the poorer classes, to come and select and make locations." Even when they did attempt to purchase clear titles, frontier settlers had great difficulty making payments. The chronicler of Steuben County observed, as "was almost unavoidable from the nature of relations, there has been no love lost between the citizens and the proprietors," and by 1818 there was widespread "clamor" in New York "against those who held large tracts of land."[37]

The Otsego area of west-central New York, on which Judge William Cooper and his associates sought to encourage development, provides a further illustration of New York's frontier during the period. The land was too hilly and rocky and had too short a growing season to attract German and Dutch settlers from older regions of New York, so Cooper (the father of novelist James Fenimore Cooper) turned for purchasers to New England's hill country, where population pressure and declining soil fertility had created a population used to farming on demanding upland areas and ready to move if offered attractive terms. They were poor, but, as Alan Taylor has noted, most "migrated to the frontier to better their position in a market society, not to drop out of it." Not everything developed as they or Cooper anticipated. On their new farms, these transplanted hill Yankees were well removed from the Mohawk and Susquehanna rivers and had to transport products overland some eighty miles to reach water routes leading to market. Harsh reality ruled out the shipment of bulky timber products that had been so important to them—and to their ancestors—in New England. To provide the settlers with a forest product to sell, Cooper launched a scheme for large-scale production of maple sugar, but his plans went awry. In the end, the settlers had to turn to manufacturing potash to supplement cattle raising and farming. Few prospered, many left, and much forestland was devastated to furnish the hardwood that went into potash production.[38]

The situation was nearly identical in the Susquehannah Land Company's domain on the upper North Branch of the Susquehanna. A company representative reported he was "encouraging New England Settlers." It was, he thought, the only way to make Luzerne County "useful to the State" or the area's proprietors: "Pennsylvanians will never settle such a Country." Indeed, it seemed that almost the only Pennsylvanians to show up in the area were land speculators.[39]

Others were also plagued by inadequate means of transportation. The Mohawk has few important tributaries; in central and western New York only areas draining into the Susquehanna or Delaware had sufficiently easy access to major markets for lumbering to develop to any significant degree before the Canal Era. Even there, development was hindered by the limitations of rafting—undependable water flows, dangerous rapids, and markets that were quickly glutted when spring floods brought down rafts in droves.

Completion of the Erie Canal hastened change, opening the door for settlers to flood out of New England into upstate New York, but the construction of feeder canals in the 1830s and after—especially the Chemung, Chenango, and Genesee—had a greater impact on lumber production. The feeder canals made commercial lumbering practical in localities where it had not been previously and reoriented much of the pre-existing lumber trade. Woodstuff that had once gone down the Delaware, the Susquehanna, or even the Allegheny now made its way eastward over the Erie Canal to Albany. Transportation costs to Albany were less than to previous outlets, prices there frequently better, and demand more constant. Thus, the Erie and its feeders ushered in a period of rapid growth for lumbering in central and western New York, and beyond in Potter County, Pennsylvania.[40]

In the 1840s shipments from Michigan also began arriving in Albany. Analysts from the Lake States have been wont to explain the cargoes as a response to the denuding of New York and Pennsylvania. Nothing could have been further from the truth. Lumbering in both states was still on the rise, not peaking until the 1870s. But the explosive growth of the Northeast that began in the 1820s was such that Glens Falls, Williamsport, and the other Mid-Atlantic centers of production could not keep up with demand. For all the output of Mid-Atlantic mills, lumbermen in Saginaw, Bay City, and elsewhere in eastern Michigan could find ready buyers in Albany, and their shipments added to the economic growth of the broad corridor traversed by the Erie Canal.[41]

The rapid growth of the area tributary to the canal was not without critics. Settlers along the Cohocton, a western tributary of the North Branch of the Susquehanna, had anticipated their valley would furnish the great route to the West; settlement and commerce would move from Baltimore up the North Branch and Cohocton and from there across the low divide to Lake Erie and the Ohio drainage. Their hopes went for naught. Guy McMaster complained that, with the Erie Canal, "Albany and New York, being stout and remorseless robbers, plundered us by force. Syracuse and Utica, being no older than we, stole our riches secretly."[42]

The area south of the Erie Canal was left off the main route of commerce, and thus away from the greatest centers of growth, but it certainly did not wither. Chemung County became the center of a great lumber-producing region. At Elmira both banks of the Chemung Canal were often "piled high with pine boards and shingles waiting shipment." Similarly, within three years of completion of the Chenango Canal to Binghamton, four million feet of lumber were being dispatched over it annually; and even before completion of the Genesee Canal an estimated fourteen million feet of lumber, as well as huge quantities of staves and shingles, sat beside its lower reaches, ready for shipment to Rochester and Albany as soon as the canal opened. Lumber prices in Rochester soon fell, saving builders there an estimated $150,000.[43]

For some twenty-five years commencing in the late 1820s much, perhaps even most, of the lumber sold in Albany—the largest lumber trade center in the United States—came from central and western New York. This region, where lumbering had begun as an adjunct of the activities of forest farmers, now had numerous lumbermen divorced from farming and a host of sawmills that existed as an end in themselves rather than as adjuncts to agrarian life. It was a transitory development. In the face of logging, Batavia's newspaper noted in 1853, "forests hereabouts are falling fast. . . . We shall soon find the supply of Wood and Lumber cut off to a great extent to supply the natural wants of our people."[44]

The large landholdings common along the Hudson were tapped for their forest wealth just as surely as were smallholdings on the frontier. Lumbering was pursued not only by the owners of estates acquired under Dutch dominion, but by later arrivals as well. In 1749, Pehr Kalm observed most Albany merchants "have extensive estates in the country and a large property in forests. If their estates have a little brook, they do not fail to erect a sawmill upon it for sawing boards and planks, which many boats take during the summer to New York, having scarcely any other cargo." In 1830 English visitor John Fowler noted the Palisades of the Hudson, which began some eight miles upstream from New York City, were "diversified only by wood slides down their sides . . . [f]or the purpose of conveying fire-wood from the top to the bottom of the rocks" from whence it could be easily transported to the city for sale. Near Albany and in many a locale further upstream, lumbering to supply both downstream cities and local markets continued apace. The effect was dramatic. As one historian put it, "[I]n the half century following the Revolution, the Hudson Valley was denuded of a great part of its forests and assumed much of its appearance of today"; it became a world of cleared and productive farms.[45]

The Mohawk, unlike the Hudson into which it flowed, was not navigable by ocean-going vessels, but construction of the Erie Canal opened its valley to commerce as never before. Extensive forests still graced the region in spite of the activities of settlers in places such as the Holland Purchase and the tracts controlled by William Cooper. "The wild land," Fowler reported, "is generally well, some of it *nobly* timbered." South of Syracuse, near Chittenango, he added, "there is one of the finest specimens of *native forest* I have seen in the country—I ever saw—tree interwoven with tree—*a dense mass of forest*—seeming to bid defiance to the footsteps, ay, even the hands of man." But lumbering was going on, pursued by farmers and others

seeking to turn landholdings to profit. "There are a number of small streams
... [which] supply most valuable mill-seats"; as a result, near Utica wooded
land was "fully as valuable as cleared." Indeed, Fowler predicted, "so rapid
are the strides of improvement and cultivation" that within a few years the
valley would be a fertile plain for husbandmen. Fowler's forecast was not
without foundation. In 1823, even before the canal was completed to Lake
Erie, over a million board feet of lumber had passed eastward through its
locks headed for the markets of Albany and New York City.[46]

Fowler overlooked a key development. Farmers and land clearing were
gradually becoming less central to New York's lumber production. In 1827,
when the Canal Commission doubled rates on lumber rafts passing through
state canals, lumbermen from northern and western New York protested.
In a petition to the legislature, supporters pointed out the importance of
the lumber business and asked that the new rate schedule be rescinded lest
lumbering operations be irreparably damaged. The petition—and its large
number of signatories—is but one of many pieces of evidence indicating a
new era was at hand. The protest was the product not of a group of forest
farmers, but of people for whom lumber production was a livelihood,
and many businessmen in New York City, as signatories to the petition,
indicated they recognized their dependence thereon. As the latter put it,
"[H]eretofore we have not, & we believe hereafter cannot, obtain by any
source of conveyance, except that of the Hudson River ... abundant supplys
of Lake Champlain Pine as a Principal means of frameing our Houses, the
perhaps unparalleled Oaks of the western Country for the Construction
of our Shipping, Hemlock for facing up our Wharves & Bridge piers, and
last & most of all Dock logs & Large Spars."[47]

Just when lumbering emerged as an end in itself is not clear, but by the
1820s it was obviously taking on a life separate from that of agriculture. In
upstate New York a lumberman's frontier was in the offing. By the end of
another decade—with the Chemung, Chenango, and Genesee canals open
and Albany booming as the nation's great lumber mart—it was in place,
although, unlike that which developed at Glens Falls, it had no single point
of focus and was thus often overlooked both at the time and since.[48]

The result of this development was more than just a new arena of
operation for the lumberman's frontier; forest devastation resulted too.
Lumbermen of the period logged without regard for their environmental
impact. Common wisdom held that farms would follow in the wake of

forest clearing, and, if they needed an argument to excuse their profligate ways, that provided it. But on the thin soils of the rocky, hilly uplands of upstate New York this was not to be. Around Beekmantown and elsewhere, farmers cleared land appearing to have promise for agriculture, hoping to enlarge their holdings thereby. They recognized that some land could never be cropped, but they might log it nonetheless if it were sufficiently convenient, and especially if it might at least make decent pasture once cleared. Farmers did the same in lands tributary to the Erie Canal, but the lumbermen who proliferated in the area after the canal's opening were less restrained. Not just potential crop and pasture land, not just tracts that were relatively convenient, but any sites with fine stands of white pine were logged—and logged without concern for reproduction or the health of the land. The end result was predictable. By 1877, Franklin Hough reported, commercial timber was gone from the drainage of the North Branch of the Susquehanna, and the end was in sight, if not already at hand, in many another part of the Middle Atlantic states too. Viewing the aftermath in 1907, James Elliott Defebaugh, America's pioneer forest historian, wrote:

> No effort has been made to preserve or renew the forests of western New York, and the streams have shrunk to mere creeks or dry beds of sand and gravel in the summer. The Allegheny, that once was large enough at Olean to promise navigation, is transformed in summer to a stream of small dimensions and is a valueless watercourse for the present generation. . . . It is estimated that only one-half of the vast region that constitutes the Allegheny watershed in southern New York is used or needed for agriculture. The remainder is now chiefly a waste of hill and valley, partly overgrown with brush and briars.

What Defebaugh said regarding lands in the Allegheny drainage might have been applied to much of the rest of the area tapped by the Erie Canal system.[49]

It is difficult to pinpoint the precise time of transition from farmer-loggers to lumbermen—indeed, it surely took place at different times in different places. It is also difficult to demonstrate all that was involved in the shift. But one thing *is* clear. Not all explanations that have been offered have merit. Speaking of the Hudson-Mohawk region, historian David Maldwyn Ellis claimed, "It was the development of the export trade that differentiated the lumberman from the farmer," and thus presumably the lumberman's from the farmer's frontier. His argument will not hold up to even the most cursory examination, whether applied to the Hudson-Mohawk region or elsewhere. Farmers along the Hudson (and countless other rivers) had been exporting products of the forest to outside markets since colonial times, yet an economy dominated by a body of men who can legitimately be called lumbermen did not appear in the area until well into the nineteenth century. Until then the quest for family farms, not the trees that graced the land, was central in luring people to the region's frontier areas.[50]

Around Lake Champlain, shipments by frontier farmers, such as those located around Beekmantown, drew outside attention. Canals and investors who erected large mills in the vicinity of Burlington soon followed. The success of these mills eventually encouraged the construction of rail lines connecting the area to the Boston market and of a line across far-northern New York from Ogdensburg on the St. Lawrence to Plattsburgh on Lake Champlain. The latter line provided Vermonters with access to the vast timber supplies on the northern slope of the Adirondacks and to the lumber the increasingly numerous mills there cut. Indeed, so closely did the area north of the Adirondacks become linked with Vermont (by kinship ties as well as the now-redirected flow of woodstuff) that it came to be referred to as New Vermont.[51]

A watershed had also been crossed in the forests tributary to Lake Champlain, although again the date cannot be pinpointed. Logging that had no real connections with agriculture—save that it provided by-employment to nearby farmers and, through its camps, an outlet for hay and other farm produce—emerged to supply mills with the raw material they needed. Unnoticed, a lumberman's frontier had materialized there. Within a generation, the Green Mountains of Vermont and, to a lesser extent, the forests on the hills immediately west of Lake Champlain had been felled. Soil erosion, siltation of streams, and rampant scrub growth followed hard on the heels of timber harvest, with the result, as one Vermonter put it, "[w]e [now] have more bushes than trees." Unlike the conifers that preceded it, this second growth had little to offer those who would combine farming with frontier forestry, and out-migration proceeded apace, leading one authority to predict glumly: "The waning of our forests will bury agriculture and the lumber industry in a common grave."[52]

In the midst of all this, pioneer ecologist George Perkins Marsh spent his early adult years as a mill owner and lumber dealer in Vermont. Troubled by what he saw, Marsh pondered inter-relationships among the developments unfolding around him. In an address to farmers, delivered in Rutland in 1847, he called for improvement "in the management of our forest lands." The denuded hills, dry streambeds, and eroded slopes of the area were the result of ill-advised agricultural clearing resulting from what Marsh called "the rage for improvement." A decade later, in a more thoroughly environmental study—an analysis of the causes of declining fish populations in the area—Marsh's focus shifted. He traced the aquatic crisis not to poor agricultural practices, but to the building of sawmills and other industrial establishments "on all the considerable streams," to the denudation of the area's mountains in the wake of large-scale lumbering, and to the degrading effects these developments had on area streams and lakes. The lumberman's frontier, it would appear, had arrived in the area, and lumbermen had supplanted farmers as the main instruments of forest depletion.[53] Thus, long before he wrote *Man and Nature*, the work that would earn him the title of "father of conservation" in the United States, Marsh was keenly aware of ecological inter-relationships. What he observed in the wake of large-scale lumbering in the Lake Champlain area seems to have led to the more sophisticated level of analysis that was to be the source of his eventual influence.[54]

What Marsh had seen was not limited to the Green Mountains and Burlington area. He might have learned his lessons as easily at any one of a number of other sites in New England or the Middle Atlantic states. Indeed, others detected many of the same deleterious effects of lumbering. Guy McMaster, writing in 1853, noted that in Steuben County, New York, the rivers had become smaller and less dependable. "The destruction of the forests has caused the drying up of multitudes of little springs. . . . Freshets can be had on shorter notice now than formerly . . . but they are of shorter duration," for when there had been good forest cover, snows melted more slowly under the trees; "perennial brooks are now 'dry runs,' except after rains, when they are filled with powerful torrents" that tear at the landscape and streamside structures but are of little use for rafting or milling.[55]

It is difficult to determine the exact time at which a lumberman's frontier emerged in many parts of the Mid-Atlantic area, but the place where it first blossomed full-blown is clear: Glens Falls, located on the Hudson some sixty miles above Albany, and in its forested hinterlands still further upstream. What developed there was not clouded by the presence of forest-farmers, whose ties to the land were more complex than those of true lumberers; nor was it obscured by a flood of imported Canadian woodstuff such as makes later developments at Burlington hard to assess. What emerged in Glens Falls, and in the Adirondacks its mills tapped, was a lumberman's frontier, pure and simple.

Abraham Wing was the first to harness the potential of the Great Falls of the Hudson. In 1762 he obtained a patent to a tract of land on the north side of the falls and moved there with a small group of fellow Quakers. Within a year he had a little water-powered sawmill in operation to take advantage of the falls' thirty-foot head of water; a grist mill quickly followed. In 1770 Wing, together with partner Daniel Jones, erected a second, larger mill. It was a "Dutch mill"; that is, instead of a single saw, the waterwheel drove several (eventually there were fourteen) set side by side so more than one board could be sawn at a time—the sort of operation that, decades earlier, Governor Bellomont had feared would denude New York if allowed to go unchecked. In 1770 John Glen received a patent to land across the river from Wing, and in 1773 Duane Parks erected a sawmill there. By then a small community, known as Wings Falls, had grown up beside the river; as many as two dozen log homes stood near Wing's mills. Although many of the settlers were part-time farmers (hence the grist mill), the falls and the sawmills they powered were the main reason for the community's existence. As economic geographer Evelyn Dinsdale put it, "[O]nly where agriculture failed in the Adirondack uplands was it possible for lumbering to develop as a specialized activity." Glens Falls and the area nearby became the hub of that activity. The record is not clear, but one suspects that by the 1780s lumber rafts were already making their way down the Hudson from sawmills at the Great Falls.[56]

The Revolutionary War hit the little settlement hard. Settlers were driven from the area, homes and mills burned; 1780 was especially bad and for decades after known simply as "the year of the burning." Persevering, Wing returned in 1783 to rebuild. Within two years Wings Falls numbered eighteen families. However, by 1788 Wing was in financial straits. In that year, according to an oft-told story, Wing agreed to rename the hamlet for John Glen if the latter would host a "wine supper" for Wing and his friends, presumably at Wing's inn, where area leaders were wont to gather. The dinner held, Glen posted public notices informing one and all of the name change. One suspects, in light of the financial difficulties in which Wing was enmeshed, that additional considerations beyond hosting a dinner were involved, but in the face of so appealing a legend alternative explanations for the name change had little chance to survive. When the little community acquired a post office in 1808, the name became official—Glens Falls it has been ever since.[57]

Growth continued until 1812, when the uncertainties of war brought economic stagnation to this exposed area, close to British-controlled

Canada, and to the country as a whole. But war was not the only problem. Lumber had to be hauled by wagon from Glens Falls' mills to sites near Fort Edward, below the falls, where it was then assembled into rafts for shipment downstream. The extra costs thus entailed undermined the competitiveness of the little community's sawmills. Even more ominous, log supplies were growing scarce and more distant. Years of cutting had depleted the limited stands in the immediate vicinity of the community.[58]

The future of Glens Falls was brighter than it appeared. In 1813 two brothers, Norman and Alanson Fox, experimented with driving free-floating logs down the Schroon River, a major tributary of the upper Hudson. These drives have frequently been described as America's first, a claim without merit, as earlier discussion of developments in Maine makes clear. In fact, there may even have been drives on the Schroon before that of the Fox brothers, for seven years earlier the state legislature had forbidden anyone from "rolling any log or logs into . . . or doing anything to obstruct said river." Such legislation would have been unlikely without the presence of drives, however small. The question of primacy aside, insofar as Glens Falls was concerned the Fox brothers' actions were seminal. They pointed the way to freeing the area's sawmills of dependence on dwindling nearby stands by showing a way to tap the forests of the Adirondacks. When prosperity returned and downriver demand burgeoned, these stands were to furnish Glens Falls' mills with the raw material for unprecedented growth.[59]

Prosperity did not arrive until the 1820s. Then the spurt in New York's economic life triggered by national prosperity and construction of the Champlain and Erie canals vitalized Glens Falls and the nearby communities of Sandy Hill (later known as Hudson Falls) and Fort Edward. Glens Falls also benefited from the Hudson River feeder to the Champlain Canal, which when widened in 1832 provided the area's mills with an all-water route to markets of Albany, New York City, and beyond. New mills sprang up, older ones enlarged. Albert Cheney built the first big mill in the late 1830s; other lumbermen soon followed, including Augustus Sherman, who in 1841 erected a large sawmill on the feeder canal a short distance outside of Glens Falls proper. Development accelerated after 1845, when Daniel W. Wing and a group of "public-spirited and far-sighted citizens" purchased the feeder canal and dam from the state and ten acres below the dam for sawmill sites. Lumbermen seized the opportunities thus offered, and numerous sawmills soon studded the tract.[60]

Central to the development of lumbering in Glens Falls was Abraham Wing, III, grandson of the community's founder. The area near the head of the Schroon that the Fox brothers had logged had fallen into the hands of parties from Troy, New York. Casting about for someone to oversee their interests, they found Wing, who built a dam and sluiceway at the outlet of Brant Lake, thus making possible the mass movement of free-floating logs down the Schroon and Hudson to Glens Falls. So successful were Wing's efforts that he moved from manager to partner to owner of the operation. As one local historian noted, "When he [Wing] took hold of the Brant Lake property, the cry . . . [in Glens Falls] was that the lumber business was finished"; the plains near town "had been stripped and denuded," but Wing gave "a new impulse . . . to the whole lumbering business of the Hudson River and its affluents."[61]

The rapid growth of lumbering in Glens Falls and nearby communities meant loggers had to move beyond Brant Lake, ever deeper into the Adirondacks, to find stands to tap and had to develop increasingly sophisticated means of getting out the sawlogs. Log drives were an important part, but more was involved. Most of the key streams originated in mountain lakes. Dams constructed at lake outlets allowed sizable heads of water to be stored; released in a flood, they flushed logs at the outlet and along downstream banks onward to Glens Falls. Logs corralled in pocket booms were winched, dragged by boat, paddled, and poled to lake outlets to await conventional driving. In winter, workmen pulled logs on sleighs across the frozen surfaces of the lakes to their outlets, there to await spring floods that would carry them downstream. Canals connected one lake to another, increasing the reach of lumbermen into the mountains. Slides moved logs down steep slopes to streams that could be used to float them to market. Elsewhere horses and oxen snaked logs to streamside on specially constructed carts and sleighs.[62]

None of the devices and techniques used in moving logs toward the sawmills was as important as what was at the receiving end: the Big Boom. Area lumbermen joined in 1849 to form the Hudson River Boom Association, which promptly constructed a log boom at Little Bay, some four miles upriver from Glens Falls. Workmen built a series of piers across the river and connected them with twenty-four-foot long, twelve-inch square pine timbers bound four together and then chained end-to-end. The vast enclosure this created could hold some two million logs; when the drives came in, logs would pile up behind the half-mile-long boom until they formed a solid mass as much as twenty feet deep. Bit by bit workers released the logs from the main boom to smaller ones downstream; there others sorted them according to their brands and then floated them to the waiting mills. It was a massive, but hardly foolproof, system: during the floods of 1859, the Big Boom failed and five hundred thousand logs were scattered downstream for forty miles.[63]

For over half a century the Hudson River Boom Association collected and sorted logs as they arrived above Glens Falls.[64] Drives increased steadily from 1851, when the association's records commence, to their peak in 1872, when over a million sawlogs reached the boom. Since Hudson River operators used a peculiar log scale and, unlike those of other areas, cut their logs thirteen feet long, it is difficult to determine the precise quantity boomed, but records indicate the drives grew from some twenty-five million board feet (Scribner scale) in 1851 to about two hundred and ten million feet in 1872. The huge lumber cut that resulted made its way downriver to the insatiable markets of New York City and other cities along the Mid-Atlantic seaboard. Spurred by the growing production in and around Glens Falls, from 1852 to 1860 New York led all states in the manufacture of lumber.[65]

To obtain stumpage to sustain the prodigious output at Glens Falls, lumbermen pushed ever deeper into the Adirondacks. They were entering an arena with a small population; no native population made permanent homes there, and, unlike on the Allegheny Plateau, few frontier farmers sought the land for agricultural pursuits. There were a few residents (such as Ned Buntline, a writer who lived at Eagle Lake and later "discovered" Buffalo Bill Cody); most lived by hunting, fishing, and serving as guides for Americans who were beginning to discover the outdoors and turn to the Adirondacks as a place to experience it. Their impact on the industry was minimal.[66]

Clashes in the Adirondacks were not primarily between older residents and newcomers, but between one lumberman and another, the most important struggle being that for control of timber around the Eckford lakes—Blue Mountain, Eagle, and Utowana. Located in Township 34 of the great Totten and Crossfield land purchase of 1772, the area lay in the heart of the Adirondacks. The lakes themselves drained northward into the Raquette River drainage and thence to the St. Lawrence, but Flow 34 (later known as Durant Lake) was only a short distance away and it drained south via Rock River into the Hudson. In the 1860s, needing fresh supplies of timber for their ever-hungry mills in Glens Falls, Ordway Jones and his partners obtained title to a major portion of the township and promptly began cutting. They carted the resulting logs to a landing on Flow 34 and then drove them down the Rock and Hudson to their mill. But Jones was dissatisfied. Seeking to reduce transportation costs and allow his crews to cut even further on the St. Lawrence side of the summit, he proposed building

Tug pulling a huge pocket boom of logs on Long Pond in the Upper Raquette Drainage. Courtesy The Adirondack Museum, #AM_P187_ref.

a dam at the outlet of Utowana Lake, digging a three-quarter-mile-long canal from Blue Mountain Lake to Flow 34, and thus redirecting the lake's outflow to the Hudson drainage. Some mill owners on the lower Raquette objected, fearing they would lose their source of raw material as well as much water on which they depended for power and transportation. Other Raquette millmen reacted differently. They proposed a diversion of their own, albeit located differently, seeing in it a chance to float logs southward to the burgeoning markets in the United States instead of being restricted to the Raquette drainage and to Burlington and Canadian outlets.[67]

The contest was remarkably similar to those in Maine over control of the headwaters of the Kennebec and Allagash, but in the end nothing came of it. In 1873 Verplanck Colvin, reporting on a topographical survey he had done for the state, analyzed and objected to Jones's proposals. Colvin protested largely on environmental grounds, for he wanted a vast forest preserve in the Adirondacks. Bit by bit others added their voices. Faced with rising opposition, both Jones and the operators from the Raquette dropped their plans. Frontier conditions were waning in the Adirondacks; lumbermen were no longer free to operate as they saw fit, expanding production with minimal interference from government or the public so long as they brought commodities into the marketplace and generated jobs.

In the years that followed, lumbermen faced further opposition to their plans for logging in the Adirondacks, but in many cases these were plans tied to railroads. Just as elsewhere, logging in the area was moving beyond the waterways. A new, more industrial order with fewer frontier overtones was set to emerge. [68]

How much New York's lumbering owed to Maine is problematic. Available records are inadequate to determine how many New York lumbermen and laborers or how much of the state's investment capital came from the Pine Tree State. It appears that neither was great. New York's lumber industry was tied to Albany, New York City, and Philadelphia, rather than Boston and overseas markets; the former would no doubt have been the primary sources of funds. Moreover, by the time the Empire State began to develop its own lumberman's frontier, the industry in Maine had already begun to move to the Lake States. There is no indication that any great number of its operators moved south to Glens Falls or the area tributary to the Erie Canal; opportunities there must have seemed too limited. Surely there was some technological transfer. The similarities between the Penobscot Boom and that at Glens Falls can hardly have been coincidental, and millmen and investors would have been fools not to tap expertise developed in the greatest lumbering area yet seen. But as Glens Falls' unique log scale suggests, even here New York seems to have marched to its own drummer. All in all, it would appear the state's lumber frontier was an independent development, and like that of Maine had grown bit by bit out of the area's colonial and early national agrarian experience.

CHAPTER FIVE

Lumber and Labor in the Pines:
New Patterns of Conflict

If Glens Falls provided the first clear manifestations in the Mid-Atlantic States of a genuine lumberman's frontier, developments at Williamsport, Pennsylvania, represented its fullest flowering. Nothing earlier, not Glens Falls, not even Bangor in its heyday, had been a larger, more vibrant, more productive lumber center. Located on the West Branch of the Susquehanna, Williamsport became preeminent for a variety of reasons. The West Branch drained a vast area of pine forest. The river was well suited for log drives and booming. The city had access to both the Pennsylvania canal system and railroads by which its mills could market their cut in New York, Philadelphia, Baltimore, and other Atlantic seaboard centers.[1]

The statistical record attests to Williamsport's importance. Its first big mill appeared in 1838, shortly after the Pennsylvania Canal gave it access to outside lumber markets, yet growth remained slow. In 1850 the population was a mere 1,615, then with construction of a large boom just upriver it quickly accelerated. By 1860 the population was 5,664, and by 1866 there were thirty sawmills in the city with a combined capacity of 995 thousand board feet per twelve-hour day (over three hundred million board feet per year).[2] Production was consistently less than capacity, but output was tremendous nonetheless. The great St. Patrick's Day flood of 1865 carried away three spans of the river bridge and some fifty million feet of lumber stacked in millyards; at its height nine-tenths of the city was under water, but the boom that was key to operations held, and production and growth quickly resumed. By 1872 there were forty sawmills employing some three thousand men. In 1876, sixty-eight million board feet left the city via the Pennsylvania Railroad, sixty-three million on the Catawissa Railroad, and forty-seven million by canal. Considerable production at Lock Haven, a few miles up the West Branch from Williamsport (and with a boom of its own), swelled the area's output further. Clinton County (of which Lock Haven was the seat) had ninety-three sawmills.[3]

Records are inadequate to quantify the forward and backward integration of the firms that produced this huge output. The absence of comment suggests there was almost no forward integration; wholesale and retail yards near the markets and the means of reaching them seem to have

101

been left to others. But those with sufficient capital engaged in backward integration from an early date. John DuBois was among them, buying his first sawmill in Lycoming County and timberland to supply it in 1838. However, limited investment capital apparently necessitated that many of the area's early lumbermen concentrated on milling and left logging and ownership of timberstands to others. Gradually this changed; owning timber seemed essential if one's mill were to be assured of sawlogs and avoid the uncertainties of purchasing logs on the open market. Local participation in building the Williamsport boom was another early step in backward integration; building railroads to tap company stands followed. Actual (or virtual) company towns, places such as DuBois and Cross Fork, emerged upstream with company stores and other adjuncts of backward integration usually present. Reinvestment of profits, coupled with an influx of capital from Maine, made such developments possible.[4]

Williamsport was more than just another great lumber-producing center. Events there, and in the hinterlands tributary to it, heralded changes in lumbering more clearly than anything that occurred elsewhere. The Clearfield County War of 1855 announced that the dominance by farmer-loggers who cut timber in winter and rafted it to market on spring floods was coming to an end. And the Williamsport lumber strike of 1872 made manifest the fact that while lumbering was still fraught with frictions, as it had been since colonial times, it had become part of America's new industrial order and was now divided not so much between those inside and those outside the industry as between capital and labor. Behind both developments lay the great Susquehanna Boom, trigger to Williamsport's explosive growth.

The first steps toward building the boom came in 1836, when John Leighton arrived from Maine to investigate the West Branch's potential for lumbering. He recognized that the miles-long stretch of deep, quiet water just above Williamsport provided an ideal location for a massive boom. Such a structure could collect logs from the vast area of the Allegheny Plateau drained by the upper West Branch and thus do for Williamsport what the Penobscot Boom had done for Bangor. At first Leighton could not find financial backers; but in 1844 he persuaded James H. Perkins of Lincoln, Maine, to visit Williamsport. Convinced by what he saw, Perkins became the main force behind efforts to get a boom constructed. In 1846 Perkins and Leighton joined John DuBois and other lumbermen from the Williamsport area to charter the Susquehanna Boom Company, a major step in the backward integration of their firms. But even then there were doubts as to the practicality of driving the West Branch, and no actual construction took place until almost the end of 1849.[5]

Drives followed, the first apparently in May 1850.[6] A violent storm four years earlier had blown down a large stand along Moshannon Creek, a tributary of the upper West Branch. The trees were too broken to furnish the long logs needed for rafts, so their owner (the Portland Lumber Company of Maine) arranged to have J. B. Wing—only twenty-six years old, but an experienced log driver—cut the timber into sixteen-foot sawlogs, such as were used in drives in Maine, and float them out on the spring floods.[7] Wing and a large force of men set to work and in the spring of 1850 drove over two million feet of logs to a temporary boom at Williamsport. A local newspaperman hailed the drive as it passed Lock Haven on May 19th as "a rare, a proud, a beautiful sight."[8]

Raftsmen had by this time been using the upper West Branch for two decades or more, but if they expected "log floating" to cease once salvage work on Moshannon Creek was complete, they soon discovered their error. Wing's drive demonstrated that the West Branch was not, as many thought, ill suited for driving; and the temporary boom at Williamsport clearly was more effective than boatmen in gathering loose logs floated down the river. A Lock Haven newspaperman put it succinctly: log drives and booms were "the cheapest way in which mills can be stocked."[9]

The Susquehanna Boom Company moved quickly to complete a permanent boom. Its heart was a series of large, stone-filled cribs down the middle of the river. Long logs (boom sticks) attached by heavy chain couplings connected the cribs. At the upstream end, a sheer boom could be extended across the river to divert logs into the boom and then withdrawn once the drive was over so that river traffic could pass. At the downstream end there were sorting works where "boom rats" separated logs according to the owner's brands and made up temporary rafts for their transit to the mills. Repeatedly enlarged, the boom came to have a capacity of three hundred million feet of logs, and extended seven miles along the river. But it was not without problems; it broke in 1860, letting fifty million feet of logs escape downstream (some all the way to Chesapeake Bay), and booming charges were a constant source of friction; but it revolutionized lumbering on the West Branch. Within two years of its completion Harris, Random & Co. built a mill that the *Lycoming Gazette* hailed as the "largest and best saw mill in the world." Others followed. A new industrial order had arrived that would last as long as there were forests to fell in Williamsport's hinterlands.[10]

Friction between raftsmen and log drivers developed almost at once, and the workers involved in the early drives contributed to these problems. As one observer put it, they "were irresponsible men, and for the damages occasioned [by their drives] no redress could be obtained." Some seem not to have been particular about what they took. The *Clearfield Republican*

The Williamsport boom filled with logs. Thirty-foot-high cribs holding boom logs in place created a storage area that stretched for seven miles along the river. The Pennsylvania Canal and Pennsylvania Railroad, key lumber carriers, are in the foreground. Courtesy James V. Brown Library, #100526dup.

complained they "cleaned the beach," adding to their drives squared timber and logs belonging to raftsmen. Wing tried to assuage local concerns through explanations of his operations in the local press and offers of cooperation with woodsmen along the river, but to no avail. Nor did protests halt once the boom was in place. Not only was rafting difficult when the stream was filled with free-floating logs, but also, when a drive was coming down, the boom's operators extended the sheer boom completely across the river to collect their logs, effectively blocking passage of rafts until its operators could be prevailed upon to open the boom to let them through. Protests mounted.[11]

Some raftsmen turned to sabotage. Their most common technique was to "iron" logs—driving old spikes, files, horseshoes, or other scrap metal into logs until the metal was hidden by the bark. When struck by high-speed saws in the mills, the metal was terribly destructive—and, when fragments began to fly, exceedingly dangerous to workmen nearby. However, mill operators soon found that peeling logs in the woods was an effective counter-measure. Peeling revealed hidden iron, but did more; because of reduced friction peeled logs were easier to handle, sliding past obstructions (and one another) more readily thus reducing the likelihood of jams; moreover, peeled logs were less susceptible to blue-stain fungi and certain wood-boring insects than unpeeled ones.[12]

The boom company began paying damages, but raftsmen still chafed at the delays the boom caused. At times raftsmen opened the boom under the cover of darkness, letting their rafts through but also allowing a good number of logs to escape downstream. At one point, John DuBois resorted to posting an armed guard on the boom to prevent a group of raftsmen who had partaken of "plenty of whiskey" from secretly opening the boom. DuBois, also armed, hid in nearby bushes to provide backup should the guard need assistance. In due course, the raftsmen arrived, confronted the guard, and, seeing the revolver sticking from his pocket, decided against a confrontation; they retreated to await the scheduled opening of a passageway the next day. DuBois was successful on this occasion, but on numerous others he and the other millmen were not, and many logs disappeared downstream as fugitive rafts slipped through the boom at night.[13]

Trying to head off conflict, in 1852 legislators from upriver introduced a bill in the state legislature to ban log drives on the Susquehanna and its tributaries. Citizens petitioned for and against the bill; after passing the House, it failed by a single vote in the Senate. William F. Packer, a key figure in the bill's defeat, explained:

> I thought the bill . . . wrong in every point. [It would have been] wrong
> if no expenditures had been made in the erection of booms in the river
> . . . but [it was] especially so, in view of the large investments of capital
> which have been made at Williamsport, Lock-Haven and elsewhere
> in the construction of booms, the erection of steam saw mills &c.,
> dependent upon that [log driving] business, as then fully recognized and
> established by law.[14]

Similar bills, introduced at the next two sessions of the legislature, met the same fate in spite of additional petitions and protest meetings in Clearfield and other rafting centers. Even a bill that would have banned log drives only on Clearfield and Moshannon creeks failed of passage.[15]

The nation's economy was slowing, however, and this—coupled with a panic on the New York Stock Exchange in the fall of 1854—led to slackened demand. Streams became less crowded, and tensions between log drivers and raftsmen eased. Under the circumstances, interest in the complaints of raftsmen waned. Even a watered-down bill designed to regulate, rather than ban, log drives not only did not pass—it failed even to win consideration in the 1855 session of the legislature.[16]

Here matters might have rested if log driving had appeared destined to continue at the same level. For some five seasons log drivers and raftsmen had shared the upper West Branch, and although drives and booms had caused problems for raftsmen, they had not forced them from the stream. But circumstances promised soon to change. New booms were abuilding, and others were planned; the number of free-floating logs on the river and its tributaries was sure to increase markedly when they commenced operation. Concerned, editor S. B. Row of the *Raftsman's Journal* called for unified action from people in the upriver area. The legislature, he argued, needed to be aware of "the great injury that may be inflicted upon the business interests of a large and hardworking class . . . by legislation authorizing construction of these booms."[17] His call had the desired effect. On March 17, 1856, a large group met in Clearfield. Those present adopted a resolution declaring "the erection of booms in the Susquehanna river impedes the navigation thereof, causes a detention and loss to our citizens, and . . . must eventually destroy the timber and board business of Clearfield county, render valueless our forests and deprive our citizens of their means of support. . . . We are opposed to any further obstructions being placed in the river, and therefore to the incorporation of more boom companies, as no boom can be constructed without injuring the descending navigation." The group named a committee to draw up a memorial to the legislature and agreed to meet again on July 4.

Spring floods commenced a few days later, temporarily turning the attention of raftsmen to the river itself. Nonetheless, it became clear that the second meeting was to go beyond merely attempting to prevent authorization of new booms; after all, the major culprit, the Susquehanna Boom, was already in place and being steadily enlarged under its existing charter. This meeting was "for the purpose of adopting measures to prevent the floating of loose logs on the Susquehanna." In other words, it was to renew the efforts of 1852, 1853, and 1854 to obtain a ban on log drives on the West Branch and its tributaries.[18]

At the appointed time, a "large and respectable crowd" gathered at the Clearfield County Courthouse and named Ellis Irvin, a local sawmill operator and businessman, its president. Judge G. R. Barrett addressed the crowd, calling for "united action . . . to the end that the rights of our lumbermen may be protected . . . without injury to the rights of others." But impatience was growing. The body adopted a resolution staking out a more militant position than Judge Barrett seemingly desired. The preamble declared:

> *The floating of loose saw logs . . . and running of rafts in the usual way, cannot be carried on at the same time. One or the other must cease, and it becomes a question only, of whether the free and uninterrupted*

navigation of these valuable highways shall continue open for the enjoyment of the mass of the people, or be monopolized by a few. . . . We will use all peaceable and lawful means first, to obtain the rights in the navigation of our public highways, in the hope of obtaining legislative action to that end, but . . . peaceably or forcibly, the nuisance must be abated. If the Legislature, to whom we have a right to appeal, turn a deaf ear to us, we must take other means to redress our wrongs. We cannot allow our mills to rot down, and our property to be rendered worthless, until we have made this last effort to save ourselves.[19]

Many may have dismissed the resolution as empty rhetoric, for words every bit as strong had been heard in 1853 and nothing had come of them. However, this time there would be no timely slackening of traffic on the river to defuse the issue.

Other meetings followed, but with no support apparent in Harrisburg those in attendance began to look to themselves for solutions. At a meeting on August 18 they appointed a committee to initiate legal action against "every person who shall hereafter put loose logs in the stream for the purposes of floating sufficient numbers to create a nuisance." Local papers published warnings headed "LOG-FLOATERS TAKE NOTICE!" They declared "proceedings shall be instituted and prosecuted against all and every person, whether owner, contractor or laborer, engaged in putting loose logs into the river or any of its tributaries in the counties of Clearfield, Elk and Centre."[20]

Matters were coming to a head. Local opposition had discouraged log drivers from operating on Chest Creek and the West Branch proper above the town of Clearfield. They had floated logs down the Moshannon since that first drive by Wing, but that stream was so tortuous it was difficult to navigate with rafts and, in any case, ran through a sparsely settled area and resultingly had weak local opposition. By the winter of 1856, however, logging contractors were at work in the woods along Clearfield and Sinnemahoning creeks, preparing to drive logs downstream on the spring floods. Both were important rafting streams located near the area's population centers.[21]

Warily, the two sides eyed one another. Opponents of log drives sent spies to determine what their rivals were doing. Uncertain how seriously to take the repeated warnings of their adversaries, loggers continued to fell trees and prepare them for driving while cautiously keeping informed of what the rafters and their supporters were doing and saying.[22]

Editor Row sensed that matters were approaching a climax. Near the end of March, he wrote:

> *Log Floating is regarded in this country in the light of a nuisance, and many efforts have been made to have it restricted by law . . . but the Legislature has been so tardy in acting on the bill before it that our raftsmen have been subjected to this annoyance for another season. Heretofore they have borne it as meekly as they could, but it seems with some "forebearance has ceased to be a virtue," and they have determined to apply a corrective themselves. Accordingly, on Clearfield creek, we understand, the logs with which the stream is literally filled are being cut up in such a manner as to render them worthless, whilst on other streams they are driven full of spikes, pieces of pot metal, &c., and it is not at all improbable that still more extreme measures may be adopted, as many of our people are in a state of high exasperation.*

Before his words were off the press, Row's prediction had become reality.[23]

On April 30 word arrived in Clearfield that the loggers were about to commence their drive. A group quickly met, formed a vigilance committee, selected officers, and divided into companies. The following day one company armed itself with whatever weapons were at hand, marched up Clearfield Creek to the site of operations, and ordered the log drivers from the woods. The latter refused to leave, so the raftsmen attacked. For a time the battle teetered in the balance, but when a second company of vigilantes arrived to reinforce the first, log drivers were driven from the field. Somehow no one was killed, but three loggers were injured by rifle fire. The victorious raftsmen proceeded to destroy equipment, boats, a cabin, and supplies belonging to the loggers, and threw what they could not destroy into the creek.

The Clearfield County War was short lived. The clash between raftsmen and log drivers had a sobering effect. Row, who from the first had supported the rafters, turned pacificatory.[24] Other community leaders appear to have done the same. For their part, the aggrieved loggers came to Clearfield and swore out complaints against forty-seven participants in the attack. Those identified were arrested and bound over for trial. Raftsmen countered by filing complaints against drivers when the latter's logs jammed, blocking Clearfield and Sinnemahoning creeks.[25] Calmer heads prevailed in the court; presiding judge James Burnside clearly sought to handle the cases so as to lessen tensions.[26]

The battle on Clearfield Creek and subsequent trials solved nothing. Fights between raftsmen and loggers still erupted, especially after the former had consumed considerable liquor during downriver stops, but nothing like the battle on Clearfield Creek occurred again. Neither side was driven from the woods, and no truce resulted, but friction was now less severe.[27]

A number of factors contributed to the reduced violence, not the least of which was fear of further court action—perhaps before a less lenient judge. In the fall of 1857, William F. Packer won the governorship. His position on log floating was clear: he had blocked a ban in the legislature and could surely be expected to veto any passed while he was chief executive. Raftsmen would have to forget about legislative relief for the duration of Packer's term.[28] In addition, depression struck that same year, lowering prices and demand, and causing the Susquehanna and its tributaries to become less crowded with logs and rafts en route to market. Moreover, as the population of the Allegheny Plateau grew, an increasing portion of the cut of small, upriver mills once floated downstream could be sold near the point of production, further reducing traffic on the river. The old concern that log drives would force the small mills of Clearfield and neighboring counties to "rot down" was proving exaggerated. In 1860 there were still sixty-eight sawmills in Clearfield County; but based on the investment capital involved they were far smaller than those in Williamsport.[29] Perhaps most important was the fact that in the wake of their battle raftsmen successfully used the courts to recover damages from log drives, splash dams, and booms; knowing that raftsmen had the legal tools to force payment and the sympathy of many potential jurors, mill operators decided the wisest course henceforth would be to settle out of court.[30]

What had happened on Clearfield Creek on that first day of May 1857 was more than just a battle between those involved in rival systems of log transport. It was a clash between an old order that was passing and a new one in its ascendancy, between the pre-industrial world of forest-farmers and the industrial world of lumbermen who had erected steam sawmills and giant booms downriver and were to go on to build, upstream, a host of sluice dams, logging railroads, and other adjuncts of large-scale, industrial production. Rafting continued on the West Branch for many years, but its dominance had passed, as the raftsmen's failure to force log drivers from the heart of their domain made clear. The lumberman's frontier had reached the Allegheny Plateau in force. Industrialists such as John DuBois and Charles and Frank Goodyear, not raftsmen like William Langdon, held the future of Pennsylvania's forests in their hands.[31]

As in Maine, the advent of industrial lumbering brought a growing division between labor and capital. Arson was one weapon aggrieved workers could turn against employers they considered unfair. One former logger recalled:

> [T]he men had a powerfull weapon, "the red-horse [fire] let loose in the slashing". . . . It happened more than once when a company foreman tried to cheat a man, for the man to reach in his pocket, get a nickel, hold it up and look the foreman in the eye and say, "that will buy a box of matches!" This would bring a satisfactory settlement.

Once, a Goodyear contractor absconded with money due the workers. Goodyear refused to pay the men, saying they should seek out the contractor to get what was due. "Fire broke out all over his slashing in Big Moore Run in Potter Co., Pa. In vain Goodyear offered four dollars per day for firefighters. The men jeered him. Helplessly he watched a million dollars go up in smoke."[32]

Even before fire became an oft-used weapon in grievances, clashes between laborers and sawmill owners were in evidence. In the years immediately following the Clearfield County War, lumbermen were beset by "Algerines," log rustlers who were notorious for stealing unattended logs along the river, removing or obliterating brands, and then selling them—often back to their rightful owners. Many were no doubt motivated by greed and opportunism, but lingering ill-will of raftsmen toward large millowners and a rising sense of alienation on the part of laborers seem to have played a role too.[33]

If there was any question as to the extent of class division in the lumber industry, it was soon answered. In 1872 the country's first major lumber strike erupted—appropriately enough, at Williamsport, where the industry itself first took modern form and where more sawmill workers were employed than anywhere else in the nation. The issues were the classic ones—hours and wages—and the rhetoric and actions of the two sides clearly revealed the deep chasm between them.

Workers in Pennsylvania had been active in the eight-hour-day movement of the post–Civil War period and in 1868 won passage of a law establishing eight hours as the legal workday in the state.[34] But the law contained no mechanism for enforcement nor penalties for non-compliance and had been amended before passage to include a provision that the law did not invalidate any agreements between employers and workers for workdays of other lengths. As a result, the law was a dead letter almost everywhere, and a twelve-to-fourteen-hour day continued to be standard in Williamsport's sawmills. Mill operators justified the long hours by the fact an entire season's log supply, floated to the Susquehanna Boom on the spring floods, had to be cut before ice closed the river for the winter.[35] To an extent, laborers acquiesced: when they went on strike in the summer of 1872, it was for a ten-hour day (paid at the same rates as the then-current, considerably longer day), rather than for the legally mandated eight hours.[36]

The National Labor Union played a major role. Under the leadership of William H. Sylvis, a Pennsylvania ironmolder, the NLU had been active in the drive for the eight-hour day. Greatly weakened by Sylvis's untimely death in 1869, the union struggled on, but failure of the various eight-hour laws to bring actual reductions in hours led to rising militancy.[37] Sylvis himself had looked on strikes as a last resort, but by the early 1870s many laborers were willing to take that step. In 1872 New York's building tradesmen, supported by numerous others in the city, went on strike for the eight-hour day; anthracite coal miners in Pennsylvania and sawmill workers in the Saginaw Valley, Michigan's rapidly rising lumber center, struck too. In the first two of these at least, and perhaps in all three, the National Labor Union played a central role. Williamsport's lumber workers were part of a broad movement of labor activism led by the NLU.[38]

The state Labor Reform convention met in Williamsport in the spring of 1872; a local of the NLU, Labor Reform Union No. 10, organized soon after. For their part, the city's lumber manufacturers formed the West Branch Lumbermen's Exchange. A confrontation between the two soon followed. On June 27, the union's local adopted a resolution proclaiming:

> [W]orkingmen in the saw mills of the City of Williamsport work from 11 and a half to 13 hours per day, a period longer than that worked by workingmen of any other city in the United States, which is an injury to the human system and an outrage upon the honest laborers of this city. . . . Workingmen in the principal cities are demanding a reduction of hours of labor from ten to eight, and we believe that if ten hours is too long a day's work for them, 12 and 13 are certainly too much for us.[39]

Union leaders appointed a committee to visit millowners to present their request for a ten-hour day starting July 1. One of the first results came when Mayor S. W. Starkweather, owner of one of the larger sawmills, fired city policeman James C. Bermingham, who had been a leader in organizing the union. But not all the millowners were so hostile. Peter Herdic, a former mayor, assured the committee the ten-hour day would be adopted at his sawmill, with extra pay when it proved essential to run longer. The Williamsport *Gazette and Bulletin*, which he controlled, reflected Herdic's moderation. On the eve of the strike, it reported the union would meet that evening and expressed hope that "prudent views" would prevail. It went on to point out the union was legal—as was the eight-hour workday—but it was unlawful to keep others from working whatever hours they agreed to. The operators and their employees, it added, "are reasonable and intelligent men," and, as such, editor John F. Meginness anticipated neither side would let pride prevent it from accepting a just settlement. Others joined in predicting early agreement.[40]

But those like Starkweather, not Herdic, carried the day in the councils of the Lumbermen's Exchange. Unused to being questioned by employees, DuBois and several other lumbermen refused to meet with the committee, and Exchange leaders sent word to the union that the mills would be operated to suit the owners, not workers. The union membership decided to wait until the July 1 date for introducing the proposed new system had passed, and then march to the sawmills to demand its inauguration. Some insisted they were not on strike, but simply demanding their rights. Be that as it may, when some two thousand members failed to report for work on Monday and instead—rallying behind the cry "Ten hours or no sawdust!"—marched on the mills, a strike was in fact under way. Fearing violence, Mayor Starkweather issued a proclamation banning the sale of alcoholic beverages and warning workers against "riotous demonstrations." Unsure this was enough, he sent a frantic wire to Governor John Geary, urging him to send militia to the city.[41]

Less hysterical observers realized Starkweather's fears were overblown. Governor Geary declined to send troops; there were, he noted, militia units in Williamsport if needed, and in any case the strike was less than ten hours old and no violence had yet occurred. As H. L. Dieffenbach, editor of the *Daily Morning Standard*, put it in discussing the first day of the strike, "the general sobriety of the men yesterday certainly gave no occasion" for the mayor's proclamation. Indeed, to ensure there was no violence, the strikers appointed twenty-two of their number to serve as policemen to oversee their march. Appropriately, they made Bermingham Chief Marshall.[42]

Other millowners, less frantic than Starkweather but no less opposed to the union, charged the strike was the work of outside agitators, complained about the rabble-rousing speeches of "demagogues," and dismissed the strikers themselves as drunken loafers.[43] In fact, some of the local's leadership did come from non-residents—for example, William Sylvis's brother James, who lived further down the Susquehanna at Sunbury, and John Siney, president of the Miners National Association and a key figure at NLU national conventions—but most came from within the community.

A. J. Whitten and Thomas H. Blake were laborers; Thomas H. Greevy, whose mother ran a modest hotel in the city, was a printer and editor of Williamsport's *Reform Journal*; Bermingham, as already indicated, was a town policeman. At the NLU local's organizational meeting, Greevy was offered the presidency, but turned it down, saying a laborer should hold the position. Whitten was then elected. It was true, however, that few *millworkers* were among the union's leadership—a fact repeatedly pointed out by their critics—and that Greevy had been active in both the state Labor Reform Union and Labor Reform Party. As to the "drunken loafers" charge, one Williamsport newspaper noted on July 11 that not a single arrest had been made for public drunkenness—or anything else—since the start of the strike.[44]

The strikers were confident. When they marched on the mills on July 2, they found few running. At some that were, they persuaded workmen to shut off the machinery and join the strike. In a few cases, when the workers refused to shut down the mills, strikers went into the plants and turned off the machinery themselves. By the end of the day virtually all Williamsport's mills were idle. The next day Thompson, Harper & Company's sawmill reopened on the ten-hour system. The strikers could hardly have imagined a more auspicious beginning. On July 4, when workers paraded to the mills again, it was simply "to see that the strike was complete."[45]

Various factors added to the strikers' optimism. The Labor Reform Union, which claimed sixty thousand members in the state, had pledged support and mass meetings filled the strikers with resolve. Membership burgeoned during the first week of the strike. Moreover, the strikers enjoyed considerable support from the community. Knowing the strikers and the conditions under which they worked, many townspeople thought the union's demands justified, and large numbers attended the almost-daily union rallies. At these gatherings unionists charged that millowners were outside capitalists who lived high at Saratoga Springs and elsewhere while "their agents here attempt to enslave the workingman." Of the Lumbermen's Exchange, one speaker said, "They breathed the same offensive doctrines against labor that had always been held by capitalists—take care of the rich, and the rich will take care of the poor." It was, he proclaimed, "nothing more than tyranny." How much effect such rhetoric had is unclear, but it is clear many millowners in fact had come from outside the area—and some of them still lived there. In any case, community support for the strikers continued. Various merchants extended credit, contributions of food and other items poured in, and some strikers even received free rent.[46]

Neither side offered concessions during the first ten days of the strike. Indeed, each seemed to be waiting for the other to take some action. A few companies broke ranks with the Lumbermen's Exchange and reopened on the ten-hour system at the earlier daily rate.

Various community leaders began mediation efforts. On July 9, H. L. Dieffenbach proclaimed the "time has come to compromise . . . for the good of the whole community" and laid out a basis for settlement, a proposal similar to one the Lumbermen's Exchange would soon produce. On the 13th a mass meeting that included many of Williamsport's leading citizens proposed a settlement along lines the editor of the *Standard* had suggested. The union promptly rejected it. A few days later, Judge James Gamble also tried to mediate, but he too was rebuffed.[47]

Then, perhaps sensing control slipping from their grasp, or perhaps believing workers' enthusiasm was waning as they approached the end of two weeks without pay, the Exchange offered a settlement. It proposed reopening the mills on an eleven-and-a half-hour a day basis (except for Saturdays, when the mills would run ten and a half hours) with an increase in pay of 25 cents a day. The union promptly rejected the proposal: the workers "fling back in the face of stranger capitalists the arrogant insults offered us and the community." It continued to stand firm for ten hours at the same pay as before and with extra pay for anything over ten hours.[48]

When sawmills attempted to reopen on the basis proposed by the Exchange, most were unable to get full crews, and on the 15th the Exchange announced the offer was rescinded. It claimed there were plenty of men who wanted to work, but threats made them afraid to step forward; the Exchange dropped its offer, it claimed, to prevent violence against those who tried to work. Sawmills, spokesmen insisted, could afford to stay closed: if they did not run, the stocks of lumber in the market would go down and prices rise, protecting them from loss. The Exchange did not stop there: in addition to the mills, it announced booming and logging operations would be closed forthwith. The impact of the strike was to be extended beyond the immediate vicinity of Williamsport to the entire drainage that supplied it with logs.[49]

As the strike ground into its third week, circumstances were changing, the relative calm nearing an end. On Friday, July 19, some strikers went to the Lutcher & Moore mill—"to enforce their notions," as the *Daily Morning Standard* put it. The county sheriff, Samuel Van Buskirk, "happening that way . . . cleared the premises of the intruders." In addition, the newspaper reported: "We are informed that it is the intention [of authorities] to arrest some of the leaders of the raid."[50] This was only the beginning.

Employers, worried by the large stocks of unsawn logs in Susquehanna Boom and by the unexpected staying power of the union, announced on Saturday, July 20, that the sawmills would reopen the following Monday on the eleven-and-a-half-hour basis offered earlier. There were, they claimed again, plenty of laborers eager to work. In fact, operators were in the process of hiring a large body of outsiders to reopen the mills, many of them workers idled by the shutting down of the boom and woods operations. Angered by the presence of these strikebreakers (and by the locals who joined them) and feeling the pinch of lost wages, union members decided to drive these "black legs" from the scene, forcing mills that had reopened to close once more.[51]

The action of owners in bringing in outsiders seems to have been a desperation move. In spite of the bluster of the Lumbermen's Exchange, millowners were hardly an unshakable phalanx. Herdic continued to waffle, four mills had already reopened on the ten-hour plan, and others seemed about to do so. All were aware of the vast store of logs—much larger than normal—awaiting in the Susquehanna Boom. A union store had just opened which promised to extend fresh credit to strikers, NLU's state central committee had offered help "if needed," and the local was able to proclaim that any needy striker had only to ask and aid would be given. There was still strong community support. In short, the union appears to have been standing firm in large part because it had reason to believe it was winning.[52]

On Monday, July 22, many sawmills did in fact reopen, as the Lumbermen's Exchange had promised, although strikers who lined the route to the mills prevented some laborers headed to work from passing and so harassed others that they turned back. Encouraged by these small victories, the strikers marched on the sawmills, determined to drive out the strikebreakers and force those mills operating to close once more. When they reached the first sawmill, that of Filbert & Otto, they found Police Chief Samuel Coder and his seven officers standing in the way, pistols drawn. Beside them stood a number of workmen and millowners deputized for the occasion. Angry words were exchanged, and a barrage of rocks followed. One policeman, struck in the jaw by a brick, lost several teeth; Chief Coder suffered a broken arm; and nearly every officer was injured to one degree or another. The strikers surged forward, pushed the defenders aside, and took over the mill. As the *Morning Standard* put it, those working there "made fast time in getting away."[53]

It is not clear who started the melee. Each side accused the other, but the fact that the strikers had refrained from violence for three weeks only to have it erupt when strikebreakers were brought in suggests the fault lay with the latter. The penchant of woods and boom workers for violent behavior was seen during the Clearfield County War and many times thereafter. Moreover, one local paper noted that most of the workers brought into the sawmills from the woods and boom were Irish. Considering the ethnic stereotypes of the day, this observation, whether or not true, seems to have been intended to suggest it was the strikebreakers, not the union members who initiated the conflict.[54]

But what followed is not in dispute. On the heels of their victory at Filbert & Otto's plant, the strikers proceeded to other sawmills. They shut the first two without major incident, but at the next the owner and several workers resisted them (as the *Clinton Democrat* reported it, the owner, "not relishing the idea that he had no control over his own property, did some 'striking' of his own"); at the fourth, that of Starkweather & Munson,[55] Mayor Starkweather reportedly led organized armed resistance. Yet in spite of the combined efforts of owners, workers, and police, the strikers swept all before them. By the end of the day, the *Sun and Lycoming Democrat* reported, the unionists had "closed all the mills and beaten and badly wounded many of the workmen." To the surprise of many, no one had been killed.

The union itself seemed stunned by the violence. At its outdoor mass meeting on the evening of the 22nd, "Uncle Jimmy" Wood and other voices of moderation replaced the usual speakers and called for a respect for law and order.

Desperately, millowners and Chief Coder turned to Sheriff Van Buskirk for help. Considering his own forces too small, Van Buskirk wired Governor Geary: "Order out national guards of the city. The rioters have overpowered the police. Answer quick." The governor had a reputation as a friend of labor, but he had no choice. He called out the guard, proclaiming: "Law and order must be sustained." But to no avail. Van Buskirk reported in a second plea to the governor, "[T]he troops at this point refuse to serve and sympathize with the mob. Send all the companies from Harrisburg." Geary responded by repeating his call on the local guard and dispatching additional units from elsewhere in the state—a total of over three hundred troops.[56]

With additional units en route, the local militia moved at last. Williamsport's Taylor Guards, a black unit, played a key role. Led by Sergeant Jim Washington, a former slave, they fixed bayonets and charged a group of marching strikers, scattering them in all directions. Recognizing that it was the militia's duty to maintain peace, rather than serve as partisans, General Jesse Merrill ordered his troops to be "moderate and temperate," but under the circumstances their actions were decidedly pro-management.

On July 24 the militia marched to the mills to prevent further clashes, but there was little for them to do, as few workmen showed up. In the hours and days that followed, militia aided civil authorities in arresting many leaders of the strike—or, indeed, anyone who seemed a threat to peace and order. Reportedly, one unionist was arrested for simply shouting, "Ten Hours!"[57]

The strike quickly crumbled. Community support disappeared in the wake of the strikers' attack on property and civil authority. Rumors swept the city. An army of workers was supposedly headed to Williamsport from the coalfields, intent upon helping their fellow laborers. As these and other alarms proved false, as arrests deprived the union of its leadership, and as the military presence kept hotheads on the two sides apart, calm returned. By July 25 the *Morning Standard* was able to proclaim: "The plain truth is THE STRIKE IS OVER." The following day editor Dieffenbach asked: "May not a conciliatory course . . . now be adopted, so that good will as well as peace may be fully restored?"

Still, hard feelings persisted. Most of those arrested were soon released, but key union leaders remained in jail. Two of their attorneys addressed a mass meeting on July 30 and "had a good effect at quieting some of the more excited," although isolated cases of harassment, rock throwing, and arson continued. Some of the more recalcitrant owners—including Starkweather and Edgar Munson, no doubt—sought to drive workers who had been active in the strike from the city, but with limited success; two-thirds of those employed in the mills following the strike reportedly were old hands.[58]

Inevitably there were postmortems. Many observers placed primary blame for the length of the strike and the eventual violence on management. In mid-July, during the strike, the editors of both the *Morning Standard* and the *Sun and Democrat* had written they considered the union's demands reasonable. A week later, a correspondent to the *Morning Standard* noted that sawmill operators claimed they would have agreed to reduced hours or an increase in pay if they had been asked by their workers, not outsiders, but "[n]obody believes that . . . and their actions betray them. It seems as if a working man was considered a mere machine by some of the employers." On July 25, as the strike came to an end, the *Morning Standard* denounced employers for trying to drive from town "old residents and good citizens, possessed of property, and blessed with families" and replace them with "strange, unknown, and untried people." Editor James Meginness was explicit. "Where does the blame belong?" he asked, and then proceeded to answer his own question: "Most of the men who have engaged in [the Williamsport lumber business] have become rich, some, we are sorry to say, have become dictatorial and somewhat arrogant." Their opulence had not gone unnoticed by employees, men who knew that their labor had produced the operators' wealth and that Pennsylvania law entitled them to an eight-hour workday and the right to organize. Under the circumstances, workers turned to the Labor Reform Union, but their every effort was rebuffed by the Lumbermen's Exchange as was "any and everything, politics not accepted, that dared to oppose or come into conflict with it." In the end, "laboring men allowed themselves to be drawn into a conflict, and by it lost the sympathy that had been extended to them previously by the community." The lumbermen, Meginness concluded, have it in their power to restore confidence and order; they should do so without vindictiveness.[59]

In spite of lingering bitterness toward lumbermen, who were seen as having treated them unfairly, most millhands apparently returned to work willingly. And well they might. Despite pending court cases that threatened the lifeblood of the union, one of its leaders noted the men were now working eleven and a half hours with an increase in pay of 25 cents a day—"so all was not lost." Not just operators and their employees, but also the larger community seems to have welcomed the return of normalcy: in May 1873, Williamsport's citizens, who had been such an important source of support for the union prior to the outbreak of violence, re-elected Starkweather to a second term as mayor.[60]

At trial most of the nearly thirty defendants were found guilty, given small fines, and released. Judge James Gamble was clearly trying to calm still-troubled waters. However, the union's four key leaders received very different treatment—even James Bermingham, who was credited with saving Chief Coder's life during the melee on July 22. Authorities considered them "agitators" who had been the primary cause of the strike and, through overheated rhetoric, of the violence that followed. Bail was set at $10,000; when Greevy posted his bail, he was promptly re-arrested on a separate warrant and another $10,000 bail was demanded. Knowing the governor's reputation as a friend of labor, Mayor Starkweather and Sheriff Van Buskirk urged Geary not to extend leniency to the four. In spite of repeated entreaties for him to intervene—including a petition bearing two thousand signatures—the governor long accepted this advice, and when they were finally tried, all four leaders were found guilty and given lengthy prison sentences. However, just before they were to enter prison, Geary pardoned them. What was behind this turnaround is not clear. Rumor credited Peter Herdic with making an eleventh-hour visit to Harrisburg and persuading the governor to pardon the strikers; that well may be the case, although no solid evidence has surfaced.[61]

Whatever the reasons for Geary's last-minute action, it rang down the final curtain on the Williamsport lumber strike—and on the National Labor Union itself. Founded in 1866, the NLU was the country's first national federation of trade unions. Its early leader, William Sylvis, abhorred strikes, believing the condition of workers could be better served through legislation. Toward that end, he emphasized political organization, lobbying, and education as the most appropriate means to improvement. He and other key leaders in the union viewed strikes as a last resort. As William's brother James put it in addressing the Williamsport local on June 25: "As regards strikes, I am opposed to them; they are knock down arguments, in which both parties lose, but God has given the laborer rights, and when capitalists attempt to destroy them, then strike!"[62] The NLU had enjoyed considerable initial success, most notably when it won passage of an eight-hour law for federal workers and similar laws in a number of states. But when these laws went unenforced—not just in Williamsport, but elsewhere as well—and as liberal reformers increasingly dominated efforts at political change to the virtual exclusion of laborers, faith in the political-legislative approach waned. Still hungering for improvement in their circumstances, sawmill workers in Williamsport had decided to strike. Had their action been crowned with success, they and workers in many another location would have been heartened and the union would no doubt have enjoyed a period of rapid growth—similar to that the Knights of Labor was to have during the following decade after a successful railroad strike. Whether this growth would have led to a lasting national union is open to question. The NLU's weak organizational structure suggests that, like the Knights, its post-strike growth would probably have been ephemeral. But the question is moot. The union had tried a political-legislative approach, but had gained nothing lasting; then in Williamsport it tried a strike and, in spite of community support and a just cause, had lost. With the end of the strike the last hope that the NLU could be a powerful voice for the working class vanished. The union hung on for a time, but like the hopes that had buttressed it, the NLU soon disappeared from the scene.[63]

Sawmill workers and their predecessors, raftsmen, were not alone in suffering from the shift to industrial lumbering. Forests suffered too. The farmer-loggers who cut and skidded pines to streamside to make up the rafts they shepherded downstream on spring floods had had a limited impact on the forest. They took only select trees, those tall enough to supply the long logs needed to give rafts their necessary rigidity and straight and solid enough to yield lumber or timbers of sufficient value to justify the per-unit costs of rafting. Moreover, available technology limited their operations to areas near rafting streams; logs could be skidded profitably up to two miles, but trees further from streams were normally safe from the axe. Finally, as part-time farmers, those engaged in rafting sought to use the agricultural slack seasons to generate as much supplementary income as possible; this too meant taking only the best trees. Clearing for crop and pasture land surely had a far greater impact on the forest than this selective, off-season logging, although it is impossible to completely separate the two, for winter logging was often an integral part of the land-clearing process even though sometimes carried out on lands with little if any agricultural potential. In contrast, those supplying log drives took any pine capable of furnishing a sixteen-foot log. When logging railroads and other technological advances extended the reach of this new breed of loggers to the farthest corners of the Allegheny Plateau, nearly every sizable pine in the forest stood in danger. Tops and limbs not suited for logs—well over half of each tree—were left on the forest floor to burn or rot.[64]

For a time hemlocks remained untouched, for they furnished inferior lumber prone to cracking, splitting, and warping. They too eventually fell before the demands of industry. Leather tanning using natural tannin from such things as hemlock bark had been practiced for centuries, but the industrial changes in the United States in the late nineteenth century required tanned leather in far greater quantities than ever before, for leather belting ran many of the machines on which the new order depended. As demand for leather burgeoned, so too did Pennsylvania's tanning industry. Laborers were soon busily at work across northern and western Pennsylvania and in neighboring portions of New York felling hemlocks and stripping them of their bark. They left limbs and tops as well as the nearly valueless logs. The result was a huge buildup of fuel on the forest floor. Forest fires, more devastating and more frequent than ever, followed. Organic material in the topsoil, young reproduction, and standing timber—all were incinerated when fire swept through an area.[65]

The sequence from rafting pine to log drives to railroad logging of pine, followed by railroad logging of hemlock, resulted in lumbering lasting an extraordinarily long time on the Allegheny Plateau. In most forest regions, logging commenced when the lumberman's frontier reached it, rose rapidly to a peak, and then quickly declined. On the Allegheny Plateau it lasted much longer. Dusenbury, Wheeler & Co. is illustrative. It commenced sawing lumber on the upper Allegheny in 1837 and continued to operate there until the 1940s. Indeed, although a steam mill was added soon after the firm commenced operations, its original water-powered plant continued cutting until 1907.[66] The result of this prolonged activity was that, by the end of the nineteenth century, a vast belt across northern and western Pennsylvania had been logged and re-logged, burned and re-burned so many times—and so devastatingly—that significant regeneration no longer took place. Scrub growth dominated where giant pines and hemlocks once grew. In local parlance the area had become the "desert of five million acres." Carl Schurz, noting that a Massachusetts firm had bought two hundred thousand acres in central Pennsylvania, clearcut to the smallest dimensions, and planned to sell the land as pasture when the trees were gone, predicted that after a few years of erosion it would "no longer furnish verdure enough to nourish a goat." Unlike in New York, where forest preserves in the Adirondacks and Catskills survived the lumbering era, Pennsylvania long had no such areas and had to endure a slow, painful recovery from its time on the lumberman's frontier.[67]

It need not have been so. As early as 1874 Governor John F. Hartranft, Geary's successor, recognized the dangers of logging in the forests of Pennsylvania. He warned the state Assembly, "an evil of considerable magnitude, which every year grows more aggravated . . . [is] the stripping of our mountains and hills of their trees." Hartranft called for "wise legislation . . . [to] rescue our descendants from the ills a perseverance in this practice will certainly entail upon them." When the legislature failed to act, Hartranft repeated his plea the following year, warning that within thirty years none of the state's forests would be left unless changes were made. He suggested that the state geological survey "make the necessary scientific and practical inquiries" to find answers to the problem of forest depletion. Again there was no legislative action.[68]

In both New York and Pennsylvania the emergence of lumbermen as an identifiable group involved a variety of economic, social, and attitudinal changes. Pioneer farmers had demonstrated the economic value of forests. Log and lumber rafts and other wood products they marketed as by-products of their struggle for an agrarian existence demonstrated that profits could be earned in the woods. This and the rural population centers that their activities brought into being attracted those who would open the interior to development. The presence of successful farmer-loggers encouraged the building of canals and railroads. If the forest could be turned to profit using crude rafts, how much more readily might it do so if the hinterlands were penetrated by improved means of transportation! Thus, though decisions to build were made in the nation's main political and economic centers, not on the frontier, they were spurred by evidence of the economic potential of America's forests that frontier farmers supplied.

Developments on this new frontier were spurred too by the arrival of men like John Leighton, who came to Pennsylvania with knowledge and capital acquired in the forests of Maine to build the sawmills, booms, and other appurtenances of this new frontier, and of J. B. Wing and countless others, their names lost to history, who also arrived from Maine, without investment capital but with expertise in abundance. The latter manned the sawmills and booms, drove the logs, and—when driven to it—provided the resistance to the abuses of sawmill owners that showed this frontier was not immune to the industrial friction marking so much of America's economic development during the Gilded Age. Men like Leighton left Maine not because the forests were running out—as yet they were not—but because they had been tied up by one rival or another. Many workers, on the other hand, arrived as a result of the great exodus from Maine that began in the 1820s and 1830s and gained momentum in the 1840s because a series of harsh winters and poor growing seasons had made farming there even less viable than previously.[69] In Maine a good portion of the lumber industry's work force still had ties to the agrarian economy—as a place of retreat if employment turned sour, if nothing else—but in New York and Pennsylvania this tie was severed. By the time the lumbering frontier was in full bloom in the Middle Atlantic States, the work force was fully industrial. If conditions turned bad, most workers had no farms to retreat to, but resorted instead either to unions or to migration to other, newer lumberman's frontiers to improve their circumstances. This pattern of migration, both of capital and of labor, was to continue until the last lumberman's frontier closed.[70]

These developments were intimately tied to the Market Revolution through which the United States passed in the early nineteenth century; indeed, they were a vital, if largely unsung, part of it.[71] As was demonstrated in discussing developments in Maine, the mindset of frontier farmer-loggers was distinctively proto- if not pre-capitalist. In the Middle Atlantic States, as in Maine, early settlers drew attention to the possibilities offered by forest resources. Because they did, a true lumberman's frontier developed in the area, at first superimposed on, but gradually largely replacing the agro-forest economy that preceded it (unless, as at Glens Falls, it developed independently with but few ties to the agrarian world from the first). The process was to repeat itself in the Lake States, the South, and the Far West, although as time passed and a succession of new frontiers was reached, the ties to agricultural forerunners became weaker. As time passed, the lumberman's frontier would be increasingly tied to America's industrialization.

CHAPTER SIX

New Mills, New Markets

In the summer of 1840, desperately seeking a new market, Ralph Wadhams dispatched a cargo of lumber from Michigan to a commission merchant in Albany, New York. According to one authority, since "freight and charges . . . ate up all the proceeds" this blind venture was not soon repeated, but the statement is suspect. Other sources maintain that $100,000 worth of lumber went from Michigan to New York the following year, making sawn wood the state's third-largest export. Be that as it may, Wadham's shipment heralded the arrival of Michigan lumber on the national scene; until then it had invariably gone to home markets.[1]

Lumbering was not new to Michigan in 1840—nor was Wadhams new to lumbering—but his shipment, more than anything earlier, heralded the commencement of a new stage in the history of the lumberman's frontier. There were many parallels between what Wadhams set in motion in Michigan and the industry in Maine, New York, and Pennsylvania, but there would be significant differences too. Much of Michigan's cut would be marketed in more distant domestic markets than those that had been supplied by the Atlantic Coast states and in interior markets that lumber from those states had rarely reached; the logs utilized by its mills would largely come not from the tracts of proprietors or other private claimants, but directly or indirectly from federal, state, and Indian land. Unlike in Maine, on the Allegheny Plateau, and in much of upstate New York, there were few settlers to draw upon for a work force, its pine belt being thinly settled; most workers would come from outside—often immigrants or experienced workers from earlier centers of lumber production. What developed in Michigan thus had as many parallels to what would follow as the lumberman's frontier moved on to new areas as it did with those that had preceded it.

Wadhams was not the first to cut lumber in Michigan. Rudimentary sawmills had been present during the periods of French and British control, but demand was limited because of Michigan's tiny, isolated population. The St. Clair area, north of Detroit in the pine belt, was the most active, having seven sawmills by 1800.[2] But as Americans moved into Michigan Territory following its opening to settlers in 1818, and especially after completion of the Erie Canal in 1825, local demand increased. Michigan Territory still had only 31,639 inhabitants in 1830, but a speculative land boom followed on the heels of the canal's completion. Settlement accelerated. By 1837, Michigan's population approached 175,000 and the then-new state's census put the number of sawmills at almost four hundred and fifty; the bulk of the settlers and nearly all the mills were located south of the pine belt.[3]

Wadhams, a Detroit merchant, was among the pioneer millmen and, by all indications, one of the most ambitious. In 1827 he purchased pine land and a mill in St. Clair County, took on a pair of partners from New York, and moved near the millsite to manage his acquisitions. Sales took place both at the mill and in Detroit, to which he shipped lumber by vessels and rafts and where one of Wadhams' partners, Henry Howard, oversaw the firm's interests. Plans ran afoul of financial realities. By 1835 the mill was deeply in debt; four years later, unable to extricate themselves from financial difficulties, the partners dissolved the firm. Wadhams' father, a wealthy New York merchant, intervened to save the investment, and the younger Wadhams continued to operate the sawmill (under arrangements that are not entirely clear); thus, it was apparently Wadhams alone who dispatched that first cargo to New York in 1840.[4]

Wadhams was not the only Detroit merchant who saw opportunity in the forests of St. Clair County. In 1835, Francis P. Browning spent $35,000 to build a steam sawmill there, the largest mill in the state at the time. When he died a year later, his estate's assets exceeded debts by a mere $2,667. A group of creditors took over the mill and incorporated it as the Black River Steam Mill Company; their timing was better than Browning's. Demand picked up in the 1840s and, selling primarily in Detroit, the firm operated successfully until 1855.[5]

Long before Wadhams' shipment, the Erie Canal was stimulating growth in the trans-Appalachian country. Following its completion, people flocked west over the canal to open farms in Ohio, Indiana, and beyond, turning what had been a trickle of settlers into a flood. Timothy Flint was in the vanguard. In Ohio he found "magnificent [hardwood] forests, which the axe has not yet despoiled," but even in remote sections "I discerned the smoke rising in the woods, and heard the strokes of the axe and the tinkling of [cow]bells and the baying of dogs," sure signs land was being taken up. "Pass this way in two years," he prophesied, and "you will see extensive fields of corn and wheat; a young and thrifty orchard, [and] fruit trees of all kinds." In ten years the "shrubs and forest will be gone."[6]

Settlement in Indiana lagged behind that of Ohio—both because it was further west and because many settlers were unwilling to move onto its extensive prairies, fearing to settle so far from sources of wood and

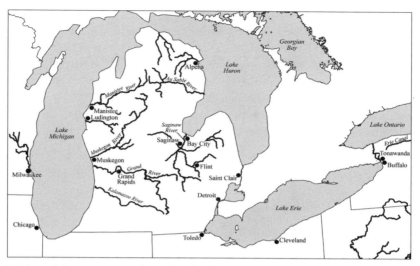

Michigan's Lower Peninsula and its lumber markets. Map by Sarah E. Hinman.

water and wanting to avoid the heavy, wet soils that dominated many of them.[7] Development proceeded nonetheless, and by 1831 Caleb Atwater could write: "The face of the country is undergoing change . . . the forest is disappearing before the industrious husbandman. . . . Indiana is only about ten, or at most, about twelve years behind Ohio." Around Indianapolis by 1837 "all of the noble old trees—walnuts, oaks, poplars, and the like of which will never be seen again—had all been cut down."[8]

Michigan followed the same pattern. In 1831 Alexis de Tocqueville and Gustave de Beaumont trekked a hundred miles north and west from Detroit to Saginaw, described to them as "the last inhabited place till the Pacific." There, in the "Siberia of Michigan," they found that four or five cabins and some thirty people "composed the whole of this little society, scarce formed." Portending its future as America's premier lumber center, Saginaw stood in a magnificent pine forest—Tocqueville and Beaumont measured one white pine twenty-two feet in circumference! Yet what they saw was not a lumber town, but an agricultural community in the making. Settlers were busily clearing land. "In a few years," Tocqueville wrote, "these impenetrable forests will have fallen, [and] the noise of civilization and industry will break the silence of the Saginaw." As Beaumont later wrote, the American "who lives in the country spends half his time fighting his natural enemy, the forest; he goes at it without respite. . . . The absence of trees is the mark of civilization, as their presence indicates barbarity."[9]

John Nowlin's family provided the archetype. The family left a rocky farm in upstate New York for the Dearborn area, and John's father promptly began felling trees "right and left until we could see the sun from ten o'clock in the morning till between one and two in the afternoon, when it mostly disappeared behind Mr. Pardee's woods." Gradually the Nowlins' clearing grew until "we could see the beautiful sun earlier." Indeed, it seemed brighter than in New York, perhaps because "the deep gloom of the forest had shaded us for so long and was now removed." By 1838, the family had cleared some sixty acres.

> We had burned the wood all up on the ground, as there was no market for it, it was worthless. . . . The grand old forest was melting away. . . . The light of civilization had dawned on us. We had cleared up what was a few years before, the lair of the wolf and the hunting ground of the red man.

Young Nowlin summarized: "Father's farm was rescued from the wilderness and consecrated to the plow and husbandry through sweat and blood."[10]

Harvey Rice was one of many applauding such activity: "[B]y dint of patient industry and the practice of rigid economy," he wrote, settlers "soon acquired a healthful homestead." Caroline Kirkland, a transplanted New Yorker living west of Detroit, was more critical of the penchant for clearing, observing pithily: "[O[urs just now is a utilitarian fanaticism of the narrowest and most short-sighted description. Whatever cannot evidently be turned to account to-day, is rejected as worthless and unprofitable. We leave the future to take care of itself." In apparent agreement, Prince Maximilian of Weid observed that if they were careful the "inhabitants of these forests would never be in want of an ample supply of wood for fuel and for timber," but careful they were not.[11]

Destruction of the vast mixed-hardwood forest stretching westward from New York and Pennsylvania was not just the work of farmers. Sawmills appeared right and left to supply settlers and the new communities that served them. By 1840, Ohio had twice as many sawmills as Maine; only Pennsylvania and New York had more, yet Maine produced $1.8 million of lumber a year, compared to only $262,000 for Ohio; production in Pennsylvania and New York also ran far ahead of Ohio's. Clearly, the state's mills were small, erected to meet the needs of a developing agricultural society, rather than part of a lumbering frontier. Indiana's were small too. Settler G. R. Taylor described "a little mill" in Scaffold Prairie that was in fact larger than average: it "cuts, as it is said, from 4 to 5 thousand feet from day[light] to dark."[12]

As Ohio's farmers turned to commercial sources for lumber, more mills appeared and older ones expanded; by 1850 Ohio was producing 6.6 percent of the nation's lumber. But with clearing proceeding at a breakneck pace and lumbering eating into the area's stands, farmers in Ohio and Indiana had to locate new sources, especially if they wanted white pine, the most widely used and easily worked wood for building. Soon enough, this meant obtaining lumber from Michigan.[13]

Forests covered some 90 percent of Michigan. Deciduous stands dominated the lower third of the state—roughly that south of the forty-third parallel. This hardwood belt, its soil well adapted for agriculture, drew most early settlers, and they, like the farmers of Ohio and Indiana, soon demanded lumber from Michigan's pineries, located further north on generally thin, leached, acidic soils with little agricultural potential. The few sawmills in the pine country were primitive water-powered affairs serving the handful of local settlers. One such was the mill of the Hubinger brothers in the German colony of Frankenmuth. A local chronicler described its operation: "[T]he saw in this mill moved so slowly . . . the men would put a log on the automatic feed carriage, set it in motion and go fishing for awhile. When the slab was cut through they would change the log over [to cut the next plank] and resume their fishing." Under such circumstances, it was farming, not lumbering that Tocqueville and Beaumont thought would spell an end to the forests around Saginaw. They were not alone. Many wondered why Gardner and Ephraim Williams built the first sawmill in Saginaw in 1832. Their wonderment was justified, for as a result of the area's poor agricultural potential, settlement in the area lagged. This and other Michigan pioneer pine mills languished until the mid-1840s.Not until lumbering developed did significant population increases take place.[14]

Timber speculators, the advanced guard of the lumberman's frontier, flocked to the pineries before any large number of farmers or sawmill operators. The circumstances they faced were new. Earlier frontiers, located in the original thirteen states, had contained no vast public domain belonging to the federal government. Claimants had obtained land from—or trespassed on—stands belonging to the states or proprietors who had been granted large tracts by the Crown. Now, the federal government was to be a major player, its policies shaped by a commitment to the Jeffersonian ideal of family farmers and a belief that this ideal could be advanced by transferring public lands to smallholders as simply and quickly as possible. A host of laws and regulations sprang from this commitment, and, ill suited though most were to timberland, they formed the context within which lumbermen now had to operate.[15]

Much of the great wave of speculation that hit Michigan in the 1830s centered on agricultural land, but some "landlookers" scouring the public domain for promising tracts urged clients to buy pine land, and a number did. In 1833 Elisha Ely of New York purchased twenty thousand acres along the Kalamazoo River for the Boston Company. About the same time, Charles Merrill of Lincoln, Maine, bought a huge block of timber on the St. Clair.[16] Others joined in. John Ball purchased twenty-five hundred acres of pine in Ottawa County; Charles Trowbridge bought over five thousand acres of timber in Allegan and Berrien counties; and Charles and William Carroll acquired thousands of acres in the pine belt, one acquisition of 1836 being forty thousand acres. In Saginaw County there were forty-one buyers of government land in 1835—most paying $1.25 per acre, although some obtained it for less by purchasing military warrants, the soldier's bounty of the age, at discounted rates. In 1836 the number of buyers increased to 155, but with plenty of land available the price remained steady.[17]

Potential town sites and mill seats, as well as prime timberland, drew speculators to the pine country. Norman Little was among them. He arrived in Saginaw in 1835 determined to make his fortune building the town, largely with Eastern capital. The Panic of 1837 brought a halt to this first wave of investment, but the way had been pointed. However slowly, development resumed, much of it along less speculative lines.[18]

The return of prosperity in the 1840s was accompanied by renewed interest in Michigan's pinelands, an interest encouraged by what Rolland Maybee aptly called the government's "land-happy generosity." The area along the Saginaw River seemed especially promising. The river emptied into Lake Huron's Saginaw Bay, giving millmen inexpensive access to markets in Detroit, Ohio, and beyond. The Saginaw's short, sluggish course boasted a plentitude of mill seats and log-storage sites; its major tributaries—the Tittabawassee, Shiawassee, Flint, and Cass—drained some six thousand square miles of pine forest, some of the finest in the state; all these streams were suited for log driving, as were many of their numerous tributaries; and the terrain made this drainage basin—a huge, low tableland—readily loggable. With the Saginaw Valley's manifest advantages, it is not surprising lumbermen gravitated there and quickly made it the leading lumber-producing center of the state and eventually the nation. The first cargo of lumber was not shipped from the Saginaw until 1841 (bound for Detroit), but by 1857 there were some fourteen mills in operation, each cutting 1.5 to 4 million feet a year; nearly all of their output was exported.[19]

Curtis Emerson was in the forefront of developments. He arrived from Vermont in 1846 and went into the malt liquor business before teaming with Charles Grant to buy a ten-year-old mill for $6,000. The partners spent another $10,000 to update the plant and expand its capacity to three million feet a year. Daniel Johnson and others followed a similar course, causing the *Detroit Free Press* to predict in 1849 that the eight mills on the Saginaw would cut twelve to twenty-five million feet that year. In the event, they sawed far less, but the area was clearly on the rise. The first Michigan mill to use gang saws successfully was in Saginaw, as was the first to use circular saws. In capital invested per plant, Saginaw County ranked first in the state. By 1854 there were forty-one steam mills in the Saginaw Valley, most of them running day and night.[20]

The advance that began in the mid-1840s was not limited to the Saginaw area. Development occurred in other parts of Michigan's pine belt as well. The collective impact was immense. Young though it was, by 1850 Michigan had become fifth among lumber-producing states, a third of its labor force employed in lumbering. Whether measured by the number of firms, the value added by manufacture, or the number of employees, lumbering was Michigan's most important industry.

Basic patterns had been established by 1850, but growth continued. Between 1850 and 1855, riding a wave of rising prices, the number of sawmills in the state increased 750 percent, and average mill size rose sharply even though many of the small, inefficient plants so common in the early years continued to operate. Large mills—and the advanced technology they incorporated, most notably steam power—dominated by 1855. So did distant sales. Indeed, the separation of mills from markets had become almost total; unlike in pioneer days, most lumber now sold in places far from the mills—and it was sales there, rather than locally, that determined prices.[21]

As production rose, purchases of timberland increased. Until the late 1840s most mills seem to have obtained the bulk of their logs from independent operators, ranging from farmers with a few trees to sell to businessmen with sizable operations.[22] For a time, the absence of aggressive buying by Michigan's millmen encouraged speculators, just as it would do later in the Gulf South. To speculators, timberland once again seemed a good investment. As Ira Davenport put it in 1849, "[T]he west has good [agricultural] land that won't be sold in 20 years, but there is no pine timber this side of Oregon but will have an owner short of that time." Investors from the East, as well as Detroit, Chicago, and points nearer to hand eagerly selected lands in a scramble that grew in intensity year by year. During the 1850s more than ten million acres of federal land in Michigan was sold or disposed of in land grants for various purposes. The United States granted so-called swamp land to the state—much of it in fact good pine land that the state then sold to private individuals for $1.25 an acre.[23]

Not everyone bought the trees he harvested; many felled what they did not own. One observer noted that "it was never considered a mortal sin" to cut across one's property line into neighboring stands. Timber was frequently sold in forty-acre plots and so many operators cut all around their property that the term "a round forty" entered industry vocabulary. A federal judge decried the situation. A thief, he wrote, is banned from "respectable social intercourse," yet for "timber which renders valuable the public lands . . . a different sentiment exists, and many, openly, and without concealment, engage in a systemized business of timber [theft] . . . building up fortunes by plundering the joint inheritance of the whole country." Local populations sided with such loggers, for they provided jobs on which their communities depended and, as a Fourth of July orator in Manistee put it, the United States is the land of the people, "we are the people, ergo the land belongs to us." Historian Lucille Kane summed up the attitude: "[T]rees had value only when men cut them down, drove them down a stream, sawed them into boards at a mill, and sold the lumber in a market." Under the circumstances, it was almost impossible to find juries that would convict timber thieves; sporadic government efforts to halt timber trespass were doomed from the start.[24]

The situation in Manistee County is illustrative. Between 1841, when lumbering commenced there, and 1849, sales of government land in the area amounted to only 842 acres, yet John Stronach operated a sizable sawmill throughout the period and by 1850 four other mills were also present. Obviously, they and their suppliers cut more timber than was on land that had been sold. A state land agent, examining forests from Grand River north to the Manistee, found state school lands and university grants in the region had been stripped two to three miles back from drivable streams. Efforts to crack down on depredations in 1853 and 1854 met strong local resistance. The attitudes that had plagued Thomas Hutchinson, David Cobb, and assorted proprietors in colonial Maine were alive and well on this new lumberman's frontier. Widespread trespass made holding land for speculative purposes less appealing than it once had been and led some who had speculated in timberland in the 1830s to sell to those planning to build sawmills. Buyers of stands who intended milling the trees became increasingly common.[25]

While lumbering flourished in Michigan in the 1850s, production was still increasing in New York, Pennsylvania, and even Maine, but only limited quantities of the cut of those states were available in trans-Appalachian markets. The lumber frontiers of the four states overlapped in time, but there was a relative, if not absolute, sequence. Moreover, their markets were distinct, none more so than those of Michigan. Jethro Mitchell's career is illustrative. In 1831, at fourteen years of age, Mitchell moved with his parents to Cincinnati, Ohio. In 1838 young Mitchell borrowed $5,000 and, with James Dunlap, entered the local lumber trade. Initially much of what they sold was rafted down the Ohio from Pennsylvania and New York, but in time these supplies proved inadequate and Cincinnati too removed from Ohio's main centers of development, so Mitchell opened a yard in Sandusky, where he received shipments from the St. Clair River, Saginaw Bay, and other sources in Michigan. Mitchell soon transferred his seat of operations to Toledo, where he continued to sell Michigan pine. Seeking to take advantage of ever-widening markets, he eventually joined the host of lumber manufacturers in Saginaw. Recognizing the need for logs to keep his mill supplied, he also became a major purchaser of Michigan timberland. New York and Pennsylvania were no longer a part of his calculations, except for Albany, which served as a secondary outlet for his cut.[26]

Beginning in the 1850s, Henry W. Sage, Henry H. Crapo, Russell Alger, and other investors joined Mitchell in recognizing the potential of Michigan's forests.[27] Some bought huge tracts that far overshadowed the purchases of earlier speculators and millmen. Many of these newcomers erected sawmills too, for with expanding markets and rising prices milling looked more and more attractive. Mitchell, Sage, and their ilk had begun as merchants; now, reflecting a general shift in American business, they moved into the realm of manufacturers.

Their timing was better than it first appeared. In 1857 the United States slipped into depression, over the following months uncertainties generated by the growing sectional conflict kept demand weak, and when fighting between North and South commenced prices fell 50 percent in some key markets, while young men marching off to war created a severe labor shortage. But soon enough, the war generated increased demand that drove up prices and kept sawmills busy, often using immigrant labor from Canada. Lumbermen now entered what Henry Sage called "eleven fat years." Taking advantage of opportunities, they built new plants in location after location and rebuilt and improved old ones. In 1869 a survey by editors of leading Saginaw and Bay City newspapers found eighty-three sawmills in the valley, seventy-seven with circular saws and forty-nine with gang saws.

These mills employed 2,909 workers (to say nothing of loggers in the woods and lumber dealers supplying the markets); they had a collective capacity of 625 million feet of lumber a year.[28]

More than wartime demand and postwar reconstruction lay behind the "fat years." Settlement of the Midwest was rushing ahead. Railroads pushed west and south, opening vast stretches of rich farmland in Iowa and elsewhere. As George Hotchkiss noted, rapid settlement of the prairies "was the necessary adjunct for bringing Michigan forests into use and developing their value." Chicago, not founded until 1832 and a mere stripling during the early years of Michigan lumbering, became the major rail hub serving the emerging agrarian empire of the prairies. As such, increasing quantities of lumber flowed to and through it: 32 million board feet in 1847, 306 million in 1856, and 647 million in 1865. By 1857 Chicago had over one hundred and fifty lumber firms, representing an investment of $60 million and employment for ten thousand workers. It had become a great lumber emporium, serving the Midwest as Albany did the Northeast.[29]

Much lumber reaching Chicago originated in Michigan, especially Muskegon, which, as the nearest lumber-producing center on Lake Michigan, had a natural advantage that soon earned it the title "Lumber Queen." Manistee was not far behind; Hotchkiss thought few "locations have exercised a greater influence in the lumber manufacture of the State than . . . the county of Manistee." Ludington and other lumbering communities on the lake shipped large quantities too, as did Saginaw and Bay City, which used rail connections to reach buyers in the Windy City.[30] At the same time, shipments to the East continued to grow, leading to the rise of major wholesaling centers at Tonawanda, North Tonawanda, and Buffalo—all near the western terminus of the Erie Canal—as well as in nearby Rochester, and to continued growth of wholesale operations in Albany, at the eastern end of the canal.[31]

As rising demand led to an increase in the number and size of sawmills, the scramble for timberland accelerated. Would-be buyers raced one another to government land offices to enter claims to choice tracts, stole information on promising stands, and resorted to skullduggery to learn where Indian reservations were to be located so they could buy reservation timber for a minimal outlay before others could. Rather than being ashamed of such behavior, lumbermen and local observers alike saw it as evidence of initiative and sagacity, the marks of a good businessman. A local chronicler wrote of one of the more successful: "With the land office at Detroit for the goal, [and] a choice section of land for the prize, it is believed that there was never a man who could beat James Fraser in the race." For his part, Charles

Hackley proudly recounted how he outwitted rivals who tried to get him drunk so they could steal information on land he had selected and then file on it before he could.[32]

Michigan's lumber industry was remarkably fragmented. There were a host of producing centers—more and more as time passed, until sawmills were present at nearly every pine-belt port along lakes Michigan and Huron. Fragmentation took place within, as well as between, operating centers. Sage, McGraw and Company, one of the largest firms along the Saginaw after completion of its mill in 1865, turned out 34.5 million feet in 1870, yet that was only about 5 percent of the area's cut. After he and Sage parted company in 1868, John McGraw built a slightly larger mill of his own.[33] Wellington Burt and Jethro Mitchell had a sawmill of similar size, but they were unable to dominate any more than had Sage. In Manistee, Muskegon, and other sawmill centers division was also the norm.[34]

Fragmentation resulted from many factors. For one, the industry's resource base was so widely scattered that central control by anyone—or even by a few—was out of the question. Moreover, there were limited economies of scale in both logging and milling. Even after 1870, by which time technological innovations made larger mills practical, a capacity of about thirty million board feet a year normally remained the upper limit for expansion of plant. Larger mills were possible, but not cost effective. For one thing, the costs of obtaining adequate log supplies rose sharply as mills grew beyond that size. In most cases it was more profitable to erect a second mill at a location nearer log sources than to bring logs considerably greater distances to supply an expanded plant. Lumber markets were as dispersed as log sources, making domination of wholesale and retail outlets difficult; being scattered, points of demand could not all be reached with equal efficiency from a central production point. In addition, marketing costs often rose with size. Harbors and docking facilities had limited capacity and could be stretched beyond natural limits only at considerable expense.[35]

The limits were human as well as physical. The industry was remarkably easy to enter, the technology sufficiently simple to be grasped by a person with but a modicum of education or experience. Over the years a large number of individuals moved from working as loggers, to being logging contractors, then mill operators. Maine, Vermont, New Brunswick, Pennsylvania, and New York had full quotas of people experienced in the woods and interested in making their way as lumbermen but who found opportunities in those older centers limited by those already operating there. Individuals from those states provided an almost inexhaustible well of potential millmen for Michigan and other Lake States, since the conditions were similar to those in older areas and required the same basic skills. At the same time, a sizable percentage of lumbermen came from modest rural backgrounds—many from near to hand—for much of what was required on the family farm was also required in the woods: skill with axes, saws, and other basic tools; ability to handle draft animals; and experience with hard physical labor.[36]

Even men from non-rural backgrounds—such as Henry Crapo, Russell Alger, and Henry Sage—found it possible to move from timber speculator to sawmill operator with relative ease. Of Crapo, his biographer noted, "Lumbering was a business about which he knew nothing, but he felt confident of his ability to learn." He was right. Crapo soon developed the largest operation in Flint. For his part, Sage can be characterized as a merchant capitalist, rather than an industrialist. Initially he was a capitalist with limited capital, but Sage was willing to gamble on the availability of credit to carry him through financial crises, and over time his faith was richly rewarded. Nor was his experience atypical. Historian Barbara Benson summarized: "[T]he ability to command working capital, either cash or credit . . . in large measure determined the fate of a business."[37]

Entry costs were modest. For $10,000 one could buy or build a sawmill large enough to enter non-local markets successfully. Such a sum, while difficult to acquire by saving alone, was within the reach of successful loggers who wanted to begin milling. Often partnerships with those they had previously supplied with logs or for whom they had worked provided start-up capital.[38]

Partnerships were long the norm. Entrepreneurs would join with one or more partners to build a sawmill, buy a tract of timber, or conduct logging operations and then, when the anticipated task was completed or accumulating profits allowed, form other partnerships for new tasks or to enlarge their operations. Thus, Charles Hackley's operations went from J. H. Hackley & Co. (1859-1866) to Hackley and Sons (1866-1877), to Hackley and McGordon (1866-1890), to C. H. Hackley & Co. (1876-1886), to Hackley & Hume (1881-1905). Similarly, Ammi W. Wright, owner of one of the largest mills in the Saginaw area, had partnerships with Charles H. Davis, Charles W. Wells, Farnum C. Stone, and Willis T. Knowlton, among others. Davis in turn developed arrangements of his own, including with members of the Weyerhaeuser network developing beyond Michigan.[39]

Ownership was not far removed from management. The emerging lumber barons, generally uncomfortable with modes of control that separated ownership and management, hesitated to embrace modern corporate forms. Corporations were becoming more widespread in the

United States from the 1880s, but Henry Sage, for one, "looked upon corporate status as a threat rather than an opportunity, as dangerous to his absolute control of the business he had built." Although Sage was willing to pursue opportunities aggressively, like many others he felt most comfortable with old, familiar forms of organization.[40]

At first, logging and sawmill technology were derivative too. Techniques perfected on earlier frontiers, especially in Maine, worked well in Michigan, easing the transfer of labor and management from older centers.[41] Log sleighs for winter skidding continued in use but of all the transferred technology, none was more important than that involved with log booms. Just as at centers in Maine, New York, and Pennsylvania, the completion of a giant boom was responsible for the rise in the Saginaw Valley of Michigan's greatest lumber-producing center. The trend began in 1856 when the Charles Merrill Company built its own boom, but it was the Tittabawassee Boom Company that revolutionized the valley's industry. Organized in 1864 by leading lumbermen of the area, the company did not have a completed boom in place until 1867. In time it came to encompass twelve miles of storage and sorting facilities. With this and booms on other branches of the Saginaw complex in place, production grew apace. By 1880 the sawmills clustered along the twenty-five-mile length of the Saginaw were cutting over a billion feet of lumber a year. Taken together, the twin towns of Saginaw and Bay City had become the nation's leading lumber-producing center. Booms appeared on other streams too, and with similar effect, although all were considerably smaller than that on the Tittabawassee.[42]

In time innovations would appear in Michigan's woods and mills. Among them were the "big wheels," an invention of Silas Overpack of Manistee in 1870. Loggers using this device would attach the butt end of one or more logs beneath the axle connecting a pair of wheels measuring as much as twelve feet in diameter. The device's slip-tongue was attached so that when horses or oxen pulled on it the butt of the logs was levered off the ground. Thus, with only their smaller ends dragging on the ground, logs could be pulled from the woods over brush and stumps to streamside landings in summer as easily as in winter. About the same time, the adoption of crosscut saws for felling also speeded woods work; previously crosscuts had only been used for cutting downed trees into log lengths. With these innovations and the spread of a network of railroads in the woods over the next two decades, summer logging became widespread, new stands could be tapped, and log supplies increased tremendously. Using logging railroads, some firms that had been cutting three to five million feet a season before long were harvesting thirty to fifty million.[43]

Logging railroads were probably the most important innovation; they brought a revolution to the timber industry. Railroads not only allowed year-round transportation of logs and opened stands well back from the waterways, but also changed basic logging practices. As the *Northwestern Lumberman* explained, with railroads "about ¼ more logs are marketed off the same lands, as poorer grades or cheaper kinds of logs can be hauled profitably." Previously loggers had taken only white pine and left even that if undersized. Now loggers "cut everything in sight . . . [even] trees as small as eight inches producing only sixteen board feet per log, which was indeed very, very small timber." Rolland Maybee summarized:

> *Year-round cutting opened a new period of the slaughter of the forests. No longer were only the large trees cut on a selective basis. Literally everything went down at the mercy of the saw. Partially cut-over areas were cut again and cleaned up once and for all time. Vast areas of untouched timber, five to ten miles back from a logging stream, were opened to systematic cutting on a take-everything basis.*

George Hotchkiss agreed: "No lumberman would today think of leaving a tree of any kind . . . providing a log can be obtained that will cut a scantling of 2x4 inches. In place of careful selection, everything is taken."[44]

Railroad logging in Michigan had its genesis in 1876, when the Flint & Pere Marquette, the state's first standard-gauge common carrier, began hauling logs to Saginaw and "succeeded beyond expectations." That same year, Winfield S. Gerrish, a young log jobber and timberland owner, visited the Centennial Exposition in Philadelphia, where he viewed a small Baldwin locomotive. This, he thought, might be the answer to how to tap some of his stands. On his return to Michigan, Gerrish formed a company to build a small narrow-gauge railroad. Loggers were skeptical, but Gerrish persevered and by 1877 had the six-mile-long Lake George & Muskegon line—built at a cost of $38,900—in operation. Its first year, the railroad hauled one-half million board feet of logs a day while other loggers were struggling because of poor sleighing conditions. Gerrish had proved his point, and other logging railroads soon followed. Gerrish died soon after, but Charles Hackley bought the Lake George & Muskegon and operated it successfully for years. By 1882, the year Hackley purchased Gerrish's line, there were thirty-two logging railroads in the state; seven years later there were eighty-nine, with a total of almost four hundred and fifty miles of track.[45]

Even after these new technologies made an appearance, winter logging camps, spring log drives, and downstream booms remained the heart of most logging operations; similarly, steam-powered sawmills using circular and sash saws, edgers, and, in time, dry kilns and band saws dominated manufacturing. Although large and complex, technologically operations were not highly sophisticated, a fact that eased entry into the industry and encouraged its spread.[46]

Similarities to Maine eased the transfer of technology and workers to the new frontier. New York and Pennsylvania were more mountainous, which reduced the number of drivable streams and encouraged logging techniques that had limited applicability in Michigan. Under the circumstances, the influence of New Englanders outstripped that of those from Middle Atlantic States even though the latter were nearer and actually supplied more workers. Rather than westward, many a Pennsylvania lumberman moved south along the Appalachians, where techniques perfected on the Allegheny Plateau were more readily applicable.[47]

Many Canadians also moved to Michigan's woods in the 1840s as Britain abandoned mercantilist trade policies, opening home markets to Baltic timber at the expense of her North American colonies. One of Canada's preeminent historians put it succinctly: "Great Britain had decided to act for her own best interest . . . and had left the colonies free to act for theirs." The flow of Canadian workers accelerated during the Civil War, when labor shortages in the states pushed wages upward, and continued strong thereafter as agricultural prices dropped in Canada, forcing many off the land. By then most immigrants were French-Canadian, but they also included a sizable contingent of Scots. Bay City, close to Canada, drew an especially large number of Canadians, but throughout the region they were the industry's largest contingent of foreign-born laborers and by 1890 made up one-fifth to one-fourth of the work force.[48]

The influx of laborers was necessitated by the fact that—unlike in Maine, Pennsylvania, and New York—there was no significant preexisting population in Michigan's pineries to draw upon for a work force. Rural settlement came, but by and large it followed rather than preceded logging, spreading as the lumberman's frontier advanced and accelerating after 1870 as railroads opened lands well back from waterways. As around New York's Beekmantown, lumbering made such settlement feasible. More and more farmers—finding good agricultural land south of the pine belt taken up or too expensive—followed the speculators and sawmill operators northward.

Far from markets, tilling poor, thin soil heavily scoured by ice-age glaciers, they struggled mightily. As in Maine, many of these back-country farmers sought to make ends meet with seasonal by-employment in nearby logging and milling operations and by selling the products of their farms, but theirs was a tenuous existence.[49]

Late in life Ulysses P. Hedrick—by then one of the country's leading horticultural experts—recalled growing up on one such Michigan farm, located near the tip of the Lower Peninsula. Although the area was north of the state's best pineries, young men from these farms found employment in woods operations, while Hedrick's father and neighbors sold them the products of their fields and forests. But as timber stands retreated before the axe, opportunities dwindled. In the end, Hedrick recalled, "We had robbed the land of its magnificent trees, and had skimmed the cream of the virgin soil, leaving Father only poor, sandy, good-for-nothing sub-marginal fields, which none of us now loved." As at Beekmantown, when the forests were gone, most of the area proved sub-marginal for agriculture.[50]

Workers from farms were the exception, rather than the rule. For the most part, the labor force in Michigan's lumber industry was made up of in-migrants who were woods and sawmill workers pure and simple. They brought with them the raw, action-oriented culture of laborers on earlier lumbering frontiers. The state's sawmill towns became centers of violence and carousing, some worse than others, but all tough enough. Indeed, although woods workers from Maine were wont to refer to themselves as "Bangor Tigers," Stewart Holbrook maintained Saginaw became tougher than Bangor had ever been: "Bangor and the Penobscot had been quiet and seemly alongside Saginaw." Bangor had a theological seminary, the Maine Temperance Society, and "the strong cultural sun that radiated from Boston and Concord"; Saginaw, "a town of the new frontier" where life "was more expansive and the tempo faster," had none of these. Holbrook's claim seems too sweeping—after all, Michigan adopted prohibition in 1853 and remained dry for twenty years—but life in the lumber towns *was* certainly rough, as various studies more careful than Holbrook's have demonstrated. As such, they echoed what had gone before—and not just in Bangor.[51]

Not all the roughness originated with laborers. As in Maine, early lumbermen contributed their share. Nineteen-year-old Charles H. Hackley worked for his passage on a schooner bound for Muskegon in 1856. Arriving with $7 in his pocket, he obtained a job as a laborer at Levi Truesdale's sawmill and that winter worked in the woods as a log scaler for $30 a month. The following spring Truesdale made him an outside foreman at the mill and, impressed by young Hackley's abilities, sent him to business school that fall. On his return, Hackley scaled logs and worked in Truesdale's new firm as bookkeeper and manager of the company store. In time Hackley would become one of Muskegon's leading lumbermen and public benefactors, but he led a lusty life and, in his early days at least, "mingled freely in the shanty boys' saloons and river dives." Even later, he acted "brashly and brazenly." Yet he was markedly successful. From 1866 he cleared more than $100,000 a year; in 1872 alone his operations earned him $365,000 profit.[52]

"The eccentric Curtis Emerson," as George Hotchkiss called him, was less successful, but even more flamboyant, his exploits dwelling in that gray area where fact and local legend mingle. The son of a wealthy Vermont merchant and banker, Emerson moved to Saginaw in 1846 and soon entered the lumber business. Crude even by Saginaw standards, he held "many wild carousels" at his home, nicknamed "the Halls of Montezuma." Reputedly snubbed in 1859 when invitations went out for a grand dinner for the town's civic and business leaders in celebration of the opening of the posh new Bancroft Hotel, Emerson was irate. On the appointed evening, he arrived on the scene inebriated, leaped onto the long table around which guests were seated, and strode its length, kicking food, crystal, and china right and left, cutting several people with flying glass and doing damage estimated at some $2,000. Not surprisingly, this broke up the soiree. Holbrook, in his typical style, concluded his account with the statement: "Next day, when he had sobered slightly, Curt willingly paid the damages. He said he was sorry that anyone was injured, but the hell with the hotel." Much if not all of this story seems to be true, but given his penchant for alcohol it should perhaps come as no surprise that Emerson was soon out of the lumber business and died not many years later in relative poverty.[53]

In spite of such occasional behavior by lumbermen, the rowdiness for which mill towns were noted was primarily a product of workers. As time passed, more and more lumbermen built pretentious mansions, supported cultural institutions, and in general distanced themselves both from such actions and from the laboring class. The ethos of nineteenth-century capitalism encouraged the process, persuading the successful they were more deserving than those who worked in the woods and mills; if only laborers would work hard and avoid the fleshpots and booze, they could rise as leading lumbermen had themselves done—and if a worker was maimed or killed on the job it was dismissed as a result of his own carelessness or intemperate life. As a Bay City attorney noted, sawmill workers "could not even stop for a drink of water, but must keep up the labor just as the inanimate machinery. The men are [but] a cog in a vast machine." Some few employers—men such as Charles Hackley—remembered from whence they had come and sought to ameliorate conditions for their workers, but most appear to have made their contributions to community betterment not because of social concerns so much as to demonstrate their status—especially to their fellow elites.[54]

Social distancing contributed to distrust by one class and resentment by the other. More basically, it produced an atmosphere in which each was ignorant of the other. Henry Crapo provides an illustration. Writing in his diary in 1864, he expressed amazement: "[M]y mill men strike!!!" Seemingly, he had little idea they were unhappy with things as they were. Henry Sage shared his views. In 1872, when his workers complained about long hours and low pay, he wrote, "We can't afford . . . to submit to the charge of an ignorant rabble . . . enterprises upon which the nation's wealth and prosperity depends." He later added, "*Never* was there so little reason for discontent—Never was labor so well paid."[55] Still, workers did not have to strike to express unhappiness with the established order. Jeremy Kilar's conclusions seem sound:

> *Public rowdiness may be interpreted as a rejection of, or a release*
> *from, the discipline and danger that lumbertown workers faced on the*
> *job. Celebration eased some of the pain of life under the exploitative*
> *economic system characteristic of nineteenth-century society . . . [while]*
> *lumbertown violence demonstrated a set of values . . . that in some ways*
> *challenged those of the economic hierarchy.*[56]

Workers displayed a certain pride in being apart from polite society when they referred to loggers as "timber beasts" and sawmill workers as "sawdust savages." It appears not all resistance came in the form of overt confrontations with management.

Be that as it may, strikes *did* occur—and not just such localized walkouts as surprised Crapo in 1864. When millworkers struck in Williamsport in 1872, so too did those in the Saginaw Valley. The goal was the same—reduction of hours from twelve or fourteen to ten—and so was the result: eventually the strike failed. Even more than in Pennsylvania, the strikers never had much chance of success. Williamsport's laborers drew inspiration and support from workers in Pennsylvania's anthracite coal mines and from champions of the eight-hour day in New York and other Eastern cities. Michigan's laborers were more isolated. Moreover, ethnic and national divisions and the transient nature of the work force made cooperation more difficult than in Williamsport and weakened community support, while the presence of numerous other producing centers in the state undermined the efforts by Saginaw Valley workers. In contrast, Michigan's employers—resident and absentee alike—formed a solid phalanx in opposition to the strike.

Wildcat strikes broke out in various mills during the first days of July 1872, and Sage and other millowners issued a joint resolution proclaiming they would "not submit to any reduction of hours of labor nor any increase of wages." Their statement was in vain; by July 5 nearly all mills in the valley were closed. Four days later, strikers belatedly formed a union, but it did little other than help keep workers' families fed. Management brought in strikebreakers, and on July 17 Sage's mill was able to restart with a partial crew; others followed suit. Within days the strike was over.[57]

Anita Goodstein, the only scholar to give the strike much attention, maintained that the workers lacked "effective organization," indeed that they were "a milling body of men with no apparent leadership." She dismisses threats to burn down the mills with the comment "after all [they] represented the only source of income to the workers" and the possibility of their forming an effective union to pursue "collective bargaining was perhaps as alien to the workers . . . as it most certainly was to employers." Considering what was transpiring in Williamsport, her analysis seems inadequate.[58] The strikers may not have gained much strength from their late-formed union, and no evidence has been unearthed showing they received aid from the National Labor Union, but the timing of the strike, coinciding as it did with that in Williamsport, suggests more planning than she admits and the possibility of NLU support. Actually, failure probably resulted more from the weaknesses in labor's position already referred to and from the absence of the sort of community support that buttressed Williamsport's strikers than from the lack of effective union activity. The Bay City *Journal* expressed a view shared by many "respectable" elements in the valley: "[T]he entire blame [for the strike] can be laid at the door of a few discontented demagogues."[59] Internally divided, without significant community or outside support, and facing uniform opposition from employers, the strikers' hopes of success were never realistic.

Although slowed by the nationwide depression that commenced in 1873, Michigan's lumber industry resumed growing in the last years of the decade and peaked in the early eighties. The spread of a network of logging railroads and other new technology helped make this final expansion possible even though stands in the river drainages, which for so long had fed the log drives that supplied mills, were almost exhausted.[60] In the 1880s, other strikes erupted, first at Au Sable, Ocada, and Muskegon and then in the Saginaw

Valley—the last of these far better organized and effective than any that had gone before; indeed, one authority has described it as "the most important strike in nineteenth-century Michigan history."[61]

By 1885 as many as seven thousand millhands worked in the seventy-seven sawmills in the Saginaw Valley; of these, some three thousand were reportedly members of the Knights of Labor.[62] As the mills opened that spring, owners announced wages would be reduced from 12 to 25 percent from those of the previous year. Although they accepted the cut—which management justified by a fall in lumber prices—workers petitioned for a reduction of the workday from eleven hours to ten to compensate. Owners ignored the petition, but since the state had passed a new ten-hour law, workers seem to have expected the shortened workday to take effect on July 1. It did not, and this combined with other complaints triggered a walkout.[63]

The strike began at W. B. Rouse's sawmill on July 6 and quickly spread. Rouse described its commencement:

My mill was closed on Monday, July 6 for . . . cleaning out the boilers. Some six or seven of the men who were about the mill took their dinner pails and started for home. One man took a [red] bandana . . . from another man's pocket, fastened it to a stick, and as they were near McEwen's mill, waived it in the air and shouted "Hurrah for ten hours." McEwen's mill was not running, some of them not having gotten over the "fourth," and the others were around the mill. The shouting of the men started them going [home] and the strike began.

By July 9 all sawmills in Bay City were shut down; a day later those in Saginaw closed as well.[64]

Lumbermen grumbled that local authorities favored the strikers. Perhaps they did, for according to the Detroit *Evening News*, in September the Knights of Labor was in "absolute control of almost every branch of the political machinery." What lumbermen seem to have wanted was not impartial enforcement of the law, but allies in their efforts to break the strike.[65] Local law-enforcement officers took steps to prevent violence and destruction of property, but refused to hire fifty additional policemen and protested when millowners brought in squads of heavily armed Pinkerton detectives. The public outcry was so strong the Pinkertons, whom the *Evening News* called "Hesians from Chicago," were quickly dismissed. Henry Sage was outraged by this capitulation to "mob rule," but he need not have worried. Saginaw's Mayor Charles Benjamin, a lumberman himself, brought in a fresh contingent of Pinkertons and prevailed upon Russell Alger,

Michigan's self-made lumberman-governor, to call out the state militia.[66] A labor journal put it succinctly: the governor called out "the militia for no purpose other than to intimidate the laborers in the interest of his brother lumber barons." Nor did he stop there. Alger issued a proclamation outlawing mass meetings and ordered the arrest of two key leaders of the strike—Daniel C. Blinn, editor of the Bay City *Labor Vindicator*, and Thomas Barry a Democratic-Greenback member of the state legislature—under Michigan's Baker Conspiracy Law, which prohibited plotting to interfere with the legitimate conduct of business.[67]

Officially the Knights of Labor played little if any part of in bringing on the strike, although Blinn and Barry, both members, were in the forefront. However, once the strike was under way the Knights exerted considerable influence. Reflecting the conservative views of the organization's national leadership, local assemblies took a moderate stance. They repudiated Blinn after one of his more inflammatory speeches—an action that did little to weaken his popularity with the rank and file—and tried unsuccessfully to mediate between millowners and strikers.[68] Terence Powderly, Grand Master Workman of the Knights, arrived in the area in late July. Never an advocate of strikes, Powderly apparently feared events in the Saginaw Valley were damaging the Knights' image, splitting its membership, and draining its resources. He made no public statements, but privately urged millhands earning over $1.50 a day to return to work at ten hours, but with proportionally reduced wages. His action undercut both the strike and Barry's leadership; it surely played a large part in the strong dislike Barry developed for him (he later stated, "I have learned to actively hate this man Powderly, and I have sworn to drive him out of the labor movement").[69]

Strikers had been dribbling back to work, especially in Saginaw, where support was never as strong as in Bay City and where boom hands, unemployed when mill shutdowns forced closure of Tittabawassee Boom, formed a ready supply of strikebreakers. By mid-August two sawmills had reopened running ten hours at the old wage rates, six on a ten-hour day with reduced pay, and eleven on an eleven-hour day. To the editor of the *Lumberman's Gazette* "the strike which has been so tenaciously adhered to for five weeks . . . was ill advised," its results disastrous for laborers, but in some ways it was actually helpful to millowners, for it drove up lumber prices $1 per thousand at a time when demand had been sluggish and prices low. By September the strike was over. "There were," Jeremy Kilar concluded, "too many logs, too many mills, too many machines, and too many available workers for the strike to succeed."[70]

Hanging over events in the Saginaw Valley in 1885, like a sword of Damocles, was the certain knowledge that lumbering there was approaching an end. Timber stands in the far reaches of Michigan's Lower Peninsula had been all but cleared, leading to a sharp decline in the quality of available sawlogs. While 40 percent had once been of the highest grade, lumbermen were now "satisfied if logs . . . [were] 20 percent 'uppers.' " Already some mills in the Saginaw Valley had cut-out their log supplies and closed. In some places, it was even worse. At Edmore, in the center of the state, the number of sawmills had dropped from five to one. Thus, when Henry Sage, faced with the strike of 1885, threatened to close his mill permanently, he was taken seriously. Even in the state's northernmost reaches, by 1893 newspapers were reporting that over the preceding decade there had been a 40 percent decrease in the size of logs available.[71]

With the decreasing availability of timber, loggers went back to re-cut stands logged earlier, taking smaller logs and species initially deemed not worth harvesting, and resorted to a more thorough cutting on whatever new stands they were able to locate. In early days clearcutting had been impractical, for profits could only be turned using the best logs; now it was a necessity—and the environmental consequences were to be felt for decades to come. The general absence of steep terrain kept soil erosion down, but the species mix was so drastically altered that—like the desert of five million acres in Pennsylvania—the remaining forest was ill equipped to return to anything more than a shadow of what it had once been.[72]

By the mid-eighties, logs were arriving in Saginaw from as far away as Georgian Bay on the Canadian side of Lake Huron. The way was pointed in August 1885 when what the *Lumberman's Gazette* aptly called "An Enormous Raft" arrived with three million feet of logs, raising "the hopes and anticipations of our mill men." Saginaw Valley's sawmills would no longer "be dependent entirely on the availability of the log supply tributary to the Saginaw River, or even on the log supply of the lower peninsula itself." Brought down at a cost of only 70 cents a thousand, rafted logs were welcome indeed, but they were only a temporary solution.[73] To make matters worse, lumber from Wisconsin and Minnesota, neither of whose stands was as depleted as Michigan's, was capturing ever-larger shares of the Midwestern market. Canadian and Southern pine was also entering outlets long served by Michiganders and at prices the latter were hard pressed to match. Production in the Saginaw Valley, which had peaked in 1882, dropped sharply during the strike year and never fully recovered. In 1890 there were still eighteen sawmills in Saginaw and twenty across the river in Bay City, but the end was in sight. Production plummeted. Signaling the end, in 1894 the Tittabawassee Boom Company, which had handled over sixteen billion feet of logs over the preceding thirty years, ceased operation. The Saginaw Valley hung on for a time by cutting Canadian logs, but clearly its end as a great lumber center was at hand.[74]

If the end of the glory days of Saginaw's lumbering was fast approaching, could those of other Michigan communities be far behind? Muskegon's output reached its highest point in 1884 and, after a brief recovery in 1887, dropped off rapidly thereafter. Muskegon soon ceased to be a major producer, its chances of continued importance killed not so much by the devastating depression that destroyed demand in the mid-nineties as by failure of its log supplies.[75] Other areas followed, including centers on rivers in the northern part of the Lower Peninsula, which, being both more tortuous and difficult to drive and more distant from markets, attracted lumbermen somewhat later than those further south. By 1900 even the pine forests of the Upper Peninsula, never extensive, were largely gone.[76] Soon Michigan became an also-ran in the ranks of softwood-lumber-producing states, but its record remained—neither Wisconsin nor Minnesota ever matched Michigan's peak annual output; indeed, not until Washington did so in 1920 did any state produce more lumber in a single year than had Michigan in its heyday.[77]

Declining population, a lack of jobs, and the disposal of cutover lands became major concerns—and sure signs that a new order had arrived.[78] The lumbering that remained involved clean-up operations rather than anything even remotely resembling Michigan's great days as a lumberman's frontier. The career of Frank Gilchrist of Alpena illustrates the situation. Once a leading producer of white pine lumber, Gilchrist shifted in turn to Norway pine, hemlock, and eventually hardwoods (turning out high-quality maple flooring). The shift, he noted, was necessitated by the fact that white pine stumpage he had once bought for 20 cents a thousand could by the turn of the century not be obtained at all, and if found "would readily command $10 to $12 a thousand." Even as he shifted to first one species and then another, Gilchrist—looking forward to operating on some new lumberman's frontier—actively invested in pineland in Canada, Minnesota, the Gulf South, and Oregon. Michigan's pineries might be gone, but Gilchrist was sure other areas would soon have lumbering frontiers of their own, and he wanted to position himself to pursue the main chance when they did. In this, he was but one of many. Russell Alger, Charles Hackley, Delos Blodgett, the Eddy family, and others followed a similar course as lumbering moved on to new stands.[79] Michigan's lumbering frontier might be over, but its lumbermen and the money they had garnered there would continue to play a role in the industry for years to come.

CHAPTER SEVEN

The Full Flowering

For three centuries Americans had been tapping the continent's forests, gradually turning fixed resources into liquid assets and accumulating the capital, technological know-how, and organizational wherewithal to make lumbering one of the United States' leading industries.[1] These developments came to full flower in the forests of Wisconsin and Minnesota. All that had gone before was but prelude to what unfolded on the St. Croix and Chippewa, at Cloquet and Beef Slough, along the Menominee, and in scores of places related thereto. Moreover, in large part what occurred subsequently in Oregon, Washington, and other far western locations, as well as in the nation's capitol, reshaping forest policy and the approaches of the forest industry, was heir to what took place in the upper reaches of the Mississippi drainage.

This full flowering was manifested in a sustained, extraordinarily high level of production, turned out by a host of sawmills at or near the optimum size for efficient operation; by a technology far more sophisticated than that of the pioneer period; by viable connections between woods, mills, and markets; by the accumulation of sufficient capital, much of it transferred from elsewhere, to finance these undertakings; and by a work force and leaders with the expertise to turn potential into reality. Underpinning all this was a magnificent wealth of forest resources. Yet much of what developed in the upper Lake States was a continuation of what had gone before. As on earlier frontiers, would-be farmers pushing westward were in the industry's vanguard. They found farmland in the southern reaches of the area and, to meet their needs, imported lumber from Pittsburgh and beyond to supplement local supplies. Some settlers even brought lumber with them down the Ohio and then up the Mississippi, but with an increase in the number of small mills and ancillary manufactories located in the wooded borderlands that angled across Wisconsin and Minnesota, separating prairies from more northerly coniferous forests, the practice became unnecessary. The earliest mills drew upon deciduous stands of the transition zone and upon local farmers for logs and labor. A settler in Carver County, southwest of St. Paul, reported:

The thick woods with which every claim in this region is more or less covered will in a few years yield not only the cash value of the timber,

149

but even now it [lumbering] already employs thousands of people who
get out logs and stack them along the river bank; even when you don't
need the cleared land, it's still worthwhile [for the farmer] to make about
$100 in this way every winter; then after several years, the stumps are
rotten and the plow is easier to handle.[2]

A traveler, discussing Wisconsin's trees in 1834, made no mention of pine. Settlement—and the focus of attention—was still on land south of the pine belt, but as trees of the transition zone disappeared and the effective opposition of Native Americans declined, milling operations moved north, pine came to dominate, and the role of farmers dwindled. What emerged drew heavily upon capital, technology, expertise, and organizational forms worked out in earlier areas of operation.[3]

As in areas further east, the coniferous forest only rarely presented solid stands of white pine, and on sandy soils, where the timber was almost exclusively white pine, quality tended to be low. Still, it was white pine that the developing market demanded, white pine that drew lumbermen to the northern woods, white pine that determined the value of stands, and white pine alone that loggers sought until depletion forced them to turn to other species or move on. All this sounds remarkably familiar.[4]

Still, there were new elements to what was transpiring. A rush to tap lead deposits in what would become southwestern Wisconsin commenced about 1825. For a time the mines were more important than the area's farms. When the rush began, Wisconsin's population stood at a mere two hundred, but by 1829 had swelled to ten thousand, leading Congress in 1836 to peel off Wisconsin Territory from Michigan, of which it had until then been a part. By 1840 the new territory was producing half the nation's lead, and Wisconsin's residents had come to be known as "Badgers," not after the animal itself, but the many miners who lived in dugouts and caves and grubbed in the earth for lead.[5]

With completion of the Erie Canal and the opening of steamboat service from Buffalo to Green Bay, Sheboygan, and Milwaukee soon after, the flow of in-migration shifted. Farmlands in southeastern Wisconsin now filled rapidly. The influx largely came from New England and upstate New York (many of the latter themselves originally New Englanders), but included an advanced guard of Germans, a group that was to play a major role in years to come. With this growth, southeastern Wisconsin took on a different character from the southwestern mining district, peopled largely from the South and Middle Border, and by 1850 had far outstripped it in population.[6]

As southeastern Wisconsin gained population, demand for lumber increased and sawmilling expanded to supply it—and there was ample opportunity, for three-fifths of the state was pineland.[7] From the mid-1830s, Chicago, growing at a breakneck pace, provided an additional, almost insatiable, demand (albeit one supplied more from Michigan than Wisconsin). Lumbering soon developed along the western shore of Lake Michigan, especially in areas tributary to Green Bay, and in Oshkosh and Fond du Lac. Isaac Stephenson estimated that as late as 1846 all the mills north of Green Bay probably "represented an investment of less than fifty thousand dollars," but by the mid-1850s the area's mills had become major suppliers of the Chicago market.[8] Serving it was far from easy; Chicago's port facilities were wretched, no tugs were present, and "for many years ships were pulled out of the [Chicago] river to the lake by hand, a headwind necessitating the use of a windlass." Daniel Stanchfield passed through in 1847 and "was disappointed in the appearance of that far-advertised city." Historians Harold Mayer and Richard Wade understood his reaction; their assessment: "The site was unpromising." But change was under way. By 1860, Wisconsin produced 355 million board feet a year, worth at an average of $6.65 per thousand nearly $2.5 million and much of it was marketed in Chicago.[9]

There were small mills scattered throughout the farm belt of southern Wisconsin. As early as 1837, Charles Goodhue built a sawmill on Rock River "to cut basswood lumber to raft down the river where new settlements were being made." Most of these mills were small, water-powered operations reminiscent of those that dominated on the Allegheny Plateau and in Ohio.[10] Nine years before, Lewis Taylor reported, the area of Beloit had been "in a state of nature," but by 1846 it had seventeen hundred inhabitants, two sawmills, two taverns, four churches, and eighteen dry-goods stores.[11]

Further west, in the new Minnesota and Iowa, early sawmills were equally modest. In 1850, the collective output of Minnesota's mills came to only $57,800. In Iowa, hardwood forests originally covered as much as 20 percent of the land area. "The river bottoms," one early writer claimed, "were covered with a virgin forest such as had never been seen by the white man." With the area's numerous watercourses, water-powered mills proliferated. By 1859 there were 540 sawmills in the state, but gradually the small mills of the two states were supplanted by larger ones, just as they had been in Wisconsin. In Iowa native forests soon ceased being the primary source of sawlogs; in time some seven-eighths of the logs used in its mills were pine floated down the Mississippi from Wisconsin and Minnesota—most from the former, and as one historian has put it, "Wisconsin and Iowa [thus] joined to form a great area of production of a product . . . vital to the uplifting of the Middle West."[12]

Noting that as time passed Wisconsin's new mills were located closer to the pineries, historian William Raney has argued that the expansion of the state's lumber industry was not to the west, but north, moving up the state's river drainages and Lake Michigan's western littoral like the fingers of a hand gradually being extended into the forested north. The argument could easily be extended to incorporate the period of railroad construction into the northland—especially the completion of the Wisconsin Central to Ashland in 1877—which added new corridors of exploitation, and to Minnesota as well (although that state lay beyond Raney's focus).[13]

The argument obscures as much as it illuminates. There *was* a westward movement to developments. Lumbering in the two-state area prospered first along Lake Michigan's western shore. In spite of superior stands, development further west lagged, for the forests were poorly located for supplying Chicago, and the huge demand that came with settlement of the Great Plains, a development that in time was to spur production on the Chippewa, St. Croix, and other forested drainages to the west, had not yet developed. Indeed, production tributary to Lake Michigan peaked while it was still rising further west; by 1875, forests in its hinterland, except for those north of Green Bay, were largely logged out. When railroads opened the way for rapid population growth on the Great Plains, production in the more westerly drainages rose sharply, for the natural flow of their commerce was to the Mississippi (and from there out onto the plains). The main centers of production moved from near Lake Michigan to western Wisconsin and then to Minnesota, production in the latter peaking after Wisconsin's was in decline. Indeed, among Minnesota's last great lumber-producing centers were Virginia and Cloquet, in the far northern portion of the state to be sure, but well west of the Chippewa and St. Croix, where Lake States lumbering centered earlier.

In any case, it was primarily logging that moved north; the centers of lumber manufacturing actually moved south as well as north. Mills downriver as far as St. Louis became major producers, sawing logs driven from the northwoods to the Mississippi and then rafted to the sawmills. Lumber from upriver—the first recorded rafts departing from Marine-on-St. Croix and Portage in 1839—competed with that of downstream producers. When he arrived in the region in 1847, Daniel Stanchfield began buying lumber from sawmills on the Wisconsin River and rafting it to Dubuque, Galena, Quincy, and St. Louis, where he earned "large profits." Rafts of logs

Rafting lumber down the Wisconsin River, which was poorly suited for log drives. Lumbermen operated mills upstream and rafted their cut downriver. Courtesy Wisconsin Historical Society, H. H. Bennett Collection, Raftsman's Series, #4268.

soon followed. In time these and similar markets became immense and rafting a major enterprise, although the Wisconsin River never became the primary source of logs from upstream—that honor fell, above all, to the Chippewa.[14]

A symbiotic relationship developed between logging and rafting, with many who in summer worked as deckhands on the steamboats that handled the rafts going up to the pineries in winter to log and in spring work the log drives; many then helped run rafts downstream to get back to their summer jobs on the raftboats. A few developed into river pilots, and some became well known, most notably Stephen Hanks, a cousin of Abraham Lincoln, who piloted rafts on the Mississippi for forty years and "knew every bend and sandbar, every towhead and crosscurrent, from Stillwater to St. Louis."[15]

The juxtaposition of major new markets served by river and rail, huge new sawmills to supply them, and vast stands of pine led to a lumber industry built on a scale and operating with a geographical sweep that was unprecedented. As a result, Wisconsin and Minnesota, each in turn, became the leading lumber-producing states, although the extent of their dominance was obscured by the millions of feet of logs floated downriver for sawing in Illinois, Iowa, and other states. Still, in these two, lumbering blossomed as never before.[16]

The new order they represented has been examined more thoroughly than any of the earlier (or, with the exception of western Washington, subsequent) centers of lumbering. Wisconsin and Minnesota's lumber industries each have been the subject of major studies, and so have the downriver mills that supplied much of the Great Plains, various individual firms, communities, and watersheds, and Frederick Weyerhaeuser—the greatest lumberman of them all. Rafting and the impact of the railroads that carried lumbering beyond the waterways have been subjects of historical examination too. Even the evolution of the legal system encouraging these developments has received major analysis. Yet a good bit can still be added, for these areas were both heirs of what had gone before and major sources of forces that shaped what followed, and existing studies do not always make this context clear.

***

Logging in the pineries did not follow immediately upon the heels of American control. Except for limited areas around Green Bay, Fort Snelling (near present-day Minneapolis), and Prairie du Chien, neither northern

Wisconsin nor areas that were to become Minnesota were legally open to white settlement—or to lumbermen—until after treaties with the Ojibwa, Lakota, and others in the 1830s (in the case of Minnesota, only the wedge of land between the St. Croix and Mississippi, the so-called "delta," was opened before 1851).[17]

Even before these treaties, there were those eyeing—and on occasion tapping—the pine stands. Residents of Prairie du Chien constructed a sawmill at the falls of the Black River in 1819 (soon destroyed by Indians resentful of the intrusion). Elsewhere, authorities allowed the building of sawmills on Indian land if tribal consent were obtained; but while this resulted in some small mills in the hinterland of Green Bay and elsewhere, these were minor exceptions to the general pattern of exclusion.[18] Then a series of treaties opened the floodgates. Only fifteen hours after the signing of the Ojibwa Treaty in 1837, Franklin Steele arrived at the falls of the St. Croix to claim a millsite, and loggers were soon cutting timber well upstream from St. Paul—also for Steele—even though they had no right to do so, the government not yet having surveyed it so it could be opened to claims. Appropriately, the treaty was widely known as the Lumberman's (or Pine Tree) Treaty.[19]

There was a great deal of boosterism in the western psyche. Henry Dodge was deeply affected. As territorial governor of Wisconsin, he envisioned the rich pine stands of the upper St. Croix valley and all the lands bordering the east side of St. Anthony Falls as Wisconsin lands. He expected them to contribute greatly to the growth of the state and in 1837 negotiated a treaty with the Ojibwa with that thought in mind.[20] Soon after, Wisconsin's territorial legislature created St. Croix County to provide a legal framework for its vast western domains; the action "was a landmark for the isolated lumbermen and traders" who had taken up residence there. But Dodge's hopes for a Wisconsin that stretched to the Mississippi were to go unfulfilled. Isolation and economic differences caused many in St. Croix County to think they should be detached from Wisconsin. The first effort to do so came in 1846, but it did not have immediate success. When the separation of Minnesota Territory from Wisconsin finally came, the forest potential of the northern belt was central in determining the boundary between the two, for residents in the former wanted the rich stands of the St. Croix to be under their control, not a government located in Madison and many in Wisconsin to keep its forest wealth—although some were frankly not interested in an area so far away. As John H. Tweedy, a Whig delegate to Wisconsin's constitutional convention, put it, he "would like to have any gentleman [in the convention] show how it was to be any profit to us to keep that portion." In the end, the boundary adopted represented a sort of compromise.[21]

Debates over the boundaries of Minnesota assumed partisan form. Republicans generally believed they could control an agricultural state with a northern boundary that would barely leave St. Paul and Stillwater within it, but Democrats wanted a larger state based on agriculture *and* lumbering, stretching from Iowa to the international border. In the end, the latter won, and it was thus Minnesota, rather than some alternative entity, within which the great forests of the western portion of the St. Croix valley and all of the areas yet further north and west were located.[22]

Minnesota was widely regarded as "an American Siberia," but it was a varied land, blessed, as William Lass has noted, with three frontiers: agriculture, mining, and lumbering. Much the same could be said of Wisconsin. The St. Croix watershed in Minnesota and Wisconsin and the Chippewa, wholly in the latter, would become two of the greatest white pine-producing drainages of all time.[23] New Englanders "laid the basis for the lumber industry in Minnesota," as they had in Wisconsin; indeed, many early immigrants to Minnesota "were lumberjacks direct from the forests of New England," but a number had worked in Michigan and lumbermen from the Mid-Atlantic states were significant contributors too.[24]

Minneapolis, located at the head of navigation on the Upper Mississippi, was destined to become the greatest lumber center of them all, and there were those who at an early date recognized its potential. A delegate in the Iowa constitutional convention of 1844, hopeful his state would be extended north to include the Falls of St. Anthony, proclaimed: "The water power there is incalculable. It will run machinery of every description and before many years it will be one of the most important spots in the western country." Although it started as a trading center, Minneapolis's economy came to rest on the twin pillars of lumber manufacturing and flour milling.[25] Other early settlements in the area ceded in the treaty of 1837 were lumber towns from the beginning, among them Marine-on-St. Croix, where the first sawmill began operating in August 1839, and Stillwater, soon labeled "the Queen of the St. Croix." But it was some time before any of these amounted to much. When Daniel Stanchfield arrived in 1847, he found only a "few weather-beaten buildings" marked the sites of Minneapolis, St. Paul, and Stillwater.[26]

Lumbering did not begin at the Falls of St. Anthony until 1848, and when it did, not everyone welcomed the development. Visiting in August 1851, Frank Mayer observed:

The falls of St Anthony extend, in a nearly strait line, across the Mississippi, being divided by an island which extends about a mile and a half up the stream. The beauty of one portion of the fall has been almost entirely destroyed by the saw mill [of Franklin Steele] which has been built immediately above, and the other portion has lost much of its wildness & beauty by the lodgement of numbers of logs (upon the rocks and between the crevices) which have come over the falls during freshets having escaped from the dam where they are collected to supply the Saw Mills.

Mayer probably realized that this was just the beginning, for to him the inhabitants presented "marked features and character which at once indicate their origin to be New England and especially 'down East from the state of Maine', raftsmen & woodsmen from the Kennebeck and Penobscot." He was right. Drawn by its rich pine stands, New Englanders were flocking to the area, and to those like Rufus King—or Caleb Cushing, who was a key underwriter of Franklin Steele's first mill there, even though he stayed on the East Coast himself—the beauty of the falls was in its productive potential. As a local historian declared: "It was largely New England energy and enterprise which put life into the manufacturing industries of Minneapolis at an early day." This was done by tapping the power of the falls.[27]

Growth continued, however sporadically. In 1855 Theodore Bost, who worked for a lumber dealer in St. Paul, wrote his parents, "St. Paul grows more attractive day by day. . . . Ravines are being filled, and regular embankments are being built along the river, whose banks are still in a primitive state: steamboats tie up to the first stump they come to or the first rock they find on shore." A few days later Bost wrote again:

The weather has been wet for the past several days; last night the rain came down in buckets and endangered the houses that have been built along the streets they have dug out to level the terrain. The weather is not at all to my boss's liking because timber from the upper Mississippi can now come downstream, the sawmills can get all the logs they want, and this will drive down the price of lumber which my man is now able to sell as dear as he pleases. How hard it is to make everyone happy at the same time![28]

Shortly after Bost wrote there were eight mills near the falls producing some twelve million feet a year. By 1870 thirteen sawmills clustered in the vicinity, and the pace of development was accelerating. Minneapolis and

St. Paul were both growing rapidly, and by 1876, having also passed St. Louis in flour production, the former was being called "the Queen City of the Northwest."[29]

The first mills were small, but some grew and larger operations from Michigan and beyond moved in. As a result, millowners had to seek ever-more-distant outlets for their cut. Historian Alice Smith observed lumbering "could by no means be regarded as a major industry in territorial Wisconsin, but certainly it was prophetic of what lay ahead." William Lass made much the same observation for the Minnesota of 1860: "While lumbering was the state's foremost economic activity, even after two decades of harvesting it was still fairly small business." In both states the old symbiotic ties between farmers and sawmills were weakening as a manufacturing frontier gradually developed alongside that of farmers; and as lumbering shifted northward, it moved well beyond the farming belt to areas where what agriculture existed was primarily ancillary to woods and sawmill operations. Rather than existing side by side with agriculture, lumbering was coming to dominate a frontier of its own. In Minnesota, where lumbering began before treaties with the Lakota opened a vast farm belt in 1851, ties between sawmills and nearby farms were never strong. Theodore Blegen observed: "Not infrequently, thanks to convenient rivers on which to float logs, and before local towns furnished markets of importance, exports preceded home community use."[30]

Iowa was similar. The first tiny mills served nearby farms, drew on them for laborers, and were often owned by people with farming backgrounds, but the larger pine mills that grew up along the Mississippi were industrial operations quite separate from farming—except insofar as farms supplied their major markets. In shipping to buyers in the developing agricultural sector, these mills were exporting from their bases of operations just as surely as were mills upriver.[31]

However unwittingly, Frederick Jackson Turner illustrated the discontinuity developing between the farming and lumbering frontiers. Turner later recalled how, during his boyhood in Portage, Wisconsin, log rafts frequently tied up along the riverfront while their crews went into town for a spree. To young Turner, it was all colorful and foreign, for his roots were firmly in the agrarian world—and when he set about writing his acclaimed studies of the American frontier, Turner gave virtually no notice of lumbering.[32]

As in southeastern Wisconsin, New Englanders, New Yorkers, and people from early-settled portions of the Lake States made up most of the early settlers of Minnesota. Although in 1840 it was still a part of Wisconsin

Territory, Lass notes settlers "on the Upper Mississippi and the St. Croix were far removed from most Wisconsinites. . . . The gap was more than geographic. The men of the Upper Mississippi were not the 'Badgers' of the lead mines or the wheat farmers of [Wisconsin's] Dane County." Most had moved to the St. Croix without even passing through the settled parts of Wisconsin, many coming directly from the forests of New England.[33] It was largely this that encouraged them to want to see the St. Croix drainage detached from Wisconsin, and it helps explain why when separation came the struggle to become territorial capital was between two lumber towns, St. Paul and Stillwater.[34]

New sawmill centers emerged in both Wisconsin and Minnesota during the 1850s. Winona, located on the Mississippi River in the southeastern reaches of the latter, was founded in 1852 on land ceded by the Lakota the year before. Steamboat captain Orrin Smith preempted the site in 1851, a community soon followed, and John C. Laird and two brothers started a lumber business there in 1855. No major timber stands grew nearby, but the river provided a ready artery for bringing logs from well-forested lands upstream, and the business prospered. In 1856, it became Laird, Norton & Company, which in time would be one of the largest components of the Weyerhaeuser syndicate and one of the leading milling centers for logs from the Chippewa drainage. At about the same time, major mills arose in Marinette, near the mouth of the Menominee River on Wisconsin's northeastern border. These too would prosper, and Marinette and Menominee (Marinette's twin city on the Michigan side of the river) in combination with other nearby centers would in time make the Menominee one of the nation's leading areas of lumber production. At these locations and numerous others scattered across the two states and downriver in Illinois, Iowa, and beyond, lumbering established a firm foothold during the decade.

In some locations—such as Fond du Lac, Oshkosh, La Crosse, and Winona—lumbering was part of a more broadly based economy (this in spite of the fact that from 1847 Oshkosh was known as the "Sawdust City"); in others, located in the heart of the pineries—places like Eau Claire, Chippewa Falls, and Marinette—it dominated. Surprisingly, much the same could be said of Clinton, Iowa; between 1870 and 1890, it turned out more lumber than any city on the Mississippi except Minneapolis. In 1876 Clinton and neighboring Lyons produced 40.5 percent of the state's cut; one year later, the editor of the *Clinton Age* reported that two-thirds of the city's population was supported by sawmills. In Iowa as a whole during the nineteenth century, only agriculture yielded products of more value than lumbering. Whether virtually alone or in places with broader economic support, the region's lumber manufacturing enjoyed tremendous growth during the 1850s—at least until the Panic of 1857.[35]

Explosive population growth during the 1850s, mostly in non-forested areas, stimulated the expansion of lumbering. Winona, for example, had but 346 inhabitants at the beginning of 1855, but over the next two years its population soared to almost three thousand; every boat bound upriver brought new settlers, and a fair proportion debarked at Winona; during 1856 alone, builders erected close to three hundred new buildings to meet the community's needs. Such expansion generated both opportunity and problems for lumbermen. Lumber was much in demand, and prices good, but Isaac Stephenson and others found it extremely difficult to fill crews to get out logs and run their mills. Settlers sought farms or opportunities in the growing agrarian communities, not forest-related employment. Moreover, there was no significant pre-existing population to draw upon in the forested area. Eau Claire County was destined to become a premier lumber center, but at its creation in 1851 it had a population of only one hundred. No doubt, mills in Iowa and Missouri, where agricultural settlement was pushing west from the Mississippi, also found it difficult to fill crews, although studies of lumbering in the downriver states are distressingly vague in their treatment of the period.[36]

Some of the earliest of the region's sawmills were built by people who, as Isaac Stephenson put it, "knew little or nothing of lumbering" and soon found themselves in difficulty as a result, but gradually men with experience arrived from Maine and New Brunswick, partly because firms like Sinclair & Wells actively recruited there. The newcomers found ample opportunity to help transform the nascent industry from the "crude . . . small establishments" they found on arrival to their "point of greatest development." Stephenson, himself from New Brunswick by way of Bangor, was only nineteen when he took over management of Sinclair & Wells's logging operations north of Green Bay and but twenty-one when he became an independent logging contractor. Some German immigrants who came seeking farms but lacked funds to acquire land right away took up employment in the woods and sawmills too. Stephenson found they "worked willingly and well," claiming they were more dependable than any other nationality. However slowly, the primitive operations of the 1840s were being replaced by more modern ones, harbingers of the great industry to come.[37]

The boom years of the 1850s were marked with failures as well as successes. Community leaders in Oshkosh and Fond du Lac pushed doggedly for construction of a canal joining the Wisconsin and Fox rivers

Wisconsin, Minnesota, and downriver. Map by Sarah E. Hinman.

to provide a water route from their locations on Lake Winnebago to the Mississippi and the emerging markets to which it gave access, but the route was challenging and the project failed to open the way for a significant traffic in lumber. The Chicago & North Western Railroad, which reached the area in 1859, proved far more important by giving the region's lumber ready access to Chicago and the markets it served.[38]

Logging was a difficult business during the early years. Shortages of capital were an even bigger concern than the lack of experienced workers. Ephraim Brown, a smalltime, independent logger, was in deep financial trouble by 1857, but struggled on. In April 1866, he complained he "had not made any money logging and that on the Chippewa only the millowners found lumbering really profitable." Moreover, according to historian Frederick Merk, during the 1860s "woodsmen were often defrauded . . . of the wages of an entire season" because of the financial irresponsibility—or dishonesty—of many logging contractors; the problem was surely present in the 1850s as well.[39]

Millowners often engaged in "bootstrap finance." Easterners invested in numerous sawmill enterprises in Wisconsin and Minnesota, but the money thus made available was often inadequate. Typically, the Daniel Shaw Company, which had a medium-size mill in Eau Claire, was "perennially short of funds for expansion and [even] for carrying current expenses." Shaw arrived from Maine via New York in 1855, by which time the Chippewa valley's sawmills were turning out some thirty million feet of lumber a year. He liked what he saw and moved quickly to order mill equipment from the East. It would travel from the manufacturer to Buffalo by railroad, by steamer to Milwaukee, from there by railroad to Prairie du Chien, then up the Mississippi by steamer to Read's Landing, and finally by keel boat up the Chippewa to Eau Claire. This was but one of many initial expenses. His sawmill was up and running by the summer of 1857, but Shaw soon found himself in financial straits, especially when the Panic of 1857 undercut prices and made sales difficult. Like many other small producers Shaw had trouble finding capital to acquire the timber or logs needed to keep sawing and resorted to buying through third parties—brokers, other lumbermen, independent loggers, Cornell University, and the state—rather than from the federal government, for this allowed him to defer payments, often until the resulting lumber was sold. For many operators, frequent fires made financial difficulties even worse. Charles Colman built a shingle mill in La Crosse in 1854 and expanded into lumber manufacturing. His sawmill burned three times, but each time he managed to find funds to rebuild. By

1886 he had, in addition to his mill, thirty-two lumberyards in the area served from La Crosse.[40]

By 1856 Chicago was the nation's leading wholesale lumber center, a development made possible by significant improvement of its harbor. Chicago sat on low-lying, boggy land that sloped gradually into a shallow anchorage. Initially, cargoes had to be off-loaded and rafted or lightered ashore, a slow, costly procedure. Then N. Ludington and Company contracted to supply square timbers with a minimum length of twenty-five feet for use in a breakwater along the waterfront. The harbor was dredged and land behind the breakwater filled. In 1848, Isaac Stephenson recalled, a ship had been lost in a storm at the foot of Lake Street, but after construction of the breakwater the site was "far inland." Changes at sawmill ports helped too. As late as 1860, the Menominee had no harbor improvements and only three and a half to four feet of water at its mouth; millowners had lumber-laden scows and rafts pulled out by hand to ships waiting in deeper water. Stephenson experimented with the use of a steam tug to pull cargoes of lumber from the Ludington mill at Marinette to waiting ships; this cut the cost of getting lumber to cargo vessels in half, made it available more cheaply in Chicago, and made that city's lumber dealers more competitive in the ever-widening circle of markets that railroads were opening in the Midwest.

Indeed, railroads made the biggest difference. In 1854, the Chicago and Rock Island reached the Mississippi, giving lumber from western Michigan and eastern Wisconsin access to river markets. Other lines followed. Favorable railroad rates to the river encouraged the flow of lumber, and Eau Claire millmen complained that Chicago's lumber often undersold theirs in the downriver markets in spite of the fact that the Chippewa, beside which their mills stood, drained directly into the Mississippi. Even those located on the Mississippi—such as W. J. Young and Company in Clinton, Iowa—found the competition hard to meet, especially since the quality of lumber arriving from the east tended to be higher than that from western mills. After completion of the Illinois and Michigan Canal in 1848, lumber also went from Chicago to St. Louis via the Illinois River, although the traffic never became what promoters had hoped, for the canal was narrow and shallow and had numerous locks. The problems of the Eau Claire operators could have been worse; as Michael Williams notes, Chicago's own explosive growth was "so great that about half of the lumber [shipped to it] was retained in the city for its own construction."[41]

In the 1850s, there were vast stretches of excellent untapped stands, and a plentitude of millsites. Moreover, sawmills were remarkably alike, for there was a limited range of available technology; thus, Isaac Stephenson argued, a millowner's competitive advantage—or simple survival—depended in large part on the efficiency of his woods operations. It was primarily in logging, he noted, "that the profits are made or the losses of operation sustained," for there individual effort, skill, and ingenuity had ample play. Philetus Sawyer's career illustrates the point. The Oshkosh lumberman opened a tract on the upper Wolf by making major improvements on the river and its tributaries, "a project his competitors thought impossible." Through this, Sawyer earned the capital he invested in the Chippewa valley and in railroads and thus acquired the fortune he rode into the United States Senate. Viewing this, Robert Nesbit wrote that most of Sawyer's "fortune thus came from shrewd timber speculations" rather than milling and marketing lumber. But the Wolf River purchase was not a speculation so much as a carefully calculated investment that illustrates the expertise of Sawyer and his minions in logging and driving. It was not always thus. W. J. Young's success was in large part a product of his extraordinary capacity as an innovative sawmill operator.[42]

Cruising—the locating and evaluating of stands—was "one of the most important aspects of lumbering," and the quality of work varied widely, for experienced "landlookers" were in short supply. Their work was simple, as John Nelligan put it, "done without much Rigmarole," although techniques improved as time passed. Nelligan reported that in the early days, "We often used to climb a tall tree . . . and from a point of vantage in the top of such a tree, usually on high ground, were able to locate and estimate timber in a large surrounding area with a fair degree of accuracy." Daniel Stanchfield provided further detail:

> *It was the custom of the cruiser to supply himself with some provisions, a blanket, a rifle or shotgun with plenty of ammunition, and a good stock of matches to start the nightly campfire, and then go alone, or with one or two companions, into the pathless forests, there to collect the information and estimates needed, remaining weeks or sometimes even months in the woods, and subsisting mostly on game, fish, and berries.*

Stanchfield had occasional confrontations with wolves while cruising, but the battle with insects was ongoing. "The mosquito, the gnat, and the moose-fly met and opposed us. They were first in the fight. The battle commenced early each morning and lasted all day . . . for days the blood flowed freely." Stanchfield and his companions returned from their first reconnaissance above St. Anthony "badly disfigured by the mosquitoes and flies . . . our necks were raw." Even for this man, who had worked in the Maine woods, notorious for its black flies, the experience was clearly daunting, and almost daily men accompanying him threatened to quit.[43]

The better cruisers gained considerable respect, and as their techniques became more sophisticated millmen depended upon them ever more heavily. Fred Burke, long active on the Menominee, recalled that Guy W. Holmes found a promising tract, cruised it, arranged an option to buy it for $750,000, and went to Chicago to find someone to make the purchase. He approached a leading lumberman and told him of his find. Holmes was "not well known to him," and the option was running out so there was no time to check his cruise, but the unnamed lumberman knew of Holmes's ability and his reputation for honesty and made the purchase sight unseen![44]

Rivalries between millmen in different localities were developing—most notably between those who shipped down the Mississippi and those who shipped to the same markets through Chicago. Other rivalries were taking shape too. Downriver lumbermen, especially those located near one another, competed for many of the same customers, creating attitudes that sometimes made it difficult for them to join in cooperative effort even when the need was manifest. F. E. Weyerhaeuser, Frederick's youngest son, later recalled, "Many members of the Mississippi Valley group were ready to fight one another upon the slightest pretext."[45]

Competition between Chippewa Falls and Eau Claire, destined to drag on for years, was especially intense. It first surfaced in 1856-1857 when each community sought the land office the federal government was planning for the Chippewa drainage, for a land office would give the city possessing it an advantage in the scramble to file on the richly forested government land of the area. Each community's leaders used connections and persuasive powers to obtain the office, but in the end money seems to have spoken the most loudly: someone reportedly paid $4,500 to have the office located in Eau Claire, and so it came to pass.[46]

In Wisconsin, Minnesota, and Iowa—as elsewhere—the Civil War temporarily interrupted the industry's growth. The Panic of 1857 undermined demand even before fighting began, while the uncertainties accompanying the outbreak of hostilities and the shortage of workers as young men marched off to war brought additional problems. But wartime needs soon revived demand, significantly aiding firms like that of Daniel Shaw, who had made large investments in land and plant just before the crash of 1857 and was in financial difficulty as a result. Wartime demand helped such firms avoid bankruptcy, but the respite was only temporary.

Meanwhile, wages went up due to the wartime shortage of workers, but the cost of living rose even faster. In response, sawmill workers in Oshkosh struck in June 1864. Their effort failed, but it was an ominous harbinger of events to come. Lumber purchases fell again immediately after the war; not until expansion in the hinterlands of the Mississippi River towns took up the postwar slack could millowners rest assured there would be ample demand for their cut.[47]

With prices up, small-time logger Ephraim Brown, in financial difficulty since 1857 and hoping to pay off his debts, operated two camps on the Yellow River in 1863-1864, cutting nearly two million feet; the next year he cut 1.3 million on the Yellow and Eau Claire, but with "too little money and incompetent men," he failed to get the logs to the mills. Others were more fortunate. In 1865 Ingram & Kennedy sent sizable shipments from its plant at Winona downriver to St. Louis, which "had been starved for lumber during recent years" but was in the market for lumber once again now that fighting had moved to more distant fields.[48]

Following the Civil War a second wave of lumbermen came to Wisconsin and Minnesota, especially to Minneapolis. This group was from Michigan, primarily the Saginaw area, and from Chicago, for manufacturers and dealers in those locales had venture capital a decade or two before most Wisconsin lumbermen were looking for investment opportunities other than in their already-established sawmills and the timberlands to feed them. Saginaw millmen fought tooth and claw as stands tributary to their mills became scarce, while Chicago's businessmen developed a speculative spirit that befitted that mushrooming city; as one historian has put it, "Chicago businessmen took every unfair advantage; they were feverishly speculative; their affairs were always unstable." The negative example of Chicagoans was common currency, and new arrivals from Saginaw were little if any better. These newcomers brought big business—and an increased level of rapacity—to lumbering in the two states, but much of what they did was remarkably familiar. Winter logging and skidding, spring drives, and the use of huge booms all echoed patterns developed earlier, especially in Maine, where conditions were similar. On the other hand, rafting lumber and logs on the Mississippi and other rivers initially utilized techniques developed on the Delaware, Hudson, and Susquehanna, although before long they were adjusted to conditions found on western rivers.[49]

After 1864 steamboats took over the handling of both lumber and log rafts. At first the boats towed rafts, but their operators soon found that pushing worked better: "In the late sixties and early seventies when the use of a steamboat in shoving and handling rafts had been successfully demonstrated," raftsman Walter Blair recalled, "every pilot wanted one . . . nearly every little boat on the Upper Mississippi and its tributaries was tried out and many of them continued in this new occupation as long as they lasted." With the addition of a smaller steamboat at the bow of the raft, maneuverability was greatly increased, no small factor on the tricky and dangerous Mississippi. Rafts soon changed too. The eastern system of rigid rafts held together by cross poles attached to pegs inserted in the outer logs was replaced by "brailed" rafts held together by an outer ring of boom logs and cross cables. Brailed rafts were easier to construct, eliminated the damage to logs from drilling holes for the pegs, and could be made larger than the old-style raft. Brailed rafts, said to be the invention of W. J. Young of Clinton, were standard by 1870; they remained so until the end of rafting. Rafting "slowly matured," Blair reported, " . . . growing larger with each yearly cycle until in the year 1880, the river traffic of rafts was reckoned one of the largest and most profitable industries in America."[50]

Sawmill operations in the region were hardly original either. Indeed, sawmill machinery was normally purchased in the East from the same manufacturers who supplied the equipment used in other locales. But imaginative sawmill operators sometimes made technological improvements. W. J. Young had his own machine shop in which he and his shop foreman worked out numerous changes in equipment design. Young never patented his improvements, and many were soon widely used. Still, these were mostly incremental changes, not major breakthroughs, and most of the region's millmen were less inventive than Young. As earlier, technological advances came in slow, small steps.[51]

For all the elements of déjà vu in the development of lumbering in Wisconsin and Minnesota, what was emerging was no carbon copy of what had gone before. For one thing, on earlier frontiers single centers had dominated, for they were located where they could control key watersheds. In many ways, Bangor was Maine's lumbering, Glens Falls New York's, Williamsport Pennsylvania's, and Saginaw-Bay City Michigan's. Other centers existed, but they were decidedly secondary. There was nothing equivalent in Wisconsin, Minnesota, and Iowa. Marinette, Chippewa Falls, Eau Claire, Oshkosh, Stillwater, La Crosse, Minneapolis, Cloquet, and others vied for dominance in the north, while downriver Rock Island, Clinton,

Davenport, Dubuque, and more added to the mix. North of Green Bay, a local newspaperman observed in 1871, "Every stream that is large enough to float a sawlog is [as] sure to breed sawmills along its banks as a swamp is to breed mosquitoes"—and as railroads extended operations away from waterways the numbers grew. Historian Randall Rohe identified forty important sawmill centers in northern Wisconsin alone. [52]

Geographical dispersion led to new elements of competition. Markets could be served from a number of different sources, forcing producers to pay as much attention to improving access to markets and reducing the cost of reaching them as to acquiring timber and logging and milling efficiently. Forward integration of operations became a major concern. As Isaac Stephenson observed, "The problem of transportation was [now] almost as important to the lumber industry as the problem of production itself." Michael Williams puts it more strongly: "Of all the improvements of the productive process, transportation was the most important factor in the acquisition of profits." Although lumber long continued to go from mill to market in rafts and barges, and to be carried over the great lakes in first sail- and then steam-powered vessels, as new lands continued to be opened further and further west of the Mississippi, marketing was increasingly done by railroad, a form of transportation that had never loomed large on earlier lumbering frontiers. [53]

The markets themselves were different too. A good portion of the cut of Maine had gone foreign, both to Europe and the Caribbean. The rest, like that of Pennsylvania and New York, largely went to long-settled East Coast areas where the growth of industry, commerce, and population was generating tremendous demand. For producers in Wisconsin, Minnesota, and downriver areas, foreign demand was negligible, that from the Atlantic states minor. Settlement and growth in agricultural lands to the south and west powered their industry; new lands, not old, were their markets—and the extent of this agricultural hinterland grew ever larger as railroads pushed west and feeder lines filled the interstices between the main lines. In these markets demand was vitally affected by the prices farmers received for their crops, especially wheat, by natural disasters such as drought and locust hordes, and by freight rates imperious railroad executives chose to charge. Such things had impinged but lightly on the industry in Maine, New York, and Pennsylvania, and not overwhelmingly even in Michigan, at least its half that faced and shipped much of its cut east.

The nature of the new order with its multiplicity of production centers and growing downriver and rail markets is perhaps best exemplified by the struggles over Chippewa Dells and Beef Slough. Chippewa Falls and

Eau Claire long fought for domination of the rich stands of the Chippewa drainage, stands as fine as American lumbermen had ever encountered; as Charles Twining has written, "[M]uch of the history of the Chippewa valley can be reduced to a description of the efforts to provide bigger and safer areas for holding sawlogs." Each community had its advantages. Chippewa Falls had unequalled sources of waterpower to drive its mills (although this dwindled in importance as sawmills shifted to steam); for its part, Eau Claire had better log storage potential than its upriver rival.[54]

Half Moon Lake was an oxbow near Eau Claire formed when the Chippewa changed course leaving a two-mile-long section cut off by a narrow, low-lying section of land. In 1857 Daniel Shaw and others formed the Half Moon Lake Company to build a wing dam and sheer boom on the river to divert logs via a short canal into the lake, which then served as a reservoir where logs could be safely stored until needed. Local leaders recognized that more storage would eventually be needed, and any new mills constructed on the river above the outlet to the canal could be served from Half Moon Lake with difficulty, if at all. A plan for a dam and other "improvements" a short distance upriver at Chippewa Dells—including a huge storage area at a big bend in the river and a mill race 1.2 miles long to connect it to Half Moon Lake—soon followed. Chippewa Falls' interests opposed the project vigorously, recognizing it would interfere with rafting their cut to market—which was difficult even under existing circumstances. Dale Peterson explained the issue succinctly: "Because the lumber industry dominated the life of the two towns, the entire communities were interested in the outcome." The editor of the *Eau Claire Free Press* did nothing to reduce tension; he reported in October 1861 that the Dells project was "to be so ingeniously constructed that all lumber from above can be taken around the dam on wheelbarrows."[55]

It would be years before the project came to fruition. In 1867 Chippewa Falls' representatives in the state legislature blocked an act granting a charter for the project, and in 1871, when Orrin Ingram and other Eau Claire lobbyists succeeded in getting a bill through, the governor vetoed it. Chippewa Falls' interests tried another tack; they sought (unsuccessfully) to have the falls declared the head of navigation on the Chippewa, which would have effectively banned log drives below their city and undermined the legality of proposed works at the Dells. When Chippewa Falls operators built a structure of their own at Eagle Rapids, a few miles above the Dells, some in Eau Claire welcomed it, thinking this might end opposition to their own plans, but the Eagle Rapids facilities had difficulties of their own, and when they washed out a second time they were not rebuilt.

Meanwhile, Eau Claire lumbermen built a network of booms and piers that extended for three-quarters of a mile along the river as a stopgap. In 1875, they again got a Dells charter bill through the legislature. This time there was no veto, but the state supreme court invalidated the franchise, saying it provided inadequate protection for the public interest—presumably meaning the movement of lumber rafts. The following year, Eau Claire's champions got yet another bill passed, this one ostensibly for an improved water supply for the city; again the governor signed, and this time the charter stood. Eau Claire voters quickly approved a $100,000 bond issue to finance construction. Deviously, Eau Claire's lumbermen used it to build the storage and sorting facilities they sought (as well as an improved water supply). The contest was over at last.[56]

In the meantime, another problem emerged for lumbermen on the Chippewa, be they from Eau Claire or Chippewa Falls: outside competition. Local operators saw the Chippewa drainage as their domain and sought to keep others out, both as buyers of timberland and of logs. But well-financed speculators moved in who could not be easily thwarted, for Orrin Ingram and the other operators in the drainage had not tied up the area's timberland, putting their funds into plants and equipment instead. Knowing of the vast stands upstream, especially along the Flambeau, the Chippewa's well-forested main tributary, they had remained confident logs would always be available. Henry W. Sage was among the interlopers. He had made a fortune in Michigan's lumber industry and, with that state's stands dwindling, was looking for new places to put his capital. He invested in railroads, ore lands, and timber, outlays that he did not consider speculative ventures, merely investments. Dorilus Morrison was another. A timber broker, Morrison attended state and federal land sales to pick up tracts for his own operations and for resale to others, be they Wisconsin operatives or outsiders.[57] Henry M. Putnam, land agent for Ezra Cornell and then for the Cornell University Land Department, was a third; indeed, Dale Peterson considered him the "most important western land agent and speculator." Such individuals were not producers seeking to sell lumber in markets served by the millowners of the Chippewa basin, but they competed for stands, drove up their price, and weakened the control of resident operators. When locals sought to prevent sales of timberland to downriver millmen, Putnam was unsupportive, believing—probably correctly—that such action would hurt the prices Cornell University received for its pineland. Indeed, he wanted to encourage outside buyers in order to increase competition and thus prices. As he wrote to an associate: "I am anxious to fasten them on our river now & draw them from the St. Croix & upper Miss[issippi] &

from the Wis[consin] & Black rivers to this river." Not all the speculators were magnates; smaller holders "performed a service by providing stumpage on credit. By agreeing to deferred payment, they made the timber more [legally] accessible to logging contractors and small time mill operators. . . . [The] federal and state governments offered no better solutions."[58]

Orrin Ingram was a leader of operators from Eau Claire and Chippewa Falls who formed rings to keep down prices by not competing at land sales and by shutting out Mississippi River millmen. In September 1883, the editor of the *Mississippi Valley Lumberman and Manufacturer* wrote: an "outsider has no more business going into the logging business on the Chippewa river waters than a small boy has to go feeding Jumbo on snuff. He is liable to get snuffed out." Such was hardly the case. The efforts of Ingram and his allies were largely unsuccessful. When Daniel Shaw needed financial aid—as he often did—he sometimes turned to downriver sources. Other operators probably did too. This encouraged the growth of the downriver foothold on the Chippewa. Moreover, there were always independents in the basin who were not parties to the collusion, government land policies aimed to encourage settlement by making sales easy and cheap, and the widely dispersed resource base made local monopolies virtually impossible. Insofar as they were successful, efforts to keep the price of timberland low probably only served to make it more attractive to outsiders.[59]

Downriver sawmill operators were even more threatening to lumbermen on the Chippewa than outside speculators. The host of mills along the Mississippi from La Crosse to St. Louis needed logs. Franklin Hough found sawmills at seventeen locations downriver, with Clinton and Davenport, Iowa, the largest producers. In the 1860s, encouraged by Henry Putnam, downriver mills turned increasingly to the Chippewa and soon became major competitors with local producers for logs. By 1877, Hough found, sawmills in Iowa alone cut 376 million board feet, and most of their sawlogs came from the Chippewa.[60]

Although far from log sources, downriver sawmills were formidable competitors for those upstream. When Daniel M. Dulany, in charge of the Empire Lumber Company's operations in Hannibal, Missouri, computed the relative expenses, he found it cost $6.32 per thousand to mill in the north and ship lumber downstream, but only $4.96 to ship logs and then manufacture in Hannibal. Figures varied over time, but log transportation was sufficiently inexpensive for downriver mills to remain competitive year after year. In 1863 it cost $2.25 per thousand to raft logs from Stillwater to Clinton; in 1874 it cost but $1.10 to raft them from Beef Slough to Clinton, and in 1881 only $1.05. In 1862, W. J. Young contracted with William

Gilmore to fell and raft logs from the St. Croix; from forest to mill Gilmore's costs totaled $7.59 per thousand; at the time, rafts of lumber sold in Clinton for $11 per thousand. Thus, Young and other downriver manufacturers could compete both with producers in Eau Claire and Chippewa Falls and those shipping by rail or canal via Chicago.[61]

The extensive plants in Eau Claire and Chippewa Falls depended upon stands Young and other outsiders were eyeing—and, before long, tapping. Moreover, if owners of Chippewa timber sold their logs to downriver buyers, the value added by manufacture would be lost to the Chippewa valley, costing the area a good half of the profit the logs might otherwise yield. Faced with these circumstances, Orrin Ingram, as noted earlier, stepped forward to lead efforts to block outside lumbermen from the Chippewa drainage.[62]

Ingram and other resident operators soon recognized the futility of trying to prevent outsiders from buying Chippewa timber, so they concentrated instead on preventing the exportation of logs to downstream mills. Control of the river—and the vital means of transportation it offered—became the focus of competition. The contest came to a head at Beef Slough, located at the mouth of the Chippewa. Indeed, Michael Williams has observed, "The history of the operations of the Beef Slough boom encapsulates the spectacular rise and fall of the Lake States lumber industry."[63]

Beef Slough brings into the picture Frederick Weyerhaeuser, a German immigrant who arrived in Rock Island, Illinois, in 1856. He soon was in charge of a lumberyard in nearby Coal Valley and then during the Panic of 1857, seeing a sawmill in Rock Island that had been idled by fire, leased and repaired it and began sawing lumber. In 1860, in partnership with his brother-in-law, F. C. A. Denkmann, Weyerhaeuser bought the mill outright. Remarkably successful, Weyerhaeuser gradually established himself as a leader among downriver millmen and over the years that followed built the largest empire of forest operations in the nation's history. At first Weyerhaeuser & Denkmann concentrated on milling and marketing, buying sawlogs on the open market rather than purchasing timberland. So too did various other downriver operatives, the bulk of the logs coming from the Black and St. Croix, from whence logs had been rafted since the late 1830s. Weyerhaeuser & Denkmann did so not because they were short on capital with which to buy timberland, but because they lacked the experience to purchase intelligently. That came in time, and by the early 1870s Weyerhaeuser was investing in timber on the Chippewa, where he found large tracts available. With experience, Weyerhaeuser found that he liked "the woods life." He became a superb evaluator of stands; as his grandson put it, the elder Weyerhaeuser "loved to buy timber. He was possessed of a deep and abiding faith in the forests and was heard by his associates to remark that 'the only mistake we ever made was in not buying pine trees whenever offered.' " Weyerhaeuser's ability to evaluate stands, his faith in timber investments, and his skill in human relations, rather than expertise as a sawmill operator, lay behind his subsequent success. Whether as a buyer of logs or timber, Weyerhaeuser was a key part of the downriver forces pitted against Orrin Ingram and his allies on the Chippewa. His "cool hand and the mutual respect members of the [downriver] pool had for each other tended to avoid the scrambles that they might otherwise have fallen into."[64]

The story of the contest is complex, details varying depending upon to whose account one turns, but historians agree on the main points if not all the particulars.[65] Logs destined for downriver operators had to be driven down the Chippewa to the Mississippi, where they were made into rafts for their final journey to the sawmills. These logs shared the Chippewa with lumber rafts from upriver mills and along the Mississippi with these plus a variety of other river traffic, all the while navigating bars, shoals, and other impediments offered by the rivers. As increasing numbers of users jostled one another, friction rose, and when one or another sought to introduce "improvements" on the river to aid his operations, the tension was palpable. Downriver interests complained the "Chippewa millmen were monopolizing the river," hardly legal since it was a public waterway. In this atmosphere, in the mid-sixties downstream operators decided to build booming, scaling, and sorting facilities at Beef Slough. There, where the Chippewa debouched sluggishly into the Mississippi, they would make up log rafts for the journey down the Mississippi to the sawmills. Ingram and his allies recognized this would make supplying logs to downriver mills easier and cheaper and thus make their owners more aggressive competitors for the timber of the Chippewa drainage. Moreover, it was evident such facilities would make the passage of lumber rafts into the Mississippi more difficult. They set out to block the project at all cost.[66]

Each side sought a charter to build works at Beef Slough—the downriver millmen to expedite their operations, the Chippewa interests to control the site to prevent its use by their rivals. Before long, the competition moved from the Wisconsin legislature to the river, and in July 1867 the so-called Beef Slough War commenced. Working through their front, the Chippewa River Improvement Company, Ingram and the upriver operators built a simple dam across the mouth of Beef Slough. It would, they claimed, force water to stay in the main channel of the Chippewa, thereby deepening it and improving navigation. Their purpose was clearly otherwise: they wanted to bar downriver interests from using the slough for storage, sorting, and raft construction. Recognizing there might be a reaction, they stationed armed guards to protect the dam—but to no avail. A group of vigilantes—or, as some would have it, a posse led by the sheriff of Buffalo County—promptly arrived and tore out the dam.[67]

Events took a decisive turn the following year. Downriver interests had been unable to wring a charter for facilities at Beef Slough from Wisconsin's legislature, but through legal legerdemain (and the shadowy activity of James H. Bacon) they managed to get control of the Chippewa River Improvement Company's franchise and, under it, promptly built the facilities they desired. However, for these to be effective, logs had to arrive from far upriver, making their way past the booms and dams of every sawmill along the route—and if the logs were halted by these upstream facilities, Beef Slough would be useless. The Beef Slough interests had a right to use the river for transportation, and boom operators were obliged to let the logs of others through with reasonable promptness, but right and practice did not always coincide, and "reasonable promptness" was open to a variety of interpretations. On most rivers, simple log exchanges and informal cooperation normally took place under such circumstances, but things were hardly normal on the Chippewa. The two sides failed to come to an agreement.[68]

Leaving nothing to chance, spokesmen for the Beef Slough group announced they expected their logs to be let through upstream booms without delay, implying that *they* would judge what was reasonable delay and not hesitate to take action if it were deemed excessive. Their warning went unheeded, so when their logs were held up at the boom in Eau Claire with the explanation that the facilities were inadequate for separating logs destined for downriver from the logs of the Eau Claire sawmills, Bacon and one hundred and fifty employees of the Beef Slough interests took matters into their own hands. Arriving in the dark of night, they cut the offending boom to release the impounded logs; upstream operators had stationed armed guards, but they were too few to halt the action. Faced with losing an entire season's logs downstream, Eau Claire operatives turned to the local sheriff, who organized a posse and arrested the boom cutters while local lumbermen scrambled to repair the damage and save their remaining logs. Bacon and his chief lieutenant had to post a $10,000 bond requiring they keep the peace for six months. For the moment things were quiet, but there was no guarantee boom cutting would not be resumed. It was a possibility Ingram, Daniel Shaw, and other Eau Claire millmen dared not ignore, and they joined their boom crews for long hours to get their logs safely into Half Moon Lake and out of the way of the rest of the drive destined for Beef Slough. Tension and bickering continued, but an uneasy truce prevailed: the Beef Slough War was over.

The drive itself was not totally successful. Downriver interests had hoped to drive some thirty to fifty million feet of logs to Beef Slough. Only ten to fifteen million actually arrived (reports vary as to the number), and the Beef Slough company faced bankruptcy. But precedent had been established and great promise remained, so in 1870 Weyerhaeuser, "not inclined to give up an undertaking which seemed to him to have great merit," joined with two others to lease the boom "to see whether they could put new life into the project." He soon persuaded an even larger group to found the Mississippi River Logging Company. By transferring his stock the following year, Weyerhaeuser effectively merged the Beef Slough operations—now with a charter granted earlier that year explicitly authorizing its activities—into the new entity. The company got off to a rocky start. Lorenzo Schricker, its first president, was a poor administrator, lacked tact, and drank too much, but late in 1872 members chose Weyerhaeuser to replace him (even though his plant was far from the largest on the Middle Mississippi). The Mississippi River Logging Company was soon prospering, providing unified control of log drives, booming, and rafting, and making purchases of timberland, the logs from which were divided among member firms. This approach was so superior to the old system of competition that within a short time Weyerhaeuser had drawn nearly all substantial operators from the boom downstream to St. Louis into the enterprise. Its members would elect him president again and again.[69]

Troubles continued, however. Chippewa basin operators persuaded federal officials to bring suit against the company for interfering with navigation, but the company prevailed in court, and when the Eau Claire Lumber Company sought a court order to close Beef Slough because its works used a type of fin boom patented by Eau Claire's Levi Pond, Beef Slough interests obtained a patent for a slightly different fin boom, forcing an out-of-court settlement that allowed them to continue to operate. It was now clear the facilities at Beef Slough would continue supplying logs to downriver mills on a regular basis. Over the years that followed, it handled more and more—in 1879 the volume reached two hundred and fifty million feet. One observer recalled, "Mr. Weyerhaeuser was seldom seen at the Slough, [but] his spirit was always evident."[70]

Gradually bigger, more powerful steamboats went into service to move log rafts from Beef Slough to the mills and to handle the lumber rafts of

Steamboats with log rafts on the Mississippi near Beef Slough. Such crowding was the bane of other users of the river. Courtesy Wisconsin Historical Society, #Whi-68937.

people like Daniel Shaw who continued to use them to send their cut to downriver markets. Walter Blair reported that during the key years of 1879-1881 the vessel he captained, the *Silver Wave*, was constantly busy moving rafts from the slough to the Mussers' sawmill in Muscatine, Iowa. There were numerous other steamboats at work as well, most notably those of J. W. and Samuel Van Sant, who built the first large steam-powered boat solely for towing logs and lumber on the Mississippi. In 1872-1873, Van Sant vessels reportedly "towed more logs and lumber to market down the river than any other line of boats ever constructed." For its part, Beef Slough became "one of the busiest river ports in the world" with up to 837 departures in a single season. During its peak, there were 125 boats regularly employed in running rafts from there to the five mills in Clinton. However, loose logs bedeviled raft boats and other craft, especially between Beef Slough's sheer boom and Reads Landing. Blair recalled they were "often too thick to run through, especially when the Chippewa was rising," and steamboats had to tie up until the heavy run was over. Wing dams (jetties) installed after 1878 helped during low water and reduced the buildup of sand bars at crucial points, but navigation on the Mississippi was never without its challenges.[71]

All this led to frequent complaints, but a *modus operandi* developed on the Chippewa and Mississippi; everyone realized they could be mightily inconvenienced by the others but that all were there to stay. Indicative of the uneasy truce that prevailed, Frederick Weyerhaeuser held up one of his drives for eight days to allow operators at Chippewa Dells time to get their logs into storage so his could pass. When periodic confrontations did occur, there was more than a bit of irony involved: in the past Eau Claire's operators had been blithely unconcerned when their facilities interfered with the downstream shipment of lumber rafts from Chippewa Falls; now they complained mightily when those at Beef Slough did the same to theirs. A sort of stalemate had developed, with neither side dominant. Indeed, as the downriver interests became firmly established on the Chippewa and the overall scale of their operations there increased, adding to the crowding on the river, toleration—even cooperation—grew more imperative, especially after a lack of snow in 1877 resulted in low water in the spring, an almost total failure of that year's drive, a short sawing season, and no profits that year for the mills in Eau Claire and Chippewa Falls.[72]

Then came the flood of 1880. In early June a series of rainstorms pounded the Chippewa drainage. At the beginning of the season log drivers had suffered from low water, now the streams began to flood. The Chippewa rose quickly—and kept rising until it crested at twenty-four feet above the low-water mark. Residents along the river had never seen anything like it. One after another, splash dams upstream washed out, adding to the flood. Eugene Shaw later recalled: "[W]ater rose so high that logs ran across the main land in the big bend of the Dells pond, mowing down trees as if they were grass." The main boom held, but 150 to 250 million feet of logs—some banked awaiting the drive, some already en route, and some stored along the river—hurtled past Eau Claire, some flushed almost to St. Louis before going aground as far as three miles from the river's normal bank. Daniel Shaw lost some two million feet of logs; others lost many more. With much of a season's log supply downstream beyond reach, Eau Claire's millmen faced disaster.

Frederick Weyerhaeuser seized the opportunity—but not in ways some upriver operators feared. Rather than forcing a vindictive settlement, he looked to the long run and worked with representatives from Eau Claire to craft a settlement that would serve their mutual interests and smooth the way for future cooperation. He addressed two problems: the recovery of logs stranded downstream from Eau Claire, and a log exchange so upriver mills could operate for the rest of the season. He worked out a salvage agreement with Orrin Ingram (the main negotiator for the Eau Claire group) stipulating that so far as practical local farmers would be hired to do the work and setting fees, payment levels, and a cut-off date for operations. Weyerhaeuser and Ingram also crafted a log-exchange agreement, the key element in their negotiations. The Mississippi River Logging Company agreed to take all logs washed down by the flood, credit them to their upstream owners (as indicated by the brands they bore), and provide an equal volume of their own logs from upriver in exchange. The agreements soon proved their worth: Ingram & Kennedy acquired 25.5 million feet of logs that otherwise would have been lost, and the board footage sawn at the upriver mills in 1880 actually exceeded the previous year's cut by some 20 percent.[73]

Even before the flood, it was clear lumbermen on the Chippewa were not going to be able to block entry of downriver interests into "their" forests, and they had been moving toward an acceptance of cooperation. In the years that followed, it became a reality. According to legal historian James Willard Hurst, Weyerhaeuser's "private treaty of 1881 . . . defined the problem as that of rationalizing the Chippewa Valley productive potential" and did a better job of working toward that end than the state's legislature and courts. As cooperation grew, the division between upriver and downriver forces became less clear: Ingram & Kennedy added a sawmill (the Standard Lumber Company) to its lumberyard at Dubuque, while Weyerhaeuser arranged a joint purchase of the big Chippewa Lumber & Boom Company of Chippewa Falls, a firm which previously had opposed cooperation and had been "the last important impediment to the unobstructed passage of logs" down the Chippewa.[74]

Before the end of 1880, those operating on the Chippewa had agreed to replace ad hoc, one-time agreements with a permanent organization. In effect the downriver Mississippi River Logging Company was expanded to include upriver lumbermen. Chartered in Wisconsin in June 1881, the Chippewa Logging Company (the "Chippewa pool") not only merged the drives of different operators, thus giving improved control and significant economies of scale, but also operated the Chippewa Lumber & Boom Company's sawmill, bought and cut timber, divided the resulting logs among the various member mills, and set quotas. Thus, in addition to logs from its own land and crews, each member got logs from the pool in proportion to the amount of stock it owned. In 1882, the Chippewa Logging Company even built 10.5 miles of railroad to provide access to the main Soo line from a large tract it had acquired from Cornell University.[75]

There was no question as to who was in charge of this diverse undertaking. Sixty-five percent of the stock went to downriver interests, only 35 percent to those upriver. Moreover, only Frederick Weyerhaeuser had authority to make purchases for the organization without consulting others, for as fellow lumberman W. J. Young put it, "Mr. Weyerhaeuser is not in the habit of making mistakes." Indeed, Bernhardt Kleven notes, "[T]his marked the real beginning of the great Weyerhaeuser lumbering empire." While upriver millmen might bridle at the Rock Island lumberman's dominance, there was little they could do about it. Knapp, Stout and Company, whose sawmills in and near Menominie made it the largest in the Chippewa drainage—and perhaps in the world—remained independent, apparently because its owners felt strong enough to operate without Weyerhaeuser's help—or interference—and because in 1872 the firm had begun marketing by rail. Knapp-Stout was the exception; over the years that followed, five of every seven logs floated down the Chippewa belonged to the pool. All in all, the arrangement was quite successful. It reduced friction among firms, including competition that drove up the price of timberland and logs, and it made long-range planning easier. Revealingly, of the four large new sawmills established on the river during the two years following creation of the pool, only the two that belonged to it prospered.[76]

The pool was not without critics. Charges of monopoly resounded, with comparisons to John D. Rockefeller's unification of refining and pipeline operations in the oil industry. In reality the attacks were absurd: in sharp contrast to Standard Oil, the pool controlled less than 2 percent of the nation's lumber industry. It provided integrated operation on only one of many major lumber-producing drainages, and even there was not fully dominant. The largest sawmill firm in the drainage (Knapp-Stout) remained outside the pool, yet it and other non-member firms used the facilities of the Chippewa Logging Company on the same terms as members. Still, controversy swirled, and the pool even became an issue in the Wisconsin election of 1882.[77]

Having come to dominance on the Chippewa, Weyerhaeuser began to look further afield. His eyes soon settled on the St. Croix. As the next major tributary of the Mississippi above the Chippewa, the St. Croix drainage's heavily forested nine million acres were a natural area of expansion for the Rock Island lumberman. Little there was new: the species, the modes of logging, and the means of getting the cut to the mills were all familiar; moreover, Weyerhaeuser had purchased logs from the St. Croix from his earliest days as a millowner in Rock Island, and his existing sawmills could be used and established markets served if he now entered the St. Croix drainage to become a timberland owner and logging operator.

Lumbering had long taken place along the St. Croix. As has been shown, it even preceded statehood, and the potential of the region's forests figured in drawing the boundary between Wisconsin and Minnesota. Potential became reality, output expanding until, as one historian put it, "St. Croix and lumber were almost synonymous." Indeed, although it yielded somewhat less than Saginaw or the Chippewa, the lumber industry on the St. Croix lasted longer; and its output was no small item—from the beginning of rafting until 1903 the St. Croix yielded an estimated 12.5 billion feet of logs. In 1892 one company there turned out over thirty-two million feet of lumber.[78]

Much of the expansion on the St. Croix was made possible by its boom. Many of its early operators were from Maine, and they soon pushed for a large boom to replace the initial system in which lumbermen collected logs from the river at their own makeshift booms, rafted them to their individual mills, and then engaged in paper exchanges to balance accounts with other millmen whose logs they had corralled with their own. Responding, in 1851 Minnesota's territorial legislature chartered a boom company for the river, the first such charter it issued. Installed near Osceola (twenty-one miles above Stillwater), the boom quickly became a focal point for sales and contracting in addition to log collection. Production expanded rapidly. Observers said, however facetiously, that if a visitor wanted to see someone from the St. Croix valley, he should go to the boom before trying the man's house. But by 1854 operators in Stillwater were cutting two-thirds of the lumber manufactured on the St. Croix, and they wanted a boom closer to their mills; among their number was Hersey, Staples & Hall, which in 1854 erected a sawmill described as the finest in the West (the firm and its successors would continue to manufacture at Stillwater into the twentieth century). Stillwater interests soon got a law passed to accommodate their needs, and in 1857 constructed a new boom three miles above Stillwater. For some years, the firm operated both booms, and when it finally closed the upriver facilities lumbermen in Osceola and Marine-on-St. Croix, left without effective service, complained mightily.[79]

The scale of operations at the St. Croix boom was tremendous. By 1854 there were already eighty-two ox-team crews operating on the St. Croix. Twenty years later, a single raft left Stillwater with 1.2 million feet of logs; in one week the following year, eight steamboats, making fifteen separate trips, departed with rafts for mills as far downriver as Burlington, Iowa. Early on, the boom company handled logs for fifty-two separate firms a year; later the volume rose to three hundred million feet of logs for over two hundred owners; and in 1890, it surpassed four hundred million feet.

Such results made the boom company the first in the Lake States to turn a profit—to say nothing of benefits it supplied to sawmill operators and the communities where their plants were located. In 1873, it returned a 32 percent profit; in spite of the onset of depression it did even better the following year.[80]

The boom was not without its problems. The original charter specified it should not interfere with navigation on the river. This was no small matter, for many communities along the stream depended on steamboats for supplies and transportation to the outside world, but log drives frequently jammed on the St. Croix and when collected behind the boom sometimes blocked it for six to ten miles upstream, making steamboat navigation impossible. Boom operators arranged for wagons to haul goods around the obstructed areas and tried to keep steamboat channels past the logs open, but their efforts were only marginally effective and complaints continued. Things got worse after 1884 when Martin Mower—"a cantankerous, penny-pinching son of the Pine Tree State"—got control of the boom and ran it without concern for navigation. As rail lines reached the river, dependence on steamboats declined, but for communities such as Franconia that were not reached by railroad the problem remained, and in the end some simply withered and died.[81]

Onto this stage stepped Frederick Weyerhaeuser, thus setting in motion the expansion beyond the Chippewa that would bring him to preeminence in the industry. The factors involved deserve analysis. What was it that brought Weyerhaeuser to the fore rather than any one of a number of others who initially were at least as well positioned?

Aside from purchases of timberland through the Chippewa Logging Company, Weyerhaeuser and various partners had gradually acquired other stands in northern Wisconsin, oftentimes in places freshly reached by railroad. Until then, river transportation had been central in determining the value of forests (which had necessitated reinventing legal rights to rivers as common carriers). For the time being, Weyerhaeuser's operations were still focused primarily on waterways, but a major shift had begun.

In 1883, in partnership with two local operators and the Mussers of Muscatine, Weyerhaeuser bought a tract on Moose River, a tributary of the upper St. Croix. Other purchases followed, and the area soon became a major source of logs not only for the Weyerhaeuser and Musser sawmills, but also for others down the Mississippi. Frustrated by haphazard operations on the St. Croix and recognizing how vital its boom was becoming, Weyerhaeuser sought to acquire it from Mower, who stoutly resisted, for he wanted nothing to do with Weyerhaeuser. When the latter, operating through a front man, finally won control of the boom in 1889, it came through lease, not purchase. As a vital link in the flow of logs to downriver operations, the boom—coupled with coordinated log drives of the sort instituted earlier by the Chippewa Logging Company—became more and more important, especially as production on the Chippewa declined. By 1892, 47 percent of the logs sawn at Weyerhaeuser & Denkmann's plant in Rock Island came from the St. Croix.[82]

In taking over the St. Croix boom, Weyerhaeuser inherited the ill will Mower had engendered. Indeed, complaints grew stronger than ever. As on the Chippewa, locals resented the intrusion of outsiders into "their" woods. Moreover, Weyerhaeuser's minions ran the boom with little concern for other users of the river; as William Rector has written, they treated it as "a giant log funnel and nothing more." The local press was unrelenting in its attacks on the result, an "octopus" that "cared not what people thought, said, or wrote."[83]

The leap from the Chippewa to the St. Croix eased the way for subsequent ones of greater distance and, in some cases, greater consequence. The huge Weyerhaeuser syndicate of later years was on its way, but further analysis is needed to understand what was transpiring. In the 1850s, Weyerhaeuser had been one of many who established sawmills along the Mississippi to manufacture lumber from logs cut far upstream. Nearer the pineries there were a host of additional mills, many appearing to have at least as much promise as Weyerhaeuser's. What was it that brought Frederick Weyerhaeuser to the fore and kept him there over the years that followed? Various explanations have been offered.

The simplest answer is that provided by Charles Edward Russell: "The manner in which he [Weyerhaeuser] was projected into the business that made him a prince among the wealthy is calculated to foster faith in the theory of luck as the controlling factor in human success. . . . Frederick Weyerhaeuser stumbled upon riches as a man might bark his shin on a log going down the lane of a dark night." To be sure, Weyerhaeuser and Denkmann were able to buy their first mill at Rock Island "for a song" because it had been damaged by fire and the owner was in financial difficulty. The purchase was fortuitous, but that alone hardly explains what followed.[84]

More was involved, and it reveals much about the industry and how it was evolving. Knapp, Stout and Company of Menomonie, Wisconsin, provides a useful starting point. The firm began about the same time as Weyerhaeuser & Denkmann, but was located nearer its source of raw materials. It had a management team with complementary talents—Henry L. Stout of Dubuque provided much of the capital and focused on marketing along the Mississippi; John H. Knapp supervised the sawmills and company interests; Andrew Tainter took care of timber purchases and logging; and William Wilson focused on rafting and lumber transportation. The firm expanded repeatedly. By the 1870s, enjoying a near-monopoly in a vast area of superb timber, it was alleged to be the largest lumber operation in the world. In 1876 it took five hundred men to conduct its spring drive. From 1875 through 1879 it was some 75 percent larger than its closest rival in the upper Mississippi drainage (the Eau Claire Lumber Company), almost triple Ingram & Kennedy's plant, and some four times larger than Weyerhaeuser's at Rock Island. In 1871 Knapp-Stout sent thirty rafts (thirty-one million feet of lumber) to markets down the Mississippi, and soon after pioneered in marketing by rail, contracting with the West Wisconsin and Sioux City lines for that purpose. For a time, this gave it an advantage over less aggressive competitors. Knapp-Stout benefited further when these lines combined with others in the late seventies to form what was popularly known as the Wisconsin Lumber Line, a combination that set rail rates low enough to allow sawmills along it to compete successfully west of the Mississippi with Chicago wholesalers and mills located on the river itself. By 1878 the company reportedly had 2,500 employees; at its height, its sawmills turned out 106 million board feet a year; by 1896, Robert Fries estimates, it had sawed two billion feet of lumber. In addition to expanding its mill repeatedly to make such production possible, the firm purchased additional timberland, buying some one hundred and twenty thousand acres of federal land between 1865 and 1888 and additional acres from Cornell University and various railroads (thirty thousand acres from Cornell alone in 1880). Moreover, Knapp-Stout had highly integrated operations with sawmills, pine lands, numerous logging camps, wholesale and retail lumberyards, steamboats for raft towing, and a bank, general merchandise stores, farms, and flour mills to serve its sawmill workers and loggers. In both 1888 and 1898, census data reveal, Knapp-Stout was the largest lumber firm in the upper Mississippi area (although by 1898 its margin over two Minneapolis companies was slight). As Joseph Shafer noted, "In all probability no other agency was more valuable in opening up, settling, and developing central western Wisconsin."[85]

Knapp-Stout was located on and dominated the drainage of the Menomonie (or Red Cedar) River, which entered the Chippewa well below

Eau Claire. Its location not only made the firm a non-participant in much of the controversy that set Eau Claire and Chippewa Falls at loggerheads, but also reduced pressure on it to work with others to find solutions to its (or the industry's) problems. Knapp-Stout's early decision to market by railroad added to this relative independence. It eventually built other mills; in addition to two plants in Menomonie,[86] by 1878 it had four others near its pineries and one each in Dubuque and St. Louis. These additions appear to have been the result of re-investing profits, not any great expansion of ownership. After its incorporation in 1878, Knapp-Stout continued under the control of the same handful of individuals as previously. This stood in sharp contrast to the industry as a whole. Robert Nesbit found that in 1897 the Wisconsin lumber industry was made up of 101 corporations and 66 partnerships, yet had a total of only 632 stockholders and 105 partners—in other words, it was characterized by a complex web of ownership with a considerable overlap and numerous multiple holdings. It was a web from which closely held Knapp, Stout and Company remained largely aloof, and as a result it was overtaken by the growing circle of Weyerhaeuser interests. Robert Fries summed it up neatly: "Knapp, Stout & Co. represented what was perhaps the maximum growth of which a single firm was capable. It came as near being a monopolistic unit as the economies of the lumber industry permitted." But by staying aloof, Knapp-Stout was gradually left behind.[87]

I. Stephenson & Company was similar, although it never dominated its area of operation north of Green Bay as completely as Knapp-Stout did its own. Isaac Stephenson acquired part ownership in the N. Ludington & Company sawmill in Marinette in 1858 after working as a timber cruiser, independent logger, and sawmill manager. He proved to be a good judge of pineland, an efficient logging operator, and an ingenious manager who devised effective solutions to the challenges of transporting lumber from his mills to Chicago and other markets. In time Stephenson invested in other sawmills in the area, including at Peshtigo, Wisconsin, and Escanaba, Michigan. His success brought him a personal fortune of over $100 million. But Stephenson was tied to Marinette and sank considerable money into its businesses and public enterprises (including the Stephenson National Bank, an opera house, and a public library[88]), rather than looking for new forests into which to expand as production in the Menominee area dwindled. Moreover, as he became a community leader, Stephenson was drawn into politics, eventually becoming a United States senator, and left the day-to-day management of his enterprises in the hands of others. Frederick Weyerhaeuser never followed this course. He was a lumberman first, last, and always, seeking to accumulate a fortune to pass on to his heirs—and thereby established a Weyerhaeuser family mantra that each generation must safeguard the financial future of the next. As custodian of the family's assets, he had little time for political diversions and always kept close personal control over his business affairs.[89]

Weyerhaeuser was not alone in careful fiscal management, and while Weyerhaeuser & Denkmann's vulnerable geographic location may have put a priority on expanding its area of operation and bringing in a widening circle of cooperating partners—thus giving it an advantage over Knapp, Stout & Co. and I. Stephenson—there were many other downriver firms similarly located and faced with similar challenges. Yet it was Weyerhaeuser, not any of the others, that came to the forefront. This requires some explanation.

Nearly all major operations, both downriver and on the Chippewa, started as partnerships. Even after firms turned to the corporate form (largely in the 1870s), ownership continued to be closely held; most were still partnerships in terms of operation, if not of law.[90] Partners can be an aid or a drag, a sort of sea anchor holding a firm back from bold expansion. In this, Frederick Weyerhaeuser was fortunate. He and Denkmann had complementary talents. Denkmann ran the Rock Island sawmill (and four others) so well Weyerhaeuser felt compelled to visit only a few times each year, thus freeing him to focus on logging and timberland acquisition and buying him time to learn the nuances of woods operations. Through this, some claimed, "Denkmann made Weyerhaeuser." Indeed, Denkmann realized how important his role was and occasionally expressed irritation when Weyerhaeuser got all the credit for their success; "Weyerhaeuser, Weyerhaeuser, always Weyerhaeuser and never Denkmann," he once blurted in frustration.[91] In spite of tensions, the two made a compatible team, and those who joined as their operations expanded brought additional strengths. Weyerhaeuser's genial personality—what a later generation would call his "people skills"—helped keep the combinations that made up the syndicate together. Although their personalities were quite different—Denkmann had a volatile temper, Weyerhaeuser was more easygoing—they both engendered an intense loyalty from those who worked with them. As the authors of *Timber and Men* observed, "Patient, shrewdly humorous [and] optimistic," after first venturing into the forests of the Chippewa Basin, Weyerhaeuser soon won the trust of "loggers, millowners and rivermen." Weyerhaeuser's ability to engender trust and loyalty continued to serve him well over the years. As historian George Sieber noted, Weyerhaeuser held the Chippewa pool "together with a personal touch which inspired confidence" and was "of greater stature as a . . . leader of sawmill men than as a sawmill operator himself."[92]

In contrast, many competitors' firms suffered from internal differences. Orrin Ingram and Alexander Dole of Ottawa—one of his original partners and the source of much of their firm's initial capital—struggled for dominance; when Ingram & Kennedy bought Dole out, it left the firm saddled with unwonted debt; and while Kennedy wanted to keep the firm firmly under the control of Ingram and himself, Ingram was more comfortable with the evolving corporate-cooperative form. Daniel Shaw and other firms dependent upon eastern capital suffered from similar differences with financial backers who were concerned with getting good returns on their investments and often sought dividends rather than plowing profits back into expansion.[93]

Again, more needs to be said, for Weyerhaeuser & Denkmann was far from alone in having a compatible and complementary management team. As Frederick Kohlmeyer shows, Laird, Norton & Co. had one too. W. J. Young and C. Lamb & Son of Clinton and the Mussers in Muscatine seem to have been similarly blessed, as was Knapp, Stout & Co. Indeed, the latter prospered, James Willard Hurst concluded, not only because it dominated a well-endowed watershed, but also through "superior leadership."[94] With neither location nor the quality of his management team sufficient to explain the increasing dominance of Frederick Weyerhaeuser, it would seem necessary to look at the man himself to determine what brought him to the fore.

Many lumbermen, Charles Twining notes, got their start because they had the mechanical skills to run a small sawmill successfully, but by 1867 the management of men was becoming as important as the mechanical demands of milling, and many never managed to make the transition; to them, desk work was "akin to retirement." Others, such as Daniel Shaw, proved excessively rigid in adhering to approaches that had served well in the past, even as they grew less appropriate.[95]

Weyerhaeuser was of a different sort. The authors of *Timber and Men*—three leading business historians, working with the help of a phalanx of graduate students—evaluated him with care. They found Weyerhaeuser a remarkably perceptive judge of business opportunities, a fact recognized by his colleagues in the Chippewa pool when they gave him sole authority to make decisions about timber purchases. The same respect carried over into subsequent undertakings. As Richard G. Lillard has noted, the indefinite yet all-powerful Weyerhaeuser syndicate that emerged was "a sort of capitalists' underground," the product of a host of ties by which "Weyerhaeuser bound his associates with gentlemen's agreements so private that many of his partners did not know who the others were." Confident in his own abilities, he was extraordinarily flexible and far seeing in devising business strategies and doggedly determined in working toward them. Furthermore, he was a good judge of people. When named president of the Mississippi River Logging Company, he asked that Thomas Irvine, a young executive with the Benjamin Harrison Company in Muscatine, be named secretary. Irvine was a superb choice, and as Weyerhaeuser's right-hand man, brought great strength to the organization. Moreover, after Weyerhaeuser and Denkmann incorporated their business in 1878, Weyerhaeuser delegated much of the responsibility for management to his eldest son, John, setting a pattern whereby "Frederick would appoint a trusted lieutenant to be in charge of a position already secured, while he went forth into new territories. Even the sons," Charles Twining has noted, "were awed and amazed at their father's daring and prowess."[96]

Daring, but hardly unprincipled. Coming onto the scene after the forests had been opened by others, Weyerhaeuser was little involved in such scandalous manipulation of land laws as marked the careers of Thomas Shevlin, Thomas B. Walker, Charles Smith, and many another. Rather than piecing together blocks of timber bit by bit from federal, state, and Indian land, as they did, he preferred what he called "deals"—major purchases from railroads, Cornell University, and others who held title to large tracts. Nor was he a plunger. He approached new opportunities carefully, hesitating—for example—before entering the South or Pacific Northwest and even turning down an opportunity to purchase the Oregon Central Military Wagon Road land grant, whose timber in time would be the backbone of the huge operations of others.[97]

These assessments obscure a less-attractive side of Weyerhaeuser. In his study of the Empire Lumber Company, based largely on manuscript sources from competitors and subordinate partners, Twining noted that Weyerhaeuser had "dictatorial tendencies" and, for all his skill in human relations, often failed to consider the interests of those with whom he was associated. Orrin Ingram, who represented the minority upstream interests in the Mississippi River Logging Company, often had opinions different from Weyerhaeuser's, but he had to express them cautiously. "A correct decision by a subordinate was one that agreed with Weyerhaeuser's own views," Twining notes; anything else was likely to require fresh discussions leading to a decision "acceptable to the one whose opinion counted." Weyerhaeuser was interested in long-term success, and plowed profits back in aggressive expansion, for he recognized two things: first, without a continuing supply of sawlogs the company would die; second, with the industry's low profit margins, his syndicate's production had to be kept expanding to generate sufficient funds to meet carrying costs and expenses. If some among his associates objected because of their immediate needs, he said he would gladly buy them out rather than change course. Yet, when he used company funds to purchase the interests of "weary and needy stockholders," this generated resentment of its own, for there were those, such as William Day, who thought the funds should have gone to pay dividends to stockholders. In short, "Weyerhaeuser was the company," and he seems to have had difficulty appreciating that what was good for him was not necessarily good for those with whom he was associated (a factor which may have contributed to some of Frederick Denkmann's grumbling). Still, often enough it *was* good for them, and those associated with Weyerhaeuser over the long haul profited—even those like Orrin Ingram who joined him reluctantly, more out of necessity than desire. Fortunately, Weyerhaeuser's considerable skill in human relations softened the impact of his tunnel vision. Self-absorption may be too strong a label for this side of the man, but under whatever label, it certainly was a key element in his eventual success.[98]

Admitting all this—his vision, his confidence, his dedication, his single-mindedness—in the final analysis there is nothing to suggest that Weyerhaeuser's rise was inevitable. Certainly he was not alone in possessing these or very similar traits. In 1899 a writer reviewing the career of Thomas Shevlin in *American Lumberman* judged:

> It is well to be successful and prosperous, but . . . the flavor is gone from the feast if it has been provided by others, wholly or in any important measure. It is this satisfaction that Mr. Shevlin possesses, for to his own foresight, business ability and pluck is due the position he now holds among the producers of white pine. To his schooling in the lumber industry in Michigan and his early association in the lumber trade should be given much credit, but back of it all was necessary there should be the man, and the man was there. Others with fully as good opportunities failed to reach the goal.[99]

Much the same could have been said of Frederick Weyerhaeuser, who rose to heights far greater than Shevlin and without using the ethically questionable tactics that repeatedly brought the latter into court. As Paul Gates notes, Henry Sage, with whom Weyerhaeuser dealt repeatedly, held Weyerhaeuser in "the highest regard" because of his "integrity, judgment, and business ability."[100]

One need not indulge in late-nineteenth-century glorification—one might even say worship—of the "self-made man" to explain Weyerhaeuser's success. There were, after all, major elements of happenstance to it. Lorenzo Schricker's failures as head of the Mississippi River Logging Company opened the door for Weyerhaeuser. Frederick Denkmann's focus on manufacturing and marketing and Thomas Irvine's on the operation of Beef Slough left Weyerhaeuser free to concentrate on timber supply and industrial expansion. If these and others had been different sorts of people, if there had been no great flood in 1880, if the Chippewa timber stands had been tied up more promptly by local operators, if the courts had ruled differently in the Beef Slough cases (as well they might have), and if any number of other things had taken a different course, Frederick Weyerhaeuser might have remained but one of several lumbermen struggling for survival in a highly fragmented industry. But none of these things did occur, and ere long Weyerhaeuser stood alone as the dominant figure in a complex syndicate of cooperating entities such as the industry had never seen before.

CHAPTER EIGHT

Actions and Reactions

In 1891 Frederick Weyerhaeuser moved from Rock Island, Illinois, to St. Paul, Minnesota, where he took up residence next door to James J. Hill, the railroad tycoon, who would soon become a close friend. Frederick's eldest son, John, stayed in Illinois to manage the sawmill at Rock Island.[1] The elder Weyerhaeuser's move was indicative of sweeping changes taking place, not only in his own operations but also in the lumber industry as a whole, changes that would alter the way Americans viewed forests and the role of both the industry and government.

The center of Lake States lumbering had long been moving westward. By the time Weyerhaeuser moved to St. Paul, Michigan had long since passed its peak of production, and, after reaching its maximum in 1892, Wisconsin would soon follow; logging in the latter's northern reaches would continue strong for some time, but further south production plummeted. Shipments of logs from the Wisconsin River ended in the mid-seventies, and the volume from the Black and Chippewa was soon falling too. Reflecting this, the great traffic in log rafts that had climbed fairly steadily until 1880, crowding the Mississippi mercilessly, began to decline. The days of downriver operations were clearly numbered.[2]

Minnesota was another matter, and the opportunities it offered lay behind Frederick Weyerhaeuser's change of residence. In 1880 Minnesota, already a major player in the industry, had 234 sawmills capitalized at $7 million; by 1890 the number had climbed to 317 and the capital invested had quadrupled. As an early historian put it: "Pine became the synonym of wealth and power. . . . [Lumber barons] with the Falls of St. Anthony as an operating center, held sway over . . . the politics of the state. . . . [and] created a formidable array of competitors." David M. Clough, who in time would be governor, was among them. By 1888, his sawmill at the falls was cutting roughly one-half million feet a year.

Within Minnesota, a geographical shift was also under way. The St. Croix valley, long a major source of lumber (as well as logs for downriver mills), did not reach its peak production until 1895, but by then the Twin Cities, located astride the Mississippi by the Falls of St. Anthony, had passed its output; four years later, Minneapolis had become the world's premier lumber-producing center—a remarkable development, for as recently as

1876 its production had lagged far behind that of Saginaw-Bay City. The area upstream from the falls was the scene of much growth during the eighties and nineties too, and it was opportunities there that attracted Weyerhaeuser. Although there had been extensive logging in the Rum River drainage, a tributary that entered the Mississippi a few miles above Minneapolis-St. Paul, on the whole the state's central and northern forests had been lightly tapped.

It was appropriate Weyerhaeuser should take up residence next door to Hill, for railroads were central to what was developing. As Agnes Larson put it, "[W]heat and lumber were the warp and woof in the weaving of the pattern that is the Northwest. And the railroad was the shuttle." In this triumvirate of influences, historian Theodore Blegen gave lumbering first place; it was "influential, through its capital, in financing the flour industry [and] in giving impetus to railroad building." In fact, each supported the others.[3]

Even before moving to St. Paul, Frederick Weyerhaeuser was thinking of expanding into forests upriver from the Twin Cities. At the annual meeting of the Mississippi River Logging Company in 1888, Iowa millman David Joyce proposed that the group invest in the St. Paul Boom Company and its timberland. The directors appointed a committee to investigate the idea, but nothing came of it. A year later, Weyerhaeuser himself pushed for expansion. His proposal was more concrete than Joyce's. Edwin C. Whitney of Minneapolis offered the company stands containing 330 million feet of quality pine, a half interest in the vital St. Paul Boom, and a controlling interest in the Mississippi & Rum River Boom, located upstream. It was tempting. Whitney asked $1.3 million, which seemed reasonable, and the purchase would guarantee a source of logs for mills of the Mississippi River Logging Company for years—a not inconsequential consideration with log production in Wisconsin dwindling.

The directors rejected the offer. Indeed, they passed a resolution aimed at heading off any further proposals of the sort, stating the company "declines to entertain the purchase of any pine . . . above the Falls of St. Anthony." A variety of reasons seems to have been behind this action, perhaps the most important being that many of the firms in the Mississippi River Logging Company were headed by men well along in years and more interested in retiring than in taking on new challenges. W. J. Young, for example, was feeling over burdened. He had gone deeply into debt to rebuild and expand his big Iowa sawmill and was having difficulty meeting financial obligations. Young insisted on making all decisions himself—as his wife commented to their son, "No one can tell him any thing"—and often paid selected bills in full before they were due in order to impress individual peers and creditors. Although he was an admirer of Weyerhaeuser, Young was in no position to join a new venture, and his wife was urging that he sell out and retire.[4]

Other factors were at work too. Although Minnesota's stands were extensive, they tended to be poorer than those of Wisconsin and Michigan. To bring inferior logs great distances downriver, past mills at the Falls of St. Anthony whose owners would like them for themselves and might devise ways of impeding their passage, seemed risky. Besides, tapping the major stands of central and northern Minnesota would require extensive financial outlays for logging railroads, outlays that might prove unwise if lumber prices fell or the timber proved poorer than anticipated. Having more experience with drives and rafting than railroad logging, many in the Mississippi River Logging Company were skeptical of projections of profits from the region.[5]

Thus, although Weyerhaeuser was soon operating in the vast area north of the Twin Cities, he did so without the extensive network of associates that had controlled the Chippewa. Indeed, although he continued to work through various combinations of partners as his complex of business enterprises grew, Weyerhaeuser never again brought together so many capable and enterprising associates as he had on the Chippewa. This is hardly surprising. The Chippewa operation had been a forced marriage that resulted when extraordinary circumstances drove together a host of competitors. Weyerhaeuser's subsequent undertakings were launched because he and others saw opportunities in them, not because of necessity.

Weyerhaeuser was ready to move into central and northern Minnesota even if the Mississippi River Logging Company was not. But he was not without allies, and in 1890, Weyerhaeuser & Denkmann—together with fellow downriver lumbermen, the Mussers of Iowa, and the Laird-Norton interests of Minnesota—bought over 212,000 timbered acres from the Northern Pacific Railroad for some $450,000. The purchase, spread across several counties, was part of the land grant the railroad had received in 1864. Other acquisitions followed (including some in far northern Wisconsin). By the end of 1892 the group owned or held cutting rights to 275,000 acres.

The new owners incorporated the Pine Tree Lumber Company to manage these lands, and widespread excitement followed news of their big purchase. Community leaders in the Mississippi River towns of Brainerd, St. Cloud, and Little Falls scrambled to attract the sawmill they expected Pine Tree to build. In the end, Little Falls, located near the very center of the state, won out. Weyerhaeuser and his partners bought a small sawmill there and began cutting while erecting a larger mill on the opposite side of the river.

Managed by Charles Weyerhaeuser and Drew Musser, sons of two of Pine Tree's founders, the new mill was a showpiece; a writer for the *Mississippi Valley Lumberman* proclaimed "there is not a sawmill in the northwest that has the modern and complete equipment that this mill has"—in this it stood in sharp contrast to the sawmills at the Falls of St. Anthony, which were technological laggards, their complacent owners kept competitive by the abundant, low-cost power provided by the falls.

Initially, there was strong demand for lumber from Little Falls; 1891 yielded an immense wheat crop west of the Mississippi, and farmers responded with a spate of building. In September 1892, Drew Musser wrote, "Our trade is all we could ask." Indeed, the thirty-two million feet sawn that year by Pine Tree's two mills exceeded the cut of any other firm north of Minneapolis. Nor was Musser alone in his sanguine assessment; as a writer in the *Mississippi Valley Lumberman* put it, the "lumber business could hardly be in more satisfactory condition than it is at the present time." Neither Musser nor the journal seem to have suspected that grinding depression was in the offing.[6]

Weyerhaeuser and his associates were not the first large operators in central Minnesota. John S. Pillsbury, David Clough, Thomas H. Shevlin, and Thomas B. Walker—among others—had, by fair means and foul, acquired huge holdings there in the seventies and eighties; and, as noted earlier, the Falls of St. Anthony had become a great center of production. Some, such as Pillsbury and Clough, although born elsewhere, were essentially home-grown industrialists; but, like Weyerhaeuser, many others moved in from other states where they had gained experience and accumulated capital. Michigan millmen were prominent in the mix. Minnesota's pioneer operators found it difficult to compete with these well-financed newcomers, and by the end of the 1880s, few oldtimers remained.[7]

Shifts in industrial leadership were accompanied by other changes. The state's pioneer lumbermen had found markets locally and downriver. Thus, direct competition with operators in Michigan and Wisconsin was limited, but as stands to the east dwindled and railroad construction gained momentum, the pattern shifted. With settlement of the plains proceeding apace, markets west of the Mississippi became increasingly important. In 1877 the Minneapolis Board of Trade predicted ten thousand new farms would be opened in the Northwest the following year; the population of Minnesota quadrupled from 1860 to 1880, most of the growth occurring in the timber-short plains and Red River valley. Railroad construction made these markets ever more accessible, but since many were also served by Michigan millmen, who marketed their cut by rail through Chicago; they were markets where competition was fierce.[8]

Few places were as affected by the spate of railroad building as Duluth, located on the western end of Lake Superior. In 1870 Jay Cooke and his associates completed the Lake Superior and Mississippi railway from Duluth to St. Paul. Construction of the line created a temporary demand for the cut of the little sawmills in and near Duluth and neighboring Superior, Wisconsin, while connections to St. Paul provided more lasting outlets. This was only the beginning, for Cooke had grander schemes. The Lake Superior and Mississippi was to be part of his Northern Pacific system, through which he planned to provide a rail link from Duluth to the Pacific Northwest. Recognizing that the Red River valley would soon be a major area of settlement, Cooke envisioned a great traffic in wheat eastward from there and of lumber westbound to it—all carried by his railroad.[9] Others could see possibilities too, and sawmill construction was soon proceeding briskly in and around Duluth, including at Cloquet, whose location above the falls on the St. Louis River gave it an advantage, for it was easier to serve with log drives than locations further downstream. Frederick Weyerhaeuser shared the vision, built sawmills in the area, and eagerly turned to marketing their cut by rail.[10]

Another factor was also at work. As the forests of Pennsylvania, Michigan, and Wisconsin approached their peaks of production, the cost of logs and timberland rose steadily, making eastbound shipments from Duluth's magnificent harbor increasingly competitive in markets those states had long served. Chicago and cities beyond depended increasingly on sawmills in northern Minnesota, and lumbermen from older centers of production began flocking there to acquire stands from which they could continue supplying their established markets. By 1882 the scramble for timberland and cutting rights in northern Minnesota had assumed epic proportions.[11]

There was an element of déjà vu to all this, but beneath the surface a sea change was taking place. Theodore Blegen, one of the founders of the Forest History Society, has observed, "As Minnesota approached its 'golden age' of lumbering, it was influenced more and more by the ability of leaders to effect concentration of ownership and syndication of lumber-milling on a large scale." Corporate forms were replacing partnerships, while the corporations themselves increasingly had interlocking boards of directors and other marks of the new industrial age. Although Frederick Weyerhaeuser's many operations were still partnerships, in other ways they reflected this trend, and his arrival was thus more than just the entry of another big-time lumberman into the forests of central and northern Minnesota. The enthusiasm with which his entry was greeted shows that, to a degree at least, community leaders in the area recognized as much.[12]

Weyerhaeuser's reception stemmed partly from the fact he seemed a sharp contrast to those who had operated in the state's timberlands previously. Over the years, one-third of Minnesota's land had come into state ownership via various grants from the federal government; and Matthias Orfield, an early student of its land-management practices, concluded that while Minnesota squandered less than some states, over time "[f]raud and trespass . . . cut deeply into the state's timber heritage." Indeed, Orfield shows, such practices were common in Minnesota from territorial days. Weyerhaeuser seemed apt to be less exploitative.[13]

The state's pioneer lumbermen, like those before them in Michigan and Wisconsin, believed they had nothing to fear from their illegalities, for "as citizens inheriting an interest in government" they had a right to enter the land, and officials would not prosecute them as trespassers since their actions helped to people the territory. Revealingly, in 1847 when Daniel Stanchfield and Caleb Dorr began cutting timber for Franklin Steele's pioneer mill in St. Anthony (later merged into Minneapolis), each negotiated payment with the area's Ojibwa chief—for, Stanchfield wrote, the pine "belonged to the red man"—but neither saw a need to approach federal authorities for permission to cut, nor paid the government for logs they took.[14]

In both Wisconsin and Minnesota such cutting was "generally conceded to be a benefit to the government." An early traveler, noting loggers at work on unsurveyed (and thus legally unopened) lands, believed they were "doing a great service," while officials of local land offices were "too influenced by public opinion to enforce the law" against such activity. Indeed, in 1851 Wisconsin's legislature asked Congress to suspend prosecutions for timber trespass until lumbermen could "supply themselves by purchases of the necessary lands" and to arrange for the immediate survey of the Wolf, Black, Chippewa, St. Croix, and Wisconsin drainages so their timber can be "brought into the market for sale." Minnesotans agreed, partly because they shared the view of the Stillwater newspaper editor who in 1855 noted of the pine forest, "There is no end of it, and it may never be exhausted." By the end of the territorial period, over four-fifths of Minnesota had been lost by the Lakota and Ojibwa, much going for only pennies an acre. This land was destined to support sawmilling on a massive scale, and already trespass was widespread. Surveyor-General George B. Sargent, noting the extent of depredations, urged rapid survey and opening of the lands to sale so "private owners might preserve what the government could not."[15]

The extent of trespass should come as no surprise. Since colonial times, rural Americans had argued they had a right to harvest the bounty of the forests, which they saw as essential both in providing necessities for everyday life and a supplemental source of income. They considered opening new areas to settlement central to America's mission, and, as has been shown earlier, in many a frontier area forests were indispensable adjuncts of the process.

In the early nineteenth century, the sentiment was as strong as ever, pushing Congress to pass the Preemption Act of 1841, legislation that gave legal standing to the claims of squatters. The act was passed with Jeffersonian dreams of a nation of rural smallholders in mind, but the line between farmers and lumberers was fuzzy, and if squatting was now legalized for one, tapping frontier forests could easily be seen as desirable for the other, especially since both ideology and experience suggested logging opened the way for agriculture. By the 1860s, Congress was sending increasingly mixed messages. Although both Congress and federal officials were beginning to show concern for depredations on public forests, the idea that opening new lands was in the public interest—and that people ought to be encouraged to do so—was as strong as ever. Passage of the Homestead Act in 1862 demonstrated the point.

If the federal government was inconsistent, frontier lumbermen were not. As Frederick Kohlmeyer has shown, early Lake States lumbermen largely came from rural backgrounds, for forests were ubiquitous and familiar to nearly every farm boy, the costs of entry low, and the technology simple and remarkably similar to that used on the farm. A part of their ideological baggage was a belief that land should be brought into production. If carving a farm from the forest was part of that process, and squatting a means to that end, so too was going into the forest to fell timber and, legal title aside, selling or milling the resulting logs. Those who sought to prevent them from doing these things often seemed to them only agents of speculators and wealthy outsiders intent upon engrossing the forests at the expense of those who lived on or near the land, people who were the real backbone of the country. Regulations coming from such sources occasioned no more respect than had the claims of colonial and early national land companies and the speculators behind them. The idea expressed by the Fourth of July orator in Manistee, Michigan, quoted in Chapter Six—"we are the people, ergo the land belongs to us"—would have been widely applauded in both Wisconsin and Minnesota. Many would have agreed with lumberman Isaac Stephenson, who said that although much of its land had been disposed of cheaply, "the government obtained the best of the bargain and . . . the returns to the country at large were of incalculable value."[16]

There was a libertarian strain to all this. Not only did the land by right belong to those who lived and worked thereon, but also outsiders who sought to regulate what could be done on it were opposed or ignored. When Minnesota's pioneer forester, C. C. Andrews, sought prosecution of those responsible for destructive wildfires, he found that even when evidence was overwhelming juries were loath to convict. One observer told Andrews, "[A] large majority of the people think that fire is a good thing . . . [keeping] this young timber killed off." In the end, community sentiment, not laws propagated and enforced by outsiders, determined how jury members voted.[17]

The attitudes of settlers were not far different from those of lumbermen. When the industry entered its period of rapid growth in the seventies, the frequency and extent of illegal and fraudulent entry increased. In 1885 Minnesota's legislature futilely tried to rein in excesses. It directed that sales of state timberland be made only if approved by the land board—a body made up of the governor, state treasurer, and state land commissioner. Lumbermen fought the reforms vigorously, especially the creation of the position of Surveyor General of the woods to oversee sales.[18]

Timber trespass was perhaps even more common than fraudulent sales. In 1874 the legislature directed Minnesota's land commissioners to seize logs cut illegally from state land and arrest the parties responsible, but there were only six land commissioners for the entire state and their income came from fees levied on lumbermen. Not surprisingly, since they were paid "by the very men whom they were directed to watch," they proceeded in ways that had little impact. The federal government did no better. In a case against Shevlin-Carpenter heard by the U.S. Supreme Court in 1893, attorneys for the defense argued that by its inaction the United States had tacitly consented to cutting on unreserved land. The court did not concede the point, but that it could seriously be made before the nation's highest tribunal suggests how widespread trespass was. Still, Minnesota's legislature continued to wrestle with the problem, passing regulations calling for payment of double damages by those found guilty of felling timber illegally. Lumbermen fought these restrictions too, the Shevlin-Carpenter Company protesting that such fines constituted deprivation of property without due process of law, but the state's supreme court disagreed and fines levied against the firm stood. John Nelligan, who spent a lifetime in the woods, saw such developments as but a part of the pattern of fraud and deceit pursued throughout the Lake States. After detailing the tricks used in gaining title to timber, he concluded: "No one was to be trusted. It was a cutthroat game of the worst sort." There is little reason to dispute the point.[19]

Management of Indian timber was no better. Under terms of the Treaty of La Pointe (1854) scrip was issued over the years to mixed-blood Lake

Superior Ojibwa, entitling a holder to select eighty acres that he could then secure in patent. By the 1860s this had been extended to include Indians living with or contiguous to the Lake Superior band and to full-blood Ojibwa regardless of place of residence, and a considerable body of scrip had been issued to people with dubious claims to eligibility—including members of other tribes. Finding people who could apply for a grant of scrip (and be induced to sell land obtained with it to lumbermen) became a widespread business. Although the scrip carried a clear statement of non-transferability, the restriction was widely ignored, and it frequently sold for nominal payments. When federal authorities began to crack down in the 1870s, many a big lumberman in Minnesota claimed to be the unknowing victim of a legal technicality. Congress responded in 1872 by making good titles gained by such "innocent" purchasers if they paid the government a fair price for the land—a price the Secretary of the Interior set at $1.25 per acre in spite of the fact that lumber company records showed that by then an acre of such land was going for $5 or more. Thus, Thomas B. Walker, Dorilus Morrison, and others secured clear title to thousands of acres "upon paying the government one fourth of the amount which it was worth, according to their own testimony."[20]

Indian land title suffered too. Although much of Minnesota had been ceded to the United States by treaty, a sizable portion of the far-northern area long remained unceded. Eventually some, but not all, was opened by treaty, yet for years logging proceeded even in the unopened portion, much of the cut going north to Canadian mills. In an effort to cope with the situation, in 1889 the United States unilaterally opened a large part of the unceded land to settlement; still, the government did a poor job of administering the area and thus failed both Indians and homesteaders while benefiting many a lumberman.[21]

The situation was similar in Wisconsin. By the early eighties lumbermen there were looking to Indian Reservations. In 1886 the Commissioner of Indian Affairs wrote: "[I]t is reported that a scheme is on foot to have the land [on the Lac du Flambeau Reservation] allotted, in order to get at the timber." There were serious irregularities on Lac Court Oreilles Reservation from the beginning. There and elsewhere the actions of loggers and local officials resulted in much criticism, leading the commissioner to appoint two special agents to investigate, but they did little to slow the inroads.[22]

Scrip of various sorts issued to non-Indians also contributed to fraud, especially since some of it allowed relocations. Many used this privilege to strip tracts of timber and then announce they had decided to change their selections to other sites. The fault lay with the law as well as the lumbermen,

Log sleigh in the Minnesota woods. Used since colonial times, sleighs made winter a key logging season. Man in the foreground is carrying hay to scatter on the ice road to slow the sleigh on downward slopes. Courtesy Minnesota Historical Society, Neg. #9057.

for legislators failed to allow for the fact the real value of timberland lay not in the land itself, but in the trees on it. As elsewhere, loggers cut "round forties," trespassing across the boundaries of land legally held to take timber from neighboring stands. By 1915 over half of Minnesota's pineland had been stripped of timber through a combination of such practices.[23]

Weyerhaeuser's huge purchase contrasted to those in central and northern Minnesota during the seventies and eighties, especially the host of small ones occurring during the scramble for timber in the Duluth area.[24] Weyerhaeuser rarely bought government tracts, and thus stood apart from the chicanery and other unseemly actions that took place at land offices when new areas were opened. Indeed, his new purchase stood in stark contrast even to the sale of blocks of timberland created when small purchases were combined to control entire townships. Like Hill (and Cooke) Weyerhaeuser was an "empire builder." He was enthusiastically welcomed in northern Minnesota because his acquisition—and the money behind it—announced a new day for the region. His subsequent purchases near Cloquet and, with Edward Hines, around Virginia and Rainy Lake reinforced the image.[25]

However positively the residents of northern Minnesota may have viewed Weyerhaeuser, a contrary vision of lumbermen was forming. The activities of the industry's leaders were being increasingly criticized both inside and outside of government. Concern was rising about an approaching "timber famine," assorted voices warning that the nation's forests would soon be gone. Minnesota's first governor, Alexander Ramsey, was among the first to raise the alarm. In his inaugural message in 1860, he "made a remarkable plea for stewardship of the state lands," and the legislature responded by following many of his suggestions. Increase Lapham and his allies in neighboring Wisconsin were less immediately successful. In 1867 the State Forestry Commission, which Lapham chaired, published a *Report on the Disastrous Effects of the Destruction of Forest Trees* calling for new policies, but the legislature was unenthusiastic, doing nothing to regulate cutting and passing only an ineffectual measure to encourage tree planting.[26]

Much of the rhetoric regarding a coming timber famine was overblown, the arguments based on faulty estimates of the nation's timber stands, but the predictions had their effect, with other factors, in shaping a new climate of opinion in which much of society came to look askance at leaders of the lumber industry—including Frederick Weyerhaeuser.

Jenks Cameron provided the first broadly based interpretation of these developments. His study, *The Development of Governmental Forest Control in the United States*, first published in 1928, reflects the historiography—and broader intellectual climate—of the times. Today Cameron's analysis seems inadequate, but he provides a useful starting point for understanding what was emerging. He argued that the gradual development of systems of forest control in the United States was a result of the triumph of Order over Adventure. Since colonial times there had been frontier forces opposed to government regulation, forces of Adventure that grew out of the attitudes and values of the Scots-Irish so numerous on the frontier and of the Scottish Borderers from whence they sprang. At the same time, there were those working, initially for the Crown and then for the national government (or for proprietors whose land claims stemmed from those sources), who sought to impose controls that would rationalize forest use. Frontiersmen were hostile to this authority that sought to regulate their activities, felt a sense of entitlement that gave them a right to utilize the forests, and possessed a strongly developed acquisitiveness. Their action-oriented value system brought them into direct conflict with authorities—the forces of Order. They long dominated in frontier forests, making Order "almost non-existent" there; yet bit by bit "the drag upon Adventure's blind rushing forward [would] become stronger" and finally in the early twentieth century bring a system of utilitarian controls to what remained of the nation's timberland.[27]

Cameron's schema can be applied to the colonial and early national periods without much violence to the facts, but after the mid-nineteenth century it becomes inadequate as an interpretive vehicle. After 1870, his image of lumbermen as neo-Borderers hostile to the forces of order and seeking untrammeled access to resources becomes less and less appropriate. In fact, lumbermen tended to be champions of order, for only through order would their sizable investments in woods and mills—as well as in banks and other key elements of the new business world—be safe. For the most part, they were staunchly Republican, some prominently so; as F. C. A. Denkmann put it, he was "a Republican, just as every good lumberman should be." They opposed unions and reformers, both threatening to the status quo, while supporting protective tariffs to keep out cheap Canadian lumber.[28] While they competed aggressively—and sometimes unscrupulously—it was not a competition designed to replace or negate the existing order, but rather one carried out within the parameters of existing law, public policy, and business values. Similarly, they championed the contemporary social order. Standing tall as community leaders, they often underwrote libraries and community-improvement projects, supported one mainline Protestant church or another, and built fine houses for their families both to reflect and to announce their elite status. In short, they were champions of the emerging new order, not adventurers operating beyond its bounds.

Frederick Weyerhaeuser's transfer to St. Paul illustrates the social distancing developing between management and labor. In St. Paul, as we have seen, he took up residence next door to fellow tycoon James J. Hill, but far from those who worked in his woods and mills (in Rock Island at least he had been close to his sawmill when not in the woods). His sons and others who now ran his sawmill and woods operations were little more than managers; the senior Weyerhaeuser continued to tightly control the financial purse strings, and in the new order control of finances was what mattered, for ultimately it meant control of decisions.

Public acceptance of the rise of corporations smoothed the way for such trends. Franchises that legislatures granted for building booms, dams, and other facilities on public waterways were in effect subsidies. The courts, taking a benign view of business, accepted such actions and thus helped lumbermen in the rapid capital accumulation necessary for their expanding operations. Speaking of Minnesota, Theodore Blegen wrote: "The state philosophy was to aid private industry to undertake jobs that would contribute to the economy of Minnesota and of the United States—a frame of mind akin to that which supported land grants for building railroads." As James Willard Hurst demonstrates, a parallel approach dominated in Wisconsin.[29]

The evolution from small proprietorships and partnerships to more complex entities, corporate and otherwise, created circumstances fraught with conflict. As we have seen, in the 1870s this led to a bitter strike in Williamsport, Pennsylvania. As lumbering moved west, similar conflicts occurred in place after place when sawmills became larger and owners more remote socially (and often geographically). Work stoppages took place in Iowa, Michigan, Wisconsin, and Minnesota as early as the 1860s.[30] Over time these became larger and more bitter. The Knights of Labor provided the vehicle for much of the protest in the 1880s, organizing strikes in Saginaw, Marinette, and elsewhere, although often the stoppages seem to have been wildcat strikes the Knights simply seized on as their own.[31]

The career of Robert Schilling is illustrative. Schilling was a familiar figure in Wisconsin's lumber centers. A leader of the state's Knights of Labor, he played a key role, especially in the drive for an eight-hour day and in the Marinette sawmill strike. Like the Knights' Terence Powderly, Schilling was not a radical, but a pragmatist who opposed strikes. In Marinette, he tried to mediate between workers and management, but was unsuccessful not only because employers adamantly refused to grant any recognition of workers' unions, but also because of his own limited vision. As Robert Nesbit has observed, Schilling was an opportunist whose "overriding fault was that he saw the Knights of Labor primarily as an instrument with which to pursue his career as a political reformer. . . . He had no conception of the Knights as an experiment in industrial unionism," and in 1892 he decamped to become national secretary of the Populists.[32]

With leadership such as Schilling's, it comes as no surprise that Wisconsin's workers, like those in Michigan and Minnesota, had little success in confrontations with management. Yet more than poor leadership was involved. The state's industrial workers came to a heightened awareness of themselves as a separate class in the 1880s, but general society seemed more sympathetic to the insecurity of employers than to the problems of workers. The Knights of Labor "enjoyed broad but shallow support," and strikes—such as the Eau Claire Sawdust War of 1881—tended to be spontaneous and poorly led, and have little chance of success. An abundance of workers depressed wages and provided ready replacements to fill the jobs of unskilled strikers.[33] Picketing and boycotts were illegal, but lockouts, blacklists, and importing scabs were not. In the strikes of 1892, Governor George Peck called out the state militia to restore order on the employer's terms. In short, neither the political and legal systems nor public opinion offered workers much leverage.[34]

This is not to say there was no sympathy for laborers, whose pay was reduced for time missed even in cases of injury on the job. In the 1880s a state inspector in Wisconsin reported: "Peter Larson got killed in the woods while in the [Knapp-Stout] company's employ. His wages were docked 20 per cent for not working his time out. His widow returned to Norway. I don't blame her." H. C. Putnam, head of Cornell's land department, showed a similar empathy, reporting during one depression:

> *It is fearful hard times for these fellows. . . . One of my [cruisers] . . . came upon a family [of a logger who was out-of-work], a wife & 5 small children alone in a log cabin in the woods & out of provisions, indeed starving. He had taken in flour & pork for himself & man for so many days—but he could not stand the sight and unloaded & then walked 15 miles to a loging camp for a fresh supply.*

Putnam clearly approved of his employee's actions.[35]

It was one thing to sympathize with victims of individual calamities, it was quite another to take steps to alleviate conditions that brought such calamities about. Legislators passed labor lien laws to protect logging contractors and woods workers from lumbermen who would fail to pay for logs and logging contractors who neglected to pay their workers, but this was not so much a humanitarian step as an effort to help rationalize the industry. It played into the hands of the industry's emerging leaders by undercutting unscrupulous rivals more than it helped workers themselves. Aside from this, little was done to address labor's problems. Indeed, as the work force came increasingly from immigrant sources and violence flared in connection with labor-management disputes, public sympathy for the plight of laborers dwindled. If reform of the industry and its practices were to come, it would have to do so from other sources.[36]

* * *

Forces of change soon appeared. The flush years following initial settlement of the plains gave way to growing agrarian distress. Discontent led to protests that evolved into the Populist movement. Railroad exploitation was the root cause of many of the farmers' difficulties and thus the focal point of most complaints, but problems were sufficiently broad for lumbermen—who from the farmers' vantage point seemed tied to the railroad interests—to be viewed as enemies too. They sold lumber to farmers and demanded payment, whether crops were good or bad. When farmers were unable to pay, lumbermen took produce, equipment, or whatever was available in lieu of cash. At one point, one of Weyerhaeuser & Denkmann's minions seized a farmer's sole cow as partial payment on a bill. But, learning of this, Denkmann ordered the cow returned; "We won't go *that* far," he said.[37] As lumbermen bought railroad land grants and shipped increasingly to rural markets by rail, the bond of identification that made them part of the target of protest grew stronger. Weyerhaeuser's well-known association with James J. Hill reinforced the view.

Minnesota stood in the forefront of events and brought Ignatius Donnelly into the picture as a critic of lumbering practices.[38] For years rumors had circulated about the theft of timber from state lands. Elected to Minnesota's legislature in 1874 as a candidate of the Anti-Monopolists (Grangers), Donnelly called for investigation of the activities of lumber interests. A committee was appointed, but results were meager. The committee found evidence that Amherst H. Wilder, using a federal permit to cut on certain Indian lands, was also logging on state school and swampland within the boundaries of tracts where he had cutting rights. The Republican press ridiculed the committee's findings; Wilder gave up the contract in question, but Minnesota recovered nothing and little else resulted.[39]

Concern did not vanish. In 1889, the state passed a law regarding use of timber on Indian land that foresters have described as the first important development of practical forestry in America.[40] However, the growing wave of rural protest had other effects and in 1893 led Minnesota's lawmakers to turn their attention once more to the mismanagement of pinelands. The legislature adopted a joint resolution calling on the governor to appoint an investigative committee. The result was the Pine Land Investigating Commission, made up of representatives from each branch of the state's government. Donnelly, back in the legislature as a Populist, was reluctant to serve on the commission, but in the end not only did so but wound up as chairman.[41] With the forces of protest stronger than ever and fresh revelations of chicanery frequent, the commission would have much greater success than its predecessor.

Commission members labored for twenty months on their "arduous, exacting, and most unpleasant" task. The resulting report was thorough— and scathing. A state scaler told the investigators his job was "to scale the logs brought to the land[ing] and to keep his eyes closed to illegal practices." Surveyor's reports were often pro forma; indeed, prior to the 1893-1894 season reports so mixed together sales it was impossible to detect what was going on, and logs were often not branded as required. The central administration was neither honest nor efficient; here, the commission reported, "we find the most palpable neglect of duty; the least regard of the state's interests; the most careless, unsystematic conduct of the business of the state; and the greatest display of either unpardonable ignorance of the duties of this office under the law, or downright dishonesty." Prior to 1891 the law requiring a state surveyor to make an estimate for a sale "was utterly disregarded." Blank estimates signed by "surveyors" were filled in by Matthew Clark, stumpage clerk at the capitol, at figures well below those reported by James Sinclair, the state's estimator. Not surprisingly, "all of the timber covered by these fraudulent estimates was speedily sold."[42]

Prosecutions followed. The first, against C. A. Smith & Co., was especially noteworthy, for popular former governor "Honest John" Pillsbury was an embarrassed partner in Smith's operations. Connections in high places were now, it seemed, no guarantee of immunity from investigation or prosecution. Judgments were won in other cases too, while—reading the handwriting on the wall—three others hastened to settle, paying $30,000 without being brought to trial. This was but the tip of the iceberg. Donnelly called the fines and payments a "mere bagatelle" compared to what Minnesota gained because lumbermen began filing honest reports regarding purchases from the state. Still, Donnelly was not satisfied. Near the end of the commission's report, he wrote: "Close the doors absolutely, and let the rascals find some other victims than the children of the state." As a biographer noted, Donnelly "favored closing the forests to private companies and creating a state monopoly"—a position consistent with the Populist call for a more activist government that would free the economy from control by the well-to-do—but neither the state nor the rest of the commission was ready for such a radical solution, and when lumberman David M. Clough succeeded Knute Nelson as governor, he ignored the report and did not press for continued investigation. However, in 1895 the legislature, guided by Charles F. Staples (who had served as secretary of the Pine Land Investigating Committee) and Harris Richardson, enacted the first partially successful general regulatory legislation.[43]

In Wisconsin nothing so dramatic was happening, although prior to 1890 Robert M. La Follette and others were speaking out against the railroad and lumber companies "seeking land grants and other special favors" from the legislature. In subsequent years, La Follette became a supporter of conservation, but he was hardly an implacable foe of lumbermen. Indeed, when he was first elected to Congress in 1900, it was with the support, financial and otherwise, of Isaac Stephenson, and he seems to have played a limited role when Wisconsin established a Forestry Commission in 1897 to begin bringing control to its timberland.[44]

Mainstream politics had effects of its own. Democrats had long campaigned against protective tariffs, seeing them as instruments that served rich industrialists while making goods more expensive for farmers and workers, but not until 1892 was the party in a position to do much about it. Then, with Grover Cleveland in the White House and a majority in both houses of Congress, the Democrats began pushing for tariff reform. The party's congressional leaders labored mightily, but gave birth to a mouse. In the end, only lumber and certain categories of wool and copper were allowed duty-free entry. Protests from lumbermen had been of no avail.[45]

When William Jennings Bryan and his allies gained control of the party in 1896 and made common cause with the Populists, they were bedeviled by the lumber schedules in the Wilson-Gorman tariff. Bryan's Nebraska background led him to see lumber as an item essential for farmers, but over-priced because of the manipulations of lumber barons. That need not have been the case. The biggest component in the value of lumber was labor, and favoring lumber interests could thus have been seen as serving the interests of laborers. Moreover, like farmers, lumbermen were often victimized by railroads; as one historian has put it, they were "sitting ducks in the game of railroad subsidies" and little able to influence the freight rates they were called upon to pay.[46] But, possessed of a pre-industrial Jeffersonian view of the economy, Bryan could not recognize such things and thus failed to find effective arguments to use in campaigning in the essential, lumber-producing swing states of the upper Midwest, just as he failed to find ways to appeal to union leaders and industrial workers elsewhere. Free silver, on which he concentrated, had limited appeal in those areas. Still, the comments of Bryan and his Populist allies about the exploitative practices of big lumber indirectly helped strengthen a growing suspicion that the industry was operating in ways inimical to the public interest and ought to be controlled.[47]

Activities of lumbermen's associations strengthened the view. When local leaders combined to provide a united front in meeting the demands of striking workers, they generated little concern among the larger public, but as their organizations became more broadly based and started addressing larger questions they seemed more ominous. By 1865 some lumbermen were echoing farmers' complaints about extortionate railroad freight rates and calling for legislative action. They soon changed their tune. In 1878 a group met with railroad officials in St. Paul and hammered out an agreement aimed at making western lumber competitive with that marketed through Chicago. So successful were the larger lumber firms in these and other negotiations with railroads that they came to see preferential freight rate agreements as essential. In 1887, when Congress was considering the bill that resulted in the Interstate Commerce Act, which would outlaw such practices, the Northwestern Lumber Manufacturer's Association came out against it and in so doing helped give its members a reputation for being more interested in profits than in the larger public welfare.[48]

Efforts by industry associations to regulate prices—either by establishing uniform price lists or by reducing production—gave the same impression. After a convention in the mid-eighties at which an attempt was made to support prices by reducing production, one lumberman complained of his colleagues:

> *Oh, yes, they want to curtail, but not a man of 'em would pledge himself to any method that would mean curtailment. . . . Men who took a prominent part in the meeting don't mean to curtail—won't curtail as long as they can sell their lumber. You couldn't bind them to any agreement with a log chain.*

Subsequent efforts were more successful, so much so that by January 1892 a federal grand jury indicted the principal officers and directors of the Mississippi Valley Lumbermen's Association for engaging in a conspiracy to set prices and thereby restrain trade, outlawed under the Sherman Antitrust Act of 1890. The defendants were found not guilty, but the indictment and trial strengthened hostile public perceptions of the industry's practices.[49]

So too did efforts to gain tariff protection against imports of cheap Canadian lumber, something industry associations sought again and again over the years. The issue came to a head in 1897 when one hundred and fifty delegates gathered in Cincinnati at a convention called for the express purpose of getting protection against imports included in the tariff legislation to which Congress was then turning its attention, and succeeded in getting protection against Canadian imports included in the Dingley Tariff that same year. Bryan and others replied to this and similar efforts by lambasting high tariffs for enriching wealthy industrialists while raising prices to consumers; in the process, they helped many reach the conclusion that the rise of lumber prices in the late nineties resulted from the success of self-serving lumbermen.[50]

Rising hostility to the "robber barons" gained impetus from other sources too, many far removed from lumbering, and as muckrakers took up the attack even Weyerhaeuser became a target. Together, these various threads of discontent paved the way for an activist state that would, among other things, protect and manage the nation's forests as never before. In this emerging climate of public opinion, the industry's widespread practice of planned obsolescence—in which sawmills became obsolete as the timber supplying them ran out, an approach that encouraged them to move repeatedly to new areas of operation—fueled a growing belief that the industry's leaders did not care about the communities where they operated, their workers, or the public interest. Critics grew increasingly vocal.[51]

Many lumbermen were baffled by the criticism. They saw themselves as engaged in honorable work, providing jobs, generating investment capital, and furnishing building materials needed by a growing nation. They believed they had operated as society had encouraged them to operate, within parameters they had not themselves established. To be sure, some among them accumulated considerable fortunes in the process, but they thought it unjust to be treated as selfish villains or even criminals. As Frederick Kohlmeyer summarized, "In their old age many lumbermen bitterly pondered the attitude that reviled and condemned them as exploiters of the public wealth for their private enrichment."[52] Their reaction had some legitimacy. Under a Minnesota law of 1895, a permit holder had to "cut the timber clean, acre by acre" and pay for all timber he did not cut and remove before the end of his permit period. Clearcutting was thus not just a result of industrial greed and shortsightedness, but required by law. Indeed, lumbermen and policy makers alike saw leaving trees uncut as wasteful; Joseph G. Thorp of Eau Claire told the National Lumbermen's Association in 1876, "We have no right to waste this rich material . . . by adopting a policy of indifference, or by failing to so manufacture and use it as to accomplish the greatest good to the greatest number." For the public good, Thorp wanted governments to speed deforestation by encouraging better facilities for the lumber business—and they did. Moreover, as stands dwindled, lumbermen took smaller and smaller trees to obtain the logs that would allow them to stay in business. In the Eau Claire area, only the best logs were taken at first, but after 1885 contracts normally required all the pine be cut; in time, hardwoods, which could be transported by train although too heavy to be floated out of the woods in drives, were felled as well. At this point, clearcutting was a mark of desperation, a means of business survival more than an indicator of wanton greed.[53]

There were social costs to these developments, and they spurred the critics. Hardwoods, lesser coniferous species (most notably hemlock), and the paper and pulp industry that moved in after large-scale lumbering departed only partially filled the void left when pine was gone. Efforts to farm the cutover largely failed. Some communities were abandoned; others struggled on plagued by underemployment and poverty. Even the forests suffered, often coming back to cedar and aspen rather than the pine of earlier years.[54]

Not everyone was caught up in the growing discontent with the changes taking place in American society—and in the forests. Many were downright hostile to the complaints of Populists, union leaders, and social critics. William Allen White's blistering editorial "What's the Matter with Kansas?" provides a classic illustration. Writing in the *Emporia Gazette*, the young Kansas newspaperman pilloried members of the Populist movement as ignorant malcontents whose problems were largely of their own making. They and other social critics ought to cease complaining and buckle down to work. In time, White would come to recognize that there had been justification for discontent during the period and a need to revise social policies, but at the time his views were sufficiently widespread to insure that the People's Party and its allies had no real chance of controlling public policy.[55]

Even many socially obtuse observers began to suspect something was wrong with the management of America's timberland as one great forest fire after another swept through the upper Lake States during the late nineteenth century, destroying whole towns and exacting a heavy toll of human casualties. In a mere four hours, the first of these, the Peshtigo fire in northern Wisconsin in 1871, burned a swath ten miles wide and forty miles long (1.28 million acres), destroyed a number of villages (including the town that lent the blaze its name), and killed upwards of fourteen hundred people (the exact number never determined). Fires burning simultaneously in Michigan destroyed an additional 2.5 million acres. Yet these blazes were eclipsed by the attention-grabbing fire that leveled Chicago at the same time and by complacency born of familiarity with the long-practiced use of fire in rural land clearing. Awareness that new conditions had developed came but slowly.[56]

Peshtigo and the great blazes that followed were not the familiar ground fires that had burned across America's forests and woodlands since colonial times and even earlier. They were holocausts seldom seen before. As had long been the practice, logging operations left limbs, tops, broken trunks, and other debris behind, but fuel loads on the ground were now greater than ever, for as logging became increasingly mechanized it became more destructive and left unprecedented quantities of potential fuel in its wake. The advent of railroad logging extended this pattern far more widely than logging tied to river drives ever had.

When immense fuel loads on the ground combined with dry atmospheric conditions, they created a tinderbox needing only a spark to set it off—and with farmers and railroads moving into the area, there were plenty of sparks. If there was too little wind to disperse the heat from the resulting blaze, the fire might jump from the ground to overhead limbs laden with resinous pine needles and then from tree to tree, spreading at a speed even the fastest horse could not outrun. These firestorms burned with such intensity the resin in trunks and needles often vaporized, rather than simply burning, and would then explode in a flash of flame from above when the buildup of flammable gases became sufficient or, if trapped inside the trunk, cause trees to explode with a force that sent huge firebrands tumbling up to a half-mile in every direction. These fires generated so much heat they created their own winds, convection currents so strong it was difficult to stand against them, and caused fires to spring ahead, skipping over whole areas to touch down again and recommence their destructive race forward. As air was sucked into the all-consuming flames, many a person hiding in the safety of a cellar or well died not from heat but from asphyxiation. Historian—and former firefighter—Stephen Pyne observed that these great fires resembled nothing so much as the firebomb raids of World War II.[57]

Other fires followed Peshtigo, including an especially destructive series that swept Michigan in 1881 (bringing the Red Cross into civilian disaster relief for the first time). Here and there concern began to be expressed. In 1884 Minnesota's state geologist wrote: "No country in the world, claiming to be a civilized and enlightened commonwealth, should permit such wanton destruction of the public domain."[58] Matthias Orfield agreed. Writing in 1911, he observed, "Perhaps the most important question before the federal government in the administration of its timber lands has been the question of the prevention of forest fires," yet not until 1897 did it take steps to control the threat of fire so as to end the "shameful waste of a priceless natural resource, such as the history of the world can scarcely parallel." The states were laggards too. Logger Louie Blanchard provided a partial explanation: "I suppose we should have burned our brush as we cut off the trees, so forest fires couldn't get going so easy. But we never knowed much about such things in those days."[59] Still, as forest conflagrations followed one after another, awareness of the need for action gradually developed.

The summer of 1894 was hot and dry and a number of serious fires erupted in northern Minnesota, but as one observer put it, "the settlers had become so accustomed to 'forest fires' that little attention was given them." That soon changed. A new fire broke out and descended on the area "with the fury and roar of the fiends in Hell." The huge fire destroyed the town of

Hinckley and various hamlets in the area, killing 418 people.[60] The death toll was less than a third that of Peshtigo, but this time there was no Chicago fire to overshadow it. Observers were stunned. Among them was C. M. Gray; almost fifty years later the fire was still indelibly etched in his mind. In Duluth, seventy-eight miles from Hinckley, Gray saw "the air . . . filled with wild ash and cinders and the ground covered by fine white ashes." He watched a Great Northern railway waybill from the line's Hinckley station "floating in the air from the fire" and rushed to retrieve it. The next day he joined a relief party that set out by train and dug some twenty-five bodies out of cellars and other places of supposed refuge. Similar stories were told many times over.[61]

The Hinckley tragedy roused concern as its predecessors had not, leading to the appointment in 1895 of C. C. Andrews as chief fire warden for Minnesota. In 1897 the legislature passed a law for fire prevention that Andrews had prepared. Public concern cooled as time passed, but new fires erupted at Chisholm (1908) and Beltrami (1910), leading to renewed interest and a strengthening of the law.[62] Other states took steps during this same period, and after yet another fire erupted in 1918, leveling Cloquet, even the federal government joined in providing relief.[63]

Fires made even those not tied to the agrarian or labor movements and not particularly concerned with industrial exploitation aware something was wrong with the way America's forests were managed. However indirectly, these forces contributed each in its own way to the view that lumbermen were operating contrary to the public interest. This opened the way for—and strengthened—the growing call for active use of government in the public interest. In time one aspect of that utilitarian movement would come to be rationalized forest management. The growth of attitudes that helped bring it about and the policies to which they led were harbingers of the end of the lumberman's frontier. Indeed, to the more prescient the end was already in sight.

Frederick Weyerhaeuser had moved to St. Paul to be closer to opportunities in new areas of forest operation, and by that time he may already have been looking at even more distant frontiers in the South and Far West. Yet much of what he dealt with in the years ahead was post-frontier. Weyerhaeuser was the great embodiment of the promise of America's forest frontier, but just as surely he embodied what was to come. Old and new, frontier and post-frontier, Frederick Weyerhaeuser stood with one foot in each.

CHAPTER NINE

Southern Beginnings

In 1608, while laying the foundations of the first permanent English settlement in North America and seeking to generate some early returns on the investments of underwriters of his colony, Captain John Smith dispatched a cargo of "Cedar wood" to Britain aboard the supply ship *Phoenix*.[1] Although Jamestown was on the edge of a vast forest belt, this initial shipment was something of an anomaly. Virginia's colonists focused on building an agricultural society—when they were not seeking a quicker road to riches—and before long found in tobacco a crop that came to dominate the colony's economy to such an extent that James I complained the settlement was "wholly built on smoke."[2] For all their potential, Southern forests would have to wait almost two and a half centuries before becoming the setting for a real lumberman's frontier.

When Smith and other whites arrived in North America, they found a great arc of forest stretching south along the Atlantic seaboard from Virginia to Florida and thence west to eastern Texas.[3] Much of this forest belt was too sandy and sterile to support plantation agriculture. William Byrd called the soil of North Carolina's pineries "near as Sandy as the Desarts of Africca," and the same could have been said of that of the Gulf South. As an early observer of the latter put it, "perpetual verdure . . . [was] only a cover for sterility, except in those spots which the course of rivers and alluvial deposits had fertilized."[4]

The first European settlements were along the Atlantic; thus forest exploitation commenced there well before it did in the Gulf South, and since these settlements were primarily agricultural, they clustered on the richer soils of the coastal plain. Thus—as in Maine, New York, and Pennsylvania—the earliest lumbering was an adjunct of agriculture, not an end in itself. Colonial authorities encouraged sawmills in order to speed local development, plantation owners found woods work a profitable way to use slaves during agriculture's slack seasons, and settlers in less-favored areas found in forest products a way to earn cash to supplement the limited support provided by herds and farms.[5] In locales such as Norfolk, Virginia, and Wilmington, New Bern, and Beaufort, North Carolina, the exportation of forest products assumed a significant level, but this was the sign of a growing, diversified, largely agricultural society in their hinterlands, not of a lumberman's frontier.[6]

Authorities in London had broader goals. Hoping to free the Royal Navy from dependence on Baltic sources of naval stores, a dependence fraught with danger, they used bounties and other incentives to encourage production in the southern colonies. These programs, had they succeeded, might have resulted in the colonies' vast forests, so well stocked with resinous pines, becoming valuable in and of themselves, but as with attempts to encourage mast and naval stores production in the northern colonies, success was limited.[7]

In spite of imperial programs, most Southerners primarily valued the woods for crop and grazing land. Plantation owners in tidewater Virginia and elsewhere acquired vast acreages of forest, not because of the anticipated value of trees but because tobacco, the economic mainstay of their export-based economy, was extraordinarily hard on the soil. Fresh land was constantly needed as older tracts lost their fertility and were abandoned (or converted to less-profitable grain production).[8]

In places ill suited for plantation agriculture—such as Virginia's Southside and much of North Carolina—forests offered a place for hogs and cows to roam, free to graze and grow fat on the mast from oaks and other deciduous trees. Such locales proved attractive to those lacking the money or connections to acquire the large tracts required for successful plantation agriculture; here they could simply squat on land not already taken. In addition to food for livestock, trees on these tracts on the fringes of society offered fuelwood and building materials and met other local needs, but forests per se were no more central to the economy of such areas than they were to the tobacco plantations. The labor shortages that encouraged colonial plantation owners to turn to slavery induced their poorer contemporaries to resort to free-range management of their herds, for it required minimal labor and capital inputs. Although well-to-do observers criticized their techniques as slothful, these settlers lacked the wherewithal to hire laborers to work their lands or manage their herds more intensively.[9]

Hogs prospered in the woods. One authority put it succinctly: swine "bred like houseflies and grew like pumpkins."[10] Cattle prospered too, if not quite so spectacularly. In winter they resorted to canebrakes along the streams and swamps for browse and cover. William Byrd reported that a settler had squatted near North Carolina's Great Dismal Swamp solely "for the Advantage of the Green Food His Cattle find there all Winter, and for the Rooting that Supports His Hogs." In spring cattle and hogs abandoned the swampy canebrakes for "the Springing Grass on the firm Land."[11]

Much of the grass pastoralists depended upon developed razor-sharp edges as it matured and soon became dry and unpalatable, but settlers found they could increase the quantities of tender new grass by burning the previous year's dry growth to "green up" the range, a process that also helped keep down the number of troublesome snakes, chiggers, and ticks. In places cattle returned to publicly supported cowpens in the evening for milking, but the range itself was unfenced and open to all; where there were no public cowpens, stock roamed even more freely. There were local variations, but a herding tradition soon developed throughout the South Atlantic colonies.[12]

Wealthy plantation owners such as William Byrd found this system of land use difficult to appreciate. "We observed few cornfields in our walks" in North Carolina, he wrote, "and those very small, which seemed strange to us, because we could see no other tokens of husbandry or improvement." Byrd soon learned people raised corn for their own use, not for fodder, as their stock "know very well how to get their own living." Indeed, he observed, "Indian corn is of such great increase, that a little pains will subsist a very large family with bread, and then they may have meat without any pains at all by the help of [the canebrakes in] the low grounds and the great variety of mast that grows on the highland." In sum, "[s]urely, there is no place in the World where the Inhabitants live with less Labour than in N[orth] Carolina."[13] To Byrd, such a life was inexcusably slothful, but attitudes to authority disturbed him almost as much as those to work. Many, he noted, had fled to North Carolina to escape the intrusive hand of Virginia's government and resented even the limited demands of local authorities. They viewed the land and its fruits as theirs for the taking; as he put it, they "make bold with the King's Land there abouts, without the least Ceremony. They not only maintain their Stocks upon it, but get Boards, Shingles and other Lumber out of it in great Abundance." Byrd contemptuously referred to the area as "lubberland," presaging generations of Southern elites (and in time Northerners as well) who applied pejorative terms to the residents of the Piney Woods: crackers, butternuts, rednecks, poor white trash.[14]

Byrd and his successors dismissed these people too readily. Their economic system was ideal for a labor-short, pastoral society with a small, ruggedly independent population—in other words, for the people along the dividing line between Virginia and North Carolina, where Byrd observed them, and subsequently in the Piney Woods of the Gulf South to which it was transferred. They were a sturdy yeomanry living a spartan existence. In terms of education and quality of life, they may have stood somewhat above the poor settlers of interior Maine—who, as we have seen, were themselves the objects of the contempt of more comfortable classes—but they shared much with them, including an emphasis on kinship and neighborhood networks, a desire to be left alone, a suspicion of official authority (dominated as it so often was by the elites), and a pre-industrial outlook fitted to life on the outer margins of the nation's market economy.[15]

Cattle and hogs (or the meat thereof) became major items in the provisioning trade with the West Indies and large overland drives to supply this commerce, as well as domestic markets, were common. By 1707 cattle raisers were so intrusive into Indian lands in South Carolina that they were a cause of the Yamasee War of 1715-1716, a war that, in addition to its human casualties, destroyed numerous stocks of cattle, drove many settlers from the colony's frontier, and struck a serious blow to West Indian trade. [16]

In the interior, beyond agricultural settlements and pastoralists, forests took on a different value: they provided habitat for deer and fur-bearing animals, trade in the hides and pelts of which was a major undertaking. So valuable was this trade with the Creeks and others that in the late seventeenth century a struggle for its control set tidewater and interior colonists—and South Carolinians and Georgians—against one another; but it was the trade in deer hides, not the trees that sheltered the game, over which control was contested. The trade continued important well into the eighteenth century. From 1699 to 1715 South Carolina exported to England an average of nearly fifty-four thousand deerskins a year; the figure had reached one hundred and sixty thousand by 1748. By the latter date, shipments of hides from Charles Town (present-day Charleston) exceeded the value of indigo, cattle, lumber, and naval stores combined. Such levels were unsustainable. Creeks often blamed the declining deer population on the inroads of cattle, especially their destructive impact on canebrakes, but over-hunting as Creek appetite for western goods increased was surely a factor too.[17]

In spite of the setbacks from the Yamasee War, raising cattle and hogs remained a major element in the frontier South—even some Creeks and Choctaws took it up—and when settlers pushed west into the Gulf South, Southern pastoral traditions went with them.[18] And well they might. William Bartram traveled through Florida and across the Gulf South to Mobile, the lower Pearl River, and New Orleans on the eve of the American Revolution and found vast areas of canebrakes and upland savannas ideally suited for livestock. Of northern Florida, he wrote, "[N]o part of the earth affords such endless range and exuberant pasture for cattle, deer, sheep, &c." Moreover, being close to the Gulf of Mexico, the area was "most conveniently located for the West Indian trade and the commerce of all the world." Livestock were already present; "the horned cattle and horses bred in these meadows," he reported, "are large, sleek, sprightly, and as fast as can be." Some no doubt belonged to Alexander McGillivray and other leading Creeks.[19]

Agriculture (plantation and otherwise), pastoral activities, and the fur and hide trade brought changes to the forests and to the native peoples who inhabited them; so too did Virginia's charcoal iron industry, which used huge amounts of wood to fire its furnaces.[20] For all this, the dominant vegetation of most of the South remained the same: trees, especially various species of pine.[21] Some few were beginning to see potential in these. In the early 1800s, Thomas Perryman, a Seminole mixed-breed, pushed the Creeks to cede a tract on the Apalachicola, hoping to build a settlement there that would engage in the exportation of lumber. Although the cession was made, nothing came of Perryman's plan.[22] Indeed, as yet there were few actual inroads into the timber itself. Only in narrow strips along larger streams and near plantations, iron smelters, or settlements was forest clearing much in evidence. None of this resulted from the forces of a lumberman's frontier; those would come later. When John F. H. Claiborne traveled through Mississippi's pine region in 1840 he still found numerous places where for "twenty miles at a stretch . . . you may ride through these ancient woods and see them as they have stood for countless years, untouched by the hand of man."[23]

As the Anglo-American population in the Gulf South grew during the early nineteenth century, herding and hunting—separately or together— became the common means of livelihood in the Piney Woods. In 1818 Estwick Evans observed thousands of cattle grazing along the banks of the Mississippi, although they were "not often fat . . . and give very little milk." At nearly the same time, Thomas Nuttall and William Darby reported huge herds in southwestern Louisiana, and Darby saw great financial opportunity in this; already, he noted, cattle from these herds were sold to feed the people of New Orleans.[24]

Anglo-American settlers trickling into the Gulf South in the first years of the nineteenth century brought with them only a limited number of cattle and hogs, for taking large herds through the land of hostile tribes was fraught with danger. However, because of earlier Spanish and French activities, there already were cattle and hogs in the area, many of the latter roaming wild. Most Anglo-Americans initially settled along the fertile margins of rivers. As the rate of in-migration increased following defeat of the Muskogees

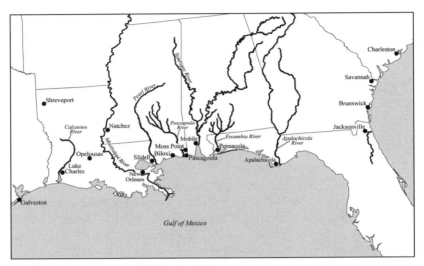

Gulf Coast pineries. Map by Sarah E. Hinman.

(Creeks) at Horseshoe Bend in 1814, stock numbers burgeoned, and settlement away from the bottomlands proceeded apace.[25]

The population of the area known as the Piney Woods not only grew rapidly because of newcomers attracted by its manifest opportunities for pastoralism, but also because many who had initially settled along the rivers moved to the Piney Woods to escape the steamy, malarial bottomlands. They were an interesting mix, described by Timothy Flint, a recently arrived New Englander, as "poor and indolent, devoted to raising cattle, hunting, and drinking whiskey." However, Flint hastened to add, the area was more healthful than the fertile lowlands and, echoing Byrd's earlier assessment of life along the Virginia-North Carolina border, he admitted that "nothing could be easier than subsistence in the Piney Woods." John M. Peck agreed. He reported that the area's forestland "produces a fine range for domestic animals and swine. Thousands are raised, and the emigrant grows wealthy, from the bounties of nature, with but little labor." John Claiborne, among the most perceptive of observers, described the people of the Piney Woods as "living in a state of equality, where none are rich and none are in want, where the soil is too thin to accumulate wealth, and yet sufficiently productive to reward industry."[26]

William Darby noted that along the Pearl River "immense forests spread themselves on both banks and reach within a few miles of the mouth of the river." Few saw opportunity in this. Pastoral activity, not lumbering, was the major undertaking; indeed, it was much more extensive throughout the Gulf South than most historians have recognized. From 1830 to 1850, one limited portion of the Gulf South alone produced a million head of cattle yearly.[27] The reasons for the rapid growth of the pastoral economy are easy to determine. Among the pines, Flint reported, "grows rank grass furnishing fine and inexhaustible summer range," while in the bottoms cane flourished providing superb winter browse. Flint waxed eloquent in describing the latter. Cane grew from fifteen to thirty feet high,

> *the richest looking vegetation that we have ever seen. The smallest sparrow would find it difficult to fly among it; and to see its ten thousand stems, rising almost contiguous to each other, and to look at the impervous roof of verdure, which it forms at the top, it has the aspect of being a solid layer of vegetation. . . . No prospect so impressively shows the exuberant prodigality of nature, as a thick cane brake. Nothing provides such a rich and perennial range for cattle, sheep and horses.*

There, as in North Carolina during Byrd's day, animals wintered in the canebrakes, roaming free to grow fat even when grass was dormant, too coarse and dry to offer much nourishment.[28]

Southern fencing practices encouraged free-range herding. If one wished to protect his crops, he had to build fences to keep animals out. The range itself was unfenced and open to all, owners depending upon brands to provide identification of their animals when the need arose.

The Piney Woods were on the frontier of white settlement; much land was still in the public domain, open to the first person to settle it. Legal, political, and social institutions that might have hindered squatters were weak, and in any case squatting had long been so common on the American frontier that many viewed it as a normal adjunct of national development. Possession of the land, not legal title, made one its owner.[29]

Under these circumstances, the people of the Piney Woods were largely independent of the planter aristocracy that dominated social, political, and economic life in the Gulf South, and before cotton became king competed with it for control of the seats of power. Like those Byrd had observed along the Virginia-North Carolina dividing line, they cherished their freedom and gained needed support from family, kin, and neighbors, not from mainstream institutions and their power brokers, whom they viewed with suspicion or outright hostility. This is not to say that pastoralists operated outside the market economy, for they participated in it directly, even enthusiastically, through the sale of animals they raised and, on occasion, crops and logs as well.[30]

As pastoralism grew in the pineries and plantations developed elsewhere, lumbering languished. The sluggishness of streams—especially as they approached the coast—limited the number of sites for water-powered sawmills, while the great distance of the fall line from the Gulf discouraged exportation of what lumber was produced. Early mills thus tended to be small, interior, and locally oriented, most erected to meet the needs of individual plantations and their neighbors. By the end of the first decade of the nineteenth century "much plank and scantling" used by settlers in Louisiana's Opelousas area was "prepared at . . . saw mills on Bayou Boeuf, and transported down the river in boats." But as people were drawn away by the cotton boom, many a community in the interior pine country withered, as did the mills that served them.[31]

In spite of its magnificent forests, lumbering was especially slow in developing in East Texas. Until after independence from Mexico, dwellings were influenced by Hispanic building traditions that used little wood or were simple log cabins whose construction depended upon the settler's axe, not the products of sawmills. In well-forested San Augustine County, the earliest sawmill apparently did not appear until 1839, while in nearby Angelina County, the first saw- and gristmill did not appear until 1853. Even then production was for local use.[32] Frederick Law Olmsted, traveling through the area in 1854, reacted much as Byrd had to North Carolina earlier; Olmsted saw "an unpleasant country and a wretched people."[33]

Elsewhere in the Gulf South sawmills appeared earlier. By the 1820s, steam-powered mills had begun to divert sawmilling from its plantation-local orientation. Steam opened the way for larger mills, made mill seats located nearer the Gulf Coast practical, and encouraged exports to New Orleans, the Caribbean islands, and even more distant markets. Available records give few details of the early coastal steam sawmills, but indirect evidence suggests considerable progress. For example, in 1830 Mississippi's legislature asked Congress to authorize construction of a lighthouse at a key coastal location because, it claimed, from New Orleans to Mobile people were engaged in the coastwise transportation "of lumber, wood, sand, lime, and cattle." Henry Gunnison was among these pioneers, erecting a mill near Mobile in 1820 that turned out twelve million feet of lumber the following year.[34]

A series of treaties with the Choctaw and Chickasaw from 1816 to 1832 opened the way to white settlement in rich lands north of the Piney Woods and set off a boom in what came to be known as the Cotton Belt. By the 1820s, Timothy Flint wrote, "Cotton is the grand staple. . . . It is, perhaps, too exclusively the object of thought, attention, and cultivation; . . . one would suppose, that it is here considered as almost the only article of much importance in . . . creation."[35]

In the flush times that followed, the Cotton Belt not only drew most of the Gulf South's new settlers, but also siphoned off many from the pineries and along the coast. Traveling through the pine country in 1840, John Claiborne found town after town in decline or virtually abandoned. The number of interior sawmills had plummeted. However, Claiborne wrote, there were those who recognized that, although they were "now scarcely thought of," eventually the area's pines would be a source of great wealth. He was not alone; already a handful of entrepreneurs had recognized that the growth in New Orleans and other cotton centers created demand for lumber, and they stayed in the pine country to supply it.[36]

As the boom in the Cotton Belt passed its peak, in-migration to the pineries resumed. Among the immigrants were a number with decidedly different backgrounds than the pioneer herdsmen. Many were New Englanders familiar with the intricacies of lumbering who turned to it in their new homes. Lumber production grew steadily thereafter. Aside from building sawmills, the newcomers seem to have had a leavening effect; as Gordon Davis—a New Englander who invested in a sawmill near Moss Point, Mississippi, and moved there to manage it—told an associate, "I am very glad to hear that some permanent Settlers are coming to the [Gulf] coast, they will add much to the improvement of the place." Another wrote, "I can hardly believe that so good a portion of old Hinsdale [New Hampshire] has been transferred to so distant a point."[37]

The scattered little sawmills of the 1830s and '40s may not have seemed like much, but they marked the emergence of a lumberman's frontier in the South, albeit a frontier operating on the fringes of and complementing the region's dominant economic order. They represented a beginning for the process of drawing people and capital to harvest the region's pines, served as harbingers of a far greater influx that was to follow, and laid important foundations. They supplied building materials for New Orleans, Biloxi, and lesser communities around the Gulf (such as Galveston and various Mexican ports); they sent lumber to Cuba to supply much of the demand for wood resulting from its growing plantation sugar economy; and they even dispatched occasional cargoes to Northern markets and thus began the familiarization of buyers there with Southern yellow pine, which, though decidedly different from the white pine that long dominated in the North, was a fine building material nonetheless.[38] Between 1850 and 1860 lumber production more than doubled. Although largely unnoticed by outsiders, by 1860 lumbering had become the second most important industry in the South (behind only flour and gristmills).[39]

The operations of Calvin Taylor and his associates typified the area's pioneer lumbering. In 1830, at the age of twenty-five, Taylor moved from New Hampshire to Yazoo County, Mississippi, where he worked as a commission merchant, dealing primarily in cotton. Reflecting the prevailing spirit, he engaged in land speculation. In time the region's economic boom ran its course; at about the same time, Taylor's partner in the business died, forcing liquidation of the overextended firm's assets in order to settle with heirs.[40] Casting about for a new means of livelihood, Taylor settled upon lumbering, and on June 1, 1846, formed a partnership with Gordon Davis to erect a steam sawmill on Bayou Bernard in Harrison County. Building the mill cost a mere $1,046.42, the millsite another $300. In spite of the smallness of the undertaking, it seemed promising. Located at Moss Point, near the mouth of the Pascagoula River, the mill was well situated for shipping to the growing New Orleans market. Taylor's brother urged him to concentrate on the sawmill and let the commission business "go to grass," for lumbering would surely be Taylor's source of future prosperity.[41]

The mill faced problems from the first. A lumber merchant in New Orleans wrote, "[I]f you can be sure of a vessel to bring lumber [here] you can sell," but getting vessels to come to Moss Point was not easy, and it turned out that lumber shipped to New Orleans did not always sell promptly or at prices that would allow a profit. Taylor and Davis soon suffered cash-flow problems. The captain of one vessel complained he had hauled lumber to market for them and "never rec'd anything from it" except promises. Some of the difficulties stemmed from the fact the mill had to shut down from time to time because its owners could not afford to hire an additional hand to clear away, sort, and stack lumber they sawed.[42]

Sawlogs were a constant worry. The partners contracted with local residents to furnish logs; Davis found the first ones delivered "small & bad" and much refuse resulted when they were sawn. Afraid the supplier would not keep them in logs, Davis contracted with a second for an additional one thousand. He explained to Taylor, "we must have plenty of logs to have the mill profitable." Three months later he was repeating the process: a local logger was getting out a raft which "I think we had better take for fear of being disappointed by Gibbons" with whom he had contracted earlier.[43] Davis purchased a "logging truck"—a heavy-duty wagon—to speed the moving of logs from the woods, but it did little to solve the basic problem of undependable suppliers.[44]

The mill ran well for a time, but soon suffered breakdowns. Repair parts arrived slowly and, even then, failed to solve the basic problem—the plant was underpowered. Davis was blunt; they needed a new, larger boiler. Yet acquiring one would be expensive, and the partners were still short on funds.[45]

In spite of problems, Taylor and Davis remained sanguine. Even before the sawmill had begun operation, Davis wrote: "I have become so partial to the Gulf coast that I feel willing to invest mor[e] capital in the Lumber Business there." He proposed adding a planing mill to finish the lumber they sawed, making it more desirable in New Orleans.[46] He also suggested the addition of a lath and shingle mill. Indeed, before the end of 1846 Davis had moved to Mississippi to join Taylor, explaining "there is an attraction there that I cannot account for."[47] Davis found two experienced millmen in Oswego, New York, whom he persuaded to move to the Gulf South to operate their plant. While Davis oversaw the manufacturing, Taylor focused on shipping and sales. Before long they took in Samuel Fowler (an in-law of Taylor and originally from New York) as a third partner and bought a schooner to help haul their cut to New Orleans and other ports.[48]

The Crescent City was a fickle market. Moreover, there seemed little chance conditions there would improve, for as the owners of one of its major lumber yards observed, there were "many mills and Schooners engaged in bringing . . . Lumber" to "the City."[49]

Seeking other outlets, Taylor dispatched Phineas Slayton to investigate the potential of Galveston, but Slayton saw little opportunity there. Its main lumber merchant bought his pine in Mobile for $8 a thousand. At such prices, by the time Taylor added transportation and other expenses, he would clear no more than in New Orleans. Besides, the market was small and business dull, "owing no doubt to the wars," making it almost impossible to sell a cargo of pine in Galveston in less than two or three weeks, a wait "which would destroy all the profits of the load."[50]

Slayton's assessment was not necessarily accurate. For years others had been shipping lumber to Galveston and beyond. Then in 1855 Captain Daniel Goos arrived in what would come to be known as Lake Charles, Louisiana, where lumbering was already the primary economic activity. Goos built a sawmill and schooner dock and began sending lumber down the Calcasieu to Texan and Mexican ports. He was markedly successful.[51]

Cypress was another matter. Slayton reported the Galveston dealer "would pay a high price for all he could get," and Samuel Fowler pushed his partners to erect a cypress mill near some stands he had located. They could purchase the land for $3 an acre, Fowler wrote, and clear $5 to $10 more per thousand milling cypress instead of pine. "I am willing to mortgage evary thing I own to raise the means," he wrote, "so sanguin am I of success." Others were becoming interested in cypress too; a correspondent reported to Taylor that swamp [i.e. cypress] land was much in demand. In spite of all this, Taylor and his partners continued sawing only pine.[52]

The sawmill of Taylor, Davis, and Fowler was but one of many along the Gulf Coast. It and other sawmills in Harrison County consumed some eighty-six thousand logs in 1849. Around Pensacola, where there had been only one sawmill in 1828, there were twenty-five by 1834. Over the next decade, many were converted from water- to steam-power, and production rose rapidly. By 1845 lumbering was Florida's leading industry. McVoy and Keyser, which during the early 1850s dominated Pensacola's lumber trade, shipped not only to New Orleans, but also to New York, Boston, Baltimore, and various lesser Gulf and Atlantic ports. Similarly, near Mobile, steam-powered sawmills gradually replaced watermills. John J. Deshon led the way. Begun in 1823 and repeatedly enlarged, by 1835 Deshon's sawmill boasted an eighty-horsepower steam engine that drove thirty-six saws and was perhaps the largest on the Gulf Coast. Mississippi's coastal mills followed a similar pattern. The first steam sawmill did not appear there until 1835—at Pascagoula in Hancock County—but within five years nine others were to be found in that county alone.[53] Even before the Civil War, some of the mills—those of Andrew Brown in Natchez and Criglar, Batchelder and Company in Pensacola, for example—had become sizable.[54]

Taylor and Davis were not the only operators from the Northeast. Asa Hursey, from Maine, had a small steam sawmill near Pearlington, Mississippi; Henry Weston, another former resident of Maine (although he came south after a brief stint in Wisconsin), worked in mills on the lower Pearl before becoming manager and then part-owner of one of them. There were also Southerners who developed sawmills—for example, Hanson Kelly, who built the first important mill in Mobile.[55] Data are sparse, but it seems clear few millowners came from the pastoral, herding economy that had long prevailed in the area.[56]

The labor that kept these little mills running was black and white, slave and free, local and in-migrant. Records are too incomplete to determine the numbers in each category, but frequent mention makes it clear slave labor was an important element, especially in unskilled positions. A number of sawmill owners, including Calvin Taylor and Andrew Brown, acquired slaves of their own; indeed, William Criglar and his partners owned 125 slaves, 76 of them males of working age. There were many others—probably the majority in light of the shortage of investment capital that plagued so many millowners—who simply hired other's slaves for $15 or so a month when they needed workers. Some slaves rose to positions of considerable responsibility.[57]

Henry Weston, transplanted New Englander, seems to have adjusted to working with slave labor with little difficulty. In 1851, before he had acquired a mill of his own, Weston told his brother he had cleared $550 in six months of sawmill work, "verry fair business for a man with out capital, but mind this is not made without hard work and close application, so close as to all most entirely exclude me from society, [until] there is nothing in my head but niggers & lumber." As a boss of slaves working in the mill, Weston reported he had to tie up and whip some of them "once in a while," but he justified his actions:

> You people think slavery a great Sin but let me tell you that they are as well of[f] as the northern labourers. The laws protect and provide for his [the slave's] feed and clothes and a Dr in case of sikness [and] every thing for his comfort, but he is made to work, if he want [i.e., won't] do his work he is whipped, a chain and ball put to his leg, put in the stocks &c. if a northern man don't show to work he has to go without bread; this is the principal difference.[58]

The ease with which Weston rationalized his behavior was symptomatic of circumstances that troubled others. English immigrant William Garland reported that, while working in a sawmill in Beaufort, North Carolina, he had roundly cursed a black "who was helping me, or rather hindering me." A relative, passing by, heard him and dressed Garland down for his profanity and for not attending church; "all *Respectable people here go* to *Church*," she said—and, one is led to believe, were not supposed to swear even when frustrated by black co-workers.[59] Lincoln Clark went further. Although he had risen to influence after moving to the Gulf South, he became convinced that living in such a society had a corrosive effect even on non-slaveholders and moved back to New England to provide a healthier social environment for his children.[60]

Slave or free, good skilled workmen were difficult to find. Many millowners in the Gulf South seem to have had experiences similar to one in Beaufort who wrote:

> I would engage an engineer [i.e., millwright] if I could be certain of his capability as well as character. . . . I expect an engineer to have a competent knowledge of sawing & the machinery appertaining thereto . . . [as well as] of mill business, as the mere attention to the engine department, constitutes but a small part of the duties I should expect.

. . . [In future hiring], I shall be particular, as I have been grossly
deceived by all the engineers I have employed since I have owned the
mill.[61]

When Alexander McVoy advertised in the Pensacola *Gazette* for a
workman "perfectly understanding the management of a single saw
in a Steam Saw Mill," he promised "liberal wages" but insisted upon
references. Obtaining adequate skilled workers, never easy, surely became
increasingly difficult during the 1850s as the number of sawmills increased
dramatically—from 1850 to 1860, the number in Mississippi more than
doubled.[62]

Henry Weston's experience is illustrative. He arrived in Mississippi in
January 1847 (after weeks of seeking employment in New Orleans) and
obtained work in J. W. Pointevent's little sawmill near the mouth of the
Pearl River. Weston's pay—$45 a month—was fairly standard, but as his
skill became known in the area, he received better offers and the following
year went to work for Judge David R. Wingate running his somewhat larger
mill. In 1849, Weston quit to return to Wisconsin, but soon returned and
was promptly rehired by Wingate. As Weston told his brother,

I am here again with my old employer who dis charged or rather
removed a man to give me a place. I am verry fortunate in having a
good name here, for without it I could not have found anything to do.
Lumbering is verry hard here now; half the mills in the country are
stopped; in St. Tanamy [sic] Parish, which is the north side of Lake
Pontchartrain, of 40 mills only 4 are now running."[63]

Both Wingate and Weston profited from their relationship. Instead of
receiving a monthly salary, Weston was paid on a piece basis: initially 50
cents a thousand board feet for lumber and 10 cents a thousand for lath.
Under Weston's direction, the mill sawed 1.1 million feet of lumber and 775
thousand lath in the first six months of 1851, enabling him to clear $550
after paying board and expenses. Near the end of the season, Weston agreed
to stay, although at a reduced rate of pay. As he explained, "[T]imes have
been verry hard but the prospects are better." Indeed, they were. Within five
years, Weston was able to buy a one-third interest in the mill.[64]

As an owner, Weston was plagued by the same shortages of skilled labor
from which he had benefited earlier. In 1856 he made a trip back East. The
man left in charge of the mill soon quit, and since Weston's two partners
were unable to find a replacement, one of them "had to come over from the

city [of New Orleans] and run the mill, and the business in the city suffered." Weston estimated the partners lost at least $1,000 as a result.[65]

The shortage of skilled laborers contributed to instability. J. W. Pointevent was not alone; holding a skilled employee could be as difficult as finding one in the first place. In the Pensacola area millmen often tried to overcome these twin problems by bringing in experienced workers from the North; in Mobile, Frederick Law Olmsted reported, the mechanics "are all from the North." Andrew Brown, on the other hand, sought a solution by training and promoting talented help from within his organization, including slaves such as Simon Gray.[66]

The fact that the South lagged in industrial development no doubt exacerbated the difficulties of attracting talented workers from outside the region and probably contributed to the shortage of skilled workers more than did low wages. Indeed, the New Orleans *Daily Picayune* claimed skilled white workers were the best paid in the country, and although there is a paucity of data with which to make systematic comparisons, skilled workers do not seem to have been paid significantly less in the Gulf South than in northern mills. [67]

Slaves, whose labor could be contracted for relatively cheaply during agriculture's slack seasons, seem to have done little to depress the wage rates for skilled workers. Even the regional fixation on cotton production, which caused much of the South's investment capital to be drawn into land and slaves instead of industrial development, seems not to have depressed the wages of skilled mechanics much below national levels.[68]

The fact remains, nowhere were the wages of skilled workers really high. Henry Weston was an anomaly. Indeed, the experiences of William Garland and his friends John Evans and Samuel Sweat, all of whom immigrated to the South from England, probably reflect the problems of skilled workers more accurately than Weston's. Evans went to Baltimore, which he soon was calling one of the worst places for a mechanic to get ahead; as he put it, "Baltimore is not the place its cracked up [to be] . . . a man of money can make money here as easy as any other place, [but] for a poor man there is no chance." A few weeks later, he added, "Baltimore is getting worse every year for the labouring Classes, so much so that in a few years they will . . . be under as much Subjugation as they are in most parts of Europe." Still, Evans's wife did not "seem altogether willing for me to go West [i.e., to the Gulf South], as she seems to think I will no[t] do any better [there] than what I have been doing" in Baltimore.[69]

Garland and Sweat had ill fortune too. Garland moved from job to job, seeking employment that would allow him to get ahead financially, but with little success. He contracted to work at a sawmill near Beaufort, North Carolina, but the owner refused to advance any money until the end of his three-month term of service for fear Garland would take it and decamp, for a former employee had "played him a similar trick." Sweat, who worked at another Southern mill, wrote he was "worse off in money matters than when I began here . . . about 30 dollars or more in debt now than when I began," and the owner was threatening to close the sawmill, a course which would have left Sweat with "nothing to do, in debt, and . . . nothing to pay it with."[70]

Although desperate for skilled workers, sawmill owners did little to make jobs more attractive. Working in sawmills was no easier in the South than elsewhere. The work was difficult and dangerous, and the treatment of laborers often left much to be desired. Frederick Ball provides a case in point. He worked for Calvin Taylor and boarded with co-owner Samuel Fowler. When Taylor complained to Ball of his attitude, the latter responded heatedly:

> *when I was eney wheres But hard at work in the mill I was where I was not wanted. . . . I often herd them [other workers] say that tha would not be hiere [hired] for any price to do as I was doing so many differint kinds of work and work so hard as I did. I eaven ben told that I was a fool for doing it, that I wold not be though[t] as mutch of and get a kick [fired] at last. It matters not of the dangers that I under go and the rest of them allso. If a Saw flies to [pieces] or a belt brakes or [a worker] gets ketch in the masheanery and cripple for life or killed all of this is nothing. We are nothing but hiard men not so good as the niggers.*[71]

Apparently widespread, such treatment helps to explain the transient nature of the industry's white labor force. Claims that, due to mechanization, all a worker had to do was "look on and see his work done as if by magic" were patently false, the product of local boosterism and the uninformed.[72]

Unlike in sawmills, work in the woods and the transportation of logs to the mills seem to have been primarily carried out by white residents of the Piney Woods. Sawmill owners sometimes dispatched slaves to the interior to get out logs, but this was the exception rather than the rule.[73]

Logging and rafting provided welcome sources of employment for the plain folk of the interior. Most seem to have viewed cutting and rafting a few logs to market much the same as they viewed hunting deer to obtain hides to sell—that is, as a source of occasional cash to buy things they could not grow, kill, gather, or make, but certainly not as a vocation or steady source of employment.

More was involved than the long-standing idea that resources of the land were free for the taking. Although the pastoral economy of the interior seemed remarkably stable to casual observers—after all, it had survived in Southern forests for one hundred and fifty years and more—it was, in fact, in trouble. Repeated burning to "green up" the grasslands had taken its toll of the sandy soil, reducing its capacity to support the lush vegetation that had attracted herdsmen. When a sizable influx of population occurred in the 1850s, the land, already stocked to (or beyond) its carrying capacity, soon showed the effects. Even canebrakes, which long seemed impervious to man or beast, began to lose their vitality as year after year too many cattle and hogs were left to feed in them for too many months. They were increasingly trampled and dry, and fires invaded them as never before. The canebrakes of southern Mississippi were indicative; in 1852 Benjamin Wailes found extensive areas of "brakes which have been destroyed by the heards [of cattle] & by the firing of the woods." Under the resulting circumstances, when lumbermen arrived in the Piney Woods in search of logs, they had no difficulty finding people willing to supply them.[74]

Piney Woods residents considered logs, like grass, theirs for the taking. Government agents and landowners alike struggled to prevent illegal cutting, but with limited success. As early as 1811, axemen were cutting illegally on government land near Mobile. When they were warned to halt their activities, a spokesman announced they would resist anyone who tried to stop them. They apparently floated out their log rafts the following spring without trouble. Similarly, in 1819 the Army commander in Mobile seized 3,800 logs he claimed had been cut on public land, but he was unable to get witnesses to testify at trial and had to release the logs.[75] In 1824 John Morris ordered timber thieves to cease cutting on his land or face "the vigor of the law," and in 1835 John Hunt, a Pensacola lumberman, published a notice warning against "cutting wood or committing further depredations upon my property." East of Pensacola, Apalachicola's town fathers set a fine of up to $200 for those convicted of illegal cutting, while the Apalachicola Land Company warned "persons who are known to be now engaged in cutting ... on the lands of said Company ... not to remove said Timber." The "wood choppers," as loggers were known in the Gulf South, and the raftsmen who got out the logs, both had reputations for being rough and independent; there is no reason to believe such warnings had much effect.[76]

Loggers were as shrewd and unscrupulous as they were hard. Charles Black reported to William Criglar that a raftsman known as "Old Sledge" had arrived with logs he had agreed to deliver. Black wrote: "It is *fair Small Timber*," the quality of which did not compare to that supplied by another logman any better "than I to Hercules." Black detailed the problems with the logs—primarily they were too short to furnish the timbers for which a buyer had contracted. Black concluded: "I write this that you may not be beaten at the game Old Sledge will try to play on you."[77]

Timber had not only to be cut, but also transported from the woods to the mills. After trees were felled, limbed, and sawed into lengths, the logs were hauled to nearby streams for floating to waiting sawmills. Log transportation to streamside was difficult—and at times impossible, for winter rains often turned the forest floor into a quagmire. Wheeled wagons, known as "caralogs" and usually pulled by four teams of oxen, were used to move logs. In the 1850s a slave named Usan Vaughan devised improvements that allowed caralogs to haul even the largest logs; they would remain at work in the Southern forests into the twentieth century, as would "big wheels," introduced from the Lake States.[78]

From streamside, most logs were floated downstream in rafts maneuvered by crews who used a long pole with a blade on the end for a rudder, employed

Big wheels with longleaf pine log. Developed in Michigan, big wheels were subsequently used in pine forests in the South and Far West. Courtesy Dolph Briscoe Center for American History, University of Texas, Austin, East Texas Collection, #di_01288.

ropes to snub them to a tree or stump to swing them around sharp bends, and at times simply poled or paddled to direct their course. On large streams without much current, rivermen sometimes used "bull pens" in moving logs, for they were easier and cheaper to assemble than rafts. Logs were floated loose on smaller streams too winding to allow rafting, but not on larger ones.[79] Nowhere did anything develop even remotely approximating the log drives of Maine, the Adirondack country of New York, or the upper Lake States. The *Gazette* crowed that the rivers flowing into Pensacola Bay made rafting from the interior easy and logs could be brought there "with the greatest facility," but such claims merely reflected editorial puffery.[80] At first rafts were simply tied up when they reached their destination, or logs floated loose or in bull pens were corralled near the millsite, but as the number of mills and rafts increased more sophisticated means were adopted, including a large boom at Moss Point.[81]

The beginnings of log rafting in the Gulf South are obscure, but it appears to have been under way by the 1820s and clearly was present by 1840 when there were already ten sawmills near the mouth of the Pearl. By the 1850s it was full blown. In 1852 Benjamin Wailes reported Biloxi's rivers were full of logs being floated to the mills; the same was surely true on the Pearl, Altamaha, and other streams as well.[82]

Calvin Taylor's operations are illustrative. Like the owners of other small mills, Taylor and his partners contracted for logs with plain folk of the interior. In 1847, Taylor paid $137 for three hundred logs purchased from Alexander Scarborough (that is, 46.5 cents per log delivered at the mill); in another contract, he paid 30 cents a log. By the late 1850s, with more mills competing for logs, the market for lumber good, and stands becoming more distant, Taylor had to pay 41 cents apiece for logs cut on his own land and 61 cents for those from contracting loggers' land or elsewhere (such as state land or the public domain). In another case, in 1859-1860, Taylor paid 53.5 cents a log. In other words, although prices varied from contract to contract and had increased by the late 1850s, Taylor paid in the neighborhood of $2.50 to $3 per thousand board feet for logs. Only the largest and best trees seem to have been acceptable. One contract from 1847 specified logs had to be at least eighteen inches in diameter at their smaller end. Although Taylor owned slaves by this time, he contracted with white loggers (whose woods crews seem also to have been white) to supply logs.[83]

Transportation costs from the delivery point at streamside to the mill were normally not included in the price of logs. Those who contracted to supply logs and those who rafted them were often different, especially as division of labor became more common with the passage of time. The cost of transportation varied with distance, the method used, and the nature of the streams on which the rafts were floated. Records are fragmentary, but costs apparently averaged in the neighborhood of 20 cents a log.[84]

Although expenses for logs and labor were low, so too were the prices of lumber. During the 1830s and 1840s, prices hovered around $8 to $12 a thousand, but even at these rates a well-run mill could turn a profit. R. E. Foster put it succinctly: "[T]o make a Steam mill pay well, much capital, much industry, and close economy are required, without which, they pay poorly." Foster pointed to W. H. Brown, who had a steam sawmill on the Pearl River, as an example of a millowner whose hard work and ability had made him a wealthy man. Andrew Brown, who specialized in cypress, did even better. In 1847 on gross sales of $56,000, he estimated he cleared $28,000. A decade later, Henry Weston reported he was helping his brother and Robert B. Carre in negotiations to buy a mill "and if we succede it will be a verry pretty business for them. Say $12 or $1500 a year for each of them."[85] By 1860 prices had climbed considerably, and Weston announced: "We have [been] doing a good business this year; we have not lost but 3 days running time since last Christmas and have cut 60,000 per week for the whole time." He and his partners were getting $18 per thousand, while logs cost "on an avarige $5.75." When Weston said that they made money like smoke, he was hardly exaggerating. By the start of the Civil War, Weston and his two partners had paid off the notes on their mill, paid for rebuilding after it burned, allowed each partner $5,000 a year in salary, and acquired $20,000 worth of slaves—a remarkable accomplishment considering Weston had arrived in Mississippi as a poor but talented workman only fourteen years before.[86]

Few millowners were so successful. Many operations suffered from poor management, inadequately skilled employees in key positions, and on occasion even arson or peculation. The record is far from complete, but it is clear bankruptcies were not uncommon. Even Robert Carre's mill, from which Weston had expected so much, foundered; Weston explained: "[B]eing green in a mill and having no good sawyer has made his business drag."[87]

Most operators' successes may have been more modest than Weston's, but a handful did even better: Andrew Brown in Natchez; Criglar, Batchelder and Company, McVoy and Keyser, and Forsyth and Simpson in Pensacola; and John J. Deshon in Mobile. The combined effect of these and other mills was dramatic.

Pensacola, long a minor port dependent upon markets in Mobile and New Orleans for the sale of its lumber, was by 1845 becoming less reliant on these markets, and by late 1850s its lumbermen were regularly dispatching cargoes to the East Coast, Caribbean Islands, Mexico, South America, and Europe. In 1857 over twenty-seven million feet of lumber left its harbor.[88] Pensacola was not alone. By 1860 there were an estimated 339 saw and planing mills in Alabama, 228 in Mississippi, and 166 in Louisiana. In spite of its late start, there were also 192 in Texas, a good portion shipping to New Orleans, the fastest-growing city in the South. Altogether these mills employed over fifty-six hundred people and produced roughly $7.4 million worth of lumber. By this time, one out of every five manufacturing establishments in Texas was a sawmill, while in Alabama some 25 percent of those engaged in manufacturing worked in sawmills. When one adds figures for indirect employment in such things as logging, rafting, and the shipping and sale of lumber, it becomes clear lumbering was of major importance in a vast swath across the Gulf South.[89]

Impressive beginnings had been made, but unlike in the Lake States they had come slowly, over a period of many decades; in 1860 most of the region's forests remained untouched. Yet there were those who recognized that whatever followed would encompass significant changes. Calvin Taylor was among them. He understood the use of waterways to move logs to sawmills could not be expanded much beyond the levels of the late 1850s, and there were vast forests that could not be reached readily from floatable streams. Railroads were being built, and Taylor foresaw that they could be used to tap new stands and open the way for unprecedented growth in Southern lumbering. Sereno Taylor agreed, telling his brother, "milling will be greatly increased and better" in Mississippi as railroad construction proceeds.[90] Those were considerations for the future. Until the Civil War brought production to a halt, millmen stayed busy using traditional practices: floating logs to their mills, sawing lumber, and shipping it in coasting vessels to New Orleans and other markets around the Gulf. The days of vast, modern mills supplied with logs by railroad and shipping their cut the same way were well in the future.

CHAPTER TEN

Bonanza Years in the Gulf South

The society of the Piney Woods was ill equipped to cope with the sweeping changes inaugurated when outsiders brought industrial forestry to the region following the Civil War. Prewar lumbermen had instituted changes, but they had been too few, their reach too limited, to launch society on a distinctly new course. Indeed, in most places what changes had occurred probably resulted more from the deteriorating condition of pastoral society than the impact of lumbering. Beginning in the 1870s all that changed. Lumbermen—and the railroads on which they depended—remade society in the Southern pineries.

Henry J. Lutcher and G. Bedell Moore were pioneers of the new order. Lutcher and Moore were self-made businessmen who owned a medium-sized sawmill in Williamsport, Pennsylvania.[1] In the late 1870s, with sawtimber in the Keystone State becoming scarce and the Williamsport strike, in which they had played a small role, fresh in their minds, they began casting about for a new area of operations. For a time, they considered Michigan and Wisconsin, but soon decided so many lumbermen had already moved there that the pine forests of Texas and Louisiana, about which they had heard good reports, might be more promising. On January 11, 1877, the two left Williamsport for the South, intent upon determining if the reports were true. En route they met in St. Louis with railroad officials, who told them about available timberlands and gave them letters of introduction. They stopped to examine timber near Pine Bluff, Arkansas, and around Texarkana, on the Texas-Arkansas border. In the latter location, they found lumbermen paid $4 to $4.50 a thousand for logs and "could sell all the lumber they could make for $10 to $12" delivered at the railroad. From Texarkana to Longview, Texas, they found extensive timberlands and a number of small mills that catered to buyers in the Dallas-Fort Worth area. Continuing south, they stopped at "a fifth rate country hotel" in Palestine and then proceeded to Houston, carefully observing the waterways, timber stands, sawmills, and railroad systems as they went. They were not impressed.[2]

Things changed as the pair moved eastward toward Beaumont and the Texas-Louisiana border.[3] In Hardin County they met Colonel J. T. Wood who had seventy-two thousand acres of fine longleaf pine, the South's premier species, that he was willing to sell for $1.50 an acre. With logs selling in Beaumont for $5.50 a thousand, the timber seemed a bargain, even though, as Moore noted, "the natives are noted for their 'skinning' propensities with travelers"—and, no doubt, with would-be Yankee timber buyers.[4]

Departing Beaumont in late January, Lutcher and Moore traveled for six days by canoe and horseback through longleaf pine forest, most of which had never seen an axe. Accompanied by James Ingalls, who served as guide, they covered some 175 miles. For lack of anything better, the trio stayed each night with local settlers, and Moore grumbled repeatedly about accommodations, food, and prices.[5]

The stands impressed Lutcher and Moore, especially those between the Neches and Sabine rivers, though it was clear that transportation would be a problem. Already logs were being floated from fifty to two hundred and fifty miles down the Neches and Angelina rivers to Beaumont. Eventually rail networks might serve to bring logs to the area's sawmills, but for some time to come they would have to be floated to the mills. Thanks to their experience in Williamsport, the two had considerable knowledge about floating logs from the woods, and Moore examined every waterway he saw with log transportation in mind.[6]

After returning to Beaumont, Lutcher and Moore continued by train to Orange, twenty-three miles to the east on the Texas-Louisiana border. There they at last found a site that met their requirements. Orange was closer to the Gulf than Beaumont, while upstream vast stands of reasonably priced, quality timber grew close to the banks of its waterway, the Sabine River (unlike along Beaumont's Neches, where cutting had already been extensive). Moreover, there was a foot more water over the bar of the Sabine than that of the Neches, making export by sea easier.[7] Good millsites were available in Orange, and local business interests encouraging. From there, they pointed out, lumber could be shipped either to Texas markets by rail or out to sea through the Sabine Pass waterway. The river itself had good current and depth and could be rafted four months a year; by digging a ditch across The Narrows, thus bypassing a bottleneck of shoal water fifteen miles upstream, it could readily be turned into a first-class waterway for log rafting. Encouraged, Lutcher and Moore began a careful evaluation of available markets and, satisfied, proceeded to buy a millsite. Lutcher stayed on in Orange, while Moore returned to Williamsport to wrap up operations there.[8]

At first the two contracted for sawlogs and things did not go well, but in 1879 they commenced buying timberland on either side of the Texas-

Louisiana border and supplying their own logs, hauling them by big wheels, cart, tram, and eventually railroad to the Sabine for rafting to the mill. The business soon prospered. By 1887 it had over ninety-three thousand acres in Louisiana's Calcasieu Parish alone and was shipping some fifty-four million feet of lumber a year, although problems with log rafting continued to bedevil them.[9]

Lutcher and Moore were not the first to manufacture lumber in Orange. In the 1850s Judge David R. Wingate left Mississippi, where he had been associated with Henry Weston, and launched operations on the Sabine. By 1877 he had the finest sawmill in the city, and unlike most Deep South millowners, who bought sawlogs from independent operators, Wingate

Felling old-growth longleaf pine near Bonami, Louisiana, for a Long-Bell affiliate. Still present was the open, grassy ground cover that long served pastoralists in the Gulf South. Courtesy McNeese State University, #1434.

owned some twenty thousand acres of timber. But with a capacity of only twenty to thirty thousand feet per day, Wingate's mill was modest compared to what Lutcher and Moore—and many other Northerners who followed them—would build.[10]

Faced with a shortage of capital and other problems, Southern millowners had difficulty rebuilding after the Civil War. In eastern Louisiana, there were fewer sawmills in 1870 than in 1850. Some Gulf South mills managed to resume operations following the war and continued to operate in the years that followed, but almost without exception they lacked the investment capital to take full advantage of emerging opportunities. The case of Calvin Taylor is illustrative. His mill was quickly back in operation after the war, but he lacked the funds to expand. Indeed, although it continued to run until his death in 1888, Taylor's mill never again reached the production level it had enjoyed on the eve of the conflict.[11] Taylor's son Samuel was forced to eke out a living as an itinerant lumber scaler. Revealingly, the younger Taylor referred to himself as "poor white trash" even though he was sufficiently well educated to conjugate Latin.[12]

Some of the more fortunate Southern mills—such as Mississippi's Pointevent-Favre Lumber Company on the Pearl River and the L. N. Dantzler and Wyatt Griffin plants at Moss Point—were able to expand to take advantage of the revived coastal trade.[13] But while their owners had sufficient capital to enlarge their sawmills and ancillary facilities, they lacked the wherewithal to make extensive purchases of timberland and build the railroads needed as logging moved away from streamside tracts and rafting was replaced by logging railroads.[14] Many of these mills were to continue operating for years, and even to prosper, but they were eclipsed in the overall scheme of Southern lumbering by the huge operations outsiders established to serve newly accessible interior markets. Only the L. N. Dantzler Lumber Company grew sufficiently to be considered one of the "big" mills. It was to continue cutting until the very end of the South's era of bonanza lumbering, not closing until 1938.[15]

Railroads were more responsible than anything else for ushering in the new era. Southern railroad building surged following the Civil War, encouraged both by state governments that considered railroads vital to the rebuilding process and by Northerners who detected investment opportunities in the defeated Confederacy. By 1872 war-damaged rail lines had been rebuilt and some thirty-three hundred miles of new ones constructed, increasing the total mileage in the South by almost 40 percent. Numerous lines built during Reconstruction went bankrupt, but by the 1880s many had reorganized and new, more soundly financed railroad companies had appeared.[16]

Rebuilding war-torn railroads and repairing other damage done during the war created demand that helped the owners of mills get back on their financial feet, while the construction of new lines internal to the South opened regional markets as never before. The Texas and New Orleans, when completed from Orange to New Orleans, was one such project, the Mobile and New Orleans another. With demand strong in the Crescent City, lumber shipments began moving over these lines almost as soon as they were completed.[17]

Just as they had with Lutcher and Moore, railroad companies actively participated in bringing Northern lumbermen and their capital south, hoping thereby to insure freight for their lines. They provided transportation, leads, introductions, and encouragement. The Illinois Central was among the most active, running special trains to carry scores of lumbermen south from Chicago to Mississippi and Louisiana to investigate possibilities.[18]

At first railroads only skirted the pineries, but soon lines penetrated the heart of the belt, opening badly needed sources of logs for coastal sawmills and making mills more feasible than ever in the interior. Foremost among these was the Houston, East and West Texas which constructed a rail network in the East Texas pineries that within a few years of Lutcher and Moore's visit had turned the area into a booming center of commercial activity. Along the sixty-six-mile length of one shortline tributary to the Texas and New Orleans, old timers later recalled sawmills being so numerous that one was never beyond the sound of a mill whistle. Other local lines and a host of crudely constructed logging railroads built by lumber firms also made the pineries increasingly accessible.[19]

Gradually railroads opened more distant markets to Southern lumber. Although white pine still dominated in the important St. Louis market, by 1875 over 20 percent of the lumber received there was Southern pine, and the percentage was rising rapidly. Other markets to the north were opening too. So great was the volume carried by the Nashville, Chattanooga & St. Louis Railway—which ran from Memphis to New Orleans via Jackson, Mississippi (incorporating the old Mobile and New Orleans line)—that management labeled it "The Great Lumber Route." Similarly, by 1885 lumber was the largest class of freight on the Illinois Central, while the Mobile and Ohio and the New Orleans and Northeastern also carried large quantities northward. In sum, as Northern prejudice against yellow pine eroded, as development proceeded in the Prairie States and beyond, and as Lake States lumber grew more costly and production there fell, Southern pine came to dominate in much of Mid-America. Favorable freight rates helped make it competitive.[20]

Developments in Virginia, North Carolina, and Georgia encouraged those in the Gulf South. Having the advantage of convenient coastwise transportation from Savannah, Brunswick, and Darien, lumbermen in those states had penetrated markets in the populous Northeast even before the Civil War. The trade recommenced soon after the return of peace and accelerated as Maine's output of white pine declined. Production in Jacksonville, located near Florida's northern Atlantic coast, burgeoned too, although its lumbermen apparently shipped more by sea than by rail. In 1875, seeing opportunity in all this, New York capitalist William E. Dodge invested in three hundred thousand acres of Georgia pine. His investment and the Northeast's growing familiarity with Southern pine, reported in the trade press, surely helped undermine the suspicions Midwestern consumers and investors had of Southern pine.[21]

Speculation in timberland was rampant when Henry Lutcher and Bedell Moore arrived in the South. Such had not always been the case. In the first years after the Civil War, most lumbermen bought logs from independent operators, just as they had before the war. Since loggers seldom bothered to obtain title to land on which they cut, they were able to provide logs at remarkably low prices; as the Pascagoula *Democrat Star* noted, a logger could not buy timber and sell the logs to millmen in competition with those with a free supply of timber. Under the circumstances, lumbermen thought it wiser to put their limited capital into milling facilities rather than timberland. Secretary of the Interior Carl Schurz found "enterprising timber thieves not merely stealing trees, but stealing whole forests . . . [and] hundreds of saw mills in full blast, devoted exclusively to the sawing up of timber stolen from the public lands."[22]

Few objected. Theft of timber from public lands was so well established in the South that taking it was widely deemed a right. As Alabama Congressman Hillary Herbert said, "The Government had permitted and . . . encouraged the people to treat the public domain as common property."[23] Schurz put the onus on the public, rather than the government. While he was head of the Department of the Interior (1877-1881), "the notion that the public forests were everybody's property, to be taken and used or wasted as anybody pleased, [was] everywhere in full operation." All the factors that

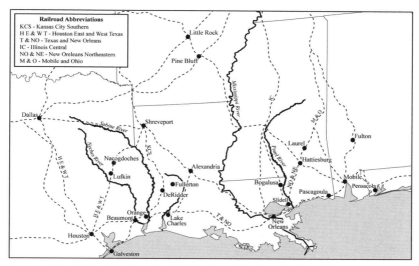

Bonanza South lumber frontier (only selected railroads shown). Map by Sarah E. Hinman.

made timber trespass common in the Lake States, plus others peculiar to the Gulf South, were at work. As noted in the previous chapter, residents of the Piney Woods, the dominant source of loggers, had long run their cattle on public lands—and had supplemented their incomes by hunting there as well. Taking logs from those same lands was but a small extension of these foraging practices and one increasingly necessary as the carrying capacity of the ranges declined. In addition, the fact that the lands supplying most of the logs belonged to the government against which Southerners had so recently fought surely served to weaken whatever limited compunctions against illegal cutting may have existed.[24]

Mississippi's loggers may not have been the worst thieves, but their story is especially well documented. In 1877, J. A. Williamson, head of the General Land Office, directed agents to confiscate logs along the Pascagoula and Pearl and at sawmills downstream, claiming they had been stolen from federal land. According to the Pascagoula *Democrat Star* the logs and lumber seized were worth over $136,000. Wyatt and E. F. Griffin were hardest hit, with $37,500 and $33,000 worth of logs and lumber taken respectively.[25]

While prosecution of the cases against the lumbermen and loggers dragged on, the flow of logs dried up and sawmill after sawmill shut down; eventually thirty-seven mills in Mississippi's coastal strip closed. Four hundred people gathered at a mass meeting to formulate a plan of resistance; all activity connected with the lumber business was at a standstill and many people were on the brink of starvation, the group proclaimed. Local authorities supported the millmen. Newspaper editors inveighed against the government's agents, and the sheriff of Jackson County backed by a posse of citizens went so far as to seize rafts of confiscated logs and return them to their "owners," who had sworn affidavits that the logs had not been taken from federal lands.

Protest reached the floor of Congress, and in 1879 Congressman Herbert introduced a bill to halt prosecution of those whose logs had been seized. It was, one opponent said, a bill to protect "individuals for conspiring . . . to defraud the United States of its property and rights" and would permit them "to hide their tracks." Herbert won support from other Southern representatives, for similar developments had occurred elsewhere—in Louisiana's Calcasieu Parish, for instance. "Deaf was Congress, and deaf the people seemed to be," Schurz lamented. Still, Herbert's proposal was watered down before passage. In the end, relief came not because of his actions, but because federal prosecution withered after Schurz, the driving force behind Williamson's efforts to halt timber trespass, left office in 1881.[26]

Forestland was gradually passing into private ownership, a development that would alter the situation dramatically. Warrants issued to veterans of the Mexican War allowing them to select acreage from the public domain (or to assign them to someone else), land grants to railroads, the Choctaw Donation Act, the Swampland Act of 1850 (which gave title to overflowed lands to the states), and the Graduation Act of 1854 (which dropped the price of federal land to as little as 12.5 cents an acre if it had been on the market, unsold, for a considerable period), combined to open the door. Through these instruments, a vast acreage would pass into private hands.[27]

Mississippi was typical. Sales by the state were slow until 1858 when it reduced the price of swampland by half (to 25 cents an acre in some counties). After the war the pace of transfer quickened as the rebuilding of damaged rail lines and the planning of new ones made it clear long-isolated timber would soon take on new value. However, with state land cheaper than the usual federal price of $1.25 an acre and with the practice of timber theft so well established, sales by the United States continued to lag.[28]

Passage of the Southern Homestead Act in 1866 halted land sales by the United States. Federal land was now reserved for entry by homesteaders, who could claim tracts of up to eighty acres. The new law did less to advance the cause of the South's agrarian smallholders (including recently freed slaves) than its sponsors had hoped, but it accomplished more than its Southern critics were wont to admit. Between 1867 and its repeal in 1876 homesteaders filed over forty thousand entries under the act; indeed, Paul

Gates points out, there was more homesteading in the South in proportion to available acreage than elsewhere in the public land states. Out of 32.4 million acres of federal land in Alabama in 1866, all but 4.6 million had passed into private hands by 1876. Even in Florida, where much of the land was too swampy to be of use without expensive draining, nearly half the available acreage of 1866 had been disposed of by 1876.[29]

The Commissioner of the General Land Office charged that numerous filings under the Southern Homestead Law were by dummy entrymen acting on behalf of lumber companies. Even many with every intention of becoming farmers soon found their sandy tracts ill suited for agriculture and abandoned or sold them to lumbermen or speculators. Florida's Surveyor General made similar charges. Thus, when lumbermen such as Lutcher and Moore and L. N. Dantzler commenced programs of timber purchase, they found many a smallholder eager to sell. A good portion, no doubt, had gained title through the Southern Homestead Act.[30]

In addition to providing a body of would-be sellers of timberland, the act gave notice to Northerners that there was still unclaimed forestland in the Gulf South. Its repeal after ten years and replacement by new legislation allowing entry to unclaimed tracts of any size for their auction price or the government minimum of $1.25 an acre (usually the latter) "opened up an orgy of speculation."[31]

Lumbermen from the Lake States were especially active in the scramble, for experience in the North had demonstrated the acquisition of timberland to be one of the surest routes to profit. One of their number noted, "Almost every man in Michigan who has made money out of pine has made it by the rise in stumpage rather than by manufacturing and selling it," while the Bureau of Corporations reported a widespread belief that "there is no profit in the sawmill, that the profit is in the timber." Articles in the Northern trade press reported Southern timberland close to water or rail transportation could be had for from $1 to $5 per acre. Cruisers sent south to evaluate opportunities confirmed the reports. The South was ripe with opportunity— Florida alone reportedly had 6.6 billion feet of standing timber—but one needed to move quickly to get title before prices climbed.[32]

Henry Lutcher's experience is illustrative. He found six thousand acres of Louisiana pine he wished to obtain with soldiers' warrants, and urged John Dibert, his key locator, to get title as fast as possible, for others were also interested. As Lutcher explained, "Our object will be to get the Large Best Bodies first & pick up the Stragling last." He went on: if land seemed "very desirable" they could take whole sections, with Dibert only riding the section lines before filing; they could "[e]xamine the Middle of sections afterwards." In light of the competition for key tracts, secrecy was vital. A broker told Lutcher & Moore: "[S]end Capt. D. your land man up here. I will ride over the Country with him and show him the lands I offer for sale. . . . We will of course not let his business be known to others until we have looked at the lands."[33] Such precautions did not insure success. Titles were often murky, thanks in part to peculiarities of Louisiana's land laws and the vagueness of old Spanish land grants. Not infrequently, conflicting claims plagued buyers.[34]

Unlike Lutcher and Moore, many of those most active in seeking control of Southern timberland were not operators of sawmills, but speculators pure and simple. Charles Goodyear, who was to erect a huge plant at Bogalusa, Louisiana, maintained that most of the timber he and other Northern millmen purchased in the 1890s came from speculators who had bought the land from the United States a decade or so before for $1.25 an acre.[35] H. L. Davis was one such.[36] Having acquired one hundred and seventy thousand acres in southern Mississippi that he described as "the finest body [of timber] in the state," Davis offered it to Lutcher & Moore for $1.50 an acre. His price was reasonable, but Lutcher & Moore turned down the offer, preferring to concentrate purchases where the logs could be milled at their plant in Texas. They directed Dibert to "look at . . . Louisiana thoroughly" before investigating lands elsewhere. For their part, Michigan lumbermen Charles Hackley and Thomas Hume—who had acquired large stands in the Carolinas, Mississippi, and Louisiana—found that treating their new holdings as investments yielded better returns than logging them.[37]

Manuscript records contain little on speculators such as Davis, but those of Robert A. Corbin provide tantalizing glimpses. Another speculator, R. L. Duvall, wrote Corbin, noting that "You[r] timber deals are very large" and then, somewhat later, informed him, "I have on deck here some tracts of very fine land, and great opportunities to make a great deal of money. . . . [W]e are now negociating to close a deal of 43,000 acres, now if you are interested . . . you must come to the front, stay with us, and help out"—financially, of course. In the end Corbin took a one-third interest in the "deal" at $1.50 an acre. The land was apparently sold to Chicago lumbermen a year later, but the price obtained is not clear.[38]

Both buyers and sellers often worked through timber brokers, paying a commission for their services. The records of brokers are fragmentary, but their role was clearly important. W. H. Howcott, a New Orleans broker active as Lutcher & Moore began acquiring timber, seems fairly typical. On a single-page handout headed "Read This Carefully," he listed nineteen tracts—one cypress, the rest pine or hardwood—all described as "heavily timbered." He also offered "a number of good mill sites in Mississippi . . . [and] a few good saw mills." The timbered tracts ranged from one thousand to one hundred thousand acres and from $1.25 to $15 an acre. Three were marked "sold": one hundred thousand acres in Georgia for $2.50 an acre; thirty-six thousand acres in Escambia County, Alabama, for $3 an acre; and twenty-three thousand acres in northern Louisiana for $1.25 an acre.[39]

Unless they were near a sawmill that needed logs, small tracts were difficult for brokers to sell. Howcott told the owner of one six hundred and forty-acre tract that the buyer he had available thought it too small and too far from his holdings. Another broker told the same would-be seller he did not think he could get the asking price of $3 an acre "for so small a tract," later adding he might be able to get $1 an acre for it. Perhaps brokers simply did not want to be bothered with small tracts, for they offered little profit even if a buyer were found. Under the circumstances, smallholders often approached sawmill operators directly when they wished to sell timberland.[40]

Size was not the only factor determining a tract's desirability; terrain was also important. Not familiar with railroad logging, Henry Lutcher initially hesitated to buy land well back from streamside, but he soon adjusted his thinking. In 1887 he wrote Dibert from Natchitoches, Louisiana, "I have been through a great deal of pine hills up here and I am not so afraid of the hills as I was before," for they could "go up the ravines with track & haul the Timber down hill to them."[41]

Previous cutting, legal or illegal, was also a consideration. After investigating one tract, Dibert reported "Hackley has . . . so little [timber] left that I don't think it advisable to take hold of any of it." The situation was not unusual, for trespass continued unabated as stands passed into private ownership. Absentee owners were especially vulnerable.[42]

In addition to their business in timberland, brokers dealt in warrants. One of them, J. L. Bradford, informed Lutcher & Moore he had two to three thousand acres of "'good valid' scrip in my office in N.O.," which the firm could use on timberlands Dibert had located for $1.20 an acre. Lutcher must have considered Bradford's proposal a bargain, for he had told his associates not long before that warrants were going for "about $4 per acre so when you get them don't locate $1.25 land with them." Such land could be acquired more cheaply by outright purchase. Given the go-ahead, Bradford proceeded to file on some twenty-three hundred acres the lumberman from Orange had selected.[43]

By the 1880s, the woods were full of timber brokers-cum-speculators, many from the Lake States and Northeast; in Mississippi from 1880 to

1888 over 85 percent of federal sales of five thousand acres or more were to Northerners. Their actions pushed the price of timberland upwards. Concerned by the rapidity of developments, the Commissioner of the General Land Office urged an end to private entry at $1.25 per acre, proposing instead that land of the United States be sold at its real value. The Pascagoula *Democrat Star* added its voice, decrying the speed with which timberland was passing into the hands of outsiders; the *Southern Lumberman* agreed; and Mississippi's state legislature, concerned over growing land monopoly, passed a law aimed at tightening controls on the sale of swamplands.[44]

The activities of Howcott, Bradford, and most other timber brokers were modest compared to those of Edward A. and Edward F. Brackenridge, Delos A. Blodgett, and James D. Lacey. The Brackenridges reportedly located over seven hundred thousand acres for their customers. Blodgett, after a successful career in lumbering in Michigan, began buying in Mississippi in 1882 and by 1906 owned 721,000 acres, much of it subsequently sold for $30 to $40 an acre.[45] But James D. Lacey was king of the lot.

Lacey first came south in 1879 as a traveling drug salesman. Recognizing opportunity in the region's almost untapped forests, he entered into partnership with others from Grand Rapids, Michigan, to purchase timberlands in southwestern Missouri and then in January 1881 went into partnership with William M. Robinson, also of Grand Rapids, to form the timber brokerage firm of Robinson & Lacey. They soon expanded the area of their activities, first into Mississippi and Louisiana and subsequently into Alabama, Georgia, Florida, and elsewhere. After Robinson's retirement in 1898, Lacey organized a successor firm, J. D. Lacey & Company, and continued acquiring timberland.

Lacey was apparently the first in Mississippi and Louisiana to recognize the potential of large-scale estimating, grouping, and entering of timberlands for resale to investors and buyers. By 1905, James Defebaugh reported, Lacey's transactions had involved over five million acres.[46] Indicative of the scale of Lacey's operations, when the Goodyears decided to relocate from Pennsylvania and New York to the Gulf South, it was Lacey who located the timberlands that allowed them to build what was heralded as "the largest lumber manufacturing proposition in the world." At one point, Charles Goodyear mailed Lacey a check for $1.25 million in payment for land he located for the new undertaking.[47]

Lacey was frank about his activities. He always maintained that greater profits could be earned by speculating in timberland than by manufacturing lumber, and he later told congressional investigators that, when he first went south, timberland "was nearly all vacant. . . . We located several million acres for northern lumber companies. We estimated those lands would cut about 6,000 feet per acre, as they were then cutting timber. They were not going above the first limbs, the balance was left in the woods and burned up." The scale of Lacey's activities and the sawmills he served was as different from the operations of men like Calvin Taylor as day from night.[48]

As title to timberland passed from speculators and brokers to lumbermen, the number of sawmills and the level of production in the Gulf South rose rapidly. Emboldened by the successes of the South's pioneer mills and driven by the dwindling supply of timber in older areas, many of the largest Northern producers began to eye opportunities in the Southern pineries. From his base in St. Paul, Frederick Weyerhaeuser joined associates in 1894 on a journey to investigate possibilities. Initially reluctant to enter the South, Weyerhaeuser was converted. As he told E. W. Durant, "I think I would better take back my ideas of this southern lumber and people." In 1902 the Denkmann Lumber Company, a Weyerhaeuser affiliate, made extensive sawmill and timberland purchases in Mississippi and Louisiana. At about the same time, Fred Herrick, who had enjoyed more modest success in Wisconsin and Minnesota, joined with logging contractor William D. Harrigan and railroader Marvin Hughuitt to take over and expand a plant in Fulton, Alabama, while between 1889 and 1902 Edward D. Wetmore and his partners, who operated in western Pennsylvania, also acquired extensive holdings. Herrick and Wetmore, and of course Weyerhaeuser, would be heard from again in the Far West.[49]

Charles and Frank Goodyear were among the largest operators attracted by the bonanza in the Gulf South. For decades they had operated sawmills in Pennsylvania and New York, but with stands there running out they were looking for fresh opportunities. Working through timber buyers such as Lacey, the brothers gradually obtained extensive holdings in Louisiana and Mississippi, usually by purchasing from speculators, but sometimes by buying directly from smallholders desirous of turning their forestland into much-needed cash. In due course, Charles Goodyear went south to examine what they had acquired and to make plans for construction of a sawmill. The area's stands, he found, grew tall and straight, logging conditions looked easy, and inexpensive labor was available. The brothers pushed boldly ahead, investing $9 million of their own capital in the venture and as much as $6 million from other sources. Not only did they construct a huge mill and ancillary facilities in Bogalusa, Louisiana, but also the New Orleans Great Northern Railroad which ran from Slidell, Louisiana, to Jackson, Mississippi, through the heart of their holdings.[50]

Charles Hines was another giant who joined the stampede. Hines operated what his letterhead described as "the Largest Lumber Yards in the World." From his yards in Chicago, he supplied individual buyers and a host of retailers throughout the upper Midwest. But Hines's sources of supply in the Lake States—his own sawmills and those of others—were running out of sawlogs, and he began seeking new stands to tap. Like so many others, Hines turned to J. D. Lacey & Co. He soon acquired vast tracts of Southern pine—one purchase alone amounted to 1.4 million acres—and erected a large plant at aptly named Lumberton to mill the logs from them. In time, Hines's operations became so extensive that James K. Vardaman, Mississippi's demagogic senator, complained that although Hines "does not own quite all the timber lands in South Mississippi yet, he wants them all." In light of Vardaman's attitude and influence, it comes as no surprise that Mississippi adopted tax policies that eventually drove Hines from the state.[51]

John Barber White was another Northerner who became a major player in the Southern pine industry. White started in Pennsylvania, but in 1880 moved to Missouri, where he established the Missouri Lumber & Mining Company. As his operations expanded, he became deeply involved in the forests of Louisiana. With capital reportedly over $1.2 million, his Louisiana Central Lumber Company was one of the largest in the state. In addition, White was a principal in the Louisiana Long Leaf Lumber Company (the "4L"), which was nearly as big. Together these two firms cut two hundred and fifty million feet of lumber a year—and they were but the most conspicuous of White's holdings. A "masterful, forceful exponent of . . . Pennsylvania grit and Pennsylvania dollars," he was an organizer of the powerful Southern Pine Association and for years one of its key leaders.[52]

These giants were not alone. By the early twentieth century the ranks of Southern lumbermen were full of men who had operated in the Mid-Atlantic or Lake states, including Frank W. Gilchrist, Thomas H. Shevlin, Edward S. Crossett, Samuel H. Fullerton, Michael J. Scanlon, Orrin Ingram, and Russell A. Alger. Herman Dierks came from Iowa to become, according to some, Arkansas's largest landowner; Crossett's holdings in the state were not much smaller.[53] Not only did many leaders of the Southern pine industry come from the North, a number continued to reside there. Indeed, so dominant were outsiders that regional spokesmen lamented seeing the opportunities offered by the Piney Woods slipping away from Southerners.[54]

Yet not all expansion was the result of the actions of Northerners. In a study of thirty-three major Texas lumbermen, Robert Maxwell found that although only five were native Texans, nine had come from other Southern states; by contrast, six were from the Middle West (including the Lake States) and seven the Northeast; six were natives of foreign countries. Of this last group, German immigrant Joseph H. Kurth, who had major lumber and railroad interests in and near Angelina County, was the most notable. Clearly, the role of outsiders was great. At least twenty-five had engaged in lumbering elsewhere before beginning operations in Texas, while a majority were absentee owners who only occasionally visited their logging and milling operations. Data on membership in the Southern Pine Association ("subscribers" as they were called) suggest the pattern was present in other parts of the Gulf South as well. Similarly, Nollie Hickman's enumeration of Mississippi's large mills around the beginning of the twentieth century is replete with the names of Northerners and Northern firms. Moreover, many Southerners lumbermen established ties to Northern financiers in order to expand operations and seize beckoning opportunities.[55]

The mills of Southerners operating in the Piney Woods were mostly small or medium sized. Lorenzo N. Dantzler's operation in the Pascagoula area was one of the rare exceptions,[56] but the few larger firms included some that would have been notable by the standards of any region. Foremost among them were those of Robert A. Long and John Henry Kirby. Both were major figures on the industry's national scene, as well as locally, although they—and their business interests—were strikingly different from one another.

A thoroughgoing Southerner, R. A. Long was nonetheless an interloper in the Gulf South. Born and reared in Kentucky, he had in the words of his biographer, "a longing to believe and live in the style and grace of the Old South Myth." He left Kentucky for Kansas in 1873, yet "for the rest of his days the South possessed him. . . . The place of his childhood, of his parents before him, would filter through his maturity like an underground spring."[57]

In 1875 Long joined two others in founding a retail lumberyard in Kansas City, his first. With railroads pushing onto the prairies from Kansas City, Omaha, and other points, settlement was proceeding rapidly, and Long found ready demand for lumber there. Using borrowed capital (Long had left Kentucky with but $700), he opened yard after yard; by 1883, he had fourteen, and the following year incorporated the whole as the Long-Bell Lumber Company. Expansion continued. In 1889, he established a wholesale division and purchased his first sawmill (in Arkansas); by 1896 he had entered manufacturing in Louisiana. By 1904 Long-Bell and its subsidiaries had sixty-one retail yards in Kansas, Oklahoma, and Indian Territory, owned 228,850 acres of timber, cut 867,319 feet of logs per year, had 3,713 employees, and owned 90 percent of the Louisiana & Pacific Railway, built to serve Long-Bell mills at Bonami, DeRidder, Longville, and Lake Charles, Louisiana. In 1906, Long added "one of the most technologically advanced mills in the country," located at Lufkin, Texas, but the plant at DeRidder, built in 1903, remained the pride of the company. Expansion paid handsomely. From 1902 to 1910 Long's personal capital rose from $500,000 to $10 million; by 1920 Long-Bell was the largest lumber manufacturer in the United States, with twelve thousand employees and $43.6 million in annual sales.[58]

Long had found his "main chance" in Kansas and Oklahoma, where he got into lumber retailing just as agriculture was being rapidly expanded, but his success was not simply a result of being in the right place at the right time. When Long entered Louisiana, the first great speculative wave had passed, but with the completion of the Kansas City Southern to Shreveport in 1897, he thought he detected an opening. Long stated, "I believe that I can truthfully and correctly say that no great body of timber has ever made or promises to make as good a percent of profits for its investors as has yellow pine," and he moved swiftly to take advantage of the opportunities Louisiana offered. His biographer observed of Long: "Embedded in his austere persona was a gambler's streak that seized the unique opportunities the age offered to men willing to take risks."[59] Long may not have been the frontiersman of popular imagination, but in many ways he was the archetype of the entrepreneurs who by his time were being drawn to the lumberman's frontier. More than ever, the lumberman's frontier had become a businessman's frontier.

John Henry Kirby was another sort. Unlike the autocratic, austere Long, Kirby was a warm, gregarious native Texan. An attorney by training, Kirby began acquiring timberlands for himself and clients soon after being admitted to the bar in 1885. He joined Boston capitalists Nathaniel D. and George Z. Silsbee to create a land company that accumulated more than two hundred and fifty thousand acres of virgin pine, and in 1893 began building the Gulf, Beaumont & Kansas City Railroad to open them for lumbering. At this point, Kirby did not think of himself as a lumberman, but as a businessman with varied interests; he was a lawyer, a railroad builder, a buyer of timberlands, and a real estate developer deeply involved in the growth of Houston—and he was a man of vision.[60]

Aware of the wave of consolidations sweeping American business around the turn of the century—especially J. P. Morgan's creation in 1901 of United States Steel, capitalized at over $1 billion—Kirby wondered if the Texas lumber industry, growing apace but still badly fragmented, was ready for similar unification. The national economy was on the upswing, and Kirby's network of contacts growing steadily; he had sold the Gulf, Beaumont, and Kansas City to the Atchison, Topeka & Santa Fe Railway in 1900, bringing the Santa Fe system into his circle of supporters. As his lawyer later put it, Kirby was to carry on "great operations, largely with other people's money." Among his major sources of funds was the Santa Fe, "which was interested in transporting the lumber" Kirby's mills produced.[61]

The great Spindletop oil strike near the Texas Gulf Coast in 1901 drove Kirby to fresh action. A group of Boston investors held huge stands of prime longleaf pine close to Spindletop, and Kirby suspected their lands might have underlying oil deposits. Pushing to take advantage of both the surface and sub-surface riches, in July 1901 Kirby persuaded New York and Boston capitalists to join him in creating two huge new companies: the Houston Oil Company, capitalized at $30 million, and the Kirby Lumber Company, capitalized at $10 million. The firms would support one another in a symbiotic relationship, the oil company making available to Kirby's mills three hundred and fifty million feet of stumpage a year, while payment for the timber would help generate needed working capital. In addition, Kirby's assets (including timberland and some fourteen sawmills) would help create the valuation base that would attract investors. Kirby himself promised to come up with $2.5 million in working capital for the lumber firm and pay $5 a thousand for logs bought from the oil company. It was a complicated arrangement, but it caught the fancy of the Houston press, which lauded the personable, forty-one-year-old Kirby as a financial wizard who in one fell swoop had created the two largest corporations in Texas. Others, less sanguine, thought $5 a thousand an exorbitant price; as one trade journal later put it, "Everyone thought he had gone crazy."[62]

All did not go as planned. Kirby could not raise the $2.5 million he had promised and had difficulty gaining title to some one hundred and eighty thousand acres of the timberland used to calculate his company's worth and potential production.[63] Officials of the two firms soon fell to squabbling. Suits and counter-suits followed, and the Kirby Lumber Company passed into receivership. With sales slumping, the receivers cut back on purchases—including such vital items as rails needed to extend the company's logging railroads—and before long had to close some of the firm's less-profitable mills.[64]

The receivers hoped a loan payable over two years would enable the company "to walk alone" by 1906, but more was needed. In November 1907 the company's treasurer wrote, "Our receipts are abominable," and although Kirby's mills had cut 1.2 billion feet of timber from Houston Oil Company lands by the end of August 1907, he reported in 1908 that continuing $120,000 a month payments to the oil company would be "disastrous" and would "so handicap the Receivers themselves for funds that they cannot operate." Default, he feared, "may destroy both the Kirby Lumber Company and Houston Oil Company."[65]

Kirby recognized what was needed. He explained to a kinsman:

> [Y]ou will remember that the receivership grew out of a dispute regarding the timber contract. That dispute has been settled and our title to the timber is now placed beyond question, but the Company owes a great deal of money which it has been unable to pay during the receivership. [It cannot get out of the red] until I can refinance the Company and get the capital with which to retire its debts and furnish it with ample working funds.[66]

However reluctantly, the Santa Fe, eager for the freight from Kirby's mills, came forth with the capital he needed—and, as problems continued, eventually assumed control.[67] Kirby stayed on as company president until his death in 1940, but during his last years he was little more than a figurehead. Throughout, however, he remained a power in the lumber industry, helping found the Southern Pine Association and serving from 1917 to 1921 as president of the National Lumber Manufacturers Association.[68]

Northerners and Southerners, large mills and small—in light of all this, the production of Southern pine rose rapidly. Output doubled between 1880 and 1890. By 1900 the Gulf South was producing over five billion board feet a year; by 1908 Louisiana was the third leading lumber producing state, and by 1910 it was second. Lumbering had become the largest industry in the South, employing one of every three wage earners. Separate statistics for the Piney Woods are not readily available, but Southern Pine Association records contain useful, if not entirely dependable, indicators. In Louisiana 60 percent of industrial wage earners worked in the lumber industry, in Mississippi and Alabama 40 percent. By 1910 the South's output had climbed to 9.5 billion board feet. The region had become the United States' leading producer of softwood lumber, turning out almost half of the national total. By 1919 there were seventeen thousand sawmills at work in the Southern pineries. Sixty-seven percent of output came from large mills, although the number of small ones grew as large tracts of untapped timber became scarce. So great had production become that the region's railroads, for all their expansion, were hard pressed to handle the volume—and additional quantities were being shipped by sea.[69]

Nothing illustrates the boom in Southern lumbering better than developments around Hattiesburg, Mississippi. When railroads opened the vast forests between the Pearl and Pascagoula rivers, new lumber towns sprang up right and left. Hattiesburg was only a small village in 1885, but by 1893 there were fifty-nine sawmills in and near it with a combined daily capacity of one million board feet. By 1905 the community had a population of over twenty thousand; nearly every major lumber wholesaler in the nation had representatives there.[70]

Hattiesburg was no Bangor, Williamsport, or Saginaw. With railroads able to tap stands in all corners of the Gulf South and enabling the shipment of lumber from a host of points, Hattiesburg had to share dominance with Laurel, Mississippi; Alexandria, Louisiana; Pensacola, Florida; and Beaumont and Orange, Texas—all of which had multiple mills—as well as with places like Bogalusa, Louisiana, which was a major center simply because of the size of its lone sawmill. A map based on data collected by the U. S. Forest Service and published in *The Timberman* in 1920 illustrates the situation. Mills cutting over ten million board feet of lumber a year were located all across the Gulf South, especially along railroads connecting to northern points. Mills cutting from one to ten million feet a year were even more numerous. From Jacksonville and the Florida panhandle west to Houston and north to Little Rock sawmills seem to have been almost everywhere.[71]

In spite of the profits and employment generated by these developments, there was a cloud on the horizon. Local resident Roy Pearce warned Charles Goodyear when the latter arrived to inspect the land Lacey had acquired for him: "[T]here'll be some ornery folks who will be tryin' to cause a heap of trouble when you start cutting down the timber. They just don't like to have furriners change the way they live." Journalist-historian John Tarver has delineated the underlying problem: "All the propaganda generated by New South advocates could not obscure the simple fact that the working people of the South were a miserable lot at best . . . cantankerous, myth-ridden, avaricious, and irretrievably ignorant."[72]

Goodyear, of course, was not the first to harvest timber in the area. For decades people had been cutting and milling pines along the Pearl River, which ran past his holdings, but earlier operations had impacted the land and its people only gradually and relatively lightly; operations on the scale Goodyear and his ilk envisioned would bring sudden, sweeping changes, not the least of which would be a huge population increase. Between 1900 and 1910, the population of St. Tammany Parish rose 41.9 percent, that of Tangipahoa 65.4 percent, and Washington (where the Goodyears built their mill) 96.2 percent. This drastically altered the lives not only of those who came to work in the sawmills and logging camps, but also of others for miles around. Tarver summed it up neatly: "The people of the piney woods, used to an independent way of living and working, had in the context of the New South to get used to an industrial sovereignty commanded by some remote and faceless person."[73]

Pearce had recognized, when he warned Goodyear of potential trouble, that the impending transformations would generate resistance, but Piney Woods people must have had mixed feelings about the growth of lumbering in their midst. On the one hand, it offered employment that provided a more reliable source of cash than traditional hunting and pastoral pursuits or cutting logs for sale to mills in Pensacola, Pascagoula, and other downstream locations. Thousands, searching for jobs in the woods and mills, flocked to the company towns that sprang up in the pine belt, and the lucky ones who had valid titles to timberlands saw their value increase rapidly.

It is not clear just how much of the industry's work force came from the pine belt, although—unlike most owners and much of management and skilled labor—the bulk clearly was from the South. Ruth Allen found that in Texas 45 percent of the workers were native-born whites and 41 percent native-born blacks. Among the whites, two-thirds were Texas-born and most of the rest Southerners. Nearly all the blacks were born in Texas, although most were probably from farming counties, rather than the Piney Woods, where previously the black population had been relatively small. In Florida blacks made up over two-thirds of the workers.[74]

For the Gulf South as a whole, one early analyst described the workforce as "homogenous and thoroughly American, whether White or Black." Others, carrying the analysis further, found a remarkable degree of social and cultural homogeneity. Most were from farming backgrounds, or at least agricultural counties rather than the Piney Woods, for the latter had too small a population to meet the industry's needs. Few were from cities. Charles Taylor wrote: "[T]he man who leaves the woods or the small mill community for the city is never coming back. Nor is the city man of much value in the backwoods. The woodsman can be spoiled by environment, but he cannot be created except by heredity." In fact, heredity had little to do with it. Only an ignorance of other opportunities—in the cities or in other regions—could lead one to accept the working and living conditions in the Southern mills and forests. The vast majority was poorly educated; indeed, the Census of 1900 classed over 20 percent as illiterate.[75] Although woods and mill workers from New England, the Mid-Atlantic, and the Great Lake states had followed the lumber industry as it moved on to new frontiers, relatively few from the South did so—this in spite of the fact Southern wages averaged well below those in newly opening areas in the West. Wages were too low to draw any great number of Northern or European workers, and those who did come seldom stayed. Religion did little to enlighten the mix. Most were fundamentalist Protestants—usually Methodist or Baptist—and given to Biblical literalism.[76]

Some, especially those on woods crews and in contract logging, were seasonal workers who farmed part of the year even though woods work could bring better financial returns. Some even opened new farms in the cutover, but the results were far from impressive. One observer reported,

> year after year these people go on and try to farm on this land. It is so poor that it will scarcely grow peanuts, but still they go in there and raise a little cotton and raise corn, and they try to raise cattle. . . . They are ignorant, they are back woodsmen, and the only way we can ever get them . . . [to change] is by example, practical demonstrations.

In spite of the presence of these part-time farmers, the backbone of the industry's labor force was increasingly made up of full-time employees.[77]

Whatever their background, the work force came to be made up of industrial laborers, a home-grown work force as poorly prepared for the wrenching changes brought by industrial forestry as were Northern industrialists for the social milieu into which they were moving. Neither understood the other. One analyst reported both men and management were so individualistic that "little effort was made to offset mutual misunderstandings and misinterpretations. . . . The foremen and the management seldom get together to discuss problems. Man talks to man, and it generally ends there." Isolation made the problem worse. The larger society, he observed, "is little understood." Mill towns and woods camps had such limited contact with the outside world that at some places where he spoke in June-August 1918, he brought the first news they had heard of World War I![78]

In both the Piney Woods communities and nearby areas from which they drew labor and supplies, industrial lumbering *was* disruptive of established ways, but it was in the former that the changes were most sweeping, the effects most clear. In the pine belt fewer people now lived on the land; although many continued to hunt and fish and raise a few cattle, this shift away from rural life weakened older folkways. Still, many traditional attitudes remained well into the twentieth century, most notably the annual firing of the woods to improve grazing. John Barber White grumbled, "It is a very expensive way to raise cattle, by burning the woods to give them sustenance," but the practice continued, and when lumbermen and government officials sought to halt it in the name of economic progress, they set off a conflict that was to continue for years.[79] In other ways, too, industrial lumbering conflicted with the old order: no longer could one run his cattle wherever he wished; no longer could one live on his small farm, supported by neighbors and kin while seeking a bit of cash from woods work when need required; and no longer could one remain largely independent of the economic mainstream controlled by outsiders. Thomas D. Clark summed up the change: "[T]he tenor of the old ways of Southern life was broken by the rise of the big lumbering industry. . . . Where backwoods Southerners had depended upon small crops, store credit and natural resources for livelihood, there was now the largely impersonal sawmill employer."[80]

Life in the mill towns contributed to discontent. There were places—such as Bogalusa and Fullerton, Louisiana; Huttig, Arkansas; and Fulton, Alabama—where conditions were better than in most,[81] and some observers claimed that, bad as they were, life in the mill towns was on the whole better than on the hardscrabble farms and settlements from which the bulk of the work force came, but still the sawmill communities were isolated, dismal places. All in all, Clark concluded, the Southern yeoman was "roughened and hardened" by work in the woods and mills.[82]

Even the best mill towns had problems. When the Goodyears began construction at Bogalusa, it quickly became "the toughest town in the county," not only as a result of the activities of construction crews, but also of "natives [who] drifted in on a Saturday night to shoot up the town." Appalled, the brothers launched a program aimed at attracting a "better class of employees," building schools and support facilities "such as were provided elsewhere in long-established and prosperous communities." Management boasted that theirs was a model town, but feudal conditions, high rents, and repressive management led to discontent, just as they did elsewhere, and eventually to attempts to bring in organized labor to help workers resolve their problems.[83]

More hastily erected, transitory communities were far from model towns. Especially in their early years, housing tended to be wretched, sanitation facilities primitive, violence endemic, and rents high. Prices at company stores usually were exorbitant, yet one who shopped elsewhere could imperil his employment. Pay was seldom in cash and often could be used immediately only if discounted severely; attempts to use company "chits" other than at the company store also necessitated discounting.[84]

As long as logging camps remained, life in them was worse than in the mill towns. Unlike in the North, logging camps were not the virtually exclusive domain of bachelors; as a result, they sported family housing—if only converted boxcars—and a modicum of support facilities. But there was nothing that smacked of permanency in these camps, which moved repeatedly, and little that was not essential to the task of production. Even more than in the mill towns, chances for self-improvement were lacking, and here as there any efforts at organizing workers to win better wages or improved living and working conditions were ruthlessly crushed. But if circumstances became too oppressive, white workers could seek employment elsewhere—there were plenty of jobs. As George Stokes put it, if a worker "was fired in the morning, he could walk down the track to the next mill and be at work again before dark."[85]

Conditions in "the Quarters," to which black employees were restricted, were even worse than in the sections where whites lived, and finding new jobs was more difficult too. Housing was segregated, but whites sometimes found themselves working beside or competing for employment with blacks, especially in the woods. Occasionally they even saw ex-slaves become foremen or win such coveted positions as woods bosses and sawyers, although worker resistance and managerial attitudes combined to insure that this was rare.[86]

Taken together, these developments fueled a rising discontent reflected in a variety of ways. In a belt of counties in southern Mississippi it contributed to the Whitecap movement, which used vigilantism and sabotage to keep ex-slaves subservient—or better, "on the farms and out of the lumber industry"—and to prevent employers from treating their white employees unfairly or acting in other ways that Whitecappers deemed unacceptable. As a secret movement utilizing illegal methods, Whitecapping is difficult to trace in detail, but the outlines are fairly clear. It combated a wide variety of social and economic changes, including the developing sharecropper system and growing power of the merchant class in country towns, but also including changes brought by industrial lumbering. Sawmills and lumber yards were frequent targets of sabotage, and the seven counties where Whitecapping was strongest were the very counties only recently traversed by the Illinois Central Railroad, that is, the heartland of Mississippi's bonanza lumber industry. Arson was a favorite weapon—not just of Whitecappers, but also of others distraught by change—and setting fires in the woods proved effective in bedeviling industrial lumbermen, just as surely as it had long been in controlling other vermin.[87]

The unhappiness manifested in Whitecapping and the considerably more widespread use of arson could be seen in other ways too. Some Whitecap leaders were active Populists, and in the 1890s when they and their allies gained control in Mississippi, they pushed through legislation limiting banks and manufacturing corporations to real estate holdings valued at not over $1 million. The limit clearly slowed the advance of the state's lumber industry, for it caused the Goodyear brothers to build the massive Great Southern sawmill at Bogalusa, Louisiana, rather than in Mississippi as originally planned.[88] In Louisiana, on the other hand, discontented lumber workers for a time sought political solutions through the Socialist party, of which they were a mainstay.[89]

Efforts at organizing labor unions were even more important indicators of discontent than vigilantism or abortive efforts at political action. The advent of industrial lumbering turned many a pastoralist-hunter-farmer into an industrial wage laborer. The crude, transitory lumber camps and towns in which most worked insured social instability, made amelioration of conditions difficult, and helped make lumber workers ripe for unionization. Initially this exploited rural proletariat turned to the Knights of Labor, but when it faltered and the American Federation of Labor did little to address their needs, workers turned to more radical leaders, created the Brotherhood of Timber Workers, and affiliated with the militant Industrial Workers of the World. Bitter strikes followed, strikes spokesmen explained and justified in class terms that would have been foreign to the Piney Woods only a few years earlier.[90]

Charles Taylor believed "[t]he I.W.W. philosophy, or one very similar to it, was native to the backwoods," creating a protest against society "made strong by the fact that society is little understood." John Henry Kirby, a thoroughgoing Bourbon Democrat, blamed federal authorities: "[Y]ou have got a Department of Labor in Washington that does not recognize one single solitary power reserved to the States . . . there is an effort by the Department of Labor to organize your saw mill employees, and mostly the colored people." Federal minions, he said, warming to his subject, were "carpet baggers just as certainly today" as those during Reconstruction and "there can be no peace—there can be no prosperity—there can be no tranquility in any community of this country where this kind of thing is

John Henry Kirby addressing the Brotherhood of Timber Workers in DeRidder, Louisiana in 1912. The crowd hardly seems the dangerous rabble Kirby and others often accused the BTW of being. Courtesy McNeese State University, #2253.

recognized or tolerated." Be that as it may, in the end the B.T.W. was broken, but the workers' sense of alienation and antagonism remained, making the area ripe for subsequent anti-capitalist demagoguery by politicians such as Louisiana's Huey Long, with his "soak the rich" program.[91]

Collective action against unions was just one way in which, by the end of the nineteenth century, Southern lumbering was moving away from the rugged individualism of its early leaders. Chronically overbuilt, the industry nonetheless cut with abandon, for so much capital was tied up in plants, railroads, and timber that income was needed to cover carrying costs. Excess production undercut prices—and profits—and lumbermen soon moved toward uniform pricing even as they tried to avoid prosecution for violation of federal anti-trust laws. Efforts to establish uniform grades and to wring rate concessions from the railroads followed.[92]

In spite of the decline of individualism among the South's leading lumbermen, theirs was at heart still a frontier industry. Drawn to the Gulf South by its forest wealth, they continued to operate as if mining the resource, turning trees into dollars with no thought for the long-term health of the forest. When the trees were gone, most expected to either cease operations or move on. John Henry Kirby saw no problem in this:

We have passed the peak of production. . . . As the lumber industry declines . . . its place . . . will be taken up by the expansion of agriculture, which will replace forests with fields, and by the advent of a general industrial era. . . . I firmly believe that the South Atlantic and Gulf states are eventually to be the heart of American industrial and international trade activities. The development of our incalculable resources has only begun.[93]

Less sweeping in his views, the manager of the Eastman-Gardiner mill in Laurel, Mississippi, simply offered to give the company's cutover lands to anyone who would pay the back taxes, which he thought amounted to more than the land was worth. Similarly, learning that his cutover would be taxed as timberland, Edward Hines abandoned efforts to reforest by leaving seed trees and directed his loggers to cut everything, leaving not a stick standing. Frustrated by the state's tax policies, Hines told a meeting of the Southern Pine Association he was "cutting out and getting out of Mississippi as fast as he could." In the face of such attitudes, efforts to persuade lumbermen to burn slash and adopt other fire-protection measures met with widespread indifference, as did attempts to get them to adopt reforestation. Even those such as Clarence D. Johnson, whose Union Saw Mill Company was as up-to-date as any and whose company town—Huttig, Arkansas—was a model community, tended to cut more and faster than their holdings could sustain. The extensive systems of rail lines millmen had built in an effort to remain competitive contributed, for only clearcutting promised a sufficient volume of logs to make the investments in railroads profitable.[94]

The gentle terrain, the vast stands, and the economic conditions of the times had all encouraged clearcut logging in the pine belt, and by the end of the 1920s nearly all the major old-growth timber stands had been felled. Small-scale operators remained, and numerous portable sawmills moved in like so many scavengers to cut the second growth, trees left where earlier high-grading had taken only the cream, and remaining scattered tracts. The number of operating mills actually rose even as production plummeted.[95]

Although the giant firms—Long-Bell, Gilchrist, Hines, and their ilk—could transfer operations to new stands in the West, the bulk of the labor force could not or would not move. They remained behind in the poverty pockets that were the cutover, working portable "peckerwood" mills, holding onto what small tracts they possessed, and, by reverting to pastoralism, returning at least partially to the patterns of the old, pre-industrial lifestyle that had been so disrupted by the advent of industrial lumbering.

Observing all this, one analyst commented: "I don't know which is the sadder, the devastation of pine lands, or the people who are trying to live on them."[96] To be sure, remaining sawmills supplied a modicum of employment, but not until the Southern paper industry took off in the 1950s did a reasonably viable forest economy return to the pine belt. Newsprint manufacturing firms at Lufkin, Texas, and elsewhere developed a system through which they contracted for logs with smallholders and even provided forest management for them. The system was far from perfect, but the people of the Piney Woods could at least live on their land while enjoying some of the fruits of the modern economic order.[97]

More than just social dislocation and loss of old-growth forests resulted from industrial forestry's activities in the Southern pineries. Longleaf pine, long the main commercial species, regenerated poorly after logging and was replaced on many sites by other species. Discouraging the use of fire to improve grazing, reducing the number of cattle, and controlling forest fires had ecological impacts too, for wildlife populations fell as pure pine stands replaced the variegated forests originally gracing much of the land; squirrels and wild turkeys—popular quarry of Piney Woods food and sport hunters—became less numerous; the magnificent ivory-billed woodpecker, dependent on old-growth forests, declined and then seemed to vanish.[98] Less readily evident changes also took place; for example, unchecked by fire, snakes, chiggers, and ticks seem to have increased.

The return of a degree of economic prosperity with the development of the Southern newsprint industry helped people of the Piney Woods, but it did nothing to restore the old landscape in which the traditional culture of the area developed and prospered. After all, paper manufacturers prefer pure pine stands as surely as did their lumbermen predecessors—and for the same reasons: they offer economies of scale, ease of operation, and other advantages that help insure profits. Moreover, theirs is an industry dominated more often than not from outside the region. There seems no chance that either the old ecological order or the old pre-industrial society will be restored. They are gone beyond recall; industrial lumbering brought the modern world to the southern pineries, and both people and nature have paid the price demanded by the intruder.

Still, the legacy is not entirely negative. As Thomas Clark noted, lumbering brought the people of the Piney Woods into the modern world, and the pine forests themselves have proven remarkably resilient, insuring a lasting heritage of opportunity and wealth for the Gulf South. It is a resiliency that was underscored in 1982 when Georgia-Pacific Corporation moved its headquarters from Portland, Oregon, back to the South, where company management detected greater potential than in the Pacific Northwest.[99]

CHAPTER ELEVEN

To the Farthest Shore—And Beyond

The reactions of early observers of North America's Pacific Coast forests differed widely. Some, intrigued by the size of trees and denseness of stands, saw great potential profit for those who would tap them. John Meares visited the north coast in 1788 and took on a cargo of spars and ships' timbers. "[T]he woods of this part of America," he wrote, "are capable of supplying, with these valuable materials, all the navies of Europe."[1] Others saw the huge, close-set trees as barriers to settlement and commerce. Bavarian botanist Charles A. Geyer, who collected in the Pacific Northwest in 1843 and 1844, was not the first to express such views, but no one did so better. Geyer saw little potential in the Northwest; he admired the "beautiful and fertile Wallamette valley," but thought it unpromising, for it flooded nearly every year and was surrounded by "mountains and high ridges . . . bristling with impenetrable pine forests." Settlers would never be able to get produce to market.[2]

Aesthetic reactions differed too. George Vancouver was entranced by the sights as he explored Puget Sound in April 1792:

> *The delightful serenity of the weather greatly aided the beautiful scenery that was now presented; the surface of the sea was perfectly smooth, and the country before us exhibited every thing that bounteous nature could be expected to draw into one point of view. . . . [The land] was bounded by a ridge of snowy mountains. . . . Between us and this snowy range, the land . . . was covered with a variety of stately trees. These, however, did not conceal the whole face of the country in one uninterrupted wilderness, but pleasingly clothed its eminences, and chequered its vallies.[3]*

Later, William Fraser Tolmie, a physician attached to Hudson's Bay Company, described scenery along the Columbia River as "of a monotonous character—a dense and unbroken forest of pines [offering] little relief to the eye tired with the sombre gloominess of the wilderness."[4] Settler George Savage put it more strongly: the "silent maddening Solitude of the unbroken forests . . . seemed to scare you and fill you with unspeakable dread and terror."[5]

Regardless of their reactions, early visitors could hardly ignore the forests that lined the continent's western shore. They were so different from those of the eastern United States or Europe! The species were unfamiliar—western red cedar, Sitka spruce, western hemlock, and, above all, Douglas fir and coast redwoods—and they grew to sizes and frequently with stand densities unprecedented in their experience.[6] From south of San Francisco to British Columbia, the great forests dominated first impressions, not only because they were so readily apparent—and different—but also because, until the great overland migrations of the 1840s, most visitors arrived by sea and spied them as soon as they hove within sight of shore. Indeed, during the early period of European and American contact, the Pacific Coast was so difficult to reach by land it might as well have been an island.[7]

Not everyone shared Geyer's gloomy view of the Northwest's economic prospects. American settlers streamed to the Pacific shore in increasing numbers in the 1840s. Until the California Gold Rush commenced near the end of the decade, most would-be settlers headed for the Willamette Valley. There they took up claims, not in the forests proper, but—like settlers in Indiana, Illinois, and elsewhere earlier—along the edges of natural prairies where grazing and cropland were available without arduous clearing and

Loggers in old-growth Douglas fir. The size of the trees made clearing such land for agriculture too expensive, while the use of springboards allowed loggers to saw and chop unhindered by the thick understory. Courtesy Oregon State University Archives, #Williams G: Ford 2.

where ample supplies of firewood and construction timber were near to hand.[8] Later arrivals, coming from the Middle Border, often settled open woodlands in foothills surrounding the Willamette, Rogue, and Umpqua river valleys. Concentrations of former Southern and Border state residents developed in Polk, Benton, Linn, Lane, and Jackson counties. They stood apart politically, socially, and economically from the settlers from New England and the Middle Atlantic states who played a central role in the towns and cities of the lower Willamette Valley (and in the mercantile community centered there). Elisha Applegate, a leading figure in southern Oregon, revealed this sharp division when he wrote during the election of 1866, "The malcontents appear very numerous—the butternuts rush in from the hills and from the heads of hollows in long lines" to vote. Southern Oregon as well as Lane, Linn, Baker, and Union counties would, he feared, be carried by "copperheads," or as he called them, "the fag end of [Confederate General Sterling] Price's long haired, dirty faced, coarse featured, hang dog looking, wild hog eating tatterdemalion host."[9] But early or late, North or South, rural settlers of pioneer Oregon came as an advanced guard of the agricultural frontier, not as lumberers. A few erected sawmills to serve local needs, but they too were a part of a farmer's frontier.[10]

Isolation plagued early settlers in both Alta California and the Pacific Northwest. They found it difficult to sell the produce of their farms, and their economies struggled. Small and distant, Pacific markets offered little relief. Settlers in Oregon shipped some grain, produce, and lumber to California and to the Sandwich islands, as Hawaii was then known; and Thomas O. Larkin, the American consul in Alta California, dispatched lumber from Monterey Bay to other California ports, to Hawaii, and to the west coasts of Mexico and South America. But shipments from Oregon were too limited to do more than keep the Willamette Valley's economy limping along, while Larkin's had little impact beyond the immediate vicinity of Monterey Bay.[11]

Around Monterey Bay, a motley group of sailors who had jumped ship found refuge over the years in nearby forested hills. They sawed lumber (largely in sawpits, but also in at least one small water-powered mill) and sold it to Larkin as a means of sustenance. Larkin was a classic example of a nineteenth-century merchant venturer, but the squatters who supplied him were of a different sort. Like many early woodsmen of Maine and the Gulf South, they belonged to the world of hunters and gatherers, rather than to the economy of business or agriculture. As yet the Far West boasted nothing that could be called a lumberman's frontier.[12]

The situation quickly changed following the discovery of gold at John Sutter's sawmill on the American Fork of the Sacramento River (or the American River, as it came to be called). At the time there were primitive sawpits around Monterey Bay and elsewhere in Hispanic California, a small steam-powered sawmill north of San Francisco near Bodega Bay, and a few water-powered mills in both California and the Pacific Northwest, but these were so crude, so limited in potential and capacity they were incapable of meeting the sudden demand that came with the Gold Rush. In 1849 there were but ten active sawmills in all California, with an estimated combined output of but five thousand board feet a day.[13] To supply the lumber needed to build the new El Dorado, additional sawmills had to be built and built quickly. Asa Simpson, Frederic Talbot, Andrew Jackson Pope, William Renton, William Carson, and a host of other entrepreneurs proceeded to do just that. Like much else in the Far West, the Pacific Coast's lumber industry can be said to have begun with the California Gold Rush.[14]

Insatiable demand for lumber in San Francisco and its hinterland quickly created a lumberman's frontier on the Pacific shore. It appeared not in the established centers of population, such as the agriculturally oriented Willamette Valley, but on (and beyond) the fringes of settlement—around Puget Sound and Grays Harbor in Washington, along the lower Columbia River and around Coos Bay and lesser bar harbors of the Oregon coast, and around Humboldt Bay and any number of dangerous little outposts on California's north coast ("dogholes," sailors called the last of these, for they were so tiny they seemed to hardly offered room enough for a dog to turn around[15]). In time, agriculture came to these scattered centers, in large part to supply woods and mill workers, but almost without exception lumbering was responsible for the initial settlement. Not surprisingly, former residents of Maine were in the forefront of this development, for Bangor was in its heyday, many from Maine joined the gold-triggered westward rush, and these immigrants soon found that, like the Pine Tree State, lumbering on the Pacific Shore demanded knowledge of the sea and ships as well as logging and manufacturing lumber.[16]

The growth in lumber production that began with the Gold Rush did not stop when California's economic bubble burst in 1854. With demand down in California, lumbermen sought other markets around the Pacific. Finding them took considerable ingenuity and perseverance, to say nothing of luck and a willingness to gamble. In the end, what emerged was an industry facing out to sea, tied to Pacific maritime markets more than domestic ones. Appropriately, the great sawmills that developed were known as "cargo mills" to distinguish them from later "rail mills" erected to ship to buyers inland.[17]

Nathaniel Crosby, Jr., was among those who pioneered the post-Gold Rush maritime trade.[18] In the fall of 1854 he wrote Joseph Lane, Oregon Territory's delegate to Congress, that he was about to depart the Columbia in his bark *Louisiana* bound for East Asia. "I have determined to try and find a [new] market for a portion of our lumber," Crosby explained, "as the present prices in California will not warant shipping to that market and proberbly thay will nearly or quite supply themselves in the future. My intention is to visit on this voyage all the ports open in China and introduce our Oregon lumber and any other of our Oregon produce that they will require also." Crosby's success was modest, but he managed to visit Hong Kong, Amoy, and Taiwan, opening the last of these to foreign trade for the first time in two centuries. Indeed, Crosby found sufficient opportunity along the China Coast to cause him to stay in Hong Kong after completion of his voyage.[19] Others followed in Crosby's wake, and in time Hong Kong became a regular outlet for West Coast lumber. George Weidler's Willamette Steam Mills, located in Portland, was an important participant in this trade, but mills on Puget Sound engaged in it too. When railroad building commenced in North China in the 1880s, considerable demand emerged there as well, and additional mills joined in the commerce.[20]

Crosby's efforts were indicative of the wide search for markets by West Coast lumbermen. Cut off from significant buyers in the interior by terrain and distance—to say nothing of a long-lasting absence of good overland transportation facilities[21]—sawmill operators turned to markets accessible by sea. Railroad construction in Mexico and Peru, the rise of plantation sugar cane production in Hawaii, and the development of mining in Australia all generated demand. By the 1880s, cargoes of railroad ties, bridge timbers, pilings, and lumber regularly cleared for trans-Pacific markets, while nearer to hand the population boom in Southern California added yet another outlet to the mix. None of these was, by itself, vital. Together they complemented, rather than replaced, demand in San Francisco and its Central Valley hinterland. But by cushioning producers against the volatility of the northern California market, and by taking sizes and grades in little demand there, they played a major role in helping the early West Coast lumber industry survive and grow. In contrast, the on-rushing development of the national economy had relatively little impact, and that mostly indirect. Nationwide depressions in the 1850s and 1870s had economic repercussions in California, but local developments—especially the end of the boom years of the Gold Rush—were more central in influencing lumber consumption in the state.[22]

In time California's economy recovered, strengthened by railroad building, the growth of agriculture, a population influx and associated business expansion, and new mining strikes, most notably the great Comstock Lode in western Nevada. The West Coast's lumber industry grew by fits and starts to take advantage of opportunities thus provided.

Asa Mead Simpson was archetypal of the entrepreneurs at the heart of the expansion the Gold Rush triggered and which resumed after the doldrums of the late 1850s passed.[23] Son of a Maine shipbuilder, Simpson arrived in California in 1850 and soon recognized that opportunities for making money selling lumber in San Francisco, Sacramento, and Stockton were better than those in the gold fields. His conclusion must have been easy to reach. Prices were extremely volatile, but often lumber sold in the Bay Area for $500 and occasionally for $750 or even $1000 per thousand board feet.[24] After only two weeks in the Sierra Nevada, Simpson abandoned mining and turned to marketing the cargo of lumber aboard the vessel on which he had sailed from Maine to the West Coast.[25] Then, in the fall of 1850, he joined a friend from Maine, S. R. Jackson, to open a lumberyard in Stockton. Simpson's affairs were soon prospering.

As sales climbed, Simpson began looking for fresh sources of supply. In the fall of 1851 he sailed north along the coast to search them out and to salvage a wrecked vessel in which he had a small interest. While in Astoria, Oregon, directing the salvage operation, Simpson purchased a partially built sawmill and arranged for its completion. Until the mill shut down two years later, having exhausted its log supply, it cut ten to fifteen thousand feet of lumber a day for shipment to California. In 1853, with his Astoria mill nearing the end of operations, Simpson made another trip northward, this time to investigate the potential for production near the mouth of Oregon's Umpqua River. Assured there were ample sources of logs there, he proceeded to open a second lumberyard, this one in Sacramento.[26]

Expansion followed. By 1856 Simpson had a mill at North Bend, on Oregon's Coos Bay. In 1857 he added a shipyard there to supply vessels to transport lumber from the Northwest to San Francisco Bay. The first product of the yard, the two-masted schooner *Blanco*, slid down the ways in 1858; dozens of others followed over the years.[27] In 1858 Simpson also put the first bar tug into service on the Oregon coast, a much-needed development on the hazardous bar harbors along that rocky shore; acquired a partial interest in a sawmill at South Bend, Washington; and had another under construction at Santa Cruz, south of San Francisco on Monterey Bay. By

1868, his mill on Coos Bay had grown so large sixteen of his vessels were kept busy hauling its cut to San Francisco, where by this time he had opened yet another lumberyard.[28]

Growth continued. By the early 1880s, Simpson had seven sawmills, and he soon made a big addition, the Northwestern Lumber Company at Hoquiam on Washington's Grays Harbor. By that point, he had both wholesale and retail yards in California, a fleet of ocean-going vessels to supply them, much of the bar tug business on the Northwest coast, and a packet line providing regular service between Portland and San Francisco. The manager of Simpson's Hoquiam facilities summed up the result: "Our fleet is adapted to cheap transportation. Owning our own tugs should give us the cheapest towage. It would seem therefore, we should be able to deliver our lumber in San F[rancisco] in competition with anything on the Pacific Coast."[29] He was surely correct.

Simpson's business empire had grown large, but management remained simple. He established the Simpson Lumber Company, which from its office on San Francisco's Market Street operated his lumberyards, managed his vessels, chartered additional ships as needed, purchased goods for his various enterprises (including company stores in the mill communities), sought out buyers, and coordinated the activities of his scattered sawmills. Yet this is misleading. Simpson's various enterprises were a maze of proprietorships and partnerships only he fully understood, and he ran the Simpson Lumber Company as he ran everything else—with a tight hand. Management, he said, rested under his hat.[30]

Simpson might lay claim to the title king of the lumber coast, at least that portion south of Puget Sound, but he was never alone. There were other lumber companies, large and small. The bigger ones were on Puget Sound, Grays Harbor, and Humboldt Bay, where decent harbors and large hinterlands made extensive operations practical. Ere long some fell victim to fire, bad management, or other problems, but others were huge, long-lived undertakings that adjusted successfully as changing circumstances placed new demands on them.[31]

Foremost among early arrivals on Puget Sound was the Puget Mill Company, founded in 1852 by three residents of East Machias, Maine, who came to San Francisco in 1849 and a fourth who remained in the Maine community. Like Simpson, two of the partners, Andrew Jackson Pope and Frederic Talbot, turned to selling lumber soon after arriving in California. Lafayette Balch, a sea captain from Maine, had obtained cargoes of pilings at Puget Sound; he told Pope and Talbot the sound was surrounded by great forests that came right down to the shore. Needing a dependable source of lumber and hearing Balch's reports confirmed by others, they decided to erect a sawmill there. Surveying the sound in 1852, Talbot located an ideal site on a deepwater anchorage local Indians called Teekalet. Recognizing the risks he and his partners were assuming, Talbot renamed it Port Gamble. By 1853 the partners had completed a sawmill there.[32]

The Port Gamble operation expanded rapidly. The sawmill was equipped with quality machinery brought out from Bangor and cut superior lumber that allowed its owners to attract and hold customers and turn good profits even when selling at competitive rates. Moreover, Pope and Talbot were cautious, conservative businessmen who plowed profits back into their business, operated insofar as possible on a cash basis, and expanded without going deeply into debt. To accommodate increased sales, in 1857 they added a second mill and additional docking facilities. Within five years their Puget Mill Company owned ten sailing vessels and was shipping some nineteen million board feet a year.[33] In 1869-1870 the company replaced its original mill with an improved plant that more than doubled capacity. By 1875, the firm was shipping forty-three million board feet annually; by the early 1880s, with the purchase of large mills at Utsalady and Port Ludlow (both also on the sound), its operations had a capacity of 335,000 board feet a day.[34]

A major factor in this expansion was the Puget Mill Company's broad market base. In its first year, with demand in California slackening, over a third of the cut of the Port Gamble mill went foreign. In 1855 the partners established W. C. Talbot and Company to handle sales and such related matters as chartering vessels and purchasing supplies; renamed Pope & Talbot in 1862, it continued to serve these functions. The firm was assiduous in cultivating the expanding Hawaiian market. By 1856 the Honolulu *Pacific Commercial Advertiser* noted trade with Puget Sound was "becoming quite important, no less than seven vessels of about two thousand tons capacity [apiece] being regularly employed." So successful was Pope & Talbot in the islands that in 1878 the Tacoma *Herald* reported the Puget Mill Company "enjoyed a monopoly of the Sandwich Island trade."[35]

The Port Blakely Mill Company was a later arrival on Puget Sound, but its roots went back even further than those of the Puget Mill Company. In 1852 Captain William Renton and C. C. Terry erected a steam sawmill on Alki Point, near Seattle. The mill commenced sawing only a few days after Henry Yesler's mill in Seattle proper, the first steam sawmill on Puget Sound,[36] but Renton's operation failed to prosper; the harbor was too exposed to be a safe all-weather anchorage. Undeterred, Renton formed a new partnership (this time with Daniel Howard) and in 1854 moved the plant to Port Orchard, a protected harbor across the sound. Until he was injured in a boiler explosion in 1857, Renton did well in this new location. He retreated to San Francisco to recover, but the mill continued under new owners until 1867 when, financially over extended due to extensive remodeling, it went bankrupt and closed permanently.[37]

Renton was not finished. Recovered from his injuries, he returned to Puget Sound and in 1863 filed on a tract at Port Blakely, a protected deepwater harbor on Bainbridge Island, just off Seattle. There Renton and Howard erected a sawmill with a capacity of fifty thousand board feet a day. When the company-owned bark *Nahumkeag* arrived on May 28 to load the first cargo from the mill, Renton began to experience success at last. Repeatedly expanded and improved, by 1882 the Port Blakely Mill Company (the name under which the sawmill was incorporated as a part of reorganization following Howard's death in 1876) had a daily capacity of two hundred thousand board feet, making it the largest single mill on the sound.[38]

When success finally came for Captain Renton, it resulted from many of the same factors that led to growth of the Puget Mill Company. Like Pope & Talbot, the Port Blakely Mill Company served a variety of markets, including California, Hawaii, South America, and Australia. It owned sailing vessels to link the mill with these scattered outlets, and it developed a marketing arm based in San Francisco—Renton, Holmes and Company—to arrange sales, charter vessels to carry lumber from the mill, and attend to the myriad other details attendant upon owning a major sawmill, ships, and a company town. Charles Holmes, who headed marketing, was so aggressive a leading official of the Puget Mill Company grumbled "I will do my best to secure . . . orders, but will make no dirty marks as . . . Blakely are constantly."[39] Unlike A. M. Simpson, Renton and Holmes did not have their own shipyard, but in 1880 the Hall brothers moved their yard from Port Ludlow to Port Blakely, giving the firm ready access to the area's leading builder of sailing ships.[40] Perhaps most important, the management team was first rate. It kept the firm away from the sort of excess debt that brought down the Port Orchard mill and at the same time arranged for steady expansion. As the Seattle *Daily Intelligencer* observed, "Capt. Renton, the guiding spirit and good genius of the place is always on hand early and late, directing every department" and everything about the facilities speaks of "solidity, system, thrift, and economy."[41]

By the 1860s there were other large operations on Puget Sound besides those of Pope and Talbot and William Renton and his associates, most notably at Port Hadlock, Seabeck, Port Madison, and Tacoma. All depended on maritime markets, were financed with capital from California, and were in large part managed from there—a fact that on occasion drew the ire of residents of the Puget Sound area. Observing developments, in 1881 a correspondent for the *Chicago Times* wrote that a quarter of the wealth of San Francisco had been "culled from the firs of Puget Sound while the government slept," and the millowners were "all residents of San Francisco" who invested their profits in the Bay city "to the perpetual hurt of Puget Sound residents."[42] But if absentee ownership and the feeling the sound was an economic colony of San Francisco were galling, the fact remained that California residents and California markets brought development far beyond what the limited agricultural potential of the Puget Sound area (and its even more limited existing agricultural settlements) could have generated.[43]

Unlike the operations of Asa Simpson, scattered along the lumber coast from Washington to California, those of companies with mills on Puget Sound tended to be concentrated in single locations (although the Puget Mill Company, which started at Port Gamble, later took over mills at other sites as well). There was no single, great lumbering center; sawmills were dispersed about the sound. Seattle was a source of supplies, labor, and entertainment and the area's only community of any size—at least, until the arrival of railroads in the 1880s transformed the village of Tacoma—but it was not a major center of lumber production. Most business not conducted at the mills transpired in San Francisco. As in the South, there was no equivalent of Bangor, Williamsport, Glens Falls, or Saginaw-Bay City. Those centers had risen to primacy because rivers flowed to them from a vast forested interior, bringing to their booms great quantities of sawlogs. Puget Sound was a vast inland sea over which huge log rafts could be towed for miles at minimal cost. No booms needed to be constructed, no log drives resorted to. There were numerous safe, deepwater anchorages, any number of millsites with ample docking and storage space, and timber in almost every direction. In such a locale, it would have been difficult for a dispersed industry not to have emerged.

In time sizable cargo mills also appeared on the better bar harbors along the coast—Grays Harbor and Shoalwater (later Willapa) Bay in Washington, Coos Bay and the lower Columbia River in Oregon, and Humboldt Bay on northern California's redwood coast—thus dispersing production even further. By and large these mills followed the patterns of Puget Sound. They were built and controlled with capital from San Francisco, shipped by sea to California and foreign markets, and acquired the cargo vessels and tugs necessary to pursue the trade. As relatively large and frequently long-lived operations, these mills were a significant presence in their communities.

Coastal mills were not always popular. Even smaller mills were controlled from San Francisco—by agents, if not by owners. This spawned complaints along the coast, just as it did around Puget Sound. J. H. Upton, editor of Oregon's *Port Orford Post*, was outspoken. San Francisco's capitalists were, he wrote, "evil birds" perched "upon the mangled and prostrate industries of our county." Warming to his subject, Upton leveled a full set of charges against E. B. Dean and Company, which he considered the worst of the lot: "They have no business in the upbuilding of the county. They evade taxes. . . . They are denuding the forests contiguous to the bay to enrich a foreign city. . . . All the proceeds from their operations are promptly invested in San Francisco."[44]

Despite these complaints, by the 1880s a lumberman's frontier was firmly established on the Pacific shore. Steam was utilized from the first; nearly all the mills were steam powered and almost from the beginning steam tugs aided sailing vessels in crossing the dangerous bars, pulled them to often-becalmed harbors such as Seabeck (located on Hood Canal, a western arm of Puget Sound), and hauled huge log rafts to millsites over the quiet waters of Puget Sound, Grays Harbor, and the lower Columbia. Initially muscle power, human and animal, dominated in the woods and wind power dominated at sea. Then, beginning in the 1880s, the use of steam power increased rapidly, revolutionizing—and greatly expanding—the industry. For all that, West Coast lumbering remained as it had been from the first, not unlike a three-legged stool, with one support in the forests of the lumber coast, one in Pacific maritime markets, and one in San Francisco where management and capital (and not a little demand) were centered.

Many of the developments along the Pacific shore were reminiscent of what had transpired earlier at Bangor and in the Gulf South, but much was distinctive as well. For one thing, the logging seasons were reversed. Unlike in the Lake States and Northeast, where snow and ice made log sleighs practical, or the Gulf South, where winter brought high water for floating out log rafts, here it brought interminable rain that turned forests into quagmires and often closed logging operations until spring. Loggers had to devise new means of moving logs to cope with these conditions. Central among them was the skid road.[45] Loggers cleared paths through the woods and every few feet placed short logs some six to twelve inches in diameter across them. They then notched these crosspieces in the middle and greased them heavily with dogfish oil or some other lubricant to create skidways over which oxen could pull logs to streamside without getting mired in the area's bottomless mud or hung up on logging refuse and other obstructions.[46]

As important as skid roads—although less noticed both at the time and since—was the use of crosscut saws in felling. Initially, crosscuts were used in bucking trees into log lengths once they were on the ground, but the actual process of felling was done with axes. Axes had been used in felling on all earlier lumbering frontiers, but driven by the immense size of Pacific Coast trees and the region's continuing labor shortages Far Western loggers needed a more efficient tool. They found it in the crosscut; "choppers" became "fellers." From the 1880s until the mid-twentieth century crosscuts were the universal felling tool in Far Western forests.[47]

Crosscut saws were not the only adaptation in felling. Underbrush was often so dense and the bases of trees (especially spruce and redwoods) so enlarged that felling was fraught with special difficulties. To cope, loggers turned to iron-tipped planks known as springboards that they inserted into notches cut in the trees' flared lower trunks. A series of springboards set like steps up the side of a trunk could take a logger several feet above the ground to give him a clear field of work—and a trunk of smaller diameter on which to saw. Loggers had to balance carefully to stand on a springboard while felling a tree, but these were a marked improvement over laboring in undergrowth at ground level while sawing through the enlarged bases of trees. Springboards were so successful they would continue in use in West Coast forests well into the twentieth century.[48]

The region's streams provided another difference between this and earlier logging frontiers. Most Far Western streams were ill suited for log drives. Spring freshets were not as abrupt as in Maine and the Lake States, and, in any case, most streams were too rocky and tortuous to drive or raft. Unlike the Penobscot, Chippewa, St. Croix, and even the Pascagoula, almost none had vast forested hinterlands from which logs could be floated. In some places, logs were floated individually rather than in drives, an approach that reduced the chance of jams. In others, splash dams were utilized—as they had been earlier in Maine, Pennsylvania, and elsewhere—to generate a sufficient head of water to flush logs out of the woods. Streams near Humboldt Bay were used to float logs to mills, sometimes in conjunction with railroads that brought them to streamside, but they were highly undependable. Indeed, in 1873 D. R. Jones had to tell his partner not to take a promising contract to supply railroad ties, for he was out of logs and until rains brought some down he saw little chance of getting any.[49] On Puget Sound, various bays, and the more sluggish streams logs were rafted

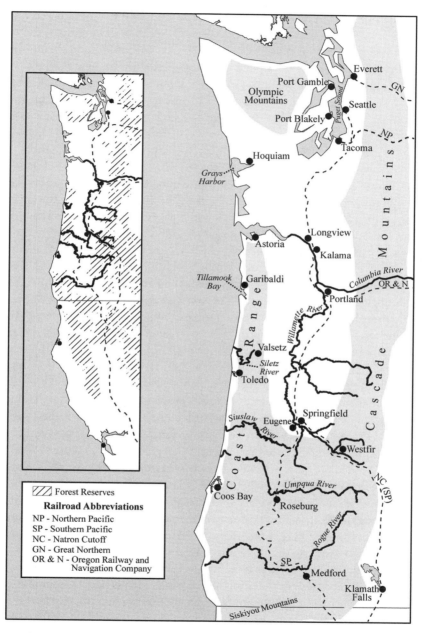

Pacific Coast forest frontier. Map by Sarah E. Hinman.

to the mills, recalling early practices in the Gulf South, although here the rafts were generally pulled by steam tugs, rather than driven by the forces of current or human muscle power.[50] Clearly, not just distance from the nation's main centers of population and dependence on new markets set this lumberman's frontier apart.

Initially present only in favored locations, West Coast lumbering gradually expanded to less well-endowed sites. Steam played a vital role. An increase in the number and power of steam-powered tugs helped sailing vessels enter and leave the area's bar harbors and made it feasible to erect sawmills on such dangerous ports as those at the mouth of Oregon's Siuslaw, Coquille, and Alsea rivers, where in better weather sailing vessels could now enter with some safety. Even at Humboldt Bay and on the lower Columbia, far better harbors where lumbering antedated the presence of bar tugs, once they were in service larger craft could enter; while the bars were still difficult, the number of vessels lost on them fell sharply.[51]

With tugs for the bar, the sawmills on Humboldt Bay grew large and the industry took on the characteristics of the great mill centers on Puget Sound; however, on less favored harbors, with their still-dangerous entries and more limited tributary forests, numerous small, second-rate, frequently ephemeral operations emerged. Of little apparent consequence other than in their immediate areas, these mills received little attention at the time and have gotten even less since. But if small and largely forgotten, they were also numerous, their collective impact considerable.

William Kyle's sawmill at the mouth of Oregon's Siuslaw River is one of the few of these mills to leave a fairly complete record, but the rough outlines of others' stories can be pieced together from local newspapers, trade journals, and assorted ephemera. What emerges is a picture of small, under-funded operations, frequently run by men whose dreams were bigger than their capacity for management.[52]

Too small and with too few financial resources to develop marketing organizations of their own, most such mills sold through commission merchants in San Francisco. These agents sold the cut of the sawmills, chartered vessels to haul it, purchased supplies and equipment for millowners, and advanced capital against future sales when special needs arose—all, of course, for a commission, normally 10 percent.[53] Commission merchants, not the lumber manufacturers themselves, dominated the trade, and they frequently ran things to their own advantage. One of William Kyle's associates put it bluntly when he wrote Kyle about their commission merchant, William Beadle & Co.: "I see now, Beadle work for Beadle as you told me once."[54]

Being under financed, most little coastal mills utilized inexpensive, used machinery and turned out low-grade products. A lumber dealer told one of them: "We are trying to work off your [Oregon] pine which is quite a different quality as compared with Puget Sound stock, and [we] do not find it easy to sell."[55]

Poor plants and an antiquated marketing system were not the only disadvantages under which these mills operated. Tugboat service was inadequate—or nonexistent—on many bar harbors, yet even a ship of extremely shallow draft could hardly enter or leave without one. The harbor at the mouth of the Umpqua, although not the worst, was illustrative. An observer wrote:

> The Ortolan *arrived a few days since, other vessels are now due. The* Ortolan *came up in four days from San Francisco. Various may be the opinions as to her entering the river, hence, a remark in point. She came in safely, but how it happened I cannot tell; the better opinion, however, is that she came in on wheels.*[56]

Not infrequently, vessels spent more time waiting to cross the bar than sailing to or from San Francisco. The barkentine *Webfoot* once waited off the Umpqua for thirty-six days before finally managing to enter; and storms kept *Sparrow*, loaded and ready for sea, at dockside for three weeks before they subsided enough for her to depart safely.[57]

Conditions were no better at Tillamook Bay. One vessel waited off its treacherous bar for thirty-five days before giving up and sailing to Portland. The captain of the shallow-draft centerboard schooner *Bella* left the bay in mid-winter, so deeply laden her decks were awash and with but sixteen inches of freeboard; still, the ship's agent grumbled that the captain would "have to load the vessel deeper . . . to make any money with her. She will carry a big load if he will only put it on." Steam-powered tugs could help, but they hardly made such places easy or safe to serve.[58]

Steam helped on California's redwood coast too, but it did not come primarily in the form of bar tugs. Except for Humboldt Bay, this area's harbors were outports, unprotected from storms and dangerously beset with rocks. Only small, nimble vessels could enter these tiny ports, and even they did so at risk. Winter storms frequently made the outports—bad enough in summer—totally unusable. James T. Smith, semi-literate captain of the schooner *Bella*, reported from Crescent City one September: "The Foremand on the Warf told my that Sailing wessels have no bisinus here this time of yare." A few days later, Smith added, "[We have] had hard time of it her[e], the sea have ben Breacket over her for Days and she dregged the moorings and Ankers and brock the vindles [windlass]. . . . Tel Beadle that yow dont vont the wessel to go Outside Port no more this year." Smith argued they might make a little money by chartering to go there, but they could lose the vessel.[59] Others shared his judgment. Millowners often found it almost impossible to get charters for mills in such locations, and even when tonnage was available costly delays were frequent.

In the 1880s shipbuilders in the Bay Area began adding steam engines to the little schooners that served the redwood coast. No longer at the mercy of the vagaries of wind and storm, captains could now enter dogholes with a modicum of safety. Repeatedly modified and improved over the years, steam schooners (as these vessels were called even after their schooner origins were far behind them) made the expansion of lumbering possible along northern California's coast. Indeed, some of its mills were to continue sawing well into the twentieth century.[60]

But even with the help of steam power, mills on bar harbors and outports faced immense problems. Located on ports that could only be visited by small vessels, owners had to market their cut in San Francisco; more distant Pacific outlets required ships large enough to yield the economies of scale necessary to turn a profit on long voyages. As William Kyle explained,

Already deeply laden, the schooner Ivanhoe *continues to take on lumber at Westport, California, while others wait in the offing. Serving such dogholes was difficult and dangerous even after steam schooners replaced sailing vessels. Courtesy San Francisco Maritime NHP, #E11.21,972pl.*

We have onley one market place, S.F. We cannot load large enough vessels to go south [i.e., to Southern California, Australia, or Latin America] or to the [Hawaiian] Islands, small vessles does not carry enough to make long trips, and large ones cant get over the bar. So we have difficulties that we cant overcome no matter how we figure it out.[61]

Restricted to the coasting trade, such mills were less insulated against market fluctuations than large cargo mills with their multiple outlets. The advent of steam-powered vessels helped these mills, but the number of bankruptcies and closures remained high.

Some of the little sawmills on the redwood coast were aided by selling through trading companies such as John Kentfield and Company. Kentfield regularly took more orders than his mill on Humboldt Bay could fill— especially orders from Hawaii, a market he cultivated assiduously. He then purchased additional lumber on the open market to make up the shortfall. Similarly, although the firm had vessels of its own, Kentfield regularly chartered additional bottoms to transport the lumber needed to fill orders, thus assuring that his mill could run at nearly full capacity and his vessels all have cargoes while he remained free to pursue new customers. The result was a long list of regular buyers, so many he could anticipate orders even when the market softened. Through Kentfield's aggressive marketing, many a small redwood mill had a portion of its cut transshipped from San Francisco to deepwater markets they could never have served directly, but for most the problem of limited outlets remained.[62]

Not all of the Pacific lumber trade's maritime adaptations involved steam. To cope with challenges of the sea, firms large and small sought vessels suited to the peculiarities of the cargo trade and the coast from which it operated. Lumbermen with a background in shipbuilding and with their own shipyards, men such as A. M. Simpson, could attack these problems directly; others turned to independent yards scattered from San Francisco northward. A host of innovations, large and small, were forthcoming. Notable was the development of two-masted, broad-beamed, single-decked schooners with huge hatches for easy loading and the ability to carry immense deckloads; schooners with retractable centerboards so they could cross all but the shallowest bars; four-, five- and six-masted schooners for the deepwater trade; and bald-headed schooners whose sail plans required smaller crews than those that carried sail on their topmasts. So different were the vessels of the lumber fleet that one leading East Coast maritime historian dismissed them as "freaks."[63]

Changes came on land as well as at sea; here too some of the most pivotal involved steam. Indeed, nothing reshaped the industry more than steam logging. In 1885 John Dolbeer of Eureka, California, taking a cue from steam-powered windlasses used to raise ship's anchors, affixed a steam engine and windlass to a heavy platform that could be moved from site to site in the woods; he then ran a long rope from the device to logs lying on the forest floor. With this so-called steam donkey, Dolbeer's loggers were able to pull logs to landings at streamside or next to railroads far more quickly than ox teams could. Moreover, donkey engines could move logs too large or too far from the landings for ox teams and could operate during the wettest months, when mud had often brought earlier operations to a halt. The Dolbeer donkey and numerous competing designs caught on quickly, especially after steel cable was substituted for rope (which had a tendency to stretch or break and was far less durable). Unfortunately, donkey engines not only speeded operations, they also increased the damage to the forest. When a donkey engine began powering a log out of the woods, anything in its way was in danger. Young trees were smashed, ground cover uprooted, and the soil gullied and broken.   In places erosion soon ran rampant.[64] Steam engines, spewing sparks in the woods, completed this unfortunate scenario. Forest fires, finding unprecedented fuel loads on the slash-strewn forest floor, burned hotter and more destructively than ever. Some of the worst forest fires in the nation's history followed.[65]

Railroads brought steam into the woods too. Initially, stands near Puget Sound, Grays Harbor, and other sawmill locations provided ample supplies of logs, but as mills grew larger and stands retreated in the face of the assault of loggers, new sources were needed. As in the Lake States and South, railroads offered the means of reaching them. By 1883, the *Northwestern Lumberman* noted, lands along streams "had been cleared of their best timber," which necessitated constructing logging railroads and drove up costs. This in turn led to the larger logging camps needed to get an adequate return on investment. At the beginning of the 1870s, the author noted, fifteen men constituted a large camp, but thirty to sixty were "now frequently employed."[66] The first logging railroad in the Pacific Northwest apparently was a narrow-gauge line from Tenino to Olympia, Washington. In 1881, during its first six months of operation, the railroad hauled "several million feet" from the woods. It operated so much more efficiently than the tramways with mule-drawn log cars previously used that within a year at least five logging railroads were in service in the vicinity.[67] The Port Blakely Mill Company followed this lead. Recognizing the advantages railroads offered, its management constructed a line into the relatively level, well-endowed timberland between Puget Sound and Grays Harbor; by 1888 some 225,000 feet of logs rolled along its tracks daily.[68]

Other companies began building railroads during the same period, and the reason was clear: as *West Shore* observed in 1884, logging railroads could haul logs ten to fifteen miles by rail for what it cost to move them one or two miles by skid roads. As a result, railroads opened tracts too far from usable waterways to be reached using earlier technology. These changes in woods operations were necessary to keep up with demand as area sawmills grew larger and more numerous and employed more and more innovations that speeded production—innovations that were themselves frequently steam powered.[69]

The 1880s was the heyday of the cargo trade. Markets boomed in Latin America, China, and Australia as mining and railroad building surged ahead, in Hawaii as plantation sugar production expanded, and in southern California as the population exploded following completion of transcontinental rail connections. To service the huge orders that resulted, steamships with much larger capacity than that of sailing vessels began calling at some of the larger mills and in their own way helped generate the demand that drove development onward.[70]

New stands were needed as production continued to rise in the 1880s, and although logging railroads enabled millmen to reach them they also introduced fresh problems. Rail lines were costly to build; one could afford to do so only if assured of a long-term supply of logs. Millmen were not interested in building common carriers for the profits they could earn from freight and passengers; they wanted railroads for their primary business, lumber production. In light of this, Port Blakely and other mill companies that built logging railroads aggressively bought up timberlands along their projected routes to safeguard their investments—and, not coincidentally, block competitors from woods that had suddenly acquired new value.[71]

Acquisition of timberland had not always been a major concern. West Coast lumbermen had built their first sawmills where they could be easily reached by seagoing vessels, which in practice meant they often located on isolated harbors where local demand was virtually nonexistent, rather than in growing population centers such as Portland or Seattle. Under the circumstances, they had little choice but to add company stores and housing to their mill towns. These expenditures—together with those on ships, tugs, mill equipment, and, in the case of larger operations, lumberyards—tied up their investment capital and necessitated that profits be plowed back into their businesses.

Under these circumstances, pioneer millowners had little money with which to finance logging operations or to purchase timberlands. Those activities were left to others. Independent loggers sold to millowners, either on the open market (such as it was, since there was often but a single buyer) or under contract. Much of their cut was illegal.[72] Land laws did not provide means for acquiring stumpage without getting title to land too, and for the latter neither lumbermen nor loggers had any use. Moreover, acquiring title to timberland was hindered by the fact the bulk of the land long remained unsurveyed and thus unavailable even if one wished to buy it. Lumbermen could acquire title to acreage in the territorial university land grant—and did so—but little else was available until 1863, when responding to public pressure President Abraham Lincoln ordered all surveyed public lands opened for sale. But there were few takers; of the three million acres offered in Washington Territory as a result of Lincoln's directive, only 2,765 sold during initial bidding.[73] It was easier to cut timber without bothering to get title; loggers simply illegally, trespassing on federal, state, and private land alike.[74]

In 1861 this practice was challenged by John J. McGilvra, the young United States district attorney for Washington Territory. Shortly after arrival in the territory, McGilvra reported to the Solicitor of the Treasury, "there are upwards of 15 saw mills on the waters of Puget Sound and Admiralty Inlet which will cut per day all the way from five to forty thousand feet of lumber. These mills are almost wholly supplied with logs from the government lands." However, McGilvra soon came to recognize that the area's economy required sawlogs for local mills and that its development was in the national interest. To reconcile these disparate facts, he proposed "a rate of stumpage should be established for this section and that it should be such a one as will ensure to the general government something more than a nominal revenue." Technically, stumpage fees would be fines, but in fact they served to open unsurveyed government land to logging without those involved having to fear their mills would be shut or logs seized by authorities. What McGilvra proposed was not to halt the cutting of timber, but to stop millmen from taking it without payment.[75]

McGilvra's approach was not without precedent. Since the early 1850s, officials elsewhere had from time to time used fines for timber trespass as a substitute for stumpage fees. It was a frequent practice in the Lake States, but had limited success there. Over a period of twenty-two years, the General Land Office spent over $150,000 to collect fines of only $250,000.[76]

With little support from the nation's capital or local courts, McGilvra was in a difficult position; nonetheless, he was able win convictions and establish a standardized fine of 15 cents per thousand board feet for logs taken. McGilvra's superiors urged him to demand more, but 15 cents was all local juries could be prevailed upon to assess. As he later wrote, he was none too happy with this, but it was the "best I could do at the time." Later agents of the General Land Office were able to get slightly larger fines, but depredations continued; between 1855 and 1870 an estimated $40 million of logs illegally passed into the hands of the area's sawmill operators. In 1880 Congress, despairing of halting the practice, passed an act allowing depredations, when detected, to be excused on payment of $1.25 an acre or stumpage fees.[77]

In the years following McGilvra's efforts, fresh log sources became available—new land grants were awarded and bit by bit public lands were surveyed and opened to entry under the Timber and Stone and Homestead acts—but illegal logging continued to plague timberland owners, public and private alike. As one observer put it, "men logged wherever they pleased . . . and this without settlement or purchase or interference from the government." Secretary of the Interior Carl Schurz found whole fleets of Pacific Coast vessels "carrying timber stolen from the public lands to be sold in foreign countries, immense tracts being devastated that some robbers might fill their pockets." For a time Hazard Stevens worked diligently to halt timber trespass on the Northern Pacific Railroad's huge land grant, but he too had limited success—causing loggers and lumbermen to be more discreet, perhaps, but certainly not halting their activities.[78]

Initially those who worked in West Coast forests were a motley group looked down upon by millowners to whom they sold logs. There was good reason for the contempt. Not only did the loggers often cut trees they had no right to fell—that proper millowners could understand—but they also broke agreements with lumbermen, failed to repay funds advanced to finance their operations, and on too many occasions simply disappeared leaving sawmills short on logs and their owners out of pocket for money advanced. One observer described loggers up the rivers and sloughs near Coos Bay as "the roughest of men"; they were hardly atypical. An observer in California described redwood loggers as having their "wages perpetually mortgaged to some rum seller," while a disgusted sawmill operator on Puget Sound wrote of one log supplier: "[H]e doesn't seem to care about his work . . . and I think it best to get his boom and then take his team and what timber he has, because I do not think we will ever get out any better."[79]

Independent loggers included many who at first glance seem a reincarnation of a type of woods worker familiar in early Maine and the pre-Civil War South. They operated on the fringes of the market economy, gathering logs much as others gathered furs or mined for gold in California's placer deposits. They viewed trees as theirs for the taking: logs belonged to the person who invested the effort to fell them and get them from the woods, not to some distant landowner (government or otherwise) who claimed title. Under the circumstances, one visitor wrote, "No one can find fault with them but uncle sam, and he is far distant."[80]

These initial impressions of West Coast woods workers overlook significant differences from their predecessors. There were, indeed, some who collected logs to provide supplemental support beyond that furnished by their cattle and agricultural land; as one resident near Coos Bay later recalled, logging and mill work enabled a family to support a small farm. But there were few such in the early years, for as Andrew Pope noted, the land was "good for nothing only for timber"; indeed, he wrote, a farmer "would starve on such land."[81]

Pope understood the situation. The size of West Coast trees made clearing slower and more arduous than in earlier forests, keeping the number of farms small, while the density of stands made the forest floor too dark to support the quantities of grass that encouraged pastoral activity in Southern pineries. Forest-dwelling farmers and pastoralists were thus too few along the Pacific shore to form the backbone of lumbering's labor force, and even if they had been numerous, the logging season conflicted with agriculture's busy months as it had not in areas where logging was primarily a winter operation.[82]

Under the circumstances, most West Coast loggers initially were in-migrants, many with experience in lumbering in New England. A good share had come west in search of gold and turned to lumbering when mining failed them.[83] They were joined by itinerant laborers drawn by higher wages than were paid in other regions. Like woods workers on earlier lumbering frontiers, they largely moved outside of polite society.[84] Proper New Englander that he was, W. H. Talbot looked upon such laborers with suspicion, if not disdain, yet not until the 1890s had his company's development proceeded to the point where he could seriously consider establishing company-run logging operations to free his firm from them. At that point, he told associates it would be better to close their mills than "tie ourselves up with irresponsible loggers and eventually get stuck."[85]

Millworkers as well as loggers were a concern. Josiah Keller and Marshall Blinn, owners of the Washington Mill Company and like Talbot New

Englanders by birth, struggled to control the laborers at their sawmill at Seabeck on Hood Canal. Their workers, one authority claimed, had a "preference for alcohol and amorous encounters with local Indian women." Initially, firms such as Pope & Talbot and the Washington Mill Company brought in laborers from Maine, but many drifted away to higher-paying jobs in Seattle, and employers had to turn to local tribesmen, erstwhile miners, sailors who had jumped ship, drifters, and others of dubious reliability. As time passed, immigrants, especially from Scandinavia, constituted an increasing percentage of the mix.[86] In 1888 the crew loading vessels at Pope & Talbot's mill at Utsalady was reportedly made up of foreigners "who cannot speak a word of English & who never saw a stick of lumber in their lives." Efforts to make a dependable work force from such material created tensions that led one resident to liken Seabeck to a penal colony. By contrast, Andrew Pope proposed making Port Gamble a model community of sorts, for his company had somehow obtained a number of good employees, and he wished to keep them: "[I]f we can make them contented . . . I think it a good investment."[87]

Model communities or not—and most were decidedly not—management had little choice but to erect company towns. With their sawmills located on isolated harbors, firms had to supply housing, stores, and other ancillary facilities if workers' needs were to be met. The layout of these communities—with housing for laborers distinct from that of management in both location and comfort—underscored social divisions and hardened attitudes of the communities' comfortable citizens toward workers. Even in Port Gamble, with its neatly painted clapboard dwellings and streets lined with elms brought around Cape Horn to give it a New England "feel," there was no question about where one stood in the community.[88]

Divisions within company towns deepened when management, faced with continuing labor shortages, turned to hiring Asians. Labor contractors advertised they could furnish Chinese workers, and any number of mill operators took up the offer, often using them as complete crews to run lath machines or at other distinctly separated tasks rather than trying to integrate them into their main crews. By 1889 Port Blakely had some thirty-five Japanese workers and the number was rising. Other mills also had a significant Asian presence, to the chagrin of many white workers, who believed they drove down wages and worsened living conditions. Encouraged by the nation's rising nativism and anti-Chinese activities elsewhere on the West Coast, virulent anti-Asian sentiments were soon in evidence and in the 1880s resulted in Asians being driven out of Tacoma and other lumber centers.[89]

Officials at Pope & Talbot saw anti-Chinese activity as a sidelight to the main issue of growing labor-management conflict. In 1885 Cyrus Walker predicted that if the Knights of Labor succeeded in driving the Chinese from Washington, its next attack would be on corporations and capital; the "better class," he reported, was against the anti-Chinese movement. Although sawmills at Port Blakely and Tacoma had been forced to discharge Chinese workers and for years Pope & Talbot had been under sporadic pressure to dismiss its Asian crews, Walker hoped the company could keep them "if we lay low." Labor's rising militancy, epitomized by the anti-Chinese movement, whipped E. G. Ames, assistant manager at Port Gamble, into a frenzy. He wrote of the Knights of Labor, "Their Chinese Hobby is only a side Issue. They are the worst of socialists and Hanging is too good for such."[90]

Ames was more outspoken than most, but his attitudes were not uncommon. When depression forced mill closures in 1893, George Emerson, manager of A. M. Simpson's mill in Hoquiam, reduced wages 10 percent and then reported in response to complaints from the Knights of Labor, still a force in the area although in sharp decline nationally:

We are inclined to think the outcome of all this trouble will be a very healthy state of affairs, and that perhaps, it is absolutely needed for readjustment of conditions that exist between capital and labor. Thus far, it has been a rich man's panic, and before spring it will be a poor man's empty stomach, which is perhaps the only way to teach a large class of our people that they cannot organize against or dictate to capital without suffering consequences.[91]

Simpson, not given to taking advice from anyone, surely approved of his manager's position.

Labor problems were not the only thing plaguing cargo mills by the late nineteenth century. Demand softened in many markets after railroad construction projects were completed or when economic depression struck, but compensating factors were at work. Steamships could carry cargoes of a size the old sailing ships could never match, making shipments to ever-more-distant ports practical. For some favorably located cargo mills, rail markets also provided new outlets to complement the old.[92] Still, by the end of the century the cargo trade was in the doldrums, and as one authoritative study put it, from 1900 to 1905 "barely kept its head above water." Rebuilding following the great San Francisco earthquake and fire of 1906 caused a welcome, if temporary, respite, but the glory days of the cargo trade were over. One result was that the Weyerhaeuser interests, which acquired a huge tract of rich forestland from the Northern Pacific Railroad in 1900, hesitated to begin milling in the Northwest but cautiously acquired and modernized a plant in Everett in 1902 to begin getting experience in manufacturing and marketing Douglas fir lumber.[93]

Yet the cargo trade would not die. The Panama Canal, completed in 1914, had a lasting impact by opening new markets on the East Coast. After a slow start, shipments from the Pacific Northwest to eastern and Gulf Coast outlets increased from 1.9 million feet in 1918 to forty-eight million feet in 1919, and they were still growing; between 1921 and 1923 shipments rose over 400 percent.[94]

Other factors were also at work. Rising domestic consumption, initiated by demand built up during World War I and carried along by a boom in housing starts that began in 1921, continued into 1927. Cargoes bound for the East Coast were but one reflection, revived shipments to California another. Early in the new century the Southern Pacific cut freight rates to California, making it possible for mills from Eugene, Oregon, south to sell in the San Francisco Bay and Central Valley areas at prices cargo mills were hard pressed to match, but cargo mills continued to supply much of the lumber needed to meet the growing demand in southern California.[95]

Coming as it did when more and more lumbermen were wrapping up in the Lake States and South, this increased demand inevitably encouraged the building of sawmills in western Oregon and Washington. Grays Harbor, blessed with one of the better ports on the coast, surrounded by some of the finest stands, and served by excellent logging streams—the Chehalis, Humptulips, Hoquiam, Wishkah, Satsop, and Wynoochee—saw lumbering flourish during the late nineteenth and early twentieth centuries. In 1895 mills on the harbor exported just over one hundred million board feet; by 1909, the annual cut exceeded five hundred million, and by 1924 shipments topped one billion. Over a twenty-seven year period, an average of five hundred and twenty deep-sea and coasting vessels called annually to carry its lumber to market. Additional quantities went inland by rail. Local boosters lauded Grays Harbor as the world's greatest lumber port; statistics are fugitive, and there were those who would have awarded primacy to Portland, but the claim may well have been true.[96]

New mills also appeared at Garibaldi on Tillamook Bay, at Toledo on Yaquina Bay, and elsewhere, while older operations (such as those of Weyerhaeuser and David Clough at Everett and Bloedel-Donovan at Bellingham) expanded. So too did lumber-carrying steamship lines (such as McCormick). Indeed, positioning itself to take advantage of the eastern trade, in 1923 Weyerhaeuser acquired steamships of its own. Federal river and harbor improvement projects supported this surge of activity—although sometimes with unexpected side effects, as when the jetty installed at the mouth of Tillamook Bay altered ocean currents and led to erosion of the peninsula between the bay and the Pacific, causing the natatorium and other developments at Bay Ocean to gradually wash into the sea.[97]

In 1920 C. D. Johnson and a group of Southerners purchased the Pacific Spruce Corporation's sawmill at Toledo on Yaquina Bay, started by the government during World War I to produce lightweight spruce for aircraft frames. Within two years they had completed the mill, docking facilities, and a logging railroad; and by 1924 were producing ninety million feet a year. Although the mill had rail access to the interior, nearly all its output was marketed by sea. Of the operation, A. W. Morgan wrote, "I do not believe there is another man except C. D. Johnson who could have nursed this operation along and held it together as he did." The mill at Garibaldi was similar. It too was started by the federal Spruce Production Division and completed by private interests after the war. Unfortunately, it had been "designed by southern lumbermen [and] was lightly built." Extensive reconstruction—an unanticipated expense—proved necessary to handle the big logs of the area.[98]

Control of the Pacific Shore's sawmills may have rested in San Francisco, but the roots of many owners were in Maine. Lumbermen and shipowners from Down East had been quick to recognize opportunities presented by the juxtapositioning of population growth in California—and later in other Pacific markets—with the richly forested lands along the northern portions of the continent's western shore, for they had seen similar circumstances enrich Bangor and other centers in the Pine Tree State. A lumber industry built on such a foundation required knowledge of ships and the sea as well as of the woods. Those who had both—and an ample supply of good business sense—soon prospered. The lumber frontier of the Pacific Coast's cargo mills was the result.

Maps of Northwestern forests, produced by the Geological Survey near the beginning of the twentieth century, reveal much about the environmental legacy of this westernmost of lumbermen's frontiers. By then narrow strips had been logged along nearly all waterways and lowlands. Though logged and—in the immediate aftermath of steam logging—tremendous eyesores, these riparian strips were not long bare of vegetation. Red alder and other pioneer species moved in where Douglas fir, cedar, spruce, and hemlock had once stood. The results were mixed. Deer and other herbivores, fattening on the abundant browse, multiplied mightily, just as they were to do in other logged-over areas in years to come, but stream pollution and degradation of water quality accompanied logging even before the donkey engine and they became worse in the years after its introduction.[99]

Still, back from the alder-dominated, logged-off strips dense forests still held sway. The way was open for a new lumberman's frontier to develop in the Far West, one that would move into these interior forests and depend more upon markets reached by rail than by sea. This new frontier would dominate West Coast lumbering in the twentieth century as that of the cargo mills had in the nineteenth. By the beginning of the new century it was that clear cargo mills represented the old order on the Pacific Coast, not a continuing frontier of opportunity. Like its predecessor, the frontier of the rail mills would bring great changes to the forests, but the new frontier's environmental impact was not to be primarily limited to narrow strips along the waterways.

CHAPTER TWELVE

Into the Mountains

On April 10, 1912, Norwegian immigrant Simon Benson gave $10,000 to the city of Portland for twenty bronze drinking fountains to be placed along streets near the waterfront—the so-called North End—where hosts of loggers gathered when in from the woods. Benson had arrived in the Pacific Northwest penniless in 1879 and parlayed hard work and an eye for the main chance into a sizable fortune. By the early twentieth century he was one of the area's leading loggers, but he had received most of his public notice by erecting a sawmill in San Diego, California, and supplying it by rafting logs eleven hundred miles by sea from the lower Columbia River. In 1912 Benson was ready to embark on two decades of public service. His fountains were a quixotic first step.[1]

Benson explained the motivation for his gift: years before he had entered one of Portland's many North End saloons on a hot summer day and asked for a glass of water. "Only beer sold here," the bartender replied curtly, so Benson ordered a beer and a glass of water, drank the water, left the beer, and departed.

> *I used to watch the workmen going into saloons with their buckets to buy beer. It seemed strange that in a city whose water is famous for its purity, workmen had no opportunity to quench their thirst except in saloons. . . . For a long time I had been getting more and more fed up with supporting the saloons, which produced nothing of value and were parasites on legitimate industry. I came to the conclusion that if a workman could get a drink of cold, pure water on a street corner, without any obligation, he probably wouldn't go into a saloon so often.*

How successful the fountains were in achieving Benson's purpose is questionable, for it was a massive undertaking: Erickson's saloon was but one of many, and its bar ran 684 lineal feet. Still, Benson claimed some saloons saw business drop 40 percent after the fountains were in place. He considered them the best investment he ever made, for they "helped knock the profit out of the saloon business and were a factor in making Oregon dry."[2]

Benson's strange gift suggests a good bit about the temperance movement in Oregon in the early twentieth century (it went "dry" in 1916)—and about

Benson himself—but it suggests at least as much about Portland's role as a lumber center as it moved toward becoming successor to Bangor, Saginaw, and their ilk.[3] Until late in the nineteenth century, Portland had been but a secondary, regional lumber producer, over one hundred miles from the sea and reached via the sandbar-strewn lower Columbia River. Would-be operators of cargo mills saw greater potential elsewhere. Now things were different. Lumber moving inland by rail challenged the volume going out to sea, and loggers were using Dolbeer donkeys and other power equipment to tap interior stands to supply the trade. Portland was ideally situated to serve the lumberman's frontier developing in its hinterlands. Benson's fountains would have served no purpose had it not been for the host of thirsty loggers and millworkers who flocked to Portland as the industry grew in and around it; forester C. M. Granger noted a few years later: "Portland's business barometer is in large part the number of unemployed loggers on Burnside Street," while logger Paul Repetto commented dryly: "Portland [was] at that time booming, or at least lively enough."[4]

What was transpiring in Portland and the Pacific Northwest was not merely the transfer of established modes of operation to new forests, nor a shift in influence from centers in Maine, the Lake States, and the South. Practices from earlier frontiers were colliding with the realities of the Far West to create a new sort of industry rather than simply repeating earlier patterns. This new frontier saw a convergence of forces set in motion by the cumulative effect of earlier ones: a growing concern for a coming "timber famine," high-ball logging as a result of new technologies (and associated increases in fire and other devastation), and larger-than-ever lumber firms as a result of accumulated capital and experience. These, when applied on the stage provided by the Pacific Northwest, a stage with its own peculiarities, would create a lumber frontier distinct from those that had gone before.

For a considerable time, the new and different were hard to discern; old practices were not. Using techniques perfected in the Lake States and Gulf South, lumbermen gained title to thousands of acres of fine timberland—as the public was to learn starting in 1904 during the widely publicized Oregon land fraud cases and, four years later, from Stephen Puter's confessional, *Looters of the Public Domain*.[5] Portland's population and production were increasing by leaps and bounds, but however much it troubled the staid New England values of some of the city's older families, these changes brought the raw elements of a resource-extracting boomtown.[6]

Portland's rise as a lumber center began with the arrival of transcontinental rail connections in the 1880s. Whenever freight rates allowed, George Weidler shipped lumber from his Willamette Steam Mills to Denver,

Omaha, and beyond. He shipped to Hong Kong as well, but it was in pioneering in the interior that Weidler made his mark. His sawmill was the largest, most modern in the city (and Simon Benson was one of those supplying it with logs).[7]

Nor was Weidler alone. On Puget Sound, the St. Paul and Tacoma Lumber Company, erected in 1889, joined in selling in the interior; others followed suit.[8] By 1899 one-sixth of Washington's lumber production was shipped east by rail; two years later the quantity had doubled, and it continued expanding. In 1899 the *Pacific Lumber Trade Journal* reported all but seven towns in western Washington depended upon lumbering, as did two-thirds of the wage earners in the state. After 1908, when Washington's lumbermen triumphed in the Portland Gateway Case, winning freight rates equal to Portland's, rail shipments from the Evergreen state rose even higher. Indeed, with something of a head start and less-challenging terrain, production in Washington long ran ahead of Oregon's. In 1905 Washington passed Wisconsin to become the nation's leading lumber-producing state and rail shipments exceeded maritime shipments for the first time. In 1911 Everett Griggs, president of the Pacific Coast Lumber Manufacturers' Association, summed up the result: "The State of Washington manufactures *more* lumber than any other state in the Union today. It is our chief industry, and when it languishes, our state does not prosper."[9] No one center stood out in Washington as Portland did in Oregon, dominating because of the many sawmills that clustered along its riverfront, because it had direct rail connections to the east, and because it was the state's center for banking, insurance, and provisioning.[10]

As in the Lake States and Gulf South, it had been the scramble for timberland, rather than sawmills themselves, that announced this newest lumberman's frontier. Timber trespass—the practice that so bedeviled John McGilvra in the 1860s—gradually gave way to acquiring title to land to supply stumpage for mills. That land was increasingly found in the mountains of the Coast Range or the well-forested western slope of the Cascades, locations that would test the ingenuity of loggers who sought to tap them.

"Landlookers"—often in the employ of eastern capitalists, but usually with an eye for their own advancement as well—were key players. Although often called timber cruisers or timber surveyors, these agents long made their living not by determining the amount and quality of timber on individual tracts—they sketched those only in rough terms—so much as by finding entrymen who would establish or already had established claims on public domain land that could be consolidated with others into tracts large enough to serve as operating units to supply mills with sawlogs. Sometimes they located promising tracts first and then found individuals who, for a small payment, would file on portions under the Homestead or Timber and Stone acts. Lumbermen would buy these blocked-up tracts, usually paying the landlooker a commission but sometimes taking him into partnership. Regardless of how they disposed of them, landlookers had to scramble to find and claim promising stands before others could do so.[11]

In 1889 when Stephen Puter came to Oregon, "the land business [was] booming, every hotel in the timbered sections of the state being crowded with timber land speculators, cruisers and locators … [and] the woods were fairly alive with timber men." In 1900 George S. Long reported to Frederick Weyerhaeuser that Portland was "full of scalawag timber brokers." Oswald West was even more damning. Oregonians, he later recalled, were so eager for economic development they turned a blind eye to what was transpiring, opening the way for "camp followers" who "like buzzards swoop[ed] down" and with the connivance of officials "through rascality and fraud gained title to thousands of acres of valuable publicly-owned timber," lands which they were later able to sell to private operators for big profits.[12]

After Congress passed the Forest Lieu Act in June 1897, entrymen did not need to file on choice timberland; claims could be on land that was isolated, lightly timbered, or of low value for other reasons and entrymen could still turn them to profit. Claims on unsurveyed land subsequently included within forest reserves could be exchanged for scrip that could be redeemed for unsurveyed federal land elsewhere. Lieu land scrip quickly became a favorite with landlookers. One could claim a tract he thought would soon be part of a reserve, profess to be a settler thereon, and after the reserve became reality exchange his claim for scrip, thus converting his claim into a readily marketable asset. A landlooker could buy scrip for a small payment and redeem it to obtain title to unreserved timber he was blocking up for clients. Since there were extensive stands outside the Pacific Northwest's forest reserves, the use of lieu land scrip was widespread. A. W. Morgan, a homesteader-turned-timber-locator, summed it up: when land claimed by homesteaders was included in reserves and scrip issued in exchange, the scrip "was soon gobbled up and sold to big corporations, usually for a small price."[13]

Oregon's school endowment lands—sections 16 and 36 of each township of the public domain, over 3.4 million acres altogether—suffered a similar fate. An Oregon law of 1887 required that the state sell unsurveyed school lands on demand for $1.25 per acre, with only one-third of the amount due as down payment. Claimants could purchase three hundred and twenty acres, rather than one hundred and sixty as under the Timber and Stone Act, and were not required to settle on the land. Since lieu privileges attached to Oregon's school land, a person could buy school land located in a reserve and then exchange it for scrip with which to obtain forested land from the remaining public domain—land that would have cost $2.50 an acre if entered directly. Fraud in connection with school lands had been common enough even before 1887; after that date, it became epidemic. As State Land Agent Timothy Davenport observed in 1896, "our laws taken as a whole might be nominated very fitly 'land monopoly made easy.' "[14]

Even these lenient requirements were subverted. As F. G. Young noted, thieves would "palm off on Oregon land office officials [claims bearing names] that cost them a dollar apiece" as well as forged signatures and counterfeited school land scrip. Presaging later efforts of federal prosecutor Francis Heney, Governor George Chamberlain appointed Oswald West as State Land Agent "with instructions to bust the . . . school land ring." In the process, the colorful West gained fame he would ride into the governorship—although his impact came more from greater honesty in filings than convictions and cancellations.[15]

The practices of entrymen and landlookers were clearly at odds with the intent of federal land laws. Congress had passed them to encourage smallholding farmers, not the lumber industry. The system that emerged frequently involved filing false affidavits stating claimants were bona fide settlers who had made "improvements" on the land. Landlookers furthered this charade by transporting train cars of "settlers" from Portland, Seattle, and various other ports to land offices where they filed dummy entries in return for a small payment. According to one oft-repeated story, much of the Puget Mill Company's timber was close to tidewater because manager Cyrus Walker used visiting sailors to file claims, and he feared they would get lost in the woods if sent any distance inland. Stephen Puter was overly sweeping, but his charge held a good bit of truth: "[T]he very cream of timber claims in Oregon and Washington were secured by Eastern lumbermen and capitalists . . . and nearly all these claims, to my certain knowledge, were fraudulently obtained." A Portland attorney tried to justify such practices to Francis Heney, sent by federal authorities to ferret out the guilty; he pointed out that land laws were poorly suited to the economic realities of lumbering, adding, "it is bad laws that make men—hum, let us say, that make such irregularities necessary." Heney exploded: such men corrupted all they touch! Indeed, Heney came to believe Oregon was "under the domination of a corrupt political ring, which hesitates at nothing to achieve its ends."[16]

Heney opposed those who would play fast and loose with the law, but others believed creating vast reserves to protect the forests was unwise, that the national interest would be better served by passing title to private citizens whose activities thereon would be regulated, if need be, by state and local governments. Such people worried little about machinations to obtain private claims to forestlands, seeing them as means of establishing family farms supported jointly by agriculture and the tapping of forest resources.

No one articulated this persisting smallholder dream better than Oregon's John Minto. He decried reserves as "unwarranted by the constitution of the nation and the compacts congress exacted from the people of Oregon as conditions of their admission as a state" and permanent government ownership and management of forests as "the entering wedge of a serious attackt on the freedom of American citizenship as we have enjoyed it," an approach that would introduce Bismarck's "socialism of the ruling class" into the United States. Minto preferred settlement of Northwestern forests by smallholding forest-farmers who would make their living by combining agricultural pursuits with tapping timber resources to supply small, local sawmills much as had been done on earlier forests in New York, Pennsylvania, and Ohio. Minto's vision came close to realization in parts of the Coast Range, but his Jeffersonian model was ill-suited for conditions in the Cascades, where markets for timber were distant, the terrain rugged, the soil poor, the growing season short, and transportation difficult and costly. The latter's forests could be tapped profitably only by large, modern mills that enjoyed economies of scale, could afford expensive logging equipment, and had the capacity to serve distant markets. Minto's claim that Oregon's forest reserves could support one hundred thousand families of forest-farmers was a chimera, as federal policy makers were by this time well aware.[17]

The drive to create reserves, the target of Minto's concern, had been long gathering. As lumbering moved west and south, it denuded first one area and then another, for forests were mined for timber, rather than managed for continuing production. The expectation that, once logged, they would be succeeded by farms was widely viewed as excusing cut-and-run practices. But the speed with which Lake States forests fell before the axe had startled even experienced lumbermen, Southern forests were rapidly following suit, and those of the Far West, it seemed, would not be far behind. With the disappearance of old-growth stands looming, fear of a timber famine grew. In an essentially wood-built country like the United States, this was no small matter, and pressure to create reserves as a hedge against such an eventuality gained force. That the bulk of the nation's unclaimed, uncut timberland was in the Far West and from the 1880s was crossed by a number of railroads with transcontinental connections—increasing the ease with which it could be tapped and marketed—made the region the stage on which much of what followed was played out.[18]

Economist James Tattersall has argued disposal of public forestland, however questionable the means, accelerated economic development in the Northwest. Disposal was "a gigantic deficit financing operation which still kept the federal budget balanced." While a more rational approach for achieving optimal use of government land might have been devised, public support for any such alternative was weak and "would have required a more competent and incorruptible civil service than in fact existed."[19] Still, fraudulent practices generated a firestorm of controversy that would shape the area's forests and their utilization from that time forward. The abuses of Gilded Age business and the painful adjustments accompanying industrialization encouraged attitudes and ideas that added force to the movement for forest reserves. When it came to fruition, the federal government would be the permanent owner—and manager—of vast tracts of timberland.

Abuses also led to the giants of the lumber industry being seen in many circles as robber barons intent upon self-aggrandizement regardless of public cost. Exposés by West, Heney, Puter, and others encouraged this view. A. W. Morgan judged most of the homesteaders on the Siletz, unlike elsewhere in Oregon, to be good, honest people (even though many eventually sold their claims), but at the time "some people thought it a crime to get any timber from the Government whether it was legal or not." Morgan, himself a successful homesteader, added, "I sometimes feel thankful that they did not get us homesteaders indicted for fraud or something of the kind." Heney called Morgan the one legitimate homesteader in his area, but Morgan "never felt very good about" the label "as I did not think I was any better than those who lost their land" when the government challenged their claims or they relinquished them out of fear of cancellation; when they had filed "most of them thought they were complying with the law."[20]

Not all Westerners reacted in the same way. John Minto saw forest reserves as undermining American values rooted in the Jeffersonian smallholding tradition; Weldon Heyburn and Henry Teller denounced them as a threat to state's rights.[21] In spite of Minto's attacks and in contrast to spokesmen from the Rockies, sentiment in favor of forest reserves was fairly widespread in Pacific Coast states, especially Oregon. There, although it had disappeared as a force on the national scene, the Grange persisted as a champion of reform, while the abuses of local banking, insurance, and transportation interests, which had long manipulated the state government, added to discontent with the status quo. More difficult to assess—but surely important—was the long-standing commitment of Oregonians to conservative, communitarian values seemingly disdained and threatened by the business community. Together these forces gave strength to protest and, in time, made the state a bulwark of progressivism. So dedicated to reform did Oregon become that an editor in Idaho, with its very different political climate, referred to it acidly as the "Freak State." The fact that sawmill operators and their minions were largely outsiders with limited local influence left the industry poorly situated to counter these developments.[22]

Reform sentiment was growing in Far Western politics, but experience suggested its influence might be ephemeral and control of state government revert to interests seeking to bend it to their own purposes. Under the circumstances, the federal government, headed by a president who talked of ending business excesses, seemed a more viable instrument than the states for ensuring forests for the future.

Gradually sentiment for reserves grew—not all of it stemming from concerns for the public interest. Some timber owners recognized reserves would reduce forestland on the market, thereby increasing the value of their stands. Similarly, various speculators, knowing rich profits could be made manipulating applicable land laws, joined the effort to have Oregon's Cascade Range set aside as a huge forest reserve. In the end, the activities of these disparate groups were crowned with success. Created by President Grover Cleveland in 1893 and subsequently enlarged by William McKinley and Theodore Roosevelt, by 1907 the Cascade Reserve encompassed some one-fourth of the total area of Oregon. Vast tracts were set aside in Washington's Cascades too—unlike in Oregon divided into three reserves—and in its Olympic Mountains as well.[23]

At 4.8 million acres, the Cascade Forest Reserve was the nation's largest; of that total, investigators for the United States Geological Survey reported 4.1 million acres were forested, but only 5,587 had been logged.[24] In 1899 and 1901, when they conducted their surveys, the USGS's agents found little evidence of false entry except in the most northerly portion. There, H. D. Langille reported, many claims were on land

> *of little or no value for agricultural purposes, and since the locations were made just prior to the inclusion of this area in the reserve, it is*

apparent the purpose of the locators was to secure the timber or to dispose of their rights to the Government for scrip which could be placed on more valuable lands elsewhere. A rough board shack 10 by 12 feet in size, with a shed roof, is usually the extent of their improvements, though some have built a few rods of fence and dug up a small patch of ground.

In the central portion of the range—an area roughly seventy-two miles by forty-five miles, encompassing nearly two million acres—Fred G. Plummer found only 245 acres in cultivation, ninety-one houses or cabins (many of them miners' or trappers' shacks used briefly each year), and nineteen barns. The only significant claims were in the Metolius River, McKenzie River, and Black Butte areas, where actual settlers have continued to live to the present day. Further south, Arthur Dodwell seemingly found even less evidence of settlement, although he did not report precise numbers.[25]

In short, during the first years of the twentieth century Oregon's Cascades were primarily a *reserve* rather than a center of activity by landlookers, speculators, and lumbermen. In 1882 a regional journal predicted Cascades timber would "in a few years prove a mine of wealth" for those seeking it, but as the nineteenth century approached its end Oregon's Coast Range provided such men with their favorite hunting grounds, for initially little of it was included in reserves; indeed, according to A. W. Morgan, by 1905 all the heavily timbered land in the northern part of the range had been filed upon and late-comers had to buy timber from title holders or claimants, including those willing to relinquish claims for a small payment rather than lose them without recompense after strict enforcement of residency requirements came into play in the wake of the timber fraud scandals— when, as Morgan put it, "the honeymoon was over." The redwood forests of California's north coast were also scoured for available stands. There was reason for this scramble for timber: speculation could pay handsomely. One tract purchased for $800 in 1891 sold for $18,500 in 1909; another, purchased for $10,000 in 1899, sold a decade later for $110,000.[26]

Yet from the beginning there were those who cast covetous eyes on timber in the Cascades, B. J. Pengra and Frank Hoberg among them. Pengra unsuccessfully petitioned to have nine townships excluded from the reserve as agricultural land—something they clearly were not. His objective seems to have been to open the way for enlarging the holdings of the Booth-Kelly Timber Company of Eugene, which controlled a vast acreage nearby that a subsidiary had obtained from the Oregon Central Military Wagon Road and Southern Pacific land grants as well as substantial additional acreage obtained under the Timber and Stone and Homestead acts.[27]

Efforts at eliminating a huge portion of the Olympic Forest Reserve in Washington were more successful, in part because much of the area in question was lowland and therefore could be more persuasively argued to have agricultural potential. Grover Cleveland created the reserve in 1897 by withdrawing 1.5 million acres of the Olympic Peninsula. Protests came almost immediately, not so much from lumbermen, many of whom recognized the reserve would increase the value of their holdings, as from local boosters. Protests were especially loud in Clallam County, located on the northern end of the peninsula; the county's development, protesters argued, would be held up by the huge withdrawal; they insisted much of the reserve ought to be restored to public domain, making it subject to homestead entry. Henry Gannett of the Geological Survey denounced such proposals, correctly noting the area's soil was better suited for growing trees than crops. Arthur Dodwell and Theodore Rixon of the same agency estimated it would cost as much as $200 an acre to clear the land for agriculture, too much to make it attractive to would-be farmers. But the final decision was not theirs. In 1900, President McKinley approved removal of some 265,000 acres from the reserve and a year later another 457,000 acres. The land carved from the reserve was among the most heavily timbered in the United States, and although there was as yet little lumbering there, much of it was well suited for logging railroads. In the end, most of this "agricultural" land went to logging or lumber companies.[28]

Thomas B. Walker and Charles A. Smith of Minnesota were, according to Kimbark MacColl, "the earliest and biggest crooks of them all." The description is not entirely accurate, for fraud had a long history in timber country, but the two certainly stood out. Using a variety of ploys, Walker increased his holdings, concentrated in northern California's pine country, until he was the second-largest private timber owner in the state (behind only the Southern Pacific) and holder of a considerable acreage in Oregon too. For his part, Smith founded the Coos Bay Lumber Company and acquired large claims in Oregon's Coos, Douglas, and Linn counties—"thousands of acres of the finest timberland in the Northwest"—as well as sizable holdings in California. Stephen Puter considered Smith's practices blatantly illegal, but he was never indicted for "the devil takes care of his own, and he was lucky enough to be saved by the statute of limitations."[29]

Frank Hoberg's activities were more modest than those of Walker, Smith, Pengra, or the opponents of the Olympic reserve, but probably more typical. In 1899, he reported to a group of Pennsylvania lumbermen that he had located a tract of thirty thousand acres on the Santiam, a major river draining westward from Oregon's Cascades. The timber fit his employers' investment needs, but Hoberg added he was also looking in the Coast Range. He had spent two years in the latter area, "putting together a deal" blocking up claims along the Necanicum River and arranging for construction of a railroad to tap it. The activities of Morgan were similar. He started out blocking up twenty-two relinquishments by fellow homesteaders in the Siletz River valley and finding a buyer. Morgan would spend the next five decades as a landlooker, surveyor, and timber cruiser.[30]

The risks of such activity were not all financial. Landlookers went into the woods armed not only against animals, but also poachers and rivals. In scouting timberlands in the Coast Range, Hoberg had to brave primitive trails, rugged terrain, and interminable rains. Not long after his report to the Pennsylvanians, he disappeared while investigating the area. When his body was finally located, he was found to have succumbed not to wild animals or foul play but to botulism from eating improperly canned food. Yet such a life appealed to some. Reminiscing, Morgan told fellow surveyor Andrew Porter, there were

> not many stands west of the Cascades in Oregon that we do not know. . . . [Y]ou pioneered in most of it as you surveyed many rugged, isolated townships and did a wonderfully good job of it under circumstances that would look impossible to the present day surveyors. I have run onto your cruiser's mark on witness trees in all the coast counties and away up in the high elevations of the Cascades. . . . No matter how tired I was, it always warmed my heart to see your mark on the trees. When we finished our day's work in the timber, we could go straight home or to camp without looking at our compass, and if it was too late to get to camp, we could lie down under a tree and sleep soundly all night long, knowing that there was some kind bear, cougar, or wildcat watching over us, guarding our slumbers so that no harm would come to us![31]

To such men, timber surveying was more than a profession, it was a grand adventure.

The activities of most landlookers are hazy at best—even their names forgotten—but those of Morgan, Stephen Puter, Willard N. Jones, and partners William Hawks and George S. Canfield can be reconstructed in some detail. It is not clear how typical any of them were, but their activities throw considerable light on an important aspect of the lumberman's frontier.

Morgan started as a logger, became a homesteader, and then moved into the sale of timberland. His many contacts among settlers in the Siletz River valley gave him an advantage in putting together blocks of timber from relinquishments, and his uncanny accuracy as a cruiser and surveyor won him many clients. Morgan loved the Siletz country. He arrived from Willapa Bay in Washington and later recalled "how thrilled I was when Fred [Stanton] and I entered that belt of lovely timber that somehow had been spared by the fires that had burned over the Yaquina and Alsea area south of it and the Tillamook area north. . . . I was through logging and had found a homestead that I wanted." When Morgan's wife induced him to move to town, "I was sorry to leave the place as it was a real home to me then, and I have never seen a place that seems so much like home to me as does that bunch of timber around Euchre Mountain." His love of the area never faltered. After moving to Portland, he went back to visit nearly every summer, and when he compiled his reminiscences in 1951 delighted in the fact that there were "still sections of it standing as green and grand as ever, and when I go up into it I feel like falling on my knees. It kinda seems like . . . [the trees] bend over toward me and wave their boughs to welcome me back among them." Page after page of Morgan's account reveals affection for the forest; timber selling had been good to him, he wrote, but never as fulfilling as simply working in the woods.[32]

Puter began his career in Humboldt County, California, where he and cohorts used dummy entrymen and false affidavits to put together a sixty-four-thousand-acre block of timber for the California Redwood Company. Then in 1888, Puter "decided to seek fresher pastures in Oregon," where accelerating development made opportunity seem unlimited. In Oregon, he put together body after body of timber using the same techniques he had utilized in California, techniques which were eventually to land him in prison.[33]

Not everyone was willing to buy the tracts Puter pieced together. Andrew B. Hammond was prepared to buy some of Puter's claims in Oregon, but backed off when clear title could not be assured. Hammond continued to expand his holdings, but largely by acquiring established firms and the timberlands they owned—most notably the Vance Lumber Company, one of the pioneers of the redwood coast—rather than parcels blocked up by landlookers.[34]

Until Puter's day, Far Western timberland normally sold by the acre, customarily in quarter-section blocks, at prices ranging from $4 to $10 an acre. Thus, stumpage could be acquired for less than 25 cents per thousand, but as the industry grew, competition increased and prices rose. In 1905 George Long asked $2 per thousand for a tract of Weyerhaeuser timber in southwestern Washington. Under the circumstances, buyers began seeking more accurate measures of the land they were considering and had cruisers estimate actual stumpage on individual tracts rather than simply assessing overall quality. With timber costing from 50 cents to $2.50 per thousand feet, cruisers took on new importance—and men like Puter and Morgan found richer opportunities than ever.[35]

For a time, Willard Jones was a partner of Puter, but the two came to a parting of the ways. Their practices were similar. Working for timber speculators more often than actual lumbermen, Jones blocked up promising tracts using scrip, school land purchases, and dummy entrymen. He was a major player in the Coast Range, Cascades, and, further east, in Oregon's Blue Mountains, and "sold a lot of timberland to some eastern friends, and made a lot of money in commissions." Like Puter, his practices resulted in his being caught in Heney's investigative web, although Morgan thought his activities relatively innocent. Of Jones and fellow indictee Ira Wade, Morgan wrote, "I never knew two better men. I would have trusted either of them with my life or purse." Still, Jones was found guilty of fraud and spent some months in jail—only to resurface later as a landlooker and sawmill manager in the Blue Mountains.[36]

Hawks and Canfield were less notorious than Puter and Jones and left nothing as romantic as Morgan's recollections, but the partners' business records show them using essentially the same practices. They charged $100 to $150 for locating Timber and Stone or Homestead Act claims and $1.25 an acre for school land "base," which when coupled with the $1.25 one had to pay the state for school land brought the cost to $2.50 an acre—the same as they had to pay for federal land.[37]

Still, while the Far Western locale was new, the practices of landlookers and their clients were not. As has been shown, false entry and other devious means of acquiring public timber had been practiced arts in the Lake States and Gulf South. Indeed, as John Ise observed, land fraud was a frontier way of life.[38]

Revelations during the Oregon timber fraud trials—coming as they did in a period of presidential and public concern over business malfeasance, frequently with the complicity of government employees—contributed to congressional reconsideration of forest policy. In 1905 Congress transferred responsibility for forest reserves from the Department of the Interior to Agriculture; gave the Forest Service (as the old Bureau of Forestry was renamed) new authority to manage them using proceeds from timber sales to fund its activities; and rescinded the oft-misused lieu land provisions of 1897. Two years later, to underscore the importance of these changes, Congress renamed the forest reserves national forests. Neither the timber thefts in the Pacific Northwest against which John McGilvra had battled earlier, nor the scandals in the Lake States and Gulf South had spurred such a response. The times had not yet been ripe.[39]

Not everything taking place in the Far West echoed what had gone before. Railroad and military road land grants opened the way for acquisitions and development as never before. To be sure, land grants had played a role earlier, especially in Minnesota, but the scale of what was now taking place was unprecedented. Most important was the grant to the Northern Pacific Railway. It was unusually generous: in addition to a two-hundred-foot-wide right-of-way, the grant included every other section for twenty miles on each side of the track for every mile built in territories (ten miles in states). Of the 7.7 million acres the line received in Washington Territory, some two million was commercial timberland. In Oregon the richest land grant went to the California and Oregon Railroad, which received some 3.7 million acres. There were also sizable grants to the Oregon Central Military Wagon Road, the Willamette Valley and Cascade Mountain Wagon Road, and the Coos Bay Wagon Road companies. Not only were these grants large, but as Jerry O'Callaghan has noted, the "large blocs embrace[d] the best, most accessible timber." All would become centers of controversy.[40]

On the whole, Northern Pacific's actions were not illegal, but its practices hardly met governmental or public expectations. Most congressmen seem to have anticipated the railroad would sell its grant piecemeal to smallholding farmers. Instead, recognizing much of it could never be farmed profitably, Northern Pacific used lieu land provisions to exchange sparsely timbered mountain acreage for rich lowland stands and to block up its forest holdings in hope of selling to lumbermen from the Lake States or South who were ready to move to the Far West. With the creation of Rainier National Park, which incorporated many sections of the Northern Pacific grant, further opportunities for profitable lieu land exchanges developed, and as a result the railroad acquired nearly one hundred and ninety thousand acres of prime timberland in western Oregon.[41] Historian Earl Pomeroy put it succinctly: this "smacked of conspiracy." Puter was less restrained. He maintained there was, indeed, a plot and devoted an entire chapter to detailing it. In the end, he charged, Mount Rainier became a national park only because "the Northern Pacific Railroad Company . . . [owned] a lot of land in the neighborhood." Robert Ficken finds Puter's argument less than convincing, but in the existing climate of anti-robber baron sentiment, it had its effect, strengthening public support for forest reserves.[42]

Sounding much like Puter, neo-progressive historian Kimbark MacColl has charged the Northern Pacific "set the pattern of speculative greed that was to be copied by lesser folk," but there was an ample supply of models for Gilded Age speculators—James J. Hill hardly invented acquisitiveness, opportunism, and self-serving—and in any case, it is a questionable value judgment to equate speculation with greed. Still, Hill's railroad *did* profit handsomely from finding buyers for many of its better stands—for example, selling two hundred thousand acres to various speculators for $8 an acre and nine hundred thousand acres to Frederick Weyerhaeuser for $6 per acre (the latter a sale the railroad's Land Department soon regretted, believing it could have received more). As Weyerhaeuser's interests in the Northwest grew, his syndicate acquired an additional one hundred and sixty thousand acres of Northern Pacific timberland in Oregon.[43]

The Southern Pacific was similar, if less successful in its maneuverings. The railroad's land grant in Oregon encompassed some of the richest stands anywhere. Originally granted to the California and Oregon, it was taken over by Ben Holladay's Oregon and California Railroad from which the Southern Pacific obtained it in turn, thus coming to own seventy million acres in Oregon, "most of it legally acquired," MacColl concedes, but "not used for the purposes for which it was granted" for little found its way into the hands of farmers. MacColl's criticism is warranted; indeed, stronger words could have been used, for in 1869 Congress had amended the original grant to require that the land be sold to "actual settlers" in quarter-section (one hundred-and sixty-acre) lots for no more than $2.50 an acre.[44]

Ignoring this requirement, first the O & C and then the Southern Pacific sold large tracts to lumber interests and speculators for more than $2.50 an acre; indeed, in 1894 some sales by the SP went for $40 an acre, and one purchaser bought forty-five thousand acres at $7 an acre. The major purchasers included A. B. Hammond, who bought forty-two thousand acres, and Booth-Kelly, which bought even more. The railroad not only brazenly ignored terms dictated by Congress, but also failed to inform buyers of them. Somehow this came to federal attention—perhaps, as the SP charged, authorities were alerted by Booth-Kelly in hopes of bringing about forfeiture of the land grant, leaving it in position to pick up choice timberland for $2.50 an acre.[45] In any case, in 1907 the Justice Department brought suit, seeking forfeiture or forced sale of the remainder of the grant. The case ground on until 1915, when the Supreme Court ruled that the entire grant, sold and unsold, was forfeit. Congress responded with the Ferris-Chamberlain Act revesting title in the United States and creating a checkerboard of some 2.3 million acres of federal forest (some forty to fifty billion board feet of timber) to be managed by the Department of the Interior's Bureau of Land Management.[46]

While the suit dragged on, Congress addressed the question of how to deal with those who had purchased from the railroad.[47] It is impossible to determine just how many purchasers were unaware of the illegality of the SP's sales. Idaho's Senator Weldon Heyburn claimed that when he was a young attorney in Oregon the requirements had been common knowledge, but by the time of the government's suit he "could not find anyone who admitted knowing about those provisions at the time." Any number came forward professing to having been duped and claiming that any forfeiture that voided purchases innocently entered into would be inequitable. An Innocent Purchasers Bill resulted, allowing those who had bought from the railroad to forfeit their titles in return for the right to repurchase from the government for $2.50 an acre, a loud echo of earlier legislation in Minnesota. During deliberations on the bill, an official of Booth-Kelly threatened: "If we do not get this . . . the first thing I will do when I get home will be to discharge our employees and close down our mills." Whether alarmed by the threat, convinced by the calls for equity, eager to put the matter behind it, solicitous of the industry's interests, or all four, in 1912 Congress passed the bill. Under its terms, Booth-Kelly, one of the biggest purchasers of SP timberland, was able to regain over seventy thousand acres it had originally bought for $40 an acre, and others did the same. Since timberland was by then worth far more than the original purchase prices, companies were glad to make additional token payments of $2.50 an acre to retain it.[48]

The upshot of all this was that a few owners came to control a good portion of the private forestland in the Northwest. In an extensive survey of the industry begun in 1909 and published in 1913-1914, the federal Bureau of Corporations found no proof of a lumber trust, but plentiful evidence of concentration—although no support for the charge that Thomas B. Walker, Charles A. Smith, and Frederick Weyerhaeuser collectively owned over half of the nation's timber. In the Pacific Northwest thirty-eight owners held one-half of privately owned timber, the Northern Pacific, Southern Pacific, and Weyerhaeuser together nearly a quarter. In Oregon, with more private forest acreage than any state, sixty-eight owners—mostly nonresidents—held 70 percent. Many holdings were speculative, acquired in expectation of a rise in stumpage value as timber grew scarce, thus allowing owners sizable unearned increments on investments without creating jobs or added production. Efforts to make smallholders the dominant possessors of forests had clearly failed.[49]

Yet the bureau's findings were misleading. Economist Wilson Compton found that while numerous tracts had been acquired for speculative purposes, carrying costs proved so high that many were forced to unload their holdings in order to pay creditors, while others had to turn to manufacturing, even in the face of existing excess production; the resulting market gluts drove down the prices of standing timber, logs, and lumber. Weyerhaeuser was among those caught in this economic vise. Although he and his associates had purchased the old Bell-Nelson mill in Everett in 1902, enlarged and modernized it, and subsequently built a sawmill at Snoqualmie Falls, they were not yet primarily interested in manufacturing in the Pacific Northwest; the syndicate followed a policy of holding most of its timber for a rise in value. But George S. Long, Weyerhaeuser's manager in the Northwest, came to recognize that conditions dictated, "We have to commence out here sooner or later to manufacture." The great day of speculative increases was over, Long believed; only by manufacturing could the company make a reasonable profit on its holdings.[50] The Forest Service agreed. In a study published in 1920, it found smallholders owned more of the Northwest's timber than the Bureau of Corporations had suggested, increasing concentration of ownership had come to a halt, and more and more owners were moving from speculation to the use of timber. John Ise summed it up: the bureau's report had been "written with the too-evident purpose of proving the existence of something approaching a monopoly condition in the timber and lumber industry," something that simply did not exist.[51]

In fact, large though its major holdings were, the industry continued to be among the country's most fragmented. With a widely dispersed resource base, with bulky raw materials that needed to be manufactured near their source (Simon Benson's San Diego sawmill to the contrary notwithstanding), with entry into the industry still fairly easy, and with economies of scale sharply decreased as sawmills grew beyond a certain point, no firm produced over 5 percent of the national total. For all the publicity about the size of Weyerhaeuser and other giants, the industry had no equivalent of Standard Oil or U. S. Steel.[52]

Land grants had made possible immense purchases by Frederick Weyerhaeuser and others with sufficient financial means, but late arrivals and those with fewer assets had to search elsewhere. However they acquired their timber, by the time of Simon Benson's gift to the City of Portland, lumbermen were erecting new sawmills throughout the Douglas fir country. In 1913 production reached a record level, 7.46 billion feet. Figures for the following year show lumber providing 55 percent of the region's payrolls and

38 percent of the value added by manufacture; estimates placed forestland capitalization at over a billion dollars. Nor did the growth end there: expansion continued apace throughout the 1920s, especially in Oregon, which had 493 billion feet of timber remaining, one-fifth of the nation's total and almost 50 percent more than Washington. In light of all this, in 1920 one authority predicted Oregon would "be the scene of the greatest lumber development in the history of the United States." Two years later, another claimed more lumber was being cut annually in Portland than in any city in the world.[53]

A number of factors combined to encourage the increased milling. Taxes and other carrying costs ate into any profit that holding timberland for long periods might generate and forced some who had not foreseen them all to liquidate early.[54] Also, the great fires of 1902 made it clear one could not hold speculative timber purchases without risk. In early September forest fires—one hundred and ten in all—burned along the Cascades from Lyman, in northern Washington, to Eugene, at the southern end of the Willamette Valley, and from the mountains to Grays Harbor and Willapa Bay on the coast. High winds drove blazes through tinder-dry forests. Soon seven hundred thousand acres were afire. On September 12, George Long reported the air so thick with smoke that Tacoma was "in a state of semi-darkness," and logger Paul Repetto later remembered it was so dark his camp had to shut down. Ashes fell in Portland, accumulating to a depth of over a half inch, while in Eugene smoke was so thick residents could not see the looming hulk of Skinner's Butte from Eighth Street, only four blocks away. A vast area in southwestern Washington burned, including some twenty thousand acres of Weyerhaeuser land. The Yacolt fire, the largest of the conflagrations, destroyed a score of settlements and $13 million of property. Thirty-five people were killed.

The great conflagrations in the Lake States—Hinckley, in particular—had awakened lumbermen to the threat of fire, but those had come where lumbering was well established and slash and other logging debris contributed to the danger. The Yacolt burn demonstrated fire was a danger in largely untapped stands too. And in case anyone had missed it, the message was driven home in 1910 when another massive fire broke out, this one in northern Idaho and neighboring areas of Washington and Montana, while in Oregon the Cobbs & Mitchell Company had a disastrous fire in holdings near the head of the Siletz and another blaze not only destroyed a considerable body of Booth-Kelly timber but also most of its company town of Wendling. The need for forest fire protection was evident, but timber owners now realized that forests could never be made wholly safe; even when the price of timber was rising, speculative purchases were fraught with danger. As pioneer forester E. T. Allen observed, under existing circumstances the lumberman "faces the danger that his investment will burn up and the practical certainty that taxes will eat up all profit before the harvest." Everett Griggs was more succinct: "Taxes and fires wait for no man."[55]

In 1922 Inman-Poulsen, the largest sawmill not just in Portland but the entire state, cut and shipped 154 million feet of lumber. Founded in 1889, by 1906 the company claimed to produce five hundred thousand feet a day; by 1924 its yearly output was two hundred million feet. At the other end of the Willamette Valley, Booth-Kelly, which had a sawmill and company town at the end of an SP spur line up the Mohawk Valley and another in Springfield, sawed 67.5 million feet in 1922 and in 1923 turned out eighty-two million.[56] Mills at Cottage Grove and further south were also growing; by 1925 the Owen-Oregon Lumber Company in Medford was cutting roughly sixty million board feet a year. For the moment, both cargo and rail mills were prospering; those that could engage in both trades were especially fortunate. The totals added up. Forester George Peavy estimated 65 percent of Oregon's industrial payroll came from sawmilling and the state's lumber industry created some $100 million in wealth annually.[57]

Booth-Kelly's rising production was a product of more than a general prosperity that fueled increased demand and of favorable freight rates to California. After years of inter-firm maneuvering, the Southern Pacific was spending $18 million constructing a rail line from Eugene to Klamath Falls. Commonly known as the Natron cutoff, the line connected with that from Klamath Falls through Weed to California's Central Valley. Roughly following the route of the old Oregon Central Military Wagon Road, the cutoff was a godsend for Booth-Kelly; it not only provided an easier route to Northern California's markets than the tortuous older route over the Siskiyous, but also ran near the extensive timberlands the company had acquired from the wagon road's land grant (after Weyerhaeuser had opted against doing so).[58]

Nor were Booth-Kelly's private holdings the only stands made accessible by the Natron cutoff. Vast areas in the Cascade (later Willamette) National Forest were too, and the Forest Service soon put up for bid a large block on the North Fork of the Willamette River, the largest sale of Douglas fir the agency had ever offered, foreshadowing the day its holdings in the Cascades would be a bulwark of Douglas fir production.[59]

Acting through his Western Lumber Company, George H. Kelly, a partner in the Booth-Kelly complex, was the successful bidder. Kelly promptly began construction of a state-of-the-art sawmill near the junction of the Middle and North forks of the Willamette and since Oakridge, the nearest community, was too small to supply the necessary housing and support facilities, added a company town, dubbed Westfir. The mill would operate for over half a century, drawing on both Booth-Kelly and national forest timber.[60]

Railroads were opening other stands in Oregon too. By 1920 there were nine hundred and thirty miles of logging railroads in the state and one hundred and fifteen sawmills in the central Willamette Valley and adjacent Cascade foothills (more than any other lumber district in the state). A good portion was dependent on feeder railroads connected to the Southern Pacific's north-south mainline. Among the leaders in 1924 was the A. B. Hammond plant at Mill City, located on an SP spur up the heavily forested drainage of the North Santiam.[61]

Not all the activity was in the Cascades. Cobbs & Mitchell Company of Portland constructed a thirty-nine-mile common carrier, the Valley & Siletz Railroad, from the Southern Pacific mainline in the Willamette Valley across the crest of the Coast Range to the headwaters of the Siletz. There the firm impounded a forty-acre log pond, erected an up-to-date sawmill (dedicated on 20 September 1920), and constructed the company town of Valsetz to provide housing and support facilities. By 1923 the community boasted a population of twelve hundred, and the mill was producing nearly sixty million feet of lumber annually. *The Timberman* proclaimed, "[N]o other section of Oregon . . . [has] a more wonderful stand of timber," this in spite of the firm's losses to fire in 1910. Like the plant at Westfir, the Valsetz mill was to continue cutting for the next half century. Paul Repetto would remember the town as "the liveliest, best know[n], most picturesque, and isolated . . . of them all."[62]

Further north in the Coast Range the Spaulding-Miami Lumber Company commenced logging in the Yamhill River drainage in the early twenties, at first shipping its logs some sixty miles by company and Southern Pacific rails to Chas. K. Spaulding's sawmills in Salem and Newberg, but soon cutting them at a big, new mill that Spaulding-Miami erected at Grand Ronde, where the Yamhill emerged from the eastern slopes of the Coast Range. There the firm also built a company town that would long remain. New sawmills were springing up elsewhere in the Coast Range—at Vernonia on the upper Nehalem River, for instance—and railroads were penetrating more and more corners of the range, which was rapidly becoming more than just the domain of timber speculators and landlookers.[63]

Impressive as these developments in Oregon's Cascades and Coast Range were, they paled in comparison to what was transpiring in Washington. There, on the north bank of the Columbia, R. A. Long was erecting a huge sawmill and accompanying planned city to be known as Longview. The undertaking dwarfed anything Long had done before, either in the South or in the pine country of the interior Far West, where he had been operating the Weed Lumber Company for some years and had acquired over one hundred and fifty thousand acres of timber in addition to the company's original holdings.

Long had settled on southwestern Washington as the scene of new operations only after careful consideration. W. F. Ryder, his timber scout on the West Coast, had traveled widely in the West and became convinced the best timber was in the Douglas fir country of Oregon and Washington. Well he might. In 1920 there were an estimated 581 billion board feet of commercial Douglas fir in the Pacific Coast states, more than the combined total of Ponderosa pine, Idaho white pine, redwood, and Western larch. James D. Lacey, operating in the Far West as he had in the South, tried to sell Long holdings on the Olympic Peninsula, but the manager of Long's Weed operation persuaded his investigators to travel to Eugene to consult with R. A. Booth, who "had a reputation for knowing as much about the fir region as anyone" and "in a business famous for its 'rough and ready' personalities . . . was conspicuous for modesty, sobriety, [and] rigid loyalty to those simple virtues which his [Methodist] circuit rider father had preached." As a nephew put it, Booth's "real fortune was the good name he [had] built."[64]

Booth suggested Long consider a large tract in Washington's Cowlitz and Lewis counties that he called "the best in the Northwest" and which its owners, the Weyerhaeuser Timber Company, were willing to sell. Long and a group of associates investigated the property in the summer of 1919 and were convinced Booth was right; the average tree scaled an amazing seven thousand board feet! Long purchased twenty-four thousand acres, paying $3.42 a thousand for fir and cedar and $1 a thousand for hemlock, a price that netted Weyerhaeuser a neat profit above what the syndicate had paid Northern Pacific (and well above the $2 a thousand A. W. Morgan had thought excessive some fifteen years earlier).

Booth served as chief negotiator for Long-Bell, and it may well have been this purchase his nephew had in mind when he recalled that Booth once refused to go into a lumber "deal" that he thought unfair even though it would have netted him a $9 million commission. When the would-be buyer replied, "Anything is fair that a man will sign his name to," which certainly sounds like Long, Booth insisted a deal must benefit both buyer and seller. In the end, the buyer acquiesced and allowed Booth to draw up an agreement based on terms he proposed. In spite of familial hagiography, one suspects Booth may have had ulterior motives. By directing Long to southwestern Washington, he may have hoped to divert Long's expansion from areas around Eugene and Klamath Falls, where Booth's interests were centered. Additional purchases followed Long's initial acquisition, bringing Long-Bell's holdings in southwestern Washington to seventy thousand acres—altogether 9.8 billion feet of timber acquired for some $17 million.[65]

Where to saw the logs had been as difficult to decide as which timber to buy, but after considering locations near Astoria and Portland, Long settled on a site at the confluence of the Cowlitz and Columbia, near the little town of Kelso, and commenced construction in 1923. The site, Long believed, would be ideal for both the cargo and rail trades. It was a decision he may later have regretted. His chief engineer estimated draining and diking the tract, bridging the Cowlitz, building a log pond, and otherwise preparing a millsite to serve the rail trade would require $1.8 million; in fact, the land alone cost far more, while draining and diking required four times the estimated amount. The huge mill—the largest in the world at the time (its capacity greater than all ten of Long's Southern mills combined)—was also expensive. And since, in that day before widespread automobile ownership, Kelso was thought too far away for millworkers to commute, a company town was judged necessary. Viewing it as a sort of monument to himself, Long insisted the town be first class, a planned city with a fine hotel, wide streets, civic buildings, and a public park (revealingly, little attention was paid to working-class housing). Before any of this was completed, Long-Bell had already spent $9 million on the site. A thirteen-mile railroad from Longview to the main logging camp at Ryderwood cost another $5.5 million. Feeling the financial pinch, the company put plans to build a second mill and port facilities to serve the cargo trade on hold, but for the sake of efficiency a second rail mill was opened in 1927 to handle smaller logs while the first plant sawed the giants. With costs continuing to escalate, Long-Bell had to sell stock and borrow from banks. Even before lumber demand and prices began to crumble in the late twenties, Long-Bell was drifting ever closer to bankruptcy.[66]

Although Weyerhaeuser's sale to Long-Bell launched the latter into the production of Douglas fir lumber, Weyerhaeuser Timber Company still owned vast stands in southwestern Washington. Some in the syndicate questioned the advisability of huge new undertakings, but having gained experience with Douglas fir through their sawmills at Everett and Snoqualmie Falls, and driven by a need to generate a larger cash flow to pay carrying costs, by the 1920s the company was ready to embark on large-scale manufacturing in its empire of fir. After considering alternative locations, the company settled on Longview, where a marvelous site was available thanks to R. A. Long's decision not to build the cargo mill originally planned and to the large area his firm had enclosed within dikes. Because of the unforeseen expenses in bringing his own plant on line, Long was eager to sell the unneeded land.[67]

F. E. Weyerhaeuser questioned the wisdom of building a mill "in Long-Bell's back yard," but others prevailed, for it was an ideal location, and in 1925 the syndicate took an option on the site. Long tried to prod Weyerhaeuser into prompt action, but with division in its ranks and the firm's daring patriarch deceased, company officials moved slowly. As Long observed, "the Weyerhaeuser crowd . . . are very deliberate in their movements." In vain he kept prodding them to exercise their option and begin building, but they kept him hanging—partly in hopes, one suspects, that Long-Bell would go bankrupt, making its assets available at bargain prices. Weyerhaeuser moved at last, but its operations in Longview would not go on line until June 1929.[68]

The size of the undertaking that finally materialized was unprecedented; Weyerhaeuser's complex at Longview dwarfed any sawmill in Oregon, on Grays Harbor or Puget Sound, and even Long-Bell's immense plant next door. It included three sawmills each designed to cut a different type of log, a shingle mill, a massive planing mill (reportedly the largest in the nation), numerous dry kilns of the latest design (a total of fifty was planned), and a central power plant to run it all. There was storage space along the Columbia for fifty million feet of logs and sheds for one hundred million feet of dried lumber. Using huge gantry cranes, the cargo dock could load four steamships at a time. Everything was mechanized using the latest equipment. No sooner was all this in place than work began on a pulp mill to use waste from Mill C, which sawed hemlock.[69]

Logs arrived at the site via railroad. Long-Bell refused to allow Weyerhaeuser to share its line, so the newcomers built their own, skirting the north edge of Longview on a boggy, difficult route because Long would not let them build through the town itself, fearing damage to its aesthetics. "My God, what a hell of a place to make us build a railroad," grumbled Al Raught, Weyerhaeuser's top man in Longview. But build it he did, and soon enough 194 miles of Weyerhaeuser logging railroads radiated out to the company's vast holdings in southwestern Washington. In 1930, its first full year of operation, Weyerhaeuser's complex turned out two hundred and thirteen million board feet of lumber and the following year cut even more before the effects of the Great Depression sent the industry into precipitous decline.[70]

⟨ ·⸝⸝⸜⸝⸜ ⟩

Logging railroads such as those that fed the new Long-Bell and Weyerhaeuser plants were necessities in the Douglas fir country. Stands along major streams had been exhausted, and splash dams, which made logging possible on smaller watercourses, only enlarged the scope of operations slightly. East of the Cascades more and more operators were turning to trucks to get out logs, but many Douglas fir logs were too large for vehicles of the period. Provided turns were not too sharp, rail cars could transport logs one hundred feet or more in length by placing independent sets of wheels under them ("disconnected trucks" loggers called them); logging trucks could do nothing of the sort.[71]

Simon Benson's operations near Clatskanie offer a case in point. There he cut huge, long sticks and transported them by railroad to the banks of the Columbia, where he used them to provide a rigid backbone in the log rafts that fed the sawmill he had erected in San Diego. When the supply of timber accessible from Benson's logging railroad gave out, he was unable to find alternative sources that would yield logs of such length, and if built with shorter logs, his ocean-going rafts would lack the structural rigidity to withstand the buffeting of the Pacific. Benson had to give up rafting to San Diego; without a source of log supply, the mill closed.[72]

Perfected in the pine country, trucks eventually came to be used on the Westside too. When they did, places like Oregon's Grants Pass and Sweet Home enjoyed a boom of their own, but this was not until after World War II.[73] However, in the 1920s some loggers were already using them on the Westside—Alex and Robert Polson, boss loggers of long standing in the Grays Harbor area, and Meiklejohn & Brown, near Monroe, Washington, for example. Polson's experimental use was an important harbinger, for their firm was one of Washington's premier independents—cutting 166 million feet of logs in 1923, a total only approached by the Simpson Logging Company. Occasional truck logging notwithstanding, during the twenties Polson's operations still primarily depended on railroads. By the end of the decade they and their allies had acquired timberland and established a network of railroads that gave them control of the rich forests of the newly opened western Olympic Peninsula, making it difficult for owners of isolated tracts to exploit their holdings and virtually forcing them to sell cheaply. In 1928 Robert Polson wrote, "The Peninsula is as well tied up now . . . as it is necessary that it should be."[74]

By 1920 *The Timberman* found two hundred and three logging railroads in Washington with a total of 1,864 miles of track and four hundred and twenty locomotives; Oregon had ninety-three railroads with nine hundred and thirty miles of track and two hundred and twenty locomotives. The number was still rising in both states in spite of difficulties presented by the mountainous terrain of the Coast and Cascade ranges. By 1929 there were four hundred and fifty lines in Oregon and over a thousand in Washington. Roughly fourteen hundred miles of new track was being laid annually in the Douglas fir region; as Nelson Brown explained, the growing number of large sawmills required "a continuous, large and reliable flow of logs daily throughout the year." Railroads dominated log transport as river drives once had elsewhere (while in 1930 only 6 percent of the Far West's log production moved by truck). Narrow-gauge lines had been important earlier, but by 1930 some 98 percent was hauled on standard-gauge lines, which as one authority soon noted "reach out to every 40-acre subdivision in the logging area." He exaggerated, but rail lines certainly were plentiful.[75]

Log train crossing a crib trestle in Oregon's Coast Range. Although sturdy and relatively easy to build, such trestles were less common than those supported by pilings. Courtesy Oregon State University Archives, #Williams G: Ford 25.

There had been logging railroads before this explosion of building in the Pacific Northwest. Nonetheless, this was something new. Railroads had a ubiquitous presence during the last years of large-scale logging in Pennsylvania, but they represented a technology that enabled lumbermen to tap remaining stands, not open a vast new frontier.[76] Railroads played a similar role in the Lake States, coming late in the area's lumbering; although they opened new stands, they can hardly be said to have been responsible for bringing large-scale lumbering to the region—river drives had done that.[77] Only in the Gulf South had railroads been essential adjuncts of the opening of a new lumberman's frontier, and even that had been different; with far gentler terrain, railroad construction was less costly in the Gulf South and demanded fewer innovations in engineering.[78]

Conditions in the Northwest tested the ingenuity as well as the pocketbooks of railroad builders, especially as lumbermen, having depleted stands tributary to Puget Sound and Grays Harbor, began shifting to more rugged mountain terrain. In the South grades seldom exceeded 2 percent; in the Douglas fir country they were frequently 6 and for short stretches sometimes even 9 percent. Routes often wound up the mountains with numerous sharp curves; horseshoe bends were not uncommon. Even with these parameters for construction, huge fills and massive wooden trestles and bridges were frequently needed (fills being preferred because they required less upkeep and would not burn if a fire swept the area).[79]

In the early twenties Daniel Strite worked on construction of a logging railroad into the mountains behind Tillamook Bay, a line designed to tap Whitney Company's eighty square miles of timber for the big new mill at Garibaldi. Strite's reminiscences make it clear that building logging roads was no simple affair. Swedish hard-rock miners were brought in to do the blasting for cuts; sub-contractors hired Yugoslavian crews to do the cut-and-fill work, paying them on the basis of cubic yards of earth moved. Of the latter, Strite wrote: "Their work was a joy to behold. The slopes of cuts were smooth as glass and the roadbed level as a pool table." Loggers struggled to clear the route: "Many of the big spruce in this area had been blown down over the right-of-way, their shallow overthrown roots rising 16 feet or more above the ground. These prone trees had to be cut in sections and rolled out of the railroad's path. . . . It was a job requiring superior woodsman's skill." The line incorporated three huge bridges; that over the Kilchis River was one hundred and fifty feet long and twenty feet high, that over Clear Creek twice as long and over twice as high. Strite confessed, "Whenever I had to walk out to see the foreman I never looked down!" The roadbed needed to be well ballasted and heavy-duty rails used if the line was to hold up under the weight of the loads expected. Not all—or even most—logging railroads were built to the standards of the Whitney line, but the difficulties Strite observed were repeated on line after line as lumbermen pushed into the mountainous back country of Oregon's westside.[80]

Logging railroads were costly—much more so than those in the Gulf South, Lake States, or interior Far West, where lighter construction would suffice and the terrain was gentler. On the Southern Pacific line from the Willamette Valley to Tillamook Bay, once the railroad crossed the summit of the Coast Range there were eight miles with "an almost unbroken series of tunnels and wooden trestles." As Everett Griggs laconically put it, "it costs something to handle timber in our country." Mainlines might run as high as $50,000 a mile. Rolling stock added more expense. Since they required a large initial capital investment—$1 million or more—logging railroads were practical only where stands would support long-term use and a large volume of logs could be carried; they were, in other words, suitable only for relatively large firms—but these were numerous in western Oregon and Washington, as the large number of logging railroads present by the late twenties attests.[81]

Moving logs to trackside was nearly as challenging as building logging railroads. Since colonial times loggers had come up with innovation after innovation for getting logs from the woods. The Northwest was heir to their efforts, but with larger trees, rougher terrain, and sawmills of unprecedented size—and appetites—new advances were necessary. Logging in western Oregon and Washington was as different from that of the Lake States and Gulf South as operations there had been from those of early Maine and New Hampshire. The adoption of crosscut saws and springboards for felling and John Dolbeer's little donkey engines for yarding were but the beginning.

By the end of the nineteenth century, power logging—a collective term for any system using mechanically powered devices for yarding—had come to stay. At first power logging utilized steam engines, but in time internal combustion and electric engines came to be used more frequently (an electric engine was reportedly in use for yarding in the Pacific Northwest as early as 1906). Although a far cry from the little steam engine Dolbeer had employed, the engines on the newer logging shows continued to be called donkey engines, perhaps because they shared the common characteristic of being stationary and pulling the logs to them (unlike bull teams and the tractors being used increasingly in the pine forests of the interior, which moved along pulling logs behind).[82]

The first major improvement over ground-lead logging—Dolbeer's system in which logs were simply winched along the forest floor—came not in the Pacific Northwest, but in the Lake States. There in the 1880s Horace Butters developed a system using a cable strung between two spar trees; to this he attached a trolley device toward which logs could be hoisted by a second cable run from the logs through a pulley to a take-up spool powered by a Lidgerwood steam engine. With at least one end of a log lifted off the ground as it was hauled to a landing, drag and chances of getting entangled with rocks and other obstructions were greatly reduced, making it possible to move logs at much greater speeds than with ground-lead techniques. Butters' system, known as skyline logging, was not widely adopted in the Lake States for ice and snow made winter skidding an inexpensive alternative, and when it was initially tried in the Far West during the first decade of the twentieth century it proved inadequate for handling the area's huge logs.[83]

Butters had pointed the way, but for many years a simpler system, known as high-lead logging, was more common in the Far West. Just who introduced the latter is not clear.[84] In high-lead logging a cable ran through a pulley system attached high on a spar tree and from there to logs to be yarded. Once the logs were attached to the cable, the engine was engaged, pulling the logs to the landing. This system was easier to install and required a smaller crew than skyline logging, but by lifting one end of logs off the ground it too greatly reduced the problems of drag and obstructions that had plagued Dolbeer and his successors. Unlike ground-lead yarding and the tractor logging of the interior pine country, high-lead logging was most effective when yarding uphill and thus was well adapted for the hilly terrain of the Coast Range. The system had its limitations—in yarding more than eight hundred feet or so, the angle of the cable from the top of the spar pole to the logs was too slight to allow them to clear obstructions and time-consuming hang-ups increased until high-lead became essentially ground-lead logging. Moreover, it was poorly suited for yarding downhill or across ravines and gullies, and with only one end clear of the ground, logs tended to bounce and twist wildly while being yarded, endangering workers and anything else in their way and often damaging the logs themselves. Still, the advantages of high-lead logging outweighed the disadvantages, and by the 1930s it was the most widely used system in the United States, annually moving over one-third of the nation's logs. By 1920, *The Timberman* reported, there were 391 high-lead installations in use in one hundred and seventy logging camps in Washington (and 1,704 donkey engines) and 191 high-lead systems in seventy-nine logging shows in Oregon (with eight hundred and fourteen donkey engines). As the Pacific Northwest's lumber industry grew, so too did these numbers.[85]

Skyline logging on a Weyerhaeuser operation in western Washington. Skyline logging was much less destructive than ground-lead logging, but as can be seen here damage to the land still resulted. Courtesy Forest History Society, Durham, NC.

High-lead logging dominated through the 1920s, but Butters' system—modified to use heavy-duty equipment—was handling more and more of the harvest. Just when skyline logging, as the system came to be known, arrived in the Far West is not clear; some claim it was introduced in the region's pineries by William K. Dyche in 1899 and subsequently adopted on the westside, first appearing there in 1904 or 1906. Whatever the case, it was well suited for many large Douglas fir operations, especially as new systems of riggings emerged for differing topography, and it was a decided improvement over its predecessors. With spar poles at either end of a "skyline," logs could be hoisted clear of the ground to avoid obstructions and easily transported across canyons, gulches, and the like. Hang-ups did not increase sharply with distance as they did with high-lead logging, and with less interference from obstructions logs could be whisked to landings at unprecedented speeds—two thousand feet a minute was not uncommon.

Moreover, the system could move logs four thousand feet or even more in some terrain, for only the sag of the skyline limited its reach. However, under most conditions the effective limit was some twenty-five hundred feet—still over three times the distance where high-lead systems ceased to be cost-effective.[86]

With the advent of overhead systems, a new elite emerged in logging camps: the high-climber. Someone had to prepare the spar trees on which high-lead and skyline systems depended, and daredevils emerged to fill the bill. They would work their way up a selected tree, chopping off limbs as they went, and then, as much as two hundred feet above the ground, top the tree by sawing through the trunk—even at that height often some two feet in diameter. The tree would buck and sway violently when its top fell free, and high-climbers had to brace their feet, push back hard into their climbing gear, and hold on for dear life while the trunk whipped back and forth like an overwrought pendulum. After the tree quieted, they calmly attached rigging to turn the topped tree into a functional spar pole. It was not a job for the fainthearted, and high-climbers earned the respect of their most hardened compatriots—and made the most of the attention they received, showing their daring-do by dancing and even standing on their heads atop trees they had just topped.

Paul Repetto recalled how he undertook his first such job at a camp near Mill City on the Santiam in 1916. The tree was five and a half feet in diameter; and he was directed to top it 165 feet from the ground. He recalled: "I had just as well admit that when I saw that [intended] spar-tree I wished I was somewhere—anywhere—else." The plan was to dynamite the top out of the tree, but some of the needed equipment was missing, so, pride on the line, Repetto informed his boss that he could chop the top out—even though 165 feet up the tree was still twenty-six inches in diameter. With jury-rigged equipment he went aloft and chopped away, even after a strong wind came up. Everyone "stopped to watch that top go out (and maybe Repp go with it as a thrill thrown in)." In subsequent years, chopping and sawing tops out became standard, but Repetto was a pioneer.[87]

There were accidents among high-climbers, of course, and some have pointed to these to demonstrate the human costs of the increasing mechanization of logging. Perhaps. But if one is to judge by the career of Paul Repetto or this author's uncle—who as a harem-scarem teenager clandestinely raced his father's auto across the countryside with friends, practicing to become the next Barney Oldfield, and then worked his way up in the woods to become a high-climber—most probably gloried in their celebrity rather than thinking themselves victims of, or even participants in, a heartless industrial system.[88]

Regardless of how high-climbers viewed themselves, power logging made woods work extraordinarily dangerous. Nothing catches the reality of conditions better than the title of Andrew Prouty's study of logging in the Northwest: *More Deadly than War!* Actually, Father Prouty's evidence does not establish that woods work *was* more dangerous than going to war—and some wars are, of course, much more deadly than others—but it does show that logging was the nation's most dangerous occupation, ahead even of coal mining. Dead limbs ("widow makers") fell silently, killing unsuspecting loggers below; if a feller miscalculated a tree's lean its butt could kick back or spin, wildly striking loggers like a giant sledge; boilers on donkey engines exploded; logs rolled, crushing choker setters connecting cables to them for yarding; cables snapped to whip like giant scythes that maimed or killed anyone in their path; while logs being yarded at great speeds by high-lead systems bounced erratically, smashing the unwary or unlucky. The list goes on and on. "Where are they now?" Paul Repetto asked late in his life of the old-timers. "Widow-makers, side swiping, flying rigging, flying chunks of timber, snapping cables or rolling logs—hazards that were, and still are, the inevitable deadly concomitants to the loggers life, have taken their heavy toll." William Manion caught the logger's reality:

> Danger walked with him at every step
> And climbed with him at every spar.
> Death rode every falling tree and rolling log
> And met him one wet morning on a hillside in the woods.

Dorothy Sherman summed it up: "There are not a great number of 'soft' jobs around a lumber camp, nor any that do not involve a goodly degree of risk."[89]

No one working in the woods was safe, yet somehow employers and employees alike seem to have accepted danger as unavoidable. Accidents were thought to result from the carelessness of workers, who, it was argued, assumed the risks attendant upon logging when they signed on to work. In 1892 a writer in the *West Coast Lumberman* proclaimed: "The carelessness of woodsmen is proverbial." That attitude long held sway, for there was some truth behind it. Careless loggers nearly crushed Emil Engstrom by felling a Douglas fir in his direction without warning. Of the incident, Engstrom later wrote: "I had been in many close escapes and been crippled up a few times, so to me it was all in a day's work. Nothing to worry about." Such fatalism was widespread, for as George Drake explained, "It was just taken for granted that you were going to be tough when you hired out as a logger."[90]

The speed-up in the woods was driven by a speed-up in the sawmills, and accidents were frequent there too. Like many others, the accident that killed Gus Smith at the Port Blakely mill was judged "due entirely to want of precaution on his own part." Courts agreed with such assessments. When an employee sued a Grays Harbor sawmill over injuries received on the job, a local judge ruled "he could not recover [damages], as the danger was known to him, and he should have used more caution in working around machinery openly known to him to be unsafe."[91]

In spite of the rising militancy of the region's labor movement, few complaints focused on the industry's abysmal safety record, perhaps because most members shared the view that accidents were often caused by carelessness or, as Washington's Department of Labor and Industries reported in 1912, over four-fifths of the accidents were considered "inherent in the trade—that is, due primarily to the nature of the work rather than to personal fault." Union leaders welcomed the passage of workmen's compensation laws, weak though they were, but social reformers and industry leaders hoping to be rid of troublesome and sometimes costly lawsuits were their main architects.[92]

As noted earlier, the Knights of Labor remained a force in the Pacific Northwest long after it had dwindled to insignificance nationally. But at the beginning of the twentieth century, lacking a national support base and plagued by internal divisions, it was poorly positioned to meet the needs of loggers and sawmill workers. The American Federation of Labor sought to fill the gap, but it too stumbled, leaving the way open for the more militant Industrial Workers of the World.[93] Violence followed, and the federal government intervened, concerned lest the production of spruce needed to build aircraft for World War I be hampered. It sent soldiers to work in the woods and encouraged the creation of the Loyal Legion of Loggers and Lumbermen, a nonviolent union substitute that brought employers and employees together in the hope that industrial cooperation would lead to improved conditions for workers while maintaining or even increasing production.[94]

Labor discontent resulted from living conditions more than high accident rates and low wages. Loggers lived a transient life without security or a sense of belonging and with death lurking ever close. Emotionally starved, they came in from the woods intent upon a carouse before going to the "slave market" to line up another job. In the process they made Portland's Burnside district and Seattle's Yesler Way notorious—folk from polite society assiduously avoided them. Father Prouty summed it up: "[L]oggers could not escape either the lethal hazards of the woods or the degrading seaminess of the 'skidroad' " districts. Logger Emil Engstrom noted that the IWW justified protest with the slogan, "We have nothing to lose but our chains." Although not an IWW member himself, Engstrom agreed: "Working from dawn to dark ten to twelve hours a day, living in dirty, ill-kept, stinking shacks, gathering grass and cedar or hemlock boughs for a bed on which to spread our blankets—in reality we were oppressed, we were in chains." The union's Joe Hill agreed, mocking those who urged patience and compliance to societal norms with "The Preacher and the Slave." Set to the tune of "In the Sweet Bye and Bye," its chorus proclaimed: "Work and slave, live on hay, you'll get pie in the sky when you die."[95]

There was some improvement over time. By 1923 *West Coast Lumberman* could argue Northwestern workers enjoyed "the shortest working day, the best living conditions and the highest wages paid anywhere in the lumber industry," but the claim was overblown. Conditions still left much to be desired, although as more and more loggers lived at home and commuted it at least became increasingly possible to escape the logging camps and still work in the woods.[96]

More was involved than a high accident rate and abysmal living conditions. In the Pacific Northwest, loggers were recipients of both managerial and middle-class contempt. This was not entirely new. As we have seen, a gap between woods workers and their employers appeared in the early days of logging in Maine and had grown as lumbering became increasingly industrialized as it moved to Pennsylvania, Michigan, and Minnesota. This division was spurred by a shift in the ethnicity of the work force during the late nineteenth century. In the Lake States, those who had risen to leadership came overwhelmingly from English-speaking stock. For French-Canadians, Scandinavians, Germans, and Finns—who as time passed supplied more and more of the workers—opportunity was less real. On the West Coast, these groups and a sprinkling of others—Asian and European—dominated the labor force. At the same time, the industry's leaders were increasingly distant from the rural roots many in the industry had once had; even those companies whose founders had humble origins were now a generation or more removed from them, and the sympathy for workers that hardscrabble beginnings had once engendered in men like Michigan's Charles Hackley was more and more rare.

By the beginning of the twentieth century half the workers in the Pacific Northwest's lumber industry were foreign born, and in the growing climate of nativism and anti-immigration sentiment, they suffered from unprecedented levels of hostility and contempt both from employers and the public. The romantic imagery of the lumberjack, which once ameliorated hostility, had now faded, replaced by that of the bindlestiff, a worker drifting from job to job with his possessions wrapped in a bedroll, his "bindle." To much of the public, bindlestiff equated roughly with tramp. Robert Ficken surveyed the letters of leaders of the Northwest's industry and found them full of derogatory references to their workers as riff-raff and worse. Thanks to the activities of the IWW, many came to see loggers not just as undependable drifters, but as dangerous and un-American as well. Such views served to dampen any interest employers might have had in improving conditions.[97]

Pennsylvanian Hiram Cranmer came to Seattle in the fall of 1914 "with the intention of working in the lumber woods." For all his experience logging on the Allegheny Plateau, what he found in the Northwest appalled him:

> *Seeing a crowd down the street aways I walked down to see what was going on. A speaker was holding forth on a soapbox in front of the I.W.W. hall. A strike was on at the time among the shingle workers. The speaker was intelligenly stating the workers wrongs. . . . Next the police rushed up and pinched the I.W.W. leaders. This in free America. Next morning I wondered at the many pack-peddlers in sight until I saw they were wearing calked shoes and were woodsmen. Then I learned that woodsmen there carried their beds with them, had to pay fifty cents per week in a lumber camp for the use of a cot to put their bed on. That a man couldn't go to a camp and hire out to the boss. He had to go first to an employment agency in Seattle and pay two dollars for a job, half of which went to the boss of the camp he was sent to. He then had to pay three cents a mile to ride a log-train out to the camp. What ever number arrived at the camp, ten or fifteen, a like number was fired to make room for them. The discharged men had to pay three cents a mile to ride the log-train back to town.*

Cranmer concluded that he "would not work under those conditions" and returned to Pennsylvania.[98]

Some employers viewed their more dependable workers as assets worth taking steps to keep. Others, fearing any concessions would undermine their authority and profits, brought pressure to hold the line on those willing to consider changes in the status quo. To them, workers were a source of inefficiencies and problems, rather than assets. Sharing the latter view, Booth-Kelly's A. C. Dixon declared in 1923 it is "more satisfactory to have the smaller crew and the machine rather than the larger crew and no machine, even if there should be no variation in cost."[99]

Roland Hartley, a principal in the Clough-Hartley sawmill in Everett, illustrates the attitude raised to the extreme. In the 1920s Hartley emerged as "an articulate and even flamboyant spokesman for the cast-iron Republican industrial conservatism he chose to defend." Fiercely individualistic, he was "determined to prevent any personal or institutional interference" in his affairs and denounced government regulation as vehemently as IWW activity. Norman Clark summed up Hartley's views:

> He was the soul of gregariousness. . . . The right words came easily for him, and he could speak without notes literally for hours, villifying labor unions, cursing socialism, or praising economic individuality and industrial freedom. There was little about progress and nothing about the Progressive Age which he could not hold up to wrath and condemnation. He detested prohibitionists, social workers, suffragettes, direct primaries, and direct legislation. He hated radicals, agitators, internationalists, pacifists, unions, taxes, and progressive legislation.

Hartley justified the Everett Massacre, in which seven Wobblies (as members of the IWW were known) were slain and forty-seven (not all of them union members) wounded; the IWW, Hartley proclaimed, "came . . . to burn Everett and to burn the mills. The citizens had to arm to repel the invasion." Mayor Hiram Gill of Seattle denounced the Everett vigilantes, but E. G. Ames, Alex Polson, and many other lumbermen agreed with Hartley. The Timberman proclaimed: "Law and order must be upheld at any cost"; to editor George Cornwall, killing Wobblies did not seem a violation of the principle. In the climate of the times, Hartley, who always had an eye for public office—and public acclaim—rode his views into Washington's governor's mansion (and, in spite of an abysmal record, subsequently won re-election).[100]

Labor was not the only problem bedeviling Northwestern lumbermen. Power logging ate into Westside forests faster than anything experienced on earlier forest frontiers and brought unprecedented damage in its wake. As Kenneth Erickson has observed, the beginning of the twentieth century inaugurated "a 30-year period of forest denudation, unequalled in the speed and volume by which timber was removed. . . . Simultaneously there came increases in . . . logging waste, damage to future stock, and danger of fires." In 1927 Thornton Munger, a regional pioneer of forestry research, decried the fact that

> [u]pon completion of "falling," logging and slash disposal, the average site is usually devoid of living trees. The smaller trees left by the fallers have for the most part been knocked down by the logging lines or burned in the slash fire, and of the few larger trees which were culled and left standing some if not all have been killed by broadcast burning.

Moreover, much of the cut never reached a sawmill. In 1926-1927, Allen Hodgson estimated, nearly 1.5 billion board feet of sawlog-size timber was wasted through breakage and uneconomic yarding and over three billion board feet (six million cords) of smaller-size wood went unused. Nor was that all. There was other, less obvious waste from erosion, destruction of seedlings and future stock, and vast quantities of slash that provided a rich breeding ground for fire and insects. The drain on the region's forests reached its apogee in the 1920s when the ratio of annual cut to growth was 10.5 to 1. Appalled, pioneer forester George Peavy pleaded for sustained yield on the region's remaining private timberland. Without it, he warned, private forests would be gone by 1947 and major inroads would have to be made on the national forests.[101] The argument that logging decadent old-growth forests opened the way for a vigorous second-growth with a much greater annual growth increment failed to quiet his concern.[102]

Far-sighted foresters like Munger and Peavy were not alone in their concern. The "automobile revolution" was under way, and Oregon entered upon a period of major highway building to accommodate it. As a result, thousands came into visual contact for the first time with the devastation wrought by forest harvests. On a trip to the Northwest, National Park Service head Stephen Mather urged preventive action. "You Oregonians," he warned,

> are so accustomed to it that you do not realize the charm of your beautiful trees to visitors from less-favored regions. The trees along your highways are a scenic asset of almost incalculable value. If you permit these trees to be cut away and your highways to traverse bare and desolate regions, you will destroy what is, in fact, your greatest tourist asset.[103]

Governor Ben Olcott was unmoved by Mather's plea, but what he saw when he inspected the new highway from Cannon Beach to Seaside spurred him to action. The Crown-Willamette Paper Company had logged along the route and left scarred, barren hillsides. Olcott was soon engaged in a major campaign to save the state's roadside timber, an effort that set in motion forces that would eventually lead not only to timbered wayside strips, but also to one of the nation's premier state parks systems.[104]

Important though they were to tourism, the efforts of Mather, Olcott, and their allies were largely cosmetic, for they concerned only narrow strips along highways. Foresters like Munger and Peavy focused on a larger, more basic picture: the health of the region's commercial forests as a whole. They found no easy answers.

At first foresters anticipated the Northwest's Douglas fir forests would restock after clearcutting. Douglas fir was not shade tolerant, and thus required open areas for seedlings to survive. In the absence of openings created by fire, windthrow, and the like, Douglas fir forests eventually gave way to shade-tolerant species such as spruce and hemlock. High-ball logging practices, although destructive of young trees, cleared the land and thus were expected to open the way for a vigorous new generation of Douglas fir.[105] But in time it became evident the forests were not restocking as expected. Alternatives to natural reseeding were needed. C. J. Buck, the Forest Service's Regional Forester for the Pacific Northwest, was among those questioning the wisdom of clearcutting followed by natural reseeding, a position that put him at loggerheads with Thornton Munger of the agency's Pacific Northwest Forest Experiment Station.[106]

Writing in the 1960s, Kenneth Erickson found the debate bewildering, for it came at a time when the costs of forest devastation were well known and Europeans were taking steps to heal the results of their own earlier destructive practices. "The reasons behind clearcutting in the Lumber Boom," he wrote, "are difficult to grasp. . . . Surely, by 1920, enough information was available to know that the scale of depletion could not continue, yet incongruously it was [in] the 1920s when clearcutting and destruction reached its most destructive heights." To Erickson clearcutting could only be explained by the presence of a "technologically well-armed, profit-seeking, and expansion-oriented industrial society supported by a ruthless 'frontier' spirit . . . a new industrialism which offered an endlessly ascending spiral of more production to give more jobs to more people who demand more production." Lumbermen, he proclaimed, "viewed the forest purely as a capital investment," and they had taxes to pay and heavy financial costs to amortize, creating pressure to liquidate their stands rapidly.

Moreover, valuation for taxes was based on standing timber, not timberland per se, a fact that exacerbated pressure to clearcut.[107]

The situation was more complex than Erickson's analysis allows. Even foresters with no economic stake in the issue differed over the best way to manage Douglas fir forests, as the differences between Munger and Buck demonstrate. Both wanted permanent forests in the Northwest, but they disagreed on the best way to achieve that end.

Fear of fire was a major factor in the debates as were tax policies that caused many to consider long-term holding of forestland economically unfeasible. Those advocating replanting after clearcutting found it hard to counter the arguments of those who claimed replanted forests would surely be destroyed by fire before they reached harvestable size. In light of the area's disastrous experience with forest fires, the fear of such conflagrations was persuasive, and as a result the nursery established in Silverton, Washington, to supply seedlings for replanting languished for years. At the same time, annual taxes added to carrying costs even though no income would be realized until stands were cut; proposals designed to defer most if not all taxes until timber was harvested long fell on deaf ears, forcing many a timber owner to log holdings sooner than he might have otherwise and led to widespread clearcutting followed by abandonment of cutover rather than holding land in anticipation of a second crop some decades later.[108]

Ubiquitous wigwam burners and fall slash burning (and smoke-filled skies) were indicators that the new lumbering frontier was fully present in the far Northwest—but it was a frontier quite different from those that had preceded it, not only because of new technologies and levels of organization, but also because the forests themselves were different. The inability of foresters to agree on how to manage Douglas fir forests was an indicator of how unlike those on earlier American frontiers they were—or, for that matter, from the European forests on which much early silvicultural knowledge was based. When foresters could not agree on how to manage Douglas fir, it is difficult—indeed, presentism in its rawest form—to criticize industry for not adopting what a later generation judges to have been the best management techniques.

Various New Western historians have argued that capitalism resulted in the commodification of resources, with the result the Far West became a "plundered province." This concept fails to explain why the result was a mining of forest resources rather than long-term sustained management or why some firms adopted management practices quite different from those of others. One cannot deny that by and large forest practices in the Far Northwest were exploitive, but as an analytical concept, the commodification of resources is a blunt instrument. It obscures the fact that commodification had been present in the forests of New England long before there was a Far West (and in Europe before that). Moreover, things had begun to change by the early twentieth century as more and more people came to question such a narrow view of forest resources. Among them were many active in the Douglas fir region, including lumbermen Simon Benson, R. A. Booth, and Henry B. Van Duzer (vice-president and general manager of what was by the 1920s Portland's largest sawmill); Forest Service officials C. J. Buck and William Greeley; and public figures, including governors Oswald West and Ben Olcott. All argued in one way or another that forests had values beyond those represented by the board feet of lumber they could produce, an argument seldom heard from those involved with earlier lumbering frontiers. Anti-capitalist interpretations fail to make allowance for the presence of such spokesmen as well as for the varieties of forest utilization, indeed even of capitalist utilization, present on the succession of forest frontiers.[109]

A narrowness of vision, exacerbated by equally narrow experience and education and widespread fear of socialism, created middle-class blinders in the 1920s that shaped actions within the lumber industry as surely as did its capitalist nature. The Wobblies and other radicals were the victims of fear and prejudice more than industrial reality. Just as Frederick Kohlmeyer had noted in the Lake States, lumbermen in the Pacific Northwest acted on the basis of the values and expectations of their times; they were captives of received knowledge and past experience that unfortunately had limited applicability in Douglas fir forests.

Lumbermen were not alone. The authors of the Bureau of Corporations study of the lumber industry (1913-1914), of the Forest Service report on timber depletion (1920), and others who wrung their hands in despair about the disappearance of virgin forests were prisoners of past experience too. They assumed that when old-growth was gone the forest (and forest industries) would be gone too—but the Douglas fir country was not Pennsylvania, Michigan, or the Gulf South; for all the cries of gloom and doom, in time a permanent (if greatly reduced) lumber industry would emerge in the forests of the Northwest, but for the time being the actions of lumbermen and foresters were shaped by ideas that had been inculcated in them by more than just the materialist forces of political economy.

Be that as it may, the Great Depression brought the rapid expansion of lumbering in the Pacific Northwest to a halt. The industry struggled simply to hang on—and in the process found occasion to re-examine some of the "truths" that had long driven it. Demand would not revive until World War II. Indeed, the tremendous demand—and unspent capital—built up during that war was to carry the industry through the heady days of the 1950s and would lead to the opening of tracts formerly too isolated or rugged to justify logging—such as Weyerhaeuser's Millicoma forest in nearly impassable mountains behind Coos Bay[110]—but this represented only a final flowering of the frontier industry present before 1929; it did not represent a new departure.

CHAPTER THIRTEEN

The Final Frontier

Since colonial times American lumbermen had moved across the continent, opening one forested area after another to exploitation. Their activity had been marked by an abundance of individual initiative and a minimum of regulation from authorities. Success required finding promising stands, establishing effective control, and logging them quickly and efficiently before control could pass to others. The others, of course, included government officials, who strove with limited success to restrain illegal cutting. All this resulted in a transitory industry that repeatedly entered new areas, cut out the timber, and then moved on to other forests to repeat the process.

By the early twentieth century, circumstances were ripe for change. Vast untapped stands remained in the mountain fastnesses and interior pine country of the Far West—on the eastern slopes of the Cascades, and in the Sierra Nevada, and on ranges east from there through the Rockies—but those, it was clear, would be the last lumberman's frontier. Alaska, distant and frigid, did not offer the opportunities to which the industry had so long been accustomed. Lumbermen looked to a future lacking in new frontiers to conquer.

Much of the forestland in this region was incorporated into the new regime of forest reserves, which in time led to programs of active management. Vast stands had been available for inclusion, for this was a late-settled, little-developed area. Moreover, it was remote from major domestic and maritime markets and, until well into the twentieth century, poorly served by transportation facilities. Rivers were few and generally undrivable; railroads, other than through routes, were late in coming.

The potential of this vast domain was immense. Included in its reserves were some of the finest stands in North America—sugar, western white, and, above all, Ponderosa pine—interspersed here and there with Douglas fir, western larch, and other less-valuable species. Extensive tracts of fine timber also lay outside the reserves. Much of the terrain was gentle, the stands open and, once reached, easy to tap—especially after truck logging became practical in the 1920s.[1]

Here and there echoes of old battles were heard. In Colorado, settlers pushing into farming and grazing lands on the periphery and occasionally even in the midst of forests often refused to report illegal logging, for they sympathized with the activity. Settlers apparently did a good bit of cutting and selling themselves. In 1897 an investigator for the United States Geological Survey was told: "This timber belongs to us settlers and we're going to get it! The government officials can't prevent us either, with an army. If they attempt to stop us we'll burn the whole region up!" Residents there and elsewhere in the Rockies regularly subverted the Free Timber Act (also known as the Timber Cutting Act), passed in 1878 to help settlers meet their domestic needs, to get control of valuable stands they then transferred to lumbermen.[2]

Farther west, many used the Timber and Stone Act—also passed in 1878 and for similar purposes—to gain control of timberland for commercial operations. In portions of the Blue Mountains and around Bend and Klamath Falls, Oregon, such activities reached a crescendo in the first years of the twentieth century as droves of opportunists arrived to establish claims before forest reserves could be established.[3] Some lands near Bend were to be irrigated by well-publicized projects, but the nearby forestland was ill suited for agriculture;[4] with some twenty-five billion board feet of timber, these lands were especially attractive to those with non-agrarian interests. When Stephen Puter arranged to take one hundred and eight dummy entrymen to land he had selected, "the concourse of vehicles resembled a Sunday turnout in Golden Gate Park." Nor was Puter alone; as he later recalled, so many people were preparing to file claims that every "vehicle or animal available was . . . pressed into service. . . . All summer long the dusty roads between [the railhead at] Shaniko and Bend were lined with travelers, and it was soon evident a large portion were under contract to convey the rights they acquired to syndicates of Eastern lumbermen." Many of the throng were school teachers dispatched by train from Minnesota by Shevlin-Hixon during the summers to establish claims to be transferred to the company, which planned a large sawmill in Bend when rail connections made it feasible. Like its parent firm, Shevlin-Hixon skated the thin edge of the law, although it did not wind up in court repeatedly as did Shevlin-Carpenter in Minnesota.[5]

Similarly, in the Blue Mountains and Oregon's Klamath country, few claimants developed farms; nearly all soon transferred title to speculators who anticipated arrival of railroads and sawmills or directly to the advance guard of various lumber interests. As around Bend, this encouraged early development of sawmills, but created a checkerboard of ownership that complicated subsequent government efforts to regulate forest use.[6]

The scramble to establish private ownership in the Western pineries was transitory. Termination of Timber and Stone Act selection in 1903 and repeal in 1905 of lieu land legislation reduced opportunities for landlookers and speculators, while by the end of 1906 much of the area's best timberland had been incorporated in forest reserves and thus placed beyond their reach. Moreover, since few farmers, ranchers, or miners resided in or near these forests, by the 1920s Forest Service employees were spending less time guarding them against trespass than devising ways of protecting them from fire and planning for regulated use.[7]

In this role, the Forest Service found itself under pressure from impatient locals who wanted timber sales to bring sawmills and jobs to their communities and who saw the Forest Service as a potential ally in insuring that development came to pass. However, in areas where a significant acreage had passed into private hands before establishment of the reserves, such lobbying was not a key factor. In Bend, for instance, community leaders focused on providing lumber companies with inducements to locate there, such as furnishing Shevlin-Hixon with a free millsite. But where most stands were within reserves, more would be needed; unless the timber was unlocked, even free millsites could not bring major sawmills. In such areas, opening stands to logging would require cooperation from the Forest Service. Contests thus often took place between two elites with different priorities, community leaders and Forest Service technocrats, rather than—as so often earlier—between a business elite that had engrossed the forest and smallholders who resisted their dominance.

The absence of a significant resident population was one of many problems faced by mill operators.[8] Local newspaper editors welcomed sawmills because they would bring employment opportunities, but actual circumstances were not so simple. The *Fossil Journal*, published in the seat of Oregon's isolated Wheeler County, predicted that building a mill at the western end of the Blue Mountains would "occupy all our surplus labor." It may have, but when the mill was built at what became the town of Kinzua its operators had to go to Spokane to complete their initial crews. Many of those recruited were single and soon quit because the mill was too far from the bright lights of the city, so the company sought married men to replace them. To obtain them it went outside the region, and for decades afterwards the soft accents of Kentucky, Arkansas, and Oklahoma dominated the streets of the little mill town—and reflecting the dominant Middle Border dialect, pronunciation of the town's name became "Kinzoo" instead of the original "Kinzuah" of Pennsylvania.[9] The situation was similar in Bend, where Shevlin-Hixon and Brooks-Scanlon brought workers from Minnesota, the previous site of their main operations. Scandinavian names such as Haglund, Hoagland, Benson, and Hansen were commonplace in the community.[10] Not just in Kinzua and Bend, but throughout the interior pine region, laborers poured in from the Lake States, the South, and elsewhere, drawn by the hope of employment.

In places such as Winlock, on the southern slope of the Blue Mountains, there were enough settlers to provide the workers for small mills, for agricultural expansion in the period around World War I had led homesteaders to push into the foothills of the range. But when a dry cycle commenced, most drifted away. The remaining users of the area were mostly cattlemen and sheepmen with ranches in the lowlands; they utilized the forested highlands for summer grazing, sometimes leasing grazing rights from forest owners and sometimes simply trespassing. They provided no labor pool—and only minor headaches—for lumbermen who moved into the area.[11]

If some of the developments of older frontiers were not much in evidence, one familiar theme *was* consistently and abundantly clear: mobility. During the early twentieth century, Far Western forests beckoned enticingly to lumbermen from Minnesota, Louisiana, East Texas, and other locales where old-growth stands were fast disappearing. Others saw potential here too: railroad builders, who had at last expanded their entrepreneurial visions to the Western pineries; land speculators, who hoped to profit from tying up key stands for re-sale to lumber barons; and local boosters, who saw a combination of pines and railroads as the route to greatness for their various crossroads communities. The lure was all the greater because it was widely recognized this was to be the last frontier for America's lumbermen. Capital, people, and ideas all soon made the leap to it.

Among the first interior stands to draw attention were those of northern Idaho. Its great forests of white pine lured the Weyerhaeusers and their allies, seeming to many of them a natural area for expansion. It lay directly west of their operations in Minnesota, was close to their vast holdings in Washington, and was endowed with white pine, which buyers preferred (albeit a western species). By Lake States' standards, Idaho timberland was cheap. Moreover, well before much of the rest of the interior Far West, the region was relatively well served by railroads, including one controlled by Frederick Weyerhaeuser's friend and neighbor, James J. Hill. One by one, the syndicate brought on line mills at Coeur d'Alene, Potlatch, Lewiston, and elsewhere. These investments were fraught with problems, but initially at least syndicate members made them with enthusiasm.[12]

In southern Idaho, the Boise, Payette, Barber, and other lumber companies also appeared early, although they tended to be smaller and less stable than those in the northern part of the state. Thanks to the construction of railroads through the Boise Basin in the 1880s and to local demand spurred by the growth of irrigation agriculture, operators of the area's mills had a nearby market. Timber sales from state land and the acquisition of federal land through the Homestead Act, lieu land provisions, and similar legislation gave them access to logs long before Forest Service timber sales became a major factor.[13]

In central and eastern Washington, production was also on the rise. Mills appeared early at Palouse City, Yakima, Wenatchee, and elsewhere. Edward D. Wetmore, who visited as a representative of a group of Eastern investors, described the Biles-Coleman plant at Omak as one of the best-run sawmills in the pine country.[14]

By the early twentieth century, growth was taking place in many other locations as well. Around Flagstaff, Arizona, the arrival of railroads encouraged sawmills and, as time passed, lumbering spread to other mountain areas in northern and eastern Arizona and northern New Mexico. Montana, Wyoming, and Colorado saw a great increase in production too, even though many stands were lodgepole pine, long considered a "weed" tree because of its small size and the low-grade lumber it yielded. Indeed, the Chief of the Forest Service noted, by the 1920s the timber industry was on the rise throughout the Rocky Mountain region, and everywhere Forest Service policies and Forest Service timber were shaping the course of development.[15]

The industry came relatively early to the northeastern portion of California. Lumbermen had been operating on a major scale in the Sierra Nevada since the 1870s, in the process familiarizing consumers with the better varieties of western pine. But early operations above Chico and in much of the Sierra took place in rugged country that required extensive systems of flumes and were otherwise costly to tap. Stands in the northeastern reaches of the state were more promising. Accessible to rail lines, closer to California's burgeoning markets than most of the Far Western pine country, and blessed with abundant sugar pine—ideal for making the packing boxes of which California's fruit growers seemed never to have enough—by the early twentieth century the area boasted numerous mills. By 1920, a reporter for *The Timberman* wrote, "from Oroville, 205 miles east of San Francisco, and following the Feather River to Portola, a distance of 116 miles, is an almost continuous series of lumber operations." Large plants existed elsewhere in northeastern California too, at locations such as Westwood, McCloud, Weed, and Susanville.[16]

Development came more slowly to forests east of Oregon's Cascades. Isolated by mountain barriers to the west and southwest, by largely unpopulated deserts to the southeast, and by torturous canyons to the north and east; bypassed by transcontinental and major regional feeder railroads; and long without significant agricultural development to spur local demand, the region's pineries long stood beckoning, but largely untapped. Sizable sawmills grew up in Baker, located in far eastern Oregon, as a combination of gold and timber drew the Sumpter Valley Railroad into the Blue Mountain country. Elsewhere there was little. By the first decade of the twentieth century, small mills had emerged in Bend and Klamath Falls, but by and large the unsurpassed ponderosa stands near these communities, and those east from Klamath Falls past Lakeview and along the low, canyon-intersected ranges of the Blue Mountains and their outriders, from Prineville northeast to the Idaho state line—hundreds of thousands of acres of first quality pine—remained untouched.[17]

Development eventually came, especially in the 1920s, and the reasons were clear enough. Although in many areas the industry was in the doldrums, sawmills in the western pineries were doing well. In 1926 E. D. Wetmore—who with others from Pennsylvania had established the Kinzua Lumber Company and through it, beginning in 1909, acquired fifty thousand acres of fine timberland near the western terminus of the Blue Mountains—joined two colleagues in touring the pine country to determine what to do with their holdings.[18] From Omak, Washington, in the north to Klamath Falls in the south, Wetmore reported, "we failed to find a plant that was not making money. Several had started with very small capital and were now prosperous and rich." Profits ran from $4 to $8 per thousand depending on the quality of timber. Wetmore queried numerous informants about prospects. The president of Northwest Bank in Portland, himself part owner of a plant in Klamath Falls, when asked if he knew of pine mills not making money, answered he did not "unless they were very badly managed." Bankers, he added, "considered the pine manufacturers good risks and were glad to take their loans." There *were*, of course, some badly managed mills. He specifically mentioned the White Pine Lumber Company in Baker, and, on the basis of other information, Wetmore added the Mt. Emily Lumber Company in La Grande. But on the whole the news was good. Encouraged, Wetmore concluded "we ought to develop the Kinzua property."[19]

Within three years Wetmore could add two other sawmills to the list of mismanaged: the Gardinier Lumber Company in Austin, in which he invested only to see it go under from peculation and poor management, and the Kinzua Pine Mills (the operating arm of the Kinzua Lumber Company), which nearly died aborning as a result of the incompetence of its first general manager, Willard N. Jones, he of earlier timber fraud fame.[20]

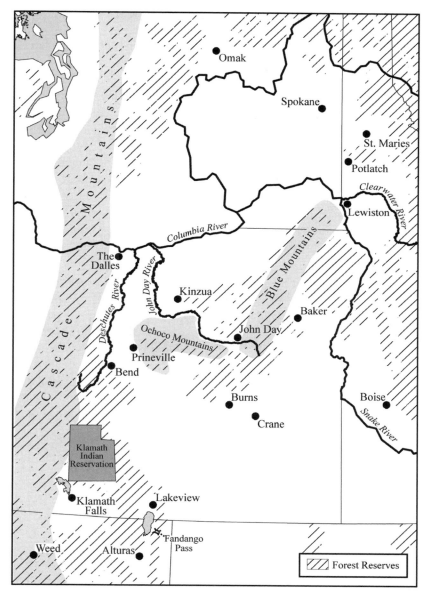

Interior Far Western pineries. Map by Sarah E. Hinman.

When development finally came, it brought large-scale logging to this last American lumberman's frontier. For those who arrived early, good stumpage was remarkably cheap. During the first decade of the century, Kinzua purchased some one hundred million feet of timber for a mere 79 cents a thousand; about the same time, the Weyerhaeuser Timber Co. paid an average of only $17.34 per acre for prime pine land near Klamath Falls. Carrying charges had driven up costs by the time the owners turned to manufacturing, but even so their timber was most inexpensive.[21]

Gradually, available stands became fewer, and the cost of timber rose. Later arrivals or those trying to expand holdings at a late date found private stumpage far more expensive than it had been a decade or two earlier—and the timber often of lower quality and more inaccessible. In light of this, Forest Service timber sales came to assume greater importance. The Gardinier Lumber Company, for example, found government timber purchased at $3.25 per thousand, delivered in its pond, cost $2.75 per thousand less than private timber acquired from the David Eccles interests. Forest Service sales prolonged the life of many a mill—in the case of Gardinier, more than doubling its timber base and, in the process, justifying the firm's original investment in plant.[22]

Even firms owning considerable acreage often came to depend on Forest Service timber. Kinzua cut on the Umatilla National Forest as well as its own lands, the Umatilla's Snowshoe Basin becoming a mainstay of its operations; and Shevlin-Hixon and Brooks-Scanlon, the twin giants that sprang up in Bend after arrival of the railroad in 1911, each bought considerable stumpage from the Deschutes National Forest even though they had major holdings of their own.

In the vast pine country of central and eastern Oregon, the old patterns of exploitation—patterns that had existed in one form or another since the days of Humphrey Chadbourne and his peers in colonial New England—ran headlong into those of post-frontier, industrial lumbering. Unrestrained, individualistic exploitation based on the principles of laissez-faire and a firm belief that progress came through maximizing production collided with regulated, planned use. Permanent operations and sustained yield were the new ideals, and with much of the timberland now not just owned, but actually controlled by the federal government, lumbermen had to adjust to the directives of Forest Service policy makers in addition to those of the marketplace.

Adjustment came more easily for some than others. The more dependent a company was on Forest Service timber, the more it had to come to immediate terms with the new age. The contrast between old and new patterns was exacerbated by the fact that, unlike in many areas opened earlier, the lands being penetrated had few residents; only in scattered locations did the frontier farmer-logger add his own complexities to developments. Frontier businessmen and the government's minions faced off, and in the end the former had to adjust, however grudgingly, to the demands of the latter. For very few did adjustment come without a degree of trauma, but no one illustrates the problems of this industry-in-transition, the dilemmas of the free-wheeling frontier lumberman on a collision course with the modern world of bureaucracy and planning, better than Fred Herrick.[23]

Herrick grew up in Michigan and at age twenty-one took a contract to deliver elm to a mill in St. Joe. The following year he began getting out hardwood logs on his own account. Soon he learned the government was planning to sell some Indian timber in northwestern Wisconsin; he took in a partner, borrowed $200,000, and bought a considerable stumpage. Over the next twenty-two years their Flambeau Lumber Company cut out the holdings, sawing more than a billion feet of white pine and clearing over $1.6 million—and in the process demonstrated the lack of concern for regulations and legalities that was to be the hallmark of Herrick's operations in the Far West. In 1903 Herrick joined W. D. Harrigan in investing in timberland and a small mill near Fulton, Alabama. The venture was spectacularly successful. Herrick followed this by buying timberland in Florida and Mississippi. Then, in 1909, he left Harrigan in charge in Alabama and headed for Idaho, lured by the Milwaukee Railroad, which hoped to induce him to build a mill beside its line across Idaho just south of Lake Coeur d'Alene. Herrick liked what he saw and not only erected the Milwaukee Lumber Company in St. Maries, but gradually acquired mills at Harrison and Coeur d'Alene, a second mill at St. Maries, the Red Collar Steamship line (which served the vicinity), and assorted other holdings. He soon became the area's largest independent operator, worth by some estimates as much as $12 million and employing some three thousand men.

Herrick was a rugged individualist of the old school. His tastes were simple, his manner direct and brusque. With pointed reference to more urbane competitors, he acidly commented, "I do my loggin' in the woods, not in the Davenport Hotel," the posh hostelry in Spokane. There was no question who was in charge of operations; an inveterate hunter, he would point to a row of stuffed mountain lion heads on his office wall and introduce visitors to his "board of directors." Gruff and demanding with employees, he nonetheless inspired loyalty and admiration. He tended to pay slightly above the going wage, but demanded hard work for it. Many stayed with him for years, and good work was rewarded with opportunities for advancement.

Herrick became a virtual folk hero to his men, who saw him as an individualist willing to buck his competitors, government agents, homesteaders, and any others who stood in his path. He asked and gave no quarter. In a struggle for control of the Marble Creek drainage southeast of St. Maries, Herrick blasted for a railroad tunnel close to streamside, tumbling huge boulders into the creek to block log drives and force competitors to use his line. Always at odds with someone, Herrick ended many a confrontation with: "Sue and be damned." Nor was it just individuals with whom he locked horns. Herrick wound up in litigation with the state of Idaho as a result of actions under a contract for logging in Heyburn State Park and his practice of mooring log rafts in the park's waters, interfering with recreational use. An investigator warned the State Land Board, which oversaw the park, to watch him closely for he was "very clever in his manipulations."[24]

When one of Herrick's ventures prospered, he invested in others, ever confident in the future of the industry and the value of the lumber in his yards. As he acquired more and more holdings, Herrick's organization remained the same: it was, he was wont to say, "under my hat." He borrowed against one enterprise to finance others, had loans from a host of different banks, and stretched lines of credit to their limit while stalling payments as long as possible. Faced with complaints, he would bellow, "I'll pay when I get damned good and ready!" His men found when they went to cash paychecks that they were sometimes asked to "wait a few days." Loggers hated receiving bad checks, but somehow they accepted it from Herrick.

In the early 1920s, already in his seventies and with more holdings than he could keep up with, Herrick embarked on the largest undertaking of his career. He won cutting rights to a huge tract—eight hundred and ninety million board feet—of national forest timber north of Burns, Oregon. In this, he was taking on a new type of venture. Under terms of the sale, he was to build some eighty miles of railroad, erect a large modern mill in Burns, and log the timber on a sustained-yield basis over a fifty-year period—all under Forest Service guidelines. In short, this rugged individualist of the old school would be required to enter the industry's new age.

The sale was the result of long-continued efforts by local interests. Burns, an old cattle town isolated on the edge of Oregon's High Desert and miles from the nearest railroad, had a narrow economic base and few prospects.[25] Fine pine forests on extensions of the Blue Mountains north of town had been withdrawn as forest reserves and incorporated into the Ochoco and Malheur national forests, but the Forest Service was loathe to open them to cutting; excess production already existed, and without a railroad or large, established sawmills in the vicinity, any logging was sure to be for small, wasteful mills. Moreover, until at least 1915, Forest Service policy reflected sentiments of the Progressive Era. Distrust of monopolies kept timber sales small, preventing the offering of tracts large enough to justify the investments in railroads and modern plants necessary to tap efficiently stands such as those north of Burns. When Balfour & Guthrie of Portland—owners of alternate sections of timber in several townships in the northeastern part of the Malheur—approached the Forest Service in 1909 about a massive timber sale to make building a large sawmill in the area feasible, the company was firmly rebuffed. "The [Chief] Forester is unwilling to consider any application for as much as a billion feet of timber," an official wrote. "It is not felt that anywhere in Washington or Oregon is there such a crying need for development" as to justify such a sale.[26]

None of this prevented local residents and their allies from pushing the Forest Service to open the forest through such sales. A headline in one regional newspaper expressed their conviction: "The Timbered Areas of Eastern Oregon Will be the Wedge that will Pry Open All the Resources."[27]

Foremost among the champions of opening the Malheur was Ephraim W. Barnes, a "timber looker" from Portland whom a contemporary described as "quite an interesting character; very crude in many ways . . . [and] always looking out for Mr. Barnes." Sometime around 1919, attracted by economic stirring in Burns—where irrigation projects and completion of a long-delayed railroad from the east were under discussion—Barnes visited the region and, recognizing the potential of forests between Burns and the twin communities of John Day and Canyon City, some one hundred miles to the north, began buying tracts. Through his contacts, Barnes sought a working relationship with an operator capable of building a large sawmill; Dwight F. Brooks, president of the Brooks-Scanlon sawmill in Bend, seems to have been interested, for by this time his firm had largely cut out its own holdings. At the same time Barnes worked to interest the local Chamber of Commerce in his plans, hoping it could persuade the Forest Service to offer a major sale on the Malheur. Through such actions, Barnes hoped for great things, both for the area and for himself.[28]

As pressure to open the forest mounted, the Forest Service's Regional Office dispatched Fred Ames and George Drake to look into the matter.

Accompanied by Barnes and others, they toured sections of the Malheur and Ochoco national forests tributary to Burns. As Drake later recalled, "I was quite impressed, frankly, with this body of timber, [both] . . . its quality and the logging conditions."[29]

Then, in January 1922, petitioners from Grant and Harney counties sent Barnes to Washington, D.C., to lobby for a bill allowing the exchange of federal and private tracts within the external boundaries of the Malheur National Forest, thus permitting blocking up of private holdings, which would in turn make building sawmills more feasible. Barnes had a personal interest; he had invested all his funds—by one report $200,000—in timber options and key millsites. President Warren G. Harding signed the resulting legislation into law on March 10, 1922, and William B. Greeley, Chief of the Forest Service, moved quickly to make the long-awaited sale available.[30]

Whether Greeley was responding to the efforts of Barnes and his allies is doubtful. The Forest Service had been edging toward larger sales as its concerns shifted from the danger of industrial monopolies to furthering the economic development of forest-dependent communities. In 1919 Greeley's predecessor, Henry S. Graves, had declared it "of the utmost importance that the industrial developments supported by National Forest stumpage be permanent." Greeley expanded on the idea the following year: "The sawdust piles and abandoned mill towns of the . . . East must not be repeated on the public forests of the West"; use must lead to permanent growth. A year later, he spelled out his ideas more explicitly: national forests should "contribute to the support of permanent industries and stable communities. The [current] policy aims also at encouraging the development of new enterprises of a kind and on a scale to utilize most effectively the raw material which the Forests can produce." He pointed to a huge sale on the Trinity National Forest in northwestern California as an example.[31] In light of all this, a major sale on the Malheur might have been forthcoming even without Ephraim Barnes, for the area was ideal for application of the policies Greeley championed.

In any case, the Forest Service called in James W. Girard to cruise the timber, and after bidding and re-bidding, the sale to Herrick went through. Barnes's attempts at self-aggrandizement had been for naught—he and Brooks-Scanlon were out[32]—but under terms of the contract Burns was to get a major sawmill, a standard-gauge common-carrier railroad with connections to the outside, and another line to Seneca, entrepot to the timber.[33] Greeley was pleased, for the sale promised the sort of stability he sought to encourage. He noted, "The capital invested in this sale originated in the Lake States in the days of white pine and has moved south and west periodically since. So far as a supply of raw material is concerned, it will never have to move again." Community leaders in Burns were pleased too, especially when on September 24, 1924, the railroad from Crane was completed, giving Burns the outside connection its residents had long desired.[34]

Details of what followed, chronicled elsewhere, need not be repeated here.[35] Suffice it to say, Herrick hired Girard away from the Forest Service to manage his undertaking, but for all Girard's expertise the project foundered. Herrick found himself financially over-extended and had difficulty meeting terms of the sale. When the deadline for completion came, the Forest Service found Herrick had spent less than half the required amount, but it granted an extension nonetheless. The editor of the *Blue Mountain Eagle*, no doubt irritated the logs were to be milled in Burns rather than John Day (which was actually closer to the timber) and an apparent confidant of Barnes, was hardly pleased: "the little scratch work" Herrick had done "is not enough to establish good faith."[36]

The *Eagle's* editor was not alone in his unhappiness. Citizens of Burns and John Day, eager for Herrick's mill to commence sawing, chafed at the repeated delays. They called on their legislators for help and in 1927 were rewarded with a memorial, passed unanimously by Oregon's legislature, asking for a congressional investigation. Senator Robert Stanfield, who had reasons of his own for wanting to embarrass the Forest Service, was more than happy to have Congress oblige. Eleven days of hearings followed. Investigators uncovered no evidence of skullduggery, despite aspersions cast by Barnes and the *Blue Mountain Eagle*, but they made Herrick's shortcomings abundantly clear. The Forest Service had no choice but to tighten the screws. Herrick was given additional extensions, but with stricter terms and a $50,000 fine for non-compliance. Herrick struggled on as best he could.[37]

Fred Herrick's problems were not simply the result of chaotic organization and a need to meet unwonted Forest Service demands. Over the years, he had prospered through expansion as timber values and lumber prices climbed steadily. Those days were past. Now there was a surplus, and lumber prices were falling. Hundreds of thousands of feet of lumber sat unsold in his yards, and when sales were made, the lumber went off at low prices. Payments from Alabama apparently ceased coming in too, Harrigan having paid off his debts to Herrick. The details are not clear, but the end result is: the income Herrick had anticipated would pay for his Malheur undertaking was not materializing. The Burns *Times-Herald* observed laconically, "Depression in the ... pine market makes the financing of large operations somewhat difficult at this time." Like R. A. Long's ambitious development at Longview, Herrick's expansion into the Blue Mountain country was falling victim to a depressed lumber market, harbinger of the general depression that would soon batter the nation.[38]

In December 1927, the Forest Service finally moved. It gave Herrick two weeks to come up with $1.5 million in additional financing. Girard protested, noting progress had been made in spite of "organized opposition with their tremendous propaganda which have blocked our financial plans in many places . . . and in the face of depressed lumber conditions, has forced Mr. Herrick to sacrifice valuable assets." Girard concluded, "We are not quitters." In spite of this bravado, the die was cast. No further investors were forthcoming, and on December 17 the Forest Service canceled Herrick's contract.[39]

Herrick appealed, claiming he had done his best, the government had lost nothing because of his failures, and cancellation would therefore be inequitable. With his appeal pending and no new investors on the horizon, Herrick maneuvered desperately to find a buyer for his Oregon interests. Frank Gardner, a timber broker from Portland, scouted for prospects. Brooks-Scanlon stayed out of the picture, apparently hoping the timber would revert to the government, leaving it in a position to pick up the timber for $2 a thousand. But others *did* take an interest. Fletcher Stark of the Lutcher & Moore interests came west to investigate; although the situation was quite different from what he was used to and he thought a mill closer to the timber would be preferable to one on the outskirts of Burns, he was tempted. But Gardner, apparently angling for a fat commission, told him Herrick had $1,800,000 tied up in the enterprise and it would take that to buy him out. Stark backed off.[40]

Herrick had reached the end of his rope, but refused to admit it. When the timber was put up for re-bid the following June, he entered the contest, bid $3 a thousand, and blithely sought to use the bond he had deposited on his original bid (and had subsequently been forced to forfeit) to meet requirements for the new round. Forest Service officials had had enough. They disqualified Herrick as a bidder, stating he lacked proof of ability to complete a proffered contract. The only other bidder was the Edward Hines Lumber Company of Chicago, which offered $2.86 a thousand. Hines received the contract, and Barnes appeared to have gotten the last laugh. It was he, the *Blue Mountain Eagle* claimed, who had interested Hines in the sale during a trip east the month before.[41]

Hines was ripe for the move. A major Midwestern lumber dealer loosely affiliated with the Weyerhaeuser interests, it had sawmills in northern Minnesota and Lumberton, Mississippi. The former had been cutting for twenty years, and its timber supply was near an end. Indeed, Hines's Virginia and Rainy Lake Company cut its last log on October 9, 1929, just over a year after Hines won the Malheur contract. Although he practiced cut-and-run forestry in the Lake States and South, the idea of sustained yield, as required on the Malheur, was hardly foreign to Edward Hines, the firm's president. As early as 1920, he had written, "[T]here is no good reason why reforestation cannot be undertaken, and the lumber business made as perpetual in America as the growing of wheat."[42]

Hines proceeded with gusto. Eager to bring the mill by Burns on line, he quickly came to terms with Herrick, buying his interests for $400,000, and rushed the railroad and sawmill to completion. The mill cut its first logs on January 27, 1930, and was soon in full operation. With this, Barnes appeared to have triumphed at last. Present when the mill sawed its first logs, Barnes was lauded by the *Times-Herald* as the "Moses who led the Grant-Harney wilderness to market."[43]

Having ingratiated himself with Hines, who lacked experience with western pine, Barnes became a key advisor. But he was in over his head. F. W. Pettibone, formerly manager of Hines's plant in Lumberton, Mississippi, replaced Girard, and at Barnes's suggestion a logging superintendent was brought in from western Oregon. Having experience only with big Douglas fir timber, he made costly changes in Girard's logging plans. As George Drake recalled, they "wasted thousands and thousands of dollars in poor railroad location"—location appropriate for Douglas fir, rather than the lighter pine. As a result, "Barnes got in the doghouse, and he and this high-priced logging superintendent left the company." As George Drake put it, "Barnes wound up without much to show for all his endeavors. . . . He was a promoter, pure and simple, without the finesse to do a good job."[44]

Hines had problems beyond those occasioned by Barnes. The company spent lavishly, seeking a first-class operation; it invested $7 million in finishing the mill and railroad and buying up privately held pine. In addition, intrigued by the promise of the Blue Mountain country, Edward Hines began looking into purchasing other mills in the area, most notably the financially troubled Kinzua operations. But before negotiations could be consummated or the company's new plant brought on line, the Great Depression struck, turning an already bad lumber market worse. Unable to move its cut, Hines, like Herrick before it, was threatened with bankruptcy. One Forest Service official later recalled "they were . . . badly busted," but under existing circumstances "the banks didn't figure it was worthwhile to take the property away from them." Somehow, Hines persevered, but the concrete skeleton of a grand hotel still stands unfinished near the millsite, a stark reminder of hopes gone awry.[45]

Herrick, Barnes, and Hines were a case unto themselves, but Burns was far from atypical. Other communities in the interior West also hungered for the Forest Service to open nearby forests. Lakeview, Oregon, was among them, although its leaders operated without the help of speculators such as Ephraim Barnes. Located some one hundred miles east of Klamath Falls, where the arrival of railroads was spurring activity, and about the same distance northeast of sizable California operations, Lakeview had extensive stands of ponderosa pine in its hinterland; with community leaders eager for growth, it seemed ripe for development.

Like those around Burns, the pineries around Lakeview had a limited population. Ranching, the mainstay of the economy, centered in the sagebrush- and bunchgrass-dominated lowlands, not in the forests (although the latter did provide summer grazing). Here and there small sawmills supplied local demand, but while their owners sometimes clashed with community and Forest Service leaders over plans for the forests they were to play a limited role in events. The key determiners of events were local business leaders and their allies on the one hand and Forest Service officials on the other. That is, developments were shaped by the interaction of two elites—one internal to the community, the other external.

Lakeview lacked adequate transportation facilities. In 1909, while Klamath Falls was beginning to boom, Lakeview remained quiescent; on the surrounding Fremont National Forest little was happening. Small mills had been cutting their own timber, but were running out and, a local Forest Service official suggested, would no doubt welcome sales of national forest timber if the prices were not prohibitive. Some, he realized, might refuse to purchase—such as C. W. Embody, who had a sawmill northwest of Silver Lake and "does not like the rules that govern timber sales, especially those affecting brush piling"—but on the whole sales seemed a good possibility. There was ample mature timber available on the Fremont, and small sales soon became a regular feature.[46]

County officials, eager to have a large sawmill constructed in the area, approached Weyerhaeuser, which had extensive holdings in Lake and neighboring Klamath counties. Jackson Kimball, key Weyerhaeuser representative in the area, was frank: "reasonable" taxes would help. The county commissioners, "indicative of their friendly attitude toward the company," responded by rebating school taxes on company lands in the Summer Lake district that had been collected in excess of needs.[47] Still, no mill materialized.

George S. Long, in charge of Weyerhaeuser's western operations, recognized the problem. The Nevada-California-Oregon Railway, which ran north from Reno, where it connected to the Southern Pacific, had reached Lakeview in 1912, but the N-C-O was an inadequate link to the outside—a lightly ballasted, under-financed, narrow-gauge line with poor equipment. Local wags asserted N-C-O stood for Narrow, Crooked, and Ornery.[48] Without an adequate railroad to get lumber to market, Weyerhaeuser's timber near Lakeview remained untapped.

By the end of World War I it appeared new rail connections would soon materialize, and Long recommended Weyerhaeuser buy tracts that would be economical to log and help block up its holdings. The timber, he said, "ought to be attractive to some moderate sized . . . operation" if Weyerhaeuser opted against building in the vicinity itself. "I think," he added, "we will want to start in a very quiet way and not be in any hurry about it."[49]

Recognizing that improved rail service was key, leaders in Lakeview hoped the Forest Service would put up a major sale to attract a large sawmill—and railroad developers as well. The Forest Service refused. In 1917 Acting Chief A. F. Potter made the agency's position clear: mature timber would be made available for "any legitimate demand which comes to the Forests in the course of normal extension of transportation facilities and the development of timber-using industries," but the Forest Service would not "sell large tracts of very inaccessible timber primarily to promote the financing and construction of a common carrier railroad. . . . It will be our policy . . . [to make sales] when the construction of the railroad is either actually completed or completely financed and unquestionably assured." If Lakeview were to get the railroad its leaders desired, it would have to do so without help from the Forest Service.[50]

Gradually things changed. In the early 1920s, major western railroad empires, jockeying for dominance, turned their attention to the untapped pine country of the interior Northwest. As they maneuvered for advantage, rumors circulated that the N-C-O would soon be taken over, upgraded to standard gauge, and completed through to Klamath Falls or The Dalles. Robert E. Strahorn, an independent, unveiled railroad-building plans of his own, and stories circulated that the Great Northern and other major lines were eyeing the area. Residents hung eagerly on every report, however unsubstantiated.[51]

Suddenly Lakeview seemed less isolated, and a scramble for nearby timberland developed. Never before, the *Lake County Examiner* observed in 1924, had so many lumbermen visited; at the beginning of November alone, fifty were present scouting out possibilities, including representatives of eighteen large operations. Sizable tracts of private timber changed hands.[52]

Forest Service policy gradually shifted too. As the agency put more and more emphasis on community development and stable forest management, its old practice of small sales to keep the tiny mills of Lake County going seemed anachronistic, and its leaders came to believe that timber on national forests should be saved for large sales. The government, George Drake explained, sought to make lumbering "a perpetual affair," and large sales of federal timber would be a means to that end. Private operators, he argued, could not afford to manage their land on a sustained-yield basis because prohibitive taxes on timberland forced owners to cut as quickly and completely as possible. Only major federal sales seemed to promise proper management.[53]

There was sufficient timber near Fandango Pass, located in the Modoc National Forest just across the California line from Lakeview, to support a relatively large mill; combined with private timber, these stands could be managed on a perpetual basis. When the Forest Service announced it had no intention of selling the Fandango timber piecemeal, operators of small mills protested, arguing they needed it to continue in business. They were joined by the chambers of commerce of Lakeview and Alturas (located a short distance south of the Fandango unit in California). Although their arguments were inconsistent with their previous efforts to get a large sawmill for the area, the chambers now maintained that such a policy constituted a locking up of resources, hurt local employment, and stood in the way of development.[54]

The Forest Service stood firm. Indeed, it now went further, announcing it would not sell the Fandango unit until a standard-gauge railroad was assured. Only with such a line, its spokesmen argued, could a sawmill capable of properly utilizing the timber be successful. Moreover, the timber would have to be harvested on a sustained-yield basis and sawn in a modern band-saw-equipped mill so as to achieve efficient use of the raw material. In the name of conservation, the agency claimed it could require no less.[55]

Protests mounted. Lakeview interests appealed to Oregon's Senator Charles McNary and Representative Nicholas Sinnott, claiming the policy was so restrictive it would dissuade millmen from investing and would result in both no sawmill *and* no standard-gauge railroad. The Forest Service gave ground, however reluctantly. Although there was as yet no standard-gauge line in place, events suggested one was in the offing, so the agency agreed to offer the Fandango tract, some two hundred million feet of timber, the following year—as a single unit to be cut on a sustained-yield basis and with its logs sawn in a modern band-saw mill. Forgetting their own inconsistencies and obstructionism, local spokesmen proclaimed the sale "the result of the combined efforts of the business interests of Alturas and Lakeview working through their Congressional representation."[56]

When the sale came up for bid only two potential buyers emerged. The Crane Creek Lumber Company won the contract with a substantial bid of $4.49 per thousand for the pine (less for other species) and announced plans to erect the modern mill required to saw it. Those who had predicted Forest Service restrictions would keep investors from bidding had been wrong, but that was not all. With the promise of a major sawmill in the area, the Southern Pacific decided to upgrade the N-C-O, which it was acquiring, to a standard-gauge line.[57]

As the date for logging the Fandango unit approached, the *Lake County Examiner* applauded its pioneering role. "Modern scientific logging is being insisted upon . . . the perpetual principle," the paper noted. "This is supposed to be the first commercial application of this principle which the government has been working out for a long time in its forest laboratories and field studies." Champions of other sales in other areas might have made the same claim, but nevertheless the newspaper had reason to welcome the commencement of milling, for it represented a major economic breakthrough for Lake County. Other mills and other large sales followed, and the area was soon a major sawmill center. Indicative of its belief that lumbering was at last firmly established, the Lake County Board of Equalization raised taxes on timberland, long kept artificially low as an inducement to outside investors.[58]

Prineville's leaders were less successful. Located in central Oregon at the western end of the Ochoco Mountains, a separated branch of the Blues, the town had a somewhat broader economic base than Burns or Lakeview. Ranching and irrigated farming were well established, although neither was centered in the forested areas. Residents dreamed of greater things, and the magnificent pine stands of the Ochocos, largely empty of people and untapped, seemed to promise them. Local newspaper editor R. H. Jonas waxed eloquent on the subject: "Few communities offer greater opportunity for the individual who would do something than does Crook County. . . . Here bounteous nature has piled natural resources in abundance that await development. . . . The largest body of yellow pine in the world lies all untouched by the lumberman's axe."[59]

Jonas exaggerated only slightly. There were some seven billion board feet of merchantable timber in the county, much of it of the highest quality and easily reached for logging. When E. D. Wetmore toured the western pine country in 1926, he found "only one tract of timber having as favorable physical conditions as our Kinzua Co. tract"; he referred to some one hundred thousand acres of timber a few miles east of Prineville that Long-Bell and other outside investors had acquired for some $28 an acre. But the Ochoco National Forest, which encompassed over half of the stands in Crook County, was among the most inaccessible in the Pacific Northwest, a federal forester reported, and its timber sales therefore were among the lowest.[60] For years local residents worked to attract a major sawmill to open these stands. Frustration was their usual reward.

The Forest Service was not the problem. Indeed, under its new policy of furthering community development, it was eager to offer a tract sufficient to justify a large modern mill in Prineville. The accessible timber, its surveys showed, would support "an operation of some size." When approached in 1922 by a firm interested in erecting a plant to cut sixty to seventy million board feet a year, the agency was encouraging. Available timber would support such a mill for six or seven decades and still leave enough for smaller operations. However, officials cautioned against a sale that would encourage construction of a mill so large as to cause "serious overcutting in the future." Their worries were unnecessary: no sawmill materialized.

Two years later, Fred Ames reiterated the Forest Service objective "to sustain one [large] operation on a permanent basis" in Prineville, but admitted that so far there had been almost no cutting on the Ochoco. Jonas recognized the fault did not lie with the Forest Service. The District Forester was interested, he reported in his *Central Oregonian*, and the agency would sell its timber "if the proper requests are made," but none had been forthcoming.[61]

As elsewhere, transportation was critical. No railroad served Prineville, and without one no big mill would come and no large timber sales would be offered. Yet railroads were so close! The main north-south line that had made large-scale lumbering possible in Bend passed less than twenty miles west of town. For years community leaders tried to get the railroad to build a branch up Crooked River to Prineville, arguing the wealth of the Ochoco forests—to say nothing of the area's farms and ranches—would make an extension profitable. Their arguments were unavailing, so with the encouragement of the Rogers interests of Minneapolis, who said they would build in Prineville if there were a railroad to it, community leaders decided to construct one themselves. The municipally owned City of Prineville Railroad was the result.[62]

Rogers failed to come through, but in 1923 sold its timberlands in the area to the Ochoco Timber Company. New assurances followed, and hope revived, only to be dashed once more. Two years later, timber owners prevailed upon county authorities to reduce assessments on timber stands, claiming development was imminent but high taxes impeded plans to build. Again no sawmills appeared. In 1927, R. A. Booth, president of the Ochoco Timber Company as well as the Booth-Kelly Lumber Company, seemed on the verge of building in Prineville; however, Booth fell seriously ill, and plans went on hold.

By this time more than one man's health was behind the lack of action. Overproduction was plaguing the industry, and investors were growing cautious. The Western Pine Manufacturers' Association insisted there was a good bit of unmet demand for pine lumber, and the *Central Oregonian* promptly echoed the report, but most operatives seemed to believe otherwise and postponed plans for major expansion. Left without traffic to make it pay, the City of Prineville Railroad—and the city itself—teetered on the brink of bankruptcy.[63]

Prineville's city fathers, like those in Lakeview, watched the railroad-building schemes of the 1920s intently. Although they already had their own little spur line, they hoped renewed railroad construction would bring additional connections and make Prineville a more appealing place for lumbermen. Plans for a major new east-west route across the state seemed especially promising, but this was a will-o'-the-wisp, and in due course the scheme collapsed. Prineville continued as before, served by the City of Prineville Railroad and nothing more.[64]

Despairing of attracting outside investors, in 1929 Prineville's Businessmen's Club tried a different ploy. It persuaded local interests—the Smith brothers and their associates—to apply to the Forest Service for some thirty-nine million board feet of timber on Canyon Creek and, with money raised locally through the sale of stock, to build a mill to saw the logs. The Canyon Creek stands, the club's leaders noted, were isolated from the Ochoco's proposed working circle. The Forest Service could sell to the Smiths without eating into the block of timber it was holding for a large mill. The Smith brothers' mill would not be what either the businessmen or the Forest Service hoped for in the long run, but it would be a start, employing some fifty men on a permanent basis, generating traffic for the city's beleaguered railroad, and demonstrating the feasibility of lumbering in Prineville. The Forest Service approved the idea, both the Canyon Creek timber and stock in the Smiths' mill were sold, and lumbering on an enlarged scale was soon under way. The *Central Oregonian* called this "only a small beginning," but hoped "it will prove the entering wedge which will result in more and more of the forest area being thrown open. . . . It looks like we may at last be at the turn of the road and that better times are in store for Prineville and Crook County."[65]

In spite of this minor victory, Prineville's leaders had failed in their years-long quest for a major sawmill. More than economic caution—and a degree of duplicity—seems to have been responsible. The *Central Oregonian* was not alone in recognizing the quality and extent of Ochoco forests. For years outside interests had been buying its stands. In addition to Booth's Ochoco Timber Company, Dant & Russell, Walter Alexander, and Charles R. Currie acquired extensive holdings. They maneuvered to keep taxes on their holdings low and added to them as opportunity afforded, but none of them seemed in any hurry to begin cutting. To both Jonas and the Grange, a force in Oregon politics long after it ceased to wield power nearly everywhere else, the message was clear: local timberlands had been engrossed by speculators who hoped to profit from rising values as untapped forests became more scarce, and such men did not care if their efforts held back development of the community. Available evidence appears to support the charge.[66]

A conviction that machinations of speculators resulted in farmers having to carry an undue portion of local taxes fueled protests. The Ochoco Irrigation District had gone deeply into debt to bring water to area farms. In financial straits, it levied special assessments on water users. This, coupled with high taxes, made local agriculture economically marginal. Timber speculators, Jonas and the Grange cried, should carry their fair share of taxes. Moreover, if high taxes forced them, these absentee owners would mill their timber as the only way to make a profit from it. In the process they would bring jobs and growth to Crook County.[67]

In other times, such protests might have led to changes in the tax structure and—as the protesters predicted—new mills, major timber sales, and economic growth. But depression was just around the corner, and when it broke President Herbert Hoover ordered a halt to large sales of national forest timber unless needed by existing plants. With industrial closures stalking the land, the last thing the government wanted was additional sawmills. Large sales on the Ochoco were thus precluded, and it would be years before Prineville developed into the lumbering center Jonas and his contemporaries had sought to make it.[68]

It was not just in Burns, Lakeview, and Prineville that new mills appeared during the twenties that depended upon national forests for sawlogs. Mills sprang up throughout the interior pine country. In Klamath Falls, lumber manufacturing dominated the city. The Algoma, Euwana Box, Pelican Bay, and Modoc lumber companies—each with a capacity of seventy-five to one hundred and fifty thousand board feet per day—as well as smaller firms, all operated in the area. The Pelican Bay Lumber Company—controlled by what Jackson Kimball called "the Mortenson crowd from Chicago"—was largest, with an investment of over $800,000 in sawmill and ancillary facilities, but it long lacked extensive timber holdings and had to rely on public timber.[69]

Inevitably, federal policies impacted such operations. In 1911 the Forest Service sold some one hundred million feet of timber to Pelican Bay. Problems resulted. Forest Service policy required removal not just of pine, but also of less-desired species. This, William B. Greeley reported, resulted in "a serious loss" to the company. The Forest Service eased requirements for cutting inferior species, but Pelican Bay still barely turned a profit on purchases of Forest Service timber. In 1916 it wound up with 45 percent of the lumber it sawed being graded rough, which was virtually unmarketable; even its higher grades of fir were hard to move. From a similar sale near Crater Lake, the W. H. Eccles Lumber Company produced 67 percent rough. Eccles must surely have lost money, for at 45 percent Pelican Bay barely broke even, and in 1917 Eccles showed a profit of only 21 cents per thousand on other federal timber it milled.[70]

Most area lumbermen depended upon timber from the huge, well-forested Klamath Indian Reservation, as well as from national forests. Indeed, in 1925 George Drake reported, "[P]ractically all the cutting of the last few years has been from the Indian Reservation." The Bureau of Indian Affairs' forestry division, rather than the Forest Service, was in charge of these stands. The policies of the two agencies differed, but both were run by professional foresters with modern ideas of timber management and both had a tremendous influence on the course of lumbering in the Klamath country.[71]

Indian timber was a special concern for R. A. Booth. Through the California and Oregon Land Company, he controlled the old Oregon Central Military Wagon Road grant that extended across the Klamath reservation. Much of it was fit only for grazing and the grant's checkerboard pattern made logging even well-timbered sections costly, so in 1906 Booth arranged a swap. He traded one hundred and ten thousand scattered acres for a block of eighty-seven thousand acres of prime timber north of Klamath Falls near Yamsey Mountain. Congress obligingly appropriated $108,750 to compensate the tribe. Observers thought the exchange profited

Booth to the tune of $2 or $3 million; they may have been right, for when the exchange was challenged, courts determined the land had been worth $2.9 million at the time of the trade and in 1918, having decided against building a sawmill in the area, Booth was able to sell the tract to Long-Bell for $3.7 million.[72]

Unlike Booth, most area lumbermen depended upon timber sales on the reservation, rather than acquiring title to portions of it. Indeed, the ready availability of Indian and national forest timber was a major reason there were so many sawmills in the Klamath district. As George Long explained, this "makes it very easy for an operator to get started." He buys at a timber sale,

> *pays a nominal amount . . . [and] then he doesn't pay [the rest due] until he cuts from month to month. . . . He has none of that initial investment [in timberland] which in the past and elsewhere have gone into the lumber business. About all he needs is enough money to build his sawmill . . . make this [initial] cash payment, [and] buy logging equipment.*

Ease of entry, Long complained, made it difficult for "the fellow who has a lot of money in timber"—such as Weyerhaeuser, R. A. Booth, and Long-Bell. Once established, small mills did not have to remain dependent upon government timber. By 1929 the Algoma Lumber Company had become "a

Fageol double-compound truck with ponderosa logs from the Klamath forest. Until the advent of pneumatic tires, solid rubber tires such as these made for a rough ride. Courtesy Oregon Historical Society, #bb006291.

large business based on the purchase of publicly controlled timber," but, like Pelican Bay and others, as its fortunes improved it acquired considerable timberland. In 1929 it cut twenty million board feet of its own, nineteen million feet of Forest Service, and 16.4 million feet of Indian stumpage. Thus, operations started on a shoestring became not just competitors in selling lumber, but in the search for private timber too.[73]

The situation created problems for the government as well as competitors. One Forest Service official complained the presence of so much Indian timber together with "the large number and size of private holdings which adjoin the Klamath Working Circle make[s] it difficult to foresee the manner in which development will take place." In addition, holdings were located so "private timber . . . practically controls U.S. timber," making it hard to regulate the cut. Worse, some smaller firms, having little invested and thus little to lose, resorted to desperate measures. When a fire broke out in Indian timber on Clover Creek, the nearly bankrupt operator in the area reportedly commented that now there "would be some cheap stumpage for sale." It was clear to Jackson Kimball that the man's partner had set the fire to create a salvage sale; Kimball commented wryly, "[T]his fire has been a gold mine for Whitcomb."[74]

The extent and quality of Klamath forests, plus the fact the area was reached by railroad near the beginning of the century, meant local leaders— unlike those in Burns, Lakeview, and Prineville—did not need to struggle to attract sawmills.[75] Indeed, at an early date Klamath politicians came to view the holdings of outside investors as fair game for levies while leaving local ranchers and farmers lightly taxed. This outlook was well developed by 1908 and, to the chagrin of lumbermen, continued through the 1920s. One way of increasing the tax yield of private forestland was to raise estimates of the stumpage thereon. Weyerhaeuser's George Long grumbled that a county cruise in 1926 had been "made with the distinct understanding that there should be found more timber."[76]

Some lumbermen had less difficulty accepting the situation than did Long and his chief local operative, Kimball. Samuel O. Johnson saw opportunity in public expenditures to build up the area. Much of the development was financed using warrants, which Johnson urged the Weyerhaeuser Company to purchase. He warned Long he should help county authorities "now when they need it, [or] you will pay a good price in the future for not coming through." Weyerhaeuser's Minot Davis observed, "[T]here is no question but that [Johnson and] his crowd are going to be a big factor in this county for some time." Kimball was equally suspicious. "The Johnson-Wendling crowd are in control," he reported, "and are encouraging a vast outlay of money in an effort to unload their town property. . . . There is graft as well as reckless waste."[77]

In spite of the political situation, development went on. With the extent and quality of stands in the area, it could hardly have been otherwise. G. W. Felts, manager of the Algoma Lumber Company, was one of the first to log in the key Pokegama area southwest of Klamath Falls. He found the trees tall, the wood soft with almost no rot or windshake, and "when the timber was down, I never saw logs so thick on the ground."[78]

Because of proximity to California (until 1926 its only rail outlet), many early Klamath millmen started with box factories. They long continued to look to California with its seemingly limitless demand for fruit boxes and thus failed to acquire experience and connections that prepared them to deal with Midwestern and Eastern markets as they opened to western pine. In this they were different not only from Weyerhaeuser, but also from the Shevlin-Hixon and Brooks-Scanlon interests in Bend.

This California orientation was partially a product of freight rates. One reason Wetmore finally decided to build at Kinzua was that, being closer, a mill there would enjoy a freight advantage over Klamath mills of some $1.50 per thousand on lumber shipped east, as well as a smaller advantage over those in Bend. Mills in Idaho enjoyed an even larger differential, and as a result, when Weyerhaeuser finally began sawing in the Klamath country, even it depended on California more than company officials would have liked. The orientation of early Klamath mills to the California box trade resulted in some inefficiency. Since timber around Klamath Falls was of the highest quality, its best use was as lumber, not box shooks.[79]

Penetrating Eastern markets required more than a sawmill, Eastern connections, and favorable freight rates. Even with the best of stands, sawmills produced a great deal of shop-grade lumber, which was hard to dispose of nearby and, being low in value, could not bear the cost of shipping to distant markets. The solution was to manufacture to get maximum value-added out of one's raw material. Besides the basic sawmills, this required planing mills, dry kilns, and cut-up plants to turn shop-grade lumber into products with sufficient value to justify shipping to distant buyers. Thus, operators had to make huge investments in plant—often well beyond initial expectations. Such outlays drove many—including Hines and Kinzua—to the brink of bankruptcy. For many of the older mills in the Klamath area, such undertakings were simply beyond their financial means.[80]

In addition to these handicaps, Klamath's pioneer lumbermen made a variety of mistakes. The Algoma Lumber Company, for example, made a costly choice of location—a marshy, lakeside millsite—driving up construction costs and making drying lumber difficult. Nearly all the pioneer mills suffered from a lack of adequate log-storage space.[81]

Eventually the limitations and mistakes of early operators opened the way to dominance in Klamath Falls of millmen closer to the industry's mainstream, most notably the Weyerhaeuser interests. But that was a long time coming. Although they had been acquiring timber in the Klamath country since 1905, not until 1929—and then only after considerable soul searching—did Weyerhaeuser build a sawmill there. For a time, the firm toyed with milling its Klamath timber in partnership with Shevlin-Hixon, which also had extensive holdings in the area, but in the end decided to buy much of Shevlin's timber and go it alone.[82]

When it came, Weyerhaeuser's Klamath mill was something of a monument to George Long, who retired on the eve of its opening. For years Long had been the chief champion within the organization of Klamath's potential. In August 1929, he predicted that within a few years, "Klamath Falls will be the largest Western pine manufacturing point in America," and for Weyerhaeuser the "handsomest pearl on the string."[83]

But Weyerhaeuser was expanding in other places, too, and had launched a major program of sawmill construction. Having acquired huge holdings in northern Idaho, it erected a large sawmill in Lewiston to complement the mill associates already were operating in nearby Potlatch. The new plant went online in 1929, just a few months before that at Klamath Falls. Weyerhaeuser's Douglas fir mill at Lewiston, even larger, started up about the same time. The plant went on line in 1929, just a few months before the Klamath Falls mill. Weyerhaeuser's Douglas fir mill at Longview, even larger than the other two, started up about the same time. With the commencement of milling in Klamath Falls and Longview, George Long noted, Weyerhaeuser had increased its capacity "possibly more than 100% . . . over what it has been doing the past ten years." Lewiston added a huge additional increment. An old friend took Long to task: "It breaks our hearts to see the Weyerhaeusers building big new mills all over the West—mammoth ones. . . . I think you will, if you keep on, put one-third of the mills in the West out of business." Yet Weyerhaeuser was not alone. Hines, Kinzua, and various other mills opened new plants at about the same time. There had been rising voices of concern about overproduction before. Now they reached a crescendo.[84]

Mills dependent upon federal timber were not the only ones being shaped by Forest Service policy. Those that owned extensive tracts in the interior pine country often had their decisions influenced too. When they bought Forest Service timber to supplement their own, they came immediately under the agency's purview, but even when they did not they frequently cooperated with it on fire prevention, grazing regulation, reforestation, and other programs, sharing technical expertise and sometimes even personnel.

Uncooperative operators tended to pay the price. These were not just small-timers: Thomas B. Walker, one of the leading lumbermen in California and holder of considerable land in the Klamath country as well, fought the Forest Service over fire prevention—Walker preferred the light-burning method, rather than the brush piling and cooperative patrols endorsed by the Forest Service. He also antagonized the Klamath County assessor; as a result, Jackson Kimball reported, "they are all watching for a chance to pounce on him." R. A. Booth was another recalcitrant, albeit one who created fewer enemies.[85]

From the mid-twenties, one of the Forest Service's greatest emphases in the pine country was selective logging. While much leadership in this campaign came from the Western Pine Association and David T. Mason, the Forest Service also played a major role. It pushed for selective cutting not only on its own pineland, but also on private holdings, served as a clearing house for information, and proselytized steadily for selective logging.[86]

Forest Service regulations had their greatest impact when timber sales on its land were involved. These not only determined what tracts would be cut and when, but also set standards for post-harvest clean-up. The regulations gradually came to address more and more details of harvest. In California, the agency tried to discourage destructive donkey and high-lead logging where other methods were applicable. On the Deschutes National Forest, George Drake bluntly ordered Jack Meister, Shevlin-Hixon's logging superintendent, to devise less-damaging methods than the tractor-logging techniques he initially used in the late 1920s.[87]

This Forest Service activity generated a certain amount of resistance, but many in the private sector had by the 1920s come to see the wisdom—even necessity—of pursuing approaches the agency advocated. But its policy of encouraging community development through new mills in places such as Burns and Lakeview was another matter. As markets became increasingly glutted in the late 1920s, criticism that the Forest Service was contributing to the problem grew. Lumbermen with sizable timber holdings had high carrying costs, putting them under pressure to bring their timber to market, a market in which they had to compete increasingly with lumber cut from Forest Service stands. The agency's timber did not represent significant financial investment by those who logged it and thus did not have the same burden of carrying costs; indeed, critics argued, there was no compelling need for the Forest Service to sell its timber until some future time when shortages had developed. In sum, through its timber sales, the Forest Service was accused of unfair competition that undermined the industry.

Forest Service spokesmen refused to accept blame for the industry's problems. They pointed with pride to their increased sales, which rose from 68.4 million feet a year in 1905 to over one billion feet in 1925 and continued to rise thereafter. The agency's policies, they insisted, contributed to the support of permanent industries and stable communities. Instead of being "undeveloped storage areas," they helped build new communities. Moreover, William B. Greeley argued, the dispersal of production that the sales brought was "essential to carry out the principle of continuous production contemplated by the organic law" under which the national forests had been set aside.[88]

Criticism mounted as overproduction grew and the price of lumber fell. At its annual meeting in 1927, the National Lumber Manufacturers' Association addressed the question. Wilson Compton, the organization's executive-secretary, argued not only that the Forest Service's sales were hurting the industry, but also that by selling timber for which there was little demand the agency was hurting the cause of conservation.[89] Greeley's annual report included a reply: the Forest Service was not forcing timber onto the market, and sales were "made only after careful consideration of the necessary balance between milling capacity and the growth of the timber and the part that Government timber should play in local economic development." Greeley's successor, Robert Y. Stuart, was more explicit. Those who called for a halt to Forest Service sales so as to save timber for the future were "short-sighted"; if the agency did as they proposed, it would be unable to provide any leadership in forestry—and, besides, "timber can not be stored indefinitely."[90]

Forest Service personnel had another reply too. They did not argue there was no glut, but rather that it was not their fault. Forest Service timber represented only a small portion of that being logged (from 1925 to 1930 it was 3.9 percent of the total in Oregon and Washington), and mills that its sales helped to bring into being—such the Hines mill outside of Burns—contributed far less to overproduction than the new Weyerhaeuser mills at Lewiston and Klamath Falls, each considerably larger and neither primarily dependent on public timber. The reply might readily have been extended to encompass a number of smaller mills too—such as that at Kinzua.[91]

There was much validity to this reply, but the private sector's contribution to the problem went beyond building new mills at a time when there was already more production than the market could readily absorb. The giant

Brooks-Scanlon and Shevlin-Hixon mills in Bend, built years before, contributed at least as much to the problem as new plants—and with considerably less justification.

Bend's sawmills were a great, final manifestation of the approach that had dominated lumbering in the Lake States, from whence their operators came. Theirs was a cut-out and get-out mentality. The owners sought to maximize profits on their investments in plant by forcing as much production from them as possible. There was no way forests around Bend could support permanent operations on the scale on which these mills operated, but no effort was made to balance the two. Indeed, when Bend's big mills were erected no one seems to have given any thought to what the area's forests could support over the long run or to the fact the interior pine country was the last of America's great forest frontiers. Both firms cut with abandon, each openly competing to outdo the other and constantly seeking new production records. In 1929, when other mills east of Oregon's Cascades were operating at a collective 64 percent of capacity, those in Bend were running double shifts and producing 130 percent of capacity based on

The Brooks-Scanlon sawmill and lumberyard in Bend in 1930. In the face of glutted markets and gathering depression, Brooks continued sawing apace. Courtesy Oregon State University Archives, #WilliamsG_CO_Brooks Scanlon1.

an eight-hour day—still cutting away as if there were no surplus and no tomorrow. In a community where not only the management, but also the bulk of the industry's workers had learned their trades in Minnesota in the days of cut-and-run forestry, few local voices questioned the wisdom of their approach.[92]

The sawmills in Bend may have represented a last flamboyant flowering of the lumberman's frontier,[93] but even in Bend there were significant differences from what had gone before. Initially, lumbermen had acquired timber in the area through such time-honored practices as dummy homestead entries and false affidavits, but the establishment of forest reserves and their increasingly intrusive administration by Forest Service personnel changed all that. Additional timber would have to be acquired through competitive bidding overseen by the technocrats of a new age. Timber harvest, fire protection, and other aspects of their operations would have to meet their mandates. Forest-farmers had no place in the emerging equation, and although people with a frame of reference established on earlier frontiers sometimes had other expectations, few with knowledge of the area seriously believed the land, once logged, was going to be turned into farms. Unlike in the Lake States, the South, and even west of the Cascades, there was no serious attempt to settle the cutover after logging cleared the area of its forest cover. This was and would remain a land of forests—but only for the moment forests on the lumberman's frontier.[94]

Differences aside, the forests of the Far West's interior represented the last phase in the long history of the lumberman's frontier of the United States. Gradually even these forest areas lost their frontier character. In some places, permanent industrial lumbering utilizing more and more second- and even third-growth timber succeeded the cutting of old-growth stands that had sustained the operations of pioneer lumbermen. In others, lumbering itself waned as recreation came to the forefront of forest uses. In yet others, the impact of ill-advised forest management policies led to a deterioration of forest quality that resulted in their becoming, if not a wasteland like Pennsylvania's desert of five million acres, degraded lands of little value for either commercial or recreational purposes. Regardless of their eventual fate, by the end of the 1920s America's last forest frontier was rapidly closing and by the 1950s, it had been so transformed that the days when it had been a vibrant, expansive center of lumbering had been relegated to the realm of history and local folk memory. The lumberman's frontier, ever-present from colonial times, was closed at last.

EPILOGUE

Whose Forests Are They?

The lumberman's frontier is closed, but there are forests still. Unlike the earlier lumbering frontiers, the Far West frontier closed not because commercial forests were gone—they were not—but because forest reserves and new management philosophies resulted in circumstances in which frontier approaches could no longer dominate. Yet echoes of old issues continue to be heard.

Conflicting claims of "ownership" of the forest have plagued Americans since before there was a United States and are with us still. Rhetoric emanating from the so-called "sagebrush rebellion" of the 1970s—whose leaders concerned themselves with forest as well as non-forest lands—had much the same tone and used arguments similar to those heard in colonial and early national times, such as those espoused by Samuel Ely. On the other side, the acid comments of critics of the movement often seemed to echo Ely's arch-enemy David Cobb.[1]

The longevity of such conflict stems in part from the fact that, unlike agricultural land, which, once settled, is recognized as the property of the farmer to use as he will with only slight interference, forestland—to a degree even that privately held—continues to be viewed as a sort of community property, the management of which the public can direct or at least regulate in rather intrusive ways. There were limits to Jeffersonian ideas about passing the public domain to smallholders; by and large the Jeffersonian vision encompassed only agricultural lands, including forestland that could be cleared for agriculture.

Today, as in earlier times, there are class overtones to conflicts over forest utilization. In a series of interviews with working-class residents of timber communities in the Far West, Beverly Brown repeatedly heard statements of despair as comfortable urbanites, in order to protect the environment and provide recreational amenities, sought to restrict or even eliminate uses that had long provided the economic backbone of forest communities. Stanley Norman, one of the interviewees, lived in Crescent City, California, when "Ladybird Johnson took a little tour and decided all this [redwood area] was going to be [a] park." Norman commented bitterly that outsiders, largely from the San Francisco Bay area, had the money and influence to push the idea through so that "*maybe* once every three or four years they could take a vacation and drive up through there and see those woods from the road." Establishing Redwood National Park "ruined a lot of lives," he maintained, and the town "died." Norman moved to Grants Pass, Oregon, and, hearing a rumor that a huge national park was proposed for *that* area too, asked sarcastically, "What will we all do? Become park rangers?"[2]

Norman was echoing a view voiced repeatedly during the 1960s. Arguments that the redwood park would create as many jobs in tourism as were lost from logging failed to alleviate disquiet. People who had spent their working lives in the woods and mills, who had accumulated expertise that provided a good living in invigorating outdoor work, and whose ambition frequently was to save enough money to buy their own logging truck or caterpillar tractor and thereby move up in the pecking order of woods workers—and sometimes had already managed to make the move—saw little appeal in service employment, perhaps running a motel or diner. Government programs to retrain displaced loggers for desk jobs were equally unattractive to people used to physical, outdoor work, who valued the independence involved in logging, and who took pride in their skill and success in dangerous jobs.[3] A logger in Washington State told Matthew Carroll, "I'd rather starve to death here and live off elk meat . . . than participate in any degrading plans to move me around and change my culture and life." A logger's wife put it bluntly with a sign in her front yard: "Retrain? If I'd wanted a CPA, I would have married one!!" In any case, as the *Grants Pass Daily Courier* observed, tourism is notable for part-time, low-paying jobs. Champions of the park seem to have little understood or sympathized with the social malaise and feelings of betrayal and despair these developments engendered—although most were not so blunt as the Reagan-era bureaucrat who dismissed the need to retrain loggers with the statement, "Anyone can find a new job; people do it all the time."[4]

Dwindling opportunities in lumbering were not limited to the redwood coast. Passage of the Wilderness Bill in 1964 and the subsequent creation of new wilderness areas, many forested, extended the pressure to loggers in other areas, but as most of the wilderness areas were in poorly accessible alpine areas where timber had slow growth rates and limited commercial value, the effect on industry was less dramatic than in the redwoods.[5] However, in the contest over wilderness status for French Pete, a heavily forested area on the west slope of Oregon's Cascades, the battle was intense.[6]

Log shipments to Japan had a wider impact. During the 1960s and 1970s, Japan entered a period of rapid economic growth and log imports from the Pacific Northwest boomed, rising from ninety-eight million board feet per year at the beginning of the period to 3.15 billion by its end. With Japanese buyers offering top dollar and timber supplies already limited, many West Coast mills were unable to obtain logs needed to remain in operation—or when they could locate them found that exports had helped drive prices out of reach (the price of No. 1 Douglas fir logs rose over 400 percent from 1950 to 1979, and the average cost of Douglas fir stumpage in westside national forests increased nine fold). Foresters and economists debated the effects of shipments, many arguing that exports created as many jobs as were eliminated in American sawmills, but to the general public—and unemployed woods and sawmill workers in particular—log exports seemed disastrous. Leading political figures, such as Oregon's Wayne Morse and Mark Hatfield, fought for an export ban similar to that enacted in British Columbia. In due course exports from federal forests *were* halted, but shipments from private forests continued—as did the bitterness of the industry's unemployed workers and their families.[7]

Loggers soon faced an additional threat: efforts to reduce or eliminate harvests in old-growth forests west of the Cascades in order to protect endangered northern spotted owls (and to a lesser degree, the marbled murrelet). Indeed, spotted owls and old-growth became icons for environmentalists, and after interminable debate the federal government implemented regulations that eliminated far more jobs in the timber industry than Redwood National Park, wilderness areas, or exports to Japan ever had. Bumper stickers and tee-shirts proliferated in forest communities suggesting among other things that spotted owls made a tasty stew. On a more intellectual level, critics of logging restrictions argued that the owl did not in fact need old growth for nesting, as was claimed—one forester told this author spotted owls were nesting in an abandoned apple orchard near his home on Bainbridge Island, Washington—and studies surfaced demonstrating that the species may be more endangered by hybridization with and competition from Alaskan barred owls and by inbreeding than by logging. Moreover, scientific advances—and a failure of the owls to rebound after restriction of logging—suggested key ecological assumptions underlying the positions of many environmentalists fighting to protect spotted owls were suspect.[8]

The problems confronting loggers were a product of structural changes within the industry as much as they were of parks, wilderness set-asides, log exports, and the protection of old-growth habitat for endangered species. With the price of logs skyrocketing, small and medium mills were increasingly unable to compete with large, integrated plants that could utilize small as well as large logs plus sawdust, slabs, and other mill residue.[9] Indicative of the situation, the number of wigwam burners—used to dispose of mill waste and long a symbol of the industry as well as a target of those who decried their contributions to air pollution—fell dramatically. Largely an adjunct of smaller mills, the number of wigwam burners in Oregon dropped 80 percent from 1968 to 1976. They soon ceased operation altogether, many remaining as silent, rusting reminders of days gone by. In the same period the number of small sawmills in the state fell from one hundred and twelve to fifty-one while large, integrated operations rose from fifty-nine to eighty-eight, increasing their share of total capacity by one-third.[10]

Meanwhile, improved highways and better trucks made it economically feasible to transport logs much greater distances, even as increased log values made transportation a declining portion of the cost of logs delivered to mills. Reflecting this, as early as 1957 the Bureau of Land Management dropped its policy of requiring logs from its land be sold to sawmills defined as in the marketing area where they were cut—a policy that had been designed to protect small, local mills. Together, these changes were more of a threat to local communities than the much-heralded restrictions on logging. Many a longtime lumber town—Westfir, Valsetz, Wendling, Sisters, and Kinzua, for example—saw their mills close, and several simply ceased to exist.[11]

Often difficulties developed at the local level even when sawmills did not close. To gain control of timberland, to eliminate competition at sales, or to furnish tax write-offs, large firms often bought small and medium-sized operations and consolidated control in corporate decision makers seemingly more concerned for the bottom line than for their employees or local conditions. The problem of insensitive, distant ownership was hardly new. As has been shown, it surfaced repeatedly in the Lake States—the mills of Bay City, Michigan, being a prime example—and in the Gulf South, but now, combined as it was with the other problems of forest communities, it engendered especially intense feelings of frustration and despair. Larry Lyon, a long-time resident of the Grants Pass area, typified the reaction; speaking of the purchaser of a local sawmill, he said "The guy . . . lives in San Francisco. . . . He doesn't care any more than the Japanese if this whole valley is stripped. He makes a fortune." Nor did all the buy-outs involve smaller companies. In Bend in 1950 Brooks-Scanlon purchased Shevlin-Hixon, while later in the decade a relatively small firm from the Southeast acquired Booth-Kelly, Coos Bay Lumber, and Pacific Spruce, all sizable Oregon operations, thereby launching the phenomenal growth that was to make Georgia-Pacific one of the nation's largest wood-products firms, but one in whose corporate thinking the interests of Oregonians played but a small part.[12]

Such developments reflected the increasing globalization of the economy. While its defenders see this as bringing more economically integrated, productive, and careful utilization of resources there are costs involved. In the process of internationalization, individual nations, citizens, and firms lose a bit of their independence; residents, workers in local (often outdated) sawmills, environmentalists, and those concerned with strictly local issues find themselves increasingly excluded from decision making. Participatory democracy and the efficacy of citizen activism suffer.

Those who struggle against these developments have often been misrepresented and misunderstood. Mark Hatfield and Wayne Morse had solid records on environmental issues, but when they argued for increasing the cut on national forests to support local, forest-dependent communities, they were castigated for pandering to voters or selling out to would-be industrial contributors. When protesters against the World Trade Organization and its policies took to the streets of Seattle in 2002, the interests of many among them were similar, but they were dismissed as hooligans and anarchists. Yet what they—and Hatfield and Morse before them—were doing was in many ways the same as the activities of locals of the Knights of Labor, of Ignatius Donnelly, and of the Populists, all of whom fought for local interests and the economically marginalized and had been misrepresented and abused for their efforts.[13]

Still, many environmentalists saw no reason to sympathize with the plight of loggers. For too long, they insisted, loggers had despoiled the land; the sooner they were gone, the better. As one said: "They're uneducated, they're crude, they're not people I would choose to be around. I don't think there's a defensible reason to keep these people doing what they're doing and keep them in their state of ignorance." Warming to his subject, he added: we need educational programs for them, "so they can spell, talk, and get along like the rest of us." Hostility showed up in other ways too. In 1977, the Forest History Society, then headquartered in Santa Cruz, California, co-sponsored a public exhibit of historic photographs of West Coast logging. Included was an enlarged photograph from the 1880s showing a pair of loggers standing beside a giant tree they were felling; across the length of their huge crosscut saw, a vandal painted "Murderers!" And words sometimes turned into action. The practice of "spiking" trees, once used by disgruntled workers in Pennsylvania and elsewhere as a weapon against unpopular or exploitive sawmill owners, now became a weapon used by environmental terrorists against workers and employers alike. Even David Cobb could hardly have exceeded such hostility.[14]

Antipathy toward loggers stemmed partially from the practices of companies that long continued to operate as if they were still in the frontier era, cutting with abandon and little concern for such things as reproduction or slash removal. In 1950, while traveling through central Oregon's Ochoco Mountains, a state forester told this author: you can always tell where the Hudspeth Lumber Company has cut, "they go through like a bear in a berry patch." When the firm went bankrupt some years later, few tears were shed—even in Prineville, where Hudspeth's sawmill was located.[15]

Similarly, William Greeley's concern for sustained-yield as a means of insuring community stability, a concern central to his efforts while Chief of the Forest Service in the 1920s, never won universal support. Repeatedly when the Forest Service or Bureau of Land management sought to bring cooperative, sustained-yield management to an area's public and private forests to support long-term community stability, the plans were defeated by private operators who insisted on going their own way. William G. Robbins refers to the idea of insuring community stability through forest management as a "naïve belief," but sustained-yield units were doomed not by the naïvete of foresters so much as by divisions within the industry. The result was often tragic. In the area around Bend a cooperative unit never emerged in spite of long-continued discussions; cutting continued apace, outstripping growth until the timber was gone and the mills closed.[16] Al Glassow, manager of Bend's Brooks-Scanlon plant, placed much of the blame for the failure on the Forest Service, whose operatives, he maintained, were more interested in enlarging the area's national forests than in establishing a cooperative sustained-yield unit.[17] Similarly, in southwestern Oregon, where there also was no cooperative sustained-yield unit, Georgia-Pacific commenced rapid cutting of its forests in the 1950s, seeking to take advantage of high prices to meet cash-flow demands and by liquidating its stands to generate capital for investment in the South, to which it was shifting its focus. Coos Bay was hard hit when Georgia-Pacific, its forestlands largely denuded, closed its big mill there in 1979—even as log exports from Coos Bay to Japan continued. Regardless of whether such things were the norm, they did nothing to assuage the feeling of many that lumbermen were not operating in the public interest.[18]

There were regional as well as class dimensions to conflicts over land use. Westerners had long felt put upon by Eastern decision makers insensitive to Western conditions and needs, while the management plans of foresters too often seemed based on theoretical knowledge gleaned from books and forestry school, rather than practical experience. As has been shown, Idaho's Weldon Heyburn and a number of leaders elsewhere in the West articulated such sentiments during the early twentieth century. Oregon's John Minto had agreed, but took a tack of his own, castigating the plans of federal foresters for being out of step with America's traditional Jeffersonian values that gave responsibility for land-use decisions to smallholders and others on or near the land. Although these ideas were not all dominant, they certainly were—and continued to be—widespread.

Discontent took many forms. In the early 1950s, Robert Smylie, Idaho's attorney-general (and soon to be governor), served as one of presidential candidate Dwight D. Eisenhower's advisors on Western affairs. Unlike Weldon Heyburn earlier, Smylie did not resort to state's-rights arguments nor maintain there was too much governmental activity. Difficulties stemmed, he argued, from a bureaucracy grown insensitive to local interests and needs. He proposed advisory committees of local people to serve as bridges between federal land management agencies and the public they served, committees with the experience to "give unbiased and technically sound advice on Departmental problems, especially in the West." The underlying idea lived on. Nearly four decades later, another Idaho official summed up the position simply: "the people . . . living in a locale of natural beauty and resources are the best stewards of the land." Dayton Hyde, a conservationist who ranched in the pine country north of Klamath Falls pinpointed part of the problem: Forest Service personnel

> *are transferred in for a few brief months or years, then transferred out, often before they have achieved an understanding of the land. Long after they are transferred on, I must live with those permanent changes they have wrought, suffer for their errors. I must live out my days as neighbor to this land, and what diminishes it diminishes me.*

To make matters worse, he argued, some of the agency's projects are undertaken not because they are truly needed, but because funds are available and would be lost if not used.[19]

Nor did attempts to combat outside control end; in 1993 Wyoming Senator Alan Simpson again gave voice to regional concerns, explaining that he and his allies were "defending a Western life style . . . [against the Clinton] Administration's war on the West." In spite of such statements, there still was no regional unanimity on the issue. Oregon's Senator Wayne Morse, for example, fought efforts to reduce federal control of the area's natural resources; and by defeating former Secretary of the Interior Douglas

McKay—whom he labeled "Giveaway Doug McKay"—in the election of 1956 made it clear to President Eisenhower and his advisors that there was considerable regional sympathy for continued federal stewardship of the land. Yet there were limits to Morse's support of federal activity. He opposed establishment of Oregon Dunes National Seashore, proposed to encompass magnificent Jessie Honeyman State Park and a sizable acreage of seaside forest, for the bill gave federal authorities power to take private property via condemnation (as he told a group of coastal residents, federal officials have "public property coming out their ears down here").[20]

Since Heyburn and Minto's day, the arguments of regional spokesmen opposing the federal role in Western affairs have been modified to make them sound more anti-bureaucratic than anti-intellectual, more libertarian than Jeffersonian, but the insistence of foresters and other experts that they know best what the forest needs continues to be widely viewed as arrogance. Both the implementation of user-fees for visitors entering various national forests and regulations on the use of snowmobiles and off-road vehicles within them are widely resented. Such regulations, often seen as catering to backpackers—on the whole, a comfortably well-off group—led to organizations, such as Idaho's Blue Ribbon Coalition, designed to push for access by motorized recreational vehicles and to bumper stickers reading "Sierra Club: Go Hike in Hell." As the agency often implementing these regulations, the Forest Service once again became a focal point for criticism. When one of this author's neighbors was confronted by a forest ranger for inappropriate activity and replied that what he was doing caused no harm, he was told: "Well, I can't allow it on *my* forest." My neighbor exploded: " 'My forest!' These aren't *your* forests, they're *mine*. They're public property!" His argument was that of the Fourth of July orator in Manistee, Michigan in 1840: the United States is the land of the people, "we are the people, ergo the land belongs to us." So common is this attitude today in Idaho that one of the state's major newspapers saw the need to run a lead editorial reminding citizens of the state "This Land Is Their Land Too." The editor was speaking not just of government forest managers but all outsiders who seek to shape policies for the West's public lands. Not everyone was convinced. In 2006, gubernatorial candidate Dan Adamson, a political newcomer, campaigned on the slogan "Idaho is for Idahoans" and, although not elected, garnered far more votes than most prognosticators had forecast.[21]

Nor is the Western sense of ownership of public lands limited to rhetoric. Stealing timber from public land—that time-honored practice of the lumberman's frontier—continues. Forest Service officials estimate that one in every ten trees cut on national forests is taken illegally, while major lumber companies claim that 3 percent of the trees felled on their lands are stolen, costing them some $350 million annually. A major black market in purloined logs has developed in the West. The thieves, officials claim, are mostly chronically unemployed men from traditional logging towns resentful over environmental restrictions that have sharply reduced logging. As one timber thief argued while incarcerated in Washington's Grays Harbor County jail, "To me it's like 'This land is your land, and this land is my land.' I'm taking my share. I don't really see it as stealing."[22]

Action took other forms as well. In 2002 residents of Grant County, Oregon, passed a ballot measure declaring, as the local newspaper put it, the "a right of citizens to participate in stewardship of natural resources on public lands." This was a matter of no little concern, for Malheur National Forest—where Edward Hines long operated—encompassed nearly 40 percent of the huge county and the Bureau of Land Management and National Park Service managed considerable additional acreage. Simultaneously, proponents pushed for a measure seeking transfer to the county of all federally owned land in Grant County and the creation of a local board to oversee forest management, a measure that essentially would have reduced the Forest Service to an advisory role. Driving all this was the fact "residents . . . feel they no longer control their lives, livelihoods or the land"—a feeling that also led them to declare the county a United Nations-free area. More was involved in the forest measures than the question of federal versus local control. Proponents saw the Forest Service as so hamstrung by environmental activists that it "hasn't been able to work as it should." Logging, thinning, and controlled burns had been so restricted the forests had become dense, with fuel loads so heavy that devastating fires were a constant threat. County Judge Dennis Reynolds, a supporter of the land management measures and former professional forester, was concerned that the United Nations measure undercut the forest proposals. He put it simply: "[W]e have to . . . remain focused on the forest and what the forest needs." Local editor David Carkhuff agreed; the vote against the United Nations illustrated how "emotional frustration can carry the day in elections," but it undermined chances the county would be taken seriously as it sought "relief from outrageous and unreasonable over-regulation" of its forests.[23]

Like other varieties, environmental politics makes strange bedfellows. The training of early-day foresters rested on a faith in science, as David Clary put it, "a technocratic outlook." Technical training and careful analysis could yield management programs that would avoid the mistakes of the past while making forest utilization efficient and sustainable. Through scientific forestry, public and private timberlands could be harvested repeatedly. Seeking to win public acceptance for this view, in the 1950s the Weyerhaeuser Timber Company launched a major advertising campaign featuring the slogan "Timber is a Crop."[24] But controversies surrounding the Viet Nam War created a new climate of opinion. Suspicion of government, of experts with their technological fixes, of absolute systems of knowledge, and of capitalism in general flourished. In this milieu, Westerners began to find new allies in their attacks on foresters and their programs. Environmental historians and others emerged who challenged the validity of many a long-held position of mainstream foresters, pointing out—among other things—flaws in their research and thus in conclusions based on it. William Robbins pinpointed the basic problem: normally "the logic of the marketplace and a production-oriented science, not the requirements of healthy ecosystems and streams, directed forest practices." Foresters, he wrote, suffer from "the overweening hubris of the profession"—although, one should add, it is a hubris shared in their own way by many of their environmental critics.[25]

The partnership of Westerners and environmentalists has never been an entirely happy one. Declensionist assumptions dominate much environmental thought, but are often not shared by Westerners who work the land, for they see it continuing productive year after year and many still hold the old idea that by bringing land into production—whether through agriculture or logging—they are implementing progress. Most seem to have rejected outright the "capture" thesis, which sees federal resource agencies as so dominated by their clients that the latter control policies. Jack Shepherd was one of the most outspoken champions of the capture thesis; by the 1960s, he maintained, the Forest Service had become a "Corporate Shill." Former Secretary of the Interior Walter Hickel launched a similar attack; as he put it, industry and the Forest Service had developed a "buddy" system. Although more scholarly, the works of Paul Hirt, William Robbins, and Richard Rajala are almost as critical—Robbins, for instance, speaking of "the close filial relationship" between big mills and the Forest Service and industry's "exclusive control" over Oregon's forest policies. The thesis has not gone unchallenged, especially by Paul J. Culhane, who subjected the idea to extended evaluation and found it wanting, and, more indirectly, by Christopher Klyza.[26] To many rural Westerners the debate is incomprehensible, for to them it seems clear "we" do not control, outsiders do. Local business interests might lobby for policies their leaders deem desirable, but usually to no avail; the seats of decision making lie elsewhere.[27]

An adversary relationship between rural Westerners and environmentalists is not inevitable. The former need not be the *bêtes noires* of the latter. In studying Orofino, Idaho, anthropologist Charlene James-Duguid found, seemingly to her surprise, that loggers love and strive to care for the woods. As one told her: "[S]how me a logger who doesn't think . . . [the woods are] the most beautiful place on earth and I'll show you a man who is not a logger." Another resident put it simply: "Loggers are environmentalists." Matthew Carroll heard much the same: most "loggers [are] much more environmentally conscious and much more concerned with the woods than the average person."[28]

Such statements make it seem there is common ground upon which environmentalists and locals could build a mutually satisfactory approach to forest management, but it has with few exceptions failed to come to pass.[29] Social distancing engenders stereotypes that make it difficult for each to hear and appreciate the arguments of the other. Even as more and more affluent Americans from urban areas moved into the timber country in search of the good life, inter-group communication remained minimal. Newcomers arrive with expectations and agendas and little appreciation for the outlook of previous residents. Local leaders might seek to attract outside investment and make their communities attractive to tourists or as a place of residence for outsiders, but they often discover, in Hal Rothman's term, that they had entered into "Devil's Bargains." Former lumber towns frequently found themselves transformed—and socially divided—by the influx of newcomers with values shaped elsewhere: Bend and Sisters, Oregon; Coeur d'Alene and McCall, Idaho; Prescott and Flagstaff, Arizona; Bainbridge Island and Port Ludlow, Washington: the list goes on and on. Speaking of southwestern Oregon, local resident Chuck Carter put it simply: "[A] lot of people . . . come in here and the first thing they'll want to do is start changing things." His wife went further. Speaking of the large influx of Californians, she said: "There's a lot of them moving in here . . . [and] they talk about, you know—the low-life Oregonians. And sort of cruelly. Like we're all backwards . . . just a bunch of dumb people . . . [from] Oregon where nothing's happening like in the Bay Area." Her bitterness was widely shared and led to such things as the bumper sticker widely seen in Oregon in the 1970s: "Don't Californicate Oregon!" Outsiders' purchases also drove up assessed land values—and thus taxes—while "No Trespassing" signs proliferated, barring old-timers from many a favorite fishing and hunting site, adding to the discontent. In such a social climate, communication between environmental champions (whether from outside the area or recent transplants) and locals with a deep-seated love of the land remained minimal. The fact locals tended to view environmentalists as interlopers with no legitimate stake in the battles over forest management and little knowledge of the forest itself exacerbated difficulties.[30]

But if there had been more communication, agreement would still have been difficult to reach. When long-time residents talked of protecting forests, their arguments usually focused on reforestation and keeping the land productive.[31] Weyerhaeuser's "Timber is a Crop" campaign took the same tack. But to environmentalists, monocultural forests, which they saw as the end product of such an approach, were undesirable. The protection of ecological diversity was one of their major goals; among other things this meant opposing the clearcutting of blocks of Douglas fir, protecting riparian stands, and saving much of the remaining old growth. Weyerhaeuser's campaign had reflected post-frontier ideas about the forest, but now it was as dated as the old cut-and-run policies of the frontier period—at least in the eyes of activists whose outlook reflected a post-industrial society.

Environmentalists and bureaucrats are not the only cause of distress for residents of forest communities. As well-to-do outsiders moved into more and more places, they valued the forests for their amenity values more than timber. Imbued with elitist assumptions and a consumption ethic that relative affluence made possible, they tended to look askance at the production ethic of an earlier age and to denigrate those who found meaning in hard, physical work, the very things that were at the heart of the value systems of many old-time residents. Few newcomers acknowledged that their post-industrial activities were as destructive of the natural qualities that had drawn them to their new places of residence as lumbering had been earlier. Foresters had long worked to try to determine what level of cutting was sustainable, but there seemed to be far less concern for the recreational carrying capacity of the land and whether the hordes of newcomers were loving it to death. As Richard White put it in connection with Island County, Washington: "In many ways it is still a pleasant place, but there is . . . no guarantee that the scenery [new] residents and visitors have discovered will survive exploitation any longer than did the other resources already depleted." One area resident, disturbed by development in and around Bend, complained bitterly to this author, insisting he would leave if he could. He was not alone in his distress. Throughout the West, alarm over runaway growth has increased, and by 2002 in state after state expenditures for open space were rising dramatically.[32]

Forests continue to draw the less affluent too. The homeless and dropouts flock to them to find a place where they can exist without falling into the maw of urban slumdom, just as many people moved to the forested outback of early Maine to find a life outside the commercial-industrial mainstream. Dee Southard recounts how thousands of "non-recreational campers" seek refuge in the woods, moving ever onward as the standard fourteen-day limit on stays drives them from one public campground to another. Others squat on vacant land or buy cheap, isolated tracts to build modest shacks for their families or a commune of like-minded individuals. There they find the means of survival—hunting and fishing, collecting forest mushrooms for sale, stealing timber for the black market in logs, or raising marijuana. Foresters report that in places this last activity has become so common, and its practitioners so militant in defense of their crops, that they fear to go into the woods alone—even when they are on their own or their employer's land.[33]

Thus, in the final analysis, America's forests are still a frontier between the settled and unsettled, a place where, just as they have from the time of the earliest European settlements in North America, rich and poor alike continue to seek meaning and a good life—however they might define it—in wild and open space. The old contests over who has a right to use those forests and how continue. There may no longer be a lumberman's frontier, but the forestlands remain a frontier nonetheless—albeit a post-industrial one. And on this, just as in earlier times, the questions of "whose forests are they" and how should they be used continues to vex American society. It is a question that seems as intractable as ever.

Notes

Frequently Cited Journals

AF	*American Forests*
Ag. Hist.	*Agricultural History*
AL	*American Lumberman*
CL	*Canada Lumberman*
FCH	*Forest & Conservation History*
FH	*Forest History*
IY	*Idaho Yesterdays*
JAH	*Journal of American History*
JF	*Journal of Forestry*
JFH	*Journal of Forest History*
JSH	*Journal of Southern History*
JW	*Journal of the West*
Mich. Hist.	*Michigan History*
Minn. Hist.	*Minnesota History*
MVHR	*Mississippi Valley Historical Review*
OHQ	*Oregon Historical Quarterly*
PHR	*Pacific Historical Review*
PNQ	*Pacific Northwest Quarterly*
SL	*Southern Lumberman*
Timb.	*The Timberman*
WHQ	*Western Historical Quarterly*
Wis. Mag. Hist.	*Wisconsin Magazine of History*

Chapter One

1. Jared Eliot, *Essays Upon Field Husbandry in New England and Other Papers, 1748-1762*, Harry J. Carman, ed. (New York: AMS Press, 1967), 7; William Cronon, *Changes in the Land: Indians, Colonists, and the Ecology of New England* (New York: Hill & Wang, 1983), 54-81, 127-56.
2. Isaac Weld, *Travels through the States of North America, and Provinces of Upper and Lower Canada, during the Years 1795, 1796, and 1797* (4th ed.; 2 vols.; London: Stockdale, 1807), 1: 32, 39-41; Markham quoted in Stevenson Whitcomb Fletcher, *Pennsylvania Agriculture and Country Life, 1640-1840* (Harrisburg: Pennsylvania Historical and Museum Commission, 1950), 2; Tycho de Boer, *Nature, Business, and Community in North Carolina's Green Swamp* (Gainesville: University Press of Virginia, 2008), 38-41, 44-46.
3. Quoted in Richard G. Lillard, *The Great Forest* (New York: Knopf, 1948), 138. See also: Charles F. Carroll, *The Timber Economy of Puritan New England* (Providence, R.I.: Brown University Press, 1973), 57-71, 123-28; Timothy Silver, *A New Face on the Countryside: Indians, Colonists, and Slaves in South Atlantic Forests, 1500-1800* (Cambridge, U.K.: Cambridge University Press, 1990), 115-16, 129-34; Michael Williams, *Americans and their Forests: A Historical Geography* (Cambridge, U.K.: Cambridge University Press, 1989), 5, 53-110.

4. John Smith, *The Complete Works of Captain John Smith (1580-1631)*, Philip L. Barbor, ed. (3 vols.; Chapel Hill: University of North Carolina Press, 1986), 1: 206, 238, 263; William Bradford, *History of Plymouth Plantation, 1620-1647*, W. C. Ford, ed. (2 vols.; Boston: Houghton Mifflin, 1912), 1: 235.

5. Silver, *New Face on the Countryside*, 116; Louis C. Hunter, *A History of Industrial Power in the United States, 1780-1930*, vol. 1: *Waterpower in the Century of the Steam Engine* (Charlottesville: University Press of Virginia, 1979), 2-3, 7-8, 29; Philip Alexander Bruce, *Economic History of Virginia in the Seventeenth Century* (2 vols.; New York: Macmillan, 1896), 2: 429-32, 491 (1st quote, p. 429; 2nd quote, p. 491); James Elliott Defebaugh, *History of the Lumber Industry of America* (2 vols.; Chicago: American Lumberman, 1906-1907), 2: 496-99, 556-59; Carl Bridenbaugh, *The Colonial Craftsman* (New York: New York University Press, 1950), 18-24; William F. Fox, *History of the Lumber Industry in the State of New York*, Sixth Annual Report, New York Forest, Fish, and Wildlife Commission (Albany: State Printer, 1901), 12-15. The Dutch had long used wind- and water-powered mills; the English, by contrast, depended upon hand-sawn planks to meet their needs. England's sawyers were largely responsible; fearing for their jobs, they discouraged sawmills through riots, sabotage, and other means. Defebaugh, *History of the Lumber Industry*, 2: 9; Hunter, *Waterpower*, 7, 15, 19, 29, 44-46; Bruce, *Economic History*, 2: 430.

6. Everett S. Stackpole, *Old Kittery and Her Families* (Lewiston, Me.: Lewiston Journal, 1903), 13, 20, 22-25, 130, 311-12; Stackpole, "The First Permanent Settlement in Maine," *Sprague's Journal of Maine History*, 14 (1926): 193; Philip T. Coolidge, *History of the Maine Woods* (Bangor, Me.: Furbush-Roberts, 1963), 21-23; Carroll, *Timber Economy*, 70-71. Numerous sources date Mason's mill from 1631, but that was the date of establishment of his plantation and building of the Great House; the sawmill was erected in 1634. In this case, the technology was Danish. Defebaugh, *History of the Lumber Industry*, 2: 6-9, 21, 63-66. On Mason, see: John W. Dean, ed., *Capt John Mason, Founder of New Hampshire* (Boston: Prince Society, 1887).

7. Leland J. Bellott, *William Knox: The Life and Thought of an Eighteenth-Century Imperialist* (Austin: University of Texas Press, 1977), 71-72, 110. However, lumbering developed slowly in the South partly because stands of longleaf pine and bald cypress, the region's best lumber species, grew on lands poorly suited for agriculture. Silver, *New Face on the Countryside*, 121; J. A. Prestridge, "Cypress from Ancient to Modern Times," *SL*, 193 (1956): 166-69; Defebaugh, *History of the Lumber Industry*, 1: 7-45, 301-331; Charles S. Sargent, *Report on the Forests of North America (Exclusive of Mexico)*, Tenth Census of the United States, Vol. 9 (Washington, DC: GPO, 1884), esp. 3-6, 494-512; Cronon, *Changes in the Land*, 19-33.

8. On the availability of waterpower, see: Hunter, *Waterpower*, 114-39.

9. Earl of Bellomont to Lords of Trade, 22 June 1700, in E. B. O'Callaghan, ed, *Documents Relative to the Colonial History of the State of New York . . .* (11 vols.; Albany, NY: Weed-Parsons, 1853-1887), 4: 668-79 (quotes, pp 670, 674). For the best attempt at quantification, see: Williams, *Americans and their Forests*, 53-110. See also: Carroll, *Timber Economy*, 62-97, 123-24, 135-36, 206; James F. Shepherd and Gary F. Walton, *Shipping, Maritime Trade,*

and the Economic Development of Colonial North America (Cambridge, U.K.: Cambridge University Press, 1972).

10. Bellomont to Lords of Trade, 22 June 1700, O'Callaghan, *Documents of New York*, 4: 668-79 (quote p 678). See also: ibid., 25 May 1700, 4: 645.

11. Carroll, *Timber Economy*, 125-28; Cronon, *Changes in the Land*, 108-26; Jamie H. Eves, "Yankee Immigrants: Ecological Crisis and the Settlement of Maine, 1763-1825" (unpub. M.A. thesis, University of Maine, 1988), 12-25, 66-67; Carl A. Bridenbaugh, "Yankee Use and Abuse of the Forest in the Building of New England," *Proceedings of the Massachusetts Historical Society*, 89 (1977): 3-35; Peter W. Dunwiddie, "Forest and Heath: The Shaping of the Vegetation on Nantucket Island," *JFH*, 33 (1989): 130-33; Silver, *New Face on the Countryside*, 107-33; Alan S. Taylor, "Liberty-Men and White Indians: Frontier Migration, Popular Protests, and the Pursuit of Property in the Wake of the American Revolution" (unpub. Ph.D. diss, Brandeis University, 1985), 37-42. For a shorter, heavily revised version of this last work, see: Taylor, *Liberty Men and Great Proprietors: The Revolutionary Settlement of the Maine Frontier, 1760-1820* (Chapel Hill: University of North Carolina Press, 1990).

12. John Nelson to Lords of Trade, 12 Dec. 1697, in Maine Historical Society, *Collections*, Second Series, *Documentary History of the State of Maine* (24 vols.; Portland: Maine Historical Society, 1869-1916 [hereafter, MHS, *Doc. Hist.*]), 10: 15; Bellomont to Lords of Trade, 2 June 1700, O'Callaghan, *Documents of New York*, 4: 668-79 (quote, p. 675).

13. Bellomont to Lords of Trade, 2 Jan. 1701, O'Callaghan, *Documents of New York*, 4: 820-27 (quote, p. 825). Earlier New York's council had ordered "no Tree bee cut for planks or other use for sale, but from the latter end of November to the beginning of March, and the tree not to bee lesse than twenty inches through." Quoted in New York, "Forest Commission Report, 1886," in *New York Assembly Documents, 1887*, no. 104 (Albany: State Printer, 1888), 29.

14. Jeremiah Drummer to David Dunbar, 26 Mar. 1729, in MHS, *Doc. Hist.*, 10: 432-33.

15. Quoted in Eves, "Yankee Immigrants," 67.

16. Ibid., 34-70. The flight from environmentally degraded areas continued during the years that followed. See: Taylor, *Liberty Men*, 61-66; Richard W. Judd, *Common Lands, Common People: The Origins of Conservation in Northern New England* (Cambridge, Mass.: Harvard University Press, 1997), 64-67.

17. Eves, "Yankee Immigrants," 1-6, 77-82, 92-144; Dunwiddie, "Forest and Heath," 130-33; Bridenbaugh, "Yankee Use and Abuse of the Forest," 32-35; William Douglass, *A Summary, Historical and Political, of the First Planting, Progressive Improvements, and Present State of the British Settlements in North America* (2 vols.; Boston: Rogers and Fowle, 1749-51), 2: 54.

18. Yasuhide Kawashima and Ruth Tone, "Environmental Policy in Early America: A Survey of Colonial Statutes," *JFH*, 27 (1983): 168-79; J. P Kinney, *Forest Legislation in America Prior to March 4, 1789*, Cornell University Department of Forestry, bulletin 370 (Ithaca, N. Y.: Cornell University, 1916), 361-63, 371-89; Lillian M. Willson, *Forest Conservation in Colonial Times* (St. Paul, Minn.: Forest Products History Foundation, 1948), 7-17; Ralph M.

Van Brocklin, "The Movement for the Conservation of Natural Resources in the United States before 1901" (unpub. Ph.D. diss., University of Michigan, 1952), 4-10; Defebaugh, *History of the Lumber Industry*, 2: 16; Douglass, *Summary, Historical and Political*, 2: 54, 68, 296 (1st quote); Thomas R. Cox et al., *This Well-Wooded Land: Americans and their Forests from Colonial Times to the Present* (Lincoln: University of Nebraska Press, 1985), 40 (2nd quote). See also: Peter Kalm, *Travels into North America*, John Reinhold Foster, trans. (Barre, Mass.: Imprint Society, 1972), 74; Weld, *Travels through the States of North America*, 32.

19. Gilbert Chinard, "The American Philosophical Society and the Early History of Forestry in America," *Proceedings of the American Philosophical Society*, 89 (1945): 484 (Vaughan quote). See also: Judd, *Common Lands, Common People*, 25-35. In other ways too, colonists sought to save labor while consuming wood. Rather than build small, fuel-efficient fireplaces and stoves, they rolled long logs into huge, open fireplaces; most of the heat went up the chimneys, thus requiring far more wood to keep a home warm than otherwise would have been the case. They thus wasted wood, but saved the labor that would have been necessary to cut the fuel smaller.

20. Warren C. Scoville, "Did Colonial Farmers 'Waste' Our Land?" *Southern Economic Journal*, 20 (1953): 178-81; Cox et al., *This Well-Wooded Land*, 34-37. Scoville's efforts at quantification have been questioned, but not his basic point. See: Roger W. Weiss, "Mr. Scoville on Colonial Land Wastage," *Southern Economic Journal*, 21 (1954): 87-90.

21. Harry J. Carman, ed., *American Husbandry* (New York: Columbia University Press, 1939), 84-85, 142, 318, 346; Tenche Coxe, *View of the United States of America* . . . (Philadelphia: Hill, 1794), 450-57; Fletcher, *Pennsylvania Agriculture and Country Life*, 326. This would long continue. Michael Williams has demonstrated that to 1860 agricultural clearing was the overwhelming cause of reduction of forest acreage. Williams, *Americans and their Forests*, 111-28.

22. The phrase is Brook Hindle's. See: Hindle, ed., *America's Wooden Age: Aspects of Its Early Technology* (Tarrytown, N.Y.: Sleepy Hollow Press, 1975); Hindle, ed., *Material Culture of the Wooden Age* (Tarrytown, N.Y.: Sleepy Hollow Press, 1981). However, see also: Charles van Ravenswaay, "America's Age of Wood," *Proceedings of the American Antiquarian Society*, 80 (1970): 49-66.

23. Carroll, *Timber Economy*, 63-65, 68-71; Hans Huth and Wilma J. Pugh, trans. & ed., "Talleyrand in America as a Financial Promoter, 1794-96: Unpublished Letters and Memoirs," *Annual Report of the American Historical Association for the Year 1941* (2 vols.; Washington, GPO, 1942), 2: 71; Silver, *New Face on the Countryside*, 116-17, 121.

24. Taylor, *Liberty Men*, 75-78 and passim; Williams, *Americans and their Forests*, 53-81; David C. Smith, "Maine's Changing Landscape to 1820," in Charles E. Clark, James S. Leamon, and Karen Bowden, ed., *Maine in the Early Republic* (Hanover, N.H.: University Press of New England, 1988), 13-25; David C. Smith, "The Harvest Cycle in Nineteenth Century Maine," in Duncan Howlett, ed., *The Small Woodland Owner in Maine*, Technical Note 85 (Orono: University of Maine, College of Forest Resources, 1982), 9-11.

25. Selectmen of Winthrop to Thomas Hutchinson and General Court, 8 Mar. 1773, MHS, *Doc. Hist.*, 14: 191.

26. John Spencer Bassett, ed., *The Writings of Colonel William Byrd of Westover* . . . (1901; reprint, New York: Burt Franklin, 1970), 75-76, 80 (1st quote, p. 75; 2nd quote, p. 80). See also: de Boer, *Nature, Business, and Community*, 40-50, 53-54.

27. Anonymous, "Reminiscences of a Former Resident of New Meadows," *Collections of the Pejepscot Historical Society*, 1 (1889): pt. 2, p. 46.

28. William Willis, ed., *Journals of the Rev Thomas Smith and the Rev Samuel Deane* . . . (2nd ed.; Portland, Me.: Bailey, 1849), 85.

29. Minutes of meetings of proprietors, 10 and 27 Sept., 28 Nov. 1716, Pejepscot Purchase Co. papers (Maine Historical Society, Portland), 1: 85 (quote, 27 Sept.). See also: Minutes of meetings of proprietors, 5 Sept. and 28 Nov. 1716, 14 Oct. 1717, 23 Apr. 1718, 11 Nov. 1719, MHS, *Doc. Hist.*, 24: 273-74, 294-95, 298, 303-304, 307; John Nelson to proprietors, 13 Sept. 1716, ibid., 288. The Pejepscot proprietors obtained their grant in 1714. It became Topsham township in 1717, giving settlers municipal rights although they could not take part in the affairs of the commonwealth of Massachusetts of which Maine was then a part. Largely abandoned during Lovell's War of 1722-1726, settlement resumed about 1730. In 1739 Topsham was divided, creating the new township of Brunswick. Harry W. Wheeler, "Brunswick at the Time of Its Incorporation," *Collections of the Pejepscot Historical Society*, 1 (1889): pt. 1, pp. 21-23.

30. Wheeler, "Brunswick at Incorporation," 24. As one settler recalled, "a sterile soil, droughts, and early frosts . . . often cut off the hopes of the husbandman, and to remedy this, recourse was had in winter to lumbering, getting out mill logs to be sawed into boards for sale." See: Anonymous, "Reminiscences of a Former Resident," 49-50.

31. Wheeler, "Brunswick at Incorporation," 33-34.

32. Belcher Noyes to Adam Hunter, 12 May 1753, Pejepscot papers, 4: 101. Protection of proprietary rights was complicated by the overlapping claims of other companies. See: Gordon E. Kershaw, *The Kennebeck Proprietors, 1749-1775* (Portland: Maine Historical Society, 1975), 150, 159-62, and passim; Alan Taylor, " 'A Kind of Warr': The Contest for Land on the Northeastern Frontier, 1750-1820," *William and Mary Quarterly*, 3rd series, 46 (1989): 3-26.

33. The Kennebeck Proprietors had already decided upon such a course. Until 1758, they recognized the king's claims to mast trees on their grant, but thereafter gave those with land they sold, although they now demanded "one half of all the wood which shall be hauled to waterside." See: Kershaw, *Kennebeck Proprietors*, 104-105.

34. Enoch Freeman to Noyes, 16 Sept. 1763, Pejepscot papers, 5: 33-36. See also: ibid., 1 and 21 Nov. 1763, 3 Apr. 1764; Noyes to Freeman, 12 Nov. 1763, ibid. Freeman was "somewhat arrogant and overbearing, [but] he was a man of great integrity and moral worth, and faithful and prompt in the discharge of the duties . . . with which he was intrusted." William Willis, *The History of Portland from 1632 to 1864* . . . (2nd ed.; Portland, Me.: Bailey and Noyes, 1865), 807.

35. Quoted in Kershaw, *Kennebeck Proprietors*, 163.

36. Noyes to Selectmen of Brunswick, 31 Mar. 1779, Pejepscot papers, 3: 199-200. See also: Adam Winthrop et al., power of attorney, 12 July 1737, ibid.,

6: 137; Henry Gibbs et al., power of attorney, 30 Nov. 1752, ibid., 3: 158-59; Isaac Royal, Belcher Noyes, and Samuel Waterhouse, power of attorney, 23 July 1763, ibid., 2: 220; Noyes to Hunter, 22 Nov. 1752, ibid, 4: 99.

37. Edward E. Bourne, *The History of Wells and Kennebunk from the Earliest Settlements* . . . (Portland, Me.: Thurston, 1875), 47.

38. Ibid., 49 (1st quote), 110, 112-14, 185, 431(2nd quote); Huth and Pugh, "Talleyrand in America," 74. See also: David R. Foster and John D. Aber, ed., *Forests in Time: The Environmental Consequences of 1,000 Years of Change in New England* (New Haven: Yale University Press, 2004), 72-82.

39. Report on new plantation at Casco Bay, 16 Aug. 1680, MHS, *Doc. Hist.*, 4: 399. See also: Leonard B. Chapman, "The First Occupancy by Europeans at Saccarappa Falls . . . " in Maine Historical Society, *Collections and Proceedings*, 2nd series (10 vols.; Portland: Maine Historical Society, 1890-99 [hereafter, MHS, *Coll. & Proc.*]), 10: 282-86.

40. Sundry inhabitants of Exeter to Francis Nicolson, 4 Dec. 1713, New Hampshire, *Provincial and State Papers* (18 vols.; Concord, N.H.: State Printer, 1867-1890), 11: 646-47. For discussions of this commerce, see: Cox et al., *This Well-Wooded Land*, 13-24; Richard Pares, *Yankees and Creoles: The Trade Between North America and the West Indies before the American Revolution* (London: Longmans Green, 1956), 38, 41-43, 154-56, 158-59; Byron Fairchild, *Messrs William Pepperell: Merchants at Piscataqua* (Ithaca, N.Y.: Cornell University Press, 1954), 36-37, 52, 54-55, 71-72, 75-76.

41. On New England's early fisheries, see: Douglass, *Summary, Historical and Political*, 1: 298-304, 537-40; Jeremy Belknap, *History of New Hampshire* . . . (2nd ed.; 3 vols.; Boston: Bradford & Read, 1812-1813), 3: 157-60, 170; Edwin A. Churchill, "A Most Ordinary Lot of Men: The Fishermen of Richmond Island, Maine, in the Early Seventeenth Century," *New England Quarterly*, 57 (1984): 184-204; William Hutchinson Rowe, *The Maritime History of Maine: Three Centuries of Shipbuilding and Seafaring* (New York: Norton, 1948), 20-32; Roger F. Duncan, *Coastal Maine: A Maritime History* (New York: Norton, 1992), 107-123.

42. On the limitations of coastal North Carolina, see: D.W. Meinig, *The Shaping of America: A Geographical Perspective on 500 Years of History*, vol. 1: *Atlantic America, 1492-1800* (New Haven, Conn.: Yale University Press, 1986), 158, 173, 177-78, 180, 183, 190; Hunter, *Waterpower*, 132-33; de Boer, *Nature, Business and Community*, 26-30.

43. Carroll, *Timber Economy*, 75-119. For more general descriptions, see: Rowe, *Maritime History of Maine*, 13-19; Duncan, *Coastal Maine*, 178-89. On the ships-forests connection, see: Robert Greenhalgh Albion, *Forests and Seapower: The Timber Problem of the Royal Navy, 1652-1862* (Cambridge, Mass.: Harvard University Press, 1926); Ronald L. Pollitt, "Wooden Walls: English Seapower and the World's Forests," *FH*, 15 (1971): 6-15.

44. Report of commissioners, 14 Dec. 1665, MHS, *Doc. Hist.*, 4: 297; Jonathan Bridger to Lords of Trade, 27 Mar. 1709, ibid., 9: 267-70; Jeremiah Dummer to David Dunbar, 26 Mar. 1729, ibid., 10: 432; Willis, *History of Portland*, 103-104, 448-50; Carroll, *Timber Economy*, 115. In 1681 forty-seven vessels entered the Piscataqua for lumber. Defebaugh, *History of the Lumber Industry*, 2: 15.

45. Bane & Nowell, agreement, 13 June 1741, Pejepscot papers, 4: 437; John Dunning, deposition, 24 May 1808, ibid., 4: 273-76 (quote, p. 273); Huth and Pugh, "Talleyrand in America," 2: 74, 80 (quote).

46. Edward Russell, "History of North Yarmouth," Maine Historical Society, *Collections*, 1st series (10 vols.; Portland: Maine Historical Society, 1865-1891[hereafter, MHS, *Coll.*]), 2: 181; Defebaugh, *History of the Lumber Industry*, 2: 85; David C. Smith, personal communication, 1 Nov. 1985. Other tide mills antedated Winslow's. See: Charles Edward Banks, *History of York, Maine* (3 vols.; Boston: Calkins, 1935), 2: 64-65, 245.

47. Robert Armstrong, defense, 6 Jan. 1724, MHS, *Doc. Hist.*, 4: 167 (1st quote); John Wheelwright, petitions, 3 Nov. 1693 and 30 May 1694, ibid., 5: 393-94, 398-99 (Wheelwright quotes); William Dummer to John Gyles, 27 May 1727, ibid., 10: 399; minutes of meeting of proprietors, 11 Nov. 1719, ibid., 24: 307; John R. Ham, *Localities of Ancient Dover* (Concord, N.H.: Republican Press, 1887), 17; Willis, "History of Portland," MHS, *Coll. & Proc.*, 1: 250-51; Samuel T. Dole, "Ancient Naquamqueeg," ibid., 7: 405; Bourne, *History of Wells and Kennebunk*, 110-11.

48. Jonathan Bridger to Lords of Trade, 26 Aug. 1718, MHS, *Doc. Hist.*, 9: 424-25; Nathaniel Jones and Nathaniel Look to Higginson & Co, 18 Jan. 1737, ibid., 11: 174-75; Taylor, *Liberty Men*, 24-29; Edward C. Cass, "A Town Comes of Age: Pownalborough, Maine, 1720-1785" (unpub. Ph.D. diss, University of Maine, 1979), 75-76; Louise Helen Coburn, *Skowhegan on the Kennbec* (2 vols.; Skowhegan, Me.: Independent-Reporter, 1941), 1: 84; warrant for seizure of lumber, 2 Nov. 1739, New Hampshire, *Provincial and State Papers*, 3: 202-203, 11: 648-49.

49. Belknap, *History of New Hampshire*, 3: 105-106; Philemon Warner to Spencer Phipps, 25 May 1751, MHS, *Doc. Hist.*, 12: 112; Andrew Burnaby, *Travels through the Middle Settlements in North America in the Years 1759 and 1760* (London: Payne, 1775), 87 (quote); Joseph J. Malone, *Pine Trees and Politics: The Naval Stores and Forest Policy of Colonial New England, 1691-1775* (Seattle: University of Washington Press, 1964), 47-56; Dole, "Ancient Naquamqueeg," 405; Ham, *Ancient Dover*, 12, 17; Mary P. Thompson, *Landmarks in Ancient Dover, New Hampshire* (1865; reprint, Durham, N.H.: Durham Historic Assoc., 1965), 127, 140-43.

50. Fox, *Lumber Industry of New York*, 35-36, is the apparent source of New York's claims to primacy. The work's author was a descendant of one of the brothers purportedly responsible for that state's first log drives.

51. [W. Woodford Clayton], *History of York County, Maine* (Philadelphia: Everts & Peck, 1880), 292, 297; Fannie Hardy Eckstorm, "Lumbering in Maine," in *Maine: A History*, Louis Clinton Hatch, ed. (5 vols.; New York: American Historical Society, 1919), 3: 689; Defebaugh, *History of the Lumber Industry*, 2: 130. For a time the Great Works was also known as Chadbourne's River. See: James Sullivan, *History of the District of Maine* (Boston: Thomas and Andrews, 1795), 20.

52. Wheelwright, petition, 30 May 1694, MHS, *Doc. Hist.*, 5: 398-99; account of losses sustained at Falmouth, Oct. 1775, ibid., 14: 305-310; George Foster Talbot, "James Shepherd Pike," in MHS, *Coll. & Proc.*, 1: 253; Charles S. Forbes, "The Story of the Presumpscot," ibid., 5: 378. Cf. Kershaw, *Kennebeck*

Proprietors, 105. Not all the action was in Maine. By 1726 logs were being driven down the Connecticut River; legislation protecting the practice soon followed. William B. Weeden, *Economic and Social History of New England, 1620-1789* (2 vols.; New York: Houghton Mifflin, 1963), 2: 578; Charles E. Clark, *The Eastern Frontier: The Settlement of Northern New England, 1610-1763* (New York: Knopf, 1970), 205; Kinney, *Forest Legislation Prior to 1789*, 399-400.

53. For an introduction to European practices, see: Raymond Viney, "L'Évolution du commerce des bois," *Revue forestière française*, 29 (1977): 27-37.

54. Thompson, *Landmarks in Ancient Dover*, 27-28.

55. Dole, "Ancient Naquamqueeg," 7: 406-407 (quote); Chapman, "The First Occupancy of Saccarappa," MHS, *Coll. & Proc.*, 10: 282-300; Clark, *Eastern Frontier*, 205. Cf. New Hampshire, *Provincial and State Papers*, 11: 539-40; Frank W. Hackett, "The Bellamy River Mill Suit," *Granite Monthly*, 5 (1882): 95; Forbes, "The Story of the Presumpscot," 5: 287, 382-83; Cotton Mather, *Magnalia Christi Americana* . . . (2 vols.; Hartford, Conn.: Andrus & Son, 1853-1855), 2: 592.

56. In any case, they were being used for these purposes well before 1789 when Maine's first boom was supposedly built on the Androscoggin. In 1790 residents of Machias reported: "[T]his spring a high freshet carried away the boom across the river, by which means 3000 logs went over the dam & the loss by this misfortune at the lowest estimate cannot be less than [£]630." The mills at Machias had been in operation for almost thirty years and had long since regularized operations. There was a boom there as early as 1776, and it may have been used to store logs from the first. Richard G. Wood, *A History of Lumbering in Maine, 1820-1861*, University of Maine Studies, 2nd series, no. 33 (1935; reprint, Orono: University of Maine Press, 1971), 130; selectmen of Machias, petition (and report thereon), 13 Jan. 1790, MHS, *Doc. Hist.*, 22: 307-308; George W. Drisko, *Narrative of the Town of Machias: The Old and the New, The Early and the Late* (Machias, Me.: Press of the Republican, 1904), 55.

57. Jonathan Bridger to William Popple, 1 July 1718, MHS, *Doc. Hist.*, 9: 395; Jonathan Dunbar to Popple, 29 Dec. 1729, ibid., 11: 4. On Dunbar, see: Malone, *Pine Trees and Politics*, 91-123 and passim; Belknap, *History of New Hampshire*, 2: 81-82, 89-93.

58. Bridger to Lords of Trade, 26 Aug. 1718, MHS, *Doc. Hist.*, 9: 424-25; Dunbar to Popple, 29 Dec. 1727, ibid., 11: 4 (quotes); documents regarding the riots at Exeter, New Hampshire, *Provincial and State Papers*, 18: 52-59; Belknap, *History of New Hampshire*, 2: 89-92; Timothy Dwight, *Travels in New England and New York*, Barbara Miller Solomon, ed. (4 vols.; Cambridge, Mass: Belknap Press of Harvard University Press, 1969), 1: 302-303; Malone, *Pine Trees and Politics*, 111-13.

59. For an early description of the use of wheels in moving mast logs, see: Belknap, *History of New Hampshire*, 3: 78-80. Mast logs were also sometimes skidded in winter and floated down the region's streams. See: Thompson, *Landmarks of Ancient Dover*, 140-44; G. T. Ridlon, Sr., *Saco Valley Settlements and Families* (Portland, Me.: by the author, 1895), 211-18; Burnaby, *Travels through the Middle Settlements*, 87.

60. Dunbar to Popple, 29 Dec. 1729, MHS, *Doc. Hist.*, 11: 3.
61. Ham, *Ancient Dover*, 12; Thompson, *Landmarks of Ancient Dover*, 127; Joseph Melcher, statement, n.d., Pejepscot papers, 5: 345; [Clayton], *History of York County*, 193-95. See also: Charles S Peterson, "Sawdust Trail," *Association for Preservation Technology Bulletin*, 5 (1973): 84-151. The first gang mill was apparently erected at Berwick, Maine, in 1650. It reportedly had as many as eighteen saws, but that was probably at a later date. See: Defebaugh, *History of the Lumber Industry*, 2: 6; Sarah Orne Jewett, "The Old Town of Berwick," *New England Magazine*, 16 (1894): 586.
62. Cape Elizabeth, Windham, Gorham, and Pearsontown, petition regarding dams, 3 Apr. 1777, MHS, *Doc. Hist.*, 15: 70; Committee on Dams, report, 23 May 1777, ibid., 100, 101; General Court, resolve on petition on dams, 20 June 1777, ibid., 129; Hackett, "The Bellamy River Mill Suit," 89-96; John Dunning, deposition, 24 May 1808, Pejepscot papers, 4: 273-76; Stackpole, *Old Kittery*, 117 (quote).
63. William Gould, "Col William Vaughan of Matinicus and Damariscotta," MHS, *Coll.*, 8: 297; Isaac Winslow to Samuel Waldo, 20 Feb. 1749, MHS, *Doc. Hist.*, 12: 43; Thompson, *Landmarks of Ancient Dover*, 223-24; Aaron Haynes, "Reminiscences of Penobscot River," *Bangor Historical Magazine*, 2 (1886-87): 101.
64. Belknap, *History of New Hampshire*, 3: 150, 197.
65. Douglass, *Summary, Historical and Political*, 2: 54.
66. Taylor, *Liberty Men*, 24-29 (quote, p. 25); Judd, *Common Lands, Common People*, 42-47. See also: Willson, *Forest Conservation in Colonial Times*, 5-7. On proprietors' problems with the Wilsons, see also: Noyes to Adam Hunter, 12 May 1753, Pejepscot papers, 4: 101; Freeman to Noyes, 1 and 21 Nov. 1763, ibid., 5: 71-72; Noyes to Freeman, 12 Nov. 1763, ibid.; Pejepscot Proprietors, minutes of meeting, 20 July 1768, ibid., 2: 18; John Dunning, deposition, 24 May 1808, ibid., 4: 273-76. Dunning's deposition deals with actions of the Wilsons ca. 1746.
67. Douglass, *Summary, Historical and Political*, 2: 7. See also: Taylor, *Liberty Men*, 1-9, 32, 61-62, 73-77, 85-86; Huth and Pugh, "Talleyrand in America," 71; Belknap, *History of New Hampshire*, 3: 194-98; Judd, *Common Lands, Common People*, 23-25. The Rev. Thomas Barnard was more explicit. In 1758 he argued free land enabled the poor to support themselves "by the spontaneous Products of Nature with Little Labour . . . [which] perpetuates Idleness, Intemperance, Ignorance, a savage Temper and Irreligion." Quoted in Taylor, *Liberty Men*, 5-6. On growing class divisions and related land issues, see: Taylor, "A Kind of Warr," 3-26.
68. Belknap, *History of New Hampshire*, 3: 197; Taylor, *Liberty Men*, 4-10, 14-18, 61-62, 73-77, 85-89.
69. Bridger to Lords of Trade, 26 Aug. 1718, MHS, *Doc. Hist.*, 9: 424-25.
70. Bridger to Popple, 17 July 1719, ibid., 10: 126-28 (quote); Richard West, "Opinion of the King's Right to the Woods in the Province of Maine," 12 Nov. 1718, MHS, *Coll.*, 2: 265-68; Malone, *Pine Trees and Politics*, 73-75 and passim; Kershaw, *Kennebeck Proprietors*, 207-211. An early historian observed, "Most people were in debt; and it has been remarked that manual laborers in the business of lumbering though fascinated with the prospect

of large emoluments, never amass wealth . . . and, therefore, many of them were more unwilling than other colonists to submit to any new or needless burden." William D. Williamson, *History of the State of Maine* (2 vols.; Hallowell, Me.: Glazier Masters, 1832), 2: 381-82.

71. Quoted in Taylor, "Liberty Men and White Indians," 48-49.

72. Ibid., 123 (quote); John Josselyn, *An Account of Two Voyages to New England* (London: Widdows, 1674), 207-212. Cf. the statement of William Allen, Jr., quoted in Taylor, *Liberty Men*, 66.

73. Stackpole, *Old Kittery and Her Families*, 13, 20, 23-24, 130, 311-31, 740; [Clayton], *History of York County*, 292, 297; John Mason to Ambrose Gibbins, 5 May 1634, New Hampshire, *Provincial and State Papers*, 1: 89; Gibbins to Mason, 6 Aug. 1634, ibid., 91-93; Francis Small, deposition, 8 Sept. 1685, ibid., 45-46; Sullivan, *History of the District of Maine*, 20; Noyes to Hunter, 12 May 1753, Pejepscot papers, 4: 101.

74. Banks, *History of York*, 2: 245-48.

75. [Clayton], *History of York County*, 2: 196-98; William S. Southgate, "The History of Scarborough from 1633 to 1783," MHS, *Coll.*, 3: 167-68 (quote, p. 167), 213; Dorothy Shaw Libbey, *Scarborough Becomes a Town* (Freeport, Me.: Bond Wheelwright, 1955), 46-47; Bourne, *History of Wells and Kennebunk*, 647; Edward C. Cass, "Settlement of the Lower Kennebec, 1620-1650" (unpub. M.A. thesis, University of Maine, 1970), 56-57.

76. Russell, *History of North Yarmouth*, 2: 181.

77. Council of New Hampshire to committee, 7 May 1681, in John Scribner Jenness, ed., *Transcripts of Original Documents in the English Archives Relating to the Early History of the State of New Hampshire* (New York: privately printed, 1876), 87.

78. Joseph Hammond et al., petition, and resolve thereon, 25 Mar 1701, MHS, *Doc. Hist.*, 9: 95-97 (quote, pp. 96-97); New Hampshire, *Provisional and State Papers*, 3: 120-21, 128, 198, 208, 211.

79. "Answers to Queries from the Right Honorable Lords of Trade and Plantations—January, 22, 1730," New Hampshire Historical Society, *Collections*, 1 (1824): 228-29.

80. For examples, see: Fairchild, *Messrs. William Pepperell*; Pares, *Yankees and Creoles*; James B. Hedges, *The Browns of Providence Plantations: Colonial Years* (Cambridge, Mass.: Harvard University Press, 1952).

81. Willis, *History of Portland*, 103, 447-50, 452; Edwin A. Churchill, "Merchants and Commerce in Falmouth (1740-1775)," *Maine Historical Society Newsletter*, 9 (1970): 93, 96-99, 102.

82. Taylor, *Liberty Men*, 154-58; Adele E. Plachta, "The Privileged and the Poor: A History of the District of Maine, 1771-1793 (unpub. Ph.D. diss., University of Maine, 1975), 13-14, 79-85, 91-92; Churchill, "Merchants and Commerce in Falmouth," 93-104.

83. Taylor, *Liberty Men*, 62-63; Bernard Bailyn, *New England Merchants in the Seventeenth Century* (Cambridge, Mass.: Harvard University Press, 1955), 98-105; Carroll, *Timber Economy*, 101-114, 116-19; James S. Leamon, *Revolution Downeast: The War for American Independence in Maine* (Amherst: University of Massachusetts Press, 1993), 4-39. The phrase is Carroll's.

Chapter Two

1. Malone, *Pine Trees and Politics*, 82-143; Cox et al., *This Well-Wooded Land*, 24-32; Kershaw, *Kennebeck Proprietors*, 201-223; Lillard, *Great Forest*, 122-37; Warren J. Gates, "The Broad Arrow Policy in Colonial America" (unpub. Ph.D. diss., University of Pennsylvania, 1951).

2. George Burgess, "A Discourse . . ." MHS, *Coll.*, 4: 73-75; Residents of Broad Bay, petition, Aug. 1757, MHS, *Doc. Hist.*, 13: 102-103; Chas. Apthorp et al., petition, 24 Mar. 1758, ibid., 13: 127-31 (quote). Cut off from their best fishing grounds and markets, fishing communities faced hard times too.

3. Williamson, *History of Maine*, 2: 364-65; Bourne, *History of Wells and Kennebunk*, 453; Catherine Fox, "The Great 'FIRE IN THE WOODS': A Case Study in Ecological History" (unpub. M.A. thesis, University of Maine, 1984), esp. 29-49, 53-58. See also: Foster and Aber, *Forests in Time*, 62-72.

4. William Brattle, James Bowdoin, and Thomas Hubbard, report of commissioners on Machias, 12 Sept. 1771, MHS, *Doc. Hist.*, 14: 138 (quote); Sullivan, *History of the District of Maine*, 39-40. On the settlement of Machias, see: Drisko, *Machias*, 10-18; Henry Smith Whittier, *East Machias, 1765-1926* ([Machias, Me.: Union-Republican, 1926-1927]; photocopied typescript, University of Maine, 1971), 1: 6 et sqq.; Eugene Alberto Mawhinney, "A Social History of Machias, Maine, prior to 1800" (unpub. M.A. thesis, University of Maine, 1949), 7 et sqq., 56-63.

5. In sash mills, saw blades were mounted within a frame to provide extra rigidity and thereby reduce the wobble that caused boards to be sawn in uneven thicknesses. Double sash mills had two saws mounted side by side, thus increasing production significantly.

6. Micah Jones Talbot, "Memoirs," quoted in Whittier, *East Machias*, 324.

7. Drisko, *Machias*, 17-18.

8. Whittier, *East Machias*, 318-20, 322 (quote, p. 319). East Machias was not officially separated from Machias until 1826.

9. Talbot, "Memoirs," quoted in Drisko, *Machias*, 14-15; MHS, *Doc. Hist.*, 14: 140-41. On Talbot, see: Edwin T. Coman, Jr., and Helen M. Gibbs, *Time, Tide and Timber: A Century of Pope & Talbot* (Stanford, Calif.: Stanford University Press, 1949), 43-45; Agnes Arline Gray, "A Social History of Machias, Maine, from 1800 to 1900" (unpub. M.A. thesis, University of Maine, 1954), 61.

10. Williamson, *History of Maine*, 2: 380-81; Drisko, *Machias*, 17, 19-22; Thomas Hutchinson to House of Representatives, 19 June 1771, MHS, *Doc. Hist.*, 14: 132-34; 21: 367.

11. Williamson, *History of Maine*, 2: 387, 396-98; Hutchinson, speech before General Court, Sept. 1770, MHS, *Doc. Hist.* 14: 104 (1st quote), 131 (2nd quote). See also: Hutchinson to General Court, 19 June 1771, ibid., 132-34; Hutchinson to Earl of Dartmouth, 13 Nov. 1772, ibid., 187. A provision in the grant requiring the petitioners not to cut or destroy any of the king's timber in the township failed to assuage Hutchinson's objections. See: Drisko, *Machias*, 21-22.

12. Brattle, Bowdoin, and Hubbard, report, MHS, *Doc. Hist.*, 14: 137-43 (quotes, pp. 137-38, 141); Williamson, *History of Maine*, 2: 363. Cf. Mawhinney, "Social History," 56, 59-60.

13. Massachusetts General Court, grant to Paul Thorndike et al., 27 Jan. 1764, MHS, *Doc. Hist.*, 13: 322-30; Francis Barnard to Earl of Halifax, 9 Nov. 1764, ibid., 385-86; Brattle, Bowdoin, and Hubbard, report, ibid., 14: 139-41; Williamson, *History of Maine*, 2: 347-48, 361-62.

14. Brattle, Bowdoin, and Hubbard, report, MHS, *Doc. Hist.*, 14: 139-40; 21: 324; Williamson, *History of Maine*, 2: 538, 544, 554; Frederick S. Allis, Jr., ed., *William Bingham's Maine Lands, 1790-1820* (Boston: Colonial Society of Massachusetts, 1954), 522-23.

15. Barnard to Earl of Halifax, 9 Nov. 1764, MHS, *Doc. Hist.*, 13: 385-86; Coolidge, *Maine Woods*, 33-47.

16. Hutchinson to Earl of Dartmouth, 13 Nov. 1772, MHS, *Doc. Hist.*, 14: 187.

17. Thomas Hill et al., memorial to General Court, 17 Aug. 1786, ibid., 21: 324; David Cobb to William Bingham, 30 Jan. 1797, Allis, *Maine Lands*, 832. The first sawmill in Ellsworth, the principal settlement on the Union River, was built about 1764. See: *Maine Historical Magazine*, 8 (1893): 207-208.

18. Hutchinson to Earl of Dartmouth, 13 Nov. 1772, MHS, *Doc. Hist.*, 14: 187.

19. Willis, *Journals of the Rev. Thomas Smith*, 204 (quote); Williamson, *History of Maine*, 2: 347-48.

20. Bourne, *History of Wells and Kennebunk*, 647-48; Folsom, *History of Saco and Biddeford*, 308; John Stuart Barrows, *Fryeburg, Maine: An Historical Sketch* (Fryeburg: Pequaket Press, 1938), 49-50. Fryeburg's first settlers arrived in 1763, built a sawmill for local needs, and within a decade were supplying logs to coastal mills engaged in the export trade.

21. John Johnston, *A History of the Towns of Bristol and Bremen . . .* (Albany, N.Y.: Munsell, 1873), 327. See also: Williamson, *History of Maine*, 2: 380-81; Moses Greenleaf, *A Survey of the State of Maine . . .* (Portland, Me.: Shirley & Hyde, 1829), 181-82.

22. Kershaw, *Kennebeck Proprietors*, 154; Henry D. Kingsbury and Simeon L. Deyo, ed., *Illustrated History of Kennebec County, Maine* (New York: Blake, 1892), 605-606 (quote).

23. Kershaw, *Kennebeck Proprietors*, 113, 116 (quote); Williamson, *History of Maine*, 2: 389; Edward Augustus Kendall, *Travels through the Northern Parts of the United States in the Years 1807 and 1808* (3 vols.; New York: Riley, 1809), 3: 80; Edward C. Cass, "A Town Comes of Age: Pownalborough, Maine, 1720-1785" (unpub. Ph.D. diss., University of Maine, 1979), 68, 113-15, 205.

24. *Bangor Historical Magazine*, 1 (1885-86): 2, 70, 103; [H.A. Ford, ed.], *History of Penobscot County . . .* (Cleveland: Williams-Chase, 1882), 517, 528-29; H. Russell Cox, *History of Orrington, Maine* (Brewer, Me.: Orrington Historical Society, 1988), 6-7; Williamson, *History of Maine*, 2: 384, 389, 554; Robert Dana Stanley, "The Rise of the Penobscot Lumber Industry to 1860" (unpub. M.A. thesis, University of Maine, 1963), 30; Ava Harriet Chadbourne, *Maine Place Names and the Peopling of Its Towns* (Portland, Me.: Bond Wheelwright, 1955), 376-77, 423-24.

25. Quoted in Kershaw, *Kennebeck Proprietors*, 219 (2nd quote), 222 (1st quote). See also: Malone, *Pine Trees and Politics*, 137-41.

26. Taylor, *Liberty Men*, 62-64, 71-74; Eves, "Yankee Immigrants," 102-119; David C. Smith, "Maine's Changing Landscape to 1820," in *Maine in the Early*

Republic, 14; Judd, *Common Lands, Common People*, 16-23. On the interior settlers, see: Eves, "Yankee Immigrants," 92-102, 120-35, 147-48; Taylor, *Liberty Men*, 66-77.

27. See: Cox et al., *This Well-Wooded Land*, 24-32; Malone, *Pine Trees and Politics*, 133-43; Albion, *Forests and Seapower*, 253-54, 269-80; Bernhard Knollenberg, *Origin of the American Revolution* (rev. ed.; New York: Free Press, 1965), 122-30.

28. Town of Machias, petition to General Court, [June 1787], MHS, *Doc. Hist.*, 21: 367-71; Mawhinney, "Social History," 7; Charles E. Clark, *Maine: A Bicentennial History* (New York: Norton, 1977), 63-64, 67; Williamson, *History of Maine*, 2: 430-32, 434, 450-52, 458-59, 461-62; John H. Ahlin, *Maine Rubicon: Downeast Settlers during the American Revolution* (Calais, Me.: Calais Advertiser, 1966).

29. Taylor, *Liberty Men*, 14-18, 62, 69-73; Leamon, *Revolution Downeast*, 40, 60-72, 135-65; Letter from Falmouth to a Gentleman in Watertown, 11 May 1775, Peter Force, ed., *American Archives . . .* (9 vols.; Washington, D.C.: Clarke & Force, 1837-1853), 4th series, 2: 553 (1st quote); Jacob Bailey to [?], 1775, MHS, *Coll.*, 5: 445-47 (2nd quote, p. 449). See also: Nathan Goold, "General Samuel Thompson of Brunswick and Topsham, Maine," ibid., 3rd series, 1: 423-58.

30. Leamon, *Revolution Downeast*, 78-80; Carl Lotus Becker, *The History of Political Parties in the Province of New York, 1760-1776*, Bulletin of the University of Wisconsin, no. 286 (Madison: University of Wisconsin, 1909), 22.

31. Clark, *Maine*, 63, 64-68; Williamson, *History of Maine*, 2: 422-27, 434-38, 453-54, 468-80, 498-99.

32. Hill, memorial, MHS, *Doc. Hist.*, 21: 324-26.

33. Williamson, *History of Maine*, 2: 482-83; Belknap, *History of New Hampshire*, 3: 22-23, 97-102; Bourne, *History of Wells and Kennebunk*, 516; Taylor, *Liberty Men*, 14-15, 64-65; Plachta, "The Privileged and the Poor," 32, 40; Smith, "Maine's Changing Landscape," 16-20.

34. Hill, memorial, MHS, *Doc. Hist.*, 21: 324-26; Machias, petition, ibid., 371-73 (quote, p. 371); *Falmouth Gazette and Daily Advertiser*, 28 May 1785; Drisko, *Machias*, 124; F. Lee Benns, *The American Struggle for the British West Indies Carrying Trade*, Indiana University Studies, no. 56 (Bloomington: Indiana University Press, 1923), 8-10.

35. Hill, memorial, MHS, *Doc. Hist.*, 21: 324-26 (quote, p. 324). Circumstances were similar at Waterborough. See: Joseph Swett et al., petition to the General Court, ibid., 20: 84; Eula M. Shorey, ed., *Bridgton, Maine, 1768-1968* (Augusta, Me.: Bridgton Historical Society, 1968), 22.

36. *Falmouth Gazette*, 29 Oct. 1785. The *Gazette*, Maine's first newspaper, commenced publication earlier that year. See: Frederick G. Fassett, Jr., *A History of Newspapers in the District of Maine* (Orono: University of Maine Press, 1932), 29-43.

37. Williamson, *History of Maine*, 2: 513-14; Belknap, *History of New Hampshire*, 3: 213.

38. Williamson, *History of Maine*, 2: 510, 517, 538, 569; William O. Raymond, ed., *Winslow Papers, 1776-1826* (St. John, N.B.: Sun, 1901), 189-90, 201,

251; Harold A. Davis, *An International Community on the St. Croix (1604-1930)*, University of Maine Studies, 2nd Series, no. 64 (1950; reprint, Orono: University of Maine Press, 1974), 53-55, 82-83, 88; Mary Priscilla Boone, "Chronicles of Calais and Vicinity: Part I: 1604-1820" (unpub. M.A. thesis, University of Maine, 1947), 47-49, 54-55; Park Holland, "Life and Diaries" (typescript copy, Special Collections, University of Maine Library, Orono), 46; Eves, "Yankee Immigrants," 133-34; Margaret Fowles Wilde, "History of the Public Land Policy of Maine, 1620-1820" (unpub. M.A. thesis, University of Maine, 1940), 127-30; Taylor, *Liberty Men*, 66-68; Moses Greenleaf, *A Statistical View of the District of Maine, More Especially with Reference to the Value and Importance of Its Interior* (Boston: Cummings & Hilliard, 1815), 103 (quote); Alexander Baring to Hope & Co., 3 Dec. 1796, Allis, *Maine Lands*, 772-73. Cf. Lawrence Donald Bridgham, "Maine Public Lands, 1781-1795: Claims, Trespasses, and Sales" (unpub. Ph.D. diss., Boston University, 1959), 23-24. Bridgham plays down land speculation at this time.

39. Williamson, *History of Maine*, 2: 506, 510, 569; Defebaugh, *History of the Lumber Industry*, 2: 11, 26-27; Taylor, *Liberty Men*, 20-21; Wilde, "Public Land Policy of Maine," 93-94 and passim; Allis, *Maine Lands*, 24-34; Coolidge, *Maine Woods*, 548-57.

40. Defebaugh, *History of the Lumber Industry*, 2: 26-27; Williamson, *History of Maine*, 2: 530-32; Falmouth *Cumberland Gazette*, cited in Eves, "Yankee Immigrants," 133-34; Robert C. Alberts, *The Golden Voyage: The Life and Times of William Bingham, 1752-1804* (Boston: Houghton Mifflin, 1969), 226, 229-31; Allis, *Maine Lands*, 27-29, 35-103. See also: Wilde, "Public Land Policy of Maine," 149-50, 152; Bridgham, "Maine Public Lands," 231 et sqq. In 1796 Bingham sold the tract to the Baring interests of London. Alberts, *Golden Voyage*, 269-76; Allis, *Maine Lands*, 592-676.

41. Leamon, *Revolution Downeast*, 198; Taylor, "Liberty Men and White Indians," 121; Ronald F. Banks, *Maine Becomes a State: The Movement to Separate Maine from Massachusetts, 1785-1820* (Middleton, Conn.: Wesleyan University Press, 1970), 15-16, 19-23, 371-72; *Falmouth Gazette*, 15 and 22 Jan., 5 and 19 Feb., 12 and 25 Mar., 9 Apr., 11 June, 10 Sept., 10 Dec. 1785; Williamson, *History of Maine*, 2: 508, 521-27, 531-32; Edward Stanwood, "The Separation of Maine from Massachusetts," Maine Historical Society, *Proceedings*, 3rd Series, 1: 129. Banks plays down the importance of lumber regulations in the early separatist movement, but contemporary sources and the role of men like Thompson suggest they were significant. See: Banks, *Maine Becomes a State*, 10-24.

42. *Falmouth Gazette*, 7 May 1785. In 1795 New Hampshire passed similar legislation. See: New Hampshire, *Provincial and State Papers*, 22: 499.

43. Massachusetts General Court, resolution, 31 Jan. 1784, MHS, *Doc. Hist.*, 20: 369; Richard Newman et al., petition to the General Court, 6 Oct. 1783, ibid., 271-73; Massachusetts General Court, Act of 15 Mar. 1784, ibid., 319-21; Williamson, *History of Maine*, 2: 507, 508, 530-31, 564, 607; Bridgham, "Maine Public Lands," 29, 36-38, 191-94, 223-30, 357-61. In their petition requesting the lottery, residents on the Saco noted: "there is a great Quantity of Timber in the State of Newhampshire, as well as in this Commonwealth" that could be floated to mills at Biddeford and Pepperellborough if the

jam near Fryeburg and the obstructions at Great Falls were removed. See: Eastman, petition, MHS, *Doc. Hist.*, 20: 271-72.

44. Baring to Hope & Co., 3 Dec. 1796, Allis, *Maine Lands*, 785; Williamson, *History of Maine*, 2: 591 (2nd quote), 593; Banks, *Maine Becomes a State*, 7-8, 366.

45. *Historical Statistics of the United States, Colonial Times to 1957* (Washington, D.C.: GPO, 1957), 13; Greenleaf, *Statistical View*, 38-40, 68.

46. Greenleaf, *Survey*, 217; William Morris to Theophile Cazenove, 9 Dec. 1792, Allis, *Maine Lands*, 194; Banks, *Maine Becomes a State*, 8 (3rd quote); Laura Fecych Sprague, ed., *Agreeable Situations: Society, Commerce, and Art in Southern Maine, 1780-1830* (Kennebunk, Me.: Brick House Museum, 1987), 18; Bourne, *History of Wells and Kennebunk*, 649.

47. Banks, *Maine Becomes a State*, 8; *Maine Historical Magazine*, 9 (1894-95): 108-122; Baring to Hope & Co., 3 Dec. 1796, Allis, *Maine Lands*, 787.

48. Sprague, *Agreeable Situations*, 25; Benjamin Lincoln to Bingham, 26 Feb. 1793, Allis, *Maine Lands*, 183.

49. Dwight, *Travels*, 2: 111-12.

50. Morris to Cazenove, 9 Dec. 1792, Allis, *Maine Lands*, 195; Baring to Hope & Co., 3 Dec. 1796, ibid., 785. Huth and Pugh, "Talleyrand in America," 78, noted that on the lower Kennebec "everything presents a spectacle of great activity and rapid growth," but Talleyrand mistakenly attributed this to the fact the trees had now been cleared and "the occupation of cutting wood has ceased to be the favorite activity of these settlers." As a summer visitor, he was unaware of the extensive logging most settlers went upriver to engage in every winter.

51. Greenleaf, *Statistical View*, 128-29; Huth and Pugh, "Talleyrand in America," 78; Kershaw, *Kennebeck Proprietors*, 37; Coburn, *Skowhegan on the Kennebec*, 1: 84; Defebaugh, *History of the Lumber Industry*, 2: 71-76 (Michaux quoted, p. 74).

52. Defebaugh, *History of the Lumber Industry*, 2: 68-70; Williamson, *History of Maine*, 1: 46; Wood, *Lumbering in Maine*, 13.

53. Garnett Laidlaw Eskew, *Cradle of Ships* (New York: Putnam, 1958), 28-30; Greenleaf, *Survey*, 228; Parker McCobb Reed, *History of Bath and Environ, Sagadahoc County, Maine* (Portland, Me.: Lakeside, 1894), 76-77 (quote), 145-46; Kendall, *Travels*, 3: 80, 142.

54. Baring to Hope & Co., 3 Dec. 1796, Allis, *Maine Lands*, 775-76; Mawhinney, "A Social History of Machias," 61-63.

55. [Ford], *History of Penobscot County*, 83, 539, 544; Eves, "Yankee Immigrants," 80-81; Huth and Pugh, "Talleyrand in America," 77; *Bangor Historical Magazine*, 5 (1889-90): 82-86. On the Penobscot country in 1793, see: Holland, "Life and Diaries," 69-83, 122-29.

56. *Bangor Historical Magazine*, 1 (1885-86): 119; 4 (1890-91): 28-34; Taylor, *Liberty Men*, 63; Eves, "Yankee Immigrants," 17-25.

57. Morris to Cazenove, 9 Dec. 1792, Allis, *Maine Lands*, 195; Lincoln to Bingham, 26 Feb. 1793, ibid., 183-84; *Bangor Historical Magazine*, 4 (1888-89): 198-99; Gray, "A Social History of Machias," 59; Arthur R.M. Lower, *Great Britain's Woodyard: British America and the Timber Trade, 1763-1867* (Toronto: McGill-Queens University Press, 1973), 175; Davis, *St. Croix*, 117. Gang mills were similar to sash mills, but mounted far more saws in a "gang."

58. Plachta, "The Privileged and the Poor," 51-53.
59. François Alexandre Frèdèric, Duc de la Rochefoucauld-Liancourt, *Travels through the United States . . .*, trans by H. Neuman (2 vols.; London: R. Phillips, 1799), 1: 424.
60. Taylor, *Liberty Men*, 6-7, 90-96.
61. Bridgham, "Maine's Public Lands," 223-24; Smith, "Maine's Changing Landscape," 15, 19; Lincoln to Bingham, 26 Feb. 1793, Allis, *Maine Lands*, 183; Cobb to Bingham, 30 Jan. 1797, ibid., 832; Kendall, *Travels*, 3: 77-78; Taylor, *Liberty Men*, 172-76.
62. Plachta, "The Privileged and the Poor," 88; Bingham, answer to queries, 19 Apr. 1796, Allis, *Maine Lands*, 741-42; Cobb to Bingham, 1 July and 18 Aug. 1795, ibid., 527, 530-31; Baring to Hope & Co., 3 Dec. 1796, ibid., 786.
63. Bingham, answer to queries, 19 Apr. 1796, Allis, *Maine Lands*, 741-42; Cobb to Bingham, 30 Jan. 1797, ibid., 832.
64. The belief they had a right to take fruits of the land for their support and sustenance continued strong among Maine's plain folk well into the twentieth century. See: Richard W. Judd, "Reshaping Maine's Landscape: Rural Culture, Tourism, and Conservation, 1890-1929," *JFH*, 32 (1988): 180-90; Edward D. Ives, *George Magoon and the Down East Game War: History, Folklore, and the Law* (Urbana: University of Illinois Press, 1988), 61-92, 288-90.
65. Plachta, "The Privileged and the Poor," 16-19, 22-24, 40-41. Plachta's analysis is flawed; she fails to appreciate the connection between commercial and lumbering operations; nonetheless, her data are valuable.
66. Sprague, *Agreeable Situations*, 16-17, 19; Plachta, "The Privileged and the Poor," 79-85, 149; Stanley, "Rise of the Penobscot Lumber Industry," 32-37; William L. Lucey, "Two Irish Merchants of New England," *New England Quarterly*, 14 (1941): 633-45.
67. Greenleaf, *Statistical View*, 88, 90; Allis, *Maine Lands*, 13, 18-19.
68. Judd, *Common Lands, Common People*, 60-63 (quote, p. 63); Taylor, "Liberty Men and White Indians," 155-56; Plachta, "The Privileged and the Poor," 13-14 and passim.
69. Cobb quoted in Robert E. Moody, "Samuel Ely, Forerunner of Shays," *New England Quarterly*, 5 (1932): 121 (1st quote); Cobb to Bingham, 9 Apr. 1797, Allis, *Maine Lands*, 844-45 (2nd quote, p. 845); Cobb to Isaac Parker, 12 Apr. 1799, ibid., 958 (3rd quote); Cobb to C. Hare, 29 Oct. 1809, ibid., 1231 (4th quote). See also: Cobb to Bingham, 5 Oct. 1795, ibid., 538-42; Kendall, *Travels*, 3: 77, 79-81, 83-84; Plachta, "The Privileged and the Poor," 85-86, 91-92; Banks, *Maine Becomes a State*, 7-10; Alberts, *Golden Voyage*, 228-31, 264-76.
70. Moody, "Samuel Ely," 119-34.
71. Banks, *Maine Becomes a State*, 48-49, 51-56, 122-25, 140-41; Willis, *History of Portland*, 777; Marion Jaques Smith, *General William King: Merchant, Shipbuilder, and Maine's First Governor* (Camden, Me.: Down East, 1980), 28-29, 130-31.
72. Morris to Cazenove, 9 Dec. 1792, Allis, *Maine Lands*, 192; Williamson, *History of Maine*, 2: 599 (quote); Greenleaf, *Statistical View*, 103-105.
73. Banks, *Maine Becomes a State*, 57; Reed, *History of Bath and Environs*, 76-77; Cyrus Eaton, *History of Thomaston, Rockland, and South Thomaston, Maine*

(Hallowell, Me.: Masters-Smith, 1865), 282; [Ford], *History of Penobscot County*, 552; Greenleaf, *Statistical View*, 89-90 (quote, p. 89); Kendall, *Travels*, 3: 155-56; Eves, "Yankee Immigrants," 148-49; Taylor, *Liberty Men*, 183, 239.
74. Williamson, *History of Maine*, 2: 664-66; Eaton, *History of Thomaston, Rockland, and South Thomaston*, 282; Taylor, *Liberty Men*, 177, 234, 239-40, 242; Wilde, "Public Land Policy of Maine," 140, 150-51; Greenleaf, *Statistical View*, 68. Some qualification of these generalizations is needed. For a summary, see: Judd, *Common Lands, Common People*, 64-67.
75. Williamson, *History of Maine*, 2: 634 (quote), 659, 662; Wilde, "Public Land Policy of Maine," 139; Sprague, *Agreeable Situations*, 30.
76. Taylor, "Liberty Men and White Indians," 770-71, 773.

Chapter Three

1. Richard S. Davis, "History of the Penobscot River: Its Use and Abuse" (unpub. M.A. thesis, University of Maine, 1972), 20; Wood, *Lumbering in Maine*, 29; Stewart Holbrook, *Holy Old Mackinaw: The Natural History of the American Lumberjack* (enlarged ed.; New York: Macmillan, 1956), 46-47; Eckstorm, "Lumbering in Maine," 690-95. Eckstorm divides lumbering in Maine into three periods: individualism (to ca. 1820); cooperation (ca. 1820-1880); and capitalism (after ca. 1880). The passing of the first stage marked a shift away from agriculture as the main objective of land use to the manufacturing and marketing of lumber as the goal. In the process, she argues, the area moved from being a farmer's to a lumberman's frontier. See also: Kingsbury and Deyo, *History of Kennebec County*, 176.
2. *Niles Weekly Register*, 27 June 1835, p. 291; Wood, *Lumbering in Maine*, 74-82; Edward Wesley Potter, "Public Policy and Economic Growth in Maine, 1820-1857" (unpub. Ph.D. diss., University of Maine, 1974), 83-85; Stanley, "Penobscot Lumber Industry," 70-74. Penobscot Indians contributed to the speculation. Needing money, they sold timber or land from time to time, and in 1833 gave up their last four townships, thus adding to the land on the market and removing a strategically located impediment to unfettered economic development. See: Wilde, "Public Land Policy of Maine," 121-22, 140-44; David Norton, *Sketches of the Town of Old Town* . . . (Bangor, Me.: Robinson, 1881), 16.
3. *Bangor Daily Whig and Courier* [hereafter *Bangor Daily Whig*], 23 Dec. 1834, 1 Feb. 1837.
4. Deborah Thompson, *Bangor, Maine, 1769-1914: An Architectural History* (Orono: University of Maine Press, 1988), 36 (quote); Wilde, "Public Land Policy of Maine," 161-62; Wood, *Lumbering in Maine*, 80-82. See also: A. M. Sakolski, *The Great American Land Bubble* (New York: Harper, 1932), 239-42; Hugh McCulloch, *Men and Measures of Half a Century: Sketches and Comments* (New York: Scribner, 1888), 214-17.
5. Potter, "Public Policy and Economic Growth," 67, 131-32; Davies, "History of the Penobscot," 25.
6. Potter, "Public Policy and Economic Growth," 80, 166-67; Thompson, *Bangor*, 6, 18, 30, 36-38 (quote, p. 36); Stanley, "Rise of the Penobscot Lumber Industry," 16, 29-31; Davies, "History of the Penobscot," 24-25; Hannah W.

Rogers, "A History of Orono, Maine" (n.p.: typescript, 1926; copy, University of Maine Library, Orono), 40.

7. *Bangor Daily Whig*, 20 Feb. 1830; 27 June 1834. See also: ibid., 4 Apr. 1834.

8. Ibid., 25 Oct. 1842, 31 Oct. and 12 Dec. 1845, 17 July 1847, 9 June 1854; Stanley, "Rise of the Penobscot Lumber Industry," 16-18; Wood, *Lumbering in Maine*, 35-36; Coolidge, *Maine Woods*, 77-80. Most shipments went domestic or to the Caribbean since Bangor's harbor could only accommodate ships up to some four hundred tons capacity. Such vessels were too small to compete effectively in the larger ports of Europe. See: *Hunt's Merchant's Magazine*, 18 (1848): 518.

9. Norton, *Sketches of Old Town*, 7-8; *Bangor Daily Whig*, 24 Apr. 1843 (1st quote), 18 Apr. 1844; Anonymous, "An Old Penobscot Lumberman, Lawrence Costigan," *Maine Historical Magazine*, 9 (1894-95): 227-28 (2nd quote). See also: Stanley, "Rise of the Penobscot Lumber Industry," 43-49; Holbrook, *Holy Old Mackinaw*, 14-28. Holbrook catches the flavor of Bangor's heyday, but he is not always dependable.

10. Thompson, *Bangor*, 109; Holbrook, *Holy Old Mackinaw*, 19-20; Norton, *Sketches of Old Town*, 19-21, 142-45; Potter, "Public Policy and Economic Growth," 82, 112-13, 116-17, 177-78. See also: Stanley, "Rise of the Penobscot Lumber Industry," 32-38; Coolidge, *Maine Woods*, 66; Chadbourne, *Maine Place Names*, 360-61.

11. Judd, *Aroostook*, 68; Holbrook, *Holy Old Mackinaw*, 36-37; Stanley, "Rise of the Penobscot Lumber Industry," 38-39; Thompson, *Bangor*, 128; Isaac Stephenson, *Recollections of a Long Life, 1829-1915* (Chicago: privately printed, 1915), 7 (1st quote), 47 (2nd quote). As Sinclair's young protégé, Stephenson was well placed to judge him. Dwinel also clashed with Samuel Veazie. See: Coolidge, *Maine Woods*, 80.

12. Wood, *Lumbering in Maine*, 38-40.

13. Rogers, "History of Orono," 26-27.

14. Potter, "Public Policy and Economic Growth," 83-85; Lloyd C. Irland, "Rufus Putnam's Ghost: An Essay on Maine's Public Lands, 1783-1820," *JFH*, 30: 60-69. The best summary of Maine's evolving land policies is David C. Smith, "Maine and Its Public Domain: Land Disposal on the Northeastern Frontier," in David M. Ellis, ed., *The Frontier in American Development: Essays in Honor of Paul Wallace Gates* (Ithaca, N.Y.: Cornell University Press, 1969), 113-37.

15. Smith, "Maine and Its Public Domain," 115-16, 126.

16. Ibid., 115-16, 118-20; Coolidge, *Maine Woods*, 565-70.

17. Smith, "Maine and Its Public Domain," 116-17, 124-25; Wood, *Lumbering in Maine*, 50; [Ford], *History of Penobscot County*, 611, 614, 619-22. Sales were largely on credit so failed to generate adequate funds for the state's needs; Maine had to depend upon poll and estate taxes for the bulk of its revenues. See: Potter, "Public Policy and Economic Growth," 46-47, 157-58, 220.

18. Quoted in Wilde, "History of the Public Land Policy of Maine," 154.

19. Potter, "Public Policy and Economic Growth," 46-47, 56-59, 83-86.

20. Judd, *Aroostook*, 30.

21. *Machias Union*, 25 Sept. 1855; Drisko, *Narrative of the Town of Machias*, 336; Ives, *George Magoon*, 50-54. How much potential farmland Washington

County had is open to question. Subsequent experience suggests it was not great.

22. Potter, "Public Policy and Economic Growth," 135, 147.
23. Although New York and Massachusetts passed general incorporation acts in the 1830s, Maine did not. Potter, "Public Policy and Economic Growth," 71, 87, 187.
24. Judd, *Common Lands, Common People*, 133-39; *Bangor Democrat*, 28 Jan. 1839 (quote).
25. [Ford], *History of Penobscot County*, 630, 633, 635.
26. Potter, "Public Policy and Economic Growth," 142-46 (quote, p. 146). Cf. Morton J. Horowitz, *The Transformation of American Law, 1780-1860* (Cambridge, Mass.: Harvard University Press, 1977).
27. [Ford], *History of Penobscot County*, 636; Potter, "Public Policy and Economic Growth," 58.
28. Edward Kirkland, *Men, Cities, and Transportation* (2 vols.; Cambridge, Mass.: Harvard University Press, 1948), 1: 204-205; Potter, "Public Policy and Economic Growth," 101-103.
29. Kirkland, *Men, Cities and Transportation*, 1: 203-206, 210, 215-22; Potter, "Public Policy and Economic Growth," 31-35, 170-74, 201-205 and passim.
30. Judd, *Aroostook*, 27-30, 59; Potter, "Public Land Policy and Economic Growth," 23-25, 44-46, 71-72, 100-101, 137-38. The roads had been built both to encourage settlement and to aid military movement in the disputed area.
31. Portland *Eastern Argus*, 16 Jan. 1829; Potter, "Public Policy and Economic Growth," 16-17, 47-51, 88-90, 91-92, 165-67.
32. Norton, *Sketches of Old Town*, 18-21, 142-45; Stanley, "Rise of the Penobscot Lumber Industry," 32-38; Potter, "Public Policy and Economic Growth," 116-17; Alfred Greer Hempstead, *The Penobscot Boom and the Development of the West Branch of the Penobscot River for Log Driving* (Orono: University of Maine Press, 1937), 17.
33. Potter, "Public Policy and Economic Growth," 16-17, 28-31, 35-38, 40-44, 49-52, 64-65, 123-28; Judd, *Aroostook*, 40-42; Kirkland, *Men, Cities, and Transportation*, 1: 215-18.
34. [Henry Putnam], *A Description of Brunswick (Maine), in Letters by a Gentleman from South Carolina . . .*(Brunswick, Me.: Griffen, 1820), 14. See also: Kendall, *Travels*, 3: 140-42.
35. On the building and operation of the boom, see: Hempstead, *Penobscot Boom*, 15-29; Wood, *Lumbering in Maine*, 132-39; Stanley, "Rise of the Penobscot Lumber Industry," 57-68. Isaac Stephenson's claim that the boom was the work of Jefferson Sinclair over-simplifies the story. See: Stephenson, *Recollections of a Long Life*, 50-51; Fred C. Burke, *Logs on the Menominee: The History of the Menominee River Boom Company* (Menasha, Wis.: Banta, 1946), 20.
36. Norton, *Sketches of Old Town*, 23 (quote); Kendall, *Travels*, 3: 78, 141-42. Under the old system, Kendall notes, roughly one-fourth of the logs sent downstream were lost, stranded, or stolen.
37. Henry David Thoreau, *The Maine Woods* (Boston: Houghton Mifflin, 1864), 4, 111. By 1852, Isaac Stephenson wrote, the river was lined with sawmills for ten miles above Old Town." Stephenson, *Recollections of a Long Life*, 52-53.

38. Wood, *Lumbering in Maine*, 128-39; Stanley, "Rise of the Penobscot Lumber Industry," 57-68; Hempstead, *Penobscot Boom*, 20-23.

39. Wood, *Lumbering in Maine*, 96-127; Hempstead, *Penobscot Boom*, 39-54; Eckstorm, "Lumbering in Maine," 693-95; Holbrook, *Holy Old Mackinaw*, 58-73.

40. Having been Anglicized from the French, the term was indeed spelled "batteaus" (or, sometimes, "bateaus").

41. Eckstorm, "Lumbering in Maine," 690-91 (Ross quoted on p. 691); Holbrook, *Holy Old Mackinaw*, 22-25; Robert E. Pike, *Tall Trees, Tough Men* (New York: Norton, 1967), 221-22; David C. Smith, *A History of Lumbering in Maine, 1861-1960* (Orono: University of Maine Press, 1972), 65-66.

42. Wood, *Lumbering in Maine*, 142-43; Rogers, "History of Orono," 85; Stanley, "Rise of the Penobscot Lumber Industry," 49-56; Potter, "Public Policy and Economic Growth," 117-18.

43. Potter, "Public Policy and Economic Growth," 15, 38, 100-101; Wood, *Lumbering in Maine*, 11-16.

44. *Bangor Daily Whig*, 1 Nov. 1845; Rowe, *Maritime History of Maine*, 119-65; William Armstrong Fairburn, *Merchant Sail* (6 vols.; Centre Lovell, Me.: Fairburn Marine Educational Foundation, 1945-55), 5: 3099-3109, 3143-54, 3194-98; Potter, "Public Policy and Economic Growth," 67, 72-73.

45. Virginia Steele Wood, *Live Oaking: Southern Timber for Tall Ships* (Boston: Northeastern University Press, 1981), esp. 106-22; Rowe, *Maritime History of Maine*, 41-42.

46. Holbrook, *Holy Old Mackinaw*, 38-40; Wood, *Lumbering in Maine*, 34, 90, 159, 162-70. Frequently described, the details of woods work need not be repeated here. For descriptions, see: John S. Springer, *Forest Life and Forest Trees . . .* (New York: Harper, 1851); Wood, *Lumbering in Maine*, 83-127.

47. Holbrook, *Holy Old Mackinaw*, 35-36; Potter, "Public Policy and Economic Growth," 79-80, 123-26, 181-82, 185; Hempstead, *Penobscot Boom*, 75-77; Eckstorm, "Lumbering in Maine," 693-94.

48. Judd, *Aroostook*, 67-71; Wood, *Lumbering in Maine*, 121-23; Coolidge, *Maine Woods*, 53-57; Eckstorm, "Lumbering in Maine," 694-95; Stephenson, *Recollections of a Long Life*, 46-48; Dean B. Bennett, *The Wilderness from Chamberlain Farm: A Story of Hope for the American Wild* (Island Press: Washington, D.C., 2001), 69-80. By the time loggers arrived from St. John, two more dams had been built north of Chamberlain Lake, extending Bangor's hinterland even further. Chamberlain Lake dam and canal continue in place, operated by the Maine Department of Parks and Lands. On logging and life on the St. John in the 1840s and 50s, see: Stephenson, *Recollections of a Long Life*, 29-39, 50-51.

49. Potter, "Public Policy and Economic Growth," 214-15; Hempstead, *Penobscot Boom*, 54-58. In 1893 two Kennebeckers succeeded where both their forerunners and Bangor's railroad promoters had failed. They built a dam on the West Branch of the Penobscot, a sluice that fed into Moosehead Lake, and a mechanical conveyor system to carry logs over the three hundred feet that separated the dammed up Penobscot waters from the sluiceway. Eight to ten million feet of logs from the Penobscot soon made their way down the Kennebec each year. It was, as Stewart Holbrook put it, "quite an engineering

feat and Maine's final great effort." Holbrook, *Holy Old Mackinaw*, 37-38; Defebaugh, *History of the Lumber Industry*, 1: 75; Hempstead, *Penobscot Boom*, 77-79; Coolidge, *Maine Woods*, 54, 75-76.

50. Potter, "Public Policy and Economic Growth," 131-32.

51. Ibid., 32-35, 104-109, 204-206; Coolidge, *Maine Woods*, 58; Willis, *History of Portland*, 567-70, 724-26; Fairburn, *Merchant Sail*, 5: 3145. By providing improved egress from the interior, the canal encouraged small sawmills around Sebago Lake and thus increased the supply of exports for Portland's merchants. Indeed, the first two boats through the canal carried cargoes of lumber. Harland Hall Carter, "A History of the Cumberland and Oxford Canal" (unpub. M.A. thesis, University of Maine, 1950), 48, 52-53; Portland *Eastern Argus*, 16 Apr. 1830. For an analysis of Portland's railroad-building efforts, see: Kirkland, *Men, Cities, and Transportation*, esp. 1: 192-222.

52. Potter, "Public Policy and Economic Growth," 26-27, 72-76, 200, 221; Willis, *History of Portland*, 560-62 (quote, p. 562), 564-67, 906-907. On the dominance of merchants during this period, see: Glenn Porter and Harold C. Livesay, *Merchants and Manufacturers: Studies in the Changing Structure of Nineteenth-Century Marketing* (Baltimore: Johns Hopkins University Press, 1971), esp. chapters II and IV.

53. Willis, *History of Portland*, 560, 731-33, 774-75 (quotes, p. 775); Rowe, *Maritime History of Maine*, 106-118; Wood, *Lumbering in Maine*," 207-213; Fairburn, *Merchant Sail*, 5: 3143; Duncan, *Coastal Maine*, 281-83.

54. Potter, "Public Policy and Economic Growth," 276-77; Wood, *Lumbering in Maine*, 204-205, 207-213; Willis, *History of Portland*, 731-32; David Demeritt, "Boards, Barrels, and Boxshooks: The Economics of Downeast Lumber in Nineteenth-Century Cuba," *JFH*, 35 (1991): 108-120. Portland dominated this trade until improved refining technology resulted in sugar containing little molasses and which, therefore, could be shipped in jute bags. When that day came, the trade—and Portland's sugar processing industry—quickly collapsed.

55. Potter, "Public Policy and Economic Growth," 16-17, 28-29, 39, 47-51, 73-75, 88-90, 165-67, 198, 219, 221.

56. Sprague, *Agreeable Situations*, 26-27.

57. Potter, "Public Policy and Economic Growth," 73, 80, 119 (quote), 122, 153-54, 166-67, 222-23, 272-73, 287-88, 299; Norton, *Sketches of Old Town*, 8; Stanley, "Rise of the Penobscot Lumber Industry," 73-74.

58. Potter, "Public Policy and Economic Growth," 151-52, 175-76, 229-30, 279-80; *Bangor Daily Whig*, 16 Feb. 1837, 14 Jan. 1841, 7 Feb. 1849 (quote). See also: Davis, *St. Croix*, 150.

59. Potter, "Public Policy and Economic Growth," 299. Potter's latter-day arguments for Whiggery have merit, but one should remember that states which followed Whig prescriptions, such as Pennsylvania and New York, spawned economic problems of their own.

60. Ibid., 249-50, 279; Wood, *Lumbering in Maine*, 23, 85 (quote); Defebaugh, *History of the Lumber Industry*, 1: 57-59. On the pulpwood era, see: Smith, *Lumbering in Maine*, 233-61; David C. Smith, "Wood Pulp Paper Comes to the Northeast, 1865-1900," *FH*, 10 (1966): 12-25; Robert D. Goode, "The Economic Growth of the Pulp and Paper Industry in Maine" (unpub. M.A. thesis, University of Maine, 1934).

61. Eckstorm, "Lumbering in Maine," 694-95; Irland, "Rufus Putnam's Ghost," 68; Smith, *Lumbering in Maine*, 190-201, 233-331; William C. Osborn, *The Paper Plantation: The Nader Report on the Pulp and Paper Industry of Maine* (Washington, D.C.: Center for the Study of Responsive Law, 1973). See also: Richard W. Judd, Edwin A. Churchill, and Joel W. Eastman, ed., *Maine: The Pine Tree State from Prehistory to the Present* (Orono: University of Maine Press, 1995), 391-419.

62. Richard W. Judd, "Lumbering and the Farming Frontier in Aroostook County, Maine, 1840-1880," *JFH*, 28 (1984): 56-67 [Judd's arguments are also presented in *Aroostook*, 81-101 and passim]; Maine, Board of Agriculture, *Annual Report* (Augusta, Me.: State Printer, 1862), 340; Davis, *St. Croix*, 151-52; Wood, *Lumbering in Maine*, 185-99; John E. Nelligan, "The Life of a Lumberman," as told to Charles M. Sheridan, *Wis. Mag. Hist.*, 13 (1929): 12-21.

63. Beatrice Craig, "Agriculture and the Lumberman's Frontier in the Upper St. John Valley, 1800-70," *JFH*, 32 (1988): 125-37 (quote, p. 137); Judd, *Common Lands, Common People*, 66-67. Attitudes toward woods workers were essentially the same on both sides of the U.S.-Canada border, see: Belknap, *History of New Hampshire*, 3: 197-98; Dwight, *Travels*, 1: 302-303, 2: 160-61; Kendall, *Travels*, 3: 72-84; Graeme Wynn, " 'Deplorably Dark and Demoralized Lumberers'? Rhetoric and Reality in Early Nineteenth-Century New Brunswick," *JFH*, 24 (1980): 168-87; Donald MacKay, "The Canadian Logging Frontier," *JFH*, 23 (1979): 8-9; Lower, *Great Britain's Woodyard*, 190-96.

64. Potter, "Public Policy and Economic Growth," 215-20, 232-33, 240, 259, 269-71, 279, 291, 298-300; Judd, *Aroostook*, 92-101; Smith, *Lumbering in Maine*, 107-108, 225-26. See also: Frank Putnam, "Maine: A Study in Land-Grabbing, Tax Dodging, and Isolation," *New England Magazine*, 36 (1907): 515-40. The growing influence of the commercial-mercantile world and the merchants at its heart was taking place in neighboring New Brunswick too. For persuasive analyses, see: Graeme Wynn, *Timber Colony: A Historical Geography of Early Nineteenth-Century New Brunswick* (Toronto: University of Toronto Press, 1981); Christopher S. Beach, "The Pulpwood Province and the Paper State: Corporate Reconstruction, Underdevelopment, and Law in New Brunswick and Maine, 1890-1930" (unpub. Ph.D. diss., University of Maine, 1991).

65. Judd, "Lumbering and the Farming Frontier," 61, 65; MacKay, "Canadian Logging Frontier," 7-15; Lower, *Great Britain's Woodyard*, 23-24, 130-32, 159-70; Stephenson, *Recollections of a Long Life*, 29-39. The strength of the hewn timber trade on the Canadian side of the border may help explain the more egalitarian patterns of land ownership and greater strength of agrarian traditions that settlement and road building patterns suggest are present there. A comparative study of patterns on the two sides of the border is warranted.

66. Fairburn, *Merchant Sail*, provides the most thorough study of shipbuilding; on fishing, although treatment of the pre-nineteenth century is brief, Wayne M. O'Leary, *Maine Sea Fisheries: The Rise and Fall of a Native Industry, 1830-1890* (Boston: Northeastern University Press, 1996), is a superior source.

Chapter Four

1. Census data on lumbering during the nineteenth century is incomplete and undependable, especially for the period prior to 1840. Figures given here should be taken as general indicators, not absolutes. Defebaugh, *History of the Lumber Industry*, 1: 474-90, 2: 496-506; Michael Williams, "Products of the Forest: Mapping the Census of 1840," *JFH*, 24 (1980): 4-23. Cf. Alexander C. Flick, ed., *History of the State of New York* (10 vols.; New York: Columbia University Press, 1933-38), 8: 82-84.

2. Flick, *History of New York*, 2: 297-98, 343, 344-45 (quote); Defebaugh, *History of the Lumber Industry*, 2: 488-89; Kawashima and Tone, "Environmental Policy in Early America," 170-71; Kalm, *Travels in North America*, 1: 298-300; Willson, *Forest Conservation in Colonial Times*, 14.

3. Sylvester K. Stevens, *Pennsylvania, Titan of Industry* (3 vols.; New York: Lewis, 1948), 1: 3-4, 14; Christopher Ward, *The Dutch and Swedes on the Delaware, 1609-64* (Philadelphia: University of Pennsylvania Press, 1930), 102-106; John R. Stilgoe, *Common Landscape of America, 1580 to 1845* (New Haven, Conn.: Yale University Press, 1982), 175-77; Israel Acrelius, *A History of New Sweden*, trans. & ed. by William M. Reynolds (Philadelphia: Historical Society of Pennsylvania, 1874), 38; Fletcher, *Pennsylvania Agriculture and Country Life*, 327 (millowner quote). In 1740 Pennsylvania County also included the area that later became Montgomery County. See also: Johan Printz, "Report of Governor Johan Printz, 1647," in Albert Cook Myers, ed., *Narratives of Early Pennsylvania, West New Jersey, and Delaware, 1630-1707* (New York: Barnes & Noble, 1912), 127.

4. Kalm, *Travels in North America*, 1: 33; Anonymous, *American Husbandry*, 75, 142-43; Carl Bridenbaugh, "The Old and the New Societies of the Delaware Valley of the Seventeenth Century," *Pennsylvania Magazine of History and Biography*, 100 (1976): 150-51, 160, 163-70; James T. Lemon, *The Best Poor Man's Country: A Geographical Study of Early Southeastern Pennsylvania* (Baltimore: Johns Hopkins University Press, 1972), 1-41 and passim; Fletcher, *Pennsylvania Agriculture and Country Life*, 328 (last quote). Cf. Flick, *History of New York*, 2: 297-98. As Michael Williams has shown, agricultural clearing was the primary cause of deforestation in the eastern colonies/states; it was especially so in Pennsylvania. See: Williams, "Clearing the United States Forests: The Pivotal Years, 1810-1860," *Journal of Historical Geography*, 8 (1982): 12-28; Williams, *Americans and their Forests*, 60-67, 111-28.

5. Kalm, *Travels in North America*, 1: 27 (1st quote), 50-51; Anonymous, *American Husbandry*, 112-13 (2nd quote); Weld, *Travels through the States of North America*, 1: 32; Stevens, *Pennsylvania*, 1: 94; Coxe, *View of the United States*, 419. Coxe's figures showed Pennsylvania's exports less than those of Massachusetts (including the Province of Maine), New Hampshire, New York, North Carolina, and Georgia, but if domestic consumption were added it probably would have stood in third place.

6. Defebaugh, *History of the Lumber Industry*, 2: 487-91; Francis B. Lee, *New Jersey as a Colony and as a State . . .* (4 vols.; New York: Publishing Society of New Jersey, 1902), 1: 282 (quote).

7. Kalm, *Travels in North America*, 1: 89 (quotes), 265. See also: Weld, *Travels through North America*, 1: 261-63; Jack McCormick and Richard T. T.

Forman, "Location and Boundaries of the New Jersey Pine Barrens," in Richard T. T. Forman, ed., *Pine Barrens: Ecosystem and Landscape* (New York: Academic Press, 1979), xxxv-xlii; Jack McCormick, "The Vegetation of the New Jersey Pine Barrens," in ibid., 229-43.

8. Kalm, *Travels in North America*, 1: 28 (quote), 118-19, 122; Anonymous, *American Husbandry*, 103; Lee, *New Jersey*, 1: 194, 284; Alfred P. Muntz, "The Changing Geography of the New Jersey Woodlands, 1600-1900" (unpub. Ph.D. diss., University of Wisconsin, 1959), 127-69; Defebaugh, *History of the Lumber Industry*, 2: 490-91, 496-506.

9. Lee, *New Jersey*, 1: 282-83, 287. See also: Willson, *Forest Conservation in Colonial Times*, 7-14.

10. Peter O. Wacker, "Human Exploitation of the New Jersey Pine Barrens before 1900," in Forman, *Pine Barrens*, 3-23; Defebaugh, *History of the Lumber Industry*, 1: 490, 2: 486-95 (quote p. 492); Harry B. and Grace M. Weiss, *The Early Sawmills of New Jersey* (Trenton: New Jersey Agricultural Society, 1968), esp. 47-89.

11. David Maldwyn Ellis, "Rise of the Empire State, 1790-1820," *New York History*, 56 (1975): 13.

12. Guy H. McMaster, *History of the Settlement of Steuben County, N. Y. . . .* (Bath, N.Y.: Underhill, 1853), 111; Franklin B. Hough, *A History of St. Lawrence and Franklin Counties, New York . . .* (Albany, N.Y.: Little, 1853), 277-79. On factors involved in such settlement, see: William T. Langhorne, Jr., "Mill Based Settlement Patterns in Schoharie County, New York: A Regional Study," *Historical Archeology*, 10 (1976): 73-92; Fox, *History of the Lumber Industry of New York*, 92-119; Evelyn M. Dinsdale, "Spatial Patterns of Technological Change: The Lumber Industry of Northern New York," *Economic Geography*, 41 (1965): 255-56. Sawmills frequently preceded gristmills, for they could be run with simple, undershot waterwheels while gristmills required more power and thus the more complex overshoot wheels. See: James Arthur Frost, *Life on the Upper Susquehanna, 1783-1860* (New York: King's Crown, 1951), 27.

13. Terry A. McNealy, "Rafting on the Delaware: New Light from Old Documents," *Bucks County Historical Society Journal*, 2 (1977): 27-29; Robert J. Wheeler, "Admiral Skinner," *Keystone Folklore Quarterly*, 3 (1958): 30-31; B. F. Falkenthal, Jr., "Improving Navigation on the Delaware River," *Papers of the Bucks County Historical Society*, 6 (1932): 110; Leslie C. Wood, *Rafting on the Delaware River* (Livingston Manor, N.Y.: Livingston Manor Times, 1935), 6-7; Harry B. and Grace M. Weiss, *Rafting on the Delaware River* (Trenton: New Jersey Agricultural Society, 1967), 8-11; William Heidt, Jr., *History of Rafting on the Delaware* (Port Jervis, N.Y.: Minisink Valley Historical Society, 1922), [1-3]; *Milford* (New Jersey) *Leader*, 10 May 1883, "Lumbering Days on the Delaware River," reprinted in New Jersey Historical Society, *Proceedings*, 71 (1953): 212-14; McMaster, *History of Steuben County*, 134-35; John C. French et al., *Rafting Days in Pennsylvania*, ed. by J. Herbert Walker (Altoona, Penn.: Times-Tribune, 1922), 54-56; C. Lee Berry, "Lumbering in Pennsylvania" ([Williamsport, Penn.], 1945; typescript on microfilm, Pennsylvania State Archives, Harrisburg, MG-262; location of original unknown; pagination supplied), 47-49; Trenton *New Jersey Gazette*, quoted in Defebaugh, *History*

of the Lumber Industry, 2: 499-500. One reliable authority suggests 1764 was originally a typographical error. He dates Skinner's first raft to 1746 and adds that it consisted of six seventy-foot pine logs intended for use as ships' masts. Fletcher, *Pennsylvania Agriculture and Country Life*, 327-28. Franklin B. Hough claimed rafting began on the Delaware in 1807. Clearly, he too was in error. Hough, *Report upon Forestry* (Washington, D.C.: GPO, 1878), 464.

14. Quoted in Defebaugh, *History of the Lumber Industry*, 2: 499-500.

15. In addition to rafts, arks were used, especially for hauling coal, but in the beginning—and always for lumber and timber—rafts were the main mode of transport connecting settlers with downstream markets. The earliest rafts were small, but as experience and expertise—as well as output and demand— grew they became larger. See: Defebaugh, *History of the Lumber Industry*, 2: 427-28; Hough, *Report upon Forestry*, 464.

16. *Milford Leader*, 10 May 1883; Thaddeus S. Kenderline, "Lumbering Days on the Delaware River," *Papers of the Bucks County Historical Society*, 4 (1917): 239, 241.

17. Defebaugh, *History of the Lumber Industry*, 2: 315, 572, 575, 582 (quote), 586-87; *Hazard's Register of Pennsylvania*, 3 (1829): 384.

18. McMaster, *History of Steuben County*, 134-36, 182-83; Elizabeth Lowman Hall and Asaph B. Hall, "Arks and Rafts on the Susquehanna" (unpub. manuscript, Historical Society of Cecil County Library, Elkton, Maryland), 1-2; Frost, *Life on the Upper Susquehanna*, 7-30, 72.

19. Hall and Hall, "Arks and Rafts on the Susquehanna," 12-16; Defebaugh, *History of the Lumber Industry*, 2: 426-27, 429-30, 432; *Hazard's Register of Pennsylvania*, 3 (1829): 400; 4 (1829): 157; 7 (1831): 315; 11 (1833): 376; McMaster, *History of Steuben County*, 26; Berry, "Lumbering in Pennsylvania," 49-50; D. F. Magee, "Rafting on the Susquehanna," Lancaster County Historical Society, *Papers and Addresses*, 24 (1920): 193-202; S. B. Row, "Clearfield County: Or, Reminiscences of the Past" (published serially in Clearfield [Penn.] *Raftsman's Journal*), 14 and 21 Sept. 1859.

20. William Lowman to Mary Beers Lowman, 29 Mar., 12 Apr., and 12 May 1848, in Hall and Hall, "Arks and Rafts on the Susquehanna," 2-9.

21. Kalm, *Travels in North America*, 1: 330 (quote), 332, 342.

22. Anne Grant, *Memoirs of an American Lady . . .* (1808; reprint, 2 vols.; New York: Dodd Mead, 1901), 2: 168-69; Defebaugh, *History of the Lumber Industry*, 2: 315, 408-23.

23. Stevens, *Pennsylvania*, 1: 17; Robert Kuhn McGregor, "Changing Technologies and Forest Consumption in the Upper Delaware Valley, 1790-1880," *JFH*, 32 (1988): 71-72. McGregor supplies the estimate of 20 per cent. For further discussions of the farm-forest nexus, see: Lillard, *The Great Forest*, 76-94 and passim; and Wayne D. Rasmussen, "Wood on the Farm," in Hindle, *Material Culture*, 15-34.

24. For further discussion, see: McGregor, "Changing Technologies and Forest Consumption," 79-81; David Maldwyn Ellis, *Landlords and Farmers in the Hudson-Mohawk Region, 1790-1850* (Ithaca, N.Y.: Cornell University Press, 1946), 112-15, 130-31, 208-211; Charles E. Brooks, "Overrun with Bushes: Frontier Land Development and the Forest History of the Holland Purchase, 1800-50," *FCH*, 39 (1995): 17-26.

25. Kalm, *Travels in North America*, 2: 388-89; Phillip L. White, *Beekmantown, New York: Forest Frontier to Farm Community* (Austin: University of Texas Press, 1979), 29-70 (quote, p. 52); H. N. Muller, "Floating a Lumber Raft to Quebec City, 1805: The Journal of Guy Catlin of Burlington," *Vermont History*, 39 (1971): 116-24; William G. Gove, "Burlington, the Former Lumber Capital," *Northern Logger and Timber Processor*, 19 (1971): 18-19, 38-43; Hough, *Report upon Forestry*, 446-53; Defebaugh, *History of the Lumber Industry*, 2: 317-18; MacKay, "The Canadian Logging Frontier," 13-15; Richard Nelson Current, *Pine Logs and Politics: A Life of Philetus Sawyer, 1816-1900* (Madison: State Historical Society of Wisconsin, 1950), 11-12. Until railroads connected Burlington with Boston, its lumber industry was linked to New York and the industry's story more a part of that of the Middle Atlantic States than of New England.

26. White, *Beekmantown*, 309, 355-62, and passim. Cf. William Joseph Griffin, oral history interview with Charles D. Bonsted (1958; typescript, Forest History Society, Durham, N.C.), 9, 16; Earl Porter, oral history interview with Elwood R. Maunder (1963; typescript, Forest History Society, Durham, N.C.), 2-6; Judd, *Common Lands, Common People*, 23-35, 93-96.

27. Joseph Riesenman, Jr., *History of Northwestern Pennsylvania* (2 vols.; New York: Lewis, 1943), 1: 343 (quote); Lewis Cass Aldrich, *History of Clearfield County, Pennsylvania* (Syracuse, N.Y.: Morris, 1887), 92.

28. Clearfield *Raftsman's Journal*, 23 Sept. 1857; William H. Egle, *Illustrated History of the Commonwealth of Pennsylvania . . .* (2nd ed.; Philadelphia: Gardner, 1880), 561; William Langdon, "A Pennsylvania Lumber Raftsman's Year: The Diary of William Langdon for 1855," ed. by Thomas R. Cox, *JFH*, 26 (1982): 124-39, esp. 136-37. Egle's report of four hundred sawmills in Clearfield County comes from William Bigler, the largest producer in the county and from 1852 to 1855 governor of the state. On Bigler, see: William C. Armor, *Lives of the Governors of Pennsylvania . . .* (Philadelphia: Simon, 1872), 413-23.

29. Langdon, "A Pennsylvania Lumber Raftsman's Year," 124-25; R. Dudley Tonkin, *My Partner, The River: The White Pine Story on the Susquehanna* (Pittsburgh: University of Pittsburgh Press, 1958), 49-54; John A. Dale et al., *History of Clearfield County, Pa.*, (published serially in Clearfield *Spirit*, 1897; copy in scrapbook, James V. Brown Library, Williamsport), 116-17; [J.H. Beers & Co., ed.], *Commemorative Biographical Record of Central Pennsylvania . . .* (2 vols.; Philadelphia: J. H. Beers, 1898), 1: 587-88.

30. Engle, *History of the Commonwealth of Pennsylvania*, 561 (1st quote); W. S. W. to S. B. Row, 19 May 1857, printed in Clearfield *Raftsman's Journal*, 27 May 1857 (2nd quote).

31. Clearfield *Raftsman's Journal*, 27 May 1857; John Blair Linn, *History of Centre and Clinton Counties, Pennsylvania* (Philadelphia: Lippincott, 1883), 91; Thomas Lincoln Wall, *Clearfield Co., Pa., Present and Past* (Clearfield: by the author, 1925), 97; Langdon, "A Pennsylvania Lumber Raftsman's Year," 124-25, 133, and passim; H. F. McCall, diary, Nov. 1837-1838 (microfilm; Pennsylvania State Archives, Harrisburg; original at Cornell University, Ithaca, N.Y.).

32. Lee Benson, *The Concept of Jacksonian Democracy: New York as a Test Case* (Princeton, N.J.: Princeton University Press, 1961), 201-205. Writing a century earlier, Franklin Hough had little to say about Burke, but described Malone in terms consistent with Benson's. "There is scarcely an inland town in the state," he wrote, "that will compare with Malone in the thrift and improvement which it has exhibited since the completion of the [Northern] railroad. . . . [It lies] in the midst of a rich and rapidly improving agricultural district." Hough, *History of St. Lawrence and Franklin Counties*, 455, 507-513 (quote, p. 509).

33. Others had similar hopes for land in the Susquehannah Land Company tract in and around Luzerne County, Pennsylvania. As one landowners' representative put it, poor settlers "prepare a way for a more wealthy Class." When these arrive, he predicted, there will be a market for local produce, and settlers will be able to pay for their farms. Robert H. Rose to Henry Drinker, 28 July (quote), 25 August 1803, *The Susquehannah Land Company Papers*, Julian P. Boyd and Robert J. Taylor, ed. (11 vols.; Wilkes Barre, Penn.: Wyoming Historical and Genealogical Society, 1930-1975), 11: 418.

34. Brooks, "Overrun with Bushes," 21-22. For further discussion, see: Charles E. Brooks, *Frontier Settlement and Market Revolution: The Holland Purchase, 1800-1845* (Ithaca, N.Y.: Cornell University Press, 1996), 82-105; H. J. Lutz, "Effects of Cattle Grazing on Vegetation of a Virgin Forest in Northwestern Pennsylvania," *Journal of Forest Research*, 41 (1930): 561-70; E. L. Jones, "Creative Disruptions in American Agriculture, 1620-1820," *Ag. Hist.*, 48 (1974): 510-28.

35. Alan Taylor, "The Great Change Begins: Settling the Forest of Central New York," *New York History*, 81 (1995): 265-90; David Maldwyn Ellis, "The Yankee Invasion of New York, 1783-1850," ibid., 32 (1951): 3-17; Ellis, "Rise of the Empire State," 6; Francis Whiting Halsey, *The Old New York Frontier . . . 1614-1800* (New York: Scribners, 1901), 337-46.

36. Ford to Samuel Ogden, 17 Dec. 1797, in Hough, *History of St. Lawrence and Franklin Counties*, 390; Ford quoted in Franklin B. Hough, *A History of Jefferson County in the State of New York . . .* (Albany: Munsell, 1854), 112 (3rd quote), 136-37 (2nd quote). On this trade, see: Lower, *Great Britain's Woodyard*, 159-70; Hough, *History of Jefferson County*, 141; MacKay, "The Canadian Logging Frontier," 8-9. On Ford, see: Hough, *History of St. Lawrence and Franklin Counties*, 589-94.

37. Hough, *History of Jefferson County*, 81; McMaster, *History of Steuben County*, 233 (quote), 235-40.

38. Alan Taylor, *William Cooper's Town: Power and Persuasion on the Frontier of the Early American Republic* (New York: Knopf, 1995), 87-92, 103, 105, 108-110 (quote, p. 103); Ellis, *Landlords and Farmers*, 112-15; Ellis, "Rise of the Empire State," 15. See also: Taylor, "The Great Change Begins."

39. Thomas Cooper to Thomas McKean, 15 Nov. 1802, *Susquehannah Land Company Papers*, 11: 342. The outpouring of poor New Englanders even reached the Allegheny Plateau, where residents of the more affluent towns and lowland farms often called them "ridge runners" in reference to their hardscrabble hill farms.

40. Timothy Flint reported that "clear and fine pine plank" was rafted down the Allegheny to buyers along the Ohio and "great quantities even to New Orleans." Wheeler, Dusenbury & Co., which shipped down the Allegheny from a mill near Olean, New York, shifted to shipping eastward with the opening of the Erie Canal and its Genesee feeder. See: Jenks Cameron, *The Development of Governmental Forest Control in the United States* (Washington, D.C.: Institute for Government Research, 1928), 101; Flint, *History and Geography of the Mississippi Valley*, (3rd ed., 2 vols.; Cincinnati: Flint, 1833), 1: 52; Walter Casler, Benjamin F. G. Kline, Jr., and Thomas T. Taber III, *The Logging Railroad Era of Lumbering in Pennsylvania: A History of the Lumber, Chemical Wood, and Tanning Companies which Used Railroads in Pennsylvania* (3 vols.; Williamsport, Pa.: by the authors, 1970-78), 3: 1101 [the chapters in this work have also been published separately under individual titles].

41. Barbara E. Benson, *Logs and Lumber: The Development of Lumbering in Michigan's Lower Peninsula, 1837-1870* (Mount Pleasant: Clarke Historical Library, Central Michigan University, 1989), 126-27; Jeremy W. Kilar, *Michigan's Lumbertowns: Lumbermen and Laborers in Saginaw, Bay City, and Muskegon, 1870-1905* (Detroit: Wayne State University Press, 1990), 21, 30. Shipments were arriving from Canada via Lake Champlain as well. Orrin Henry Ingram, *Autobiography* (Eau Claire, Wis., by the author, 1912), 19, 24-27.

42. McMaster, *History of Steuben County*, 108; Halsey, *The Old New York Frontier*, 388-91.

43. Defebaugh, *History of the Lumber Industry*, 2: 408-428, 432-34 (quote, p. 432); Neil Adams McNall, *An Agricultural History of the Genesee Valley, 1790-1860* (Philadelphia: University of Pennsylvania Press, 1952), 100, 183-91; Irwin W. Near, *A History of Steuben County, New York, and Its People* (2 vols.; Chicago: Lewis, 1911), 1: 246-49; Henry Perry Smith, *History of Broome County* . . . (Syracuse, N.Y.: Mason, 1885), 76-77; Hough, *Report upon Forestry*, 441-42, 447-50; Ronald E. Shaw, *Erie Water West: A History of the Erie Canal, 1792-1854* (Lexington: University of Kentucky Press, 1966), 239-41 and passim; Carol Sheriff, *The Artificial River: The Erie Canal and the Paradox of Progress, 1817-1862* (New York: Hill & Wang, 1996), 53-54, 64-68; See: Noble E. Whitford, *History of the Canal System of the State of New York* . . . Supplement to the Annual Report of the State Engineer (2 vols.; Albany: Brandow, 1906), esp. 1: ch. 19. The Genessee connected to the upper Allegheny, but with production rising further west this provided little fresh demand for lumber from upstate New York.

44. Batavia *Republican Advocate*, 12 Apr. 1853, as quoted in McNall, *Agricultural History of the Genesee Valley*, 183; Frost, *Life on the Upper Susquehanna*, 82-83; McMaster, *History of Steuben County*, 231. The list of pioneer New York lumbermen compiled by William Fox is replete with the names of producers from the central and western parts of the state. See: Fox, *History of the Lumber Industry of New York*, 91-119.

45. Ellis, *Landlords and Farmers*, 14, 75, 112-13; Kalm, *Travels in North America*, 1: 343; John Fowler, *Journal of a Tour through the State of New York in the*

Year 1830 . . . (London: Whittaker, Treacher, and Arnot, 1831), 40; Nelson Greene, ed., *History of the Valley of the Hudson, River of Destiny, 1609-1930* (5 vols.; Chicago: Clarke, 1931), 2: 630 (3rd quote).

46. Fowler, *Journal of a Tour*, 76, 79-80, 85 (italics in original); Ellis, *Landlords and Farmers*, 130-31; Shaw, *Erie Water West*, 135-36, 202.

47. Peter Sharpe et al., petition to New York State Legislature regarding duties on lumber rafts on state canals, 26 February 1827 (New York State—misc. file, box 2, canals; Manuscript Department, New York Historical Society, New York); Shaw, *Erie Water West*, 248. The petition has been referred to as being from 146 New York lumbermen, but careful reading shows it to be from businessmen cognizant of the "cry of complaint & prayer for relief" of "our fellow Citizens ranking in the order of Lumbermen & residing in the Northern and Western Sections of this State."

48. For example, Stewart Holbrook in his classic history of the lumber industry totally ignores activities in central and western New York (and barely mentions those centered at Glens Falls). See: Holbrook, *Holy Old Mackinaw*, 76.

49. Defebaugh, *History of the Lumber Industry*, 2: 443-44; Hough, *Report upon Forestry*, 453, 455; Shaw, *Erie Water West*, 239-41; McNall, *Agricultural History of the Genesee Valley*, 188. Shipments from Olean started as early as the 1820s, and when Wisconsin built its first capital the lumber used came from the Allegheny, rather than the state's well-forested northern reaches. See: Flint, *History and Geography of the Mississippi Valley*, 1: 52; Casler, Kline, and Taber, *Loggine Railroad Era in Pennsylvania*, 3: 1101; Wyman, *Wisconsin Frontier*, 41; Robert F. Fries, *Empire in Pine: The Story of Lumbering in Wisconsin, 1830-1900* (Madison: State Historical Society of Wisconsin, 1951), 8.

50. Ellis, *Landlords and Farmers*, 112. Fletcher claims that after 1840 lumbering in Pennsylvania was "more specialized—a business by itself instead of a sideline of farming." This also serves as a rough indicator of when the transition to a lumberman's frontier occurred in New York. See: Fletcher, *Pennsylvania Agriculture and Country Life*, 327.

51. Hough, *History of St. Lawrence and Franklin Counties*, 285-86, 556-62; Franklin B. Hough, *A History of Lewis County in the State of New York . . .* (Albany: Munsell & Rowland, 1860), 110, 119; Lewis Stillwell, "Migration from Vermont, 1776-1860," *Proceedings of the Vermont Historical Society*, 20 (1916): 352. See also: Dwight, *Travels*, 3: 266-67.

52. Gove, "Burlington," 18-19, 38-43; Judd, *Common Lands, Common People*, 91-93 (quotes pp. 92, 93); Current, *Pine Logs and Politics*, 13-15. Burlington's lumber industry continued after the 1850s, although much of Vermont's accessible forestland had been cut; rough Canadian lumber, brought by water and finished in plants in Burlington, became a mainstay as did lumber cut in sawmills in New York that drew on the still-timbered north slope of the Adirondacks.

53. For the most part, those who continued farming shifted to specialized commercial agriculture and no longer depended upon the forest and its products. However, as wood products rose in value and railroads made sales

in distant markets possible, some turned attention to their farm woodlots, frequently second-growth stands. On the other hand, hill farmers seeking to continue the older, semi-subsistence agrarian system apparently made up much of the region's out-migration, although some among them, such as Philetus Sawyer, had enjoyed some success as lumbermen. For discussions, see: Judd, *Common Lands, Common People*, 64-67, 85-89; Fred A. Shannon, *The Farmer's Last Frontier: Agriculture, 1860-1897* (1945; New York: Harper & Row, 1968), 245-61; Current, *Pine Logs and Politics*, 10-15.

54. George Perkins Marsh, *Address Delivered before the Agricultural Society of Rutland County, Sept. 30th, 1847* (Rutland, Vt.: Rutland Herald, 1848), 6, 9, 17-19 (quotes); Marsh, *Report Made under Authority of the Legislature of Vermont, on the Artificial Propagation of Fish* (Burlington, Vt.: Free Press, 1857), 13-15. On Marsh, see: David Lowenthal, *George Perkins Marsh, Prophet of Conservation* (Seattle: University of Washington Press, 2000), 4-7, 95-99, 182-86, 296-98; Jane Curtis, *The World of George Perkins Marsh, America's First Conservationist* (Woodstock, Vt.: Woodstock Foundation, 1982). In his own day Marsh's impact was limited. *Man and Nature* was too massive and technical for widespread appeal. Marsh urged his publishers to print an inexpensive abridged edition, such as was done in Italy, but to no avail. As he put it, "[N]either I nor my books have ever found favor" at Scribners, "& my wishes were ignored." Marsh to [?], 6 February 1875 (Ferdinand J. Dreer Collection, Manuscript Division, Historical Society of Pennsylvania, Philadelphia), vol. 961.

55. McMaster, *History of Steuben County*, 36-37.

56. Bill Gove, "Glens Falls—The Queen City Built by the Lumber Industry," *Northern Logger and Timber Processor*, 24 (Apr. 1976): 8; [Gresham Publishing Co., ed.], *History and Biography of Washington County and of the Town of Queensbury* . . . (Chicago: Gresham, 1894), 143; Austin Welles Holden, *History of Queensbury* . . . (Albany, N.Y.: Munsell, 1874), 55-57, 73; Fox, *History of the Lumber Industry of New York*, 27; Defebaugh, *History of the Lumber Industry*, 2: 318; Dinsdale, "Spatial Patterns," 256. The numerous rafts reported by Anne Grant came from not far downstream.

57. [Gresham Publishing Co.], *History and Biography of Washington County*, 143-44 (quote, p. 144); Holden, *History of Queensbury*, 40, 57; Benson J. Lossing, *The Hudson, from the Wilderness to the Sea* (New York: Virtue & Yoston, 1866), 68-69; Gove, "Glens Falls," 8; Harold K. Hochschild, *Lumberjacks and Rivermen in the Central Adirondacks, 1850-1950* (Blue Mountain Lake, N.Y.: Adirondack Museum, 1962), 1-2.

58. The problem was faced by many sawmills in northern New York. Only those with river access to sizable hinterlands prospered. See: Dinsdale, "Spatial Patterns," 259-60, 262-63.

59. Fox, *History of the Lumber Industry of New York*, 35; William Chapman White, *Adirondack Country* (New York: Knopf, 1968), 90; Gove, "Glens Falls," 8-9, 30; Hough, *Report upon Forestry*, 437-39; Hochschild, *Lumberjacks and Rivermen*, 2; Dinsdale, "Spatial Patterns," 258; Defebaugh, *History of the Lumber Industry*, 2: 316. See: Fox, *History of the Lumber Industry of New York*, 36; J. P Kinney, *The Essentials of American Timber Law* (New York: Wiley, 1917), 210-13.

60. Gove, "Glens Falls," 9, 30, 36; Defebaugh, *History of the Lumber Industry*, 2: 407; Hough, *Report upon Forestry*, 440; Lossing, *The Hudson*, 65-66; Dinsdale, "Spatial Patterns," 256-58; George Rogers Taylor, *The Transportation Revolution, 1815-1860* (New York: Rinehart, 1951), 32-36; Shaw, *Erie Water West*, 414; [Gresham Publishing Co.], *History of Washington County*, 53-54, 84-88, 95-98 (quote, p. 98).

61. Holden, *History of Washington County*, 78-79.

62. Hochschild, *Lumberjacks and Rivermen*, 8-26, 49-63; Dinsdale, "Spatial Patterns," 258-59.

63. Gove, "Glens Falls," 40; Defebaugh, *History of the Lumber Industry*, 2: 316-17; Hough, *Report upon Forestry*, 439; Lossing, *The Hudson*, 65-66.

64. Some time after 1862 log drives began being managed by the association, but an agreement that year shows they were regulated through a separate agreement of many of the same lumbermen who had joined to form the boom association. See: Hochschild, *Lumberjacks and Rivermen*, 22, 73-88.

65. Ibid., 68; Defebaugh, *History of the Lumber Industry*, 2: 316-17; Gove, "Glens Falls," 30, 38, 40; Lossing, *The Hudson*, 68-71; Philip G. Terrie, *Contested Terrain: A New History of Nature and People in the Adirondacks* (Syracuse, N.Y.: Adirondack Museum and Syracuse University Press, 1997), 85-86.

66. Hans Huth, *Nature and the American: Three Centuries of Changing Attitudes* (reprint ed.; Lincoln: University of Nebraska Press, 1972), 81, 96-100, 110-11; Roderick Nash, *Wilderness and the American Mind* (rev. ed.; New Haven, Conn.: Yale University Press, 1973), 61-62, 103-104, 116-18; Hochschild, *Lumberjacks and Rivermen*, 2-4; Alfred L. Donaldson, *A History of the Adirondacks* (2 vols.; New York: Century, 1921), 1: 190-201; Russell M. L. Carson, *Peaks and People of the Adirondacks* (Garden City, N.Y.: Doubleday Page, 1927), 157-58; Frank Graham, Jr., *The Adirondack Park: A Political History* (New York: Knopf, 1978), 15-44; Dinsdale, "Spatial Patterns," 256. The few old-style farmer-loggers present sometimes clashed with lumbermen and preservationists. See: Porter, oral history interview, 2-9; Karl Jacoby, *Crimes Against Nature: Squatters, Poachers, Thieves, and the Hidden History of American Conservation* (Berkeley: University of California Press, 2001), 17-78.

67. Hochschild, *Lumberjacks and Rivermen*, 1, 4-5, 7, 11, 32-34. See also: Charles W. Bryan, Jr., *The Raquette, River of the Forest* (Blue Mountain Lake, N.Y.: Adirondack Museum, 1964), 104-107.

68. Terrie, *Contested Terrain*, 84-95, 107; Graham, *Adirondack Park*, 65-78; Carson, *Peaks and People of the Adirondacks*, 218-22; E. R. Wallace, *Descriptive Guide to the Adirondacks . . .* (5th ed.; New York: Forest and Stream, 1876), 227, 232-37; Van Brocklin, "The Movement for the Conservation of Natural Resources," 51-54; Marvin Wolf Kranz, "Pioneering in Conservation: A History of the Conservation Movement in New York State, 1865-1903" (unpub. Ph.D. diss., Syracuse University, 1961), 43-64, 127-47, 179-80; Verplanck Colvin, *Report on a Topographical Survey of the Adirondack Wilderness of New York* (Albany, N.Y.: Argus, 1873), 155-56.

Chapter Five

1. After considerable bickering between railroad and canal advocates, Pennsylvania commenced construction of a cross-state canal in 1826. With a trans-Allegheny portage railroad connecting its two ends, the mainline canal was completed in 1834. The canal was sold to the Pennsylvania Railroad in 1857, and although portions were closed in following years, the section serving Williamsport continued in operation. Canals, however, had less impact on Pennsylvania's lumber industry than on New York's. See: Julius Rubin, "An Imitative Improvement: The Pennsylvania Mainline," in Carter Goodrich et al., *Canals and American Economic Development* (New York: Columbia University Press, 1961), 67-114; Taylor, *Transportation Revolution*, 43-45.

2. There were 198 sawmills in Lycoming County, many of those not in Williamsport clustered close by. *Eighth Census of the United States: 1860*, Vol. 3: 516.

3. Pennsylvania, Bureau of Industrial Statistics, *Third Annual Report, 1874-1875* (Harrisburg: State Printer, 1876), 538; Hough, *Report upon Forestry*, 464-65; *Eighth Census of the United States: 1860*, 3: 503-504; Defebaugh, *History of the Lumber Industry*, 2: 591-607; Pennsylvania, Department of Agriculture, *First Annual Report, 1895, Part 2: Forestry Division* (Harrisburg: State Printer, 1896), 344; James C. Humes, "The Susquehanna Boom: A History of Logging and Rafting on the West Branch of the Susquehanna River," *Now and Then*, 14 (1962): 4-14; John F. Meginness, *Otzinachson: or, A History of the West Branch Valley . . .* (Philadelphia: Ashmead, 1857), 438-40, 447-51; Meginness, *Lycoming County: Its Organization and Condensed History for One Hundred Years* (Williamsport: Gazette and Bulletin, 1895), 61, 77-78; Williamsport *Lycoming Gazette*, 5 Feb. 1868; Williamsport *Gazette and Bulletin*, 4 Jan. 1870; Thomas W. Lloyd, "When Lumber was King" ([Williamsport], n.d.; typescript, James V. Brown Library, Williamsport), 1-2, 27-28. Lock Haven was also a major center of the spar and timber trade, which depended on rafting even after log drives and booms made their appearance on the river. See: Defebaugh, *History of the Lumber Industry*, 2: 602-603; Stevens, *Pennsylvania*, 1: 273-74.

4. Casler, Kline, and Taber, *Logging Railroad Era in Pennsylvania*, 3: 1201-1206; Hiram Cranmer, "Harvesting the Hemlock: The Reminiscences of a Pennsylvania Wood-Hick," ed. by Thomas R. Cox, *Western Pennsylvania Historical Magazine*, 67 (1984): 121-22; [James Elliott Defebaugh, ed.], *American Lumbermen: The Personal History and Public and Business Achievements. of . . . Eminent Lumbermen of the United States* (3 vols.; Chicago: American Lumberman, 1905-1906), 1: 67-69. With the advent of company towns and of logging railroads that tapped stands not accessible from the river, much production moved away from Williamsport.

5. Lock Haven *Clinton Democrat*, 29 Apr., 24 June 1851; Egle, *History of the Commonwealth of Pennsylvania*, 465-67; Defebaugh, *History of the Lumber Industry*, 2: 593, 596-98, 600-601; Berry, "Lumbering in Pennsylvania," 87-124; George S. Banger, *History of the Susquehanna Boom Company from 1846 to 1876* (Williamsport: Gazette and Bulletin, 1876), 2; Thomas W. Lloyd, *History of Lycoming County, Pennsylvania* (2 vols.; Topeka, Kans.: Historical

Publishing, 1929), 1: 343-58. Some sources incorrectly credit Perkins with originating the idea of a boom at Williamsport. See: Banger, *History of the Susquehanna Boom*, 1-2; James Myers, "Recollections of the Susquehanna Boom," *Journal of the Lycoming County Historical Society*, 8 (1972): 14; Lewis Edwin Theis, "Lumbering and Rafting on the West Branch," Northumberland County Historical Society, *Proceedings*, 21 (1957): 101-102; Lloyd, "When Lumber Was King," 17-21.

6. There is some question as to the date of the drive, usually acknowledged to have been the first on the upper West Branch. John B. Rumberger gives the question the fullest coverage and sets the date at 1852; however, both the *Clinton Democrat* and Rumberger's own internal evidence indicate 1850, a much more probable date. See: Rumberger, "Loggers against Rafters," *Lock Haven Express* (reprinted from Philadelphia *North American*), 17 June 1915; Lock Haven *Clinton Democrat*, 28 May 1850; [Beers & Co.], *Commemorative Biographical Record*, 1: 565.

7. Wing's connection, if any, to Abraham Wing of Glens Falls or to his descendants is unclear. He was born in Maine, not New York. Manuscript census records, Clinton County, Pa., 1860 (National Archives, microcopy #432, roll 768), p. 405.

8. Lock Haven *Clinton Democrat*, 28 May 1850. Construction of the temporary boom began the previous year; a permanent boom did not go into operation until 1851, which accounts for the varying dates given for the beginning of the Susquehanna Boom.

9. Ibid., 24 June 1851 (quote); Lloyd, "When Lumber Was King," 30-35; Lloyd, *History of Lycoming County*, 1: 343, 508-512; Berry, "Lumbering in Pennsylvania," 90. For good descriptions of log drives in the area, see: Joseph Reisenman, Jr., *History of Northwestern Pennsylvania* (3 vols.; New York: Lewis, 1943) 1: 349-55; Samuel A. King, "A Log Drive to Williamsport in 1868," *Pennsylvania History*, 29 (1962): 155-56; Nelligan, "Life of a Lumberman," 25-30.

10. Williamsport *Lycoming Gazette*, 23 June 1852, 5 Feb. 1868; Williamsport *West Branch Bulletin*, 21 Jan. 1865; Lock Haven *Clinton Democrat*, 24 June, 12 Aug., 2 Sept. 1851, 6 Jan. 1852; Myers, "Recollections," 15; Casler, Kline, and Taber, *Logging Railroad Era in Pennsylvania*, 1: 404-405; Roland D. Swoope, Jr., *History of Clearfield County . . .* (Chicago: Richmond & Arnold, 1911), 632; Banger, *History of the Susquehanna Boom*, 2-9; [Defebaugh], *American Lumbermen*, 1: 68. Booms at Lock Haven and near the mouth of Pine Creek followed, that at Lock Haven was built soon after Williamsport's. Hough, *Report upon Forestry*, 465-66.

11. Row, "Clearfield County," 12 Oct. 1850 (1st quote); *Clearfield Republican*, 6 May 1853; Wing and Getchell, statements in Lock Haven *Clinton Democrat*, 12 Aug., 2 Sept. 1851, 6 Jan. 1852. See also: Clearfield *Raftsman's Journal*, 23 Sept. 1859; John Blair Linn, *History of Centre and Clinton Counties, Pennsylvania* (Philadelphia: L. H. Everts, 1883), 93.

12. Row, "Clearfield County," 12 Oct. 1859; Tonkin, *My Partner*, 25-26; D. S. Maynard, *Historical View of Clinton County from Its Earliest Settlement to the Present Time* (Lock Haven, Penn.: Enterprise, 1875), 55; French et al., *Rafting Days*, 24; Gladys Tozier, "The Ring of the Axe and the Whir of the Saw," *Journal of the Lycoming County Historical Society*, 2 (1961): 18.

13. Lloyd, "When Lumber Was King," 14-15. DuBois owned considerable timberland in Clearfield County, from which he supplied his mill in Williamsport via log drives. He was thus a major participant in the struggle between raftsmen and log drivers. [Defebaugh], *American Lumbermen*, 1: 67-68.

14. *Clearfield Republican*, 4 Feb. 1853. See also: ibid., 14 Jan. 1853. As published, Packer was replying to a resolution thanking him for "defending" the ban on log drives. This was a typographical error; from the context it is clear "defeating" was meant.

15. Pennsylvania, *Legislative Journal, House*, 1853, 1: 138, 157, 233, 435, 627, 679-80; ibid., *Senate, 1854*, 217, 244, 345; Lock Haven *Clinton Democrat*, 15 Feb. 1, 8, and 15 Mar., 19 Apr. 1853, 7 Mar. 1854.

16. *Clearfield Republican*, 29 Nov. 1854; Clearfield *Raftsman's Journal*, 21 Feb., 2 and 9 May, 21 Nov. 1855, 13 Feb. 14 May 1856; Tonkin, *My Partner*, 27. In February 1855 the *Raftsman's Journal* reported that the regulatory bill "will in all probability pass," but the *Legislative Journals* show it was never considered.

17. Clearfield *Raftsman's Journal*, 19 Mar. 1856. Tonkin, *My Partner*, p. 24, incorrectly states this meeting was on 17 Mar. 1855. Since Pennsylvania's general incorporation law did not apply to transportation, each new boom company had to obtain a charter from the legislature. See: Louis B. Hartz, *Economic Policy and Democratic Thought: Pennsylvania, 1776-1860* (Cambridge, Mass.: Harvard University Press, 1948), 40-42.

18. Clearfield *Raftsman's Journal*, 25 June 1856.

19. Ibid., 9 July 1856 (quote); Tonkin, *My Partner*, 24-25. Cf. "Remarks of [Seth A.] Backus Relative to Log Floating," Pennsylvania, *Daily Legislative Record, 1857*, no. 80, pp. 3-4. On Irvin, see: Dale et al., *History of Clearfield County*, 116-17; [Beers & Co.], *Commemorative Biographical Record*, 1: 587-88.

20. Among other places, the notice appeared in Clearfield *Raftsman's Journal*, 18 Feb. 1857.

21. Row, "Clearfield County," 12 Oct. 1859; Dale et al., *History of Clearfield County*, 131; Rumberger, "Loggers against Rafters"; John Quigley, paper on lumbering (Ross Library, Lock Haven), pamphlet file.

22. Rumberger, "Loggers against Rafters." This is the fullest extant description of the confrontation. Although unfootnoted, it is clearly solidly based on contemporary newspapers, court testimony, and the recollections of participants. Rumberger was a long-time resident of the area.

23. Clearfield *Raftsman's Journal*, 6 May 1857. Row's statement was apparently written on 29 or 30 Apr. or 1 May. By 2 May, he had received news of a clash on Clearfield Creek, which he published immediately below his original piece.

24. For example, on 20 May, Row refused to print a letter received relative to the battle, saying it would only serve to "embitter the parties against each other." See: Clearfield *Raftsman's Journal*, 20 May 1857.

25. Ibid., 6 and 20 May 1857.

26. Ibid., 26 Aug. 1857.

27. Pennsylvania Writers Project, *Pennsylvania Cavalcade*, 381; Works Progress Administration, *Pennsylvania: A Guide to the Keystone State* (New York:

Oxford University Press, 1940), 562; clipping from *New York World*, July 1860 (Ross Library, Lock Haven), pamphlet file.

28. Row, "Clearfield County," 12 Oct. 1859; Tonkin, *My Partner*, 26-27; James Mitchell, *Lumbering and Rafting in Clearfield County, Pennsylvania, on the West Branch of the Susquehanna River* (Clearfield: n. p., [c. 1922]), 41. See also: William Packer Clarke, *The Life and Times of the Hon. William Fisher Packer, Resident of Williamsport, Governor of Pennsylvania* (Williamsport: Lycoming County Historical Society, 1937); Armor, *Governors of Pennsylvania*, 433-49. Packer was from Clearfield and a leading lumberman in his own right.

29. *Clearfield Republican*, 4 Feb. 1853, 21 May 1858, 16 Mar. 1859; Clearfield *Raftsman's Journal*, 9 July 1856, 23 and 30 Sept., 7 Oct., 11 Nov. 1857, 10 Mar., 23 June 1858; *Eighth Census of the United States: 1860*, Vol. 3: 503-504, 516; Tonkin, *My Partner*, 10-22. During the period, some of the county's small mills did close, at least temporarily, but this appears to have been caused by depression more than log drives. See: Clearfield *Raftsman's Journal*, 12 Jan. 1859.

30. Aldrich, *History of Clearfield County*, 97; Lloyd, "When Lumber Was King," 12-15; Tonkin, *My Partner*, 36; Nelligan, "Life of a Lumberman," 29-30. See also: Samuel Caldwell et al., petition to Senate and House, n.d., and Brown, Allen & Co. et al., statement to Senate and House, 18 Mar. 1872 (copies in Lycoming County Historical Society Museum, Williamsport, manuscript file); David Baird to V. Tonkin, 4 Sept 1883, and Fred J. Dyer to Tonkin, 24 July 1891 and 5 Mar. 1892 (Pennsylvania State Archives, Harrisburg, Tonkin manuscripts, MG-127, business corres.).

31. On DuBois, see: Defebaugh, *History of the Lumber Industry*, 2: 600-601; [Defebaugh], *American Lumbermen*, 1: 66-69; Swoope, *History of Clearfield County*, 630-34; John F. Meginness, ed., *History of Lycoming County, Pennsylvania* (Chicago: Brown Runk, 1892), 1098-99; Casler, Kline, and Taber, *Logging Railroad Era in Pennsylvania*, 3: 1201-26.

32. Cranmer, "Harvesting the Hemlock," 124-26 (quotes, p. 124).

33. Clearfield *Raftsman's Journal*, 16 Mar. 1856; W. J. McKnight, *A Pioneer Outline History of Northwestern Pennsylvania* . . . (Philadelphia: Lippincott, 1905), 355-57; *American Digest* (50 vols.; St. Paul: West, 1897-1904), 33: 1574, paragraphs 48 h-l; 1575, paragraph 49 c-h; Pennsylvania Writer's Project, *Pennsylvania Cavalcade*, 381. Algerines got their name from Algerian pirates, whose behavior was supposedly similar to that of log rustlers.

34. On the eight-hour movement, see: Marion Cotter Cahill, *Shorter Hours: A Study of the Movement since the Civil War*, Studies in History, Economics and Public Law, no. 380 (New York: Columbia University Press, 1932); George E. McNeill et al., *The Labor Movement: The Problem of Today, Comprising a History of Capital and Labor, and Its Present Status* (New York: Hazen, 1888), 124-45, 173-74; Terence Powderly, *Thirty Years of Labor, 1859 to 1889* (rev. ed.; Philadelphia: n. pub., 1890), 29, 43-44, 241; E. L. Godkin, "The Eight-Hour Muddle," *The Nation*, 4 (1867): 374.

35. Williamsport *Daily Morning Standard* [hereafter *Morning Standard*], 18 July 1872.

36. The strike has received only undependable, cursory treatments. See: Defebaugh, *History of the Lumber Industry*, 2: 601-602; Lloyd, "When Lumber Was King," 43-46; Nancy Lee Miller, "Sawdust War: Labor Strife in the Sawmills," *Pennsylvania Forests*, 72 (Mar.-Apr. 1982): 6-8, 13; Berry, "Lumber in Pennsylvania," 167-79; Marshall R. Anspach, "The Saw Dust War of 1872," *Now and Then*, 10 (1953): 277-84; Holbrook, *Holy Old Mackinaw*, 78-80.

37. Unions were legalized in Pennsylvania in 1869 (although Clearfield and Centre counties were excluded from coverage, probably because of memories of the Clearfield County War). Literature on Sylvis and the National Labor Union is scanty and often dated. See: Powderly, *Thirty Years of Labor*, 33-58; James C. Sylvis, *The Life, Speeches, Labors and Essays of William H. Sylvis . . .* (Philadelphia: Claxton, Remsen & Haffelfinger, 1872); Gerald Grob, "Reform Unionism: The National Labor Union," *Journal of Economic History*, 14 (1954): 126-40; Jonathan Grossman, *William H. Sylvis: Pioneer of American Labor* (New York: Columbia University Press, 1945); Philip S. Foner, *History of the Labor Movement in the United States* (5 vols.; New York: International Publishers, 1947-80), 1: 370-82, 429-32; Charlotte Todes, *William Sylvis and the National Labor Union* (New York: International Publishers, 1942); David Montgomery, "William H. Sylvis and the Search for Working-Class Citizenship," in Melvyn Dubofsky and Warren Van Tine, ed., *Labor Leaders in America* (Chicago: University of Illinois Press, 1987), 3-29. For a step toward fresh analysis, see: Stephen Edward Freund, "The National Labor Union's Antebellum Labor Crusade" (unpub. M.A. thesis, San Diego State University, 1993).

38. Sylvis, *Life of William Sylvis*, 207-208, 265-69, 276; Freund, "The National Labor Union's Crusade," 18-25; McNeill, *The Labor Movement*, 128-33, 138, 142-45; Cahill, *Shorter Hours*, 32-43, 68-72, 137-52; Todes, *William H. Sylvis*, 8, 20, 54-60, 108; John R. Commons et al., *History of Labour in the United States* (4 vols.; New York: Macmillan, 1918-1935), 2: 47, 87-110, and passim; Kilar, *Michigan's Lumbertowns*, 217-18.

39. Chicago *Workingman's Advocate*, 20 and 27 May, 8 July, 5 Aug. 1871, 27 Apr., 11 and 18 May 1872; Williamsport *Epitomist*, 11 July 1872 (quote), reprinted in New York *Sun*, 26 July 1872; Anspach, "Saw Dust War," 278; Hough, *Report upon Forestry*, 465. See also: Pennsylvania, Bureau of Statistics of Labor and Agriculture, *Second Annual Report, 1873-1874* (Harrisburg: State Printer, 1874), 497. The *Workingman's Advocate* was the official organ of the NLU. Labor Reform Union, the name used by NLU locals in Pennsylvania, reflected ties to the Labor Reform Party, through which the NLU hoped to push its political and legislative programs; however, because of the NLU's weak organizational structure and the fact its records burned in the great Chicago fire, details of the ties between the two organizations are difficult to determine. See: Chicago *Workingman's Advocate*, 20 and 27 May, 8 July, 5 and 19 Aug., 11 Nov. 1871.

40. Williamsport *Gazette and Bulletin*, 29 June 1872; Williamsport *Morning Standard*, 3 July 1872; Anspach, "Saw Dust War," 278-79; Meginness, *History of Lycoming County*, 381. On Herdic, see: Lloyd, "When Lumber Was King," 21, 23-24, 28, 56-58; New York *Sun*, 4 Mar. 1877; George Strayer Maxwell, "Peter Herdic, 1824-1888," Williamsport *Sun*, 23 Jan. 1926.

41. Geary was considered a friend of labor. The Pennsylvania delegation pushed him for the Labor Reform Party's presidential nomination in 1872. See: Chicago *Workingman's Advocate*, 17 Feb. 1872; Armor, *Governors of Pennsylvania*, 466-89.

42. Williamsport *Morning Standard* 1and 2 July (quote, 2 July) 1872; Williamsport *Epitomist*, 11 July 1872; Miller, "Sawdust War," 6-8; Anspach, "Saw Dust War," 279; Berry, "Lumbering in Pennsylvania," 167-70. Within a few days workers at some of the mills in Lock Haven were on strike too. See: Lock Haven *Clinton Democrat*, 4 July 1872; Philadelphia *Public Ledger*, 6 and 8 July 1872; Williamsport *Morning Standard*, 6, 9, and 19 July 1872.

43. Williamsport *Epitomist*, 11 July 1872; Williamsport *Daily Morning Standard*, 16, 18, 20, and 22 July 1872; Anspach, "Saw Dust War," 279; Miller, "Sawdust War," 8.

44. Philadelphia *Public Ledger*, 31 July 1872; Chicago *Workingman's Advocate*, 18 May, 15 June 1872; Williamsport *Epitomist*, 11 July 1872; Williamsport *Sun and Lycoming Democrat* [hereafter *Sun and Democrat*], 11 July 1872; Williamsport *Morning Standard*, 16 and 18 July 1872; Berry, "Lumber In Pennsylvania," 168-70; Miller, "Sawdust War," 7; Anspach, "Saw Dust War," 278. Cf. Williamsport *Morning Standard*, 19 July 1872, on leadership in Lock Haven.

45. Williamsport *Sun and Democrat*, 11 and 18 (quote) July 1872.

46. David R. Roediger and Philip S. Foner, *Our Own Time: A History of American Labor and the Working Day* (New York: Greenwood Press, 1989), 118-19; Berry, "Lumber in Pennsylvania," 170; Anspach, "Saw Dust War," 282; Williamsport *Gazette and Bulletin*, 12 and 17 July, 3 Aug. 1872; Williamsport *Morning Standard*, 1, 2, 3, 4, and 22 July 1872; Williamsport *Sun and Democrat*, 11, 18 (quotes), and 25 July 1872; Chicago *Workingman's Advocate*, 14 Sept. 1872. The *Epitomist*, 11 July 1872, claimed strikers lost support on the first day when they took control of various mills and turned off the machinery. Other sources make it clear much support continued until violence broke out on July 22. This was a familiar pattern. In smaller communities in the late nineteenth century strikers frequently enjoyed local sympathy unless or until violence and destruction of property put in an appearance. See: Herbert G. Gutman, "The Worker's Search for Power: Labor in the Gilded Age," in H. Wayne Morgan, ed., *The Gilded Age* (rev. ed.; Syracuse, N.Y.: Syracuse University Press, 1970), 31-53; Michael J. Cassity, "Mechanization and Social Crisis: The Knights of Labor and a Midwestern Community, 1885-1886," *JAH*, 66 (1979): 41-61.

47. Williamsport *Morning Standard*, 9, 13, 16 July 1872; Williamsport *Gazette and Bulletin*, 14 July 1872; Williamsport *Epitomist*, 11 July 1872; Anspach, "Saw Dust War," 279; Meginness, *History of Lycoming County*, 282.

48. Williamsport *Morning Standard*, 6, 11, and 12 (quote) July 1872; Williamsport *Gazette and Bulletin*, 15 July 1872; Williamsport *Epitomist*, 11 July 1872.

49. Berry, "Lumbering in Pennsylvania," 170-71; Williamsport *Morning Standard*, 15, 16, and 19 July 1872.

50. Williamsport *Morning Standard*, 22 July 1872.

51. Williamsport *Morning Standard*, 18 July 1872; Williamsport *Epitomist*, 11 July 1872; Berry "Lumbering in Pennsylvania," 171. There is no way of estimating how many workers returned to their jobs at this point or how widespread the desire to do so was. Various sources refer to the presence of those who wanted to return to work on the owners' terms, but none provide any quantification. Berry, whose uncle was among local laborers who returned to work, suggests the numbers were high, but his pro-management biases make Berry a suspect source. See: Williamsport *Epitomist*, 11 July 1872; Williamsport *Morning Standard*, 15 July 1872; Anspach, "Saw Dust War," 279; Miller, "Sawdust War," 8; Berry, "Lumbering in Pennsylvania," 171-72. From the first, unionists worried about the possibility millowners would hire outsiders as strikebreakers, a common practice at the time. On July 2, the union adopted a resolution proposed by James Sylvis calling on workmen from elsewhere not come to Williamsport as strikebreakers. Williamsport *Sun and Democrat*, 11 July 1872.

52. Williamsport *Gazette and Bulletin*, 15 and 17 July 1872; Williamsport *Epitomist*, 11 July 1872; Williamsport *Sun and Democrat*, 12 and 18 July 1872; Anspach, "Saw Dust War," 283; Miller, "Sawdust War," 8. Herdic's actions, one paper suggested, were judged by many to be an effort to regain popularity; certainly, there were influential people who distrusted his motives. E. W. Capron, editor of the *Epitomist*, told a fellow editor that Herdic had frequently told him, "I'm for Pete, every time!" to which the second editor responded, "That's Pete, natural as life, sure!" See: Williamsport *Epitomist*, 11 July 1872; Lock Haven *Clinton Democrat*, 15 Aug. 1872 (quote).

53. There are several contemporary and near-contemporary accounts of the "riot." They tend to agree in general, but differ on details. There is no reason to question the accuracy of any, for they were written for an audience that included many with first-hand knowledge of events. Even accounts of those reporting to the *Workingman's Advocate* and of Berry, who represented the opposite political pole, are in essential agreement. The following is a composite account based on Williamsport *Morning Standard*, 23 July 1872; Williamsport *Sun and Democrat*, 25 July 1872; Williamsport *Gazette and Bulletin*, 22 and 23 July 1872; Lock Haven *Clinton Democrat*, 25 July 1872; Chicago *Workingman's Advocate*, 27 July (misdated 20 July), 17 Aug., 14 Sept. 1872; Philadelphia *Public Ledger*, 23 July 1872; Berry, "Lumbering in Pennsylvania," 171-74.

54. Williamsport *Sun and Democrat*, 1 Aug. 1872; Chicago *Workingman's Advocate*, 17 Aug., 14 Sept. 1872; Anspach, "Saw Dust War," 281-83; Miller, "Sawdust War," 8.

55. Lock Haven *Clinton Democrat*, 25 July 1872. Edgar Munson was president of the Lumbermen's Exchange. See: Williamsport *Morning Standard*, 16 July 1872.

56. For documents by principals involved in the actions of the guard, see: John W. Geary, "Proclamation Relative to Labor Disturbances at Williamsport," 22 July 1872, in George Edward Reed, ed., *Pennsylvania Archives*, 4th Series, vol. 9, *Papers of the Governors, 1871-1883* (Harrisburg: State Printer, 1902), 53-54; Geary, "Annual Message to the Assembly, 1873," ibid., 161-62; Williamsport

Morning Standard, 24 and 25 July 1872; Williamsport *Sun and Democrat,* 25 July 1872; Chicago *Workingman's Advocate,* 27 July 1872.

57. Williamsport *Sun and Democrat,* 1 Aug. 1872; Williamsport *Gazette and Bulletin,* 12 Nov. 1885; Williamsport *Morning Standard,* 24 (Merrill quote) and 25 July 1872; D. S. Maynard, *Biographical Sketches of Prominent Citizens and Business Men of Clinton County, Pa.* (Lock Haven, Penn.: Enterprise, 1877), 22-26.

58. Williamsport *Morning Standard,* 30 and 31 (quote), July, 3 Aug. 1872.

59. Ibid., 16 and 22 July 1872; Williamsport *Sun and Democrat,* 18 July 1872; Williamsport *Gazette and Bulletin,* 3 Aug. 1872; Lock Haven *Clinton Democrat,* 25 July 1872. See also: Anspach, "Saw Dust War," 282.

60. Williamsport *Morning Standard,* 25, 26, and 30 July, 1, 2, 3, and 7 Aug. 1872; Chicago *Workingman's Advocate,* 14 Sept. 1872 (quote); Meginness, *History of Lycoming County,* 344.

61. Williamsport *Morning Standard,* 29 and 30 July 1872; Williamsport *Sun and Democrat,* 1 Aug. 1872; Chicago *Workingman's Advocate,* 17 Aug., 14 Sept. 1872; Philadelphia *Public Ledger,* 27 and 30 July 1872; Frederic A. Godcharles, *Daily Stories of Pennsylvania* (Milton, Penn.: by the author, 1924), 474; Anspach, "Saw Dust War," 284; Berry, "Lumbering in Pennsylvania," 173, 175-78. See also: Lycoming County Bar, *A Testimonial to the Hon. James Gamble . . .* (Williamsport, Penn.: Gazette and Bulletin, 1879). Sources differ on the precise number of defendants.

62. Quoted in Williamsport *Sun and Democrat,* 11 July 1872.

63. This interpretation differs from that dominating earlier scholarship (see note 36, above), which emphasized the elements of polite reform in the NLU while largely ignoring its use of strikes in its struggle with capitalists. When both sides of its activity are considered, it seems evident that the NLU deserves a more prominent place in American labor history than it has enjoyed heretofore.

64. Casler, Kline, and Taber, *Logging Railroad Era in Pennsylvania,* provides a useful, if antiquarian, overview of the impact of railroads and related technologies. See also: Cranmer, "Harvesting the Hemlock," 116-123. Most studies of Pennsylvania's industrial development ignore the lumber and tanning industries.

65. Casler, Kline, and Taber, *Logging Railroad Era in Pennsylvania,* 3: 1001-1099; Craig A. Newton and James R. Sperry, *A Quiet Boomtown: Jamison City, Pa., 1889-1912* (Bloomsburg, Penn.: Columbia County Historical Society, 1972); Gale Largey, "The Brunswick Tannery," *Pennsylvania Heritage,* 6 (1980): 10-13; Homer Tope Rosenberger, *Mountain Folks: Fragments of Central Pennsylvania Lore* (Lock Haven, Penn.: Ross Library, 1974), 120-24; Ellis, *Landlords and Farmers,* 211-12; Griffin, oral history interview, 16. On the changing nature of forest fires, see: Stephen J. Pyne, *Fire in America: A Cultural History of Wildland and Rural Fire* (Princeton, N.J.: Princeton University Press, 1982), 181-218.

66. Casler, Kline, and Taber, *Logging Railroad Era in Pennsylvania,* 3: 1101-29. Williamsport's eclipse as a lumber-producing center was thus delayed and came almost simultaneously with that of Saginaw, Michigan, which was

viewed by Holbrook as its "successor" as the nation's lumber capital. In 1890, lumber and planing mills still constituted 55.3 percent of business investment and paid out 29.4 percent of wages earned in the Pennsylvania city. See: Holbrook, *Holy Old Mackinaw*, 80 et sqq.; *Eleventh Census of the United States: 1890*, 12: *Census of Manufactures*, pt. 2: 614-17.

67. Carl Schurz, address to American Forestry Association and Pennsylvania Forestry Association, 1 Oct. 1889 (AFA Papers, Forest History Society, Durham, N.C.), box 7, AFA hist. 1889 file, pp. 8-9; Van Brocklin, "The Movement for the Conservation of Natural Resources," 38, 55-56; Casler, Kline, and Taber, *Logging Railroad Era in Pennsylvania*, vi-vii; French et al., *Rafting Days*, 85; Ralph Widner, ed., *Forests and Forestry: A Reference Anthology* (Missoula, Mont.: National Association of State Foresters, 1968), 24-25.

68. John Frederick Hartranft, "Annual Message to the Assembly, 1874," *Pennsylvania Archives*, 4th Series, 9: 308; Hartranft, "Annual Message to the Assembly, 1875," ibid., 433-34. In spite of Hartranft's pleas, it took considerable time before Pennsylvania took steps toward forest protection and renewal. Studies of these subsequent developments ignore Hartranft's role. See: J. T. Rothrock, "On the Growth of the Forestry Idea in Pennsylvania," *Proceedings of the American Philosophical Society*, 32 (1893): 332-42; Henry Clepper, "Rise of the Forest Conservation Movement in Pennsylvania," *Pennsylvania History*, 12 (1945): 200-216; Clepper, "Forest Conservation in Pennsylvania: The Pioneer Period, from Rothrock to Pinchot," ibid., 48 (1981): 41-50.

69. Holbrook, *Holy Old Mackinaw*, 72-78; Stewart H. Holbrook, *The Yankee Exodus: An Account of the Migration from New England* (New York: Macmillan, 1950), 10-24; Ellis, "Yankee Invasion of New York," 3-17; Harold Fisher Wilson, *The Hill Country of Northern New England: Its Social and Economic History* (New York: AMS Press, 1967), 27-94.

70. Some authorities claim few Pennsylvania lumbermen migrated to other regions as their timber ran out. This is incorrect, as the careers of the Goodyears, Henry M. Lutcher, and John DuBois, among others, show. Some went south along the Appalachian chain, using logging techniques perfected in the mountains of Pennsylvania and New York; others migrated west to the Lake States and beyond. Workmen as well as capitalists migrated, including many who subsequently returned to apply their experience in the forests of their home states. See: Casler, Kline, and Taber, *Logging Railroad Era in Pennsylvania*, 1: 574-80, 3: 1222-25; Cranmer, "Harvesting the Hemlock," 127; Fred W. Kohlmeyer, "Northern Pine Lumbermen: A Study in Origins and Migrations," *Journal of Economic History*, 16 (1956): 529-38; George B. Engberg, "Who Were the Lumberjacks?" *Mich. Hist.*, 32 (1948): 238-46.

71. On the market and transportation revolutions, see: Taylor, *Transportation Revolution*, esp. 207-398; Porter and Livesay, *Merchants and Manufacturers*; Thomas C. Cochran, "Early Industrialization in the Delaware and Susquehanna River Areas: A Regional Analysis," *Social Science History*, 1 (1977): 283-306.

Chapter Six

1. George W. Hotchkiss, *History of the Lumber and Forest Industry of the Northwest* (Chicago: Hotchkiss, 1898), 48; Benson, *Logs and Lumber*, 11, 126, 135.

2. Jane M. Kinney, "Pioneers of St. Clair County," Michigan Pioneer and Historical Society, *Collections*, 29 (1901): 170-71; William Lee Jenks, *St. Clair County, Michigan: Its History and Its People . . .* (2 vols.; Chicago: Lewis, 1912), 1: 362-72; George Newman Fuller, *Economic and Social Beginnings of Michigan: A Study of the Settlement of the Lower Peninsula during the Territorial Period, 1805-1837* (Lansing: Wynkoop-Hallenbeck-Crawford, 1916), 162-63; Benson, *Logs and Lumber*, 38; Hotchkiss, *Lumber and Forest Industry*, 43-59.

3. Benson, *Logs and Lumber*, 37-41, 101-102; Hotchkiss, *Lumber and Forest Industry*, 33-34, 37, 47; Fuller, *Economic and Social Beginnings*, 65-66, 116-117, 134-36; F. Clever Bald, *Detroit's First American Decade, 1796-1805* (Ann Arbor: Michigan State University Press, 1948), 26, 73, 86, 133; George Newman Fuller, "Early Settlement in Southern Michigan, 1805-1837," *Mich. Hist.*, 19 (1935): 182-83, 188; Carl Addison Leach, "Paul Bunyan's Land and the First Sawmills of Michigan," ibid., 20 (1936): 73; Rolland H. Maybee, "Michigan's White Pine Era, 1840-1900," ibid., 43 (1959): 394-95, 422-23; Larry B. Massie, "Plows, Ships, and Shovels: Economic Development in Michigan, 1836-1866," in *Michigan: Visions of Our Past*, ed. by Richard J. Hathaway (East Lansing: Michigan State University Press, 1989), 97; Milo M. Quaife and Sidney Glazer, *Michigan: From Primitive Wilderness to Industrial Commonwealth* (New York: Prentice-Hall, 1948), 146, 150.

4. Benson, *Logs and Lumber*, 42, 101; Jenks, *St. Clair County*, 1: 123-24, 235, 243-44, 257, 368, 489; Hotchkiss, *Lumber and Forest Industry*, 51, 53-54. James Mills incorrectly credits Curtis Emerson with making the first export shipment in 1847. See: James Cook Mills, *History of Saginaw County, Michigan* (2 vols.; Saginaw, Mich.: Seaman & Peters, 1918): 1: 396.

5. Benson, *Logs and Lumber*, 42, 55, 66-67, 101-102, 128; Jenks, *St. Clair County*, 1: 143, 255, 271, 366, 368-71; Hotchkiss, *Lumber and Forest Industry*, 48. Partial records of Wadhams' mill and the Black River Steam Mills are in the William Lee Jenks Papers (Burton Historical Collection, Detroit Public Library, Detroit, Mich.), D3, J8, L4.

6. Timothy Flint, *Recollections of the Last Ten Years . . .* (Boston: Cummings Hilliard, 1826), 22, 27-28 (1st quote), 39-40, 43-44, 52-53 (2nd and 3rd quotes). See also: Morris Birkback, *Notes on a Journey in America, from Virginia to Illinois* (London: Ridgway, 1818), 34, 70-72; R. Carlyle Buley, *The Old Northwest: Pioneer Period, 1815-1840* (2 vols.; Indianapolis: Indiana University Press, 1975), 2: 43-49; James E. Davis, *Frontier Illinois* (Bloomington: Indiana University Press, 1998), 201-219; Malcolm J. Rohrbough, *The Land Office Business: The Settlement and Administration of American Public Lands, 1789-1837* (New York: Oxford University Press, 1968), 102, 127-32, 234.

7. Richard L. Power, "Wet Lands and the Hoosier Stereotype," *MVHR*, 22 (1935): 33-48; Terry Jordan, "Between Forest and Prairie," *Ag. Hist.*, 38 (1964): 205-216; David E. Schob, *Hired Hands and Plowboys* (Urbana:

University of Illinois Press, 1975), 21-42. The pattern was similar in Illinois. See: William D. Walters, Jr., "Initial Field Location in Illinois," *Ag. Hist.*, 57 (1983): 289-96; William D. Walters, Jr., and Jonathan Smith, "Woodland and Prairie Settlement in Illinois," *FCH*, 36 (1992): 15-21.

8. Buley, *Old Northwest*, 2: 49-53; Harlow Lindley, ed., *Indiana as Seen by Early Travelers* (Indianapolis: Indiana Historical Commission, 1916), 530-31 (1st quote); Shirley S. McCord, ed., *Travel Accounts of Indiana, 1679-1961* (Indianapolis: Indiana Historical Bureau, 1970), 142-43 (2nd quote).

9. George Wilson Pierson, *Tocqueville and Beaumont in America* (New York: Oxford University Press, 1938), 230-31, 250 (1st quote), 262-79 (3rd quote, p. 271; 4th quote, p. 278); Buley, *Old Northwest*, 2: 80-99 (2nd quote, p. 92), 162-64; Kilar, *Michigan's Lumbertowns*, 19 (last quote); Mills, *History of Saginaw*, 1: 66-78; Albert Millerm, "The Saginaw Valley," Michigan Pioneer and Historical Society, *Collections*, 7 (1886): 239-41; Fuller, "Economic and Social Beginnings," 364-400. See also: Jeremy W. Kilar, "Tocqueville's Companion Traveler: Gustave de Beaumont and the Journey into Michigan Wilderness, 1831" *Mich. Hist.*, 68 (1984): 34-39.

10. John Nowlin, *The Bark Covered House, or Back in the Woods Again*, ed. by Milo M. Quaife (Chicago: Lakeside, 1937), 28 (1st quote), 41-42, 46-50 (2nd quote, pp. 49-50), 166-71 (3rd quote, pp. 166, 170), 180 (4th quote); Buley, *Old Northwest*, 2: 94-96; Bernard C. Peters, "Michigan's Oak Openings: Pioneer Perceptions of a Vegetative Landscape," *JFH*, 22 (1978): 18-23. Apparently seeking to avoid the hard work of clearing, Pardee settled an oak opening and left wooded portions of his claim uncut. The elder Nowlin took consolation in the fact Pardee's approach failed, for the soil on his claim was too poor to support profitable agriculture.

11. Harvey Rice, *Sketches of Western Reserve Life* (Cleveland, Ohio: Williams, 1885), 79; Caroline S. Kirkland, *Forest Life* (2 vols.; New York: Francis, 1842), 1: 216; Maximilian, Prince of Weid, *Travels in the Interior of North America*, trans. by H. Evans Lloyd (London: Ackermann, 1843), 68, 72, 75-76 (quote, p. 76); Defebaugh, *Lumber Industry of America*, 1: 323-24. On agricultural clearing, see: Williams, "Clearing United States Forests," 23-25; Michael Williams, "Ohio: Microcosm of Clearing in the Midwest," in *Global Deforestation in the Nineteenth-Century World Economy*, ed. by Richard P. Tucker and J. F. Richards (Durham, N.C.: Duke University Press, 1983), 3-13.

12. Emmett A. Conway, "History of Sawmilling in Ohio," *Woodlands*, 13 (1976): 20-23; Donald A. Hutslar, "Ohio Waterpowered Sawmills," *Ohio History*, 55 (1975): 5-56; Williams, "Products of the Forest," 7; G. R. Taylor to Calvin Taylor, 6 Feb. 1850 (Calvin Taylor Papers, Hill Memorial Library, Louisiana State University, Baton Rouge [hereafter, Taylor Papers]), box 3, file 7.

13. Henry B. Steer, comp., *Lumber Production in the United States, 1799-1946*, USDA, Misc. Pub. no. 699 (Washington, D.C.: GPO, 1948), 11; Williams, *Americans and their Forests*, 160-67; Defebaugh, *Lumber Industry of America*, 1: 489-91.

14. Mills, *History of Saginaw*, 2: 304 (quote); Benson, *Logs and Lumber*, 1-13, 59-62, 69-70; Maybee, "Michigan's White Pine Era," 395-98; Kilar, *Michigan's Lumbertowns*, 20-21; Defebaugh, *Lumber Industry of America*, 1: 311; Hotchkiss, *Lumber and Forest Industry*, 30-32, 46, 94, 97, 104; Fuller,

Economic and Social Beginnings, 36-38. For more detailed views, see: B. E. Quick, "A Comparative Study of the Distribution of Climax Association of Southern Michigan," *Papers of the Michigan Academy of Science, Arts and Letters,* 3 (1924): 215-40; Eric A. Bourdo, Jr., "The Forest the Settlers Saw," in Susan L. Flader, ed., *The Great Lakes Forest: An Environmental and Social History* (Minneapolis: University of Minnesota Press, 1983), 3-16. On Saginaw's first mills, see: Miller, "Saginaw Valley," 241-43; Hotchkiss, *Lumber and Forest Industry,* 94-97; Mills, *History of Saginaw,* 1: 92-93, 128, 142, 168, 393-96.

15. Mills, *History of Saginaw,* 2: 349, 423; Benson, *Logs and Lumber,* 15-36; Cox et al., *This Well-Wooded Land,* 138-42; Williams, *Americans and their Forests,* 396-99; Defebaugh, *Lumber Industry of America,* 1: 342-94; John Ise, *The United States Forest Policy* (New Haven, Conn.: Yale University Press, 1920), 45-78; Roy M. Robbins, *Our Landed Heritage: The Public Domain, 1776-1970* (2nd ed.; Lincoln: University of Nebraska Press, 1976), 72-116. See also: Paul W. Gates, "Homestead Law in an Incongruous Land System," *American Historical Review,* 41 (1936): 652-81.

16. Merrill would become one of Michigan's leading millmen—unlike Ely, whose firm foundered during the Panic of 1837—but he did not transfer milling operations from Maine until 1854. Benson, *Logs and Lumber,* 114, 269; Mills, *History of Saginaw,* 1: 415-16; 2: 18; Hotchkiss, *Lumber and Forest Industry,* 104-105.

17. Benson, *Logs and Lumber,* 19-26, 34, 41; Kilar, *Michigan's Lumbertowns,* 21, 27, 32-36; Williams, *Americans and their Forests,* 224-27; Fuller, *Economic and Social Beginnings,* 66-67; Caroline Kirkland, *Western Clearings* (New York: Wiley & Putnam, 1845), 4-6; George M. Blackburn and Sherman L. Ricards, "A Case Study in Local Control: The Timber Industry in Manistee County, Michigan," *JFH,* 18 (1974): 15-16. See also: Defebaugh, *Lumber Industry of America,* 1: 378-80; Rohrbough, *Land Office Business,* 241-46, 248.

18. Kilar, *Michigan's Milltowns,* 28-33; Buley, *Old Northwest,* 2: 147-59; Blackburn and Ricards, "Timber Industry in Manistee," 18-19; Fuller, *Economic and Social Beginnings,* 68-69, 400; Mills, *History of Saginaw,* 1: 148-50; Maybee, "Michigan's White Pine Era," 394-95.

19. Benson, *Logs and Lumber,* 4, 9-10, 62, 69-70; Kilar, *Michigan's Lumbertowns,* 21-23; Maybee, "Michigan's White Pine Era," 398 (quote), 401-402; [H.R. Page & Co.], *History of Bay County, Michigan* (Chicago: Page, 1883), 41, 64.

20. Benson, *Logs and Lumber,* 70-71, 106, 113-16; Mills, *History of Saginaw,* 1: 183, 393; 2: 322; [Page & Co.], *History of Bay County, Michigan,* 41-43; Anonymous, "A Pioneer Michigan Lumber City," *Timb.,* 29 (June 1928): 60-61; Massie, "Plows, Ships, and Shovels," 105; Hotchkiss, *Lumber and Forest Industry,* 94-97; Michigan Pioneer and Historical Society, *Collections,* 7 (1884): 290.

21. Benson, *Logs and Lumber,* xii, 57-59, 71-72, 101-108, 116-18, 137, 160-64; Williams, *Americans and their Forests,* 201-203, 218-20; Mills, *History of Saginaw,* 1: 397.

22. Delos A. Blodgett's operations were probably the largest by an independent logger, but he did not begin his harvests until 1850. Benson, *Logs and Lumber,* 82-83; [Defebaugh], *American Lumbermen,* 2: 209-212; Hotchkiss,

Lumber and Forest Industry, 177-79; Anonymous, "Profiting by Advantage," *AL*, 70 (15 July 1905): 1, 3.

23. Benson, *Logs and Lumber*, 19-23, 25-26 (quote, p. 26), 81-83; Maybee, "Michigan's White Pine Era," 398-99.

24. Hotchkiss, *Lumber and Forest Industry*, 37 (1st quote); Benson, *Logs and Lumber*, 18-21; Blackburn and Ricards, "Timber Industry in Manistee," 16-17 (2nd quote, p. 16); Lillard, *Great Forest*, 156-60; [Page & Co.], *History of Manistee County*, 24 (3rd quote); Mills, *History of Saginaw*, 1: 424, 425; Lucille Kane, "Federal Protection of Public Timber in the Upper Great Lake States," *Ag. Hist.*, 23 (1949): 135-39 (quote, p. 139).

25. Blackburn and Ricards, "Timber Industry in Manistee County," 17; Kane, "Federal Protection of Public Timber," 136-37, 139; Benson, *Logs and Lumber*, 16-18; Lillard, *Great Forest*, 161-69; Cameron, *Development of Forest Control*, 144-55. On considerations that led one timberland owner to undertake sawmilling, see: Martin D. Lewis, *Lumberman from Flint: The Michigan Career of Henry H. Crapo, 1855-1869* (Detroit, Mich.: Wayne State University Press, 1958), 32-37.

26. [Defebaugh], *American Lumbermen*, 1: 135-37. On Toledo, Sandusky, and Cleveland as lumber markets, see: Hotchkiss, *Lumber and Forest Industry*, 361-70.

27. Alger, an attorney from Cleveland, first went into the shingle business, then lumber. See: Rodney Ellis Bell, "A Life of Russell Alexander Alger, 1826-1907" (unpub. Ph.D. diss., University of Michigan, 1975), 24-29.

28. George F. Lewis and Charles B. Headley, *Saginaw Valley* (Bay City, Mich.: Bay City Courier, 1869); Benson, *Logs and Lumber*, 168-70; Hotchkiss, *Lumber and Forest Industry*, 101-103, 679; Herbert Brinks, "The Effect of the Civil War in 1861 on Michigan Lumbering and Mining," *Mich. Hist.*, 44 (1960): 100-107; Anita Shafer Goodstein, *Biography of a Businessman: Henry W. Sage, 1814-1897* (Ithaca, N.Y.: Cornell University Press, 1962), 38-39, 66, 77-78 (quote, p. 77); Lewis, *Lumberman from Flint*, 18, 21-29, 44-50, 104-113; Bell, "Alger," 38.

29. Anonymous, "Pioneering in the Michigan-Chicago Lumber Trade," *AL*, n.v. (22 Dec. 1906): 28-29; Benson, *Logs and Lumber*, 11-12, 46, 55, 56, 73, 122-24, 130-32, 182-83; Williams, *Americans and their Forests*, 179-82, 183-86; George Barclay, "Chicago—The Lumber Hub," *SL*, 193 (15 Dec. 1956): 177-80; Hotchkiss, *Lumber and Forest Industry*, 44 (quote), 661-79, 685; Chauncey M. Depew, ed., *1795-1895: One Hundred Years of American Commerce . . .* (2 vols.; New York: Haynes., 1895), 1: 198; Constance McLaughlin Green, *American Cities in the Growth of the Nation* (New York: DeGraff, 1957), 100-115; Fred W. Kohlmeyer, "Lumber Distribution and Marketing in the United States," *JFH*, 27 (1983): 85; Frederick Merk, *Economic History of Wisconsin during the Civil War Decade* (Madison: State Historical Society of Wisconsin, 1916), 81; Arthur Charles Cole, *The Era of the Civil War, 1848-1870* (Springfield: Illinois Centennial Commission, 1919), 348-50; Bessie Louise Pierce, *A History of Chicago* (2 vols.; New York: Knopf, 1937-40), 2: 38, 67, 103-105.

30. Kilar, *Michigan's Lumbertowns*, 20-21, 45-46, 88; Frederick L. Honhart, "The Hackley & Hume Papers," *JFH*, 23 (197): 136-39; Blackburn and Ricards,

"Timber Industry in Manistee," 15, 20-21; Hotchkiss, *Lumber and Forest Industry*, 219-24, 244-84 (quote, p. 261), 291-316.

31. Hotchkiss, *Lumber and Forest Industry*, 350-66; Defebaugh, *Lumber Industry of America*, 2: 445-65; Williams, *Americans and their Forests*, 179-83.

32. Benson, *Logs and Lumber*, 13, 17-18, 26, 34; Lewis, *Lumberman from Flint*, 18, 21; Louis P. Haight, *The Life of Charles Henry Hackley, Drawn from Old Public and Family Records* (Muskegon, Mich.: Dana, 1948), 28-30; [Page & Co.], *History of Bay County*, 67-68 (quote, p. 68); Mills, *History of Saginaw*, 405, 423-24; Maybee, "Michigan's White Pine Era," 399-400; Bell, "Alger," 116-17.

33. Goodstein, *Biography of a Businessman*, 68-70; Hotchkiss, *Lumber and Forest Industry*, 101-102, 143; [Page & Co.], *History of Bay County*, 51-52, 170-71; Kilar, *Michigan's Lumbertowns*, 40-42, 55; Mills, *History of Saginaw*, 1: 397, 410; Maybee, "Michigan's White Pine Era," 425-28. See also: *Bay City Journal*, 8 Dec. 1866, 16 Nov. 1867; Bay City *Lumberman's Gazette*, 3 Nov. 1877. Both Sage and McGraw also had extensive timberlands in Wisconsin, and in 1875 McGraw acquired half-interest in W. J. Young & Co., the largest sawmill in Clinton, Iowa. See: George Wesley Sieber, "Sawmilling on the Mississippi: The W. J. Young Company, 1858-1900 (unpub. Ph.D. diss., University of Iowa, 1960), 143-46.

34. Kilar, *Michigan's Lumbertowns*, 54-55, 154-55; Jeremy Kilar, "From Forest and Field to Factory: Michigan Workers and the Labor Movement," in Hathaway, *Michigan: Visions of our Past*, 239; Anonymous, "Profiting from Experience, *AL*, 75 (25 Sept. 1904): 1, 55; [Defebaugh], *American Lumbermen*, 1: 179-80; Blackburn and Ricards, "Timber Industry in Manistee," 19-21; Kohlmeyer, "Northern Pine Lumbermen," 529-30. Kilar's *Michigan Lumbertowns* is good, but by limiting his study to three cities he obscures the extent of fragmentation. In addition to Saginaw, Bay City, and Muskegon, a number of other centers deserved attention including Au Sable, Alpena, Manistee, Ludington, and Flint.

35. Benson, *Logs and Lumber*, 167-68, 174-77; Williams, *Americans and their Forests*, 217; Sieber, "Sawmilling on the Mississippi," 281-85.

36. Benson, *Logs and Lumber*, 53-55, 110, 113, 212-19; Kilar, *Michigan's Lumbertowns*, 136-45; Kohlmeyer, "Northern Pine Lumbermen," 531-32; George B. Engberg, "Who Were the Lumberjacks?" *Mich. Hist.*, 32 (1948): 238-45.

37. Lewis, *Lumberman from Flint*, 22; Goodstein, *Biography of a Businessman*, 39, 49; Hotchkiss, *Lumber and Forest Industry*, 89-93, 96; Benson, *Logs and Lumber*, 108 (quote), 173-80, 221-22.

38. Benson, *Logs and Lumber*, 84-85, 104-111; Kohlmeyer, "Northern Pine Lumbermen," 531-34.

39. Hotchkiss, *Lumber and Forest Industry*, 111-14; Mills, *History of Saginaw*, 2: 1-17; Dan Peters, "The Hackley and Hume Papers, 1859-1955: A Narrative Sketch" (unpub. typescript account, 1976; Archives and Manuscripts Dept., Michigan State University Library, Ann Arbor), 4.

40. Goodstein, *Biography of a Businessman*, 68, 70-71 (quote, p. 71), 75-77, 159-60; Kohlmeyer, "Northern Pine Lumbermen," 529-30, 532-34.

41. Michael Williams notes the dominance of people from the Northeast, but oddly emphasizes the changes they implemented rather than continuities, even though the changes he describes were implemented in Maine and New York as well as the Lake States. Williams, *Americans and their Forests*, 201-216.

42. Kilar, Michigan's *Lumbertowns*, 15, 21-25, 31, 36-42; Benson, *Logs and Lumber*, 2-4, 8-10, 69-72, 160-61; Holbrook, *Holy Old Mackinaw*, 83-84, 91; Mills, *History of Saginaw*, 1: 319-403, 411; [Page & Co.], *History of Bay County*, 41, 46-47; Maybee, "Michigan's White Pine Era," 414-16; Goodstein, *Biography of a Businessman*, 99-102. Both Saginaw and Bay City had smaller neighbors along the river, some ephemeral, some not. The terms Saginaw and Bay City, as used here, refer not just to the two cities proper, but also to their immediate neighbors.

43. Roy M. Overpack, "The Michigan Logging Wheels," *Mich. Hist.*, 35 (1951): 222-25; William G. Rector, "Railroad Logging in the Lake States," ibid., 36 (1952): 351-62; Raymond D. Burroughs, "The Big Wheels," *AF*, 59 (1953): 16-18, 43; Haight, *Hackley*, 37-39, 105-106; Benson, *Logs and Lumber*, 112-19, 139-40, 146-47, 149, 153-55; Holbrook, *Holy Old Mackinaw*, 101-102; Lillard, *Great Forest*, 148-55; Kilar, *Michigan's Lumbertowns*, 212; [Page & Co.], *History of Bay County*, 47; Williams, *Americans and their Forests*, 205, 206-216, 228; Maybee, "Michigan's White Pine Era," 407, 417-22. Big wheels were later used in the Gulf South and Far West; crosscuts were probably first used in felling on the West Coast.

44. Chicago *Northwestern Lumberman*, 6 and 20 Jan. 1883 (1st quote, 20 Jan.); Maybee, "Michigan's White Pine Era," 397, 407 (2nd quote), 417-22 (3rd quote, p. 417); Hotchkiss, *Lumber and Forest Industry*, 378.

45. Hotchkiss, *Lumber and Forest Industry*, 329; Maybee, "Michigan's White Pine Era," 417-20; William G. Rector, *Log Transportation in the Lake States Lumber Industry, 1840-1918 . . .* (Glendale, Calif.: Clark, 1953), 218-24; Haight, *Hackley*, 37-39, 105-106; Lake George & Muskegon Railroad materials, Charles H. Hackley Papers (Historical Collections, Michigan State University Archives, East Lansing), box 3, files 27-28. Ironically, Gerrish did not employ a Baldwin locomotive on his line, but a Porter.

46. Maybee, "Michigan's White Pine Era," 423-26; Kohlmeyer, "Northern Pine Lumbermen," 533; Benson, *Logs and Lumber*, 110, 168-73; Mills, *History of Saginaw*, 1: 397-99; [Page & Co.], *History of Bay County*, 42, 45-46. On the evolution of technology, see: Hotchkiss, *Lumber and Forest Industry*, 649-60; Thomas R. Cox, "Logging Technology," *Encyclopedia of American Forest and Conservation History*, ed. by Richard C. Davis (2 vols.; New York: Macmillan, 1983), 1: 347-54; William G. Rector, "Log Transportation," ibid., 1: 357-62.

47. Engberg, "Who Were the Lumberjacks?" 239-40; Benson, *Logs and Lumber*, 85-91, 196-97, 212-16; Massie, "Plows, Ships, and Shovels," 97; Kohlmeyer, "Northern Pine Lumbermen," 530, 534-36; Hotchkiss, *Lumber and Forest Industry*, 300, 485; Williams, *Americans and their Forests*, 201; Casler, Kline, and Taber, *Logging Railroad Era in Pennsylvania*, 1: 574-80. Stewart Holbrook and David Smith make it sound as if Maine supplied the bulk of the Michigan industry's labor force, but analyses by Engberg and others demonstrate this was not the case, although as Maine's forests became

increasingly depleted out-migration from there did increase. Holbrook, *Holy Old Mackinaw*, 72-78; David C. Smith, "The Logging Frontier," *JFH*, 18 (1974): 98-99, 101-103, 106. See also: Fuller, *Economic and Social Beginnings*, 170-71, 468-88; Holbrook, *Yankee Exodus*, 85-86, 108-111; J. Horace Stevens, "The Influence of New England in Michigan," *Mich. Hist.*, 19 (1935): 351-52.

48. Engberg, "Who Were the Lumberjacks?" 241-42; Kilar, *Michigan's Lumbertowns*, 180-81, 184, 196; Wynne, *Timber Colony*, 52-53; Lower, *Great Britain's Woodyard*, 88-95 (quote, p. 91). Perhaps the most important Canadian immigrant was Robert Dollar, who emigrated from Scotland to Canada in 1858 and then in 1882 to Michigan, where he took up lumbering. Dollar later moved to California, where he became a leading lumberman and merchant fleet operator. See: Robert Dollar, *Memoirs of Robert Dollar* (4 vols.; San Francisco: by the author, 1917-1925), 1: 2-27; 3: 23; Gregory Charles O'Brien, "The Life of Robert Dollar, 1844-1932" (unpub. Ph.D. diss., Claremont Graduate School, 1969).

49. Engberg, "Who Were the Lumberjacks?" 244-45; Rohrbough, *Trans-Appalachian Frontier*, 244; Kilar, *Michigan's Lumbertowns*, 63-64; Michigan State Agricultural Society, *Annual Report for 1855* (Lansing: Homer & Fitch, 1856), 828-29; Benson, *Logs and Lumber*, 50-53, 82. "Conversely," Barbara Benson notes, "a 'professional' logger might supplement his earnings through agricultural day labor during the summer and fall." Ibid., 198.

50. U. P. Hedrick, *The Land of the Crooked Tree* (New York: Oxford University Press, 1948), 236-51, 350 (quote); Maybee, "Michigan's White Pine Era," 430.

51. Holbrook, *Holy Old Mackinaw*, 83-88 (quote, p. 83); F. B. Streeter, "History of Prohibition Legislation in Michigan," *Mich. Hist.*, 2 (1917): 289-309; Mills, *History of Saginaw*, 1: 233-34, 407-408; Kilar, *Michigan's Lumbertowns*, 50, 71-75, 91-93, 102-106, 112-34 (quote, p. 134) [for an earlier version, see: Kilar, "Great Lakes Lumber Towns and Frontier Violence," *JFH*, 31 (1987): 71-85]; George M. Blackburn and Sherman L. Ricards, "A Demographic History of the West: Manistee County, Michigan," *JAH*, 57 (1970): 600-618; Theodore M. Karamanski, *Deep Woods Frontier: A History of Logging in Northern Michigan* (Detroit, Mich.: Wayne State University Press, 1989), 103-117.

52. Kilar, *Michigan's Lumbertowns*, 51, 143, 147-48 (quotes, p. 148); Holbrook, *Holy Old Mackinaw*, 112-13; [Defebaugh], *American Lumbermen*, 1: 223-26; Hotchkiss, *Lumber and Forest Industry*, 224-28; Haight, *Hackley*, 20, 22-23, 25-26, 33, 65-66. See, also: correspondence files, Hackley Papers.

53. Holbrook, *Holy Old Mackinaw*, 82-83 (quote, p. 83); Kilar, *Michigan's Lumbertowns*, 52, 148; Michigan Pioneer and Historical Society, *Collections*, 7 (1886): 279; Benson, *Logs and Lumber*, 213-14; Hotchkiss, *Lumber and Forest Industry*, 114; Mills, *History of Saginaw*, 1: 144-48; 2: 322. Mills's version of the incident differs from Holbrook's in several respects, but he also details other escapades by Emerson.

54. Kilar, "From Forest and Field to Factory," 240 (quote); Kilar, *Michigan's Lumbertowns*, 143-53, 176-77. See, also: Karamanski, *Deep Woods Frontier*, 103-104; Goodstein, *Biography of a Businessman*, 71-74, 80-81, 86, 92-93; Lewis, *Lumberman from Flint*, 194-97.

55. Benson, *Logs and Lumber*, 203-204; Lewis, *Lumberman from Flint*, 192-94 (1st quote, p. 193); Goodstein, *Biography of a Businessman*, 80-83 (2nd quote, p. 81; 3rd quote, p. 83). Benson's view that mill and woods workers

were generally happy with conditions seems based on a simplistic view of the evidence.

56. Kilar, *Michigan's Lumbertowns*, 132-34 (quote, p. 134). Kilar demonstrates that social distancing was especially acute in Bay City, where much of the industry was controlled by absentee owners removed geographically as well as socially and economically from their workers, ibid., 153-63; Kilar, "A Comparative Study of Lumber Barons as Community Leaders in Saginaw, Muskegon, and Bay City," *Mich Hist.*, 74 (1990): 35-42. See, also: Maybee, "Michigan's White Pine Era," 385-94.

57. Bay City *Daily Journal*, 3 (quote), 9, 17, and 19 July 1872; Kilar, *Michigan's Lumbertowns*, 232.

58. Goodstein, *Biography of a Businessman*, 83-86 (quote, p. 84). See, also: Kilar, *Michigan's Lumbertowns*, 217; Doris B. McLaughlin, *Michigan Labor: A Brief History from 1818 to the Present* (Ann Arbor: Institute of Labor and Industrial Relations, University of Michigan, 1970), 33; Vernon H. Jensen, *Lumber and Labor* (New York: Farrar & Rinehart, 1945), 58-59. For an earlier version of Goodstein's study, see her "Labor Relations in the Saginaw Valley Lumber Industry, 1865-1885," *Bulletin of the Business Historical Society*, 27 (1953): 206-211; in both accounts, she draws heavily on the papers of Henry Sage, but as an absentee owner he was poorly positioned to evaluate what was transpiring in Saginaw Valley's working-class circles.

59. Bay City *Daily Journal*, 19 July 1872. In elections that fall, the Republican strategy centered on identifying the Democratic candidate with the union, which suggests a greater importance for it than the *Journal* was willing to concede. Goodstein, *Biography of a Businessman*, 126.

60. Kilar, Michigan's *Lumbertowns*, 212; Williams, *Americans and their Forests*, 200, 206-208; Rector, *Log Transportation*, 168-69, 218-24; Rector, "Railroad Logging in the Lake States," 351-62.

61. Kilar, *Michigan's Lumbertowns*, 218-45; Kilar, "From Forest and Field to Factory," 242-43; Jensen, *Lumber and Labor*, 59-63; Goodstein, *Biography of a Businessman*, 87-92; Haight, *Hackley*, 71-72, 96-97; McLaughlin, *Michigan Labor*, 32-49 (quote, p. 32). Kilar, "Community and Authority Response to the Saginaw Valley Lumber Strike of 1885," *JFH*, 20 (1976): 67-79, is an earlier version of the chapter on the strike in *Michigan's Lumbertowns* and is cited below only when it differs from the later analysis.

62. Kilar, *Michigan's Lumbertowns*, 229; Kilar, "Community and Authority Response," 71; Goodstein, *Biography of a Businessman*, 87; Michigan Bureau of Labor and Industrial Statistics, *Third Annual Report* (Lansing: State Printer, 1886), 119; Bay City *Daily Tribune*, 14 July 1885. Estimates of the number of millhands in the valley range upwards from 4,232, a figure clearly too low.

63. Kilar, Michigan's *Lumbertowns*, 229-30; Goodstein, *Biography of a Businessman*, 88; Jensen, *Lumber and Labor*, 62; McLaughlin, *Michigan Labor*, 33-35; Pittsburgh *Journal of United Labor*, 25 Sept. 1885; Bureau of Industrial and Labor Statistics, *Third Annual Report*, 110; Bell, "Alger," 179-80. In fact, the ten-hour law was not to take effect until September.

64. Bureau of Industrial and Labor Statistics, *Third Annual Report*, 93 (quote); McLaughlin, *Michigan Labor*, 36; [Page & Co.], *History of Bay County*,

53; Kilar, *Michigan's Lumbertowns*, 229-36; Bell, "Alger," 180. Goodstein, *Biography of a Businessman*, 88, has the strike commence at "the Rust mills."

65. Detroit *Evening News*, quoted in Bell, "Alger," 188, 192; Kilar, *Michigan's Lumbertowns*, 234, 235-37; Sidney Glazer, "Labor and Agrarian Movements in Michigan, 1876-1896 (unpub. Ph.D. diss., University of Michigan, 1932), 96. Other community leaders were even more sympathetic to the strikers, if not to their leaders. See: Kilar, *Michigan's Lumbertowns*, 232, 236, 238, 240-41, 243-44; Goodstein, *Biography of a Businessman*, 89-90, 92; McLaughlin, *Michigan Labor*, 44, 45.

66. Bell, "Alger," 181-89, 193-94. Alger lived his first years in poverty in a shanty in the forest and was orphaned at age eleven or twelve. He rose to wealth and influence, serving as a general in the Civil War, governor of Michigan, and then Secretary of War under President William McKinley. In addition to Bell's dissertation, see: [Defebaugh], *American Lumbermen*, 2: 41-44; Hotchkiss, *Lumber and Forest Industry*, 75-77; George N. Fuller, ed., *Governors of the Territory and State of Michigan*, Bulletin no. 16 (Lansing: Michigan Historical Commission, 1928), 131-36.

67. Goodstein, *Biography of a Businessman*, 89 (1st quote); Kilar, *Michigan's Lumbertowns*, 237-40 (2nd quote, p. 238); McLaughlin, *Michigan Labor*, 38, 41-45; Bell, "Alger," 183-85.

68. Kilar, *Michigan's Lumbertowns*, 231-34; Goodstein, *Biography of a Businessman*, 88, 90; Goodstein, "Labor Relations in the Saginaw Valley Lumber Industry," 216; McLaughlin, *Michigan Labor*, 33-34, 36, 40, 43-44; Bell, "Alger," 180-81.

69. Kilar, *Michigan's Lumbertowns*, 241, 339 (quote); McLaughlin, *Michigan Labor*, 47-48. Kilar has Powderly urging "ten hours and old wages," but this is surely mistaken, for laborers were paid on a daily, not an hourly basis, and "old wages" would thus have constituted the raise workmen were seeking all along. Kilar, "Community and Authority Response," 76; Kilar, *Michigan's Lumbertowns*, 241. Cf. Goodstein, *Biography of a Businessman*, 88, 91-92.

70. Kilar, *Michigan's Lumbertowns*, 241-43; Kilar, "From Forest and Field to Factory," 243-45 (quote, pp. 244-45); Goodstein, *Biography of a Businessman*, 91; Jensen, *Lumber and Labor*, 61-62; Bay City *Lumberman's Gazette*, reprinted in *CL*, 5 (15 Aug. 1885): 276; Bell, "Alger," 191, 192. The greater strength of strikers in Bay City seems largely to have resulted from the distancing of workers and absentee owners, who made up some 60 percent of the city's lumbermen. The lack of mutual understanding that resulted from the absence of day-to-day contact encouraged intransigence on both sides.

71. *CL*, 5 (15 June 1885): 235; Williams, *Americans and their Forests*, 227, 229 (quote); Goodstein, *Biography of a Businessman*, 90; Karamanski, *Deep Woods Frontier*, 141.

72. Although rooted in the experience of Michigan's lumbering frontier, the environmental consequences of this deforestation are a part of the story of post-frontier times and thus beyond the scope of this study.

73. Bay City *Lumberman's Gazette*, reprinted in *CL*, 5 (1 Aug. 1885): 266; Robert C. Johnson, "Logs for Saginaw: The Development of Raft Towing on Lake Huron," *Inland Seas*, 5 (1949): 373-41, 83-90; Johnson, "Logs for Saginaw: An

Episode in Canadian-American Tariff Relations," *Mich. Hist.*, 34 (1950): 213-23; A. R. M. Lower, W. A. Carrothers, and A. A. Saunders, *North American Assault on the Canadian Forest*, ed. by Harold A. Innes (Toronto: Ryerson Press, 1938), 148-49, 153-55.

74. *Eleventh Census of the United States: 1890*, Vol. 8, pt. 2: 424-26, 434-36; Mills, *History of Saginaw*, 1: 403-404, 411-13; Maybee, "Michigan's White Pine Era," 424, 428-29; Williams, *Americans and their Forests*, 228; Hotchkiss, *Lumber and Forest Industry*, 143-44, 147, 159, 679-85; [Page & Co.], *History of Bay County*, 43-45, 57; Anonymous, "Logs Driven in the Saginaw District, 1864-1892," *Northwestern Lumberman*, n.v. (18 Feb. 1893): 16.

75. Maybee, "Michigan's White Pine Era," 424; Kilar, *Michigan's Lumbertowns*, 262-63; Haight, *Hackley*, 69-70, 78-79. In 1890 sawmills represented 78.6 percent of business investment in Muskegon and 49.4 percent of wages earned; by 1900 the figures (including both saw and planning mills) had fallen to 41.2 and 25.3 percent respectively. The figures for Saginaw and Bay City were similar. See: *Eleventh Census of the United States: 1890*, Vol. 12: *Census of Manufactures*, pt. 2: 54-55, 58-59, 354-55, 502-505; ibid., *1900*, vol. 8, pt. 2: 424, 426, 434, 436.

76. Karamanski, *Deep Woods Frontier*, 16, 18, 123, 141-42; Maybee, "Michigan's White Pine Era," 429. Hardwoods dominated the Upper Peninsula, pine making up but 15 percent of stands.

77. Williams, *Americans and their Forests*, 228; Lewis, *Lumberman from Flint*, 6-7; Maybee, "Michigan's White Pine Era," 422; United States, Forest Service, *Lumber Production, 1869-1934* (Washington, D.C.: USDA, Forest Service, Division of Forest Economics, 1936), 7, 8, 9, 10, 44.

78. Williams, *Americans and their Forests*, 230-37; Maybee, "Michigan's White Pine Era," 430; Norman J. Schmaltz, "The Land Nobody Wanted: The Dilemma of Michigan's Cutover Lands," *Mich. Hist.*, 67 (1983): 32-40; Hotchkiss, *Lumber and Forest Industry*, 373-79. See, also: Richard H. Harms, "Life after Lumbering: Charles Henry Hackley and the Emergence of Muskegon, Michigan" (unpub. Ph.D. diss., Michigan State University, 1984).

79. Anonymous, "A Plain Exponent of Commerce," *AL* , 67 (27 Sept. 1902): 1; Anonymous, "Appreciation of Opportunity," ibid., 72 (26 Dec. 1903): 1, 19; Anonymous, "A Doer of Big Things," ibid., 76 (8 Oct. 1904): 1, 53 (quote); Anonymous, "True to His Traditions," ibid., 77 (18 Mar. 1905): 1, 35; Anonymous, "Profiting by Advantages," ibid., 79 (15 July 1905): 1, 63; [Defebaugh], *American Lumbermen*, 1: 171-73, 223-26; 2: 159-62, 209-213; Hotchkiss, *Lumber and Forest Industry*, 75-77, 167, 177-80, 224-28.

Chapter Seven

1. By 1860, of all branches of manufacture, lumber ranked second in value added (behind only cotton goods), third in value of product, and fourth in employment. Near the beginning of the new century, Bernhard Eduard Fernow, America's first professionally trained forester, ranked it even higher: "[F]orest products as second only in importance to agriculture, wood crops second to food crops, both equally indispensable." B. E. Fernow, "American Lumber," in Robert M. LaFollette, ed., *The Making of America*, Vol. 3:

Industry and Finance (Chicago: Making of America Company, 1906), 355; *Eighth Census of the United States: 1860,* Vol. 3: *Census of Manufactures,* 733-42; Williams, *Americans and their Forests,* 193-97; Perloff et al., *Regions, Resources and Economic Growth,* 118-19, 157-58.

2. Ralph Henry Bowen, ed. and trans., *A Frontier Family in Minnesota: Letters of Theodore Bost, 1851-1920* (Minneapolis: University of Minnesota Press, 1981), 177.

3. Mark Wyman, *The Wisconsin Frontier* (Bloomington: Indiana University Press, 1998), 181-83, 250-51; John Milton Holley, "Waterways and Lumber Interests of Western Wisconsin," *Proceedings of the State Historical Society of Wisconsin, 1906* (Madison: State Historical Society of Wisconsin, 1907): 209. For a more detailed, nuanced analysis, see: Margaret Walsh, *The Manufacturing Frontier: Pioneer Industry in Antebellum Wisconsin, 1830-1860* (Madison: State Historical Society of Wisconsin, 1972), esp. 5-6, 15-16, 19-21, 53-56, 104-111, 125-40.

4. Dale Arthur Peterson, "Lumbering on the Chippewa: The Eau Claire Area, 1845-1885" (unpub. Ph.D. diss., University of Minnesota, 1970), 37-38; Filibert Roth, *On the Forestry Conditions of Northern Wisconsin,* Department of Agriculture Bulletin no. 16 (Washington, D.C.: GPO, 1898), 3, 10-15, 20-21; Agnes M. Larson, *History of the White Pine Industry in Minnesota* (Minneapolis: University of Minnesota Press, 1949), 4-8; Williams, *Americans and their Forests,* 198-200. Of the upper Lake States, Minnesota was most forested. With thirty-three million acres, it had some 10 percent more than Michigan and 33 percent more than Wisconsin, but its stands tended to be of lesser quality. See: E. G. Cheney, "The Development of the Lumber Industry in Minnesota," *Journal of Geography,* 14 (1916): 194-95; Bourdo, "The Forest the Settlers Saw," 3-16; Clifford E. Ahlgren and Isabel F. Ahlgren, "The Human Impact on Northern Forest Ecosystems," in Flader, *Great Lakes Forest,* 33-44.

5. Wyman, *Wisconsin Frontier,* 131-32, 135-40; William F. Raney, *Wisconsin: A Story of Progress* (New York: Prentice-Hall, 1940), 89-91, 138-42; Joseph Shafer, *The Wisconsin Lead Region* (Madison: State Historical Society of Wisconsin, 1932); Reuben Gold Thwaites, "Notes on Early Lead Mining in the Fever (or Galena) River Area," *State Historical Society of Wisconsin Collections,* 13 (1895): 287-92; Alice E. Smith, *The History of Wisconsin,* Vol. 1: *From Exploration to Statehood* (Madison: State Historical Society of Wisconsin, 1973), 183-84, 187, 523, 529-30. Wisconsin Territory encompassed the future state as well as what would become Minnesota, Iowa, South Dakota, and part of North Dakota.

6. Smith, *History of Wisconsin,* 378-79, 466-70; Richard N. Current, *History of Wisconsin,* Vol. 2: *The Civil War Era, 1848-1873* (Madison: State Historical Society of Wisconsin, 1976), 42-48; Raney, *Wisconsin,* 110-11, 199-200; Guy-Harold Smith, "The Settlement and Distribution of Population in Wisconsin," *Transactions of the Wisconsin Academy of Sciences, Arts, and Letters,* 26 (1929): 53-108; Stephenson, *Recollections of a Long Life,* 79-80, 87, 104-106. Guidebooks and pamphlets encouraged immigration. The first sizable work was Increase A. Lapham, *A Geographical and Topographical Description of*

Wisconsin (1844); it was widely circulated in the East in this and later editions (with somewhat altered title).

7. Raney, *Wisconsin*, 91-96; Robert C. Nesbit, *The History of Wisconsin*, Vol. 3: *Urbanization and Industrialization, 1873-1893* (Madison: State Historical Society of Wisconsin, 1985), 46.

8. In areas further south development came sooner. By 1851, there was an estimated investment of $6 million in lumbering in the Wisconsin River Valley alone. Hurst, *Law and Economic Growth*, 126.

9. Daniel Stanchfield, "History of Pioneer Lumbering on the Upper Mississippi and Its Tributaries, with Biographical Sketches," *Minnesota Historical Society Collections* (17 vols.; St. Paul: Minnesota Historical Society, 1872-1920 [hereafter *MHSC*]) 9: 326; Fries, *Empire in Pine*, 18-19; Williams, *Americans and their Forests*, 183-85; Current, *Pine Logs and Politics*, 16-24, 27-28; Stephenson, *Recollections of a Long Life*, 74, 82-83, 92 (1st quote); Burke, *Logs on the Menominee*, 7-9; Harold M. Mayer and Richard C. Wade, *Growth of a Metropolis* (Chicago: University of Chicago Press, 1969), 3 (2nd quote).

10. Lucius G. Fisher, "Pioneer Recollections of Beloit and Southern Wisconsin," *Wis. Mag. Hist.*, 1 (1916): 271-72; Cheyney, "Development of the Lumber Industry," 194-95; Bourdo, "Forest the Settlers Saw," 7-14.

11. Lewis Taylor to Calvin Taylor, 6 Oct. 1846, Taylor Papers. On early Beloit, see: Fisher, "Pioneer Recollections," 271-86.

12. Nathan H. Parker, *Iowa as It Is in 1855 . . .* (Chicago: Keen & Lee, 1855), 35 (1st quote); George B. Hartman, "The Iowa Sawmill Industry," *Iowa Journal of History and Politics*," 40 (1942): 54-65, 68 (2nd quote); Lyda Belthuis, "The Lumber Industry of Eastern Iowa," ibid., 46 (1948): 120-26, 132, 134-35; Hough, *Report upon Forestry*, 530; Theodore C. Blegen, *Minnesota: A History of the State* (rev. ed.; Minneapolis: University of Minnesota Press, 1975), 328; Fries, *Empire in Pine*, 86-88; Larson, *White Pine Industry*, 361-63; Paul W. Gates, "Weyerhaeuser and Chippewa Logging Industry," in *The John H. Hauberg Historical Essays*, ed. by O. Fritiof Ander (Rock Island, Ill.: Denkmann Memorial Library, 1954), 51. See also: Jacob A. Swisher, *Iowa, Land of Many Mills* (Iowa City: State Historical Society of Iowa, 1940).

13. Raney, *Wisconsin*, 206.

14. Stanchfield, "History of Pioneer Lumbering," 326 (quote); Sieber, "Sawmilling on the Mississippi," 109-111, 203-205; Williams, *Americans and their Forests*, 186-89; Edward W. Durant, "Lumbering and Steamboating on the St. Croix River," *MHSC*, 10: 657-62; Wilbur H. Glover, "Lumber Rafting on the Wisconsin River," *Wis. Mag. Hist.*, 25 (1941-42): 155-77, 308-24; Charles E. Twining, *Downriver: Orrin H. Ingram and the Empire Lumber Company* (Madison: State Historical Society of Wisconsin, 1975), 262; Ceylon C. Lincoln, "Personal Experiences of a Wisconsin River Raftsman," *Proceedings of the Wisconsin State Historical Society, 1910* (Madison: by the society, 1911), 181-89; Simon Augustus Sherman, "Lumber Rafting on the Wisconsin River," ed. by Albert H. Sanford, ibid., 58 (1918): 171-80; Hough, *Report upon Forestry*, 528-31; Holley, "Waterways and Lumbering Interests of Western Wisconsin," 210, 213. Holley notes that because of the difficulty of driving the Wisconsin, sawmills were scattered along it rather than concentrated near its mouth.

15. Walter A Blair, *A Raft Pilot's Log: A History of the Great Rafting Industry on the Upper Mississippi, 1840-1915* (Cleveland: Clark, 1930), 25, 33-46, 204, 211-16; Belthuis, "Lumber Industry of Eastern Iowa," 130 (quote); Charles Edward Russell, *A-Rafting on the Mississip'* (New York: Century, 1928), 81-93, 109-20, 130-47, 313-17.

16. Williams, *Americans and their Forests*, 195-200, graphically illustrates the situation. On downriver mills, see especially: Hartman, "Iowa Sawmill Industry," 64-83; Fred W. Kohlmeyer, *Timber Roots: The Laird, Norton Story, 1855-1905* (Winona, Minn.: Winona County Historical Society, 1972), 182-203; Belthuis, "Lumber Indusrty of Eastern Iowa," 126-36; Sieber, "Sawmilling on the Mississippi," 46-104; Hidy, Hill, and Nevins, *Timber and Men*, 17-18, 21-22, 29-31.

17. Treaties with the Menominee and Winnebago opened some of the more southerly stands, but pinelands were primarily opened by treaties with the Ojibiwa (Chippewa) and Lakota (Sioux). For maps showing the various cessions and their dates, see: Raney, *Wisconsin*, 76, 78; Blegen, *Minnesota*, 172.

18. For examples, see: Alice Elizabeth Smith, *James Duane Doty: Frontier Promoter* (Madison: State Historical Society of Wisconsin, 1954), 69-70, 73-76; Holley, "Waterways and Lumber Interests of Western Wisconsin," 208-211.

19. Anthony Godfrey, *A Forestry History of Ten Wisconsin Indian Reservations . . .*, Report Prepared for Bureau of Indian Affairs, Forestry Branch, Minneapolis (Washington, D.C.: GPO, 1997), 6-9.

20. Louis Pelzer, *Henry Dodge* (Iowa City: State Historical Society of Iowa, 1911), 128-33, 139-40.

21. Lass, *Minnesota*, 74, 77 (quote); Raney, *Wisconsin*, 124-28; Folwell, *History of Minnesota*, 1: 393-412; Smith, *History of Wisconsin*, 510; Reuben Gold Thwaites, "The Boundaries of Wisconsin," *State Historical Society of Wisconsin, Collections* , 11 (1899): 451-501; Alexander N. Winchell, "Minnesota's Eastern, Southern, and Western Boundaries," *MHSC*, 10: 680-84; Lawrence Martin, *The Physical Geography of Wisconsin* (2nd ed.; Madison: State Printer, 1932), 481-87.

22. Lass, *Minnesota*, 20, 73-99, 100-101; Blegen, *Minnesota*, 217, 220; Winchell, "Minnesota's Boundaries," 484-87.

23. Lass, *Minnesota*, 114, 128; Peterson, "Lumbering on the Chippewa," 4, 26-27, 29, 706-707. The bulk of the lumber production on the St. Croix was in Minnesota, especially at Stillwater, but some took place in Hudson, Wisconsin, and other locations on the east side of the river.

24. Larson, *White Pine Industry*, 229 (1st quote); Lass, *Minnesota*, 76-77 (2nd quote, p. 77); Blegen, *Minnesota*, 321-22; Peterson, "Lumbering on the Chippewa," 68-69; Kohlmeyer, "Northern Pine Lumbermen," 530, 535-36; Engberg, "Who Were the Lumberjacks?" 239-40. For a contemporary account, see: E. S. Seymour, *Sketeches of Minnesota, the New England of the West . . .* (New York: Harper, 1850).

25. Blegen, *Minnesota*, 160 (quoting Iowa delegate); Lucille M. Kane, *The Waterfall that Built a City: The Falls of St. Anthony in Minneapolis* (St. Paul: Minnesota Historical Society, 1966), 14-29, 57-61; Folwell, *Minnesota*, 1: 486-89; Winchell, "Minnesota's Boundaries," 680-82.

26. Stanchfield, "History of Pioneer Lumbering," 328. See also: William H. C. Folsom, *History of Lumbering in the St. Croix Valley . . ,*. in *MHSC*, 9: 291-324; Augustus B. Easton, ed., *History of the St. Croix Valley* (2 vols.; Chicago: Cooper, 1909), 1: 18-22; 2: 974-77.

27. Bertha L. Heilbron, ed., *With Pen and Pencil on the Frontier in 1851: Sketches of Frank Blackwell Mayer* (St. Paul: Minnesota Historical Society Press, 1986), 243 (1st quote), 245 (2nd quote); Atwater, *History of Minneapolis*, 1: 84, 527 (3rd quote); Rufus King, "Milwaukee to St. Paul in 1855," *Wis. Mag. Hist.*, 11 (1927): 183-84; Stanchfield, "History of Pioneer Lumbering," 327-28, 329, 339; Loehr, "Franklin Steele," 311-14; Folwell, *History of Minnesota*, 1: 229, 356.

28. Bowen, *Frontier Family in Minnesota*, 59 (1st quote), 64 (2nd quote).

29. Lass, *Minnesota*, 76, 98, 145-46; Loehr, "Caleb Dorr," 134-38; Loehr, "Franklin Steele," 309-318; Atwater, *History of Minneapolis*, 1: 387-91, 536-39, 542-44; Kane, *The Waterfall that Built a City*, 98-99; Blegen, *Minnesota*, 320; Stanchfield, "History of Pioneer Lumbering," 347-50. Stanchfield's larger numbers of lumbermen are explained by the fact most firms had multiple owners at any one time and different owners over time.

30. Smith, *History of Wisconsin*, 512 (1st quote); Lass, *Minnesota*, 76-77, 142-44 (quote, p. 144); Blegen, *Minnesota*, 316 (3rd quote); Walsh, *The Manufacturing Frontier*, 15-16, 39, 46-47, 53-57; Wyman, *Wisconsin Frontier*, 251-52, 263-71; Williams, *Americans and their Forests*, 128-33, 160-67; Gates, "Weyerhaeuser and Chippewa Logging," 51-52; Kohlmeyer, "Northern Pine Lumbermen," 531-32.

31. Belthuis, "The Lumber Industry of Eastern Iowa," 136, 140-41; Hartman, "Iowa Lumber Industry," 64-68, 82-83. For a detailed discussion of the marketing problems of a large river mill, see: Sieber, "Sawmilling on the Mississippi," 317-471.

32. Ray Allen Billington, *The Genesis of the Frontier Thesis: A Study in Historical Creativity* (San Marino, Calif.: Huntington Library, 1971), 11-12; Charles E. Twining, "The Lumbering Frontier," in Flader, *The Great Lakes Forest*, 128; Smith, "The Logging Frontier," *JFH*, 18 (1974): 96-98.

33. Lass, *Minnesota*, 76-77 (quote), 120-21; Blegen, *Minnesota*, 201-205.

34. Lass, *Minnesota*, 101-104; Folwell, *Minnesota*, 1: 489-95; Winchell, "Minnesota's Boundaries," 682-85.

35. Kohlmeyer, *Timber Roots*, 23-25, 31; Sieber, "Sawmilling on the Mississippi," 46-53, 58; Peterson, "Lumbering on the Chippewa," 200; Belthuis, "Lumber Industry of Eastern Iowa," 140-41; Hartman, "Iowa Lumber Industry," 64-68, 87-88; Fries, *Empire in Pine*, 16-23; Larson, *White Pine Industry*, 26-28, 40-44; Merk, *Economic History of Wisconsin*, 60-61.

36. Kohlmeyer, *Timber Roots*, 37-38; Reynolds, *Daniel Shaw*, 6-8, 13, 46-50; Peterson, "Lumbering on the Chippewa," 40-98; Walsh, *Manufacturing Frontier*, 126-27; Sieber, "Sawmilling on the Mississippi," 66, 68-69, 92-94; Engberg, "Lumber and Labor," 154-55; Hauberg, *Weyerhaeuser & Denkmann*, 51, 57. See also: Smith, *Doty*, 350-53.

37. Stephenson, *Recollections of a Long Life*, 50-51, 63-65, 74, 79-81 (2nd quote, p. 79), 87, 104-105 (1st quote, p. 104; 3rd quote, p. 105), 134-35; Peterson,

"Lumbering on the Chippewa," 175-77; Reynolds, *Daniel Shaw*, 44-45; Hartman, "Iowa Sawmill Industry," 79.

38. Current, *Pine Logs and Politics*, 25-28, 45-46, 51-54, 216-17; Smith, *Doty*, 186-89, 308-325; Merk, *Economic History of Wisconsin*, 85-87; Matthias Nordberg Orfield, *Federal Land Grants to the States with Special Reference to Minnesota*, Studies in the Social Sciences, no. 2 (Minneapolis: University of Minnesota, 1915), 97. In subsequent years, Congressman Philetus Sawyer—who had large lumber interests in the Oshkosh area—pushed for federal funds to build a major ship canal along the Fox-Wisconsin route. Sawyer was an accomplished Congressional log roller, but his efforts failed to open a significant trade. Current, *Pine Logs and Politics*, 184-88, 190; Nesbit, *Urbanization and Industrialization*, 137-38. For an example of Sawyer's sharp business practices, see: John E. Nelligan, "The Life of a Lumberman," as told to Charles M. Sheridan, *Wis. Mag. Hist.*, 13 (1929): 283-84.

39. Peterson, "Lumbering on the Chippewa," 126, 131-34; Stephenson, *Recollections of a Long Life*, 63-65, 79-81, 90-91, 104-105; Merk, *Economic History of Wisconsin*, 109.

40. Peterson, "Lumbering on the Chippewa," 88, 125-26, 199-200 (1st quote); Reynolds, *Daniel Shaw*, 3, 6-10 (2nd quote, p. 10), 53-54, 130-36; William W. Bartlett, *History, Tradition, and Adventure in the Chippewa Valley* (Eau Claire, Wis.: by the author, 1929), 187; Blegen, *Minnesota*, 322-24; Nesbit, *Urbanization and Industrialization*, 54-58; Twining, *Downriver*, 35-37, 42-51; Hurst, *Law and Economic Growth*, 309-21; Albert H. Sanford, "The Beginnings of a Great Industry at La Crosse," *Wis. Mag. Hist.*, 18 (1935): 375, 387-88; Hidy, Hill, and Nevins, *Timber and Men*, 25-26; Ellis B. Usher, *Wisconsin, Its Story and Biography* (8 vols.; Chicago: Lewis, 1914), 7: 1935-37. Colman had other problems as well. Although La Crosse grew following the Civil War, Franklin Hough notes that the Black River, from which Colman's logs came, was "very difficult. . . . Sometimes several seasons pass before logs started on the upper waters reach the boom at La Crosse. Very few reach the mills till the second summer after they have been banked." Hough, *Report on Forestry*, 530. See also: Usher, *Wisconsin*, 1: 153-219; Sieber, "Sawmilling on the Mississippi," 4-5, 12-14; Holley, "Waterways and Lumber Interests of Western Wisconsin," 210-11; John Shaw, "Shaw's Narrative," *Collections of the State Historical Society of Wisconsin*, 2: 197-232.

41. Stephenson, *Recollections of a Long Life*, 82-84, 92, 94, 96, 102, 124-26, 171, 173; Peterson, "Lumbering on the Chippewa," 196; Larson, *White Pine Industry*, 30-31; Williams, *Americans and their Forests*, 184-86 (quote, p. 185), 188; Sieber, "Sawmilling on the Mississippi," 345-49; James Parton, "Chicago," *Atlantic Monthly*, 19 (1867): 325-45; Mayer and Wade, *Chicago*, 16-17, 20, 26, 28; Russell, *A-Rafting on the Mississip'*, 64-65, 70-72. See also: George W. Sieber, "Railroads and Lumber Marketing, 1858-78: The Relationship between an Iowa Sawmill Firm and the Chicago and North Western Railroad," *Annals of Iowa*, 39 (1967): 33-46. Milwaukee was also a major market for lumber and had similar problems with its harbor, but with a smaller hinterland it never assumed Chicago's importance to the industry. See: Stephenson, *Recollections of a Long Life*, 82-83, 92.

42. Stephenson, *Recollections of a Long Life*, 85 (quote), 88-89, 120; Nesbit, *Urbanization and Industrialization*, 70; Sieber, "Sawmilling on the Mississippi," 261-84, 592-94. For a full treatment of Sawyer's career, see: Current, *Pine Logs and Politics*.

43. Stephenson, *Recollections of a Long Life*, 77-78, 88-89 (1st quote); Nelligan, "Life of a Lumberman," 45-46 (2nd quote); Stanchfield, "History of Pioneer Lumbering," 330-31, 333 (4th quote), 338, 353-54 (3rd quote); Loehr, "Caleb Dorr," 127-29, 133-34; Russell, *A-Rafting on the Mississip'*, 42-44. According to one authority, landlooker James Beckey "logged, farmed, trapped, hunted, and looked for pineland, but he was unable to write"—a sort of successor to the *coureur de bois*. He was atypical; most were average men whose only distinctive characteristic was knowledge of timber. Since there were few settlers in the northwoods, not many were available to serve as landlookers. See: Peterson, "Lumbering on the Chippewa," 218-22.

44. Reynolds, *Daniel Shaw*, 20; Burke, *Logs on the Menominee*, 10, 73-74 (quote). The incident Burke reports was long after Stanchfield's early work, but the respect for the skill of the better cruisers was of long standing.

45. Hidy, Hill, and Nevins, *Timber and Men*, 34, 37-38, 42 (F. E. Weyerhaeuser quote), 53; F. K. Weyerhaeuser, *Trees and Men* (New York: Newcomen Society of North America, 1951), 9; Sieber, "Sawmilling on the Mississippi," 13, 55-58, 112-14, 317-21, 590-91, 595, 602.

46. Peterson, "Lumbering on the Chippewa," 203-205.

47. Merk, *Economic History of Wisconsin*, 59-109; Current, *Pine Logs and Politics*, 27-30; Reynolds, *Daniel Shaw*, 13-14; Kohlmeyer, *Timber Roots*, 65; Twining, *Downriver*, 69-70, 71-75, 79; Sieber, "Sawmilling on the Mississippi," 31-35, 69-70, 94; Williams, *Americans and their Forests*, 187.

48. Peterson, "Lumbering on the Chippewa," 125-26 (1st quote); Twining, *Downriver*, 85-88 (2nd quote); Sieber, "Sawmilling on the Mississippi," 94, 128-30. Log rafts got the most attention, but lumber rafts were numerous too. In 1871 Knapp-Stout alone dispatched thirty rafts, containing thirty-one million board feet of lumber downstream. Peterson, "Lumbering on the Chippewa," 491.

49. The new arrivals included Thomas Shevlin, destined to be a major player not only in Minnesota, but also in the Gulf South and Far West. See: Anonymous, "The Maker of Opportunities," *AL*, n.v. (9 Dec. 1899): 1, 20; Anonymous, "White Pine Pioneer at Rest," ibid., (20 Jan. 1912): 1, 69.

50. Sieber, "Sawmilling on the Mississippi," 203-230; Blair, *A Raft Pilot's Log*, 23-46, 51-53, 69-76, 185 (1st quote), 191-92, 221-22, 265 (2nd quote), and passim; Rector, *Log Transportation in the Lake States*, 151-62; Larson, *White Pine Industry*, 94-98; Belthuis, "Lumber Industry of Eastern Iowa," 127-32, 136-39; Hartman, "Iowa Sawmill Industry," 72-77; Bernhardt J. Kleven, "Rafting Days on the Mississippi," *Proceedings of the Minnesota Academy of Science*, 16 (1948): 53-56; Russell, *A-Rafting on the Mississip'*, 100-109, 154-56; Marie E. Meyer, "Rafting on the Mississippi," *Palimpset*, 8 (Apr. 1927): 121-31; Peterson, "Lumbering on the Chippewa," 72-74, 86, 185-93, 479-93.

51. Hartman, "Iowa Lumber Industry," 57-63, 77-79; Reynolds, *Daniel Shaw*, 40, 43-45; Sieber, "Sawmilling on the Mississippi," 265-81; Williams, *Americans and their Forests*, 201-203; Hauberg, *Weyerhaeuser & Denkmann*, 33, 52-53.

52. Randall Rohe, "Lumbering: Wisconsin's Northern Urban Frontier," in *Wisconsin, Land and Life*, ed. by Robert C. Ostergren and Those R. Vale (Madison: University of Wisconsin Press, 1997), 222-25 (*Green Bay Advocate* quoted, p. 222).

53. Stephenson, *Recollections of a Long Life*, 82-83, 92 (1st quote), 168-69; Williams, *Americans and their Forests*, 203 (2nd quote); Peterson, "Lumbering on the Chippewa," 72-74, 86, 185-93; Sieber, "Sawmilling on the Mississippi," 250-52, 334-36, 414-18. Lake Michigan's routes were vital to eastern Wisconsin's lumber industry, cheap water rates being affected by rail rates from Marinette and other centers and Chicago being served by water and rail at a ratio of three to two. However, the lumber trade "got the rag, tag, and bobtail of the Great Lakes fleet—even derelicts." In 1873 sailing vessels outnumbered steam two to one, but the latter averaged larger by half; by 1888 there were more steam-powered than sailing vessels. See: Nesbit, *Urbanization and Industrialization*, 130-33 (quote, p. 132).

54. Hurst, *Law and Economic Growth*, 227; Larson, *White Pine Industry*, 235, 237; Merk, *Economic History of Wisconsin*, 97-99; Twining, *Downriver*, 32.

55. Twining, *Downriver*, 172-73 (*Eau Claire Free Press*, 31 Oct. 1861, quoted p. 173); Fries, *Empire in Pine*, 71-73; Reynolds, *Daniel Shaw*, 12-13, 93-100, 105-111; Peterson, "Lumbering on the Chippewa," 14, 79-80, 84, 189 (2nd quote), 200, 274-78, 293 (3rd quote), 479-93; Ingram, *Autobiography*, 49-51; Merk, *Economic History of Wisconsin*, 97-99; Robert K. Boyd, "Up and Down the Chippewa River," *Wis. Mag. Hist.*, 14 (1931): 243-52, 256-58. For maps and diagrams showing features at Eau Claire, see: ibid., 256, 258; Peterson, "Lumbering on the Chippewa," 154.

56. Ingram, *Autobiography*, 50-52, 58-59; Twining, *Downriver*, 173-79; Reynolds, *Daniel Shaw*, 79-81; Fries, *Empire in Pine*, 50-51, 71-72; Peterson, "Lumbering on the Chippewa," 283-85, 296-317, 335-38, 346-49, 506-41; Hurst, *Law and Economic Growth*, 165, 170, 172, 232, 244-45, 259, 264, 268-69, 417.

57. Goodstein, *Henry W. Sage*, 182; Peterson, "Lumbering on the Chippewa," 211-17, 225-26, 242-43; Reynolds, *Daniel Shaw*, 23. On Morrison, see: Atwater, *History of Minneapolis*, 2: 614-18; Stanchfield, "History of Pioneer Lumbering," 358-59; Larson, *White Pine Industry*, 36, 38, 58-59, and below, Chapter 8.

58. Twining, *Downriver*, 128-29, 166-67, 169-70; Peterson, "Lumbering on the Chippewa," 212-13, 217, 548-49 (1st quote); Gates, *Wisconsin Pine Lands of Cornell University*, 60-61, 93; Gates, "Weyerhaeuser and Chippewa Logging," 54-58; Nesbit, *Urbanization and Industrialization*, 523 (3rd quote); Sieber, "Sawmilling on the Mississippi," 159-61; Hidy, Hill, and Nevins, *Timber and Men*, 43-45; Current, *Pine Logs and Politics*, 122 (Putnam quote).

59. Peterson, "Lumbering on the Chippewa," 233-38, 598-99 (*Mississippi Valley Lumberman* quoted p. 598); Reynolds, *Daniel Shaw*, 131, 136; Hartman, "Iowa Sawmill Industry," 69-70; Sieber, "Sawmilling on the Mississippi," 169-70. Richard Current claims rings "were common." See: Current, *Pine Logs and Politics*, 121-23.

60. Hough, *Report upon Forestry*, 568-69. On the relative production of various upstream and downstream sites, see: Williams, *Americans and their Forests*, 227; for lists of downriver mills, see: Hidy, Hill, and Nevins, *Timber and*

Men, 34-38; Weyerhaeuser, *Trees and Men*, 10; and Hartman, "Iowa Sawmill Industry," 78-81.

61. Hartman, "Iowa Sawmill Industry," 72-73; Sieber, "Sawmilling on the Mississippi," 126-27, 216.

62. Twining, *Downriver*, 104-106, 247-48; Rector, *Log Transportation in the Lake States*, 33-34; Hartman, "Iowa Sawmill Industry," 68-70; Sieber, "Sawmilling on the Mississippi," 130-32; Hidy, Hill, and Nevins, *Timber and Men*, 44-45, 48; Ingram, *Autobiography*, 52-55, 72.

63. Williams, *Americans and their Forests*, 206; Sieber, "Sawmilling on the Mississippi," 169-70; Fries, *Empire in Pine*, 142-43.

64. Hidy, Hill, and Nevins, *Timber and Men*, 5-10, 22-24, 28-32 (1st quote, p. 32), 34-38, 41-42, 60; Weyerhaeuser, *Trees and Men*, 14 (2nd quote); Hauberg, *Weyerhaeuser & Denkmann*, 46, 53; Gates, "Weyerhaeuser and Chippewa Logging," 55-56, 58-62 (3rd quote); Richard G. Lillard, "Timber King," *Pacific Spectator*, 1 (1947): 15-16, 21; Blair, *A Raft Pilot's Log*, 77; Bernhardt J. Kleven, "The Mississippi River Logging Company," *Minn. Hist.*, 27 (1946): 194; Ingram, *Autobiography*, 51, 53-55; Peterson, "Lumbering on the Chippewa," 375-76; Sieber, "Sawmilling on the Mississippi," 164-65, 170-72; Fries, *Empire in Pine*, 146.

65. Cf. Merk, *Economic History of Wisconsin*, 91-95; Weyerhaeuser, *Trees and Men*, 9-12; Hauberg, *Weyerhaeuser & Denkmann*, 118-20; Peterson, "Lumbering on the Chippewa," 317-33, 338-46, 541-52, and passim; Twining, *Downriver*, 106-113, 171-72; Fries, *Empire in Pine*, 142-54, 156; Richard N. Current, *Wisconsin, A Bicentennial History* (New York: Norton, 1977), 112-15; Current, *Pine Logs and Politics*, 125-27; Reynolds, *Daniel Shaw*, 17-19; Kohlmeyer, *Timber Roots*, 82-116; Williams, *Americans and their Forests*, 205-206, 221, 228; Hidy, Hill, and Nevins, *Timber and Men*, 31, 38, 41-42; Wyman, *Wisconsin Frontier*, 266-71; Rector, *Log Transportation in the Lake States*, 131-33, 146-47, 274-75; Blair, *A Raft Pilot's Log*, 47-54; Kleven, "Mississippi River Logging Company," 191-202.

66. Kleven, "Mississippi River Logging Company," 194-96 (quote, p. 194-95); Hartman, "Iowa Sawmill Industry," 71-72; Lillard, "Timber King," 16-18.

67. Peterson, "Lumbering on the Chippewa," 298; Twining, *Downriver*, 106-112; Wyman, *Wisconsin Frontier*, 268.

68. Hurst, *Law and Economic Growth*, 195-97, 227-28, 266-68; Fries, *Empire in Pine*, 147-49.

69. Weyerhaeuser, *Trees and Men*, 10-11; Kohlmeyer, *Timber Roots*, 84-86; Sieber, "Sawmilling on the Mississippi," 172-74, 189, 194-200; Hartman, "Iowa Sawmill Industry," 65-68, 78-79. There were cooperative drives on the Chippewa earlier, but the Mississippi River Logging Company formalized and perfected the system. See: Peterson, "Lumbering on the Chippewa," 428-34.

70. Twining, *Downriver*, 111-12; Kohlmeyer, *Timber Roots*, 84-87, 101-103; Fries, *Empire in Pine*, 147; Hidy, Hill, and Nevins, *Timber and Men*, 47-54; Matthew G. Norton, *The Mississippi River Logging Company: An Historical Sketch* (n.p.: by the author, 1912), 13-14 (1st quotes); Sieber, "Sawmilling on the Mississippi," 170-81; Blair, *A Raft Pilot's Log*, 47-54, 69 (last quote);

Lillard, "Timber King," 17-19. Fin booms were retractable sheer booms fixed with a series of movable fins extending down from the body of the boom into the river. When the fins were rotated to catch the current, the boom would be forced out into the river to stop approaching logs; when they were subsequently turned parallel to the current, the boom could be withdrawn to allow traffic to pass.

71. Blair, *A Raft Pilot's Log*, 27-28, 48 (1st quote), 51-53, 77-93, 140-45, 195-201, 221-23, 250-54, and passim; Belthuis, "Lumber Industry of Eastern Iowa," 136-39; Twining, *Downriver*, 132-35; Kohlmeyer, *Timber Roots*, 103-104, 106; Rector, *Log Transportation in the Lake States*, 147-70, 272-76 (2nd quote, p. 275); Larson, *White Pine Industry*, 94-95; Hartman, "Iowa Sawmill Industry," 74-76; Sieber, "Sawmilling on the Mississippi," 216-17; Peterson, "Lumbering on the Chippewa," 72-74, 86, 185-93, 479-93; Russell, *A-Rafting on the Mississip'*, 152-56; James H. Baker, *Lives of the Governors of Minnesota*, *MHSC*, 13: 400-401 (3rd quote p. 401). Samuel Van Sant became a prominent figure in Minnesota and served as governor from 1901 to 1905.

72. Hurst, *Law and Economic Growth*, 268; Twining, *Downriver*, 182-84; Hidy, Hill, and Nevins, *Timber and Men*, 49-51; Peterson, "Lumbering on the Chippewa," 298, 350, 536-37, 541-54; Reynolds, *Daniel Shaw*, 12-13, 75-76, 93-100, 105-111; Kleven, "Mississippi River Logging Company," 196-97. For extended discussions, the first by an insider, the other an historian, see: Norton, *Mississippi River Logging Company*, and Robert F. Fries, "The Mississippi River Logging Company and the Struggle for the Free Navigation of Logs," *MVHR*, 35 (1948): 429-48.

73. Twining, *Downriver*, 182-83, 185-93, 204-205; Peterson, "Lumbering on the Chippewa," 557-68; Reynolds, *Daniel Shaw*, 77-78 (quote), 122; Hidy, Hill, and Nevins, *Timber and Men*, 72-74; Kohlmeyer, *Timber Roots*, 99-100; Ingram, *Autobiography*, 67-68; Kleven, "Mississippi River Logging Company," 198-200; Sieber, "Sawmilling on the Mississippi," 181-83.

74. Hurst, *Law and Economic Growth*, 196-97, 268-69 (1st quote, p. 269); Peterson, "Lumbering on the Chippewa," 561-65; Twining, *Downriver*, 170-71, 203, 206-207 (2nd quote); Kohlmeyer, *Timber Roots*, 171-74; Hidy, Hill, and Nevins, *Timber and Men*, 73-74, 77, 79-80; Fries, *Empire in Pine*, 154-55; Ingram, *Autobiography*, 53-55; Sieber, "Sawmilling on the Mississippi," 278-79, 183-84. Chippewa Lumber & Boom Co. was the only producer on the river that refused to be party to the exchange and salvage agreements, choosing "for purposes of its own . . . to use its strategic site to make things difficult for all below." Twining, *Downriver*, 190-91 (quote, p. 190); Kleven, "Mississippi River Logging Company," 197, 199.

75. For details on the pool, see: Peterson, "Lumbering on the Chippewa," 561-643.

76. Peterson, "Lumbering on the Chippewa," 566-631, 649-51, 661; Twining, *Downriver*, 205-209, 213-18; Kohlmeyer, *Timber Roots*, 100, 125, 158-66, 171; Hidy, Hill, and Nevins, *Timber and Men*, 74, 77-78, 80-82, 84; Sieber, "Sawmilling on the Mississippi," 186-200 (1st quote, p. 200); Kleven, "Mississippi River Logging Company," 196 (2nd quote), 198-200; Lillard, "Timber King," 19-21; Rector, *Log Transportation in the Lake States*, 266-70,

279; [Joseph Shafer], "The Knapp-Stout & Co. Lumber Company," *Wis. Mag. Hist.*, 3 (1920): 470; Fries, *Empire in Pine*, 89, 126-27, 155-56; Hotchkiss, *Lumber and Forest Industry*, 416, 489-90. William Rector errs when he states that in 1888 most of Knapp-Stout's output was rafted to Dubuque, Fort Madison, and St. Louis. Rector, *Log Transportation in the Lake States*, 33.

77. Hidy, Hill, and Nevins, *Timber and Men*, 78-79; Peterson, "Lumbering on the Chippewa," 589, 632, 641-43; Kohlmeyer, *Timber Roots*, 158, 164-65. In time Beef Slough silted up and, after a new round of controversy, facilities moved across the Mississippi to West Newton Slough; from there, the pool continued operating essentially as before. Blair, *A Raft Pilot's Log*, 53-54.

78. William G. Rector, "Rise of the St. Croix Octopus," *Wis. Mag. Hist.*, 40 (1957): 171 (quote); Blair, *A Raft Pilot's Log*, 289-90; Larson, *Empire in Pine*, 18-24, 52, 107-108, 132, 222-24, 238.

79. William G. Rector, "From Woods to Sawmill: Transportation Problems in Logging," *Ag. Hist.*, 23 (1949): 239-42; Rector, "St. Croix Octopus," 173; Rector, *Log Transportation in the Lake States*, 119-25; Fries, *Empire in Pine*, 48-49, 51; Larson, *White Pine Industry*, 19-22, 24, 60, 151; Hotchkiss, *Lumber and Forest Industry*, 525. Michael Williams errs when he makes the boom nearer Stillwater the first on the river and that built on the Black in 1854 the first in Wisconsin. See: Williams, *Americans and their Forests*, 204.

80. Rector, "St. Croix Octopus," 171, 175-76; Rector, "From Woods to Sawmill," 242; Larson, *White Pine Industry*, 24-25, 130-33. See also: Rector, *Log Transportation in the Lake States*, 112-25, 134-35, 142-44.

81. Rector, "St. Croix Octopus," 174, 176-77 (quote, p. 177); Rector, *Log Transportation in the Lake States*, 119-20; Hidy, Hill, and Nevins, *Timber and Men*, 97. The last-named source erroneously renders the name "Mowrer."

82. Hidy, Hill, and Nevins, *Timber and Men*, 95-97; Kohlmeyer, *Timber Roots*, 129-31; Rector, "St. Croix Octopus," 177; Larson, *White Pine Industry*, 24-26, 132-33. See also: Twining, *Downriver*, 163-64, 262.

83. Rector, "St. Croix Octopus," 177 (quotes); Rector, "From Woods to Sawmill," 242; Hidy, Hill, and Nevins, *Timber and Men*, 97-98; Lillard, "Timber King," 14, 21.

84. Russell, *A-Rafting on the Mississip'*, 181-82.

85. *Chitek* (Wis.) *Alert*, 8 and 15 Sept. 1916; *Rice Lake* (Wis.) *Chronotype*, 21 Sept. 1927; *Eau Claire Leader-Telegram*, 4 July 1976; Hotchkiss, *Lumber and Forest Industry*, 123-26, 476; Hurst, *Law and Economic Growth*, 473; Kohlmeyer, *Timber Roots*, 162-63; Fries, *Empire in Pine*, 21, 89, 101, 124-27, 172, 223; Peterson, "Lumbering on the Chippewa," 549-52 and passim; Nesbit, *Urbanization and Industrialization*, 51, 53-54, 71-73, 80, 83; Current, *Pine Trees and Politics*, 105, 123, 132-34; Larson, *White Pine Industry*, 26-27, 100-101, 134-35; Reynolds, *Daniel Shaw*, 154, 162-63; Gates, *Wisconsin Pine Lands of Cornell University*, 71, 111-12, 125-26, 133-34, 136, 231-33; Merk, *Economic History of Wisconsin*, 74-75; Blair, *A Raft Pilot's Log*, 34; Rector, *Log Transportation in the Lake States*, 97; [Shafer], "Knapp-Stout & Co.," 469-71 (quote pp. 470-71). Unfortunately, there is no full study of Knapp-Stout.

86. Not to be confused with Menominee, Michigan.

87. Nesbit, *Urbanization and Industrialization*, 51, 53-54; Fries, *Empire in Pine*, 89, 101, 124-28 (quote, pp. 127-28), 172, 209; Williams, *Americans and their Forests*, 218-20; Current, *Wisconsin*, 115; Hidy, Hill, and Nevins, *Timber and Men*, 55.

88. Early lumbermen in Eau Claire seem to have been similar. Echoing Earl Pomeroy's pivotal argument of several years ago, Dale Peterson observed they "came from well-established communities in the East and had no desire to endure, at least for long, the absence of schools, churches, and other aspects of culture." Peterson, "Lumbering on the Chippewa," 89-91 (quote, p. 89); Pomeroy, "Toward a Reorientation of Western History," 579-600.

89. Krog, "Marinette: Origin and Growth," 400, 403; Krog, "Marinette becomes a City," 25, 30-31, 32; Carl E. Krog, "Rails across the Water," *Inland Seas*, 29 (1973): 170-76; Stephenson, *Recollections of a Long Life*, 77-78, 82-85, 88-89, 105-106, 134-36, 137-39, 161-62, 168-69; Fries, *Empire in Pine*, 222-23, 225, 228; Gates, *Wisconsin Pine Lands of Cornell University*, 71, 107-20; Merk, *Economic History of Wisconsin*, 75; Nelligan, "Life of a Lumberman," 297-98; Current, *Wisconsin*, 190.

90. Ingram & Kennedy was the only major Eau Claire firm not to incorporate in the 1870s. See: Peterson, "Lumbering on the Chippewa," 439-40.

91. Hauberg, *Weyerhaeuser & Denkmann*, 52-53 (1st quote, p. 53), 57-58 (2nd quote); John Henry Hauberg, Jr., *Recollections of a Civic Errand Boy . . .* (Seattle: Denkmann Pacific, 2003), 187.

92. Hauberg, *Weyerhaeuser & Denkmann*, 51-52, 57, 61-63, 65-66, 120-22, 128; Hidy, Hill, and Nevins, *Timber and Men*, 53, 60-61 (1st quote); Sieber, "Sawmilling on the Mississippi," 189 (2nd quote); Sieber, "Lumbermen at Clinton," 783-84; Lillard, "Timber King," 24-26.

93. Twining, *Downriver*, 37-41, 78-80, 91; Reynolds, *Daniel Shaw*, 133-35.

94. Kohlmeyer, *Timber Roots*, 182-91 and passim; Hidy, Hill, and Nevins, *Timber and Men*, 34-37; George W. Sieber, "Sawlogs for a Clinton Sawmill," *Annals of Iowa*, 37 (1964): 348-59; Sieber, "Wisconsin Pineland and Logging Management," *Transactions of the Wisconsin Academy of Arts, Sciences, and Letters*, 56 (1968): 65-72; Hurst, *Law and Economic Growth*, 473. See also: Hartman, "Iowa Sawmill Industry," 71-72, 75-78, 80-82.

95. Twining, *Downriver*, 91 (quote), 93; Reynolds, *Daniel Shaw*, 146-51; Kohlmeyer, "Northern Pine Lumbermen," 531, 533-34.

96. Hidy, Hill, and Nevins, *Timber and Men*, 53-54, 59-61; Lillard, "Timber King," 21; Charles E. Twining, *Phil Weyerhaeuser, Lumberman* (Seattle: University of Washington Press, 1985), 5.

97. Hidy, Hill, and Nevins, *Timber and Men*, 62, 84, 96-97, 208, 212; Lillard, "Timber King," 14-15. See also: Peterson, "Lumbering on the Chippewa," 375-76; Orfield, *Federal Land Grants*, 92-93.

98. Twining, *Downriver*, 213-218 (1st quotes, p. 215; last two quotes, p. 217), 253; Ingram, *Autobiography*, 51-55, 72; Lillard, "Timber King," 20, 26.

99. *AL*, n.v. (9 Dec. 1899): 1.

100. Gates, "Weyerhaeuser and Chippewa Logging," 64. For examples of Shevlin's approach, see: Orfield, *Federal Land Grants*, 172, 174, 211.

Chapter Eight

1. Hidy, Hill, and Nevins, *Timber and Men*, 207; Twining, *Phil Weyerhaeuser*, 5-7; Lillard, "Timber King," 21.

2. Blair, *Raft Pilot's Log*, 265, 291; Reynolds, *Daniel Shaw*, 154; Nesbit, *Wisconsin*, 47; Larson, *White Pine Industry*, 220-28. In Davenport, Iowa, in 1890 the lumber industry still represented 21.9 percent of investment and 10.5 percent of wages, but by 1900 the percentages had fallen to 0.8 percent and 2 percent respectively. *Eleventh Census of the United States: 1890*, Vol. 12: *Census of Manufactures*, pt. 2: 180-81; ibid.: *1900*, Vol. 8: pt. 2: 248-49.

3. Blegen, *Minnesota*, 319 (3rd quote), 324-29; Atwater, *Minneapolis*, 1: 542-44; J.C. Ryan, "Minnesota Logging Railroads," *Minn. Hist.*, 27 (1946): 300-308; Baker, *Lives of the Governors*, 359-63 (1st quote, p. 360); Larson, *White Pine Industry*, 105-124 (2nd quote, p. 124), 162-63, 242-45, 361-63; Hidy, Hill, and Nevins, *Timber and Men*, 104-105; Hough, *Report upon Forestry*, 541-51. Hough's report was published in 1878 before lumbering was in full swing in Minnesota; he gives only general information on the state. See: ibid., 531-40.

4. Hidy, Hill, and Nevins, *Timber and Men*, 103-105 (1st quote, p. 103); Sieber, "Sawmilling on the Mississippi," 561 (2nd quote), 567-73 (3rd quote, p. 569).

5. Hidy, Hill, and Nevins, *Timber and Men*, 104, 105; Larson, *White Pine Industry*, 8; Twining, "The Lumbering Frontier," 124-25; Williams, *Americans and their Forests*, 198-200.

6. *Mississippi Valley Lumberman*, 22 (July 22, 1892): 7 (3rd quote); 23 (July 21, 1893): 6 (1st quote); Hidy, Hill, and Nevins, *Timber and Men*, 104-108, 111-13 (2nd quote, p. 113), 165-68; Weyerhaeuser, *Trees and Men*, 12-13; Larson, *White Pine Industry*, 230-31, 233-34, 238, 245-46, 253; Kohlmeyer, *Timber Roots*, 273-76.

7. Larson, *White Pine Industry*, 37-38, 156-57, 229-31, 251-52, 274-82, 389; Baker, *Lives of the Governors*, 359-63; Blegen, *Minnesota*, 326-27; Kohlmeyer, "Northern Pine Lumbermen," 535-36; *AL*, 56 (Dec. 9, 1899): 1, 20; n.v. (Oct. 16, 1909): 1, 33. See also: Williams, *Americans and their Forests*, 227-30; Kilar, *Michigan's Lumbertowns*, 262-65. C. A. Smith and Company was the most notable exception. Pillsbury had been active in lumbering since 1857— it provided much of the capital that made possible his early activity in flour milling, for which he is primarily remembered. In 1878, he was a founder of the Smith firm, destined to be a prominent player not only in Minnesota, but also on the West Coast.

8. Larson, *White Pine Industry*, 105-107, 110-14, 120; Fries, *Empire in Pine*, 86-87; Reynolds, *Daniel Shaw*, 100-104, 127; Blegen, *Minnesota*, 340-47.

9. Lass, *Minnesota*, 147-48. Cooke's ambitions were greater than his financial capacity. His line had only reached Bismarck, Dakota Territory, before his investment bank was forced to close in 1873; the Northern Pacific struggled on until failing in 1875. Henry Villard rescued the NP with fresh capital, but it was another decade before it reached the Pacific Northwest. On Cooke, see: Henrietta Larson, *Jay Cooke, Private Banker* (Cambridge, Mass.: Harvard University Press, 1936).

10. Hidy, Hill, and Nevins, *Timber and Men*, 116-20; Lillard, "Timber King," 21; Bell, "Alger," 407. In time Cloquet would pass Minneapolis to become the world's largest lumber-manufacturing center.

11. Larson, *White Pine Industry*, 105-107, 112-24, 247-52, 267-82; Blegen, *Minnesota*, 326-27; Hidy, Hill, and Nevins, *Timber and Men*, 116-18, 171; Ise, *Forest Policy*, 80; Anonymous, "Cloquet, Home of White Pine," *AL*, 75 (9 July 1904): 35-46.

12. Blegen, *Minnesota*, 324-29 (quote, p. 327); Hidy, Hill, and Nevins, *Timber and Men*, 106.

13. Orfield, *Federal Land Grants*, 138,145-52 (quote, p. 147), 168-75, 207-218.

14. Loehr, "Caleb Dorr," 129; Stanchfield, "History of Pioneer Lumbering," 328-29, 231-32 (quote, p. 331), 335-38, 344-45. Stanchfield's narrative gives no reason to doubt the genuineness of his solicitude for Native Americans—as he put it at one point, "Fifty four years have passed since I first dealt with the Indians. In all my experience, they have been found more true and honorable than most of the white men with whom they have come in contact on the frontier" (ibid., p. 332). However, paying Chief Hole-in-the-Day for trees taken also guaranteed freedom from harassment and panhandling by the chief's people.

15. Folwell, *Minnesota*, 1: 159-60, 217-23, 351, 356-58 (1st and 2nd quotes and Sargent quote, p. 357); Hurst, *Law and Economic Growth*, 126 (3rd quote); Blegen, *Minnesota*, 316-18 (4th quote, p. 317); Peterson, "Lumbering on the Chippewa," 40-48, 65-66 (5th quote, p. 66); Raney, *Wisconsin*, 199-206; Wyman, *Wisconsin Frontier*, 161-63, 250; Fries, *Empire in Pine*, 9-10; Smith, *History of Wisconsin*, 1: 510-11; Reynolds, *Daniel Shaw*, 6; Cameron, *Development of Forest Control*, 135-36, 224-31; Lass, *Minnesota*, 76, 90, 92-93; Larson, *White Pine Industry*, 13-14. Robert Nesbit observed: "Natural hazards and socially acceptable timber theft certainly discouraged early speculation in remote timber." Nesbit, *History of Wisconsin*, 3: 51.

16. Kohlmeyer, "Northern Pine Lumbermen," 531-32, 537-38; Engberg, "Who Were the Lumberjacks?" 244-45; Stephenson, *Recollections of a Long Life*, 63-65 (quote, p. 65), 90-91; Hurst, *Law and Economic Growth*, 20-47, 93-117. Timber fraud may thus be similar to the actions of squatters, but most historians have treated them quite differently, decrying the former and accepting, if not applauding, the latter—a difference in which the strength of the Jeffersonian and Turnerian influences seems evident.

17. R. Newell Searle, "Minnesota Forestry Comes of Age: Christopher C. Andrews, 1895-1911," *FH*, 17 (July 1973): 17-18 (Wilson quote, p. 18); Lass, *Minnesota*, 203-205; Larson, *White Pine Industry*, 330-31.

18. Orfield, *Federal Land Grants*, 172, 174, 176-79, 207-218; William G. Rector, "Lumber Barons in Revolt," *Minn. Hist.*, 31 (1950): 33-39; Blegen, *Minnesota*, 324-29.

19. Orfield, *Federal Land Grants*, 139-40, 168-79 (1st quote, pp. 177-78), 209-211; Nelligan, "Life of a Lumberman," 280-84 (2nd quote, p. 283); Russell, *A-Rafting on the Mississip'*, 45-50. See also: Hough, *Report upon Forestry*, 12-17; Lucile Kane, "Federal Protection of Public Timber in the Upper Great Lake States," *Ag. Hist.*, 23 (1949): 135-39; Peterson, "Lumbering on the Chippewa," 259-69, 590-97. For the Supreme Court case, see: *U.S. v. Mock*, 149 U.S., 273. The claims of Frederick Kohlmeyer, Fred Burke, and D. C. Everest that timber thievery was uncommon are belied by too much evidence to be taken seriously. See: Kohlmeyer, *Timber Roots*, 140-42; Burke, *Logs on*

the *Menominee*, 13-14, 73-74; D. C. Everest, "A Reappraisal of the Lumber Barons," *Wis. Mag. Hist.*, 36 (Autumn 1952): 21.

20. Orfield, *Federal Land Grants*, 189-206 (quote, p. 206); Grace Lee Nute, *Rainy River Country: A Brief History of the Region Bordering Minnesota and Ontario* (St. Paul: Minnesota Historical Society, 1950), 52-56, 58; Cameron, *Development of Forest Control*, 227-29.

21. Nute, *Rainy River Country*, 56-58; Peterson, "Lumbering on the Chippewa," 377-82; J. P Kinney, *Indian Forest and Range: A History of the Administration and Conservation of the Redman's Heritage* (Washington, D.C.: Forestry Enterprises, 1950), 6-8; Kinney, *A Continent Lost—A Civilization Won: The Indian Land Tenure in America* (Baltimore: Johns Hopkins University Press, 1937), 255-62, 337; Cameron, *Development of Forest Control*, 224-31.

22. Current, *Pine Logs and Politics*, 211-12 (1885), 217-18 (1890); Peterson, "Lumbering on the Chippewa," 377-82, 590-97 (quote, pp. 590-91); Godfrey, *Forestry History of Ten Wisconsin Indian Reservations*, 23-26, 44, 57, 85. Some were eyeing Indian reservations even earlier. In 1869-1870, Philetus Sawyer introduced a bill in Congress to open the Menominee Reservation; it did not pass, but efforts continued. In 1870 the Acting Commissioner of Indian Affairs announced he would receive bids for Menominee timber in township lots via sealed bids in Washington, D.C. Objections that this would shut out all but the largest buyers and insiders caused the plan to be revoked, as was a separate ploy a year later. Current, *Pine Logs and Politics*, 72-74, 115; Duncan A. Harkin, "The Significance of the Menominee Experience in the Forest History of the Great Lakes Region," in Flader, *Great Lakes Forest*, 98.

23. Orfield, *Federal Land Grants*, 168, 178-79 and passim.

24. For a description of some of the practices used to get timber in the Duluth area, see: Ise, *Forest Policy*, 80.

25. Robert H. Wiebe, *Businessmen and Reform: A Study of the Progressive Movement* (Chicago: Quadrangle, 1968), 12-13; Hidy, Hill, and Nevins, *Timber and Men*, 115-18, 183, 186; Nute, *Rainy River Country*, 91-94, 96-99; Larson, *White Pine Industry*, 235, 284-85; James G. Lewis, "Edward Hines (1863-1931)," *Forest History Today*, n.v. (spring/fall 2004): 64-65; C. M. Oehler, *Time in the Timber* (St. Paul, Minn.: Forest Products History Foundation, 1948), 3.

26. Baker, *Lives of the Governors*, 16, 42 (for Ramsey's career, see ibid., 3-46); Orfield, *Federal Land Grants*, 153; Increase A. Lapham, J. G. Knapp, and H. Crocker, *Report on the Disastrous Effect of the Destruction of Forest Trees, Now Going on so Rapidly in the State of Wisconsin.* (1867; reprint, Madison: State Historical Society of Wisconsin, 1967); Milo M. Quaife, "Increase Allen Lapham: Father of Forest Conservation," *Wis. Mag. Hist.*, 5 (1921): 104-108; Current, *History of Wisconsin*, 116, 472-73. See also: Graham P. Hawks, "Increase A. Lapham, Wisconsin's First Scientist" (unpub. Ph.D. diss., University of Wisconsin, 1960); Quaife, "Increase A. Lapham: First Scholar of Wisconsin," *Wis. Mag. Hist.*, 1 (1916): 3-15.

27. Cameron, *Development of Forest Control*, 120 and passim. John Ise anticipated Cameron. "The western people, like frontiersmen everywhere" he wrote, "were impatient of delay, and always wanted *rapid development*." He

added, "Speculation and frauds have always characterized the frontier. . . . The West has always been too much saturated with the idea of rapid exploitation. . . . [Westerners] were, as indeed they still are, 'boosters' of the most enthusiastic brand." If regulation—Cameron's Order—were to come, it would have to originate elsewhere. Ise, *Forest Policy*, 166, 371-72 [italics in original]. For antidotes to such ideas, which reflect the influence of Frederick Jackson Turner and emphasize the differences between East and West, see: Pomeroy, "Toward a Reorientation of Western History," and Wallace D. Farnham, "'The Weakened Spring of Government': A Study in Nineteenth-Century History," *American Historical Review*, 68 (1963): 662-80.

28. Current, *Pine Logs and Politics*, 146-53, 195-200; Baker, *Lives of the Governors*, 359-63; Anonymous, "Russell Alexander Alger," *AL*, n.v. (3 Mar. 1906): 1, 53; Hurst, *Law and Economic Growth*, 476-77; Larson, *White Pine Industry*, 261-63, 392-93; Fries, *Empire in Pine*, 113-121; Cox et al., *This Well-Wooded Land*, 161-63 (Denkmann quote, p. 162).

29. Peterson, "Lumbering on the Chippewa," 58-59; Blegen, *Minnesota*, 324; Hurst, *Law and Economic Growth*, passim; Williams, *Americans and their Forests*, 216-17.

30. Current, *Pine Logs and Politics*, 28-29; Merk, *Economic History of Wisconsin*, 109-110; Peterson, "Lumbering on the Chippewa,"458-60; Sieber, "Sawmilling on the Mississippi," 95-98; and above, Chapter 6.

31. Current, *Pine Logs and Politics*, 243-44; George B. Engberg, "The Knights of Labor in Minnesota," *Minn. Hist.*, 22 (1941): 367-90; Engberg, "Lumber and Labor in the Lake States," ibid., 36 (1959): 153-66; Engberg, "Collective Bargaining in the Lumber Industry of the Upper Great Lakes States," *Ag. Hist.*, 24 (1950): 205-211; Fries, *Empire in Pine*, 212-18; Jensen, *Lumber and Labor*, 58-63; Ise, *Forest Policy*, 144-45; Charles R. Lamb, "Sawdust Campaign," *Wis. Mag. Hist.*, 22 (1938): 6-14; Reynolds, *Daniel Shaw*, 88-92; Krog, "Marinette," 222-26; Ware, *Labor Movement in the United States*, 123-25, 139-45; Peterson, "Lumbering on the Chippewa," 670-82; Hauberg, *Weyerhaeuser & Denkmann*, 109-111; Kilar, *Michigan's Lumbertowns*, 229-36; Bell, "Alger," 181-82, 184, 187, 190, 192.

32. Nesbit, *Wisconsin*, 73-76, 384-417 (quote, p. 417); Milton M. Small, "The Biography of Robert Schilling" (unpub. M.A. thesis, Univ. of Wisconsin, 1953), esp. 64-65, 191-205, 273, 337.

33. At Knapp, Stout & Co. wages declined from $1.31.5 per day in 1868 to $1.15^{1}/$_{2}$ in 1874-1876 and $1.00 in 1878-1879, these for an eleven-hour day in winter and eleven and a half hours in summer. *Tenth Census of the United States: 1880*, Vol. 20: 485.

34. Nesbit, *Wisconsin*, 77, 380-83 (quote, p. 382); Peterson, "Lumbering on the Chippewa," 461-63, 607-612, 669-70; Reynolds, *Daniel Shaw*, 89-92; George B. Engberg, "The Knights of Labor in Minnesota," *Minn. Hist.*, 22 (1941): 388-90; Jensen, *Lumber and Labor*, 58-63; Hurst, *Law and Economic Growth*, 487-90. George Engberg argues there was a labor shortage, but low wages and other evidence suggest otherwise. See: Engberg, "Lumber and Labor in the Lake States," *Minn. Hist.*, 36 (1959): 153-66.

35. Wisconsin, Bureau of Labor and Industrial Statistics, *Biennial Report, 1887-1888*, 113; Peterson, "Lumbering on the Chippewa," 36-37, 392 (Putnam quote); Nesbit, *Wisconsin*, 75.

36. Peterson, "Lumbering on the Chippewa," 131-34; Jensen, *Lumber and Labor*, 57-58, 62-65; Larson, *White Pine Industry*, 356-59; Hurst, *Law and Economic Growth*, 391-409, 479-80.

37. Hauberg, *Weyerhaeuser & Denkmann*, 107; Hidy, Hill, and Nevins, *Timber and Men*, 39 (quote; italics added).

38. Wisconsin lagged. In 1864 the state's land commission called upon the citizenry to condemn the stealing of timber from Wisconsin's lands and Increase A. Lapham actively championed new policies, but the legislature did not establish a forestry commission until 1897. Fries, *Empire in Pine*, 199-201, 246-47; Van Brocklin, "Movement for the Conservation of Natural Resources," 23-24, 36, 61-62.

39. Martin Ridge, *Ignatius Donnelly: The Portrait of a Politician* (Chicago: University of Chicago Press, 1962), 156; Blegen, *Minnesota*, 323-24; Folwell, *Minnesota*, 3: 207, 506-507.

40. Anonymous, "Highlights in the History of Forest Conservation," FS 12 (mimeographed; Washington, D.C.: Forest Service, 1948; copy in American Forestry Association Papers, Forest History Society, Durham, N.C., box 7, file 1), 2. Cf. Searle, "Minnesota Forestry Comes of Age," 14-25; Searle, "Minnesota State Forestry Association, Seedbed of Conservation," *Minn. Hist.*, 44 (spring 1974): 16-29; Blegen, *Minnesota*, 404-407; Lass, *Minnesota*, 202-205; Larson, *White Pine Industry*, 263-64, 317-18, 343.

41. Larson, *White Pine Industry*, 336; Folwell, *Minnesota*, 3: 206-207; Ridge, *Donnelly*, 316.

42. Orfield, "Federal Land Grants," 211-28 (commission quote, p. 212); Folwell, *Minnesota*, 3: 507-512 (1st quote, p. 507); Ridge, *Donnelly*, 315-19. See also: Pine Land Investigating Committee, *Report . . . to the Governor of Minnesota . . .* (St. Paul: Pioneer Press Printing, 1895), esp. 4-8, 20-24, 57, 79.

43. Ridge, *Donnelly*, 317-19 (quotations, p. 318); Orfield, *Federal Land Grants*, 207-208; Larson, *White Pine Industry*, 336-38; Folwell, *Minnesota*, 3: 512-14. On Pillsbury, see: Baker, *Lives of the Governors*, 227-50 (esp. 232), 359; on Clough, 359-72.

44. Nancy C. Unger, *Fighting Bob La Follette: The Righteous Reformer* (Chapel Hill: University of North Carolina Press, 2000), 97; Robert S. Maxwell, *La Follette and the Rise of Progressivism in Wisconsin* (Madison: State Historical Society of Wisconsin, 1956), 62-63, 165.

45. Michael Kazin, *A Godly Hero: The Life of William Jennings Bryan* (New York: Knopf, 2006), 32-35.

46. Nesbit, *Wisconsin*, 112 (quote); Sieber, "Sawmilling on the Mississippi," 373-77.

47. Paolo E. Coletta, *William Jennings Bryan* (3 vols.; Lincoln: University of Nebraska Press, 1964-1969), 1: 60; Kazin, *A Godly Hero*, 65-69, 76-79. Literature on the tariff is voluminous, but most says little about lumber. However, see: Thomas R. Tull, "The Shift to Republicanism: William L. Wilson and the Election of 1894," *West Virginia History*, 37 (1975): 17-33; Defebaugh, *History of the Lumber Industry*, 1: 445-63; Johnson, "Logs for

Saginaw: Tariff Relations," 213-23; *CL*, July 1892-Apr. 1896. The last-named source reports views from both sides of the international border. See esp.: ibid., 15 (Sept. 1894): 4-5; (Oct. 1894): 4-5.

48. Fries, *Empire in Pine*, 93-99; Larson, *White Pine Industry*, 393-97; Peterson, "Lumbering on the Chippewa," 702-705.

49. Fries, *Empire in Pine*, 113, 129-38 (quote, pp. 132-33; italics in original); Larson, *White Pine Industry*, 240-41, 254, 390-91; Hidy, Hill, and Nevins, *Timber and Men*, 174-76; Kohlmeyer, *Timber Roots*, 164, 215.

50. Defebaugh, *History of the Lumber Industry*, 1: 453-61; *CL*, 18 (Jan. 1897): 4; ibid., (Feb. 1897): 1-2, 5; Fries, *Empire in Pine*, 113-21; Larson, *White Pine Industry*, 261-63, 392-93. Not all lumbermen favored protection from Canadian logs and lumber. Russell Alger thought the former essential for Michigan's declining industry. Bell, "Alger," 406.

51. For example, see: Gustavus Myers, *History of the Great American Fortunes* (1907-1910; reprint, New York: Modern Library, 1937), 689-91.

52. Kohlmeyer, "Northern Pine Lumbermen," 537-38 (quote p. 538).

53. Orfield, *Federal Land Grants*, 174 (1st quote); Fries, *Empire in Pine*, 227 (Thorp quote); Current, *Wisconsin*, 114; Peterson, "Lumbering on the Chippewa," 359-61, 589; Reynolds, *Daniel Shaw*, 64-65; Nesbit, *Wisconsin*, 86.

54. Nesbit, *Wisconsin*, 86; Reynolds, *Daniel Shaw*, 28-29, 61-62, 114-16; Nelligan, "Life of a Lumberman," 249; Williams, *Americans and their Forests*, 193-94; Wyman, *Lumberjack Frontier*, 79-80. See also: Norman J. Schmaltz, "The Land Nobody Wanted: The Dilemma of Michigan's Cutover Lands," *Mich. Hist.*, 67 (1983): 32-40; Vernon R. Carstenson, *Farms or Forests: Evolution of a State Land Policy for Northern Wisconsin, 1850-1932* (Madison: University of Wisconsin, College of Agriculture, 1958); Ahlgren and Ahlgren, "Human Impact on Northern Forest Ecosystems," 38-44; Lynn Sandberg, "The Response of Forest Industries to a Changing Environment," in Flader, *Great Lakes Forest*, 197-201; Hazel H. Reinhardt, "Social Adjustments to a Changing Environment," ibid., 206-214.

55. White's views then and later can be traced in the *Autobiography of William Allen White* (New York: Macmillan, 1946), 280-85, 292, 509-510. See also: Gene Clanton, *Populism: The Humane Preference in America, 1890-1900* (Boston: Twayne Publishers, 1991), 156-59.

56. Fries, *Empire in Pine*, 105, 245-46; Current, *Wisconsin*, 22; Nelligan, "Life of a Lumberman," 38-42; Stephenson, *Recollections*, 175-85; Merk, *Economic History of Wisconsin*, 101-104; Orfield, *Federal Land Grants*, 138-40; Williams, *Americans and their Forests*, 232; Pyne, *Fire in America*, 200-211; Joseph Shafer, "Great Fires of Seventy-One," *Wis. Mag. Hist.*, 11 (1927): 96-106; Josephine Sawyer, "Personal Reminiscences of the Big Fire of 1871," *Mich. Hist.*, 16 (1932): 422-30; Stewart H. Holbrook, *Burning an Empire: The Story of American Forest Fires* (New York: Macmillan, 1943), 61-76, 94-102. For more extended treatment, see: Robert W. Wells, *Fire at Peshtigo* (Englewood Cliffs, N.J.: Prentice-Hall, 1967).

57. Pyne, *Fire in America*, 19-29, 204, 211-13; Williams, *Americans and their Forests*, 447-48; Searle, "Minnesota Forestry Comes of Age," 17-18.

58. Quoted in Orfield, *Federal Land Grants*, 180.

59. Ibid., 138-40 (1st quote, p. 138); Wyman, *Lumberjack Frontier*, 46-47 (Blanchard quote); Holbrook, *Burning an Empire*, 102-107.

60. C. M. Gray, "The Appalling Hinckley (Minn.) Fire of 1894—A True Incident Relative to One of America's Major Catastrophes," (typescript, 1941; Special Collections, San Diego State University library, San Diego, Calif.), Hinckley fire folder, pp. 1-8 (quotes pp. 1 and 5); Holbrook, *Burning an Empire*, 77-86.
61. C. M. Gray, "Note on the Hinckley Fire," Los Angeles, Calif., 20 Sept. 1941 (Special Collections, San Diego State University library, San Diego, Calif.). Gray's accounts were prepared for Holbrook as part of the latter's research for *Burning an Empire*, but Holbrook neither cites nor acknowledges them.
62. Orfield, *Federal Land Grants*, 138, 179-80, 184-88; Larson, *White Pine Industry*, 340-42; Pyne, *Fire in America*, 213; Holbrook, *Burning an Empire*, 87-93; Searle, "Minnesota Forestry Comes of Age," 15-20.
63. Defebaugh, *History of the Lumber Industry*, 1: 402-403; Pyne, *Fire in America*, 213-16; Fries, *Empire in Pine*, 249-50; J. Alfred Mitchell, "Accomplishments in Fire Protection in the Lake States," *JF*, 37 (1939): 748-50; J. P Kinney, *The Development of Forest Law in America* . . . (New York: Wiley, 1917), 28-46; Williams, *Americans and their Forests*, 232-33, 449-50; Van Brocklin, "Movement for the Conservation of Natural Resources," 54-55, 61-62; Francis M. Carroll and Frank B. Raiter, "The People versus the Government: The 1918 Cloquet Fire and the Struggle for Compensation," *JFH*, 29 (1985): 4-21.

Chapter Nine

1. John Smith, "A True Relation . . ." in *The Complete Works of Captain John Smith (1580-1631)*, ed. by Philip L. Barbour (3 vols.; Chapel Hill: University of North Carolina Press, 1986), 1: 97; John Anthony Eisterhold, "Lumber and Trade in the Seaboard Cities of the Old South, 1607-1860" (unpub. Ph.D. diss., University of Mississippi, 1970), 1-2.
2. As quoted in Cox et al., *This Well-Wooded Land*, 29.
3. Often thought of as simply a pine belt, these forests were in fact remarkably diversified. See: Sargent, *Report on the Forests of North America*, 3-6, 494-512; Defebaugh, *History of the Lumber Industry*, 1: 324-31; Silver, *A New Face on the Countryside*, 16-25; Richard W. Massey, Jr., "A History of the Lumber Industry in Alabama and West Florida, 1880-1914" (unpub. Ph.D. diss., Vanderbilt University, 1960), 9-23.
4. Bassett, *Writings of Colonel William Byrd*, 74; C. F. Volney, *View of the Climate and Soil of the United States* . . . (Philadelphia: Conrad, 1804), 7. The British edition (London, 1804) offers a more awkward translation of Volney's French. On the Gulf South, see also: Flint, *History and Geography of the Mississippi Valley*, 1: 218-24, 228-35, 239-48, 250-63; Laurence C. Walker, *The Southern Forest: A Chronicle* (Austin: University of Texas Press, 1991), 1-32, 37, 42-45.
5. Mart A. Stewart, *"What Nature Suffers to Groe": Life, Labor, and Landscape on the Georgia Coast, 1680-1920* (Athens: University of Georgia Press, 1996), 71-72; Eisterhold, "Lumber and Trade in the Old South," 1-23.
6. Bassett, *Writings of Colonel William Byrd*, 28; Eisterhold, "Lumber and Trade in the Old South," 97-100; William S. Powell and Hugh T. Lefler, *Colonial North Carolina: A History* (New York: Kraus, 1973), 151-74; Lawrence Lee, *The Lower Cape Fear in Colonial Days* (Chapel Hill: University of North Carolina Press, 1965), 145-81; H. Roy Merrens, *Colonial North Carolina in the Eighteenth Century* (Chapel Hill: University of North Carolina Press, 1964),

149-55; de Boer, *Nature, Business, and Community*, 52-54, 60-61. In time sawmills emerged near Beaufort and elsewhere in the Atlantic South that were quite separate from plantations and farms; they provided broadened economic opportunities, but did little to draw people to the area and thus hardly represented a lumberman's frontier.

7. Malone, *Pine Trees and Politics*, 28-56, 124-43; Cox et al., *This Well-Wooded Land*, 16-19, 25-29; Justin Williams, "English Mercantilism and Carolina Naval Stores, 1705-1776," *JSH*, 1 (1935): 169-85; Lewis C. Gray, *History of Agriculture in the Southern United States to 1860* (2 vols.; Washington, D.C.: Carnegie Institution, 1933), 1: 151-60; G. Melvin Herndon, "Naval Stores in Colonial Georgia," *Georgia Historical Quarterly*, 52 (1968): 426-33. See also: Walker, *Southern Forest*, 39-40, 75; G. Melvin Herndon, "Forest Products of Colonial Georgia," *JFH*, 23 (1979): 131-35; de Boer, *Nature, Business, and Community*, 50-53.

8. Avery O. Craven, *Soil Exhaustion as a Factor in the History of Virginia and Maryland, 1606-1860* (Urbana: University of Illinois Press, 1926); Aubrey C. Land, "The Tobacco Staple and the Planter's Problems: Technology, Labor, and Crops," *Ag. Hist.*, 43 (1969): 69-82; Harold B. Gill, Jr., "Wheat Culture in Colonial Virginia," ibid., 52 (1978): 380-93; G. Melvin Herndon, "The Significance of the Forest to the Tobacco Plantation Economy of Antebellum Virginia," *Plantation Society*, 1 (1981): 430-39; Gray, *History of Agriculture in the Southern United States*, 1: 166-69; Walker, *Southern Forest*, 33-36, 56-57, 60-62, 65.

9. Stewart, *What Nature Suffers to Groe*, 72-86; Cox et al., *This Well-Wooded Land*, 34-35. On labor-saving efforts in colonial land use, see: John Solomon Otto, *The Southern Frontiers, 1607-1860: The Agricultural Evolution of the Colonial and Antebellum South* (New York: Greenwood, 1989), 15, 66-67, 132-34. Grady McWhiney traces the extensive herding practices used here and, subsequently, in the Gulf South to Celtic origins; the interpretation is suspect. See: McWhiney, *Cracker Culture: Celtic Ways in the Old South* (Tuscaloosa: University of Alabama Press, 1988); David Hackett Fischer, *Albion's Seed: Four British Folkways in America* (New York: Oxford University Press, 1989), 620; Otto, *Southern Frontiers*, 64.

10. Rasmussen, "Wood on the Farm," 15-34; Williams, *Americans and their Forests*, 55-57, 67-74; Lillard, *The Great Forest*, 18-19 (quote).

11. Bassett, *Writings of Colonel William Byrd*, 28, 54, 62 (1st quote), 66 (2nd quote), 74-76. See also: Walker, *Southern Forest*, 49-52, 85-86. "Cane" was actually various species of bamboo, especially *Arundinaria tecta*.

12. Stewart, *What Nature Suffers to Groe*, 68-69, 72-77, 85-86; Pyne, *Fire in America*, 143-49; G. S. Dunbar, "Colonial Carolina Cowpens," *Ag. Hist.*, 35 (1961): 125-30; Gray, *History of Agriculture in the Southern United States*, 1: 147-48; Susan L. Yarnell, *The Southern Appalachians: A History of the Landscape*, Forest Service, General Technical Report SRS-18 (Asheville, N.C.: United States Forest Service, Southern Research Station, 1998), 9-11; Otto, *Southern Frontiers*, 42-44; Walker, *Southern Forest*, 85-86. Fires set by pastoralists did not burn hot enough or spread far enough into the damper bottomlands to be a threat to mature hardwoods that supplied mast or the canebrakes that furnished winter feed and cover, but they did have a negative

impact on the sandy soil of the pineries, reducing its ability to support the lush vegetation that originally made them attractive to herdsmen. See: Stewart, *What Nature Suffers to Groe*, 68-69, 72-86; Walker, *Southern Forest*, 34-36, 85.

13. Bassett, *Writings of Colonel William Byrd*, 43, 44 (1st quote), 75 (remaining quotes), 76, 80.

14. Ibid., 28 (1st quote), 47, 60-61, 63, 75 (2nd quote), 76, 79-81. See also: Walker, *Southern Forest*, 84-85.

15. Bassett, *Writings of Colonel William Byrd*, 43, 47, 60-61, 63, 79-81. Historians long reflected Byrd's negative view of these "poor whites." A more balanced view emerged with Frank Owsley and the so-called Vanderbilt school. See, especially: Frank L. Owsley, "The Pattern of Migration and Settlement on the Southern Frontier," *JSH*, 11 (1945): 147-76; Owsley, *Plain Folks of the Old South* (Baton Rouge: Louisiana State University Press, 1949); Herbert Weaver, *Mississippi Farmers, 1850-1860* (Nashville, Tenn.: Vanderbilt University Press, 1945); James C. Bonner, "Plantation and Farm: The Agricultural South," in *Writing Southern History: Essays in Historiography in Honor of Fletcher M. Green*, Arthur S. Link and Rembert W. Patrick, ed. (Baton Rouge: Louisiana State University Press, 1965), 147-74.

16. Verner W. Crane, *The Southern Frontier, 1670-1732* (New York: Norton, 1981), 163, 184-85; Otto, *Southern Frontiers*, 37-39.

17. Yarnell, *Southern Appalachians*, 6-8; Crane, *Southern Frontier*, 108-112, 120-36; Claudio Saunt, *A New Order of Things: Property, Power, and the Transformation of the Creek Indians, 1733-1816* (Cambridge, UK: Cambridge University Press, 2003), 46-49, 177. See also: Lillard, *The Great Forest*, 34-42; R. K. MacMaster, "The Cattle Trade in Western Virginia, 1760-1830," in Robert D. Mitchell, ed., *Appalachian Frontiers: Settlement, Society, and Development in the Pre-Industrial Era* (Lexington: University Press of Kentucky, 1991), 127-49; Amos J. Wright, Jr., *The McGillivray and McIntosh Traders on the Old Southwest Frontier, 1716-1815* (Montgomery, Ala.: New South Books, 2001), 41.

18. For analyses of Southern herding traditions, see: Gray, *History of Agriculture in the Southern United States*, 1: 138-51, 200-212; Owsley, "Population and Settlement on the Southern Frontier," 147-54; James C. Bonner, "The Open Range Livestock Industry in Colonial Georgia," *Georgia Review*, 17 (1963): 85-92; John S. Otto, "Open-Range Cattle-Herding in Southern Florida," *Florida Historical Quarterly*, 65 (1987): 317-34; James Taylor Carson, "Native Americans, the Market Revolution, and Cultural Change: The Choctaw Cattle Economy, 1690-1830, *Ag. Hist.*, 71 (1997): 1-18; Terry G. Jordan, "The Origin of Anglo-American Cattle Ranching in Texas: A Documentation of Diffusion from the Lower South," *Economic Geography*, 45 (1969): 65-71; Forrest McDonald and Grady McWhiney, "The Antebellum Southern Herdsman: A Reinterpretation," *JSH*, 41 (1975): 147-66; Thomas D. Clark and John D. W. Guice, *Frontiers in Conflict: The Old Southwest, 1795-1830* (Albuquerque: University of New Mexico Press, 1989), 99-116.

19. William Bartram, *Travels through North and South Carolina, Georgia, East and West Florida . . .* (London: Johnson, 1792), 167, 205-206 (2nd quote), 232-33 (1st quote), 394, 396, 400, 422-23; Saunt, *New Order of Things*, 47-

50, 70-74, 88, 173-74, 257-59, 272; Otto, *Southern Frontiers*, 113-15; James E. Fickle, *Mississippi Forests and Forestry* (Jackson: Mississippi Forestry Foundation and University Press of Mississippi, 2001), 21-26; Jeffrey Drobney, *Lumbermen and Log Sawyers: Life, Labor, and Culture in the North Florida Timber Industry, 1830-1930* (Macon, Ga.: Mercer University Press, 1997), 13-14. Anticipating later American practices, French settlers dispatched wood products to Caribbean markets. John Hebron Moore, *Andrew Brown and Cypress Lumbering in the Old Southwest* (Baton Rouge: Louisiana State University Press, 1967), 3-8; Fickle, *Mississippi Forests*, 29, 51; Clarence P. Gould, "Trade between the Windward Islands and the Continental Colonies of the French Empire, 1683-1763," *MVHR*, 25 (1939): 473-75.

20. Yarnell, *Southern Appalachians*, 13; Williams, *Americans and their Forests*, 147-52; Cox et al., *This Well-Wooded Land*, 15-16; Albert E. Cowdrey, *This Land, This South: An Environmental History* (Lexington: University Press of Kentucky, 1983), 65-80, 89-101; Massey, "History of the Lumber Industry of Alabama and West Florida," 11, 15, 16-17, 19-20; Drobney, *Lumbermen and Log Sawyers*, 21-22; Bassett, *Writings of Colonel William Byrd*, 345, 348-49, 350.

21. Longleaf pine would be the most commercially important species, but loblolly, short-leaf, and other species were also present, all marketed as Southern or yellow pine. Cypress was also much valued from an early date, for it resisted rotting, an important factor in warm, humid climes; however, cypress was difficult to log because of the swampy terrain on which it grew. See: de Boer, *Nature, Business, and Community*, 26-27, 38-39; Philip L. Buttrick, "Commercial Use of the Longleaf Pine," *AF*, 25 (1915): 896-908; Thomas C. Croker, Jr., "The Longleaf Pine Story," *JFH*, 23 (1979): 32-38; Nollie Hickman, *Mississippi Harvest: Lumbering in the Longleaf Pine Belt, 1840-1915* (Oxford: University of Mississippi, 1962), 2-5; Moore, *Andrew Brown*, 9-11; Massey, "History of the Lumber Industry of Alabama and West Florida," 7-24; Fickle, *Mississippi Forests*, 22-26.

22. Saunt, *A New Order of Things*, 225-26.

23. Wright, *McGillivray and McIntosh Traders*, 79; John F. H. Claiborne, "A Trip through the Piney Woods," *Publications of the Mississippi Historical Society*, 9 (1906): 523. In spite of statements by Claiborne and others, forests of the Gulf South were much shaped by Native American practices. See: Fickle, *Mississippi Forests*, 7-13; Silver, *A New Face on the Countryside*, 36-66.

24. Estwick Evans, *A Pedestrious Tour*, in Reuben Gold Thwaites, ed., *Early Western Travels, 1748-1846* (32 vols.; Cleveland: Clark, 1904-1907), 8: 330-31; Thomas Nuttall, *Journal of Travels into Arkansa Territory*, ibid., 13: 311; William Darby, *A Geographical Description of the State of Louisiana . . .* (Philadelphia: John Melish, 1816), 85-86. See also: Otto, *Southern Frontiers*, 122-24; Flint, *History and Geography of the Mississippi Valley*, 1: 261.

25. William Warren Rogers et al., *Alabama: The History of a Deep South State* (Tuscaloosa: University of Alabama Press, 1994), 54-60; Hickman, *Mississippi Harvest*, 7, 9-13; W. H. Sparks, *The Memories of Fifty Years* (3rd ed.; Macon, Ga.: Burke, 1872), 331-32; Otto, *Southern Frontiers*, 116-17; Fickle, *Mississippi Forests*, 14-15. See also: Weaver, *Mississippi Farmers*, 26-33; John Haskins

Napier III, *Lower Pearl River's Piney Woods: Its Land and People* (Oxford: University of Mississippi Center for the Study of Southern Culture, 1985), 26-27, 40-41, 44-45. In 1814 the Creeks ceded a huge swath of land extending from Georgia to north of Mobile.

26. Flint, *History and Geography of the Mississippi Valley*, 1: 153-54, 201-203, 220-22, 223-24, 231-32, 260-61; Flint, *Recollections*, 260, 305, 306 (1st quote); John M. Peck, *A New Guide for Emigrants to the West. . .* (2nd ed., Boston: Gould, Kendall & Lincoln, 1837), 41 (2nd quote); John F. H. Claiborne, "Rough Riding down South," *Harper's New Monthly Magazine*, 30 (6 June 1862): 29 (3rd quote); Frederick L. Olmsted, *A Journey in the Seaboard Slave States, with Remarks on their Economy* (New York: Dix & Edwards, 1856), 348-51. Olmsted's observations reflected what Frank Owsley called the "traditional" view of the people of the pineries. For more sensitive early descriptions, see: Claiborne, "A Trip through the Piney Woods," 514-16, 521-23, 530-33; Sparks, *Memories of Fifty Years*, 331-33.

27. Darby, *Description of Louisiana*, 176; *Report of the Commissioner of Patents for the Year 1850,* Part II: *Agriculture* (Washington, D.C.: GPO, 1851), 260; McDonald and McWhiney, "Antebellum Southern Herdsman," 148-55. See also: Nollie W. Hickman, "The Yellow Pine Industries in St. Tammany, Tangipahoa and Washington Parishes, 1840-1915," *Louisiana Studies*, 5 (1966): 75-76.

28. Flint, *History and Geography of the Mississippi Valley*, 1: 53-54, 56. See also: Weaver, *Mississippi Farmers*, 20, 42, 45, 58-61; Owsley, "The Pattern of Migration and Settlement on the Southern Frontier," 149-53; Claiborne, "A Trip through the Piney Woods," 521-22; Hickman, "Yellow Pine Industries," 76-77; Sir William Dunbar, "Report . . . at the Conclusion of His Services in Locating and Surveying the Thirty-First Degree of Latitude," *Mississippi Historical Society Publications*, 3 (1900): 188-89, 193-94.

29. Weaver, *Mississippi Farmers*, 42, 59, 60; Napier, *Lower Pearl River's Piney Woods*, 64-65; Fickle, *Mississippi Forests*, 21. For examples of institutional weakness during the boom period, see: Joseph G. Baldwin, *The Flush Times of Alabama and Mississippi: A Series of Sketches* (1853; reprint, New York: Hill & Wang, 1957), esp. pp. 36-43, 59-65; Napier, *Lower Pearl River's Piney Woods*, 53-56.

30. Napier, *Lower Pearl River's Piney Woods*, 40-44; Hickman, *Mississippi Harvest*, 11-13; Lacy K. Ford, "Popular Ideology of the Old South's Plain Folk: The Limits of Egalitarianism in a Slaveholding Society," in Samuel C. Hyde, Jr., ed., *Plain Folk of the South Revisited* (Baton Rouge: Louisiana State University Press, 1997), 207-208, 218-21; Bradley G. Bond, "Herders, Farmers, and Markets on the Inner Frontier: The Mississippi Piney Woods, 1850-1860," in ibid., 73-82, 85-94; Drobney, *Lumbermen and Log Sawyers*, 13, 61-62.

31. Moore, *Andrew Brown*, 11-13, 61-62; Hickman, *Mississippi Harvest*, 7-8; Hunter, *Waterpower*, 130-39; John Hebron Moore, ed., "South Mississippi in 1852: Some Selections from the Journal of Benjamin L. C. Wailes," *Journal of Mississippi History*, 18 (1956): 20, 21-22, 24; Drobney, *Lumbermen and Log Sawyers*, 20-22; Darby, *Description of Louisiana*, 105.

32. James M. McReynolds, "Family Life in a Borderland Community: Nacogdoches, Texas, 1779-1861" (unpub. Ph.D. diss., Texas Tech University,

1978), 3-4, 38, 47-48, 51, 55-56, 59; George Louis Crockett, *Two Centuries in East Texas: A History of San Augustine County and Surrounding Territory from 1685 to the Present Time* (Dallas, Tex.: Southwest Press, 1932), 88; Bob Bowman, ed., *Land of the Little Angel: A History of Angelina County, Texas* (Lufkin, Tex.: Lufkin Printing, 1976), 182; Robert S. Maxwell and Robert D. Baker, *Sawdust Empire: The Texas Lumber Industry, 1830-1940* (College Station: Texas A&M University Press, 1983), 10, 16-18. As late as the 1840s, buyers in Galveston imported lumber from Mobile rather than interior Texas. See: P. Slayton to C. Taylor, 21 Mar. 1847, Taylor Papers, 3: 3.

33. Quoted in Witold Rybczynski, *A Clearing in the Distance: Frederick Law Olmsted and America in the Nineteenth Century* (New York: Scribners, 1999), 125.

34. Mississippi State Assembly, *Laws of Mississippi* (Jackson, Miss.: State Printer, 1830), 204-205; Mobile *Register*, 17 Dec. 1821; Hickman, *Mississippi Harvest*, 16-17; Napier, *Lower Pearl River's Piney Woods*, 45-48; Eisterhold, "Lumber and Trade in the Old South," 145-46, 170-77; Hickman, "Yellow Pine Industries," 77; Drobney, *Lumbermen and Log Sawyers*, 17, 23; Fickle, *Mississippi Forests*, 52; Brian Rucker, "Arcadia and Bagdad: Industrial Parks of Antebellum Florida," *Florida Historical Quarterly*, 67 (1988): 147-65. See also: Rucker, "Blackwater and Yellow Pine: The Development of Santa Rosa County, 1821-1865" (unpub. Ph.D. diss., Florida State University, 1990). The first steam-powered mill in the Gulf South was apparently erected in 1802— using the boiler from a wrecked steamboat. In what is clearly a typographical error, Eisterhold dates the mill from 1862, instead of 1802; Stanley F. Horn, long-time editor of the *Southern Lumberman*, has it as 1803. The mill was an isolated (and not particularly successful) case. For practical purposes, the beginnings of steam-powered sawmills in the area came in the 1820s (not the 1830s as James Fickle asserts). See: Eisterhold, "Lumber and Trade in the Old South," 201-202; Moore, *Andrew Brown*, 13-14; Horn, *This Fascinating Lumber Business* (Indianapolis, Ind.: Bobbs-Merrill, 1943), 100-101; Fickle, *Mississippi Forests*, 59.

35. John K. Bettersworth, *Mississippi, A History* (Austin, Tex.: Steck, 1959), 176 and passim; Flint, *History and Geography of the Mississippi Valley*, 1: 221. For an extended discussion, see: John Hebron Moore, *Agriculture in Ante-Bellum Mississippi* (New York: Bookman Associates, 1959).

36. Claiborne, "A Trip through the Piney Woods," 491, 510, 512, 523-24 (quote), 528-30; Fickle, *Mississippi Forests*, 57-58.

37. Davis to Calvin Taylor, 10 Aug. 1846, Taylor Papers, 3: 2 (1st quote); Preston Pond to C. Taylor, 20 Jan. 1850, ibid., 3: 7 (2nd quote); Napier, *Lower Pearl River's Piney Woods*, 51-52, 57; Hickman, *Mississippi Harvest*, 7-8, 9-13, 19, 22, 28-30, 32; Hickman, "Yellow Pine Industries," 77-78; Fletcher M. Green, *The Role of the Yankee in the Old South* (Athens: University of Georgia Press, 1972), 122-23.

38. Napier, *Lower Pearl River's Piney Woods*, 56; Eisterhold, "Lumber and Trade in the Old South," 145-51, 158-68, 182-93, 226-31; Hickman, *Mississippi Harvest*, 14, 26-27, 31-34, 42-43. On trade with Cuba, see also: Demeritt, "Boards, Barrels, and Boxshooks," 108-110, 113-115; Drobney, *Lumbermen and Log Sawyers*, 14-20.

39. Clement Eaton, *The Growth of Southern Civilization, 1790-1860* (New York: Harper, 1961), 238; *Eighth Census of the United States: 1860,* Vol. 3, 73; United States, *Preliminary Report of the Eighth Census* (Washington, D.C.: GPO, 1862), 176-77. See also: Eisterhold, "Lumber and Trade in the Old South," 191-92, 229-31.

40. Undated statement, Taylor Papers, 3: 1; E. Ordway to C. Taylor, 14 Jan. 1847, ibid., 3: 3. Taylor's commission business, Ordway wrote, "presents a horrible picture of the evils of indiscriminate credit." In addition to Ordway's letter, box 3 contains considerable other material on the financial problems of the commission business.

41. Sereno Taylor to C. Taylor, 10 Jan. 1846, Taylor Papers, 3: 2.

42. J. W. Arthur & Co. to C. Taylor, 31 Aug. 1846, ibid. (1st quote); Spencer Taylor to C. Taylor, 19 Jan. 1847 2nd quote); Davis to C. Taylor, 22 Jan. 1847, ibid. 3: 3. Cf. C. D. Bonney to C. Taylor, 2 Oct. 1850, ibid., 3: 8. The size of the mill is not clear. A nephew claimed it sawed ten thousand board feet a day; initially it seems to have cut closer to twenty-five hundred feet. See: Spencer Taylor to C. Taylor, 19 Jan. 1847, ibid., 3: 3; G. R. Taylor to C. Taylor, 6 Feb. 1850, ibid., 3: 7. For accounts of the Taylor-Davis operations (and its successor firm), see: Hickman, *Mississippi Harvest*, 34-42; Fickle, *Mississippi Forests*, 61-62. Some details in Hickman differ from this account.

43. Buying from multiple log suppliers was common. One millman purchased from twenty-five different logmen during 1858-1860. See: Hickman, "Logging and Rafting in South Mississippi," 164.

44. Davis to C. Taylor, 10 Aug. 1846, ibid., 3: 2; ibid., 22 Jan. 1847, 3: 3; ibid., 26 Dec. 1847, 3: 4; Hickman, *Mississippi Harvest*, 38-40; Fickle, *Mississippi Forests*, 70-71. On logging, see also: Hickman, "Logging and Rafting Timber in South Mississippi," 158-59, 163-68; Drobney, *Lumbermen and Log Sawyers*, 64-65.

45. Davis to C. Taylor, 26 Dec. 1847, Taylor Papers, 3: 4; ibid., 13 Sept. 1848.

46. There is considerable correspondence on the partners' efforts to locate and purchase an adequate planing machine. See, especially, ibid., 3: 8.

47. Davis to C. Taylor, 10 Aug. (quote), 6 Oct. 1846, ibid., 3: 2.

48. Gordon Davis to C. Taylor, 26 Dec. 1847; Sereno Taylor to C. Taylor, 30 Dec. 1847, ibid., 3: 4; Lewis Taylor to C. Taylor, 5 May 1853, ibid., 3: 9.

49. Sereno Taylor to C. Taylor, 30 Dec. 1847, ibid., 3: 4; Chase & Ludlow to Taylor & Fowler, 22 and 25 June, 28 Sept. (quote) 1850, ibid., 3: 8. On the New Orleans market, see: Eisterhold, "Lumber and Trade in the Old South," 214-22; Eisterhold, "Lumber and Trade in the Lower Mississippi Valley and New Orleans, 1800-1860," *Louisiana History*, 13 (1972): 71-91.

50. Slayton to C. Taylor, 21 Mar. 1847, Taylor Papers, 3: 3. See also: Eisterhold, "Lumber and Trade in the Old South," 183, 186, 192-93. Slayton thought a mill would only pay if located nearer the Galveston market in the east Texas woods. Asa Hursey, owner of a mill on the Pearl, considered chartering a vessel to haul lumber to New York, and received similar advice: "[T]he high rates of freight from Pearl River . . . would be your greatest obstacle." R. E. Foster to Hursey, 1 Sept. 1849 (Asa Hursey Papers, Hill Memorial Library, Louisiana State University, Baton Rouge), folder 1.

51. Eisterhold, "Lumber and Trade in the Old South," 183, 186, 189-90, 192-93;

Donald J. Millet, "The Lumber Industry of 'Imperial' Calcasieu," *Louisiana History*, 7 (1966): 59-60.

52. Slayton to C. Taylor, 21 Mar. 1847, Taylor Papers, 3: 3; S. Fowler to C. Taylor, 21 July, 23 Sept. (quote) 1847, ibid., 3: 4; J. R. Richards to C. Taylor, 12 Jan. 1850, ibid., 3: 7. There were major problems with cypress operations too. Flint, *History and Geography of the Mississippi Valley*, 42.

53. Hickman, "Logging and Rafting in South Mississippi," 164; Eisterhold, "Lumber and Trade in the Old South," 145-53, 165, 171-78; Napier, *Lower Pearl River's Piney Woods*, 57; Dorothy Dodd, "Florida in 1845," *Florida Historical Quarterly*, 24 (1945): 15; Herbert J. Doherty, "Antebellum Pensacola: 1821-1860," *Journal of Florida History*, 37 (1959): 337-57; Pensacola *Gazette* 26 Mar. 1834, 5 June 1852; Drobney, *Lumbermen and Log Sawyers*, 16-20.

54. Eisterhold, "Lumber and Trade in the Old South," 159-64; Drobney, *Lumbermen and Log Sawyers*, 22-23; Moore, *Andrew Brown*. In time Brown's firm became the R. F. Learned Lumber Company. It operated under one name or another for well over one hundred years. See: Charles W. Crawford, "A History of the R. F. Learned Lumber Company, 1865-1900," (unpub. Ph.D. diss., University of Mississippi, 1968); Bolling A. Johnson, "Story of the Learned Mill—Longest Continuous Operation in the United States," *Lumber World Review*, 38 (Jan. 10, 1920): 28-30; M. B. Peabody, "125 Years of Sawmilling," *SL*, 193 (Dec. 15, 1956): 151-52.

55. Anonymous [unidentified grandson of Henry Weston], "The History of the H. Weston Lumber Co.," 3-10A, 19-21 (undated typescript, Weston Family Papers, J. D. Williams Library, University of Mississippi, University), folder 1; Eisterhold, "Lumber and Trade in the Old South," 146-47, 160, 196, 201, 203-207; Hickman, *Mississippi Harvest*, 18-19, 21-22; Napier, *Lower Pearl River's Piney Woods*, 57-59; Hickman, "Yellow Pine Industries," 77-78; Fickle, *Mississippi Forests*, 59-60; Drobney, *Lumbermen and Log Sawyers*, 15; Green, *Role of the Yankee in the Old South*, 122-23.

56. Napier, *Lower Pearl River's Piney Woods*, 57, 58; Hickman, *Mississippi Harvest*, 13-14, 19-22.

57. Mobile *Register*, 5 Oct. 1824, 4 July 1826, 4 May, 1 and 23 Sept. 1835; Moore, "South Mississippi in 1852," 18-32; Eisterhold, "Lumber and Trade in the Old South," 175, 177, 191-92, 196-201, 205, 207-211, 225; Hickman, *Mississippi Harvest*, 18, 20, 24, 25, 37, 40-42, 278-80; Moore, *Andrew Brown*, 124-48; Hickman, "Yellow Pine Industry," 78; William Criglar, deed to Louisiana Criglar, 5 July 1862, William Criglar Papers (Southern Historical Collection, University of North Carolina, Chapel Hill); Drobney, *Lumbermen and Log Sawyers*, 20, 22-23; John Hebron Moore, "Simon Gray, Riverman: A Slave Who Was Almost Free," *MVHR*, 49 (1962): 472-84; Harnett T. Kane, *Natchez on the Mississippi* (New York: Bonanza, 1947), 134-35; Anonymous, "History of the H. Weston Lumber Co.," 30.

58. Weston to Levi Weston, 1 June 1851, Weston Papers, folder 1. See also: ibid., 8 Nov. 1851; Anonymous, "History of the H. Weston Lumber Co.," 30.

59. William H. Garland to Harriet Garland, 11 Nov. 1841 (Garland Papers, Southern Historical Collection, University of North Carolina, Chapel Hill).

60. Clark to parents, 22 Sept. 1846 (Clark Papers, Huntington Library, San

Marino, Calif.). If Fletcher Green is correct, men like Weston were more typical than Clark. See: Green, *Role of the Yankee in the Old South*, 131-32.

61. Samuel P. Reed to W. Garland, 4 Oct. 1841, Garland Papers.

62. Pensacola *Gazette*, 9 Mar. 1850. See also: Mobile *Register*, 29 Apr. 1823, 2 Nov. 1842; Eisterhold, "Lumber and Trade in the Old South," 178-79, 191-92, 207-208.

63. H. Weston to S. W. Weston, 15 Dec. 1850, as quoted in Anonymous, "History of the H. Weston Lumber Co.," 13 [punctuation added]. See also: Hickman, "Yellow Pine Industries," 77-78. Many of the closed mills in St. Tammany Parish must have been interior mills; while times were trying for sawmills able to engage in the seaboard trade, closures among them were less numerous.

64. H. Weston to L. Weston, 1 June and 8 Nov. 1851, Weston Papers, folder 1; Fickle, *Mississippi Forests*, 59.

65. H. Weston to L. Weston, 9 Nov. 1856, Weston Papers, folder 1.

66. John S. C. Abbott, *South and North: Or, Impressions Received during a Trip to Cuba and the South* (New York: Abbey & Abbot, 1860), 201-202; Frederick Law Olmsted, *The Cotton Kingdom . . .*, ed. by Arthur M. Schlesinger (New York: Knopf, 1953), 220; Eisterhold, "Lumber and Trade in the Old South," 151, 157, 178-79, 199, 203-204, 207-208; Moore, "Simon Gray," 472-73, 483-84; Anonymous, "History of H. Weston Lumber Co.," 30.

67. New Orleans *Daily Picayune*, 16 Nov. 1852.

68. Eisterhold, "Lumber and Trade in the Old South," 226; Moore, *Andrew Brown*, 131-33. Neither of these sources nor the New Orleans *Daily Picayune* presents significant evidence in support of these generalizations.

69. John W. Evans to W. Garland, 30 June, 6 Aug. 1847, Garland Papers. On Baltimore as a lumber center, see: Eisterhold, "Lumber and Trade in the Old South," 125-44.

70. W. Garland to H. Garland, 11 and 27 Nov. (1st quote) 1841, Garland Papers; Sweat to W. Garland, 11 July 1842 (3rd quote), 30 June 1847 (2nd quote), ibid. See also: ibid., 15 Aug. 1841, 27 Jan. 1842.

71. Ball to C. Taylor, 25 Feb. 1850, Taylor Papers, 3: 7. Ball may have been one of the skilled workmen Gordon Davis earlier reported recruiting in the Northeast. He does not appear to have been a common laborer.

72. Pensacola *Gazette*, 17 Mar. 1849.

73. Eisterhold, "Lumber and Trade in the Old South," 179, 199, 208-209; Moore, *Andrew Brown*, 60-61.

74. Eugene Hilgard, *Report on the Geology and Agriculture of Mississippi* (Jackson, Miss.: State Printer, 1860), 361; Napier, *Lower Pearl River's Piney Woods*, 57; Hickman, *Mississippi Harvest*, 13-14, 42, 276; Hickman, "Logging and Rafting in South Mississippi," 154; Moore, "South Mississippi in 1852," 22 (quote); Fickle, *Mississippi Forests*, 56-58.

75. Samuel Brown to Governor Holmes, 24 June 1811, in Clarence Edwin Carter, ed., *Territorial Papers of the United States* (28 vols.; Washington, D.C.: GPO, 1956), 6: 206-207; George Peters to John C. Calhoun, 2 Feb. 1819, ibid., 18: 551-77, 22: 809-810. See also: Ibid., 6: 205-206, 224; 9: 456-57, 19: 428; Fickle, *Mississippi Forests*, 52-53.

76. Mobile *Register*, 5 Oct. 1824; Pensacola *Gazette*, 25 Apr. 1835; Eisterhold,

"Lumber and Trade in the Old South," 155, 209, 213-14; Hickman, "Logging and Rafting in South Mississippi," 155, 170-72. John Eisterhold—"Lumber and Trade in the Old South," 156 and 180—blames illegal logging on smalltime operators, saying owners of large mills had too much at risk to engage in such practices and, in any case, sufficient timberland of their own. His claim is suspect. Available records, although scanty, do not demonstrate widespread timber ownership by operators of the area's larger mills, and the financial limitations with which many wrestled raise questions about their ability to purchase sufficient timber stands to keep their mills financed. Until at least the 1870s, it would appear large operators contributed to trespass as much as small ones, for they depended on independent loggers for sawlogs to keep their plants running.

77. Black to [W. Criglar], n.d., Criglar Papers.
78. Hickman, "Logging and Rafting in South Mississippi," 56-59; Etienne William Maxson, *The Progress of the Races* (Washington, D.C.: Murray Brothers, 1930), 10; Fickle, *Mississippi Forests*, 70-71; Drobney, *Lumbermen and Log Sawyers*, 64-65.
79. Hickman, "Logging and Rafting in South Mississippi," 163-67; Cyril Edward, *Four Centuries on the Pascagoula* (2 vols.; Starkville, Miss.: privately printed, 1953), 1: 146; Drobney, *Lumbermen and Log Sawyers*, 62, 69-71. "Bull pens" were more lightly constructed than rafts, being made by connecting several logs end-to-end to form an enclosure that was then filled with a hundred or so loose logs. These were essentially the same as the brails (pocket booms) used on the Mississippi and, less often, in the Adirondacks.
80. Pensacola *Gazette*, 19 Dec. 1835.
81. Hickman, *Mississippi Harvest*, 13-14, 38-42; Hickman, "Logging and Rafting in South Mississippi," 164; Walker, *Southern Forest*, 127-28; Fickle, *Mississippi Forests*, 53.
82. *Sixth Census of the United States: 1840* (Washington, D.C.: Thos. Allen, 1841), 236; Moore, "South Mississippi in 1852," 30; Napier, *Lower Pearl River's Piney Woods*, 46-48, 56-57, 60-63; Hickman, *Mississippi Harvest*, 5-6, 17-18; Hickman, "Logging and Rafting in South Mississippi," 163-64; Fickle, *Mississippi Forests*, 52-53; Rucker, "Blackwater and Yellow Pine," 163 and passim; Benjamin L. C. Wailes, *Report on the Agriculture and Geology of Mississippi* (Jackson, Miss.: State Printer, 1854), 349.
83. Hickman, *Mississippi Harvest*, 20, 38-40.
84. Ibid., 20, 38-40; Hickman, "Logging and Rafting Timber in South Mississippi," 163-68; Hilgard, *Report on the Geology and Agriculture of Mississippi*, 382, 385.
85. Pensacola *Gazette*, 26 Mar. 1834; G. Davis to C. Taylor, 22 Jan. 1847; Slayton to C. Taylor, 21 Mar. 1847, Taylor Papers, 3: 3; S. Taylor to C. Taylor, 30 Dec. 1847, ibid., 3: 4; Chase & Ludlow to Taylor & Fowler, 22 and 25 June 1850, ibid., 3: 8; Foster to Asa Hursey, 29 Oct. 1848, Hursey Papers, folder 1; H. Weston to L. Weston, 18 Oct. 1857, Weston Papers, folder 1; Eisterhold, "Lumber and Trade in the Old South," 187; Hickman, "Yellow Pine Industries," 78; Moore, *Andrew Brown*, 56; Fickle, *Mississippi Forests*, 59-60.
86. H. Weston to L. Weston, 15 July 1860, as quoted in Anonymous, "History

of H. Weston Lumber Co.," 29 (quote); Anonymous, "History of H. Weston Lumber Co.," 30.

87. Eisterhold, "Lumber and Trade in the Old South," 151-53, 174, 177-78, 186-87, 202, 211-12; H. Weston to L. Weston, 15 July 1860, as quoted in Anonymous, "History of H. Weston Lumber Co.," 29.

88. Pensacola *Gazette*, 12 Dec. 1846; Eisterhold, "Lumber and Trade in the Old South," 164-68, 181-83; Drobney, *Lumbermen and Log Sawyers*, 23; Fickle, *Mississippi Forests*, 63-64.

89. *Eighth Census of the United States: 1860*, Vol. 3: *Census of Manufactures*, 14, 203, 294, 594; Vera Lea Dugas, "Texas Industry, 1860-1880," *Southwestern Historical Quarterly*, 59 (1955): 154; Hickman, "Yellow Pine Industries," 79; Eisterhold, "Lumber and Trade in the Old South," 192, 221. Eisterhold provides a useful overview of the importance of Gulf South lumbering in this period. See: ibid., 223-31.

90. Hickman, *Mississippi Harvest*, 31; S. Taylor to C. Taylor, 21 Sept. 1859, Taylor Papers, bound letters, v. 5. See also: John Hebron Moore, "Railroads of Antebellum Mississippi," *Journal of Mississippi History*, 41 (1979): 53-56.

Chapter Ten

1. Lutcher was a son of German immigrants, Moore of an Episcopal minister of modest means. Both went to work in the industry at a young age and rose through talent and hard work. See: "Henry J. Lutcher," in [Defebaugh], *American Lumbermen*, 2: 377-80; [Mrs. Bedell Moore], "Sketch of the Life of Gregory Bedell Moore" (G. T. B. Moore Papers, East Texas Research Center, Stephen F. Austin State University, Nacogdoches, Texas), 1: 6-9.

2. [G. Bedell Moore], "Henry J. Lutcher and G. Bedell Moore's Trip to Texas, 1877," photocopy of diary, Moore Papers, 3: 2-8 [original in possession of Carolyn Negley, San Antonio]; Robert S. Maxwell, "The First Big Mill: The Beginnings of Commercial Lumbering in Texas," *Southwestern Historical Quarterly*, 86 (1982): 13; John Reed Tarver, "The Clan of Toil: Piney Woods Labor Relations in the Trans-Mississippi South, 1880-1920" (unpub. Ph.D. diss., Louisiana State University, 1991), 3-4. See also: [Defebaugh], *American Lumbermen*, 2: 362-63.

3. [Moore], diary, 15-17. The Texas and New Orleans was completed from Houston to Orange (on the Texas-Louisiana border) before the Civil War and thence to New Orleans in 1881. St. Clair G. Reed, *A History of Texas Railroads and of Transportation Conditions . . .* (Houston: St. Clair, 1941), 84-87, 229.

4. [Moore], diary, 9-11, 16-17 (quote, p. 11).

5. Ibid., 18-32; Maxwell, "First Big Mill," 16-20.

6. [Moore], diary, 18; Maxwell, "First Big Mill," 9-11, 13, 17, 20.

7. Ship captains did not consider the Sabine inviting. An agent later informed Lutcher & Moore he was trying to find tonnage to load at Sabine Pass, the river's port, "but all the Shipbrokers seem to have a dread of the . . . place, as they believe they will have to load some miles from shore & in the open," using lighters to take cargo to waiting vessels. Harbor improvements had by then made lighters were no longer necessary, but the reputation the Sabine earned while Lutcher and Moore were getting established in the area persisted. Thomas Sutherland & Co. to Lutcher & Moore, 29 Nov. 1895

(Lutcher and Moore Papers [hereafter LMP], East Texas Research Center, Stephen F. Austin State University, Nacogdoches, Tex.), box 2.

8. [Moore], diary, 33-37, 61-68, 75; Maxwell, "First Big Mill," 20-25, 27-28; [Moore], "Gregory Bedell Moore," 22. See also: Walker, *Southern Forest*, 127-28; Robert S. Maxwell, "Lumbermen of the East Texas Frontier," *FH*, 9 (1965): 13-14.

9. "Lands Owned by Lutcher & Moore in Calcasieu Parish, La.," undated clipping, LMP, box 1; "The Lutcher & Moore Lumber Company," undated clipping, in [Moore], "Gregory Bedell Moore," 22; M. S. Morris, oral history interview by R. S. Maxwell, Sabine County, 5 Aug. 1958 (Forest History Collection [hereafter FHC], East Texas Research Center, Stephen F. Austin State University, Nacogdoches, Tex.), OH-30; James H. McNamara, Robert P. Turpin, and B. C. McDonough, oral history interview by R. S. Maxwell, Orange, 13 Aug. 1963, ibid., OH-25; Tarver, "Clan of Toil," 50-51, 53, 56. See also: Donald J. Millet, "The Economic Development of Southwestern Louisiana, 1865-1900" (unpub. Ph.D. diss., Louisiana State University, 1964); Daniel Dennett, *Louisiana As It Is* . . . (New Orleans: Eureka, 1876), 15, 19, 28-31, 34, 36, 129-32; William H. Harris, *Louisiana: Products, Resources and Attractions* (New Orleans: Brandao, 1885), 18-20, 58.

10. [Moore], diary, 33; Maxwell, "First Big Mill," 8, 20; Maxwell and Baker, *Sawdust Empire*, 53; Dennett, *Louisiana As It Is*, 111; Millet, "The Lumber Industry of 'Imperial' Calcasieu," 51-69; Fickle, *Mississippi Forests*, 59.

11. Hickman, *Mississippi Harvest*, 44, 47, 52, 55; Hickman, "Yellow Pine Industries," 79; Massey, "History of the Lumber Industry in Alabama and West Florida," 41-42; Maxwell and Baker, *Sawdust Empire*, 20-21; Drobney, *Lumbermen and Log Sawyers*, 25.

12. S. Taylor to Ray Taylor, 19 Nov. 1883, Taylor Papers, 4: 7; S. Taylor to C. Taylor, 9 July 1886, 2 Feb. 1888; S. Taylor to Eva Taylor, 6 Dec. 1886, ibid., 4: 8; 6 Aug. 1890, ibid., 5: 1; S. Taylor to Lulu Taylor, 16 May 1888, 29 Mar., 2 Nov., 22 Dec. 1889, ibid., 4: 8; 28 Sept. 1892 (quote), ibid., 5: 1; 13 Feb. 1902, ibid., 5: 2.

13. The data are incomplete, but Nollie Hickman maintains that by the mid-seventies mills on the Pascagoula and at Moss Point had expanded so much the area became the second-largest lumber-manufacturing center on the Gulf Coast, behind only Pensacola; Jeffrey Drobney notes that by 1870 Florida's sawmills had surpassed prewar production. Hickman, *Mississippi Harvest*, 48; Drobney, *Lumbermen and Log Sawyers*, 25-27. See also: Hickman, "Yellow Pine Industries," 80; Fickle, *Mississippi Forests*, 86.

14. The high cost of building logging railroads drove lumbermen to buy tributary timberland to insure a satisfactory return on their investments. This barred nearly all old-time Southern operators from the opportunities offered as the bonanza era entered its heyday. See: Massey, "History of the Lumber Industry in Alabama and West Florida," 52.

15. Hickman, *Mississippi Harvest*, 50-54, 119-20, 168-75; Fickle, *Mississippi Forests*, 86; Napier, *Lower Pearl River's Piney Woods*, 80-82; Massey, "History of the Lumber Industry in Alabama and West Florida," 27-28; Maxwell and Baker, *Sawdust Empire*, 20-21; Jerrell H. Shofner, "Negro Laborers and the Forest Industries in Reconstruction Florida," *JFH*, 19 (1975): 185-88.

16. Drobney, *Lumbermen and Log Sawyers*, 74. For discussions, see: Mark W. Summers, *Railroads, Reconstruction, and the Gospel of Prosperity: Aid Under the Radical Republicans, 1865-1877* (Princeton, N.J.: Princeton University Press, 1984); John F. Stover, *The Railroads of the South, 1865-1900* (Chapel Hill: University of North Carolina Press, 1955).

17. Hickman, *Mississippi Harvest*, 44-45, 48-54; Fickle, *Mississippi Forests*, 71-75. See also: Phil D. Muth, "New Orleans—Important Lumber Center," *SL*, 193 (15 Dec. 1956): 241-42; James Boyd, Southern Pine Association history [hereafter SPA history], typescript files, ca. 1940 (Southern Pine Association Papers [hereafter SPAP], Hill Memorial Library, Louisiana State University, Baton Rouge) X-70, box 5, file 10-a, 1-2.

18. Williams, *Americans and their Forests*, 241; Hickman, *Mississippi Harvest*, 48, 57, 58-59, 83-84; Fickle, *Mississippi Forests*, 83; Massey, "History of the Lumber Industry in Alabama and West Florida," 40; Hidy, Hill, and Nevins, *Timber and Men*, 207-209; Drobney, *Lumbermen and Log Sawyers*, 38.

19. Hickman, *Mississippi Harvest*, 48-49, 53, 55-58; Maxwell and Baker, *Sawdust Empire*, 34-39, 200; Williams, *Americans and their Forests*, 252-54; Napier, *Lower Pearl River Piney Woods*, 74; Fickle, *Mississippi Forests*, 71-73; Walker, *Southern Forest*, 103-105; McNamara, Turpin, and McDonough, oral history interview; W. I. Davis, oral history interview by R. S. Maxwell, n.p., 20 Mar. 1956, FHC, OH-19; Boyd, SPA history, SPAP, X-70, box 5, file 10-a, 1-3. See also: Louisiana Board of Commissioners for the Louisiana Purchase Exposition, *A Handbook of Louisiana* (Baton Rouge: Louisiana Board of Agriculture & Immigration, 1904), 84-85, 203-204; Joel Campbell DuBose, *Alabama History* (Richmond, Va.: Johnson, 1908), 287-88; Hilton Watson, "Alabama's Sawmill Industry," *SL*, 193 (15 Dec. 1956): 158-61; Bowman, *Land of the Little Angel*, 182; Flora G. Bowles, *A History of Trinity County, Texas, 1827-1928* (Groveton, Tex.: Groveton Independent School, 1966), 47-52.

20. Larson, *White Pine Industry*, 129, 220-21, 224, 375, 397; Maxwell and Baker, *Sawdust Empire*, 87-95; Williams, *Americans and their Forests*, 238-41; Massey, "History of the Lumber Industry in Alabama and West Florida," 28-29; Hickman, *Mississippi Harvest*, 45, 58-59, 61, 63-65, 281; Fickle, *Mississippi Forests*, 73-75, 80-81; Horn, *This Fascinating Lumber Business*, 102-105; Boyd, SPA history, SPAP, X-70, box 5, file 10a, 2-4; Fred E. Dickinson, "Development of Southern and Western Freight Rates on Lumber," *SL*, 185 (15 Dec. 1952): 230-34.

21. Horn, *This Fascinating Lumber Business*, 102-104; I. James Pikl, *A History of Georgia Forestry*, Research Monograph no. 2 (Athens: University of Georgia, Bureau of Business and Economic Research, 1966), 7-8; Walker, *Southern Forest*, 88-89. See also: W. McKee Evans, *Ballots and Fence Rails: Reconstruction on the Lower Cape Fear* (Chapel Hill: University of North Carolina Press, 1966), 199-200, 275-76; John and Ina Woestemeyer van Noppen, "The Genesis of Forestry in the Southern Appalachians: A Brief History," *Appalachian Journal*, 1 (1972): 64-66; de Boer, *Nature, Business, and Community*, 87-92.

22. Pascagoula *Democrat Star*, 4 Jan. 1878; Massey, "History of the Lumber Industry in Alabama and West Florida," 27-34, 54; Williams, *Americans and their Forests*, 240; Schurz, address to AFA (AFA Papers), box 7, AFA hist. 1889 file, 5.

23. *Congressional Record*, 46th Cong., 2nd sess., 1564.
24. Schurz, address to AFA (AFA Papers), box 7, AFA hist. 1889 file, 5; Massey, "History of the Lumber Industry in Alabama and West Florida," 27-32; Shofner, "Negro Laborers and the Forest Industries in Florida," 190-91; Cameron, *Development of Forest Control*, 170-78; Drobney, *Lumbermen and Log Sawyers*, 6-7, 27, 30.
25. Pascagoula *Democrat Star*, 30 Nov. 1877.
26. *Congressional Record*, 46th Cong., 2nd sess., 1564-67 (1st quote, p. 1566, 3128-29, 3577-85, 3627-32); U.S. Congress, *Senate Exec. Doc. 9 (1877-78)*, Part 1: 64-65; Part 2: 8-9, 38-41; Schurz, address to AFA (AFA Papers), box 7, AFA hist. 1889 file, 7; Millett, "The Lumber Industry of 'Imperial' Calcasieu," 55-58; Ise, *Forest Policy*, 88-90; Cameron, *Development of Forest Policy*, 170-78; Hickman, *Mississippi Harvest*, 49, 53, 54, 74-81; Napier, *Lower Pearl River's Piney Woods*, 80; Lillard, *The Great Forest*, 170-75. The Pascagoula *Democrat Star*, 1877-1879, reported from the local viewpoint. Oddly, although this was a major event, it is unmentioned in James Fickle's *Mississippi Forests*.
27. Fickle, *Mississippi Forests*, 82. For fuller discussions, see: Paul W. Gates, "Federal Land Policy in the South, 1866-1888," *JSH*, 6 (1940): 303-330; Hickman, *Mississippi Harvest*, 68-87.
28. Hickman, *Mississippi Harvest*, 68-69, 81, 88-93; Orfield, *Federal Land Grants to the States*, 112-14, 118. See also: Henry Lewis Coles, "A History of the Administration of Federal Land Policies and Land Tenure in Louisiana, 1803-1860" (unpub. Ph.D. diss., Vanderbilt University, 1949).
29. Gates, "Federal Land Policy in the South," 309-310; Massey, "History of the Lumber Industry in Alabama and West Florida," 34-39; Hickman, *Mississippi Harvest*, 69-72; Fickle, *Mississippi Forests*, 82-83; Drobney, *Lumbermen and Log Sawyers*, 36-37. See also: Warren Hoffnagle, "The Southern Homestead Act: Its Origins and Operation," *Historian*, 32 (1972): 612-29; Roy M. Robbins, *Our Landed Heritage: The Public Domain, 1776-1970* (2nd ed.; Lincoln: University of Nebraska Press, 1972), 212-16.
30. *Report of the Commissioner of the General Land Office*, 1877 (Washington, D.C.: GPO, 1878 [hereafter *Report*, with year]), 16-21; Lillard, *The Great Forest*, 101; Hickman, *Mississippi Harvest*, 85-86, 95; Walker, *Southern Forest*, 40-41; Fickle, *Mississippi Forests*, 85.
31. Massey, "History of the Lumber Industry in Alabama and West Florida," 29-48 (quote, p. 39); Hickman, *Mississippi Harvest*, 68-72; Drobney, *Lumbermen and Log Sawyers*, 37-40; Gates, "Federal Land Policy," 303-330. Identifying these smallholders is beyond the scope of this study; however, L. N. Dantzler's Land Ownership Journals (L. N. Dantzler Papers, John Davis Williams Library, University of Mississippi, Oxford) provide insight; they list the original buyers and date of sale of all lands acquired by the company.
32. *Northwestern Lumberman*, 5 (9 Oct. 1880): 2; ibid., 12 (25 June 1887): 3-6; Massey, "History of the Lumber Industry in Alabama and West Florida," 26-27; Drobney, *Lumbermen and Log Sawyers*, 38-44; Williams, *Americans and their Forests*, 241-44 (1st quote, p. 240); Hickman, *Mississippi Harvest*, 61-63, 81-84; Fickle, *Mississippi Forests*, 82-85, 94 (2nd quote); Hickman, "Yellow Pine Industries," 80-81; Hidy, Hill, and Nevins, *Timber and Men*, 207-209; C. W. Goodyear, *Bogalusa Story* (Buffalo, N.Y.: privately printed, 1950), 27-

30; Tarver, "Clan of Toil," 3-5; Horn, *This Fascinating Lumber Business*, 102-103; Gates, "Federal Land Policy," 316-21; *Tenth Census of the United States: 1880*, Vol. 9: *Census of Manufactures*, 519-24.

33. Lutcher to Dibert, 1 Mar. 1887, LMP, box 1; H. C. Howard to Lutcher & Moore, 4 May 1887, ibid.

34. Mrs. H. C. Wilson to Dibert, 29 Sept. 1885; Dibert to Wilson, 22 Sept. 1885, ibid. This box has other correspondence regarding land-claims conflicts. See also: Lewis & Lewis to J. E. Hawkins, 6 and 24 Oct. 1907 (Hawkins Papers, Hill Memorial Library, Louisiana State University, Baton Rouge), C-85, box 7, 1907 file.

35. Goodyear, *Bogalusa Story*, 29-30. Much had also been bought from the states for even less.

36. Not the Oregon writer of the same name.

37. Davis to Lutcher & Moore, 22 Apr. 1887; H. C. Howard to Lutcher & Moore, 4 May 1887; Lutcher & Moore to Dibert, 3 Dec. 1888, LMP, box 1; Goodyear, *Bogalusa Story*, 29-30; Honhart, "Hackley & Hume Papers," 140. It is not clear if the tract offered Lutcher & Moore was part of the immense timberlands later acquired by Edward Hines or the Goodyear brothers (see below), but it seems likely.

38. Duvall to Corbin, 6 Apr. (1st quote), 15 May 1891 (2nd quote) (Robert A. Corbin Papers, Hill Memorial Library, Louisiana State University, Baton Rouge), box 3, folder 12; 13 Feb., 17 Mar., 6 Apr., 8 July 1892, ibid., 3: 14; agreement of R. A. Corbin, Sam Johnson, and R. L. Duvall, 6 Mar. 1891, ibid., 3: 13.

39. Howcott, "Timber Lands, Mill Sites, Etc.," n.d., copy in LMP, box 1.

40. Howcott to Mrs. J. M. B. Tucker, 3 Oct. 1890; H. M. Loomer & Co. to Tucker, 3 Sept. 1890 (quote), 5 Apr. 1892; Yates & Noble to Tucker, 22 and 27 Nov. 1890 (Tucker Papers, Hill Memorial Library, Louisiana State University, Baton Rouge), box 1, file 9.

41. Lutcher to Dibert, 1 Mar. 1887, LMP, box 1.

42. Dibert to Lutcher & Moore, 27 June 1888, ibid.; Massey, "History of the Lumber Industry in Alabama and West Florida," 29, 33; Roy Dudley and W. L. Avery, oral history interview by R. S. Maxwell, Groveton, Tex., 15 Mar. 1960, FHC, OH-20. See also: Nat Wasey to Lutcher & Moore, 8 June 1886, LMP, box 1; M. P. Boyd to Lutcher & Moore, 10 Jan. 1887, ibid; B. F. Bonner to S. A. McNeely, 17 Oct. 1904, (Kirby Lumber Company Papers [hereafter KLCP], East Texas Research Center, Stephen F. Austin State University, Nacogdoches, Tex.), box 11.

43. Bradford to Lutcher & Moore, 26 Apr. (1st quote), 13 May 1888; Lutcher to Lutcher & Moore, 26 May 1885 (2nd quote), LMP, box 1.

44. Commissioner of General Land Office, *Report* (1883), 9; Pascagoula *Democrat Star*, 16 Apr. 1886; Hickman, *Mississippi Harvest*, 94; *SL*, n.v. (1 Apr. 1883): 10; ibid., (July 1, 1883): 9; Goodyear, *Bogalusa Story*, 37; Albert D. Kirwan, *Revolt of the Rednecks: Mississippi Politics, 1876-1925* (Gloucester, Mass.: Peter Smith, 1964), 54-57; Fickle, *Mississippi Forests*, 82, 84-85, 86, 91. Thomas D. Clark, late dean of Southern historians, described these speculators as "timberland carpetbaggers," but James Fickle insists that at the time they were not viewed that way. See: Clark, *The Greening of the South: The*

Recovery of Land and Forest (Lexington: University Press of Kentucky, 1984), 14-20 (quote, p. 16); Fickle, *Mississippi Forests*, 80-81.

45. Hickman, *Mississippi Harvest*, 81-84, 99, 100, 283-84; Fickle, *Mississippi Forests*, 82, 84, 85; Gates, "Federal Land Policy," 316-21; Williams, *Americans and their Forests*, 241-43; Napier, *Lower Pearl River's Piney Woods*, 72-73; [Defebaugh], *American Lumbermen*, 2: 211, 215.

46. [Defebaugh], *American Lumbermen*, 1: 235-38; Bolling A. Johnson, "A Short History of the James D. Lacey Co.," *Lumber World Review*, n.v. (Aug. 15, 1915): 17-20; Anonymous, "James D. Lacey," *AL*, 54 (May 13, 1899): 1, 19; Hickman, *Mississippi Harvest*, 82-83; Massey, "History of the Lumber Industry in Alabama and West Florida," 40-41; Goodyear, *Bogalusa Story*, 38. The voluminous Lacey papers are housed at the Forest History Society, Durham, N.C.

47. Goodyear to Lacey, 8 Mar. 1905, in Goodyear, *Bogalusa Story*, 37; Anonymous, "The Largest Lumber Manufacturing Proposition in the World," *AL*, 86 (4 July 1908): 53-68; [Defebaugh], *American Lumbermen*, 3: 182. See also: Michael Curtis, "Early Development and Operations of the Great Southern Lumber Company," *Louisiana History*, 14 (1973): 347-68; Casler, Kline, and Taber, *Logging Railroad Era in Pennsylvania*, 1: 574-78.

48. Gates, "Federal Land Policy" 316; Lacey, testimony before Ways and Means Committee, U.S. House of Representatives, 20 Nov. 1908, as quoted in Bureau of Corporations, *The Lumber Industry*, 1: pt. 1, 184-85. See also: Goodstein, *Biography of a Businessman*, 177-78.

49. Hidy, Hill, and Nevins, *Timber and Men*, 207-211; Fickle, *Mississippi Forests*, 84 (Weyerhaeuser quote), 88; Hauberg, *Recollections of a Civic Errand Boy*, 188; Hickman, "Yellow Pine Industries," 81-82; Paige Reeves and Virginia S. Harrigan, "The Scotch Lumber Company History" (typescript, 1988; in possession of V. Harrigan, Fulton, Ala.); [James Boyd], "Scotch Lumber Company, Fulton," sawmill descriptions, historical data working files, SPAP, box 77c; Anonymous, "Father and Son," *AL*, 12 (28 Oct. 1911): 3, 71; Edward D. Wetmore Papers (Warren County Historical Society, Warren, Pa. [hereafter WP]), box 58.

50. Goodyear, *Bogalusa Story*, 47, 50, 59, 73-81; Curtis, "Early Development of the Great Southern Lumber Company," 348-55; Fickle, *Mississippi Forests*, 76, 82; Hickman, "Yellow Pine Industries," 83-85; Casler, Kline, and Taber, *Logging Railroad Era in Pennsylvania*, 1: 574-75; Anonymous, "The Largest Lumber Manufacturing Proposition," 54, 64, 68; a map of Goodyear's holdings in 1908 appears on p. 56.

51. *AL*, 5 (19 Mar. 1904): 1; Edward Hines Lumber Company, *Fifty Years, Edward Hines Lumber Company* (Chicago: Hines, 1929); Burns (Oregon) *Times-Herald*, 8 May 1930; Larson, *White Pine Industry*, 260, 373, 380; Hickman, *Mississippi Harvest*, 182; Fickle, *Mississippi Forests*, 88, 91, 92, 101; Napier, *Lower Pearl River's Piney Woods*, 110; Kirwan, *Revolt of the Rednecks*, 213-14 (quote). Weyerhaeuser had become a major stockholder in Hines, which perhaps helps explain his initial hesitancy about expanding into the South.

52. [Defebaugh], *American Lumbermen*, 1: 359-62; Anonymous, "Story of a Great Enterprise," *AL*, 70 (May 9, 1903): 43-90 (quote, p. 44); James Boyd, SPA history, SPAP, X-70, box 5, file 10-a, 3; Tarver, "Clan of Toil," 57-68,

73-80, and passim; John A. Galloway, "John Barber White: Lumberman" (unpub. Ph.D. diss., University of Missouri, 1961); Leslie G. Hill, "History of the Missouri Lumber and Mining Company, 1880-1909" (unpub. Ph.D. diss., University of Missouri, 1949).

53. Fickle, *Mississippi Forests*, 83-85, 88; [Defebaugh], *American Lumbermen*, 1: 171-73, 327-30, 395-98; 2: 41-44, 81-84; Anonymous, "Manufacturer and Dealer," *AL*, 55 (July 8, 1899): 1, 14; [Boyd], "Fordyce Lumber Company, Fordyce, [Arkansas]," sawmill descriptions, historical data working files, SPAP, box 77c; [Boyd], "Crossett Lumber Company, Crossett, [Arkansas]," ibid.; [Boyd], "Bradley Lumber Company of Arkansas, Warren", ibid.; [Boyd], "Alger-Sullivan Lumber Company, Century, [Florida]" ibid.; subscribers to Southern Pine Association, 1924, ibid., P-2, box 39(a), SPA folder; Ingram, *Autobiography*, 80-81; Drobney, *Lumbermen and Log Sawyers*, 44-60; Baynard Kendrick and Barry Walsh, *A History of Florida Forests* (Gainesville: University Press of Florida, 2007), 237-47; John M. Collier, *The First Fifty Years of the Southern Pine Association* (New Orleans: Southern Pine Association, 1965), 19, 21; Bell, "Alger," 407; Anonymous, "Herman Dierks," *AL*, (May 24, 1913): 1, 73; F. McD. Dierks, Jr., *The Legacy of Peter Henry Dierks, 1824-1972* (Tacoma, Wash.: by the author, 1972). Walker mistakenly gives Dierks's first name as Hans.

54. Dudley and Avery, oral history interview; Southern Forestry Congress, "Proceedings of the Second Forestry Congress," New Orleans, Jan. 28-30, 1920, SPAP, X-69, box 4, file 11a, p. 46; list of subscribers, Sept. 1, 1920, and June 1, 1924, ibid., P-2, box 39(a), SPA folder; Massey, "History of the Lumber Industry in Alabama and West Florida," 42, 47; Fickle, *Mississippi Forests*, 82-85.

55. Maxwell and Baker, *Sawdust Empire*, 166; list of subscribers, Sept. 1, 1920, and June 1, 1924, SPAP, P-2, box 39(a), SPA folder; Hickman, *Mississippi Harvest*, 178-82. On Kurth, see: Maxwell and Baker, *Sawdust Empire*, 105-111; Simon W. Henderson, Jr., oral history interview by R. S. Maxwell, n.p., 10 Aug. 1964, FHC, OH-23.

56. Hickman, *Mississippi Harvest*, 50-51, 119-20, 153, 168-75; Fickle, *Mississippi Forests*, 86.

57. Lenore K. Bradley, *Robert Alexander Long: A Lumberman of the Gilded Age* (Durham, N.C.: Forest History Society, 1989), xi-xiv, 1-16 (1st quote, p. xiv; 2nd quote, p. 16). See also: Anonymous, "From Tree to Trade in Yellow Pine," *AL*, 75 (July, 2, 1904): 47-116; and Fickle, *Mississippi Forests*, 83.

58. Bradley, *Long*, 17-31, 50-51, 175-79, 181; Maxwell and Baker, *Sawdust Empire*, 93-95. Although Long's first yard was in Kansas City, Kansas, and early sales were largely in that state, when he incorporated in 1884, he did so in Missouri, and in 1891 he moved his corporate headquarters to Kansas City, Missouri.

59. *Lumber Trade Journal*, n.v. (15 Mar. 1902): 23 (1st quote); Bradley, *Long*, xi (2nd quote), 32-35, 52.

60. On Kirby, see Maxwell and Baker, *Sawdust Empire*, 98-105, Tarver, "Clan of Toil," 49-50, 70-71, 158-61, 918-19; Mary Lasswell, *John Henry Kirby, Prince of the Pines* (Austin, Tex.: Encino Press, 1967); Jack Dionne, *A Brief Story of the Life of John Henry Kirby* (Houston, Tex.: Kirby Lumber Company, 1940);

and Anonymous, "Timber Resources of East Texas, Their Recognition and Development by John Henry Kirby . . . ," *AL*, 68 (Nov. 22, 1902): 43-78.

61. John W. Minton, oral history interview by R. S. Maxwell, n.p., 13 May 1956 and 5 Aug. 1958, FHC, OH-27.

62. *Houston Chronicle*, 13 Nov. 1901; *Timb.*, 21 (Feb. 1920): 51. See also: Maxwell, "Lumbermen of the East Texas Frontier," 14-15; Anonymous, "Timber Resources of East Texas," 43-78; John O. King, *The Early History of the Houston Oil Company of Texas, 1901-1908* (Houston: Texas Gulf Coast Historical Assoc., 1959); Arthur M. Johnson, "The Early Texas Oil Industry: Pipelines and the Birth of an Integrated Oil Industry, 1901-1911," *JSH*, 32 (1966): 516-28.

63. Kirby's personal finances were as strained as his lumber company's. See: Analysis of John H. Kirby—Personal Account, 31 Dec. 1901 and 31 Mar. 1904, KLCP, box 7.

64. F. A. Helbig to C. A. Lyon, 26 Mar. 1904, KLCP, box 7; manager, mills & logging to R. L. Weatherby, 2 Apr. 1904, ibid.; O. H. Pennock, Jr., to J. S. Rice, 17 June 1904, ibid.; Rice to D. Woodhead, 20 June 1904, ibid.; B. F. Bonner to F. G. Pettibone, 5 Oct. 1907, ibid., box 38. Kirby tried to avoid closing mills by "passing pay-days, which act was misunderstood and for which I was roundly abused." Kirby to A. L. Harris, 22 Nov. 1907, ibid.

65. Helbig to Lyon, 26 Mar. 1904, ibid., box 7; Bonner to Pettibone, 5 Oct. 1907, ibid., box 38; KLC treasurer to Lyon, 19 Nov. 1907 and 11 June 1908, ibid.; KLC, statement of lumber cut from Houston Oil Company lands, July 1, 1901 to Aug. 31, 1907, n.d., ibid.

66. [Kirby] to J. W. Hammond, 14 Aug. 1908, ibid.

67. Without control, the Santa Fe could not be assured of Kirby's freight. In spite of friction with KLC's management, the Orange & Northwestern Railway, associated with Lutcher & Moore, hauled a portion of Kirby's cut. See: B. F. Bonner to W. W. Yeatman, 15 June 1907, ibid.; Maxwell and Baker, *Sawdust Empire*, 31.

68. Lasswell, *John Henry Kirby*, 186-200; Collier, *First Fifty Years of the Southern Pine Association*, 44-45, 171; James E. Fickle, *The New South and the "New Competition": Trade Association Development in the Southern Pine Industry* (Urbana: University of Illinois Press, 1980), 95-103; Keith L. Bryant, Jr., *History of the Atchison, Topeka and Santa Fe Railway* (New York: Macmillan, 1974), 189, 364.

69. [SPA], "Survey 1913 Values of Southern Pine," SPAP, X-69, box 4; Southern Forester's Conference, "Proceedings of the Southern Forester's Conference," Jacksonville, Fla., 3-4 Jan. 1919, ibid., file 13c, esp. pp. 48-57; Southern Pine Association, "Proceedings of the Fourth Annual Convention . . . ," New Orleans, 25-26 Feb. 1919, ibid., box 73b, p. 173; Boyd, SPA history, SPAP, X-70, box 5, file 10-a, 3-5; J. E. Rhodes, testimony, c. 1924, ibid., X-67, box 2, file 9a, pp. 2-3, 13-14; Walker, *Southern Forest*, 100-101; Drobney, *Lumbermen and Log Sawyers*, 2-3, 7-8, 209; Fickle, *Mississippi Forests*, 86, 91; Horn, *This Fascinating Lumber Business*, 31-32, 100. Most descriptions of the bonanza era in the Southern pineries focus on individual states. However, see: Williams, *Americans and their Forests*, 238-85. In spite of his all-inclusive

title, Defebaugh's *History of the Lumber Industry* does not deal with the post-colonial South.

70. Hickman, *Mississippi Harvest*, 177; Fickle, *Mississippi Forests*, 88. The growth of nearby Laurel was almost as impressive. John Kemper started development by building a small mill at its key railroad junction. Others followed, including the Eastman-Gardiner Lumber Company, whose annual capacity had expanded by 1899 to sixty million board feet; by 1904 it was shipping 3,530 carloads of lumber a day and employed one thousand workers. By 1915 Laurel was the largest lumber-producing center in the state. See: Hickman, *Mississippi Harvest*, 177-83; Jo Dent Hodge, "The Lumber Industry in Laurel, Mississippi, at the Turn of the Nineteenth Century," *Journal of Mississippi History*, 35 (1973): 361-79.

71. Anonymous, "When Will the South Cease to be a Factor?" *Timb.* 21 (Feb. 1920): 49-50 (map, p. 50).

72. Goodyear, *Bogalusa Story*, 3, 16, 18, 27-30, 44 (1st quote); Tarver, "Clan of Toil," 8-12 (2nd quote, pp. 8-9); Casler, Kline and Taber, *Logging Railroad Era in Pennsylvania*, 1: 574, 576-78.

73. Hickman, "Yellow Pine Industries," 85; Tarver, "Clan of Toil," 12; Drobney, *Lumbermen and Log Sawyers*, 8-9, 61-62, 102-105.

74. Ruth A. Allen, *East Texas Lumber Workers: An Economic and Social Picture, 1870-1950* (Austin: University of Texas Press, 1961), 51-59; Drobney, *Lumbermen and Log Sawyers*, 84, 104. S. S. Henry, a native Southern lumberman, thought blacks were the best sawmill workers, but the opinion was not universally shared. See: Hickman, *Mississippi Harvest*, 241-45.

75. This was not just true of common laborers. This author's grandfather, listed in the Louisiana census as an "engineer," was in fact a millwright, and at his wedding in 1882 signed the marriage record with an X.

76. Maxwell and Baker, *Sawdust Empire*, 117-18, 140-42; Hickman, *Mississippi Harvest*, 233-34, 245-46; Shofner, "Negro Laborers and the Forest Industries in Florida," 189; Charles F. Taylor, "Special Report on Industrial Conditions in the Mills and Camps of the Southern Pine Association" (typescript, 1918), (SPAP), Q-22, file 69b, p. 3 (1st quote), 11 (2nd quote). James Tarver paints a more complex picture. See: Tarver, "Clan of Toil," 29-30, 43-44, 75-76, 110-11, 118-20, 122, 134, 137-38, 165-55, 195-96, 253-54. Although wages were rising in the South, the gap between it and the rest of the nation widened following the Civil War. For comparative regional data, see: Perloff et al., *Regions, Resources and Economic Growth*, 170-80, 184-90.

77. Denman quoted in Southern Forestry Congress, "Proceedings of the Second Forestry Congress," (SPAP), X-69, box 4, file 11-d, p. 66-67; Tarver, "Clan of Toil," 9-10, 15-16, 21-23, 28-30, 49, 57-58, 83-84, 101; Drobney, *Lumbermen and Log Sawyers*, 61-62, 102-104, 177. The Southern Pine Association saw sale of cutover to would-be farmers as a way of relieving members of denuded lands and—in spite of the arguments of Frank Gilchrist and others that the soil lacked the nutrients for successful agriculture—encouraged establishing these hardscrabble farms. Cutover Lands Committee, minutes, 14 Dec. 1916, SPAP, R-4, box 70b, 1916 board minutes file, pp. 21-23; ibid., 2 Apr. 1917, 1917 board minutes file, pp. 17-20; ibid., 11 Oct. 1917, pp. 9-11; ibid., report to board of directors, 9 July 1920, 1920 board minutes file, p. 14; [National Forestry Conference], "Report of Forestry Conference," Chicago,

24 Oct. 1919, ibid., X-69, box 4, file 8, pp. b11-b12, i3. See also: Maxwell and Baker, *Sawdust Empire*, 196; Hickman, *Mississippi Harvest*, 261-65.

78. Taylor, "Special Report," 28 (2nd quote), 33 (3rd quote), 35 (1st quote).

79. Thomas D. Clark, "The Impact of the Timber Industry on the South," *Mississippi Quarterly*, 25 (1972): 158-60; SPA, "Pine and Patriotism: Official Report of the Second Annual Meeting," New Orleans, 19-20 Feb. 1917, SPAP, S-10, box 85b, p. 219 (quote); Pyne, *Fire in America*, 143-60; John Shea, "Our Pappies Burned the Woods," *AF*, 46 (1940): 159-62. For an analysis of the continuing problem, see: Thomas Hansbrough, "A Sociological Analysis of Man-Caused Fire in Louisiana" (unpub. Ph.D. diss., Louisiana State University, 1961).

80. Clark, "The Impact of the Timber Industry on the South," 158-59. Many did not foresee how permanent changes would be. One resident recalled: locals took jobs in mill and woods operations viewing "the cutting of great tracts of woods as an inevitable but temporary intrusion into their self-sufficient and largely uncommercial livelihood; . . . all knew that after a few years Gulf and the other companies would have 'cut out' and Calcasieu Parish would be theirs again." Otis Dunbar Richardson, "Fullerton, Louisiana: An American Monument," *JFH*, 27 (1983): 200.

81. Curtis, "Early Development of the Great Southern Lumber Company," 353-55; Richardson, "Fullerton," 198-99; Reeves and Harrigan, "Scotch Lumber Company History," passim; Bradley, *Long*, 48-49; Thad Sitton and James H. Conrad, *Nameless Towns: Texas Sawmill Communities, 1880-1942* (Austin: University of Texas Press, 1998), 35; Defebaugh, *American Lumbermen*, 2: 331.

82. Clark, "Impact of the Timber Industry on the South," 160 (quote); N. B. Weatherford, oral history interview by R. S. Maxwell, Camden, Tex., 13 Oct. 1959, FHC, OH-39, 54; George F. Middlebrook, oral history interview by R. S. Maxwell, Caro, Tex., 15 Oct. 1959, ibid., OH-26, 28-30; Clyde J. Woodward, oral history interview by R. S. Maxwell, Nacogdoches, Tex., 16 Jan. 1960, ibid., OH-43, 64-67; Taylor, "Special Report," 5-7, 13, 23-25, 33-35; Peter A. Speek, "Notes on Investigations of Three Texas Lumber Towns," U.S. Department of Labor, Reports of the Commission on Industrial Relations, 1914 (microfilm copy, Stephen F. Austin State University Library, Nacogdoches, Tex.); Hickman, *Mississippi Harvest*, 249-53; Fickle, *Mississippi Forests*, 113-17; Tarver, "Clan of Toil," 14, 126; William T. Chambers, "Life in a Southern Sawmill Community," *Journal of Geography*, 30 (1931): 181-89. For extended studies, see: George Alvin Stokes, "Lumbering in Southwest Louisiana: A Study of the Industry as a Culturo-Geographic Factor" (unpub. Ph.D. diss., Louisiana State University, 1954); Allen, *East Texas Lumber Workers*; Sitton and Conrad, *Nameless Towns*, esp. 34-126; Maxwell and Baker, *Sawdust Empire*, 136-54; Tarver, "Clan of Toil," 92-151.

83. Goodyear, *Bogalusa Story*, 83-85 (1st quote, p. 83), 87, 107 (2nd quote); Lillard, *The Great Forest*, 301-308; Curtis, "Early Development of the Great Southern Lumber Company," 357-58; Casler, Kline, and Taber, *Logging Railroad Era in Pennsylvania*, 1: 575. See also: Hickman, *Mississippi Harvest*, 251-52; Sitton and Conrad, *Nameless Towns*, 51. Jeffrey Drobney is less critical. See: Drobney, *Lumbermen and Log Sawyers*, 177-94, 199-203.

84. Sitton and Conrad, *Nameless Towns*, 80-84, 92-102; I. R. Palmer, oral
    history interview by R. S. Maxwell, n.p., 15 Aug. 1958, FHC, OH-32, p. 41;
    Tarver, "Clan of Toil," 14, 126. See also: Kendrick and Walsh, *History of
    Florida Forests*, 287-303; Harry Weaver, "Labor Practices in the East Texas
    Lumber Industry" (unpub. M.A. thesis, Stephen F. Austin State University,
    Nacogdoches, Tex., 1961); Richard W. Massey, Jr., "Labor Conditions in the
    Lumber Industry in Alabama, 1880-1914," *Journal of the Alabama Academy
    of Science*, 37 (1966): 172-81; Drobney, *Lumbermen and Log Sawyers*, 182,
    194-98.
85. Maxwell and Baker, *Sawdust Empire*, 53, 55, 65, 128-33, 141-42; Sitton and
    Conrad, *Nameless Towns*, 52-55, 113-126, 148-52; George T. Morgan, Jr., "The
    Gospel of Wealth Goes South: John Henry Kirby and Labor's Struggle for
    Self-Determination, 1901-1916," *Southwestern Historical Quarterly*, 75 (1971):
    186-97; Morgan, "No Compromise—No Recognition: John Henry Kirby,
    the Southern Lumber Operators' Association, and Unionism in the Piney
    Woods, 1906-1916," *Labor History*, 10 (1969): 193-204; James E. Fickle, "The
    Louisiana-Texas Lumber War of 1911-1912," *Louisiana History*, 16 (1975): 59-
    85; Grady McWhiney, "Louisiana Socialists in the Early Twentieth Century:
    A Study of Rustic Radicalism," ibid., 20 (1954): 315-36; Stokes, "Lumbering in
    Southwest Louisiana," 3-4.
86. Taylor, "Special Report," 12, 14-15, 23; Maxwell and Baker, *Sawdust Empire*,
    123, 145-47; Shofner, "Negro Laborers and the Forest Industries in Florida,"
    183; Sitton and Conrad, *Nameless Towns*, 71-77, 105-107; Allen, *East Texas
    Lumber Workers*, 54, 56-59, 86-87; Hickman, *Mississippi Harvest*, 238-39;
    Fickle, *Mississippi Forests*, 104-113; Drobney, *Lumbermen and Log Sawyers*,
    84-85.
87. William F. Holmes, "Whitecapping in Mississippi: Agrarian Violence in
    the Populist Era," *Mid-America*, 55 (1973): 134-47; Napier, *Lower Pearl
    River's Piney Woods*, 84 (quote); Hickman, *Mississippi Harvest*, 239-40;
    Fickle, *Mississippi Forests*, 108. Night riders sometimes adopted such tactics
    elsewhere. See: Shofner, "Negro Laborers and the Forest Industries in
    Florida," 185; Tarver, "Clan of Toil," 110-11, 149-50, 153-58, 257.
88. Goodyear, *Bogalusa Story*, 37, 42; Curtis, "Early Development of the Great
    Southern Lumber Company," 351-52. See also: Hickman, *Mississippi Harvest*,
    88-100, 254-59; Taylor, "Special Report," 13.
89. McWhiney, "Louisiana Socialists," 315-36. See also: James R. Green, *Grass-
    Roots Socialism:: Radical Movements in the Southwest, 1895-1943* (Baton
    Rouge: Louisiana State University Press, 1978).
90. Maxwell and Baker, *Sawdust Empire*, 128-33; Morgan, "No Compromise—
    No Recognition," 193-204; Fickle, "Louisiana-Texas Lumber War," 59-85;
    Hickman, *Mississippi Harvest*, 235-39; Bradley, *Long*, 66-72; Jensen, *Lumber
    and Labor*, 86-94; Fickle, *Mississippi Forests*, 107-109; Drobney, *Lumbermen
    and Log Sawyers*, 111, 124-47; Casler, Kline, and Taber, *Logging Railroad Era
    in Pennsylvania*, 1: 576-78. See also: James R. Green, "The Brotherhood of
    Timber Workers, 1910-1913: A Radical Response to Industrial Capitalism
    in the Southern U.S.A.," *Past and Present*, 60 (1973): 161-200; Merl E. Reed,
    "Lumberjacks and Longshoremen: The I.W.W. in Louisiana," *Labor History*,
    13 (1972): 41-59; papers on strikes, 1891-93 (Alexander Gilmer Papers,

University of Texas, Austin), box 2N39. For a full if rather disjointed account, see: Tarver, "Clan of Toil," 23-25, 107-108, 151-750.

91. Taylor, "Special Report," 28; SPA, minutes of meeting, 5 Dec. 1919, SPAP, R-4, box 70b, 1919 board minutes file; Kirby, statement in "Proceedings of a Mass Meeting of Manufacturers of Southern Pine Lumber," New Orleans, 2-3 Apr. 1919, ibid., Q-22, box 67b, 38-47 (quotes pp. 43, 44-45); Maxwell, "Lumbermen of the East Texas Frontier," 15; Tarver, "Clan of Toil," 445-569, 855-84; Drobney, *Lumbermen and Log Sawyers*, 142-47. See also: James E. Fickle, "Management Looks at the 'Labor Problem': The Southern Pine Industry during World War I and the Postwar Era," *JSH*, 40 (1974): 61-76.

92. Southwestern Lumbermen's Association, report of meeting, Galveston, Tex., 21 July 1888, SPAP, R-17, box 77a; Boyd, SPA history, SPAP, X-70, box 5, file 9g, 1-2; 9i, 1; 9j, 1-2; SPA, "Official Report of the First Annual Meeting," 19, 20, 23; "Official Report of Mass Meeting," 16-17, 49, 91-92; SPA, "Pine and Patriotism," 11; "Report of Forestry Conference," M-7; J. E. Rhodes, Congressional testimony, ca. 1924, SPAP, X-67, file 9a; Kirby to J. E. Defebaugh, 24 Feb. 1908, KLCP, box 38; W. C. Jones, oral history interview by R. S. Maxwell, n.p., 8 Jan. 1965, FHC, OH-24, 26. For full discussion of SPA activities, see: Fickle, *The New South and the New Competition*.

93. *Timb.*, 21 (Nov. 1919): 46.

94. Southern Foresters Conference, "Proceedings," 6-7, 61, 118-19; Hickman, *Mississippi Harvest*, 260-63; "Meeting of Southern Foresters," New Orleans, 18-19 Jan. 1918, transcript; SPAP, X-69, box 4, file 10a, pp. 62-63, 79, 81; [Defebaugh], *American Lumbermen*, 2: 331-32; Fickle, *Mississippi Forests*, 101-104 (quote, p. 101); Tarver, "Clan of Toil," 88-89; George A. Stokes, "Lumbering and Western Louisiana Cultural Landscapes," *Annals of the Association of American Geographers*, 47 (1957): 250-66. There were exceptions. See: Maxwell and Baker, *Sawdust Empire*, 168-80; Clark, *Greening of the South*, 48-50.

95. F. V. Dunham, "How the Small Mills are Affecting the Southern Pine Industry," in SPA, "Official Reports of the Proceedings of the Semi-Annual Meeting of the Subscribers to the Southern Pine Association," Memphis, 27 June 1924 (SPAP), Q-24, box 68b, 18-25; SPA, "Pine and Patriotism," 8; ibid., "Report of Forestry Conference," 6; Boyd, SPA history, SPAP, X-70, box 5, file 10-a, 3-5; SPA, "Lumber and Liquidation: Official Report of the Sixth Annual Meeting," New Orleans, 5-6 Apr. 1921, SPAP, S-10, box 85b, 17-18; Anonymous, "Probable Life of the Texas Pine Industry," 21 *Timb.* (Feb. 1920): 51; Anonymous, "When Will the South Cease to be a Factor?" 49-50; Maxwell and Baker, *Sawdust Empire*, 159-60; 197-99. The Southern pine industry's labor force doubled from 1880 to 1909 and then began a steady contraction. See: Tarver, "Clan of Toil," 237.

96. Fickle, *Mississippi Forests*, 117-19; Denman, quoted in Southern Forestry Congress, "Proceedings of Second Forestry Congress," 66-67.

97. Jack P. Odem, "Charles Holmes Herty and the Birth of the Southern Newsprint Paper Industry, 1927-1940," *JFH*, 21 (1977): 77-89; Elwood R. Maunder, ed., *Voices from the South: Recollections of Four Foresters* (Santa Cruz, Calif.: Forest History Society, 1977), passim; Clark, *Greening of the South*, 102-132.

98. Mikko Saikku, "Home in the Big Forest: Decline of the Ivory-billed Woodpecker and Its Habitat in the United States," in *Encountering the Past in Nature: Essays in Environmental History*, Timo Myllyntaus and Mikko Saikku, ed. (Helsinki, Finland: University of Helsinki Press, 1999), 87-119. See also: Michael K. Steinberg, *Stalking the Ghost Bird: The Elusive Ivory-Billed Woodpecker in Louisiana* (Baton Rouge: Louisiana State University Press, 2008). Long thought extinct, the ivory-billed woodpecker was spotted again in 2005.

99. Clark, *Greening of the South*, 131-47; Clark, "The Lasting Heritage: Land and Trees," in Lucius F. and Linda V. Ellsworth, eds., *The Cultural Legacy of the Gulf Coast, 1870-1940* (Pensacola, Fla.: Gulf Coast History and Humanities Conference, 1976), 17-35; Clark, "Impact of the Timber Industry on the South," 157-60; Fickle, *Mississippi Forests*, 120-94; Portland *Oregonian*, 26 Jan. 1981; William G. Robbins, *Landscapes of Conflict: The Oregon Story, 1940-2000* (Seattle: University of Washington Press, 2004), 173-75. See also: Douglas W. MacCleery, *American Forests: A History of Resiliency and Recovery* (Durham, N.C.: Forest History Society, 1993), esp. 39-46.

Chapter Eleven

1. John Meares, *Voyages made in the Years 1788 and 1789 from China to the North West Coast of America* . . . (London: Logographic Press, 1790), 224.

2. Charles A. Geyer, "Notes on the Vegetation and General Character of the Missouri and Oregon Territories, Made during a Botanical Journey . . . 1843 and 1844," *London Journal of Botany*, 5 (1846): 198-201 (quote, p. 199).

3. George Vancouver, *A Voyage of Discovery to the North Pacific Ocean* . . . (3 vols.; London: Robinson and Edwards, 1798), 2: 227-28. On Vancouver in Puget Sound, see: Robert B. Whitebrook, "Vancouver's Anchorages on Puget Sound," *PNQ*, 44 (1953): 115-28; Murray Morgan, *Puget's Sound: A Narrative of Early Tacoma and the Southern Sound* (Seattle: University of Washington Press, 1979), 3-17.

4. William Fraser Tolmie, *The Journals of William Fraser Tolmie, Physician and Fur Trader* (Vancouver, B.C.: Mitchell Press, 1963), 166-67.

5. Quoted in Robert Bunting, *The Pacific Raincoast: Environment and Culture in an American Eden, 1778-1900* (Lawrence: University Press of Kansas, 1997), 26. Bunting over-simplifies early reactions to the forests of the Pacific Coast.

6. The names used illustrate the newness of the flora. Douglas fir was not a fir, nor as Tolmie and (on occasion) Geyer called it, a pine, but in a genus of its own. The tree's long-used scientific name *Pseudotsuga taxifolia* (now replaced by *P. menziesii*) translates as yew-leaved false hemlock—clearly, even its botanical describer did not know quite what to make of it. Similarly, Western red cedar did not belong to any of the genera commonly called cedar—it merely resembled some of them.

7. Geyer provides a useful illustration. When he returned east with the botanical specimens he had gathered, he did so by sea, for his overland journey to the Northwest had made him aware of the difficulties of that route. In returning by sea, Geyer chose to ignore his earlier promise to turn his finds over to George Engelmann of St. Louis, who had outfitted him, and to brave the

ire of Asa Gray, Sir William Jackson Hooker, and the period's botanical establishment. He considered a broken bond and disapproval of leading botanists a lesser danger than returning east by land. On Geyer, see: Thomas R. Cox, "Charles A. Geyer: Pioneer Botanist of Upper Oregon," *IY*, 43 (1999): 11-32.

8. Peter G. Boag, *Environment and Experience: Settlement Culture in Nineteenth-Century Oregon* (Berkeley: University of California Press, 1992), 28-41; Bunting, *Pacific Raincoast*, 73-75; William A. Bowen, *The Willamette Valley: Migration and Settlement on the Oregon Frontier* (Seattle: University of Washington Press, 1978), esp. chapters 5 and 6; Harlow Zinser Head, "The Oregon Donation Land Claims and their Patterns" (unpub. Ph.D. diss., University of Oregon, 1971).

9. Elisha L. Applegate to Mrs. Lindsay Applegate, 4 June 1866 (O. C. Applegate Papers, University of Oregon Library, Eugene), box 2, folder 6; Earl Pomeroy, *The Pacific Slope: A History of California, Oregon, Washington, Idaho, Utah, and Nevada* (New York: Knopf, 1965), 135-38; Jesse S. Douglas, "Origins of the Population of Oregon in 1850," *PNQ*, 41 (1950): 95-108; Robert W. Johannsen, *Frontier Politics and the Sectional Conflict: The Pacific Northwest on the Eve of the Civil War* (Seattle: University of Washington Press, 1955), 197-201, 209-210, 216-18; Jerry C. Towle, "Changing Geography of Willamette Valley Woodlands," *OHQ*, 83 (1982): 66-87. See also: Towle, "Woodland in the Willamette Valley: An Historical Geography" (unpub. Ph.D. diss., University of Oregon, 1974).

10. Eugène Duflot de Mofras, *Travels on the Pacific Coast*, trans. by Marguerite Eyer Wilbur (2 vols.; Santa Ana, Calif.: Fine Arts, 1937), 2: 111; Edmond S. Meany, Jr., "History of the Lumber Industry of the Pacific Northwest to 1917" (unpub. Ph.D. diss., Harvard University, 1935), 80-83, 89-93; John A. Hussey, *Champoeg: Place of Transition* (Portland: Oregon Historical Society, 1967), 68.

11. Arthur L. Throckmorton, *Oregon Argonauts: Merchant Adventurers on the Western Frontier* (Portland: Oregon Historical Society, 1961), 53-69; Dorothy O. Johansen and Charles O. Gates, *Empire of the Columbia: A History of the Pacific Northwest* (rev. ed.; New York: Harper & Row, 1967), 211-21; Bunting, *Pacific Raincoast*, 91-92. For a more positive view of Oregon's prospects, see: James R. Gibson, *Farming the Frontier: The Agricultural Opening of the Oregon Country, 1786-1846* (Seattle: University of Washington Press, 1985), 135-47.

12. Robert J. Parker, "Larkin, Anglo-American Businessman in Mexican California," in Adele Ogden and Engel Sluiter, ed., *Greater America: Essays in Honor of Herbert Eugene Bolton* (Berkeley: University of California Press, 1945), 415-29.

13. Forest Service, California Forest and Range Experiment Station, *A Century of Lumber Production in California and Nevada*, Forest Survey Release no. 20 (Berkeley: California Forest and Range Experiment Station, 1953), 12. On earlier lumbering operations, see: C. Raymond Clar, *California Government and Forestry from Spanish Days until the Creation of the Department of Natural Resources in 1927* (Sacramento: California Division of Forestry,

1959), 3-52; Alan K. Brown, *Sawpits in the Spanish Redwoods* (San Mateo, Calif.: San Mateo County Historical Assoc., 1966); Sherwood D. Burgess, "Lumbering in Hispanic California," *California Historical Society Quarterly*, 41 (1962): 237-48; Meany, "History of the Lumber Industry," 47-83.

14. Robert E. Ficken, *The Forested Land: A History of Lumbering in Western Washington* (Seattle: University of Washington Press, 1987), 21-26; Clar, *California Government and Forestry*, 42-44.

15. On these outports, see: Karl Kortum and Roger Olmsted, " '. . . it is a Dangerous-Looking Place': Sailing Days on the Redwood Coast," *California Historical Society Quarterly*, 50 (1971): 43-58; Gordon Newell and Joe Williamson, *Pacific Lumber Ships* (New York: Bonanza Books, 1960), 138-46; Lynwood Carranco, *Redwood Lumber Industry* (San Marino, Calif.: Golden West, 1982), 104-115.

16. Even around California's Humboldt Bay, which had more nearby land suitable for agriculture than most West Coast lumber ports, farming followed rather than preceded lumbering and was continually overshadowed by it. On its early development, see: Daniel A. Cornford, *Workers and Dissent in the Redwood Empire* (Philadelphia: Temple University Press, 1987), 7-23; Owen C. Coy, *The Humboldt Bay Region, 1850-1875: A Study in the American Colonization of California* (Los Angeles: California State Historical Assoc., 1929).

17. For a fuller account of the cargo mills, see: Thomas R. Cox, *Mills and Markets: A History of the Pacific Coast Lumber Industry to 1900* (Seattle: University of Washington Press, 1974).

18. Originally from Brewster, Mass., Crosby had brought supplies from New York to Oregon in 1845 and stayed on to engage in the trade between California and Oregon. See: Arthur L Throckmorton, *Oregon Argonauts: Merchant Adventurers on the Western Frontier* (Portland: Oregon Historical Society, 1961), 57, 90, 101.

19. Nathaniel Crosby to Joseph Lane, 22 July (quote), 13 Aug. 1854 (Joseph Lane Papers, Oregon Historical Society, Portland); San Francisco *Daily Herald*, 28 July 1855; Crosby to T. J. Dryer, in Portland *Oregonian*, 18 Aug. 1855. Cf. A. J. Pope to Wm. Pope & Sons, 23 Jan. 1855 (A. J. Pope Papers, Pope & Talbot Archives, Port Gamble, Wash.).

20. For context, see: Thomas R. Cox, "Harbingers of Change: American Merchants and the Formosa Annexation Scheme," *PHR*, 42 (1973): 167-73.

21. Development in Puget Sound's hinterland was limited until completion of transcontinental rail connections in the 1880s; mills on the Oregon and northern California coasts had to wait even longer for rail lines from outside. Only the difficult, sandbar-strewn Columbia offered a useable water route through the Coast Range; other streams that crossed it—the Klamath, Rogue, and Umpqua—were not navigable, but the absence of good transmontane transportation did protect coastal operators from competition from the interior.

22. This argument is developed further in Cox, *Mills and Markets*, 71-100, 109, 114, 214-26, and, more broadly, in Cox, "The Passage to India Revisited: Asian Trade and the Development of the Far West, 1850-1900," in John A.

Carroll, ed., *Reflections of Western Historians* (Tucson: University of Arizona Press, 1969), 85-103. See also: Dorothy Marie Sherman, "A Brief History of the Lumber Industry in the Douglas Fir Belt of Oregon" (unpub. M.A. thesis, University of Oregon, 1934), 10-12, 41-44.

23. On Simpson, see: Hubert Howe Bancroft, *Chronicles of the Builders of the Commonwealth* . . . (8 vols.; San Francisco: History Company, 1891-92), 4: 432-39; Thomas R. Cox, "Lumber and Ships: The Business Empire of Asa Mead Simpson," *FH*, 14 (1970): 14-26; Stephen Dow Beckham, "Asa Mead Simpson: Lumberman and Shipbuilder," *OHQ*, 68 (1967): 259-73; Beckham, *The Simpsons of Shore Acres* (Coos Bay, Ore.: Arago Books, 1971), 1-19.

24. Caspar T. Hopkins, "The California Recollections of Caspar T. Hopkins," *California Historical Society Quarterly*, 25 (1946): 339; John Brown, *Reminiscences and Incidents of Early Days of San Francisco (1845-1850)* (San Francisco: Grabhorn Press, 1933), 106-107.

25. There were numerous lumber shipments from Maine to California during this period. See: Brian H. Smalley, "Some Aspects of the Maine to San Francisco Trade, 1849-1852," *JW*, 6 (1967): 593-603.

26. The Umpqua community where Simpson expected to obtain lumber proved ephemeral; he soon turned to other sources. See: Verne Bright, "The Lost County, Umpqua," *OHQ*, 51 (1950): 211-26; A. G. Walling, *History of Jackson, Josephine, Douglas, Curry and Coos Counties in Oregon* (San Francisco: Walling, 1884), 401-404; Harold A. Minter, *Umpqua Valley, Oregon, and Its Pioneers* (Portland, Ore.: Binfords & Mort, 1967), 75-83.

27. Robert E. Johnson, "Schooners Out of Coos Bay" (unpub. M.A. thesis, University of Oregon, 1953).

28. Portland *Oregonian*, 1 Aug. 1868.

29. George Emerson to Samuel Perkins, 25 July 1892, Emerson letterbooks (Henry Suzzalo Library, University of Washington, Seattle).

30. Cox, "Lumber and Ships," 22-24.

31. There are several accounts of such mills, a number solidly based on manuscript material. See: Edwin T. Coman, Jr., and Helen M. Gibbs, *Time, Tide and Timber: A Century of Pope & Talbot* (Stanford, Calif.: Stanford University Press, 1949); Andrew Price, Jr., *Port Blakely: The Community Captain Renton Built* (Seattle: Port Blakely Books, 1989); Murray Morgan, *The Mill on the Boot: The Story of the St. Paul & Tacoma Lumber Company* (Seattle: University of Washington Press, 1982); Howard Brett Melendy, "One Hundred Years of the Redwood Lumber Industry, 1850-1950" (unpub. Ph.D. diss., Stanford University, 1952).

32. Coman and Gibbs, *Time, Tide and Timber*, 6-13, 30-35, 51-55; Ficken, *Forested Land*, 27-36; E. L. Riddell, "History of Port Gamble," in Poulsbo (Wash.) *Kitsap County Herald*, 10 and 17 July 1931.

33. To free sawmill managers to focus on the manufacture of lumber, the partners incorporated Puget Sound Commercial Company in 1876 to own and operate their growing fleet of sailing vessels and tugboats. Coman and Gibbs, *Time, Tide and Timber*, 115.

34. Ibid., 103-105, 110-11; Ficken, *Forested Land*, 36.

35. Coman and Gibbs, *Time, Tide and Timber*, 80-81, 118-19; Honolulu *Pacific Commercial Advertiser*, 4 Sept. 1856; Tacoma *Herald*, 17 May 1878. The

Herald's claim was an over-statement, but Puget Mill's market share was clearly substantial and dependable.

36. On Yesler, see: John R. Finger, "Seattle's First Sawmill, 1853-1869: A Study in Frontier Enterprise," *FH*, 15 (1972): 24-31.

37. Price, *Port Blakely*, 8-15; Iva L. Buchanan, "An Economic History of Kitsap County, Washington, to 1889" (unpub. Ph.D. diss., University of Washington, 1930), 89, 237-39, 279-80.

38. Price, *Port Blakely*, 16-27; Buchanan, "Economic History of Kitsap County," 269-76; *West Shore*, 8 (1882): 55, 183.

39. E. G. Ames to Cyrus Walker, 16 Apr. 1890 (E. G. Ames Papers, Henry Suzzalo Library, University of Washington, Seattle), Walker, personal corres.

40. Buchanan, "Economic History of Kitsap County," 173-89; Price, *Port Blakely*, 69-88; Thomas R. Cox, "Single Decks and Flat Bottoms: Building the West Coast's Lumber Fleet, 1850-1920" *JW*, 20 (1981): 70-72; Seattle *Daily Intelligencer*, 18 Aug. 1877; Henry Hall, *Report on the Shipbuilding Industry of the United States*, U.S. Bureau of the Census, Tenth Census (1880), 8: part 4, 132; Gordon Newell, ed., *The H. W. McCurdy Marine History of the Pacific Northwest* . . . (Seattle: Superior, 1966), 21.

41. Seattle *Daily Intelligencer*, 28 Nov. 1877 (quote), 13 July 1877; Richard C. Berner, "The Port Blakely Mill Company, 1876-1889," *PNQ*, 57 (1966): 158-71; Robert E. Ficken with William R. Sherrard, "The Port Blakely Mill Company, 1888-1903," *JFH*, 21 (1977): 202-217; Price, *Port Blakely*, 28-51.

42. Olympia *Columbian*, 10 Dec. 1853; Olympia *Pioneer and Democrat*, 25 Mar., 10 June 1854; Seattle *Daily Intelligencer*, 11, 17, and 21 Oct. 1876, 2 Mar., 16 and 30 May 1877, 22 Jan. 1878; *Chicago Times* reprinted in *CL*, 1 (15 Mar. 1881): 9 (quote); (1 Apr. 1881): 3; Donald Hathaway Clark, "An Analysis of Forest Utilization as a Factor in Colonizing the Pacific Northwest and in Subsequent Population Transitions" (unpub. Ph.D. diss., University of Washington, 1952), 54-55; Ficken, *Forested Land*, 33-34; Bunting, *Pacific Raincoast*, 131-33.

43. San Francisco *Journal of Commerce*, reprinted in *CL*, 3 (15 Oct. 1883): 307; San Francisco *Alta California*, 1 Jan. 1886; Clark, "Forest Utilization as a Factor in Colonizing the Northwest," 37 and passim; William H. Hutchinson, "California's Economic Imperialism: An Historical Iceberg," in Carroll, *Reflections of Western Historians*, 67-83.

44. *Port Orford Post*, reprinted in *Coos Bay News*, 2 June 1880. See also: Portland *Oregonian*, 23 Apr. 1865; Stephen Dow Beckham, *Coos Bay: The Pioneer Period, 1851-1890* (Coos Bay, Ore.: Arago Books, 1973), 40-44; William G. Robbins, *Hard Times in Paradise: Coos Bay, Oregon, 1850-1986* (Seattle: University of Washington Press, 1988), 12-20. Robbins (p. 20) mistakenly identifies A. M. Simpson as the target of Upton's attack.

45. The term evolved into "skid row" and came to refer to the sleazy districts of brothels, bars, and cheap lodging houses that were the center of much of a logger's off-season life. Yesler Way in Seattle was the archetype, but initially skid roads had more practical purposes. See: Walter F. McCulloch, *Woods Words: A Comprehensive Dictionary of Loggers Terms* (Portland: Oregon Historical Society, 1958), 167.

46. *West Shore*, 5 (Jan. 1877): 68; Kenneth A. Erickson, "The Morphology of Lumber Settlements in Western Oregon and Washington" (unpub. Ph.D. diss., University of California, Berkeley, 1965), 27-28; Holbrook, *Holy Old Mackinaw*, 172-83; Bunting, *Pacific Raincoast*, 135-36; Meany, "History of the Lumber Industry," 245-46; [Edgar Cherry & Co.], *Redwood and Lumbering in California* ... (San Francisco: Edgar Cherry, 1884), 34-50.

47. *West Shore*, 9 (1982): 136; Erickson, "Morphology of Lumber Settlements," 23; Sherman, "Lumber Industry in the Douglas Fir Belt," 18; Nelson C. Brown, *Logging: The Principles and Methods of Harvesting Timber in the United States and Canada* (New York: John Wiley, 1949)), 93, 95; Andrew Mason Prouty, *More Deadly than War!: Pacific Coast Logging, 1827-1981* (New York: Garland, 1985), 54, 56-57. Crosscuts were soon in use in the Lake States and South too.

48. J. D. Young, "Changes in a Half-Century of Coast Logging Methods and Equipment," *Proceedings Pacific Logging Congress* (1912): 35; Prouty, *More Deadly than War!*, 53-54; Brown, *Logging*, 96-98; Steve Conway, *Logging Practices: Principles of Timber Harvesting Systems* (San Francisco: Miller Freeman, 1976), 104.

49. D. R. Jones to John Kentfield, 2 Feb. 1873, C. Nelson to Kentfield & Co., 21 Jan., 12 Feb. 1873 (Kentfield Company Papers, Bancroft Library, University of California, Berkeley), box 1, file 1; Nelson to Kentfield & Co., 12 Dec. 1878, ibid., box 3-6; J. W. Henderson to Kentfield & Co., 8 June 1876, ibid., box 2-1.

50. Helen M. Gibbs, "Pope & Talbot's Tugboat Fleet," *PNQ*, 42 (1951): 3-23; Gordon R. Newell, *Pacific Tugboats* (Seattle: Superior, 1957); Stephen Dow Beckham, *Swift Flows the River: Log Driving in Oregon* (Coos Bay, Ore.: Arago Books, 1990); Ruth Busse Allingham, "Splash Dams, etc.: A Conversation with Frank Oman," *Sou'wester*, 30 (1995): 3-24; Edwin van Syckle, *They Tried to Cut It All: Grays Harbor, Turbulent Years of Greed and Greatness* (Aberdeen, Wash.: Friends of Aberdeen Public Library, 1980), 150-56.

51. Carranco, *Redwood Lumber Industry*, 85; Coy, *Humboldt Bay Region*, 118, 120-22; Melendy, "One Hundred Years of Redwood Industry," 146, 151-52; David Jones to John Kentfield, 2 Feb. 1872 (Kentfield Papers), box 1-1; C. Nelson to John Kentfield, 25 Mar. 1875, box 1-4; C. Nelson, 5 Oct. 1875; Charles Reed to Kentfield & Co., 6 Nov. 1875, ibid., box 1-7; James McIntyre to Kentfield, 8 and 19 Nov. 1875, ibid., box 1-2; W. J. Woodley to Kentfield & Co., 19 June 1878, ibid., box 3-3; Woodley to Kentfield, 27 Nov. 1878, ibid., box 38; James A. Gibbs, Jr., *Pacific Graveyard: A Narrative of Shipwrecks where the Columbia River Meets the Pacific Ocean* (3rd ed., Portland, Ore.: Binfords & Mort, 1964). The problems of the Columbia were not limited to its bar. See: *West Shore*, 7 (1881): 16-17.

52. For fuller treatments see: Thomas R. Cox, "William Kyle and the Pacific Lumber Trade: A Study in Marginality," *JFH*, 19 (1975): 4-14; Melendy, "One Hundred Years of the Redwood Lumber Industry," 118-32, 179-80, 232-35, 241-49. Bunting overlooks this trade, claiming Oregon's mills only sold in local markets. His statement only applies in the Willamette Valley. See: Bunting, *Pacific Raincoast*, 130-31.

53. Sometimes small coastal mills marketed through lumber companies in San Francisco that functioned as their commission merchants, rather than through commission merchants per se. The disadvantages remained.

54. J. T. Smith to Meyer & Kyle, 9 Aug. 1898 (William Kyle & Sons Papers, Lane County Historical Society, Eugene, Ore.), box 150.

55. S. H. Harmon Lumber Company to Florence Lumber Co., 6 Oct. 1899 (Kyle Papers), box 150. Oregon pine was the trade name long used for Douglas fir.

56. Salem *Oregon Statesman*, 25 Apr. 1853.

57. Roseburg (Ore.) *Plaindealer*, 16 Feb., 2 Mar. 1887. There were difficulties even at the better ports of Grays Harbor, the lower Columbia, and Humboldt Bay. At one point, George Emerson reported nothing had been able to get over Grays Harbor's bar for two weeks and thirteen vessels were backed up, loaded and ready for sea; another time, Charles Nelson reported fog so thick captains could hardly find the bar to enter Humboldt Bay; and from Knappton on the Columbia a captain reported conditions so bad "I have no rest while I lay here." Emerson to A. Simpson, 17 Dec. 1894, Emerson letterbooks; C. Nelson to J. Kentfield (Kentfield Papers), box 1-7; James McIntyre to Kentfield, 8 and 19 (quote), Nov. 1875, ibid., box 1-2.

58. J. T. Smith to Meyer and Kyle, 14 Feb. 1898 (Kyle Papers), box 148; Beadle to Meyer and Kyle, 9 Feb. 1898 (quote), ibid., box 145; Ada M. Orcutt, *Tillamook: Land of Many Waters* (Portland, Ore.: Binfords & Mort, 1951), 78-99. Even larger firms on better harbors were plagued by the question of how much freeboard to allow. When a marine surveyor refused to issue Pope & Talbot's vessels certificates for insurance unless the firm loaded vessels less deeply, company officials threatened to find another surveyor, for they believed leaving so much freeboard "would be ruinous": lumber schooners "are built to take deck loads, and if they are not allowed to take same, their profits are necessarily lost." E. G. Ames to W. H. Talbot, 5 July 1885; Pope & Talbot to Puget Mill Co., 23 May 1891 (quote, Ames Papers). See also: Adams, Blinn & Co. to Washington Mill Co., 1 Apr. 1859 (Washington Mill Co. Papers).

59. Smith to Meyer and Kyle, 22 and 30 Sept. 1898 (Kyle Papers), box 148. Ironically, *Bella* was lost in 1906 off the bar harbor of the Siuslaw, for whose trade she had been designed and built, not at one of the outports of the redwood coast. At certain seasons, her remains can still be seen on the beach near Florence.

60. David W. Dickie, "The Pacific Coast Steam Schooner," *Historical Transactions, 1893-1943* (New York: Society of Naval Architects and Marine Engineers, 1945), 39-46; Jack McNairn and Jerry MacMullen, *Ships of the Redwood Coast* (Stanford, Calif.: Stanford University Press, 1945), 14-20, 100-108, 117; Newell and Williamson, *Pacific Lumber Ships*, 61-108.

61. Kyle to P. Snodgrass, 22 Aug. 1899 (Kyle Papers), box 174.

62. Dorothy Weidberg, "The History of John Kentfield & Co., 1854-1925" (unpub. M.A. thesis, University of California, Berkeley, 1940), 5-29. The little-used Kentfield Papers, especially boxes 16-22, are replete with details of the company's trade in Hawaii.

63. For discussions of vessels used in the coasting and deepwater trades, see: Cox, "Single Decks and Flat Bottoms," 65-74; McNairn and MacMullen, *Ships of the Redwood Coast*, 21-25, 100-108, and passim; F. W. Hibbs, "Shipping and Shipbuilding of Puget Sound," Society of Naval Architects and Marine

Engineers, *Transactions*, 12 (1904): 264, 274-75; Robert A. Weinstein, *Grays Harbor, 1885-1913* (New York: Viking, 1978), 148-90; Buchanan, "Economic History of Kitsap County, Washington," 172-89; Fairburn, *Merchant Sail*, 3: 1654, 1657; 4: 2605-2606, 2609 (quote).

64. Carranco, *Redwood Lumber Industry*, 60-69; Melendy, "One Hundred Years of the Redwood Industry," 28-48; Peter J. Rutledge and Richard H. Tooker, "Steam Power for Loggers: Two Views of the Dolbeer Donkey," *FH*, 14 (1970): 20-28; Meany, "History of the Lumber Industry," 246-49; Asa S. Williams, "Logging by Steam," *Forestry Quarterly*, 6 (Mar. 1908): 1-33; Prouty, *More Deadly than War!* 59-61; Nelson Courtlandt Brown, *Logging-Transportation: The Principles and Methods of Log Transportation in the United States and Canada* (New York: Wiley, 1936), 79-99; Emil Engstrom, *The Vanishing Logger* (New York: Vantage, 1956), 15.

65. William T. Cox, "Recent Forest Fires in Oregon and Washington," *Forestry & Irrigation*, 8 (1902): 462-70; George T. Morgan, "The Fight Against Fire: The Development of Cooperative Forestry in the Pacific Northwest," *IY*, 6 (winter 1962): 20-30; Holbrook, *Burning an Empire*, 109-114; Ficken, *Forested Land*, 118-19, 123-31. See also: Bob Zybach, "The Great Fires: Indian Burning and Catastrophic Forest Fire Patterns of the Oregon Coast Range, 1491-1951" (unpub. Ph.D. diss., Oregon State University, 2004).

66. *Northwestern Lumberman*, reprinted in *CL*, 3 (1 Jan. 1883): 11.

67. *West Shore*, 8 (1882): 182 (quote); Portland *Oregonian*, 1 Jan. 1882; Meany, "History of the Lumber Industry," 259-64; *CL*, 2 (15 Sept. 1882): 278. Earlier railroads in the Pacific Northwest were not primarily used in logging.

68. *West Shore*, 13 (1887): 264; 14 (1888): 619; Berner, "Port Blakely Mill Company," 158, 161-64; Price, *Port Blakely*, 89-94.

69. *West Shore*, 10 (1884): 73.

70. As time passed, steamships became increasingly common; although sailing vessels continued to haul lumber into the 1920s, by that time steamships dominated—indeed, the decade of the twenties saw steamship lines acquiring mills of their own to insure cargoes for their vessels. Coman and Gibbs, *Time, Tide and Timber*, 281-303; Ted Wurm, *Mallets on the Mendocino Coast: Caspar Lumber Company Railroads and Steamships* (Glendale, Calif.: Trans-Anglo Books, 1986); Newell and Williamson, *Pacific Lumber Ships*, 153-67.

71. Ficken, "Port Blakely Mill Company," 211-12; Berner, "Port Blakely Mill Company," 161-64; Price, *Port Blakely*, 89-91; Ficken, *Forested Land*, 55, 63, 71-72. See also: Alvin Hovey-King, "The Lumber Industry of the Pacific Coast," *American Monthly Review of Reviews*, 27 (1903): 317-23.

72. Coman and Gibbs, *Time, Tide and Timber*, 68-69, 111; Ficken, *Forested Land*, 32; E. T. Allen, statement, Southern Pine Association, "Proceedings, Fourth Annual Convention . . . 1919," 54, 152 (SPAP), R-10, box 73b.

73. Charles M. Gates, *The First Century at the University of Washington, 1861-1961* (Seattle: University of Washington Press, 1961), 21-26; Coman and Gibbs, *Time, Tide and Timber*, 111-12; Ficken, *Forested Land*, 41-42; Fred J. Yonce, "Lumbering and the Public Timberlands in Washington: The Era of Disposal," *JFH*, 22 (1978): 6-8. The Pope & Talbot interests were an exception and began acquiring timberland at an early date, including much from the

university grant. In spite of initial reluctance (or inability) to buy, by 1868 almost forty-three thousand acres of university land had been sold, with Pope & Talbot's Puget Mill Co. by far the largest buyer. See: Coman and Gibbs, *Time, Tide and Timber*, 111-12.

74. Few studies deal with developments in the Oregon and California coastal forests, but there is nothing to suggest the patterns of trespass and false entry that characterized the Puget Sound area were not prominent there as well. For examples, see: Stephen A. D. Puter, *Looters of the Public Domain* (Portland, Ore.: Portland Printing House, 1908), 16-20, 22-35, 417; Carranco, *Redwood Lumber Industry*, 146-48.

75. McGilvra as quoted in Ivan Doig, "John J. McGilvra & Timber Trespass: Seeking a Puget Sound Timber Policy, 1861-1865," *FH*, 13 (1970): 6-17 (quotes, p. 10). On McGilvra, see also: Doig, "John J. McGilvra: The Life and Times of an Urban Frontiersman, 1827-1903" (unpub. Ph.D. diss., University of Washington, 1969); Ficken, *Forested Land*, 42-44; Yonce, "Lumbering and the Public Timberlands in Washington," 8-13.

76. Lillard, *The Great Forest*, 169; Fries, *Empire in Pine*, 190-92.

77. Doig, "John J. McGilvra & Timber Trespass," 17 (quote); Yonce, "Lumbering and Public Timberlands in Washington," 12; Bunting, *Pacific Raincoast*, 137-39; Meany, "History of the Lumber Industry," 169-75; Tattersall, "Economic Development of the Pacific Northwest," 154.

78. Ficken, *Forested Land*, 40, 44-47 (quote, p. 44); Yonce, "Lumbering and Public Timberlands in Washington," 10-17; Schurz, address to AFA and PFA (AFAP), box 7, AFA historical 1889 file, 5; Joan Carson, *Tall Timber and the Tide* (Poulsbo, Wash.: Kitsap Weeklies, 1971), 37; Bunting, *Pacific Raincoast*, 139-41.

79. Coman and Gibbs, *Time, Tide and Timber*, 68-69; Ficken, *Forested Land*, 32; Royal A. Bensell, *All Quiet on the Yamhill: The Journal of Royal A. Bensell . . .*, ed. by Gunter Barth (Eugene: University of Oregon Books, 1959), 145-46 (1st quote); S. P. Blinn to R. Hoyoke, 14 Sept. 1870; Washington Mill Co. to J. Adams, 11 Aug. 1883 (2nd quote) (Washington Mill Company Papers, Henry Suzzalo Library, University of Washington, Seattle); *CL*, 5 (15 June 1885): 235 (3rd quote). Some sympathized with the loggers, noting millowners formed combines to keep log prices low and in other ways took advantage of them—which left "logging to that class of men who are eternally in debt to the mill stores, and are not a whit better off with logs at six dollars than at present rates." Seattle *Daily Intelligencer*, 21 July, 12 Sept. 1877 (quote), 7 Jan. 1878.

80. Quoted in Ficken, *Forested Land*, 32; Bunting, *Pacific Raincoast*, 142. See also: Frederick J. Yonce, "Public Land Disposal in Washington" (unpub. Ph.D. diss., University of Washington, 1969), 229 and passim; Coman and Gibbs, *Time, Tide and Timber*, 111.

81. Robbins, *Hard Times in Paradise*, 19; Pope to Pope & Sons, 30 Nov. 1860 (Pope Papers). See also: Carson, *Tall Timber and the Tide*, 37-38; Clark, "Forest Utilization in the Pacific Northwest," 18; William Joseph Bilsland, "An Historical Comparative Analysis of the Economies of Grays Harbor and

Pacific Counties, Washington, to 1920" (unpub. M.A. thesis, University of Oregon, 1966), 44-45.

82. Ficken, *Forested Land*, 25-26; Bunting, *Pacific Raincoast*, 75-77. Not everyone realized the forest's agricultural limitations. For example, see: Seattle *Daily Intelligencer*, 21 Nov. 1876, 5 Sept. 1877.

83. Not just mines in California shaped events. In the late 1850s, the Fraser River gold rush in British Columbia drew many who had failed to strike it rich in California, and when riches there proved illusory drifted back to the coast and into employment in logging and lumbering, especially in the area of Vancouver and nearby Puget Sound. Ficken, *Forested Land*, 32; Coman and Gibbs, *Time, Tide and Timber*, 68; Joseph Collins Lawrence, "Markets and Capital: A History of the Lumber Industry of British Columbia" (unpub. M.A. thesis, University of British Columbia, 1960).

84. Daniel Cornford provides a useful analysis of the labor force in Humboldt County, California. There is nothing to suggest the Puget Sound area was different other than in minor ways. Cornford, *Workers and Dissent in the Redwood Empire*, 18-20. On regional wage patterns, see: Perloff et al., *Regions, Resources and Economic Growth*, 25-27.

85. Talbot to Cyrus Walker, 17 Jan. 1894 (Ames Papers), Pope & Talbot, incoming corres. See also: Seattle *Daily Intelligencer*, 12 Sept. 1877; W. Adams to R. Holyoke, 10 Sept. 1883 (Washington Mill Co. Papers); Ficken, *Forested Land*, 70-71.

86. Ficken, *Forested Land*, 31-32 (quote, p. 32); Coman and Gibbs, *Time, Tide and Timber*, 52, 68-70, 172-73; Price, *Port Blakely*, 52-60; Carson, *Tall Timber and the Tide*, 32-69.

87. Edward Clayson, Sr., *Historical Narratives of Puget Sound: Hood's Canal, 1865-1885: The Experience of an Only Free Man in a Penal Colony* (Seattle: R. L. Davis, 1911), 6-8 and passim; Thomas F. Gedosch, "Seabeck, 1857-1886: The History of a Company Town" (unpub. M.A. thesis, University of Washington, 1967), 55-56, 59, 63-65; Coman and Gibbs, *Time, Tide and Timber*, 134; F. C. Talbot to W. H. Talbot, 13 May 1888 (1st quote); Pope to Pope & Sons, 21 Feb. 1859 (2nd quote, Pope Papers); Newell and Williamson, *Pacific Lumber Ships*, 111-12. Iva Buchanan considered Clayson's picture of Seabeck overdrawn, claiming conditions no worse than in other sawmill communities on the sound. On the one hand, she seems to have accepted too readily the glowing accounts in area newspapers, badly infected by boosterism, and on the other to have missed the fact that conditions were bad for workers throughout the industry. Buchanan, "Economic History of Kitsap County," 117-20, 253.

88. Buchanan, "Economic History of Kitsap County," 279-97; Clark, "Forest Utilization in the Pacific Northwest," 18; Price, *Port Blakely*, 37-42; Coman and Gibbs, *Time, Tide and Timber*, 70, 163-73; Carson, *Tall Timber and the Tide*, 9-15.

89. Washington Mill Co. to W. J. Adams, 13 May 1884; Wa Chong & Co. to Adams, Blinn & Co., 28 Apr. 1875 (Washington Mill Co. Papers); Seattle *Daily Intelligencer*, 29 Aug. 1870, 18 Aug., 2, 3, 9, and 15 Oct. 1876; Price, *Port Blakely*, 130-43; Cox, "Lumber and Ships," 24; Meany, "History of the

Lumber Industry," 324-26; Lynwood Carranco, "Chinese Expulsion from Humboldt County," *PHR*, 8 (1961): 329-40; B. P. Wilcox, "Anti-Chinese Riots in Washington," *Washington Historical Quarterly*, 20 (1929): 204-212; Jules A. Karlin, "The Anti-Chinese Outbreaks in Seattle, 1885-1886," *PNQ*, 39 (1948): 103-130; Morgan, *Puget's Sound*, 212-52. For the broader context, see: Robert E. Wynne, "Reaction to the Chinese in the Pacific Northwest and British Columbia" (unpub. Ph.D. diss., University of Washington, 1964); Lorraine Barker Hildebrand, *Straw Hats, Sandals, and Steel: The Chinese in Washington State* (Tacoma: Washington State American Revolution Bicentennial Commission, 1977); Carlos A. Schwantes, "From Anti-Chinese Agitation to Reform Politics: The Legacy of the Knights of Labor in Washington and the Pacific Northwest," *PNQ*, 88 (1997): 174-84.

90. A. J. Pope to Cyrus Walker, 8 Feb. 1878; Walker to W. H. Talbot, 26 and 31 Oct., 6 Nov. 1885; Ames to W. H. Talbot, 10 Nov. 1885 (Pope Papers).

91. Emerson to Simpson, 1 Sept. 1893 (quote), 1 and 2 June 1894 (Northwest Mill Company Papers, Henry Suzzalo Library, University of Washington, Seattle).

92. The St. Paul & Tacoma mill reversed the process. Built for the rail market, it found maritime outlets useful while developing interior contacts and awaiting favorable rail rates. In 1902 the firm bought the Northwestern Lumber Company's cargo mill on Grays Harbor to aid it in the maritime trade. Charles E. Twining, *George S. Long, Timber Statesman* (Seattle: University of Washington Press, 1994), 42; Morgan, *Mill on the Boot*, 144-53; Robert E. Ficken, "Weyerhaeuser and the Pacific Northwest Timber Industry, 1899-1903" *PNQ*, 70 (1979): 151-52.

93. Williams, *Americans and their Forests*, 314; Hidy, Hill, and Nevins, *Timber and Men*, 221-24 (quote, p. 222), 234-35; Ellis Lucia, *Head Rig: Story of the West Coast Lumber Industry* (Portland, Ore.: Overland Press, 1965), 58-59; Ficken, "Weyerhaeuser and the Pacific Northwest Timber Industry," 147-51. Norman Clark overstates the importance of Weyerhaeuser's mill in Everett. See: Clark, *Mill Town: A Social History of Everett . . .* (Seattle: University of Washington Press, 1970), 59.

94. J. H. Bloedel, "The Panama Canal—Its Relation to the Lumber Industry of the Pacific Coast," in National Lumber Manufacturers' Association, *Problems Affecting the Lumber Industry*: Official Report Ninth Annual Convention … (Chicago: National Lumber Manufacturers' Association, 1911), 173-82; Ralph Clement Bryant, "The Panama Canal and the Lumber Trade," *AF*, 20 (1914): 81-91; Anonymous, "Where the Lumber is Shipped," *Timb.*, 25 (Oct. 1924): 98-100; Ficken, *Forested Land*, 156, 160-62; Erickson, "Morphology of Lumber Settlements," 53-54; Meany, "History of the Lumber Industry," 147, 158-61; Arthur E. Rockwell, "The Lumber Trade and the Panama Canal, 1921-1940," *Economic History Review*, 2nd series, 24 (1971): 445-62. Stanley Horn's figures differ, but tell the same story. In 1913 78 percent of the Douglas fir cut was consumed west of the Mississippi, by the 1940s the figure had fallen to 50 percent, thanks largely to new markets opened by the canal. Horn, *This Fascinating Lumber Business*, 77-78.

95. *Timb.*, 5 (Nov. 1903): 7; 26 (Aug. 1925): 130-32; 29 (Apr. 1928): 48-50; Meany, "History of the Lumber Industry," 163-64; Barbara Amy Breitmayer

Vatter, *A Forest History of Douglas County, Oregon, to 1900: A Microcosmic Study of Imperialism* (New York: Garland, 1985), 203, 253; Archie W. Mbogho, "Sawmilling in Lane County, Oregon: A Geographical Examination of Its Development." (unpub. M.A. thesis, University of Oregon, 1965), 24-33; Dickinson, "Freight Rates on Lumber," 240-41; John H. Cox, "Organizations of the Lumber Industry in the Pacific Northwest, 1889-1914" (unpub. Ph.D. diss., University of California, Berkeley, 1937), 137-41; Erickson, "Morphology of Lumber Settlements," 54-58, 160, 168.

96. Portland *Oregonian*, 1 Jan. 1882; *Timb.*, 26 (Dec. 1924): 233; Meany, "History of the Lumber Industry," 128-29; Erickson, "Morphology of Lumber Settlements," 211-20, 226-28; Ficken, *Forested Land*, 57-58, 138-40; Williams, *Americans and their Forests*, 304, 325, 327; Wall, *Log Production in Washington and Oregon*, 6. See also: Robert A. Weinstein, "Grays Harbor County, 1880-1920," *The Record*, 35 (1974): 5-44.

97. Clough was a former governor of Minnesota, and his transfer to the Pacific Northwest encouraged others to do the same. See: Clark, *Mill Town*, 59-63. On Bay Ocean and the jetty problem, see, Orcutt, *Tillamook*, 230-33.

98. *Timb.*, 24 (Jan. 1923): 32; (Feb. 1923): 50; 26 (Dec. 1924): 232; 54 (1949): 102-104; Daniel D. Strite, "Hurrah for Garibaldi!" *OHQ*, 77 (1976): 213, 215-19; Portland *Oregonian*, 20 Aug. 1922; Anonymous, "Pacific Spruce Corporation and Subsidiaries," *Lumber World Review*, 46 (10 Feb. 1924): 35-124; Morgan, *Fifty Years in Siletz Timber*, 25-27 (quote, p. 27); Erickson, "Morphology of Lumber Settlements," 142-43, 156-57, 183-84, 196-98; Strite, "Up the Kilchis, Pt. I," 312 (quote); Orcutt, *Tillamook*, 131. On Johnson, see also: Anonymous, "Light in a Dark Corner," *AL*, 77 (28 Jan. 1905): 51-82; [Defebaugh], *American Lumbermen*, 2: 329-32.

99. Bunting, *Pacific Raincoast*, 144-47; Arthur R. Kruckeberg, *The Natural History of Puget Sound Country* (Seattle: University of Washington Press, 1991), 152-54, 268-69; George H. Plummer, F. G. Plummer, and J. H. Raveine, *Map of Washington Showing Classification of Lands* (Washington, D.C.: GPO, 1902), in National Archives, Conservation Branch, Record Group 57. Unlike other maps produced by the Geological Survey during the period, no written report seems to have accompanied this one. For a simplified version, see: Williams, *Americans and their Forests*, 306 (and cf. 326).

Chapter Twelve

1. Alice Benson Allen, *Simon Benson, Northwest Lumber King* (Portland, Ore.: Binfords & Mort, 1971), 15-35, 49-56, 85-103; Fred Lockley, *History of the Columbia River Valley from The Dalles to the Sea* (3 vols.; Chicago: Clarke, 1928), 1: 628-30; Oliver Greeley Hughson, "When We Logged the Columbia," *OHQ*, 60 (1959): 183-85; W. T. Evenson, "Ocean Log Rafts," *Timb.*, 27 (July 1926): 37-38; Anonymous, "Forty Years of Raft Building: Career of John A. Fastabend," ibid., 34 (Oct. 1933): 16-17, 24-26; Bea Evenson, "The Benson Raft" (typescript, n.d.; San Diego Historical Society Archives, San Diego, Calif.); Holbrook, *Holy Old Mackinaw*, 89-91; Kramer Adams, "Blue Water Rafting: The Evolution of Ocean Going Log Rafts," *FH*, 15 (1971): 16-27; Brown, *Logging-Transportation*, 164-68; Meany, "History of the Lumber Industry," 254. Some called the mill Benson's Folly, but it proved successful,

earning some $400,000 in profits in three years before Benson sold it to a business associate; after the sale, he continued to supply the mill's logs.

2. Allen, *Simon Benson*, 104-106 (1st quote, p. 105); George M. Cornwall, "Colorful Career of Simon Benson," *Timb.*, 42 (Dec. 1940): 46-48; Fred Lockley, *Visionaries, Mountain Men & Empire Builders* (Eugene, Ore.: Rainy Day Press, 1982), 343-47 (2nd quote, p. 343); Holbrook, *Holy Old Mackinaw*, 172-74. See also: E. Kimbark MacColl, *The Shaping of a City: Business and Politics in Portland, Oregon, 1885-1915* (Portland, Ore.: Georgian Press, 1976), 209, 213, 236, 258, 327-28, 345, 403-412.

3. Williams, *American and their Forests*, 326-28; Woodrow R. Clevinger, "Locational Change in the Douglas Fir Lumber Industry," *Yearbook of the Association of Pacific Coast Geographers*, 15 (1953): 23-31. In ways the city was more like Portland, Maine, or Minneapolis-St. Paul than Saginaw or Bangor, rather than a single-industry city; it had a broad range of support for its growth; the exportation of wheat, which burgeoned as dryland farming expanded in the interior, contributed to development.

4. C. M. Granger, "Keeping the Forests at Work," *Four L Lumber News*, 9 (no. 1, 1927): 8; Paul Repetto, *The Way of the Logger* (Chehalis, Wash.: Loggers World, 1970), 4; Meany, "History of the Lumber Industry," 251-53. There were other indicators of the crudeness that accompanied the expansion of lumbering in the Pacific Northwest. For example, the theft of log rafts—not individual logs, but entire rafts containing upwards of three million feet—became a practiced art on the lower Columbia and Puget Sound. Holbrook, *Holy Old Mackinaw*, 222-29; Stewart H. Holbrook, "Log Pirates on Puget Sound," *AF*, 43 (Jan. 1937): 22-25; Anonymous, "Defeat of Log Piracy," *Timb.*, 39 (Dec. 1937): 16-18.

5. Johansen and Gates, *Empire of the Columbia*, 401-402; MacColl, *Shaping of a City*, 288-98. See also: Jerry A. O'Callaghan, "Senator Mitchell and the Oregon Land Frauds, 1905," *PHR*, 21 (1952): 255-61; John Messing, "Public Lands, Politics, and Progressives: The Oregon Land Fraud Trials, 1903-1910," ibid., 35 (1966): 35-66.

6. Abner Baker, "Economic Growth in Portland in the 1880s," *OHQ*, 67 (1966): 105-123; Johansen and Gates, *Empire of the Columbia* (2nd ed.), 316-17, 322, 328-32; Donald Macdonald, "Portland Points the Way," *Sunset*, 17 (June 1907): 50. Cf. John S. Cochran, "Economic Importance of Early Transcontinental Railroads: Pacific Northwest," *OHQ*, 71 (1970): 26-98; Tattersall, "Economic Development of the Pacific Northwest," 86-104, 137-38, 141-42, 183, 186.

7. Cox, *Mills and Markets*, 146, 159-60, 200, 203-207, 209, 230, 232; Thomas R. Cox, "Lower Columbia Lumber Industry, 1880-1893," *OHQ*, 67 (1966): 160-78; Ficken, *Forested Land*, 58-64; Bancroft, *History of Oregon*, 2: 759; Allen, *Simon Benson*, 24; Lucia, *Head Rig*, 41. Weidler's mill was built in the 1870s to supply construction material to Ben Holladay's Oregon & California Railroad. Ellis Lucia, *The Saga of Ben Holladay, Giant of the Old West* (New York: Hastings House, 1959), 256-57; Erickson, "Morphology of Lumber Settlements," 114-15.

8. [Defebaugh], *American Lumbermen*, 3: 14-15; Cox, *Mills and Markets*, 206-207, 287-91; Ficken, *Forested Land*, 56, 59-60, 86, 106; George F. Cornwall,

"Fifty Years: History of St. Paul & Tacoma Lumber Company," *Timb.*, 39 (May 1938): 16-30; Anonymous, "A Story of the Development of One of America's Greatest Lumbering Manufacturing Institutions," *AL*, n.v. (21 May 1921): 1, 67-138; Morgan, *The Mill on the Boot*, 5-7, 48-65.

9. Forest Service, *Lumber Production, 1869-1934*, 14; Everett G. Griggs, "The Lumber Industry in its National Scope," in National Lumber Manufacturers' Association, *Problems Affecting the Lumber Industry*, 125 (quote); J. Cox, "Organizations of the Lumber Industry," 141-65. On the Pacific Coast Lumber Manufacturer's Association and its successor, the West Coast Lumbermen's Association, see: Lucia, *Head Rig*, 3-11, 66-85, and passim. More generally, see: William G. Robbins, *Lumberjacks and Legislators: Political Economy of the U.S. Lumber Industry, 1890-1941* (College Station: Texas A&M University Press, 1982), 90-111; Bureau of Corporations, *Lumber Industry* (4 vols.; Washington: GPO, 1913-1914), 4: 355-75, 383-86.

10. *Pacific Lumber Trade Journal*, 4 (1899): 11-12; Lucia, *Head Rig*, 60-63; Williams, *Americans and their Forests*, 326-27; Alexander Norbert MacDonald, "Seattle's Economic Development, 1880-1910" (unpub. Ph.D. diss., University of Washington, 1959), 95-106, 150, 166-68, 170-76, 182-87; Tattersall, "Economic Development of the Pacific Northwest," 179-88; Erickson, "Morphology of Lumber Settlements," 90-91, 116-21, 127-33, 139-42; Meany "History of the Lumber Industry," 125-27, 164-67; Dickinson, "Freight Rates on Lumber," 239-42. In 1920 Oregon passed Louisiana to become the second-largest lumber producer; by that year, ninety billion feet of timber had been cut in western Washington, compared to only thirty billion in western Oregon. Oregon would not out-produce Washington until 1938. Brian R. Wall, *Log Production in Washington and Oregon in Historical Perspective*, USDA, Forest Service Resources Bulletin, PNW 42 (Portland, Ore.: USDA, Forest and Range Experiment Station, 1972), 1-3, 26.

11. Meany, "History of the Lumber Industry," 175-78, 203-204; Ficken, *Forested Land*, 48-53. Fraudulent practices are detailed in United States, Public Lands Commission, *Report of the Public Lands Commission*, House Exec. Doc 46, 46th Cong., 2nd sess. (Washington, D.C.: GPO, 1880). In 1892, the Supreme Court virtually legalized using dummy entrymen to gain title to public land. Harold H. Dunham, *Government Handout: A Study in the Administration of the Public Lands, 1875-1891* (1941; reprint, New York: DaCapo, 1970), 268-70.

12. Puter, *Looters of the Public Domain*, 20 (1st quote); Hidy, Hill, and Nevins, *Timber and Men*, 223 (Long quote); Oswald West, "Reminiscences and Anecdotes of Oregon History," *OHQ*, 50 (1949): 108-109 (3rd quote). By 1921 the situation had changed but little. C. L. Starr approached A. W. Morgan regarding timber for the Cobbs-Mitchell firm of Portland, but Morgan thought he "seemed a little distrustful . . . [for] he had no doubt been deviled by many timber brokers, for Portland was full of [them] . . . and they were trying to make sales, and all knew he had plenty of ready money." Morgan, *Fifty Years in Siletz Timber*, 69 (quote), 81.

13. Johansen and Gates, *Empire of the Columbia*, 461-62; Ise, *Forest Policy*, 331-32; Puter, *Looters of the Public Domain*, 20, 73-74; Orcutt, *Tillamook*, 129-30; O'Callaghan, *Disposition of the Public Domain in Oregon*, 74-80, 85-92; Morgan, *Fifty Years in Siletz Timber*, 10 (quote). Like the so-called Forest

Management (or Organic) Act, the Forest Lieu Act was, in fact, a section of the Sundry Civil Appropriations Act of 1897.

14. *Hill's Annotated Laws of Oregon, 1887,* sections 3595-3612, 3617-20; Bancroft, *History of Oregon,* 2: 654-58, 660-62; Lon L. Swift, "Land Tenure in Oregon," *OHQ,* 10 (1909): 38; F. G. Young, "Financial History of the State of Oregon: Part III, Oregon's Public Domain," ibid., 11 (1910): 122-24, 130-31, 133-52; Puter, *Looters of the Public Domain,* 21, 234, 315-38; Lawrence Rakestraw, "A History of Forest Conservation in the Pacific Northwest, 1891-1913" (unpub. Ph.D. diss., University of Washington, 1955), 26-27, 47; O'Callaghan, *Disposition of the Public Domain in Oregon,* 64-66; MacColl, *Shaping of a City,* 294, 396-98. Rakestraw, p. 47, states one-fourth of the price was required as down payment. Actually, 50 percent was needed for timberland and one-third for other land, but as the state seldom investigated claims, most entrants attested entries were for agricultural land and thus avoided the larger payment.

15. Young, "Financial History of Oregon," 145-51; Burton J. Hendrick, "'Statement No. 1': How Oregon Democracy, Working under the Direct Primary, has Destroyed the Political Machine," *McClure's Magazine,* 37 (1911): 504-506, 516-19; Rakestraw, "Forest Conservation in the Pacific Northwest," 159-60; Puter, *Looters of the Public Domain,* 334-36; Robert E. Burton, *Democrats of Oregon: The Pattern of Minority Politics, 1900-1956* (Eugene: University of Oregon Books, 1970), 31-32; West, "Reminiscences and Anecdotes," 107-110 (quote, pp. 107-108). Oregon later tightened policies regarding school lands, but disposal continued until little timbered school land remained. Its approach contrasted with Washington's. Largely through the efforts of William Henry Harrison Beadle, its constitution required that school lands be sold at appraised value, but for not less than $10 per acre. Subsequent legislation forbade sale if the timber cruised over a million feet per quarter section. As a result, Washington kept 78 percent of its school land. See: Meany, "History of the Lumber Industry," 209-212.

16. Meany, "History of the Lumber Industry," 179-205; Ficken, *Forested Land,* 237-38; Puter, *Looters of the Public Domain,* 21 (1st quote); Lincoln Steffens, "The Taming of the West," *American Magazine,* 24 (1907): 590-91 (2nd quote, p. 590); Portland *Oregonian,* 3 Jan. 1905 (3rd quote); Elmo R. Richardson, *The Politics of Conservation: Crusades and Controversies, 1897-1913* (Berkeley: University of California Press, 1952), 19, 55.

17. Minto, "From Youth to Age as an American," *OHQ,* 9 (1908): 140-42, 154, 164-72, 374-87; Minto, *Rhymes of Early Life in Oregon . . .* (Salem: Statesman, 1915), 25 (1st quote); Minto to F. G. Young, 20 Dec. 1908, Minto Papers (Oregon Historical Society, Portland), box 2 (2nd quote); Minto to editor, Portland *Oregonian,* 10 May 1911 (3rd quote); Morgan, *Fifty Years in Siletz Timber,* 2-4, 11-14. See also: Thomas R. Cox, "The Conservationist as Reactionary: John Minto and American Forest Policy," *PNQ,* 74 (1983): 146-53. On earlier patterns in the Willamette Valley, the possible genesis of Minto's plan, see: Meany, "History of the Lumber Industry," 80-83, 89-93, and maps following 128; Sherman, "Lumber Industry in the Fir Belt," 8-9, 12-13; Mbogho, "Sawmilling in Lane County," 20-22, 40.

18. The literature is voluminous. Useful overviews are: Cameron, *Development of Governmental Forest Control,* 179-260; Steen, *Forest Service,* 26-86; David A.

Clary, *Timber and the Forest Service* (Lawrence: University Press of Kansas, 1986), 3-125; Rakestraw, "Forest Conservation in the Pacific Northwest," 1-68; Ise, *Forest Policy*, 92-95, 109-142. See also: Harold K. Steen, ed., *Origins of the National Forests: A Centennial Symposium* (Durham, N.C.: Forest History Society, 1992), 3-18, 259-75, 287-332; Steen, *The Beginning of the National Forest System*, USDA, Forest Service, FS-488 (Washington, D.C.: GPO, 1991).

19. Tattersall, "Economic Development of the Pacific Northwest," 148-56 (1st quote, p. 153), 159-61 (2nd quote, p. 161).

20. Ficken, *Forested Land*, 51-52; Morgan, *Fifty Years in Siletz Timber*, 2-4, 7 (2nd quote), 10 (1st quote), 11-14, 17. As earlier, such attacks confused and angered many lumbermen who saw themselves as having opened vast areas while acting within parameters endorsed by the age. See: NLMA, *Problems Affecting the Lumber Industry*, 17-20, 33, 44-47, 53-54, 108-109, 123-24, 183-89.

21. Cameron, *Development of Governmental Forest Control*, 207-208, 244-45; R. G. Cook, "Senator Heyburn's War against the Forest Service," *IY*, 14 (winter 1970-71): 12-15; Elmer Ellis, *Henry Moore Teller, Defender of the West* (Caldwell, Ida.: Caxton, 1941), 97, 367-84; Lawrence Rakestraw, "The West, States Rights, and Conservation: A Study of Six Public Lands Conferences," *PNQ*, 47 (1957): 89-99; G. Michael McCarthy, "The Forest Reserve Controversy: Colorado under Cleveland and McKinley," *JFH*, 20 (1976): 80-90; Gifford Pinchot, *Breaking New Ground* (New York: Harcourt Brace, 1947), 257-58, 299-301; Harold T. Pinkett, "Western Perceptions of Forest Conservation," *JW*, 18 (1979): 72-74.

22. *West Shore*, 14 (1888): 239; Richardson, *Politics of Conservation*, 37, 101-102, 121, 158; Lancaster Pollard, "The Pacific Northwest," in Merrill Jensen, ed., *Regionalism in America* (Madison: University of Wisconsin Press, 1951), 187-212; Dodds, *Oregon*, 71-114; Johansen and Gates, *Empire of the Columbia*, 352-60, 430-37; Rakestraw, "The West, States Rights, and Conservation," 23-24; MacColl, *Shaping of a City*, 185-92, 280-88; *Coeur d'Alene Evening Press*, 9 January 1911 (quote); West, "Reminiscences and Anecdotes," 109-110.

23. Gerald W. Williams, "John B. Waldo and William G. Steel: Forest Reserve Advocates for the Cascade Range of Oregon," in Steen, *Origins of the National Forests*, 314-32; Rakestraw, "Forest Conservation in the Pacific Northwest," 26-27, 45-53, 159-69, 176-77, 213; Bancroft, *History of Oregon*, 2: 654-58; Fred G. Plummer, *Forest Conditions in the Cascade Range, Washington . . .*, United States Geological Survey Professional Paper no. 6 (Washington, D.C.: GPO, 1902); Lawrence and Mary Rakestraw, *History of the Willamette National Forest* (Eugene, Ore.: Willamette National Forest, 1991), 2-3. Eventually Oregon's Cascade Reserve was divided into a number of national forests.

24. H. D. Langille et al., *Forest Conditions in the Cascade Range Forest Reserve, Oregon*, United States Geological Survey, Professional Paper no. 9 (Washington, D.C.: GPO, 1903), 15-18, 24-26.

25. Langille et al., *Forest Conditions in the Cascade Reserve*, 37, 42 (quote), 71, 74-76, 92, 148-49. Speculation in timber by "agricultural" entrymen was more widespread in Washington, perhaps because lumbering was more developed

there and opportunities thus more manifest. See: Rakestraw, "Forest Conservation in the Pacific Northwest," 137, 140-43.

26. *West Shore*, 8 (Jan. 1882): 2; Wilson M. Compton, *The Organization of the Lumber Industry* . . . (Chicago: American Lumberman, 1916), 69-70; Johansen and Gates, *Empire of the Columbia*, 462-63; Morgan, *Fifty Years in Siletz Timber*, 2 (quote), 5, 7-8. On speculation in the redwoods, see: Puter, *Looters of the Public Domain*, 16-20; Duane D. Fischer, "The Short, Unhappy Story of the Del Norte Company," *FH*, 11 (Apr. 1967): 12-25; Fischer, "Owen Enterprizes," 558-64, 568-75, 585-87; John M. Eddy, *In the Redwood's Realm* (San Francisco: Stanley, 1893), 79.

27. Rakestraw, "Forest Conservation in the Pacific Northwest," 162-66; Puter, *Looters of the Public Domain*, 446; Langille et al., *Forest Conditions in the Cascade Reserve*, 184-85, 192; O'Callaghan, *Disposition of the Public Domain in Oregon*, 50-52, 81-82; Ise, *Forest Policy*, 329; Bureau of Corporations, *The Lumber Industry*, 1: 75-76; Vatter, *Forest History of Douglas County*, 265, 347, 350; [Defebaugh], *American Lumbermen*, 3: 59. The land Pengra wanted eliminated was east of the Cascades in the upper Deschutes watershed. Rakestraw mistakenly places it on the westside along the Middle Fork of the Willamette, even though his accompanying map locates it correctly. On Pengra, see: Bancroft, *History of Oregon*, 2: 458, 651-52, 705. Booth-Kelly's origins are traced, somewhat chaotically, in Vatter, *Forest History of Douglas County*, 161-62, 171, 265, 295, 301, 306-307, 309-310, 324-27, 342, 344-50. See, also: Mbogho, "Sawmilling in Lane County," 27-31; Randall V. Mills, *Railroads down the Valleys* (Palo Alto, Calif.: Pacific Books, 1950), 104, 118-19; [Defebaugh], *American Lumbermen*, 3: 57-60.

28. Rakestraw, "Forest Conservation in the Pacific Northwest," 67-68, 126-36; Ficken, *Forested Land*, 124; Arthur Dodwell and Theodore F. Rixon, *Forest Conditions in the Olympic Forest Reserve, Washington*, United States Geological Survey, Professional Paper no. 7 (Washington, D.C.: GPO, 1902), 11-14, 18, 20-21; Richardson, *Politics of Conservation*, 9. Dodwell and Rixon did their field work in 1898-1900, before reduction of the reserve; the eliminated sections were therefore included in their report.

29. MacColl, *Shaping of a City*, 185-92, 280-88 (1st quote, p. 288); Puter, *Looters of the Public Domain*, 9-10, 20, 21, 33-35, 42-44, 185-86, 196-211 (3rd quote, p. 211), 295-314 (2nd quote, p. 295), 419-20, 426; Robbins, *Hard Times in Paradise*, 31-34; Rakestraw, "Forest Conservation in the Pacific Northwest," 168, 208; California State Conservation Commission, *Report of the Conservation Commission, State of California, 1 Jan. 1913* (Sacramento: State Printing Office, 1913), 51, 430. See also: Larsen, *White Pine Industry*, 282-85.

30. Frank Hoberg to C. W. Stone, 28 Apr. 1899; E. R. Kreiger to Stone, 2 May 1899, Thos. Struthers estate, Oregon property file, WP, box 65; Morgan, *Fifty Years in Siletz Timber*, 5, 7-8, 17-21, 33-39. Hoberg's activity near the coast apparently was in behalf of Andrew B. Hammond, who was buying in the area. On Hammond, see: George M. Cornwall, "The Passing of a Stalwart Lumberman," *Timb.*, 35 (Jan. 1934): 62; Carranco, *Redwood Lumber Industry*, 99, 101, 138, 149, 155-59; Cornford, *Workers and Dissent*, 153-54, 164-66, 172; Gage McKinney, "A. B. Hammond, West Coast Lumberman," *JFH*, 28 (1984): 196-203, esp. 198-200.

31. Morgan, *Fifty Years in Siletz Timber*, 33-39, 52-53 (quote), 59-63, 69-81. On difficulties faced by surveyors and landlookers, see also: Arthur V. Smyth, *Millicoma: Autobiography of a Pacific Northwestern Forest* (Durham, N.C.: Forest History Society, 2000), 22-23; Anonymous, "Surveyors of the Wilderness," *Timb.*, 49 (July 1948): 52-53; Donald H. Clark, *Eighteen Men and a Horse* (Seattle: Metropolitan Press, 1949), 25-26.

32. Morgan, *Fifty Years in Siletz Timber*, 3-4 (1st quote), 17 (2nd and 3rd quotes), 69-82.

33. Eureka (Calif.) *Humboldt Daily Times*, 14 Mar. 1888; *Report of the Commissioner of the General Land Office, 1888* (Washington, D.C.: GPO, 1889), 47; *Timb.*, 29 (Dec. 1927): 106; Dunham, *Government Handout*, 263-68; Puter, *Looters of the Public Domain*, 16-20 (quote, p. 20), 22-32, 174-75; Carranco, *Redwood Lumber Industry*, 146-48; Melendy, "One Hundred Years of Redwood Lumber Industry," 86.

34. Puter, *Looters of the Public Domain*, 89-90, 299-300; Carranco, *Redwood Lumber Industry*, 155-57; McKinney, "Hammond," 198-99; Cornwall, "Passing of a Stalwart Lumberman," 62. Hammond was not alone in holding to such a policy. See: Clark, *Eighteen Men and a Horse*, 110-11.

35. Puter, *Looters of the Public Domain*, 388-94; Morgan, *Fifty Years in Siletz Timber*, 2-3.

36. Puter, *Looters of the Public Domain*, 22-27, 30-32, 175, 347-56; Morgan, *Fifty Years in Siletz Timber*, 2, 10 (quote); O'Callaghan, *Disposition of the Public Domain in Oregon*, 92-93. On Jones's later career, see below, Chapter 13. The Wetmore Papers contain considerable material detailing Jones's methods and activities; Wetmore and his associates may well be the "eastern friends" to whom Jones refers.

37. William Hawks and George S. Canfield, business records, Nov. 1902-Jan. 1903, Hawks & Canfield Papers (Oregon Collection, McKnight Library, University of Oregon, Eugene). John A. Benson and F. A. Hyde operated a similar partnership, first in California then in Oregon, until exposed and brought to trial by Heney. See: Puter, *Looters of the Public Domain*, 317, 320, 329, 483-87; Young, "Financial History of Oregon," 151; Messing, "Public Lands, Politics, and Progressives," 46-48, 55, 58, 60; Stephens, "Taming of the West," 491-505.

38. Ise, *Forest Policy*, 79.

39. Cameron, *Development of Forest Control*, 238-40; Steen, *Forest Service*, 70-76; Pinchot, *Breaking New Ground*, 244-50, 254-62; Messing "Public Lands, Politics, and Progressives," 62-64; O'Callaghan, *Disposition of the Public Domain in Oregon*, 85-92; Morgan, *Fifty Years in Siletz Timber*, 2, 7-8, 10-11. The Oregon land fraud trials did not conclude until 1910, but by 1905 they had received sufficient publicity to have a major impact.

40. Ficken, *Forested Land*, 44-47; Elmo Richardson, *BLM's Billion-Dollar Checkerboard: Managing the O & C Lands* (Santa Cruz, Calif.: Forest History Society, 1980), 2-7; O'Callaghan, *Disposition of the Public Domain in Oregon*, 37-47, 50-52, 55-56, 58, 78 (quote); Johansen and Gates, *Empire of the Columbia*, 370-76; Meany, "History of the Lumber Industry," 216-30; W. Turrentine Jackson, "Federal Road Building Grants for Early Oregon," *OHQ*, 50 (1949): 23-28; Vatter, *Forest History of Douglas County*, 193-97, 243-44, 248-52; Orfield, *Federal Land Grants to the States*, 92-93; H. S. Bruce, "A

History of the Oregon Central Military Wagon Road Company . . ." (unpub. M.A. thesis, University of Oregon, 1936).

41. Since the NP had track in Oregon—albeit a mere thirty miles connecting Kalama, on the Columbia, to Portland—the company's exchange privileges could be exercised there as well as in Washington.

42. Pomeroy, *Pacific Slope*, 209 (quote); Puter, *Looters of the Public Domain*, 68-85 (quote, p. 318); Ficken, *Forested Land*, 119-21; Ise, *Forest Policy*, 331-32; "Forest Conservation in the Pacific Northwest," 146-52. See also: O'Callaghan, *Disposition of the Public Domain in Oregon*, 78-80; Smyth, *Millicoma*, 11-13; Roy E. Appleman, "Timber Empire from the Public Domain," *MVHR*, 26 (1939): 201-203; Ross Ralph Cotroneo, "History of the Northern Pacific Land Grant, 1900-1952" (unpub. Ph.D. diss., University of Idaho, 1966), 35-54, 357. Puter, *Looters of the Public Domain*, 378-80, lists lands NP obtained in Oregon in exchange for its holdings within Rainier park. As these exchanges were authorized by separate legislation, they continued even after 1905 when Congress repealed the general forest lieu provisions.

43. Cotroneo, "History of the Northern Pacific Land Grant," 246-56; Ross R. Cotroneo, "Timber Marketing by the Northern Pacific Railway, 1920-1952," *JFH*, 20 (1976): 121-22; Albro Martin, *James J. Hill and the Opening of the Northwest* (New York: Oxford University Press, 1976), 465; Ficken, *Forested Land*, 93-96; Hidy, Hill, and Nevins, *Timber and Men*, 207, 211-15; Meany, "History of the Lumber Industry," 221-27; J. Cox, "Organizations of the Lumber Industry," 16. See also: Cotroneo, "Western Land Marketing by the Northern Pacific Railway," *PHR*, 27 (1968): 299-320; Ficken, "Weyerhaeuser and the Northwest Timber Industry," 146-54; Smyth, *Millicoma*, 12-13.

44. MacColl, *Shaping of a City*, 291-94 (1st quote, p. 292; 2nd quote, p. 291); Bancroft, *History of Oregon*, 2: 747-48; L. E. Bean, *The Oregon and California Land Grant* . . . (Salem: State Printer, 1917), 9. Congress's action in 1869 was in step with the times. The Homestead Act had been passed in 1862 and sentiment favoring settlement of the frontier by farmers was strong. For its part, the NP sought to sell to farmers, for management believed only in that way could a sufficient population be built up along the line to make it pay. See: Cotroneo, "History of the Northern Pacific Land Grant," 36-50, 53-54.

45. The charge is probably untrue. Booth-Kelly's sawmill at Wendling depended on timber from former SP land and had to close for two years when its titles came into question. It is unlikely the firm would have knowingly risked such an eventuality.

46. Richardson, *Billion-Dollar Checkerboard*, 3-18, 25-30; O'Callaghan, *Disposition of the Public Domain in Oregon*, 37-47; Bancroft, *History of Oregon*, 2: 651, 653-54; Ise, *Forest Policy*, 328; Vatter, *Forest History of Douglas County*, 351. See also: John Ganoe, "History of the Oregon and California Railroad," *OHQ*, 25 (1924): 236-83; David M. Ellis, "The Oregon and California Railroad Land Grant, 1866-1945," *PNQ*, 39 (1948): 253-83.

47. By 1903 when the SP halted sales, 28 percent of the grant had been sold. With its remaining holdings the railroad was still one of the state's largest landowners. O'Callaghan, *Disposition of the Public Domain in Oregon*, 80-82; Meany, "History of the Lumber Industry," 214-17. See also: Dunham, *Government Handout*, 86-100, 272-86.

48. Richardson, *Billion-Dollar Checkerboard*, 13-18 (quote, p. 14).
49. Bureau of Corporations, *Lumber Industry*, especially, Part II: *Concentration of Timber Ownership in Important Selected Regions* and Part III: *Land Holdings of Large Timber Owners*; Hidy, Hill, and Nevins, *Timber and Men*, 305-309; Cameron, *Development of Governmental Forest Control*, 284-86; Ise, *Forest Policy*, 315-17, 327-32, 328-29; Meany, "History of the Lumber Industry," 178-79; Charles P. Norcross, "Weyerhaeuser—Richer than Rockefeller," *Cosmopolitan*, 42 (1907): 252-59. See also: Appleman, "Timber Empire from the Public Domain," 193-208. Walker attacked claims as to the amount of land he, Smith, and Weyerhaeuser held, maintaining they only had some one-half of one percent of the nation's stands. See: Minneapolis *Journal*, 20 and 21 May 1909.
50. Compton, *Organization of the Lumber Industry*, 107-125; Twining, *George S. Long*, 41-45 (Long quote, p. 42), 63-66, 88-89, 145-50, 169-75, 186-87; Ficken, "Weyerhaeuser and the Pacific Northwest Timber Industry," 146-47, 151, 152, 154; J. Cox, "Organizations of the Lumber Industry," 15; Erickson, "Morphology of Lumber Settlements," 238, 240-42. In addition to commencing manufacturing in the Pacific Northwest, by 1917 Weyerhaeuser had sold 215,000 acres of timberland to reduce carrying costs and finance construction of new mills. Hidy, Hill, and Nevins, *Timber and Men*, 278-79; Twining, *George S. Long*, 265, 371; Bradley, *Long*, 122; John M. McClelland, Jr., *R. A. Long's Planned City: The Story of Longview* (Longview, Wash.: Longview Publishing, 1976), 4.
51. Forest Service, *Timber Depletion, Lumber Prices, Lumber Exports, and Concentration of Ownership*, Report on Senate Resolution 311 (Washington, D.C.: GPO, 1920), 62-66; NLMA, *Problems Affecting the Lumber Industry*, 53-54, 106-107, 183-89; O'Callaghan, *Disposition of the Public Domain in Oregon*, 82; Ise, *Forest Policy*, 316. See also: Steen, *Forest Service*, 111-13; Hidy, Hill, and Nevins, *Timber and Men*, 307-309.
52. Twining, *George S. Long*, 44-45; NLMA, *Problems Affecting the Lumber Industry*, 106-107, 186-88; Sherman, "Lumber Industry in the Douglas Fir Belt," 88-89; Hidy, Hill, and Nevins, *Timber and Men*, 290-309.
53. Johansen and Gates, *Empire of the Columbia*, 460, 464-65; Forest Service, *Timber Depletion*, 23-24; E. G. Crawford, address, in "Proceedings of the Fifth Annual Convention of the Southern Pine Association," New Orleans, 16-18 Mar. 1920, SPAP, R-10, box 73b, 35-46 (quote, p. 37). See also: Oregon Conservation Commission, *Annual Report* (Salem: State Printer, 1912), 17.
54. William B. Greeley, *Some Public and Economic Aspects of the Lumber Business* (Washington, D.C.: GPO, 1917); Tattersall, "Economic Development of the Pacific Northwest," 155.
55. Hidy, Hill, and Nevins, *Timber and Men*, 213, 229-31 (1st quote, p. 229); Twining, *George S. Long*, 52-55; Ficken, *Forested Land*, 118-19; Ficken, "Weyerhaeuser and the Northwest Timber Industry," 153; Holbrook, *Burning an Empire*, 108-33; Alden H. Jones, *From Jamestown to Coffin Rock: A History of Weyerhaeuser Operations in Southwest Washington* (Tacoma, Wash.: Weyerhaeuser, 1974), 6-18; Repetto, *Way of the Logger*, 36; Cotroneo, "History of the Northern Pacific Land Grant," 262; Morgan, *Fifty Years in Siletz Timber*, 43-51; Shannon Kracht, "Wendling, A Company Town," *Lane*

County Historian, 20 (spring 1975): 13-14; E. T. Allen, *Practical Forestry in the Pacific Northwest: Protecting Existing Forests and Growing New Ones* . . . (Portland, Ore.: Western Forestry and Conservation Association, 1911), 14-21 (2nd quote, p. 20), 91-92; NLMA, *Problems Affecting the Lumber Industry*, 35-36, 125 (3rd quote); William T. Cox, "Recent Fires in Oregon and Washington," *Forestry & Irrigation*, 8 (1902): 462-70; Henry S. Graves, "The Protection of Forests from Fire," *AF*, 19 (Sept. 1910): 509-518; William G. Morris, "Forest Fires in Western Oregon and Western Washington," *OHQ*, 35 (1934): 313-39; George T. Morgan, Jr., "Conflagration as Catalyst: Western Lumbermen and American Forest Policy," *PHR*, 47 (1978): 167-87; Pyne, *Fire in America*, 239-59. Wendling was named after George X. Wendling of San Francisco, a partner in some of Booth's enterprises. See: Kracht, "Wendling," 5-6; [Defebaugh], *American Lumbermen*, 3: 59, 61-64.

56. Details of Booth-Kelly's operations are not clear, but the owners had other sawmills besides these two. Production figures for Booth-Kelly seemingly do not include its smaller mills at Coburg, Saginaw, Harrisburg, etc. See: Vatter, *Forest History of Douglas County*, 161-62, 171, 265, 310, 344-50; Mbogho, "Sawmilling in Lane County," 24-30, 31; Kracht, "Wendling," 3-16; James E. Sprague, reminiscences, Eugene *Register-Guard*, 23 July 1950; Erickson, "Morphology of Lumber Settlements," 167-68; [Defebaugh], *American Lumbermen*, 3: 58-59.

57. *Pacific Lumber Trade Journal*, 5 (Apr. 1900): 5; 9 (Nov. 1900): 12-13; 11 (May 1905): 16; Anonymous, "Marvelous Growth and Development of City of Smokestacks," *AL*, n.v. (5 Mar. 1910): 56-57; Anonymous, "Bloedel-Donovan Lumber Mills," ibid., n.v. (19 July 1913): 43-57; *Timb.*, 24 (Feb. 1923): 50-51; [Defebaugh], *American Lumbermen*, 3: 46-47; [Southern Lumberman], *Southern Lumberman's Directory of American Saw Mills and Planing Mills* (Nashville, Tenn.: Southern Lumberman, 1928), 822; J. Cox, "Organizations of the Lumber Industry," 59-60, 65-68; Ficken, *Forested Land*, 101-102, 116; Hidy, Hill, and Nevins, *Timber and Men*, 234, 281-82; Coman and Gibbs, *Time, Tide and Timber*, 200-209, 253-62, 265-80, 284-86; Clark, *Eighteen Men and a Horse*, 35-46, 63-68, 73-74, 137-50; Strite, "Hurrah for Garibaldi," 213-19; Orcutt, *Tillamook*, 134-35; Richardson, *Billion-Dollar Checkerboard*, 35-36, 39-40; Jeffrey M. LaLande, *Medford Corporation: A History of an Oregon Logging and Lumber Company* (Medford, Ore.: Klocker, 1979), 27-49; Fischer, "Owen Enterprizes," 577-82; Mills, *Railroads down the Valleys*, 106-107; George W. Peavy, "What About Oregon's Timber?" *Four L Lumber News*, 8 (no. 28, 1926): 5.

58. *Timb.*, 23 (June 1922): 28-29; (July 1922): 94; 24 (Apr. 1923): 108; (Sept. 1923): 144; (Oct. 1923): 56; 25 (July 1924): 80; 26 (Oct. 1925); Hidy, Hill, and Nevins, *Timber and Men*, 212; Rakestraw and Rakestraw, *Willamette National Forest*, 30; Meany, "History of the Lumber Industry," 164; Earl Pomeroy, *The American Far West in the Twentieth Century* (New Haven: Yale University Press, 2008), 154.

59. *Timb.*, (May 1923): 26; William B. Greeley, "Report of the Chief Forester," *Annual Reports of the Department of Agriculture, 1924* (Washington, D.C.: GPO, 1925 [hereafter "Report of the Forester" and year]), 16-17.

60. *Timb.*, 24 (Sept. 1923): 144; (Oct. 1923): 56; 25 (May 1924): 216; 26 (Aug. 1925): 56-59; 29 (Apr. 1928): 48-50; Vatter, *Forest History of Douglas County*, 347; Erickson, "Morphology of Lumber Settlements," 181, 309-311.
61. *Timb.*, 21 (Aug. 1920): 35; 22 (May 1921): 38; 26 (Dec. 1924): 232; 29 (Apr. 1928): 48-50; Erickson, "Morphology of Lumber Settlements," 179, 182. In spite of rich timber stands, there was no railroad up the South Santiam until 1931, so milling lagged well behind that on the North Santiam. Margaret Standish Carey and Patricia Hoy Hainline, *Sweet Home in the Oregon Cascades* (Brownsville, Ore.: Calapooia Publications, 1979), 79-80, 83-84.
62. *Timb.*, 24 (May 1923): 38-39 (quote, p. 38); 26 (Dec. 1924): 232; Morgan, *Fifty Years in Siletz Timber*, 33, 48; Erickson, "Morphology of Lumber Settlements," 356-59; Repetto, *Way of the Logger*, 31 (quote), 39.
63. *Timb.*, 23 (Mar. 1922): 32; (May 1922): 33; 24 (May 1923): 39; 25 (July 1924): 40, 55-62; George M. Cornwall, "Logging Clatsop County: Oregon Coast Region Illustrated Evolution of Logging Methods," ibid., 37 (Sept. 1936): 18-24; Wall, *Log Production in Washington and Oregon*, 7; Erickson, "Morphology of Lumber Settlements," 183-84.
64. McClelland, *Long's Planned City*, 4 (1st quote); *Eugene Register-Guard*, 30 Apr. 1944 (2nd quote); Barbara Booth Davis and John Booth Peterson, *The Robert Booth Family of Oregon* (mimeographed; n.p., 1948), 37 (3rd quote).
65. *Timb.*, 21 (Feb. 1920): 34-39; McClelland, *Long's Planned City*, 2-4, 33; Bradley, *Long*, 122; Twining, *George S. Long*, 234, 239, 242-43, 246, 248-49, 371; Davis and Peterson, *Booth Family*, 38 (quote).
66. *Timb.*, 23 (Oct. 1922): 36-38; 24 (Apr. 1923): 34-35; (June 1923): 42-43; 25 (Mar. 1924): 5-7; (Aug. 1924): 49-58, 144; Leith Abbott, "Longview—The Miracle City," *Export & Shipping Journal*, 4 (Sept. 1923): 9, 15; McClelland, *Long's Planned City*, 4-6, 8-10, 12-27, 33-37, 129-30, 200-201, 231; Twining, *George S. Long*, 334, 371-72, 392; Bradley, *Long*, 123-24, 131, 135, 143-44, 156, 158-59; Ficken, *Forested Land*, 174-75, 184; Erickson, "Morphology of Lumber Settlements," 153-54, 255-64, 339-42; Pomeroy, *Far West in the Twentieth Century*, 110.
67. Twining, *George S. Long*, 276-77, 281, 331-32, 343, 349; Hidy, Hill, and Nevins, *Timber and Men*, 403, 406-410, 414; Bradley, *Long*, 131-35, 152-54, 165, 181-83; McClelland, *Long's Planned City*, 130-37; Ficken, *Forested Land*, 176.
68. Twining, *George S. Long*, 276-77, 281-82, 301-302, 303-304, 311-12, and passim; Hidy, Hill, and Nevins, *Timber and Men*, 407-408; McClelland, *Long's Planned City*, 132-37 (quotes, p. 132); Bradley, *Long*, 152-54; Jones, *Jamestown to Coffin Rock*, 30-46.
69. *West Coast Lumberman*, 56 (July 1929): 43; *Timb.*, 29 (May 1928): 40; Jones, *Jamestown to Coffin Rock*, 47-56, 62-63; Hidy, Hill, and Nevins, *Timber and Men*, 408-410; McClelland, *Long's Planned City*, 136-38.
70. Williams, *Americans and their Forests*, 318; McClelland, *Long's Planned City*, 136-37 (quote, p. 137); Hidy, Hill, and Nevins, *Timber and Men*, 410; Jones, *Jamestown to Coffin Rock*, 153. Over 12.4 billion board feet of logs were cut in the Douglas fir region in 1929. Weyerhaeuser's Longview operations added some 15 percent at a time when excess production was already a major problem (precise percentages cannot be calculated since some of the cut at

Longview was hemlock and apparently was not included in Forest Service statistics). See: Wall, *Log Production in Washington and Oregon*, 3.

71. H. H. Peed, "The Motor Truck and Its Relation to the Northwest Log Market," *West Coast Lumberman*, 34 (1 Apr. 1918): 34; *Timb.*, 21 (Jan. 1920): 44; Carl C. Jacoby, "Motor Truck Logging," ibid., 22 (May 1921): 99-100; Erickson, "Morphology of Lumber Settlements," 180, 225; Brown, *Logging-Transportation*, 189-93, 215, 225; Strite, "Up the Kilchis, Pt. II," 16.

72. Allen, *Simon Benson*, 87-88; Erickson, "Morphology of Lumber Settlements," 343-46; Evenson, "Benson Raft," 16.

73. Erickson, "Morphology of Lumber Settlements," 314-15, 325-26; Tattersall, "Economic Development of the Pacific Northwest," 86-104, 137-38, 141-42, 183, 186; Carey and Hainline, *Sweet Home*, 79-80, 83-84.

74. Prouty, *More Deadly than War!*, 80-81; E.H. Meiklejohn, "Truck Logging," *Timb.*, 21 (Oct. 1920): 85-86; ibid. (Feb. 1920): 98-99; 22 (May 1921): 99-100; (Aug. 1921): 97; 24 (May 1923): 130-32; van Syckle, *They Tried to Cut It All*, 99-103, 268-69; Ficken, *Lumber and Politics*, 151, 152; Erickson, "Morphology of Lumber Settlements," 170, 180, 227-28, 314-15, 325-26; Ficken, *Forested Land*, 170 (quote), 180. See also: Anonymous, "Robert Polson, Master Logger," *Timb.*, 37 (Mar. 1936): 34-36; [Defebaugh], *American Lumbermen*, 3: 34-36.

75. *Timb.*, 21 (Aug. 1920): 35; Anonymous, "Railroad Logging in the West," ibid., 50 (Oct. 1949): 63-78; Williams, *Americans and their Forests*, 318-19; Brown, *Logging-Transportation*, 201, 203-204 (1st quote, p. 203); Axel J. F. Brandstrom, *Analysis of Logging Costs and Operating Methods in the Douglas Fir Region* (Seattle, Wash.: Charles Lathrop Pack Forestry Foundation, 1933), 8 (2nd quote). See also: Prouty, *More Deadly than War!*, 78-80. By 1930, the peak had been reached; a decade later, trucks handled half the output.

76. Pennsylvania had few logging railroads prior to 1885, but many after; at least three hundred and seventy logging railroads operated at one time or another. By 1906 most sawmills cutting three million feet a year or more depended on logging railroads; the largest firm was the Central Pennsylvania Lumber Co., with sixteen mills at fourteen sites. Its last mill closed in 1941, marking the end of large-scale lumbering in Pennsylvania. Casler, Kline, & Tabor, *Logging Railroad Era in Pennsylvania*, 1: vii-viii, 490-92.

77. Rector, "Railroad Logging in the Lake States," 351-62; Rector, *Log Transportation*, 194-205, 218-35, 281-85.

78. Williams, *Americans and their Forests*, 254-60; Richard W. Massey, "Logging Railroads in Alabama, 1880-1914," *Alabama Review*, 14 (1961): 41-50; Brown, *Logging-Transportation*, 209. See also, above, Chapter 10.

79. Brown, *Logging-Transportation*, 206-209, 212-14.

80. Strite, "Up the Kilchis, Pt. I," 294-314 (1st quote, p. 313; 2nd quote, p. 310); "Up the Kilchis, Pt. II," 6-10 (3rd and 4th quotes, p. 9). See also: *Timb.*, 19 (Nov. 1917): 49-50; 23 (Mar. 1922): 38; 25 (Nov. 1923): 64-66; 26 (Nov. 1924): 82; (Aug. 1925): 50-53, 174; 28 (Jan. 1927): 37; 29 (Nov. 1927): 52-54; Orcutt, *Tillamook*, 118-19; Brown, *Logging-Transportation*, 209-214.

81. Griggs, "The Pacific Coast Lumber Manufacturers' Association," in NLMA, *Problems Affecting the Lumber Industry*, 130 (quote); Brown, *Logging-Transportation*, 191-93, 200, 203-205, 212-21, 223-25; Williams, *Americans and their Forests*, 318-19; Meany, "History of the Lumber Industry," 259-65;

Henry E. Haefner, "Reminiscences of an Early Forester," *OHQ*, 76 (1975): 61-
63; Donald G. Mackenzie, "Logging Equipment Development in the West,"
oral history interview with Elwood R. Maunder, *FH*, 16 (1972): 31; *Timb.*, 32
(Nov. 1930): 46-49; 33 (July 1932): 26, 46; 34 (Nov. 1932): 28-29; *AL*, n.v. (28
July 1928): 46-47; Brandstrom, *Logging Costs and Operating Methods*, 66.

82. Brown, *Logging-Transportation*, 33-80; *Timb.*, 7 (Mar. 1906): 26; W. F.
McCulloch, "The 'Firstest' Logger," *AF*, 58 (1952): 11, 12, 33-34; Engstrom,
Vanishing Logger, 11-12, 14-15.

83. Richard A. Rajala, *Clearcutting the Pacific Rain Forest: Production, Science,
and Regulation* (Vancouver: University of British Columbia Press, 1998),
20-22; Steve Conway, *Logging Practices: Principles of Timber Harvesting
Systems* (San Francisco: Miller Freeman, 1976), 190-91, 200-210; Rector, *Log
Transportation*, 244-45, 300; Brown, *Logging-Transportation*, 104-111; Prouty,
More Deadly than War!, 61-62, 64-65, 67-70; Williams, *Americans and their
Forests*, 317-19; Brandstrom, *Logging Costs and Operating Methods*, 10-11.

84. Michael Williams credits Butters with developing high-lead logging, but his
evidence shows Butters' system was an early form of skyline logging, not high
lead; Andrew Prouty, in spite of extensive knowledge of the woods, lumps the
two under "overhead logging." Williams, *Americans and their Forests*, 216,
315-16; Prouty, *More Deadly than War!*, 61-78.

85. Williams, *Americans and their Forests*, 216, 315-17; Brown, *Logging-
Transportation*, 79-104; Conway, *Logging Practices*, 192-200; Meany,
"History of the Lumber Industry," 249-50, 286-87; Strite, "Up the Kilchis,
Pt. II," 18-19; George M. Cornwall, "The Logging Industry in Retrospect
and Prospect," ibid., 27 (Nov. 1925): 50-53; Prouty, *More Deadly than War!*,
64-78; Brandstrom, *Logging Costs and Operating Methods*, 10-12, 38, 41, 55,
62-63; H. B. Gardner, "Ground Skidder or High Lead," in *Proceedings of the
Pacific Logging Congress*, (1916): 13. Donkey engines outnumbered high-lead
systems since some of the latter used more than one engine and donkeys were
also used in skyline systems and for loading rail cars.

86. W. S. Taylor, "Different Stages in the Evolution of the Overhead System of
Logging," *Timb.*, 15 (Jan. 1914): 30-31; *West Coast Lumberman*, 29 (1916):
34; *Proceedings of the Pacific Logging Congress*, (1921): 35; R. W. Vinnedge,
"Overhead Logging Systems," ibid., (1922): 14; Meany, "History of the
Lumber Industry," 250-51; Anonymous, "Skyline Methods Used in Logging,"
Timberbeast, 9 (spring 1996): 26-29; McCulloch, "Firstest Logger," 32; Prouty,
More Deadly than War!, 68, 69-70, 75-76; Brandstrom, *Logging Costs and
Operating Systems*, 10-11; Mackenzie, "Logging Equipment," 30-33; Strite,
"Up the Kilchis, Pt. I," 185-86.

87. Repetto, *Way of the Logger*, 1, 10, 13, 18, 34, 38 (quote); Strite, "Up the
Kilchis, Pt. II," 23-25. Even after Lidgerwood introduced a movable steel
tower attached to a railroad car to replace one of the spar trees in a skyline
system, high-climbers continued to be needed. Rajala, *Clearcutting the Pacific
Rain Forest*, 26-29, 50; Williams, *Americans and their Forests*, 317; Conway,
Logging Practices, 190, 234-40. See also: Anonymous, "Lidgerwood vs.
Mundy: Origin of Steel Skidder," *Timb.*, 50 (Oct. 1949): 54-55.

88. Prouty, *More Deadly than War!*, 65, 67, 72-78; Rajala, *Clearcutting the
Pacific Rain Forest*, 26; Giles French, interview by the author, Portland, Ore.,
September 26, 1970.

89. Prouty, *More Deadly than War!*, 59-64, 87-132, 136-37, 143, 157-59; William Manion, "To a Logger," quoted in ibid., 156; Repetto, *Way of the Logger*, 6; Sherman, "Lumber Industry in the Fir Belt," 22; Norman F. Coleman, "Men in the Camp," *Proceedings of the Pacific Logging Congress*, (1923): 43. Manion's verse was written for a memorial plaque in Seaside, Oregon; the plaque was subsequently moved to a local logging museum.

90. *West Coast Lumberman*, 3 (June 1892): 2; Engstrom, *Vanishing Logger*, 105; George L. Drake (with Elwood R. Maunder), "Pacific Logging Congress: An Inside View," *FH*, 16 (Oct. 1972): 27; Prouty, *More Deadly than War!*, 130-32.

91. Prouty, *More Deadly than War!*, 122 (1st quote); *West Coast and Puget Sound Lumberman*, 13 (1902): 293.

92. Ficken, *Forested Land*, 131-32, 135-56; Prouty, *More Deadly than War!* 133-59 (quote, p 143); Drake, "Pacific Logging Congress," 28. See also: NLMA, *Problems Affecting the Lumber Industry*, 73-97, 255.

93. The Northwest lumber industry's labor history has been studied extensively; only a bare outline needs repeating here. See: Jensen, *Lumber and Labor*, 117-47; Robert E. Ficken, "The Wobbly Horrors: Pacific Northwest Lumbermen and the Industrial Workers of the World, 1917-18," *Labor History*, 24 (1983): 325-41; Ficken, *Forested Land*, 131-56, 162-63; Harry W. Stone, "The Beginnings of the Labor Movement in the Pacific Northwest," *OHQ*, 47 (1946): 155-64; H. E. Tobie, "Oregon Labor Disputes, 1919-1923," ibid., 48 (1947): 7-24, 195-213, 309-21; Robert L. Tyler, "I.W.W. in the Pacific Northwest: Rebels of the Woods," ibid., 55 (1954): 3-44; Tyler, *Rebels in the Woods: The I.W.W. in the Pacific Northwest* (Eugene: University of Oregon Books, 1967). See also: Engstrom, *Vanishing Logger*, 38-63.

94. Cloice Howd, *Industrial Relations in the West Coast Lumber Industry*, United States Bureau of Labor Statistics, Misc. Pub. 349 (Washington, D.C.: GPO, 1924); Hidy, Hill, and Nevins, *Timber and Men*, 337-51; Ficken, *Forested Land*, 138-56; Clark, *Mill Town*, 140-56, 173-231; Norman H. Clark, "Everett, 1916, and After," *PNQ*, 57 (1966): 57-64; David C. Botting, Jr., "Bloody Sunday," ibid., 49 (1958): 162-72; John M. McClelland, Jr., "Terror on Tower Avenue," ibid., 57 (1966): 65-72; Robert L. Tyler, "Violence at Centralia, 1919," ibid., 45 (1954): 116-24; Tyler, "The United States Government as Union Organizer: The Loyal Legion of Loggers and Lumbermen," *MVHR*, 47 (1960): 434-51; Harold M. Hyman, *Soldiers and Spruce: Origins of the Loyal Legion of Loggers and Lumbermen* (Los Angeles: University of California, Institute of Industrial Relations, 1963); Claude W. Nichols, Jr., "Brotherhood in the Woods: The Loyal Legion of Loggers and Lumbermen, A Twenty Year Attempt at 'Industrial Cooperation'" (unpub. Ph.D. diss., University of Oregon, 1959). Centralia, where one of the most violent clashes occurred, had mills of its own, but was primarily the railhead for eastbound shipments from Grays Harbor.

95. Jensen, *Lumber and Labor*, 105-106, 107, 111; Howd, *Industrial Relations in the West Coast Lumber Industry*, 24; Tyler, *Rebels of the Woods*, 93; Prouty, *More Deadly than War!* 22-36, 43-49 (quote, p. 44); Engstrom, *Vanishing Logger*, 18-20, 38-39 (quote); Edith Fowlke and Joe Glazer, ed., *Songs of Work and Protest* (New York: Dover, 1973), 157 (Hill quote); Clark, *Eighteen Men and a Horse*, 91-95. Cf. Rajala, *Clearcutting the Pacific Rain Forest*, 29-30.

In spite of Joe Hill's words, food was generally plentiful in logging camps; it was other living conditions that were notoriously bad. See: Joseph R. Conlin, "'Old Boy, Did You Get Enough Pie?': A Social History of Food in Logging Camps" *JFH*, 23 (1979): 164-85; Prouty, *More Deadly than War!*, 36-43.

96. *West Coast Lumberman*, 32 (Nov. 1917): 39; 44 (1 May 1923), 33; Engstrom, *Vanishing Logger*, 72-73, 81-85; Sherman, "Lumber Industry in the Fir Belt," 45, 57-58, 65; Howd, *Industrial Relations in the West Coast Lumber Industry*, 38; Pomeroy, *Far West in the Twentieth Century*, 107; Stewart H. Holbrook, *The American Luumberjack* (enlarged ed. of *Holy Old Mackinaw*; New York: Collier, 1962), 219-24, 230-31.

97. Ficken, *Forested Land*, 72-73, 133; Clark, *Eighteen Men and a Horse*, 92; Prouty, *More Deadly than War!*, 26-27, 43-44; Repetto, *Way of the Logger*, 33.

98. Hiram M. Cranmer, reminiscence, 3 July 1947 (typescript; Forest History Society, Durham, N.C.), 1. Cf. Clark, *Mill Town*, 178-79, 181-82. The portion of Cranmer's account dealing with the Pacific Northwest was not included in the version published as "Reminiscences of a Pennsylvania Wood-Hick," in the *Western Pennsylvania Historical Magazine* and cited earlier.

99. Ficken, *Forested Land*, 142-44, 148-49; Rajala, *Clearcutting the Pacific Rain Forest*, 10 (quote). Simon Benson was among the more enlightened; he established Benson Polytechnic High School in Portland to provide training for industrial jobs and thus undercut the attraction of the IWW to youth who could only look forward to menial jobs. See: William R. Lindley, "Lumber King Countered Wobblies with Portland Trade School," *JW*, 32 (1993): 69-75. See also: Clark, *Eighteen Men and a Horse*, 92-107.

100. Clark, *Mill Town*, 63-64 (1st quote, p. 63; 2nd quote, p. 64), 163-65 (3rd quote, p. 164), 202-226 (4th quote, p. 202), 238-39; Ficken, *Forested Land*, 140, 141, 144-45, 148; *Timb.*, 18 (Nov. 1916): 80P (quote); (July 1917): 71; Prouty, *More Deadly than War!*, 26-27. On Hartley, see: Albert Francis Gunns, "Roland Hill Hartley and the Politics of Washington State" (unpub. M.A. thesis, University of Washington, 1963); Herbert Hunt and Floyd C. Kaylor, *Washington West of the Cascades* (3 vols.; Chicago: Clarke, 1917), 2: 172-77; Robert E. Ficken, *Lumber and Politics: The Career of Mark E. Reed* (Seattle: University of Washington Press, 1979), 93-131.

101. Peavy was prescient. By the 1950s, private stands were so depleted lumbermen turned increasingly to Forest Service timber. For analyses of the shift, see: Paul W. Hirt, *Conspiracy of Optimism: Management of the National Forests since World War Two* (Lincoln: University of Nebraska Press, 1994), and Thomas Parry, Henry J. Vaux, and Nicholas Dennis, "Changing Conceptions of Sustained-Yield Policy on the National Forests," *JF*, 81 (1983): 150-54.

102. Erickson, "Morphology of Lumber Settlements," 95-98 (quote, p. 97); Thornton T. Munger, *Timber Growing and Logging Practice in the Douglas Fir Region*, USDA Bulletin no. 1493 (Washington: GPO, 1927), 13-14; Forest Service, *Timber Depletion*, 32; Allen H. Hodgson, *Logging Waste in the Douglas Fir Region* (Portland: West Coast Lumberman, 1930), ix-x; George W. Peavy, *Oregon's Commercial Forests*, Oregon State Board of Forestry Bulletin no. 2 (Salem: State Printer, 1922), 15. On Munger, see also: Rajala, *Clearcutting the Pacific Rain Forest,* passim.

103. Quoted in Portland *Oregonian*, 5 Sept. 1920. See also: Thomas R. Cox,
     The Park Builders: A History of State Parks in the Pacific Northwest (Seattle:
     University of Washington Press, 1988), 32-36.
104. Cox, *Park Builders*, 36-37. Lumbermen Simon Benson, R. A. Booth,
     and John Yeon joined Olcott in his preservationist campaigns. See: Cox,
     Park Builders, 40, 54, 191, 193, 208; Lockley, *History of the Columbia River
     Valley*, 1: 630, 832; Michael J. Evers, "John Yeon and the Construction of the
     Columbia River Highway" (unpub. M.A. thesis, San Diego State University,
     1992), 10-15, 47-48, 94.
105. Allen, *Practical Forestry*, 39-48; Forest Service, *Growth and Management
     of Douglas Fir in the Pacific Northwest*, Circular 175 (Washington, D.C.:
     GPO, 1911); Munger, *Timber Growing and Logging Practice in the Douglas
     Fir Region*; Munger, "The Cycle from Douglas Fir to Hemlock," *Ecology*, 21
     (1940): 451-59; Rajala, *Clearcutting the Pacific Rain Forest*, 92-94, 110-11. See
     also: Allen, "America's Transition from Old Forests to New," *AF*, 29 (1923):
     67-71, 106, 163-68, 235-40, 307-311; John F. Preston, "Silvicultural Practice
     in the United States during the Past Quarter Century," *JF*, 23 (1925): 236-44;
     Leo A. Isaac, *Reproductive Habits of Douglas Fir* (Washington, D.C.: Forest
     Service, 1943).
106. Rajala, *Clearcutting the Pacific Rain Forest*, 123-24, 139-42; Anonymous,
     "Selective Logging and Its Application in the Douglas Fir Region," *Timb.*, 30
     (June 1929): 38-42; Anonymous, "The Application of Selective Logging in
     the Douglas Fir Region," *West Coast Lumberman*, 57 (1930): 27-28; "Selective
     Logging in the National Forests of Douglas Fir Region," *JF*, 29 (1931): 768-74;
     Thornton T. Munger, "A Look at Selective Cutting in Douglas-Fir," ibid., 48
     (1950): 97-99; Bruce E. Hoffman, *Management Possibilities in Douglas Fir
     Forests* (Washington, D.C.: Charles Lathrop Pack Forestry Foundation, 1941).
107. Erickson, "Morphology of Lumber Settlements," 88-89, 100-102 (quotes, pp.
     100-101).
108. David A. Cameron, "The Silverton Nursery: An Early Experiment in
     Pacific Northwestern Reforestation," *JFH*, 23 (1979): 122-29; Erickson,
     "Morphology of Lumber Settlements," 104-107; Allen, *Practical Forestry*,
     18-21, 33-35, 70-76, 113-28; Steen, *Forest Service*, 92, 110, 130; White, *Land
     Use, Environment, and Social Change*, 97-105, 113-41; Williams, *Americans
     and their Forests*, 304-305, 455-56; Hidy, Hill, and Nevins, *Timber and Men*,
     381-85, 388-89. Abandoning cutover repeated patterns seen in the Lake States
     and Gulf South; it reflected received knowledge ill fitted for the Northwest.
     Such practices had been ill suited to earlier frontiers too, but the expectation
     of being able to farm cleared forests continued because of the persistence of
     Jeffersonian concepts that existed more in the American mind than in reality.
109. Robbins, *Colony and Empire: The Capitalist Transformation of the American
     West* (Lawrence: University Press of Kansas, 1994), 3-21, 128-31; Robbins,
     "The 'Plundered Province' Thesis and Recent Historiography of the
     American West," *PHR*, 55 (1986): 577-97; Erickson, "Morphology of Lumber
     Settlements," 102-103; Thomas R. Cox, "The Stewardship of Private Forests:
     The Evolution of a Concept," *JFH*, 25 (1981): 188-96; Cox, *Park Builders*,
     8-13, 32-78. Robbins repeats his charge implicitly or explicitly in other works
     as well. The phrase "plundered province" originated with Bernard DeVoto,

"The West: A Plundered Province," *Harper's*, 169 (1934): 355-63. See also: Patricia Nelson Limerick, *The Legacy of Conquest: The Unbroken Past of the American West* (New York: Norton, 1987).
110. Smyth, *Millicoma*, 28-42, 48-53.

Chapter Thirteen

1. Unlike the Douglas fir abundant from the Cascades to the sea, that in the interior yielded hard, brittle, inferior lumber. Trade journals have much information on log truck development. See, for examples: J. P. Drissen, "Time Study of Motor Truck Logging of Yellow Pine," *Timb.*, 22 (Aug. 1921): 97; 23 (Dec. 1921): 1-2; Hamilton L. Hintz, "Motor Truck Logging in Northern California," ibid., 24 (May 1923): 130-32; Truman W. Collins, "Evolution of Logging Trucks," ibid., 40 (Aug. 1939): 15-16. See also: Myron E. Krueger, "Forestry and Technology in Northern California, 1925-1965," oral history interview by Amelia R. Fry, 1968 (Bancroft Library, Regional Oral History Office, Berkeley, Calif.), 5-8.

2. United States Geological Survey, *Twentieth Annual Report, 1898-1899* (7 vols.; Washington, D.C.: GPO, 1900), 5: 143. The governor of Idaho Territory expressed similar sentiments in 1879: "[T]he people must consume the timber growing on the public lands or abandon the country. . . . Even an army could not protect the timber from depredation" (quoted in Dunham, *Government Handout*, 59). See also: G. Michael McCarthy, *Hour of Trial: The Conservation Conflict in Colorado and the West, 1891-1907* (Norman: University of Oklahoma Press, 1977), 26-28, 63-66; Richardson, *Politics of Conservation*, 53, 86-90, 153-56 and passim; Robert L. Matheny, "The History of Lumbering in Arizona before World War II" (unpub. Ph.D. diss., University of Arizona, 1975), 172, 188-94.

3. Rakestraw, "Forest Conservation in the Pacific Northwest," 174-92, 207-208;   Philip Cogswell, Jr., "Deschutes Country Pine Logging," in Thomas Vaughan, ed., *High & Mighty: Select Sketches about the Deschutes Country* (Portland: Oregon Historical Society, 1981), 236-38; Ronald L. Gregory, "Life in Railroad Logging Camps of the Shevlin-Hixon Company, 1916-1950," *Anthropology Northwest*, 12 (2001): 16-18.

4. Land to be irrigated lay north and east of Bend, timber south and west. See: Anonymous, *An Illustrated History of Central Oregon . . .* (Spokane, Wash.: Western Historical Publishing, 1905), 129; Phil F. Brogan, *East of the Cascades* (Portland, Ore.: Binfords & Mort, 1964), 97-201.

5. U.S. Public Lands Commission, *Report*, 58th Cong., 3rd sess., 1905, S. Doc. 189, pp. vi, xvi; U.S. National Conservation Commission, *Report*, 60th Cong., 2nd sess., 1909, S. Doc. 676, 3: 389; Puter, *Looters of the Public Domain*, 81 (1st quote), 84 (2nd quote). Shevlin's huge mill in Minneapolis closed in 1907, so it was ready for a new seat of operations. See: Larson, *Empire in Pine*, 399.

6. F. P. Deering to Weyerhaeuser Timber Co., 5 June 1907, Weyerhaeuser Timber Co., incoming corres., 1900-1938, Deering file, Weyerhaeuser Timber Company Papers (Weyerhaeuser Company Archives, Federal Way, Wash. [hereafter WTCP]), box 44; Brogan, *East of the Cascades*, 248-49; Rakestraw, "Forest Conservation in the Pacific Northwest," 47-53, 159-61, 206-208, 267; Puter, *Looters of the Public Domain*, 80-88; O'Callaghan, *Disposition of*

the Public Domain in Oregon, 13-15, 61-66, 71-80, 92; Gregory, "Railroad Logging Camps of Shevlin-Hixon," 18-22.

7. Recent literature has depicted the Forest Service as playing a custodial role with little active timber management until after World War II. This is a distortion, even though the Forest Service *did* become more active in timber sales after the war than before. Cf. Hirt, *Conspiracy of Optimism,* 27-43; Clary, *Timber and the Forest Service,* 29-93; Nancy Langston, *Forest Dreams, Forest Nightmares: The Paradox of Old Growth in the Inland West* (Seattle: University of Washington Press, 1995), 108-113, 157-200.

8. Thanks to a cycle of wet years, there was considerable homesteading on desert lands of Central Oregon in the first decades of the twentieth century. As settlers were "dusted out" when normal rainfall returned, they often went to work in the woods and mills, as did railroad-construction workers once lines to the area had been completed, but there was still a relatively small local labor supply. Gregory, "Railroad Logging Camps of Shevlin-Hixon," 33-37.

9. *Fossil* (Oregon) *Journal,* 8 Apr., 21 Oct. 1927; Wetmore to Chapel, 18 July 1930, Wetmore, incoming corres., WP, box 4; observations by the author in the summers of 1949 and 1950. Wetmore considered building the mill in Condon, located in the wheat country at the end of a Southern Pacific spur line, but finally decided to build a twenty-four-mile common carrier from Condon to a site nearer their timber.

10. Holbrook, *Holy Old Mackinaw,* 156, 187; Gregory, "Railroad Logging Camps of Shevlin-Hixon," 39; Paul Hosmer, *Now We're Loggin'* (Portland, Ore.: Metropolitan Press, 1930), 39-46. The Minnesota-Scandinavian influence was common knowledge when the author lived in the area in the 1940s and 1950s. Brooks-Scanlon also had major operations in Louisiana during the period and (after 1917) in Florida, but while Minnesotans often filled supervisory positions there, the firm's mills there drew largely on Southern sources for laborers. See: Drobney, *Lumbermen and Log Sawyers,* 55-58, 103-104.

11. Kinzua Lumber Co. to W. S. Jackson, 31 July 1909; Butte Creek Land, Live Stock & Lumber Co. to W. C. Calder, 14 and 28 Feb., 5 Mar. 1918; Calder to Butte Creek Land, Live Stock, & Lumber, 18 Feb., 2 Mar. 1918; Calder to Wetmore, 2 and 28 Mar. 1918, Kinzua Lumber Co., outgoing corres., 1909-1918 file, WP, box 97; F. Smith Fussner, ed., *Glimpses of Wheeler County's Past: An Early History of North Central Oregon* (Portland, Ore.: Binfords & Mort, 1975), 61-65; Rakestraw, "Forest Conservation in the Pacific Northwest," 96-124, 174-76. The penchant of sheepmen for setting fires to "green up the range," a major problem in California, was less common in the inland Northwest.

12. Weyerhaeuser, *Trees and Men,* 14-15; Hidy, Hill, and Nevins, *Timber and Men,* 207-208, 248-72; Kohlmeyer, *Timber Roots,* 296-306, 313; Twining, *Phil Weyerhaeuser,* 3-55; Keith C. Petersen, *Company Town: Potlatch, Idaho, and the Potlatch Lumber Company* (Pullman: Washington State University Press, 1987), 1-34; John Fahey, *The Inland Empire: Unfolding Years, 1879-1929* (Seattle: University of Washington Press, 1986), 188-213; Clarence C. Strong and Clyde S. Webb, *White Pine: King of Many Waters* (Missoula, Mont.: Mountain Press, 1970), 1-34; C. Edward Behre, "Stumpage Prices in Lake States and Inland Empire," *Timb.,* 22 (Aug. 1921): 65-66S; Blair Hutchinson,

"A Century of Lumbering in Northern Idaho," ibid., 39 (Sept. 1938): 14-15; (Aug. 1938): 20-21.

13. Kohlmeyer, *Timber Roots*, 294-98; J. B. Lafferty, *My Eventful Years* (Weiser, Ida.: Signal American, 1963), 31, 44-45; Harry C. Shellworth, oral history interview with Ralph W. Hidy, 1955 (Forest History Society, Durham, N.C.), 45-46; ibid., interview with Elwood R. Maunder, 6 June 1966, 1-9; Merle W. Wells, "Timber Frauds on Crooked River," *IY*, 29 (Summer 1985): 2-13; Boise *Idaho Herald*, 2 Apr. 1915; Anonymous, "The Two Modern Plants of the Boise Payette Company," *Timb.*, 21 (Mar. 1920): 41.

14. William H. Kensel, "Early Spokane Lumber Industry, 1871-1910," *IY*, 12 (Spring 1968): 25-31; Edith E. Erickson, "Lumbering in Whitman County," *Bunchgrass Historian*, 8 (Summer 1980): 13-17; Robert W. Swanson, "A History of Logging and Lumbering on the Palouse River, 1870-1905" (unpub. M.A. thesis, Washington State University, 1958); A. W. Moltke, oral history interview with Elwood R. Maunder and George T. Morgan, 2 July 1960 (Forest History Society, Durham, N.C.), 1-2, 5; Orrin H. Sinclair, oral history interview with John Larson, 1954, ibid., 6-9; A. C. White, "Lumber Industry of the Inland Empire," *Timb.*, 22 (Mar. 1921): 129-32; A. W. Cooper, "The Inland Empire Lumber Industry," ibid., 25 (Mar. 1924): 52-55; Anonymous, "A Survey of Inland Empire Conditions," ibid., 25 (Oct. 1924): 130; Anonymous, "Sawmills of North Central Washington," ibid., 25 (Oct. 1924): 135; Wetmore to J. P. Jefferson, 29 May, 11 July, 5 Sept. 1925, 26 Oct. 1926, Jefferson incoming corres., 1925-27 file, WP, box 46.

15. Robert L. Matheny, "Lumbering in the White Mountains of Arizona, 1919-1942," *Arizona and the West*, 18 (1976): 237-46; Matheny, "History of Lumbering in Arizona," 212-13, 233-34 and passim; Duane A. Smith, "A Social History of McPhee, Colorado's Largest Lumber Town," in *Forests Under Fire: A Century of Ecosystem Mismanagement in the Southwest*, Christopher J. Huggard and Arthur R. Gomez, ed. (Tucson: University of Arizona Press, 2001), 42-46; L. J. Colton, "Early Day Timber Cutting upon the Upper Bear River," *Utah Historical Quarterly*, 25 (1967): 202-208; Clarence C. Strong and Judy Schutza, "The Birth of Montana's Lumber Industry," *Pacific Northwest Forum*, 3 (winter 1978): 11-21; Anonymous, "National Forests of New Mexico," *Timb.*, 24 (Apr. 1923): 40-41; Anonymous, "Developing New Mexico's Lumber Wealth," ibid., 25 (Apr. 1924): 62; Greeley, "Report of the Forester (1925)," 25, 26.

16. Bradley, *Long*, 177; W. H. Hutchinson, "The Sierra Flume & Lumber Company of California, 1875-1878," *FH*, 17 (Oct. 1973): 14-20; Philip M. McDonald and Lona F. Lahore, "Lumbering in the Northern Sierra Nevada: Andrew Martin Leach of Challenge Mills," *Pacific Historian*, 28 (Summer 1984): 19-31; Anonymous, "Feather River Scene of New Mill Activities," *Timb.*, 21 (Aug. 1920): 39 (quote); C. Stowell Smith, "California White and Sugar Pine Industry," ibid., 23 (Feb. 1922): 124-26; Anonymous, "Weed Lumber Co.," ibid., 24 (Apr. 1923): 103; Anonymous, "California Sugar Pine," ibid., 26 (Jan. 1925): 50-51; Anonymous, "Pioneer California Pine Company: History of Madera Sugar Pine Co.," ibid., 30 (June 1929): 180-82; [Defebaugh], *American Lumbermen*, 3: 62-64; W. H. Hutchinson, "The California Investment of the Diamond Match Company" (typescript, 1957;

copy, Forest History Society Library, Durham, N.C.), 31-62; James T. Stevens, oral history interview with Elwood R. Maunder, 1957 (Forest History Society, Durham, N.C.), 27-29; Swift Berry, *Lumbering in the Sugar and Yellow Pine Region of California*, U.S. Dept. of Agriculture, Bulletin no. 440 (Washington, D. C.: GPO, 1917).

17. Thornton T. Munger, *Western Yellow Pine in Oregon*, U.S. Department of Agriculture Bulletin no. 418 (Washington, D.C.: Dept. of Agriculture, 1917); George L. Drake, *A Forester's Log: Fifty Years in the Pacific Northwest*, oral history interview with Elwood R. Maunder, 1975 (Forest History Society, Durham, N.C.), 94-95; W. C. Geddes, oral history interview with John Larson, 1953 (Forest History Society, Durham, N.C.), 3; Brogan, *East of the Cascades*, 234-56; Gregory, "Railroad Logging Camps of Shevlin-Hixon," 15-16; Leonard Arrington, *David Eccles: Pioneer Western Industrialist* (Logan: Utah State University Press, 1975), 83-95; Anonymous, "A Vigorous Lumber Center of the Far West," *AL*, n.v. (24 Aug. 1912): 38-40; Anonymous, "Pioneer Lumbering in Klamath . . ." *Timb.*, 29 (July 1928): 42-49; Anonymous, "Pioneer Eastern Oregon Lumber Firm," ibid., 34 (Sept. 1933): 48-49; W. E. Lamm, *Lumbering in Klamath* (Klamath Falls, Ore.: Lamm Lumber Co., n.d.), 32-34. Large mills came to Klamath after a rail line reached it from Weed in 1909 and to Bend after completion of rail construction through the Deschutes River canyon in 1911. Lamm, *Lumbering in Klamath*, 12-17; Cogswell, "Deschutes Country Pine Logging," 237-42.

18. Wetmore had a number of partnerships, many with overlapping membership, and holdings in both Southern and Far Western pineries. Several were operated out of the same office in Baker, Oregon. Most were timber speculations without operating mills. In time he added a dairy farm, a newspaper, orange groves, and other enterprises. Money for these ventures came from the oil and timber industries of western Pennsylvania. Wetmore's voluminous but little-utilized papers detail his many business interests.

19. Wetmore to Jefferson, 29 May, 11 July, 5 Sept. 1925, 26 Oct. 1926 (quotes), Jefferson, incoming corres., 1925-27 file, WP, box 46; Wetmore to D. B. Turner, 21 Aug. 1926, Turner-Wetmore incoming corres., 1919-33 file, ibid., box 13. See also: David Townsend Mason, *Timber Ownership and Lumber Production in the Inland Empire* (Portland, Ore.: Western Pine Manufacturers Association, 1920), 64-73. Mason had been less sanguine; he noted that from 1905 to 1915 that costs of production outstripped prices realized, but by Wetmore's survey things had improved markedly.

20. Chapel to Wetmore, 25 and 28 May, 2 Nov. 1927, Wetmore incoming corres., 1927 and no date file, WP, box 4; Wetmore to Jones, 25 Oct. 1927, ibid., outgoing corres., 1927-28 file, ibid., box 6; Wetmore to Chapel, 28 and 31 Oct., 2 Nov. 1927, ibid.; Wetmore to Chapel, 19 and 24 May 1927, Chapel outgoing corres., 1927-33 file, ibid., box 10; F. C. McColloch to Chapel (and accompanying clipping), 16 July 1933, ibid.; Wetmore to Chapel, 9 Nov. 1927, Wetmore outgoing corres., 1927-28 file, ibid., box 47; *Fossil Journal*, 18 Feb., 8 Apr., 16 Sept., 28 Oct. 1927, 9 Nov. 1928. See also: Puter, *Looters of the Public Domain*, 350.

21. Kinzua Lumber Co. to Jackson, 31 July 1909; Wetmore, report to stockholders, 21 Oct. 1916, Kinzua Lumber Co., outgoing corres., 1909-18 file, WP, box 97; Hidy, Hill, and Nevins, *Timber and Men*, 241. Willard

Jones had been an associate of Puter and the Blue Mountains were an area where timber fraud took place, but no evidence has been located indicating the firm's acquisitions were illegal. Jones bought scrip on the open market and used it to file on land for Kinzua. This was within the letter if not spirit of the law, and correspondence of Jones and Wetmore gives no hint either considered it improper.

22. Kinzua Lumber Co. to Jackson, 31 July 1909, Kinzua Lumber Co. outgoing corres., 1909-18 file, ibid., box 97; Jones to Wetmore, 9 Sept. 1912, ibid., incoming corres., 1909-18 file; Morris Shelton to Wetmore, Wetmore, incoming corres., 1923-24 file, ibid., box 3; Gardinier Lumber Co., minutes of annual stockholders' meeting, 26 Oct. 1925, ibid.; "List of Mills in Oregon and Washington Established Primarily to Cut National Forest Timber," 31 Jan. 1927, S-Sales Policy, 1915-1926 file, Record Group 95, Forest Service, Pacific Northwest Regional Office, Historical Records (National Archives and Records Service, Seattle [hereafter PNW Hist. Rec.]), box 14. Not long after the Kinzua purchases, government timber in the area was going for $3.10 per thousand for pine and $1 per thousand for other species. See: Kinzua Lumber Co. to Jones, 8 Apr. 1913, Kinzua Lumber Co. outgoing corres., 1909-1918 file, WP, box 97.

23. Material on Herrick is fragmentary. See: Spokane *Spokesman-Review*, 22 July 1910; Wilbur W. Hindley, "His 20 Log Started $12,000,000 Fortune," ibid., 26 May 1929; Anonymous, "A Lumberman with Hobbies," *Timb.*, 24 (June 1923): 31; J. M. Pond, "Fred Herrick: The Story of One of the Most Colorful Careers in the Lumber Industry of this Country," *Four-L Lumber News*, 12 (1 Sept. 1930): 18, 42-43; Arthur Earl Victor, "Fred Herrick and Bill Grote: Idaho's Paul Bunyan and His Bull of the Woods," *Pacific Northwesterner*, 16 (1972): 33-48; Harry C. Shellworth, oral history interview with Elwood R. Maunder, 1963 (Forest History Society, Durham, N.C.), 4-5; Strong and Webb, *White Pine*, 143-47; Godfrey, *Forestry History of Ten Wisconsin Indian Reservations*, 119-21.

24. H. A. Bergh to State Land Commissioners, 18 Feb. 1918, Heyburn State Park files, Dept. of Parks and Recreation Papers (Idaho State Archives, Boise), folder 7. This folder, labeled "Logging/Export Lumber Co.," contains voluminous records on the suits. For a summary, see: F. G. Miller and Henry Schmitz, "A Report on Heyburn Park," (typescript; 2 vols.; Moscow, Ida., 1920), 2: 16-20 (copy in Heyburn Park files).

25. *Timb.*, 21 (Oct. 1920): 49; George Francis Brimlow, *Harney County, Oregon, and Its Range Land* (Portland, Ore.: Binfords & Mort, 1957); Peter K. Simpson, *The Community of Cattlemen: A Social History of the Cattle Industry in Southeastern Oregon, 1869-1912* (Moscow: University of Idaho Press, 1987), 5-14, 86-115, 152-54; E. R. Jackman and R. A. Long, *The Oregon Desert* (Caldwell, Ida.: Caxton, 1973), 1-15.

26. Wm. T. Cox to District Forester, 30 Jan. 1909, S-Sales, Policy, 1908-1914 file, PNW Hist. Rec., box 14 (quote); George H. Cecil to Forester, 14 Feb. 1911, ibid., box 13; Cox to Cecil, 25 Feb. 1911, ibid.; Henry S. Graves to James Wilson, 8 July 1912, S-Sales, General, 1909-14 file, ibid., box 13; F. E. Ames to Forest Officers, 30 Mar. 1915, General, 1915-23 file, ibid.

27. Canyon City (Ore.) *Blue Mountain Eagle*, 30 Mar. 1923.

28. Drake, *Forester's Log*, 95-96 (quote, p. 95), 109; David T. Mason, oral history interview with Elwood R. Maunder, 26 July 1967 (transcript; Forest History Society, Durham, N.C.), tape no. 349, p. 47; Ira Jenckers Mason, oral history interview with Elwood R. Maunder, 10 Jan. 1968 (Forest History Society, Durham, N.C.), 3; Brimlow, *Harney County*, 237; Canyon City *Blue Mountain Eagle*, 20 Nov. 1925; Jerry L. Mosgrove, *The Malheur National Forest, An Ethnographic History* (John Day, Ore.: Malheur National Forest, 1980), 178, 183. Barnes may have visited the area as early as 1910 and interested the Edward H. Hines Company of Chicago in it soon thereafter; Barnes also may have been behind Balfour & Guthrie's application. As with many things regarding him, the record is not clear. See: Lakeview (Ore.) *Lake County Examiner*, 25 Oct. 1928; Cecil to Forester, 14 Feb. 1911, S-Sales, Policy, 1908-14 file, PNW Hist. Rec., box 14.

29. Drake, *Forester's Log*, 95-96.

30. Ibid.; Brimlow, *Harney County*, 237-38; Canyon City *Blue Mountain Eagle*, 9 Nov. 1923.

31. Henry S. Graves, "Report of the Forester (1919)," 10; Greeley, "Report of the Forester (1920)," 10; ibid. [1921], 18-19; Walter H. Lund, "Timber Management in the Pacific Northwest Region, 1927-1965," oral history interview with Amelia R. Fry, 1967 (Bancroft Library, Regional Oral History Office, Berkeley, Calif.), 16-17; Cox to Greeley, 25 Feb. 1911, PNW Hist. Rec. box 14. On Greeley's policies, see: George T. Morgan, Jr., *William B. Greeley, A Practical Forester, 1879-1955* (St. Paul, Minn.: Forest History Society, 1961), 32-58; Robbins, *Lumberjacks and Legislators:*, 90-97, 101-102, 105-106, 109-111.

32. Its original timberland largely cut, Brooks would continue as a major operator by purchasing the large Hill family holdings west of Bend.

33. Drake, *A Forester's Log*, 97, 99-100; Greeley, "Report of the Forester (1922)," 23; Edward Hines Lumber Co., "Memorandum to the United States Forest Service, Department of Agriculture," 10 July 1961 (copy; Edward Hines Lumber Co., vertical file, Forest History Society, Durham, N.C.), 3, 10-11, 20-23, 25, A.2-A.9. On Girard, see: Rodney C. Loehr, ed., *The Man Who Knew Trees: The Autobiography of James W. Girard*, (St. Paul, Minn: Forest Products History Society, 1949), 24; Anonymous, "James W. Girard: Patriarch of National Forest Timber Cruising . . ." (typescript; U.S. Forest Service History Collection, logging: timber cruising file, Forest History Society, Durham. N.C). Although large, the sale was to be only the opening wedge. Working plans encompassed some eleven billion feet of timber tributary to Burns, five-sixths of it in public ownership. See: E. J. Hanzlik, "Working Plan Report for the Burns Working Circle," 6 July 1922, S-Plans, Timber Management, Malheur, Burns W.C. (1922-50) file, Forest Service, Pacific Northwest Regional Office Records (National Archives and Records Service, Seattle [hereafter PNW Records]); B. E. Hoffman, "Report Concerning Factors Affecting Plan of Management of Timber Tributary to Burns," 1 Feb. 1926, ibid.; Walt L. Dutton, "Management Plan, Silvies Working Circle, Malheur National Forest," May 1928, ibid.

34. Greeley, "Report of the Forester (1923)," 26. See also: E. D. Kneipp to District Forester, 23 May 1928, S-Plans, Timber Management, Malheur, Burns

W. C., PNW Records, box 82; Hanzlik, "Working Plan Report," ibid. As Hanzlik put it, "Timber developments in this circle will be a means of aiding all established communities in the region." For Forest Service views, see: Jno. D. Guthrie, "Development of New Oregon Pine Section," *Timb.*, 25 (Oct. 1924): 49-51, 127-29.

35. For details, see: Thomas R. Cox, "Frontier Enterprise vs. the Modern Age: Fred Herrick and the Closing of the Lumberman's Frontier," *PNQ*, 84 (1993): 19-29; Langston, *Forest Dreams, Forest Nightmares*, 175-87; Langston, "Forest Dreams, Forest Nightmares: An Environmental History of a Forest Health Crisis," in Char Miller, ed., *American Forests: Nature, Culture, and Politics* (Lawrence: University Press of Kansas, 1997), 257-63; Mosgrove, *Malheur National Forest*, 183-89.

36. Greeley, "Report of the Forester (1926)," 26; Drake, *Forester's Log*, 102-103; Brimlow, *Harney County*, 238-39; Canyon City *Blue Mountain Eagle*, 27 June, 17 Oct. 1924 (quote), 30 Jan., 21 Aug. 1925, 9 Apr. (Girard quote), 25 June 1926, 4 Mar. 1927; Burns *Times-Herald*, 18 July (quote) and 21 Aug. 1925; Anonymous, "Girard: Patriarch of National Forest Timber Cruising," 9. See also: S-Sales, Appraisals, Fred Herrick Lmbr. Co. file, PNW Records, box 141.

37. Burns *Times-Herald*, 20 Mar., 24 Apr., 26 June 1926, 1, 15, and 29 Jan., 5 Feb., 8 Oct., 3 Dec. 1927; Canyon City *Blue Mountain Eagle*, 25 June, 15 Oct. 1926, 14 and 28 Jan., 1 Apr. 1927; Portland *Oregon Journal*, 9 Jan. 1927; *Herrick Timber Contract, Malheur National Forest, Oreg.*, Senate Report 1695, 69th Cong., 2nd sess.; Drake, *Forester's Log*, 105-106; I. J. Mason, oral history, 3-4; Brimlow, *Harney County*, 239-40.

38. Drake, *Forester's Log*, 102; Burns *Times-Herald*, 8 Oct. 1927.

39. Burns *Times-Herald*, 3 and 17 Dec. 1927.

40. Drake, *Forester's Log*, 103-105; C. M. Granger to Forester, 12 May 1928, S-Plans, Timber Management, Malheur, Burns W.C., 1922-50 file, PNW Records, box 82. In the end, Lutcher & Moore "bought into an outfit down in Arizona on one of the Indian reservations which turned out to be a lemon. Afterwards . . . they were kind of regretful that they hadn't spent their money at Burns." Drake, *Forester's Log*, 104.

41. Burns *Times-Herald*, 28 Jan., 2 and 9 June 1928; Canyon City *Blue Mountain Eagle*, 8 June 1928; Prineville *Central Oregonian*, 14 June 1928; Lakeview *Lake County Examiner*, 12 Jan., 2 Feb. 1928; Drake, *Forester's Log*, 104; Mosgrove, *Malheur National Forest*, 189.

42. Hines as quoted in [Anonymous], *Fifty Years, Edward Hines Lumber Company* (Chicago: Edward Hines Lumber Co., 1942), 5, and in [Anonymous], "Forest to Factory to You: Edward Hines Lumber Co., Seventy-Fifth Year" (typescript; n.p., [c. 1967], 5; *AL*, n.v. 24 July 1909): 42-43; ibid. (19 Oct. 1929): 60; Lewis, "Edward Hines," 64-65. See also: Larson, *White Pine Industry in Minnesota*, 235, 260, 373, 380, 400; Hidy, Hill, and Nevins, *Timber and Men*, 195-96; Oehler, *Time in the Timber*, 56; Nute, *Rainy River Country*, 91-94, 96-99.

43. *AL*, 30 (7 Sept. 1929): 56; ibid. (19 Oct. 1929): 60; ibid. (14 Dec. 929): 74; ibid. (28 Dec. 1929): 50; Anonymous, *Fifty Years*, 5-21; Drake, *Forester's Log*, 105-106; Prineville *Central Oregonian*, 14 June 1928; Lakeview *Lake County Examiner*, 4 Oct., 27 Dec. 1928; Burns *Times-Herald*, 22 and 29 Sept. 1928,

2, 10, 24, and 31 Jan. (quote), 7 and 14 Feb., 28 Mar., 8 May 1930. The special edition of the *Times-Herald* published on dedication day is replete with information on Hines, his companies, the mill, and its key personnel.

44. Burns *Times-Herald*, 31 Jan. 1930; Drake, *Forester's Log*, 106-108 (quotes), 110.

45. Brimlow, *Harney County*, 240-42; Mosgrove, *Malheur National Forest*, 189-95; I. J. Mason, oral history, 4; Hines, "Memorandum to United States Forest Service," 3, 23-25; Edward Hines Lumber Company, *1982 Annual Report*, 3; S-Sales, Appraisals Edward Hines Lmbr. Co. file, PNW Records, box 141; Jefferson to Chapel, 5 Aug. 1929, Wetmore incoming corres., 1928-29 file, WP, box 4; Jefferson to Wetmore, 13 Mar. 1930, Jefferson outgoing corres., 1927-30 file, ibid., box 47. On Hines's situation, see also: Luce to Wetmore, 10 Mar. 1929, Wetmore incoming corres., 1929 file, ibid., box 4; Drake, *Forester's Log*, 145-46; Lewis, "Edward Hines," 64-65.

46. Scott Leavitt, oral history interview with Elwood R. Maunder and George T. Morgan, 6 July 1960 (Forest History Society, Durham, N.C.), 2-4; Guy M. Ingram to District Forester, 20 Mar. 1909, S-Sales, Policy, 1908-14 file, PNW Hist. Rec., box 14. There is considerable discussion of slash/brush piling in Policy files, ibid., boxes 13-14. Ingram was obviously thinking of a number of small sales, not the sort of major offering that attracted development to Burns.

47. J. F. Kimball to George S. Long, 27 Mar. 1910, Kimball 1910 file, WTCP, incoming corres., box 52.

48. The N-C-O had reached Alturas, California, some fifty miles south of Lakeview, in 1908. David Myrick, "Nevada-California-Oregon Railway," *Western Railroader*, 18 (June 1955): 2-20.

49. George S. Long, "Memorandum Regarding a Block of Timber We Own in Modoc County," 14 Aug. 1919, timber assessments file, Long, office files (Weyerhaeuser Company Archives, Federal Way, Wash. [hereafter, LPO]), box 3; Long to Kimball, 14 Aug. 1919, ibid. Modoc County is in California, immediately south of Oregon's Lake County.

50. A. F. Potter, policy statement, 20 Feb. 1917, S-Sales, General, 1915-23 file, PNW Hist. Rec., box 13.

51. Lakeview *Lake County Examiner*, 28 Feb., 13 and 20 Mar., 4 Sept. 1924, 19 Mar. 1925, 25 Aug., 10 Nov. 1927; David F. Myrick, "Strahorn System: Oregon, California, & Eastern," *Western Railroader*, 21 (Apr. 1958): 3-9; *Timb.*, 21 (Aug. 1920): 39; Anonymous, "The O. C. & E. Railroad," ibid., 43; Anonymous, "Oregon-California Pine Development," ibid., 25 (Aug. 1924): 60-62; Anonymous, "Railroads Battle for Klamath Basin Timber," ibid., 26 (Oct. 1925): 230-35. During the first half of 1925 almost every issue of the *Lake County Examiner* reported railroad-building schemes and rivalries. In 1924, in anticipation of the coming of a railroad, a large Forest Service timber sale seemed imminent, but nothing came of it. See: Lakeview *Lake County Examiner*, 9 Oct., 20 Nov. 1924.

52. Lakeview *Lake County Examiner*, 24 Jan., 28 Feb., 13 and 20 Mar., 29 May, 6 Nov. 1924.

53. Quoted in ibid., 20 Nov. 1924. See also: *Timb.*, 25 (Oct. 1924): 100.

54. Lakeview *Lake County Examiner*, 16 and 23 Oct., 13 and 20 Nov. 1924. *The Timberman* misunderstood the Forest Service's position and thus

misrepresented the controversy over Fandango and other Forest Service sales in the area. See: *Timb.*, 26 (Apr. 1925): 120.

55. Lakeview *Lake County Examiner*, 26 Feb. 1925, 24 Apr., 25 Oct. 1925. On the comparative efficiency of band saws and circular saws, see: Rodney C. Loehr, "Saving the Kerf: The Introduction of the Band Saw Mill," *Ag. Hist.*, 23 (1949): 168-72.

56. Lakeview *Lake County Examiner*, 3 Dec. 1925.

57. Ibid., 5 Feb., 7 and 21 May 1925, 10 Nov. 1927, 24 and 26 Apr. 1928.

58. Ibid., 13 Sept., 25 Oct. 1928 (quote), 18 Apr. 1929, 30 May, 29 Aug., 5 and 30 Dec. 1929, 2 and 16 Jan. 1930; *Timb.*, 40 (Jan. 1939): 61. Growth followed. In 1938, hardly a banner year, Lakeview's mills would cut fifty-eight million board feet; the community's largest sawmill cut sixteen million feet. *Timb.*, 40 (Jan. 1939): 61.

59. Prineville *Central Oregonian*, 28 Apr. 1927 (quote), 16 Feb. 1928.

60. Wetmore to Jefferson, 26 Oct. 1926, Jefferson incoming corres., 1925-27 file, WP, box 46; Assistant District Forester, "Supplemental Statement of Policy, Ochoco National Forest," 11 Mar. 1921, S-Plans, Timber Management Policy Statements, Ochoco-Olympic, 1915-36 file, PNW Records, box 2. See also: Prineville *Central Oregonian*, 23 Aug. 1928. The timber was less isolated than the Forest Service suggested. It was some twenty miles from Prineville to the beginning of timber and an additional twenty miles from the town to existing rail lines. This was less than half the distance of the Malheur timber from railroads at the time of Fred Herrick's purchase.

61. A. B. Greeley to District Forester, 7 Jan. 1920, S-Sales, Policy, 1915-26 file, PNW Hist. Rec., box 14; Assistant District Forester, "Supplemental Statement of Policy"; E. J. Hanzlik, "Memorandum," 13 July 1922, S-Plans, Timber Management, Ochoco, General, 1922-51 file, PNW Records, box 83; Fred E. Ames, "Management Plan, Prineville Working Circle, Ochoco National Forest," 28 Oct. 1924, Crooked River W. C., 1924-49 file, ibid.; Prineville *Central Oregonian*, 3 Feb. 1927, 19 Jan. 1928 (quote).

62. John F. Due and Francis Juris, *Rails to the Ochoco Country: The City of Prineville Railway* (San Marino, Calif.: Golden West, 1968), 49-101; Mills, *Railroads down the Valleys*, 122-28. As the editor of a local newspaper put it, the community "begged, pleaded and prayed for many years that somebody would come to its rescue" with a railroad. Prineville *Crook County Journal*, 12 Mar. 1914.

63. Due and Juris, *Rails to the Ochoco Country*, 103-146; John F. Due, "The City of Prineville Railway and the Economic Development of Crook County," *Economic Geography*, 43 (1967): 170-81; Mills, *Railroads down the Valleys*, 128-32; Randall V. Mills, "Prineville's Municipal Railroad," *OHQ*, 42 (1941): 256-62; Cogswell, "Deschutes Country Pine Logging," 254-55; Prineville *Crook County Journal*, 16 Sept. 1915, 2 Mar., 1 June 1916; Prineville *Central Oregonian*, 3 and 10 Feb. 1927, 19 Jan., 2 Feb., 15 Mar. 1928; H. C. Obye to Regional Forester, 23 Aug. 1934, S-Plans, Timber Management, Ochoco, General, 1922-51 file, PNW Records, box 83. At first Jonas seems to have been persuaded by claims that market conditions prevented the building of new mills. See: Prineville *Central Oregonian*, 7 Apr. 1927.

64. Prineville *Crook County Journal*, 12 Mar. 1914, 11 Nov. 1915; Prineville *Central Oregonian*, 12 and 26 July, 16 Aug. 1928, 14 Mar., 28 Nov., 5 and

19 Dec. 1929. On plans for an east-west line across the state, see: Myrick, "Strahorn System," 3-9; Mills, *Railroads down the Valleys*, 32-70.

65. Prineville *Central Oregonian*, 25 Oct. 1928, 3, 10, and 24 Jan., 28 Feb., 13 June (quote) and 20 June, 25 July, 21 Nov., 5 Dec. 1929; "Briefs of Policy Statements, 1930," S-Plans, Timber Management Policy, 1912-34 file, PNW Records, box 80.

66. Prineville *Central Oregonian*, 19 Jan., 2 and 16 Feb., 8, 15, and 29 Mar. 1928. See also: C. J. Buck to Robert Y. Stuart, 28 Apr. 1931, S-Sales, Policy, 1927-33 file, PNW Hist. Rec., box 15.

67. Prineville *Central Oregonian*, 16 and 23 Feb., 8 and 15 Mar. 1928.

68. Buck to Stuart, 28 Apr. 1931, S-Sales, 1927-33 policy file, PNW Hist. Rec., box 15; Stuart to Charles L. McNary, 18 May 1931, ibid.; D. T. Mason, oral history interview, tape 349, pp. 47-48; Due and Juris, *Rails to the Ochoco Country*, 143-57; Cogswell, "Deschutes Country Pine Logging," 254-56. Nationally, lumber production fell from thirty-six billion board feet in 1929 to 10.1 billion in 1932. See: Forest Service, *Lumber Production, 1869-1934*, 74. In addition to the timber east of Prineville, the "beautiful, flat pine timber country" near Sisters, the north slope of the Blue Mountains tributary to Pilot Rock, and timber on the Warm Springs Indian Reservation also came on line late. See: Moltke, oral history interview, 2: 3 (quote).

69. E. J. Hanzlik, "A Study of the Timber Situation in the Klamath Working Circle, South-Central Oregon," 21 Feb. 1922, S-Plans, Timber Management, Fremont, East Klamath W. C., 1922-49 file, PNW Records, box 81; appraisal facilities, S-Sales, Appraisals, Pelican Bay Lumber Co. file, ibid., box 141; "List of Mills in Oregon and Washington Established Primarily to Cut National Forest Timber," 31 Jan. 1927, S-Sales, Policy, 1915-26 file, ibid., box 14; Lamm, *Lumbering in Klamath*, 13-17. See also: H. D. Mortensen, "History of the Klamath County Lumber Industry," *Timb.*, 24 (July 1923): 154-55; Anonymous, "Oregon-California Pine Development," ibid. (Aug. 1924): 60-62; Greeley, "Report of the Forester (1921)," 19. The Baker, Fentress & Co. manuscripts, housed at the Knight Library, University of Oregon, Eugene, contain records of the Algoma Lumber Company (twenty-five boxes); they are a vast store of information on lumbering in the Klamath country.

70. Kimball to Long, 12 Apr. 1911, Kimball 1911 file, incoming corres., WTCP, box 54; Greeley to Forester, 21 Nov. 1914, S-Sales, Policy, 1908-14 file, PNW Hist. Rec., box 14; Edwin C. Erickson, "Report on the Grades, Size, and Defects in Yellow Pine Logs on All Pine Sales during . . . 1916," 3 Mar. 1917, General, 1915-33 file, ibid., box 13; appraisal of 1910, 1913, 1914, and 1916 sales, S-Sales, Appraisals, Pelican Bay Lumber Co. file, PNW Records, box 141; H. D. Mortensen to Bruce Hoffman, 12 Feb. 1918, ibid. Pelican Bay's problems were exacerbated when, to log the Bear Creek sale of 1914, it had to build a railroad from Kirk, a line nearly as long as Herrick's to the Malheur timber.

71. Hanzlik, "Timber Situation in the Klamath Working Circle," S-Plans, Timber Management, Fremont, East Klamath W. C., 1922-49 file, PNW Records, box 81; Drake, "Memorandum for FM and Mr. Granger," 23 Apr. 1925, ibid.; Elwood R. Maunder, ed., *J.P Kinney, The Office of Indian Affairs: A Career in*

Forestry (New Haven, Conn.: Forest History Society, 1969), 28, 33. See also: Theodore Stern, *The Klamath Tribe: A People and their Reservation* (Seattle: University of Washington Press, 1965), 147-48, 152-53, 236; Anonymous, "Saw Timber Resources of Indian Reservations," *Timb.*, 26 (Jan. 1925): 62. According to this last source, the Klamath reservation had an estimated seven billion board feet of standing timber (considerably more than any other), of which 90 percent was the highly valued ponderosa pine.

72. O'Callaghan, "Klamath Indians and the Oregon Wagon Road Grant," 21-28; O'Callaghan, *Disposition of the Public Domain in Oregon*, 80-81; Stern, *Klamath Tribe*, 176; Bradley, *Long*, 121; Twining, *George S. Long*, 90-94; [Defebaugh], *American Lumbermen*, 3: 57-60.

73. Long, "Testimony at ICC Hearings," railroad development plans file, LPO, box 3; E. E. Carter to E. J. Grant, 17 Jan. 1929, S-Sales, Policy, 1927-33 file, PNW Hist. Rec., box 15; appraisals, 1929, S-Sales, Appraisals, Pelican Bay Lumber Co. file, PNW Records, box 141; Bob J. Lewis et al., "Algoma Lumber Co.," *Timberbeast*, 6 (spring-summer 1987): 8-31.

74 R. W. Putnam, "Klamath Working Circle, Fremont Division," July 1930, S-Plans, Timber Management, Fremont, East Klamath W. C., 1922-48 file, PNW Hist. Rec., box 81 (1st quote); Drake, "Memorandum for FM and Mr. Granger," ibid.; "Briefs of Policy Statements, 1930," ibid., 1912-34 file, box 80 (2nd quote); Kimball to Long, 5 Sept. 1910, Kimball, incoming corres., 1910 file, WTCP, box 52.

75. After the Southern Pacific reached Klamath Falls from Weed in 1909, local leaders kept campaigning for connections to the north. George Long joined them. He did not want to build a mill in Klamath Falls if it would be dependent upon a single line from the south. Having two railroads come to Bend, he noted, had helped it "considerably" and extension of the northern lines to Klamath Falls would "enable us to begin to manufacture our own timber" there. Long, "Testimony to ICC Hearing," railroad development plans file, LPO, box 3; Long to Paul S. Shoup, 3 Oct. 1925, ibid.; Twining, *George S. Long*, 291, 302, 308-309, 340-41.

76. The evidence is too extensive to cite in full. However, see: Kimball to [Long], 3 June 1908, Kimball, Jan.-May 1908 file, incoming corres., 1900-38, WTCP, box 47; ibid., 9 May, 24 Oct., 5 Nov. 1910, box 52; ibid., 11 Oct. 1911, box 54; Charles Graves to Long, 20 Apr. 1912, K, 1912 file, ibid., box 56; Long to W. P. Hopkins, 6 Jan. 1913, ibid.; Kimball to Long, 17 Feb. 1927, Timber assessments file, LPO, box 3; Long to Kimball, 17 Feb. 1927, ibid. (quote); Twining, *George S. Long*, 303.

77. Johnson to Long, 23 Sept. 1911, Kimball, 1911 file, incoming corres., 1900-1938 file, WTCP, box 54 (quote); Minot Davis to Long, 1 Dec. 1911, D, 1911 file, ibid.; Kimball to Long, 27 Jan. and 23 Apr. 1912, Kimball, 1912 file, ibid., box 56; R. N. Day to W. L. McCormack, 15 Mar., 22 Sept., 20 Nov., 24 Dec. 1913, D-Del, 1913 file, ibid., box 59; Johnson to Long, 27 Mar., 12, 14, and 15 May 1913; Long to Johnson, 26 May 1913, K-J, 1913 file, ibid. See also: Twining, *George S. Long*, 76, 162-63.

78. Felts to Long, 7 July 1908, A, 1908 file, incoming corres., ibid., box 46. See also: Deering to Weyerhaeuser Timber Co., 5 June 1907, incoming corres., 1900-1938, Deering file, WTCP, box 44.

79. Long, "Testimony at ICC Hearings," railroad development plans file, LPO, box 3; R. R. McCartney to C. H. Ingram, 19 May 1931, Klamath Falls Branch, 1930-32 file, Ingram Office Files, box 1; Wetmore to Jefferson, 26 Oct. 1926, Jefferson, incoming corres., 1925-27 file, WP, box 46; Jefferson to Wetmore, 27 Aug. 1928, ibid., outgoing corres., 1927-1930 file, box 47. See also: Shellworth, oral history interview (1966), 1-33, 38. Most box shook sales were handled through California Pine Box Distributors; thus even in California, Klamath's manufacturers had little need to give much attention to marketing. See: Jim Bryant and Jim Cooper, "1932: Operations of the Fruit Growers Supply Company," *Lassen Ledger*, 2 (May 1982): 19-26; Anonymous, "Wooden Box Review," *Timb.*, 43 (1942): 11-64; Anonymous, "Half a Century of Box Making," ibid., 50 (1949): 218-26.

80. Wetmore to Luce, 15 Aug. 1928, Wetmore, outgoing corres., 1927-28 file, WP, box 7; Chapel to Wetmore, 25 Feb. 1931, 31 Mar. 1932, ibid., incoming corres., 1931 file, box 4; Luce to Wetmore, 10 Oct., 25 Nov. 1932, ibid., 1932 file; Wetmore to Jefferson, 14 Aug. 1928, 7 Oct. 1932, Jefferson, incoming corres., 1928-30 file, ibid., box 46; Jefferson to Conrad, 20 Aug. 1928, ibid., outgoing corres., 1927-30 file, box 47; Jefferson to Wetmore, 27 Aug. 1928, ibid.; Jefferson to Wetmore, 27 Aug. 1928, ibid.; Jefferson to Wetmore, 13 Mar. 1930, ibid.; Hines, "Memorandum to the United States Forest Service," 23-24, A-3; I. J. Mason, oral history, 4.

81. Long, "Testimony at ICC Hearings," railroad development plans file, LPO, box 3; W. M. Bray to Long, 27 Sept. 1927, Timber assessments file, ibid.

82. Long to Kimball, 12 Nov. 1923, 31 Mar. 1925, Klamath Falls transactions file, legal, LPO, box 1; F. E. Weyerhaeuser to Long, 15 Jan., 11 and 16 June, 21 July 1927, St. Paul office, 1927 file, incoming corres., WTCP, box 104; Kimball to F. E. Weyerhaeuser, 6 May 1927, Kimball, 1927 file, ibid., box 102; Long to T. J. Humbird, 18 July 1928, lumber business matters, misc. file, LPO, box 2; Long to W. M. Bray, 20 Sept. 1927, timber assessments file, ibid., box 3; Long to F. S. Bell, 19 Jan. 1929, Mill business-admin.-personnel file, ibid.; Long, "Testimony at ICC Hearings," railroad development plans file, ibid.; McCartney to Ingram, 19 May 1931, Klamath Falls branch, 1932 file, Ingram Office Files, box 1; *AL*, 30 (2 Nov. 1929): 65; Hidy, Hill, and Nevins, *Timber and Men*, 403-406; Harry J. Drew, *Weyerhaeuser Company: A History of People, Land and Growth* (Klamath Falls: Weyerhaeuser Company, Eastern Oregon Region, 1979), 6-25; Lamm, *Lumbering in Klamath*, 12, 20-21; Twining, *George S. Long*, 313, 320-21. When Weyerhaeuser decided to build in Klamath Falls, William Bray reminded Long of past mistakes and warned him to be careful. Large companies, he wrote, "often make quite as bad mistakes as small ones." See: Bray to Long, 15 Sept. 1927, timber assessments file, LPO, box 3.

83. Long, "Testimony at ICC Hearings," railroad development plans file, LPO, box 3; Long to F. G. Wisner, 19 Oct. 1923, ibid.; Twining, *George S. Long*, 313, 364.

84. Long to F. S. Bell, 19 Jan. 1929, mill business-admin.-personnel file, LPO, box 2 (1st quote); Twining, *George S. Long*, 327-39, 350 (2nd quote); Twining, *Phil Weyerhaeuser*, 56-76; Hidy, Hill, and Nevins, *Timber and Men*, 406-410,

512-18; Bradley, *Long*, 131-35, 152-54, 156, 181-83; Anonymous, "Lumber Manufacture Commences in America's Greatest Remaining White Pine Timber . . ." *Timb.*, 28 (July 1927): 146-47.

85. Kimball to Long, 27 Jan., 1 Feb., 12 Aug. 1911; Kimball to D. P. Simons, 17 Feb. 1911, incoming corres., Kimball, 1911 file, WTCP, box 54; Fred Ames, "Memorandum of Inspection Trip to District 5 during September 1920," 4 Oct. 1920, S-Sales, Policy, 1927-33 file, PNW Hist. Rec., box 15; *AL*, 30 (2 Nov. 1929): 65-66; [Brooks-Scanlon], *Deschutes Pine Echoes*, 9 (Mar. 1926): 12-13; (Apr. 1928): 15. On debates over light burning, see: Pyne, *Fire in America*, 100-112; Clar, *California Government and Forestry*, 342-43, 464, 488-94; Allen, *Practical Forestry*, 14-17, 44-46, 57, 91-98.

86. For examples, see: Henry S. Graves to District Forester, 7 Mar. 1912, S-Sales, "Limitation of Cut," 1911 folder, PNW Hist. Rec., box 13; Selective logging, 1930-38 file, PNW Hist. Rec., box 17 (esp. Fred Ames to Kinzua Pine Mills, 7 Mar. 1930); I. J. Mason, oral history interview, 3; Wetmore to Luce, 21 Feb. 1930, Wetmore, outgoing corres., Jan.-June 1930 file, WP, box 97; Luce to Wetmore, 26 Feb. 1930, ibid., incoming corres., 1930 file, box 4; Lakeview *Lake County Examiner*, 25 Oct. 1928. Mason was more interested in sustained yield than selective logging; he carefully pointed out they were not the same. See: D. T. Mason, oral history interview, 1, 5-6, 15-17, 29; William G. Robbins, "Lumber Production and Community Stability: A View from the Pacific Northwest," *JFH*, 31 (1987): 189-92.

87. Fred Ames, "Memorandum of Inspection Trip to District 5 during September 1920," 4 Oct. 1920, S-Sales, Policy, 1927-33 file, PNW Hist. Rec., box 15 (this box contains additional materials on this subject); Drake, *Forester's Log*, 10-12, 154-58. See also: *Deschutes Pine Echoes*, 8 (Jan. 1927): 13; 9 (Aug. 1928): 3; 11 (Jan. 1930): 15; (Apr. 1930): 12.

88. Greeley, "Report of the Forester (1922)," 22 (1st quote); ibid. (1925), 25 (2nd quote).

89. Willard L. Marks to Charles L. McNary and enclosures, [c. Mar. 1927]; C. J. Buck to Forester, 28 Apr. 1931, S-Sales, Policy, 1927-33 file, PNW Hist. Rec., box 15; State of Oregon, Thirty-Fourth Legislative Assembly, Regular Session, *Senate Joint Memorial No. 12* (Salem: State Printer, 1927); National Lumber Manufacturers Association, news release, 20 July [1927], copy in S-Sales, Policy, 1927-33 file, PNW Hist. Rec., box 15.

90. Greeley, "Report of the Forester (1927)," 22; Robert Y. Stuart, ibid. (1928), 29.

91. J. D. Guthrie, memorandum for Mr. Granger, 10 Mar. 1927; W. M. Jardine to Sam A. Kozer, 15 Mar. 1927; E. E. Carter to E. J. Grant, 17 Jan. 1929; Fred Ames, "Memorandum for Lands," 11 Aug. 1930, Buck to Forester, 28 Apr. 1931, S-Sales Policy file, 1927-33, PNW Hist. Rec., box 15; Long to T. J. Humbird, 18 July 1927, lumber business matters, misc. file, LPO, box 2; Long to F. S. Bell, 19 Jan. 1929, mill business, administration and personnel file, ibid.; R. A. Booth to Long, 19 Sept. 1929, "B" 1929 file, WTCP, box 101; Stuart, "Report of the Forester (1929)," 30. See also: Wall, *Log Production in Oregon and Washington*, 2, 15-22, 30, 40-41, 44-45.

92. Fred Ames, "Memorandum for District Forester," 23 Dec. 1925; Allen H. Hodgson, "Possibilities for Stabilizing and Indefinitely Prolonging

Community Life in the Deschutes Timber Production Area of Central Oregon," 1 May 1934, S-Plans, timber management, Deschutes, general, 1920-50 file, PNW Records, box 80; "Timber Volume, Mill Capacity, Mill Cut, by Production Units," n.d. [c. 1930], timber management, 1912-34 file, ibid.; E. A. Sherman to Regional Forester, 17 Feb. 1934, timber management, Deschutes Plateau W. C., 1926-1936 file, ibid.; [Paul Hosmer], "A Brief Sketch of the Oregon Operations of one of America's Greatest Lumber Manufacturing Institutions," *Deschutes Pine Echoes*, 3 (Jan. 1922): 1-17; Rodney C. Loehr, ed., *Forests for the Future: The Story of Sustained Yield as Told in the Diaries and Papers of David T. Mason, 1907-1950* (St. Paul: Forest Products History Foundation and Minnesota Historical Society, 1952), 195-97; Anonymous, "Production of Bend Mills," *Timb.*, 22 (May 1921): 48D; Anonymous, "Where Two Big Companies Manufacture 400,000,000 Feet of Pondosa Pine Yearly," *AL*, n.s., 30 (30 Nov. 1929): 34-35; Phil F. Brogan, *East of the Cascades* (Portland, Ore.: Binfords & Mort, 1964), 255-57. The Brooks-Scanlon Papers (Oregon Historical Society, Portland) contain considerable material on overcutting by the two mills. Pondosa was a trade name briefly used for ponderosa pine. Material on eventual protests is in Robert W. Sawyer Papers, University of Oregon library, Eugene. See also: Robbins, *Landscapes of Conflict*, 156-65; Robbins, "Lumber Production and Community Stability," 192, 193.

93. Here and there other sawmills would appear later—for example, in 1938 Frank Gilchrist built a sawmill and company town some fifty miles south of Bend—but such latecomers soon became essentially post-frontier operators living in a world where the Forest Service dominated. See: Brogan, *East of the Cascades*, 259; Cogswell, "Deschutes Country Pine Logging," 256-57.

94. Northeastern California was an exception; farms replaced some eighty-three thousand acres of forests, at least for a time. See: California Conservation Commission, *Report, 1913*, 67-71.

Epilogue

1. On the sagebrush rebellion, see: Richard D. Clayton, "The Sagebrush Rebellion: Who Should Control the Public Lands?" *Utah Law Review*, n.v. (1980): 505-533; John D. Leshy, "Unraveling the Sagebrush Rebellion: Law, Politics and Federal Lands," *University of California Davis Law Review*, 14 (1980): 317-55; Richard M. Mollison and Richard W. Eddy, "The Sagebrush Rebellion: A Simplistic Response to the Complex Problems of Federal Land Management," *Harvard Journal on Legislation*, 19 (1982): 97-142; William L. Graf, *Wilderness Preservation and the Sagebrush Rebellion* (Savage, Md.: Rowman and Littlefield, 1990); R. McGregor Cawley, *Federal Land, Western Anger: The Sagebrush Rebellion and Environmental Politics* (Lawrence: University Press of Kansas, 1993).

2. Beverly A. Brown, *In Timber Country: Working People's Stories of Environmental Conflict and Urban Flight* (Philadelphia: Temple University Press, 1995), 63-72, 123-33, 183-230 (quotes, pp. 189, 190, 194). See also: Susan Schrepfer, "Conflict in Preservation: The Sierra Club, Save-the-Redwoods League, and Redwood National Park," *JFH*, 24 (1980): 60-76. Historian Harry McDean's comment on proposals to take cattle off the

northern plains and create a "buffalo commons" is apropos: they want to turn the West into "a Yuppie playground," he said. Frank J. and Deborah Popper, "The Reinvention of the American Frontier," paper presented to Western Historical Association (with comment by McDean), Reno, Nevada, 18 Oct. 1990. On the Poppers' argument and McDean's reply, see: *Christian Science Monitor*, 18 Dec. 1990, p. 13. See also: Frank J. Popper and Deborah E. Popper, "Great Plains: Checkered Past, Hopeful Future," *Forum for Applied Research and Public Policy*, 9 (1994): 90-91; Doug Coffman, Charles Jonkel, and Robert Scott, "The Big Open: A Return of Grazers of the Past," *Western Wildlands*, 16 (1990): 40-44.

3. Early in the twenty-first century, television's History Channel began a series called "Axmen" that depicts the values and actions of a number of contemporary small gyppo-logging operators in Oregon's northern Coast Range. Without explicitly addressing the subject, the series demonstrated the huge attitudinal gap between today's woods workers and most environmentalists.

4. *Grants Pass* (Ore.) *Daily Courier*, 30 Jan. 1993; "Retrain for What?" *The Nation*, 257 (1993): 519-20; Norman Hayner, "Taming the Lumberjack," *American Sociological Review*, 10 (1945): 217-25; Matthew S. Carroll, "Taming the Lumberjack Revisited," *Society and Natural Resources*, 2 (1989): 91-106; Matthew S. Carroll and Robert G. Lee, "Occupational Community and Identity among Pacific Northwestern Loggers: Implications for Adapting to Economic Changes," in Robert G. Lee, ed., *Community and Forestry: Continuities in the Sociology of Natural Resources* (Boulder, Colo.: Westview Press, 1990), 141-55; Matthew S. Carroll, *Community and the Northwestern Logger: Continuity and Change in the Era of the Spotted Owl* (Boulder, Colo.: Westview Press, 1995), 70, 91-99, 123 (3rd quote), 125-26, 148 (1st and 2nd quotes), 157-58; Brown, *In Timber Country*, 34-35, 70, 189, 209. See also: David H. Williamson, "Give 'er Snoose: A Study of Kin and Work among Gyppo Loggers of the Pacific Northwest" (unpub. Ph.D. diss., Catholic University of America, 1976); Susan Clayton and Susan Opotow, ed., *Identity and the Natural Environment: The Psychological Significance of Nature* (Cambridge, Mass.: MIT Press, 2004).

5. The literature on the Wilderness Bill is voluminous. For introductions, see: Christopher McGrory Klyza, *Who Controls Public Lands? Mining, Forestry, and Grazing Policies, 1870-1990* (Chapel Hill: University of North Carolina Press, 1996), 76-93; Roderick Nash, *Wilderness and the American Mind* (rev. ed.; New Haven, Conn.: Yale University Press, 1973), 200-236; Craig W. Allin, *The Politics of Wilderness Preservation* (Westport, Conn.: Greenwood Press, 1982), 102-169; Kevin R. Marsh, *Drawing Lines in the Forest: Creating Wilderness Areas in the Pacific Northwest* (Seattle: University of Washington Press, 2007); Harold K. Steen, *The Chiefs Remember: The Forest Service, 1952-2001* (Durham, N.C.: Forest History Society, 2004), 17-19, 33-34.

6. Kevin R. Marsh, " 'This is Just the First Round': Designating Wilderness in the Oregon Cascades, 1950-1964," *OHQ*, 103 (2002): 210-33; Marsh, *Lines in the Forest*, 19-37, 50-64, 99-120.

7. Alice H. Ulrich, *U.S. Timber Production, Trade, Consumption, and Price Statistics, 1950-80*, USDA Forest Service Misc. Publications no. 1408

(Washington, D.C.: GPO, 1981), 19-21, 33; Brown, *In Timber Country*, 47, 89, 109, 138-39, 239; Robbins, *Hard Times in Paradise*, 134-35, 167, 169; Smyth, *Millicoma*, 76-77; William Deary, "Log Exports: Is the Tide Turning?" *AF* (Mar.-Apr. 1993): 49-52; Thomas R. Cox, "The North American-Japan Timber Trade: A Survey of Its Social, Economic, and Environmental Impact," in *World Deforestation in the Twentieth Century*, ed. by John F. Richards and Richard P. Tucker (Durham, N.C.: Duke University Press, 1988), 164-86; Cox, "The North American-Japan Timber Trade: The Roots of Canadian and U.S. Approaches," *FCH*, 34 (1990): 112-21. See also: Mayme Elizabeth Smith, "Penetrating the Japanese Market: The Weyerhaeuser Experience" (unpub. M.B.A. thesis, San Diego State University, 1984), 5-18.

8. Interagency Scientific Committee, *A Conservation Strategy for the Northern Spotted Owl* (Portland, Ore.: Forest Service, Bureau of Land Management, Fish and Wildlife Service, and National Park Service, 1990); ibid., *Draft Supplemental Environmental Impact Statement on Management of Habitat for Late-Successional and Old-Growth Forest Related Species within the Range of the Northern Spotted Owl* (Washington, D.C.: GPO, 1993); *Grants Pass Daily Courier*, 18 Nov. 1986, 7 and 24 June 1989, 19 Feb. and 10 Mar. 1992; Darrell Palmer to the author, 17 Dec. 1992 (Cox, personal corres.); Brown, *In Timber Country*, 29-33, 48, 71, 191, 227; Steen, *The Chiefs Remember*, 79-81, 93-94, 111-13; Stephen G. Boyce and Chadwick D. Oliver, "The History of Research in Forest Ecology and Silviculture," in Harold K. Steen, ed., *Forest and Wildlife Science in America: A History* (Durham, N.C.: Forest History Society, 1999), 431-32, 436-38, 440; Thomas E. Hamer et al., "Hybridization between Barred and Spotted Owls," *Auk*, 111 (1994): 487-92; Elizabeth G. Kelly et al., "Recent Records of Hybrization between Barred Owls (*Strix varia*) and Northern Spotted Owls (*S. occidentalis caurina*)," ibid., 121 (2004): 806-810; W. Chris Funk, Eric D. Forsman, Thomas D. Mullins, and Susan M. Haig, *Genetics Show Current Decline and Pleistocene Expansion in Northern Spotted Owls*, Open-File Report 2008-1239 (Reston, VA: U.S. Geological Survey, 2008); Shannon Peterson, *Acting for Endangered Species* (Lawrence: University Press of Kansas, 2002), 81-118.

9. The closing of small, inefficient plants was speeded by the collapse of lumber prices in the early 1980s. Having contracted for expensive timber, firms found themselves financially squeezed, encouraging them to phase out marginal plants. Pomeroy, *Far West in the Twentieth Century*, 111; Joe P. Mattey, *The Timber Bubble that Burst: Government Policy and the Bailout of 1984* (New York: Oxford University Press, 1990), 3-6, 19, 30-32.

10. James O. Howard and Bruce A. Hiserote, *Oregon's Forest Products Industry, 1976*, USDA Forest Service Resources Bulletin PNW-79 (Portland, Ore.: Pacific Northwest Forest and Range Experiment Station, 1978), 5-6, 9-12, 24-25; PEDCo-Environmental Specialists, *Control and Alternatives: Combustion of Wood Residue in Conical (Wigwam) Burners*, Report prepared for the Environmental Protection Agency (Washington, D.C.: Environmental Protection Agency, 1975).

11. Richardson, *Billion-Dollar Checkerboard*, 144-47; Robbins, *Landscapes of Conflict*, 153-54; Rajala, *Clearcutting the Pacific Rain Forest*, 207. In Central Oregon, the Forest Service had a similar program of reserving timber sales

for mills in the area, thus protecting sawmill-dependent communities, but during the high demand following World War II the program fell by the wayside. See: H. J. Andrews to A. J. Glassow, 13 Feb. 1948, forestry—Brooks-Scanlon folder, SP, box 8. For an example of a mill that sought integration to remain competitive, see: LaLande, *Medford Corporation*, 123-42.

12. Brown, *In Timber Country*, 48 (quote), 85, 191-92, 217-18, 226; Brogan, *East of the Cascades*, 256; John MacDonald, "Georgia-Pacific: It Grows Big on Trees," *Fortune*, 65 (1962): 111-17; Owen R. Cheatham and Robert B. Pamplin, *The Georgia- Pacific Story* (New York: Newcomen Society of North America, 1966); John R. Ross, *Maverick: The Story of Georgia-Pacific* (n.p.: Georgia-Pacific, 1980), 58-61, 88, 95, 96, 100-103, 306-312; Dennis C. LeMaster, *Mergers among the Largest Forest Products Firms, 1950-1970*, Research Bulletin no. 854 (Pullman: Washington State University, College of Agriculture Research Center, 1977); Pomeroy, *Far West in the Twentieth Century*, 111.

13. Susan R. Fletcher, "Environment and the World Trade Organization (WTO) at Seattle: Issues and Concerns," Report for Congress (Washington, D.C.: Library of Congress, Congressional Research Service, 1999), 4-5; Anup Shah, "WTO Protests in Seattle, 1999," *Free Trade and Globalization: Global Issues*, Web site, 18 Feb. 2001; Nigel Sizer, David Downes, and David Kaimowitz, "Free Trade: Liberalization of International Commerce in Forest Products: Risks and Opportunities," *Forest Notes* (Nov. 1999): 1-23; Lynn Walsh, "WTO under Siege," *Socialism Today*, 44 (Jan. 2000). See also: Robert C. Paehlke, *Democracy's Dilemma: Environment, Social Equity, and the Global Economy* (Cambridge, Mass.: MIT Press, 2003).

14. Harold K. Steen, "The Forest History Society and Its History" (typescript; Forest History Society records, Durham, N.C.; revised 1996), 10-11; *Grants Pass Daily Courier*, 26 May, 13 and 22 June 1987; Carroll, *Community and the Northwestern Logger*, 153-54 (quote); Peter Wild, *Pioneer Conservationists of Western America* (Missoula, Mont.: Mountain Press, 1979), 184-97; Dave Foreman and Bill Haywood, *Ecodefense* (Tucson, Ariz.: Ned Ludd, 1987), 14-15 and passim; Judi Bari, "Earth First! In Northern California: An Interview with Judi Bari," *Capitalism, Nature, Socialism*, 4 (Dec. 1993): 1-29; Brown, *In Timber Country*, 141, 199, 227.

15. District Forester William Wren, comment to the author, near Mitchell, Oregon, summer 1950.

16. F. A. Silcox, "Report on Sustained-Yield Timber Operations," [1937], forestry—Silcox folder, SP, box 8; C. J. Buck to Shevlin-Hixon, [June 1937], Shevlin-Hixon folder, ibid.; Bend Chamber of Commerce to Harold L. Ickes, petition, 1 Aug. 1945, Bend Chamber of Commerce folder, ibid.; H. J. Andrews to A. J. Glassow, 13 Feb. 1948, Brooks-Scanlon folder, ibid. Additional material on sustained-yield efforts is in SP, box 8. See also: Roy O. Hoover, "Public Law 273 Comes to Shelton: Implementing the Sustained-Yield Forest Management Act of 1944," *JFH*, 22 (1978): 87-101; Paul W. Bèdard and Paul N. Ylvisaker, *The Flagstaff Federal Sustained Yield Unit*, Inter-University Case Program no. 37 (Tuscaloosa: University of Alabama Press, 1957); Robert G. Lee, "Sustained-Yield and Social Order," in Harold K. Steen, ed., *History of Sustained-Yield Forestry: A Symposium* (Santa Cruz,

Calif.: Forest History Society, 1984), 90-100; Richardson, *Billion-Dollar Checkerboard*, 95-107, 111-14, 119-27; Gerald W. Williams, "Community Stability and the Forest Service," paper presented at Oregon Planning Institute, Eugene, 1987 (rev. ed., Portland, Ore.: Forest Service, Pacific Northwest Region, 1995).

17. A. J. Glassow to Robert W. Sawyer, 22 June 1953, forestry—Brooks-Scanlon folder, SP, box 24; Glassow to Sawyer, 8 Apr. 1950, forestry—Brooks-Scanlon folder, SP, box 8; Bend Chamber of Commerce meeting, notes on discussion, 24 Nov. 1950, Bend Chamber of Commerce folder, ibid.; Glassow to Edward Brooks, 5 June 1950, Brooks-Scanlon Papers, box 32, folder 11; Klamath Falls *Herald and News*, 16 Dec. 1944, 8 and 9 Jan. 1945.

18. Robbins, *Hard Times in Paradise*, 116-19, 133-34, 157-58; Robbins, *Landscapes of Conflict*, 148-56 (quote p. 154), 166-67, 173-75; Richardson, *Billion-Dollar Checkerboard*, 5-64, 100-107; Brown, *In Timber Country*, 47, 48, 191-92, 217, 239, 241; Pomeroy, *Far West in the Twentieth Century*, 110-11. Log exports from Coos Bay continued until 2005. Pocatello *Idaho State Journal*, 19 July 2005; Seattle *Post-Intelligencer*, 16 Aug. 2005.

19. Elmo Richardson, *Dams, Parks, and Politics: Resource Development & Preservation in the Truman-Eisenhower Era* (Lexington: University Press of Kentucky, 1973), 71-73, 77-78 (1st quote, pp. 72-73); Cox, *The Park Builders*, 108-109; Charlene James-Duguid, *Work as Art: Idaho Logging as an Aesthetic Moment* (Moscow: University of Idaho Press, 1996), 36 (2nd quote); Dayton Hyde, *Yamsi: A Year in the Life of a Wilderness Ranch* (1971; reprint, Corvallis: Oregon State University Press, 2001), 87-95 (3rd quote, p. 87), 213-14.

20. Klyza, *Who Controls Public Lands?*, 2-4, 12-14 (1st quote, p. 3); Dodds, *Oregon*, 204-206 (2nd quote, p. 204); Carroll, *Community and the Northwestern Logger*, 159-61. For a recent example, see: Langston, *Forest Dreams, Forest Nightmares*, 252-57. See also: Derek R. Larson, "Preserving Eden: The Culture of Conservation in Oregon, 1960-1980" (unpub. Ph.D. diss., Indiana University, 2001).

21. Boise *Idaho Daily Statesman*, 17 Dec. 2002; 25 May 2006; Brown, *In Timber Country*, 28; John Prebbanow, comments to the author, June 2000. See also: Marion Clawson, *Forests, For Whom and For What?* (Baltimore, Md.: Resources for the Future, 1975).

22. Pocatello *Idaho State Journal*, 3 June 2002; 19 May 2003 (quote).

23. John Day *Blue Mountain Eagle*, 26 June (1st, 2nd, and 4th quotes), 11 Sept. (3rd quote) 23 Oct. 2002 (last quotes); Grant County, General Election Ballot, 5 Nov. 2002; Kathy McKinnon, Grant County Clerk, "Measure Detail Report," 8 Nov. 2002 (copies in Cox, personal corres.). See also: Michael Hibbard, "Issues and Options for the Other Oregon," *Community Development Journal*, 24 (1989): 145-53.

24. Hays, *Conservation and the Gospel of Efficiency*, 28-35, 264-66, 271-76; Clary, *Timber and the Forest Service*, 6-17 (quote, p. 16); Cox, "The Stewardship of Private Forests," 188-96; Albert Arnst, "Planning a Public Information Program," *JF*, 49 (1951): 427-30; Hidy, Hill, and Nevins, *Timber and Men*, 568.

25. Langston, *Forest Dreams, Forest Nightmares*, 97-99, 296-300; Hirt, *A Conspiracy of Optimism:*, 1-26, 142-44, 284-90; Rajala, *Clearcutting the Pacific Rain Forest*, 88-124, 128, 131, 140-42, 150, 18, 205-206; Robbins, *Landscapes of Conflict*, 34-37, 148-52, 158-59, 177 (1st quote), 181-205; Robbins to the author, 4 Oct. 2005 (2nd quote; Cox, personal corres.); F. Dale Robertson and George M. Leonard, "Traditional Forestry Hits the Wall," excerpts of oral history interviews by Harold K. Steen, *Forest History Today* (spring 2000): 2-8; F. L. Bunnell, "The Myth of the Omniscient Forester," *Forest Chronicle*, 52 (1976): 150-52. For overviews, see: Francis Sandbach, *Environment, Ideology and Policy* (Montclair, N.J.: Allanheld, Osmun, 1980); Samuel P. Hays, *Wars in the Woods: The Rise of Ecological Forestry in America* (Pittsburgh: University of Pittsburgh Press, 2007).

26. Jack Shepherd, *The Forest Killers: The Destruction of the American Wilderness* (New York: Weybright & Talley, 1975), 345-64 (the term is used in the title of Chapter 11, but the interpretation appears throughout); Walter J. Hickel, *Who Owns America?* (New York: Paperback Library, 1972), 126 and passim; Robbins, *Landscapes of Conflict*, 158 (1st quote), 169-73 (2nd quote, p. 169), 178-88; Hirt, *Conspiracy of Optimism*, 105-113, 131-50, 216, 220-29; Rajala, *Clearcutting the Pacific Rain Forest*, 167-89, 219-21; Paul J. Culhane, *Public Lands Politics: Interest Group Influence on the Forest Service and the Bureau of Land Management* (Baltimore, Md.: Johns Hopkins University Press, 1981); Klyza, *Who Controls Public Lands?*, 6-8, 75-76, 93-107. For the broader context, see: Martin Nie, *The Governance of Western Public Lands: Mapping the Present and Future* (Lawrence: University Press of Kansas, 2008).

27. Nancy Langston suggests the positions of local and outside interests, as well as economic and non-economic interests, could be reconciled through "a dialogue between people and land; it means people knowing the place they work." But she seemingly fails to appreciate the depth of the anger locals direct toward meddlesome non-resident "experts," an anger that would make such understanding difficult to achieve, if not impossible. See: Langston, *Where Land and Water Meet: A Western Landscape Transformed* (Seattle: University of Washington Press, 2003), 117-18, 151-69.

28. James-Duguid, *Work as Art*, 9 (1st quote), 15, 36 (2nd quote), 45-46, 59, 70, 103-106, 113, 120; Brown, *In Timber Country*, 119-20, 169, 191-92; Carroll, *Community and the Northwest Logger*, 131-32 (3rd quote). See also: Lawrence M. Lipin, *Workers and the Wild: Conservation, Consumerism, and Labor in Oregon, 1910-1930* (Urbana: University of Illinois Press, 2007).

29. The success of *High Country News*, published in rural Colorado, suggests this sort of communication can in fact occur; however, only a small portion of its content focuses on forests and just how many of its readers are long-time, rural Westerners is open to question.

30. Hal K. Rothman, *Devil's Bargains: Tourism in the Twentieth-Century American West* (Lawrence: University Press of Kansas, 1998); Brown, *In Timber Country*, 45-46, 51-52, 55-56, 78, 86 (1st quote), 101, 109 (2nd quote), 140, 147, 150-51, 159, 187, 200, 201, 214-15, 240; Carroll, *Community and the Northwest Logger*, 102-107, 128-30; William G. Robbins, *Colony and Empire: The Capitalist Transformation of the American West* (Lawrence: University Press of Kansas, 1994), 190-97; Robert Chandler, "Deschutes Country: Recent

Times," in Vaughan, *High & Mighty*, 261-72. Rothman focuses on Rocky Mountain and Southwestern areas, and on mining and ranching rather than lumber towns, but the forces he discusses certainly apply to them too.

31. Brown, *In Timber Country*, 46-47; James-Duguid, *Work as Art*, 51, 104-106.

32. Ellen Watterston, "What One Thing?" *Oregon Quarterly*, 86 (winter 2006): 15-19; Robbins, *Colony and Empire*, 194-96; Chandler, "Deschutes Country," 262-63, 266-69; Richard White, *Land Use, Environment, and Social Change: The Shaping of Island County, Washington* (Seattle: University of Washington Press, 1980), 142-54, 159-60 (quote); Leo Lemon, comment to the author, Bend, Ore., 15 Sept. 2006; Pocatello *Idaho State Journal*, 18 Dec. 2002.

33. P. A. Dee Southard, "Looking for Sanctuary: Staying on Publicly Owned Lands as a Response to Homelessness" (unpub. Ph.D. diss., University of Oregon, 1998); Brown, *In Timber Country*, 5-6, 44, 110-11; Lawrence Millman, *Lost in the Arctic: Explorations on the Edge* (New York: Thunder Mouth's Press, 2002), 209-212; Robbins, *Land of Conflict*, 211, 325; Howard Meadowcroft, comment to the author, Santa Cruz, Calif., October 1977.

A Note on Sources

As the attendant notes make clear, this study rests on a wide variety of sources. Reflecting the state of existing scholarship as well as available materials, the dominant types vary from area to area. Ronald J. Fahl, *North American Forest and Conservation History: A Bibliography* (Santa Barbara, Calif.: A.B.C. Clio Press, 1977), and, for more recent works, the Biblioscope sections of the *Journal of Forest History* and *Environmental History* provide essential beginning points in a search for material.

Few works cover the sweep of American forest history. The most valuable is Michael Williams, *Americans and their Forests: A Historical Geography* (Cambridge, U.K.: Cambridge University Press, 1989). Covering much the same ground, but with sometimes fresher interpretations is Thomas R. Cox, Robert S. Maxwell, Phillip Drennon Thomas, and Joseph J. Malone, *This Well-Wooded Land: Americans and their Forests from Colonial Times to the Present* (Lincoln: University of Nebraska Press, 1985). Reflecting the influence of Frederick Jackson Turner, Jenks Cameron, *The Development of Governmental Forest Control in the United States* (Baltimore, Md.: Johns Hopkins University Press, 1928), and Richard G. Lillard, *The Great Forest* (New York: Alfred A. Knopf, 1948), focus more directly on frontier aspects. Both are useful, if dated. In spite of its title, James Elliott Defebaugh, *History of the Lumber Industry of America* (2 vols.; Chicago: American Lumberman, 1906-1907), covers only the colonial period and the New England and the Middle Atlantic areas in detail; treatment of other regions is limited to general issues and national policies.

Chapters on New England benefit from a host of local studies and published collections of letters, reminiscences, other primary documents. Among the more valuable are Gordon E. Kershaw, *The Kennebeck Proprietors, 1749-1775* (Portland: Maine Historical Society, 1975); Frederick S. Allis, Jr., ed., *William Bingham's Maine Lands, 1790-1820* (Boston: Colonial Society of Massachusetts, 1954); Maine Historical Society, *Documentary History of the State of Maine* (24 vols.; Portland: Maine Historical Society, 1869-1914); and New Hampshire, *Provincial and State Papers* (18 vols.; Concord: State Printer, 1867-1890). Among unpublished manuscript collections, the papers of the Pejepscot Purchase Company, located at the Maine Historical Society in Portland, are especially revealing.

Secondary works are also essential. Richard G. Wood, *A History of Lumbering in Maine, 1820-1861* (Orono: University of Maine Press, 1935), is flawed, but useful. Better, although dealing largely with the post-frontier period, is David

C. Smith, *A History of Lumbering in Maine, 1861-1960* (Orono: University of Maine Press, 1972). Recent scholarship has provided useful context and helped shape interpretations. Key works include Charles E. Clark, *The Eastern Frontier: The Settlement of Northern New England, 1610-1763* (New York: Alfred A. Knopf, 1970); Charles F. Carroll, *The Timber Economy of Puritan New England* (Providence, R.I.: Brown University Press, 1973); William Cronon, *Changes in the Land: Indians, Colonists, and the Ecology of New England* (New York: Hill & Wang, 1983); Alan S. Taylor, *Liberty Men and Great Proprietors: The Revolutionary Settlement of the Maine Frontier, 1760-1820* (Chapel Hill: University of North Carolina Press, 1990); and Edward Wesley Potter, "Public Policy and Economic Growth in Maine, 1820-1857" (unpub. Ph.D. diss., University of Maine, 1974).

Considerably less is available on forest history in the Middle Atlantic area. Useful documentary sources are E. B. O'Callaghan, ed., *Documents Relative to the Colonial History of the State of New York* (11 vols.; Albany.: Weeds, Parsons & Co., 1853-1887), and Julian P. Boyd and Robert J. Taylor, ed., *The Susquehannah Land Company Papers* (11 vols.; Wilkes Barre, Penn.: Wyoming Historical and Genealogical Society, 1930-1975). William F. Fox, *A History of the Lumber Industry in the State of New York* (Washington, D.C.: GPO, 1902), is a short but valuable source by a participant. Walter Casler, Benjamin F. G. Kline, Jr., and Thomas T. Taber, III, *The Logging Railroad Era of Lumbering in Pennsylvania: A History of the Lumber, Chemical Wood, and Tanning Companies which Used Railroads in Pennsylvania* (3 vols.; Williamsport, Penn.: by the authors, 1970-1978), is more detailed, but antiquarian. Much of the story can be retrieved from local histories and publications of county historical societies. Newspapers are invaluable, especially those from Clearfield and Williamsport, Pennsylvania. Context and interpretive insights are provided by Phillip L. White, *Beekmantown, New York: Forest Frontier to Farm Community* (Austin: University of Texas Press, 1979), and Charles E. Brooks, *Frontier Settlement and Market Revolution: The Holland Purchase, 1800-1845* (Ithaca, N.Y.: Cornell University Press, 1996).

For what the industry calls the Lake States—Michigan, Wisconsin, and Minnesota—there are a number of valuable secondary studies. George W. Hotchkiss, *History of the Lumber and Forest Industry of the Northwest* (Chicago: George W. Hotchkiss, 1898), is full of detail, but disjointed. More valuable are Barbara E. Benson, *Logs and Lumber: The Development of Lumbering in Michigan's Lower Peninsula, 1837-1870* (Mount Pleasant: Clarke Historical Library, Central Michigan University, 1989); Robert F. Fries, *Empire in Pine: The Story of Lumbering in Wisconsin, 1830-1900* (Madison: State Historical Society of Wisconsin, 1951); Agnes M. Larson, *History of the White Pine Industry in*

Minnesota (Minneapolis: University of Minnesota Press, 1949); and Jeremy W. Kilar, *Michigan's Lumbertowns: Lumbermen and Laborers in Saginaw, Bay City, and Muskegon, 1870-1905* (Detroit: Wayne State University Press, 1990). Studies of individual firms abound. Among the better are: Ralph W. Hidy, Frank Ernest Hill, and Allan Nevins, *Timber and Men: The Weyerhaeuser Story* (New York: Macmillan, 1963); Fred W. Kohlmeyer, *Timber Roots: The Laird, Norton Story, 1855-1905* (Winona, Minn.: Winona County Historical Society, 1972); and Charles E. Twining, *Downriver: Orrin H. Ingram and the Empire Lumber Company* (Madison: State Historical Society of Wisconsin, 1975). The histories of all three firms extend beyond the Lake States. Specialized studies rich with insights include: Paul W. Gates, *The Wisconsin Pine Lands of Cornell University: A Study in Land Policy and Absentee Ownership* (Ithaca, N.Y.: Cornell University Press, 1943); Vernon R. Carstenson, *Farms or Forests: Evolution of a State Land Policy for Northern Wisconsin, 1850-1932* (Madison: College of Agriculture, University of Wisconsin, 1958); James Willard Hurst, *Law and Economic Growth: The Legal History of the Lumber Industry in Wisconsin, 1836-1915* (Cambridge, Mass.: Belknap Press of Harvard University Press, 1964); William G. Rector, *Log Transportation in the Lake States Lumber Industry, 1840-1918* . . . (Glendale, Calif.: Arthur H. Clark, 1953); and Matthias Nordberg Orfield, *Federal Land Grants to the States with Special Reference to Minnesota*, Studies in the Social Sciences, no. 2 (Minneapolis: University of Minnesota, 1915). Among the more useful doctoral dissertations are: George Wesley Sieber, "Sawmilling on the Mississippi: The W. J. Young Lumber Company, 1858-1900" (unpub. Ph.D. diss., University of Iowa, 1960), and Dale Arthur Peterson, "Lumbering on the Chippewa: The Eau Claire Area, 1845-1885" (unpub. Ph.D. diss., University of Minnesota, 1970). Autobiographies, reminiscences, and biographies provide further insights, especially Walter A Blair, *A Raft Pilot's Log: A History of the Great Rafting Industry on the Upper Mississippi, 1840-1915* (Cleveland, Ohio: Arthur H. Clark, 1930); Daniel Stanchfield, "History of Pioneer Lumbering on the Upper Mississippi and Its Tributaries, with Biographical Sketches," *Minnesota Historical Society Collections*, 9 (1899); Isaac Stephenson, *Recollections of a Long Life, 1829-1915* (Chicago: privately printed, 1915); Richard N. Current, *Pine Logs and Politics: A Life of Philetus Sawyer, 1816-1900* (Madison: State Historical Society of Wisconsin, 1950); John E. Nelligan, "The Life of a Lumberman," as told to Charles M. Sheridan, *Wisconsin Magazine of History*, 13 (1929-1930); and sketches in the trade press, especially [James E. Defebaugh], *American Lumbermen* (3 vols.; Chicago: American Lumberman, 1905-1906). First-rate state histories by Theodore Blegen, Robert Nesbit, Richard Current, and others treat the industry in context, as do Margaret Walsh, *The Manufacturing Frontier: Pioneer Industry in Antebellum Wisconsin, 1830-1860* (Madison: State

Historical Society of Wisconsin, 1972); Mark Wyman, *The Wisconsin Frontier* (Bloomington: Indiana University Press, 1998); and Lucille M. Kane, *The Waterfall that Built a City: The Falls of St. Anthony in Minneapolis* (St. Paul: Minnesota Historical Society, 1966). All in all, the Lake States are the most thoroughly studied portion of the lumberman's frontier.

Traditionally Southern historiography has focused on other issues, but in recent years attention has turned to the environment. Key works include Timothy Silver, *A New Face on the Countryside: Indians, Colonists, and Slaves in South Atlantic Forests, 1500-1800* (Cambridge, U.K.: Cambridge University Press, 1990); Mart A. Stewart, *"What Nature Suffers to Groe": Life, Labor, and Landscape on the Georgia Coast, 1680-1920* (Athens: University of Georgia Press, 1996); and Albert E. Cowdrey, *This Land, This South: An Environmental History* (Lexington: University Press of Kentucky, 1983). In some ways the environmental perspective was anticipated by the so-called Vanderbilt school. See especially Frank L. Owsley, *Plain Folks of the Old South* (Baton Rouge: Louisiana State University Press, 1949); Herbert Weaver, *Mississippi Farmers, 1850-1860* (Nashville, Tenn.: Vanderbilt University Press, 1945); and Forrest McDonald and Grady McWhiney, "The Antebellum Southern Herdsman: A Reinterpretation," *Journal of Southern History*, 41 (1975). The observations of this group, if not their sympathy for poor whites, were anticipated in the colonial period by William Byrd, for whose views see John Spencer Bassett, ed., *The Writings of Colonel William Byrd of Westover in Virginia Esqr.* (New York: Doubleday, Page & Co., 1901).

The forest history of the South has been a relatively recent concern. Leading published works include Nollie Hickman, *Mississippi Harvest: Lumbering in the Longleaf Pine Belt, 1840-1915* (Oxford: University Press of Mississippi, 1962); Robert S. Maxwell and Robert D. Baker, *Sawdust Empire: The Texas Lumber Industry, 1830-1940* (College Station: Texas A&M University Press, 1983); Jeffrey A. Drobney, *Lumbermen and Log Sawyers: Life, Labor, and Culture in the North Florida Timber Industry, 1830-1930* (Macon, Ga.: Mercer University Press, 1997); and James E. Fickle, *Mississippi Forests and Forestry* (Jackson: Mississippi Forestry Foundation and University Press of Mississippi, 2001). Doctoral dissertations also provide essential information, especially those of George Alvin Stokes, "Lumbering in Southwest Louisiana: A Study of the Industry as a Culturo-Geographic Factor" (unpub. Ph.D. diss., Louisiana State University, 1954); Richard W. Massey, Jr., "A History of the Lumber Industry in Alabama and West Florida, 1880-1914" (unpub. Ph.D. diss., Vanderbilt University, 1960); and John Anthony Eisterhold, "Lumber and Trade in the Seaboard Cities of the Old South, 1607-1860" (unpub. Ph.D. diss., University of Mississippi, 1970). Labor conditions have received considerable attention. Especially useful are

Ruth A. Allen, *East Texas Lumber Workers: An Economic and Social Picture, 1870-1950* (Austin: University of Texas Press, 1961); John Reed Tarver, "The Clan of Toil: Piney Woods Labor Relations in the Trans-Mississippi South, 1880-1920" (unpub. Ph.D. diss., Louisiana State University, 1991); and Thad Sitton and James H. Conrad, *Nameless Towns: Texas Sawmill Communities, 1880-1942* (Austin: University of Texas Press, 1998). Also valuable are John Hebron Moore, *Andrew Brown and Cypress Lumbering in the Old Southwest* (Baton Rouge: Louisiana State University Press, 1967); and James E. Fickle, *The New South and the "New Competition": Trade Association Development in the Southern Pine Industry* (Urbana: University of Illinois Press, 1980). Unlike with the Lake States, it is essential to consult manuscripts in order to piece together much Southern forest history. Key collections include the Calvin Taylor, Asa Hursey, and Southern Pine Association papers in the Hill Memorial Library at Louisiana State University; the Weston family papers in the J. D. Williams Library at the University of Mississippi; and the G. T. B. Moore and Kirby Lumber Company papers, as well as transcripts of numerous oral histories, in the East Texas Research Center, at Stephen F. Austin State University.

Sources on the Far West's forest frontiers have a dual personality. There are a number of good secondary studies dealing with westside forests, but few on the interior pine country. For context for both areas, see: Earl Pomeroy, *The Pacific Slope: A History of California, Oregon, Washington, Idaho, Utah, and Nevada* (New York: Knopf, 1965), and James Neville Tattersall, "Economic Development of the Pacific Northwest to 1920" (unpub. Ph.D. diss., University of Washington, 1960). On the westside, Robert Bunting, *The Pacific Raincoast: Environment and Culture in an American Eden, 1778-1900* (Lawrence: University Press of Kansas, 1997), provides environmental insights. On lumbering there, see: Edmond S. Meany, Jr., "History of the Lumber Industry of the Pacific Northwest to 1917" (unpub. Ph.D. diss., Harvard University, 1935); Thomas R. Cox, *Mills and Markets: A History of the Pacific Coast Lumber Industry to 1900* (Seattle: University of Washington Press, 1974); and Robert E. Ficken, *The Forested Land: A History of Lumbering in Western Washington* (Seattle: University of Washington Press, 1987). The best study of the redwood industry continues to be Howard Brett Melendy, "One Hundred Years of the Redwood Lumber Industry, 1850-1950" (unpub. Ph.D. diss., Stanford University, 1952), but see also Owen C. Coy, *The Humboldt Bay Region, 1850-1875: A Study in the American Colonization of California* (Los Angeles: California State Historical Assoc., 1929), and C. Raymond Clar, *California Government and Forestry from Spanish Days until the Creation of the Department of Natural Resources in 1927* (Sacramento: California Division of Forestry, 1959). Policies and attendant controversies are traced in Lawrence Rakestraw, "A History of

Forest Conservation in the Pacific Northwest, 1891-1913" (unpub. Ph.D. diss., University of Washington, 1955); Jerry O'Callaghan, *The Disposition of the Public Domain in Oregon* (Washington, D.C.: GPO, 1960); Elmo R. Richardson, *The Politics of Conservation: Crusades and Controversies, 1897-1913* (Berkeley: University of California Press, 1952) and *BLM's Billion-Dollar Checkerboard: Managing the O & C Lands* (Santa Cruz, Calif.: Forest History Society, 1980); and G. Michael McCarthy, *Hour of Trial: The Conservation Conflict in Colorado and the West* (Norman: University of Oklahoma Press, 1977). Labor's travails are traced in Robert L. Tyler, *Rebels in the Woods: The I.W.W. in the Pacific Northwest* (Eugene: University of Oregon Books, 1967); Andrew Mason Prouty, *More Deadly than War!: Pacific Coast Logging, 1827-1981* (New York: Garland, 1985); and Daniel A. Cornford, *Workers and Dissent in the Redwood Empire* (Philadelphia: Temple University Press, 1987). For insights into key industrial leaders, see: Edwin T. Coman, Jr., and Helen M. Gibbs, *Time, Tide and Timber: A Century of Pope & Talbot* (Stanford, Calif.: Stanford University Press, 1949), and Charles E. Twining, *George S. Long, Timber Statesman* (Seattle: University of Washington Press, 1994). For the context of developments in the interior, see John Fahey, *The Inland Empire: Unfolding Years, 1879-1929* (Seattle: University of Washington Press, 1986), and Nancy Langston, *Forest Dreams, Forest Nightmares: The Paradox of Old Growth in the Inland West* (Seattle: University of Washington Press, 1995). Robert L. Matheny, "The History of Lumbering in Arizona before World War II" (unpub. Ph.D. diss., University of Arizona, 1975), is suggestive of developments and problems beyond its area of focus. Also broadly suggestive is Keith C. Peterson, *Company Town: Potlatch, Idaho, and the Potlatch Lumber Company* (Pullman: Washington State University Press, 1987). However, for much of the story of the pine country, manuscript sources are essential. Among the most important are the previously untapped Edward D. Wetmore papers, Warren County Historical Society, Warren, Penn.; the historical records of the Forest Service's Pacific Northwest Regional Office, National Archives and Records Service Center, Seattle; and the Weyerhaeuser Timber Company archives, Federal Way, Wash. Oral histories conducted by the Forest History Society and by the Bancroft Library, Berkeley, Calif., are also vital, especially George L. Drake, *A Forester's Log: Fifty Years in the Pacific Northwest*, oral history interview with Elwood R. Maunder (Santa Cruz, Calif.: Forest History Society, 1975). Local newspapers provide other perspectives and much-needed information, the most essential being those from Burns, Lakeview, and Prineville, Oregon. Both here and for the westside, trade publications, especially *The Timberman,* provide vital information and insights.

Index